Enrich Series on China's Economic Issues

Enrich Series on China's Economic Issues

This series emphasizes the employment of modern economics methods to explore and research hot-spot issues and difficulties in the reform, opening-up and economic development facing China today. It covers a wide variety of economic issues ranging from monetary policy, fiscal policy, regional economy to industrial and banking development.

Vol. 1 China's Opening-up: The Impact on Monetary Policy Choice

Vol. 2 Growth of the Service Sector in the Yangtze River Delta

Vol. 3 Foreign Trade Growth and Economic Development in China: Retrospective and Future Prospects

Vol. 4 A Study of the Macroeconomic Effects of China's Financial Deficits

Vol. 5 Competition, Concentration and Efficiency of Commercial Banks in Korea, Mainland China and Taiwan

Enrich Series on China's Economic Issues Vol. 2

Growth of the Service Sector in the Yangtze River Delta

Liu Zhibiao

Zheng Jianghuai

Enrich Professional Publishing

Published by

Enrich Professional Publishing (S) Private Limited
16L, Enterprise Road,
Singapore 627660
Website: www.enrichprofessional.com
A Member of Enrich Culture Group Limited

Hong Kong Head Office:
1/F., Lemmi Center, 50 Hoi Yuen Road, Kwun Tong, Kowloon, Hong Kong, China

Beijing Office:
Rm 1108A, Culture Plaza, No. 59 Zhongguancun St., Haidian District, Beijing, China

Translated by Zhang Wei and Tang Zhou

ISBN (Hardback)	978-981-4298-20-9
ISBN (ebook)	978-981-4298-21-6 (pdf)
	978-981-4298-55-1 (epub)

Enrich Professional Publishing is an independent globally minded publisher focusing on the economic and financial developments that have revolutionized new China. We aim to serve the needs of advanced degree students, researchers, and business professionals who are looking for authoritative, accurate and engaging information on China.

Contents

Preface to the Series

The development and change of economic theory is closely associated with economic practice. With the transition of China to a socialist market economic system, practice requires the development and prosperity of economics; at the same time, practice is creating the conditions for the development of economics.

Market-oriented reform in China is unprecedented and no ready-made economic theory can be used for guidance. This is a major challenge for Chinese scholars. "By other's faults, wise men correct their own." With the translation and introduction of a large quantity of Western economic theories to China and the growth of many skills in modern economics attainment, brand-new tools and perspectives are available for the understanding and solving of the economic problems of China. Theory and practice are interactive. While using modern economic theory as reference, China, as an unparalleled "test field," will certainly inject new vitality into the development of economic theory and become an important driving force for its development. Only in this way may economics based on researches on Chinese economic problems be established. It is against this backdrop that Chinese economic issues are endowed with special significance.

The fundamental purpose of planning for and publishing the Series on Economic Issues in China is to encourage economists' spirit of innovation and exploration, further promoting the development and prosperity of economics research in China, and to establish a platform that is suitable for the growth of new ideas among economics works in China, providing a theoretical economic circle on China and explorers in real sectors a space for presentation of high-level research findings, thus enabling this series to be indispensable reading for readers at home and abroad to learn about the development of economics and the economy in China.

The distinctness and urgency of economic issues in China will provide Chinese scholars with a broad space for development. Using economic issues in China as the breakthrough point, this series emphasizes the employment of modern economics methods to explore and research hot-spot issues and difficulties in the reform and opening-up and economic development of China. For the purpose of development of the Chinese economy and economics, on an academic basis, this series has employed a "double-blind review system" integrated with solicited manuscripts from experts so as to cultivate a number of Chinese academic pioneers with the spirit of rationality and exploration in the field of economics. China is an ideal country for economic research, where the diligent may make plentiful and substantial achievements.

Preface

The Modern Service Industry and Its Rise in the Global Value Chain

Introduction

After nearly three decades of continuous and rapid economic growth, the Yangtze River Delta is now facing one of its most pressing problems—its rise in the industrial value chain in an overall manner, and the conversion of the extensive economic development model, which are the key issues for future sustainable development of the Yangtze River Delta. In order to transform the economic development model we need to fundamentally change the development path of high input, high consumption and high pollution supporting economic growth and take a new path of industrialization with Chinese characteristics that enjoys high technological content, good economic returns, low resources consumption, little environmental pollution, and gives full play of human resources. Only in this way can we realize sustainable development. This book is one of the outcomes of our long-term studies on the economic development of the Yangtze River Delta. Although the essays in this book are written separately by writers from their own points of views, they are always united with a guiding principle, namely that we should analyze the relationship between the service industry and other economic variables in the Yangtze River Delta in an overall manner, and from the angle of the service industry, especially the modern service industry in this region, to disclose the mechanism, behavior and performance of the modern service industry in the industrial value chain, so taking a new road of industrialization, conversion of the development model and harmonious economic development.

In writing the preface for this book I would like first of all to talk about the relationship between the development of the modern service industry and China's rise in the global value chain. I choose this topic because it is closely related to my understanding of the modern service industry on the new road of industrialization. My basic view is that: in the modern economy, the competitiveness of non-service industry (primary industry and manufacturing) is determined by the service industry, and the development of the service industry also depends on the input from modern advanced producer service (APS). So I chose the upgrade of industries in China in the Global Value Chain

(GVC) as the starting point for my analysis.

In recent years, studies on the international division in the trend of globalization and on the "North-South trade" division between developing countries and developed countries have moved on from whether or not to join the GVC to two profound issues: firstly, which way of joining the GVC can best help countries at the low-end of the division system to update their industries; secondly, since the vast majority of companies which join the GVC also join local industrial clusters, the focus of research has shifted onto how to overcome the homogeneous competition of local industrial clusters and how to make use of cluster-supporting enterprises to constantly rise to the high-end of GVC.

Gereffi (1999) believes that after joining the GVC division system dominated by developed countries, developing countries will automatically upgrade the value chain of local enterprises because through learning and catching up with the technology, management capability and institutional system of developed countries, local enterprises in developing countries in the buyer-driven GVC will benefit from rapid escalation and "automatic" realization of mechanism: assembling imported spare and component parts → independently operating the entire production process → designing their own products → selling products of their own brand in regional or global markets. This optimistic view is strongly criticized by Humphrey, Schmitz (2004) and others, who believe that in this kind of GVC the upgrading process of enterprises in developing countries is suppressed or "captured" at the low-end of the GVC by big buyers in developed countries, and so it is difficult for those enterprises in developing countries to rise to the higher end of the value chain, not to mention the so-called "automatic" realization mechanism during the upgrading process. Cramer (1999) put forward pessimistic "fatalism" of industrial upgrading under the conditions of globalization: limited by its own comparative advantages, the less-developed country is forced to engage in production activities of primary products in the GVC, which activities are all determined by the behavior, structures and systems of the multinational companies in OECD countries. Therefore the less-developed countries are locked into the "low-end path" of development for a long time and suffer cruel exploitation which is hard to reverse in terms of income distribution.

These arguments, on the one hand, warn countries such as China which adopt the export-oriented development mode based on international OEM, and on the other hand remind us that we should study our rise up the value chain from a dynamic perspective and gradually get rid of the control of transnational enterprises on local enterprises in developing countries through their dominance in the GVC. In fact, pessimism and fatalism on the issue of industrial upgrading are both incorrect. It is important to adhere to the methodology of dynamism and to break through the traditional practice of continuously basing future competitive advantage on primary production factors and gradually eliminate the dependence on the "low-end path" using the input of advanced factors. Specifically, to increase investment in the modern producer service of the existing manufacturing sector is the key to the "automatic transfer" order of industrial upgrading mentioned by Gereffi.

Our analysis is focused on the functioning mechanism and implementation method of the input in modern producer service in the GVC. We believe that the reason why the developed countries can occupy the high-end of the GVC and be engaged in non-entities activities, thus obtaining dissymmetrical distribution of global benefits, is that in industrial restructuring, the continuous input of technology, knowledge and human capital included in modern producer services enable the industrial structure to "soften." Reeve (2006) found from his recent study that investment in human capital and education has a significant and unique effect on the evolution of the industrial structure of the OECD countries. He pointed out that in the new economic situation almost all manufacturing industries are heavily dependent on capital and workforce with a secondary educational level. But on the other hand, a workforce with a high educational level leads to a decrease in production costs of the manufacturing industry. It is well known that the level of technology, knowledge and human capital depends on education. Therefore, the development of high-quality education (including high-quality vocational and technical education) is the basis for the industrial upgrading of a China with export-oriented characteristics.

The service industry in the GVC, particularly the modern producer service, is an extremely realistic and highly valuable issue in the study of the GVC. At present, domestic studies on all aspects of the GVC have mainly concentrated on manufacturing. In fact, the experience of developed countries shows that the time consumed and the added value produced in the entire industrial chain of manufacturing are both limited. The associated service sectors including finance, R&D, design, technical services, logistics, marketing and branding activities are the links of high added value. In addition enterprises in China's coastal areas, especially in the Yangtze River Delta, join in local industry clusters while joining in the GVC, that is to say that the enterprises' joining in the GVC is supported by their joining in local industrial clusters. The manufacturing of local industrial clusters also needs to be supported by the modern service industry, and therefore paying close attention to the service industry and in particular ANote in the GVC is also important in the attempt to achieve overall upgrading of local industrial clusters.

The Investment of Producer Services

The producer service industry, as an independent industrial sector, is a driving force for the growth of manufacturing with its strong supporting function. Theoretically speaking, the active effect of producer services on industrial competitiveness is related to the high-level factors which are intensive, highly competitive, irreplaceable and can sustainably create value in the output of the industry. On this matter, Canadian economists Gruber and Walker (1989) concluded that: the producer service is the flywheel which imports increasingly professional human capital and knowledge capital into the goods and services production process, and to a considerable extent, the producer service constitutes the channel of these capitals into the production process, so that it can not only improve the operation efficiency as well as the operation scale during the production process of goods and services but also enhance the productivity of other input factors while increasing the output value. This conclusion has been proved by the empirical researches of Guerrieri (2003) and other researchers. They took the OECD countries in the 1990s as samples to study the decisive issue of international competitiveness and international specialization in the producer service, and found that there exists an important positive correlation between the development of manufacturing industry and producer service in a country.

In particular, the development of modern ANote in the modern producer service has laid the foundation for the competitiveness of manufacturing and other service sectors. ANote is composed of those industries which are closely related to knowledge production, dissemination and application, such as finance, insurance, information and communication technology, business services (including R&D services, design services, creative services, engineering services, business consulting services, knowledge property services etc.). The function mechanism of ANote's optimization of manufacturing structures and upgrading of industrial chain can be analyzed on four levels covering material, behavior, management and system.

Firstly, from the aspect of input materials, a variety of invisible implicit knowledge embodied in ANote are specifically reflected in the input cost of the manufacturing industry.[1] (1) This input has improved the product performance of the equipment manufacturing industry and the market competitiveness of the products manufactured through software-embedding in hardware, in particular, in machine tools such as machinery equipment. In this pattern of modern international division of labor, the manufacturing industry's competitiveness does not lie in the manufacturing process itself, but rather in the quantity and quality of advanced producer services which are input during the manufacturing process. (2) A variety of products research and development services involved in ANote, such as pre-production market and positioning research services, design services in research and development, creative services, tooling services, engineering and technical services in production, equipment rental services, logistics services in marketing, network brand services and export services can strongly enhance the differentiation degree of products and competitors, thus strengthening a company's pricing power and market controlling power. (3) Various types of producer services for manufacturing enterprises in production and capital operations, such as financial services, enterprise management consulting services, legal and intellectual property rights services etc. often play a decisive role in improving the clarity of business strategy and increasing market share, merger, acquisition and growth.

Secondly, from the aspect of enterprises' behavior, in general, there is a "customer–supplier" relationship between the manufacturer and producer services producer. Not only does there exist an "adjacency" effect between the two, but also the organizational structure of ANote has an influence on the demand of manufacturing industry for these services while the organizational structure of the manufacturing industry affects the supply of producer services (Marshall, 1982). Therefore the cost of acquiring services from service providers, such as the travel time and frequency (O'Farrell and Hitchens, 1990) of conference, rises as the distance between the two sides increases. Coffey and Bailly (1991) stressed that in developed countries, "intermediate demand service production is potentially the most expensive part because it includes not only the cost of maintaining face-to-face exchange with service providers but also the inputs of service and market costs." This theory indicates that the manufacturers can get huge benefits from cooperative location with the production of producer services. Goe (1990) pointed out that producer services manufacturers can also get huge profits from positioning themselves "adjacent" to manufacturers, as manufacturers create a market for them.

Thirdly, judging from the evolution of the modern enterprise management model, modern manufacturing enterprises are turning "flat," "flexible" and "fine," in accordance with the principle of international division of labor within products. In this global labor division system within product, industrial upgrading is no longer an overall upgrading of industry and complete upgrading of the product value chain, but upgrading of a certain function, a certain production stage, a certain process, and a certain technical feature in the value chain of a certain product. If this statement is true, in the conditions of globalization and outsourcing, we must strive to realize large-scale economy of a certain function, a certain production stage, a certain process, and a certain technical feature in the value chain of a certain product on the basis of specialization, in order to promote industrial upgrading. If a company outsources business at which it is not good or in which it lacks comparative advantage, and is more focused on its core business, then professional outsourcing companies can provide more professional and excellent services, and the costs of the company are therefore reduced. Then manufacturing industry is further promoted. A developed manufacturing industry, in turn, will put more demanding requirements on producer services and cause a "push-pull effect," thus forming a mutually reinforcing development trend, and making this area superior to other areas in terms of knowledge spillover, labor quality, and environmental facilities and become a key selected area for manufacturing investment, particularly foreign investment, ultimately realizing a win-win situation.

Fourthly, since a benign institutional arrangement reduces transaction cost, ANote is the most important part of a manufacturing enterprise system and also creates a new system environment suitable for competition of manufacturers, so advanced producer services are embodied in system costs and transaction costs of manufacturing enterprises. It is not difficult to understand that financial services, legal services, logistics services, and other producer services are transaction costs of manufacturing companies. When a local industrial cluster has excellent producer services, namely the transaction cost of producer services is lower than the management cost of the company, the company will outsource part of its business. If the information service sector develops ANote and makes the Internet become mature, leading to a decline in information and communication costs, thus reducing the transaction costs of companies for access to services from the market, it will be helpful for companies to adopt outsourcing. Manufacturing enterprises through outsourcing not only can reduce transaction costs and overcome the lack of motivation to improve quality of commodities and services, but also can effectively control risks. Companies greatly promote the development of the producer services by adopting outsourcing. Moreover, with the detour and flexibility of the production process, experts in related fields are needed to carry out planning, control, and evaluation in every stage of production in order to make production as efficient as possible. As financial, consulting, law, engineering and other fields become increasingly specialized, the extent of specialization means that large-scale manufacturing enterprises are unable to provide these services themselves. Scientific and technological progress has promoted professional division of labor and means that producer services are separate from manufacturing. The development and expansion of manufacturing has provided great space for the development of producer services.

In other words, input of ANote in the manufacturing industry is equivalent to the specialized "advanced factors" mentioned in the Porter theory (Porter, 1998). It can greatly improve national productivity, thus becoming the key factor in upgrading the development level of China's manufacturing industry in the GVC.

The Implementation Mechanism of ANote

Since the reform and opening up, the effect of China's strong manufacturing export capacity on economic growth has been significant and very compelling. From 1980 to 2006, exports of Chinese goods rose at an annual average growth rate of 25.66%, exceeding the average export growth rate of the world over the same period by 18.32% and contributing 27% to the growth of the GDP on average.[2] Over the 10 years from 1993 to 2002, exports soared from US$91.76 billion to US$325.57 billion, a 2.55-fold increase. The proportion of the GDP accounted for by exports rose from 15.3% to 26.3% and the proportion of total global volume of exports accounted for by the volume of Chinese exports increased from 2.5% to 5.1%. From 2003 to 2006, exports respectively amounted to US$438.2 billion, US$593.3 billion, US$761.9 billion, and US$968.9 billion, with the annual average growth rate reaching 31.4%.[3] We believe that this impressive performance is mainly attributable to the comparative advantage of low-level factor input rather than international competitiveness reflected by input "high-level factors."

This conclusion has been confirmed by our recent empirical study which is based on a large-scale questionnaire survey.[4] Our study has confirmed that after effective control of the industrial and geographical factors, product division of labor, firm size, business location and other traditional factors have a positive effect on exports of domestic manufacturers, while technological innovation, human capital, high capital intensity and other factors which are emphasized in classic trade theory do not become decisive factors in the exports of domestic manufacturers. In the context of economic restructuring, institutional factors have a significant influence on export expansion of domestic manufacturers. This influence may be mainly reflected in incentives to export of small-scale companies. The export competitiveness of domestic manufacturing enterprises is mainly based on integration of multiple factors arising from the cluster effect.

At present, China's domestic manufacturers are generally suppressed or locked into the low-end part of the GVC labor division system, affecting continuous improvement of export capacity.

The conclusion from empirical research fully explains that: on the one hand, since the reform and opening up, the international competitiveness of China's manufacturing industry has been enhanced, mainly through improving the productivity of low-level factors input via system reform; on the other hand, the advanced factors and specialized factors (capital intensity, human capital, technological innovation and other factors) mentioned by Porter cannot play their due role due to the lack of a real embedding mechanism during the international competitiveness-forming process of China's manufacturing. In reality, we believe that it is difficult for modern advanced factors to be embedded in China's manufacturing industry. The main reasons are as follows:

Firstly, the factor endowment difference in Heckscher and Ohlin (H-O) neo-classical theory holds that the international trade theory with a decisive role played by inter-country specialization tools on the whole can possibly still be applied to China's current stage of development. China's manufacturing in general still belongs to labor-intensive industry which relies on factor endowments of low-cost labor to obtain export competitiveness. Therefore the use of mature factor input to enhance industrial competitiveness should be closely combined with the economic development stage of a country. At the low stage of economic development, advanced factor input often cannot effectively exploit the comparative advantages or enhance industrial competitiveness. On the contrary, it is more likely to deviate from a country's comparative advantages, distort the real development process, and exert a negative effect because of massive consumption. But it should be considered that long-term restriction on input of low-level factors easily makes China fall into the "comparative advantage trap."[5] Therefore the nature of the problem is not whether or not to pay attention to high-level factor input but rather, under the existing development constraints, how to utilize the factor endowment difference between China and developed countries so as to not only obtain real trade benefits to promote economic stability and full employment but also gradually improve input structure in dynamic development, remove the temptation of the "comparative advantage trap," and achieve industrial upgrading objectives. This requires a realistic embedding mechanism of advanced factors consistent with the development requirements at the current stage.

Secondly, according to our observation of the practice in China, at present most domestic companies do not seek to rely on high-level factors to build high-end competitiveness but pursue means such as OEM to shift to the GVC labor division system dominated by big buyers from developed countries, and basically shift to low-end manufacturing or processing and assembly in the GVC. As long as Chinese companies participating in the GVC labor division system try to build their core technical capabilities, brands and sales terminals, they form challenges to the monoNoteony power of multinational corporations in most developed countries. As contract issuing parties in the GVC labor division system, they will adopt various means to hinder Chinese enterprises from forming an independent innovation capacity, thus forcing Chinese enterprises to be "locked" or "captured" in the low-end link of the GVC.[6] Therefore technological innovation and other factors are found in our empirical analysis to be not the decisive factor in exports of domestic enterprises. PerhaNote it is not a voluntary act or independent selection by domestic enterprises but instead is forced passive selection in the benefit game with enterprises from developed countries in the current GVC labor division pattern. Hence there is the problem of how to change the prerequisite of determining the balance in the benefit game in the current GVC labor division pattern. On this issue, we cannot expect the automatic elimination of monoNoteony power of companies from developed countries; instead, we can only rely on continuous innovation and upgrading of our input factors. The monoNoteony power of companies from developed countries is not inherent but formed through continuous investment in advanced factors. Therefore we should work out an embedding mechanism of "advanced factors" which can compete with mono Noteony power.

Thirdly, according to our on-site research, local manufacturers in local industrial clusters in China are interested in low-level factors-oriented export, which is closely related with the single function configuration of manufacturing clusters in China and lack of specific ways for embedding of advanced factors into the manufacturing industry. Most of the existing manufacturing industry clusters in China are simple gatherings of similar industries or parts and components supporting industry in a particular space. These manufacturing clusters with a single function lack intellectual support from ANote, the function of reducing transaction costs and the function of strengthening product differentiation. In improving production capacity in a large-scale manner and reducing direct manufacturing costs, they are basically separate from ANote with regard to advanced factors. Therefore, between clusters, there is fierce competition between regions with local government as the main body and administrative boundaries as the characteristic, while within the cluster there are the following problems: first, brutal price competition among enterprises driven by product homogeneity; second, competition for existence among enterprises in the cluster featured by "fighting for skills" (especially the disorderly flow of senior technicians and management personnel); third, imitation and infringement competition caused by inadequate protection of intellectual property rights and implied knowledge. Due to this intense competition, manufacturing clusters in the Chinese coastal areas do not pay attention to R&D expenditure or invest in human capital, but only practice high-consumption with low-cost competition. While this brings "China price"[7] fear to the global manufacturing industry, it has induced overall recession of some manufacturing clusters which are localized in low-level factors to a large extent.[8] Therefore, if an "advanced factors" embedding mechanism is unavailable, a large number of manufacturing clusters in China with a single function will disappear in the foreseeable future, particularly after the developing countries whose other factors are more superior to those of China join in the global competition.

The Joint Development Mechanism

Through practice we have observed that currently in coastal areas of China, especially the Yangtze River Delta, some gathering areas of the service sector with ANote as the main content have been formed. Advanced manufacturing and modern service companies can provide composite products and related services at the fastest pace with the most efficient input of advanced factors, having formed not only a differentiated competition pattern among enterprises within the cluster, but also a embedding mechanism of co-location and collaboration between the service industry and manufacturing industry in the cluster.

The target of our on-site investigation is Jintong International Industrial Park[9] inside the Changzhou Wujin High-tech Industrial Development Zone, where manufacturing is developed. The park has been developed and built by Jiangsu Jintong Construction Co., Ltd., covering an area of 1000 mu and a planned construction area of 900,000 square meters. Currently, 17 high-standard industrial workshoNote, one production service center, and one life service center covering nearly 30 million square meters have been built. In addition, standard workshoNote and R&D buildings covering more than 100,000 square meters will be officially put into use.

Jintong International Industrial Park is a new high-tech industrial park and serves as an "integrated service provider for enterprises" integrating a scientific research incubation center, manufacturing center, and modern service center into one. With the modern service industry as the core, it has the environmental characteristics of a circular economy and a garden-style community. With "two-wheel drive of modern service industry and advanced manufacturing" as its logo, it provides enterprises settled there with an integrated international industry operating platform. The producer services that it deploys for manufacturing mainly include: (1) Technology services, such as industrial design, engineering simulation, patent services, technical design, software development and testing etc. The state-level "International Science and Technology Cooperation Base," state-level "High-tech Innovation Service Center," and state-level "Overseas Students Pioneer Park" in the park give priority to eligible enterprises for the provision of "seed money," to reduce the time from scientific and technological "incubation" to "industrialization." (2) Manufacturing services, including human resources, logistics, international freight forwarding, bonded warehouses, leasing, certification etc, are comprehensive services integrating plant construction, equipment installation and supervision, industrial engineering, logistics, business management and property management. (3) Business services, such as financial, legal, tax, advertising and exhibition services etc. (4) Logistics services, such as catering, accommodation, and posts and telecommunications. The modern service factors of "Jintong Service System" can provide enterprises in the park with a variety of high-efficiency but low-cost other services other than its core process.

As a new carrier of large efficient domestic and foreign enterprises and an interactive platform of fast-growing SMEs, since its opening in 2005 the Jintong International Park has attracted more than 20 internationally renowned modern service enterprises from Fortune 500. The entry of leading international enterprises has also attracted many returned overseas students starting their own businesses and some large domestic enterprises. The phase-I occupancy rate of the project has reached 80%. Currently the park has become a demonstration area for modern service industry cluster and manufacturing service process outsourcing, with Changzhou as the core area and with influence in Southern Jiangsu, which is known as an international manufacturing base, and even influencing whole Yangtze River Delta.

The initial experience in investment in and construction of the Jintong International Industrial Park is a major inspiration in finding a realistic embedding mechanism of "advanced factors" consistent with the development requirements of China at the current stage.

First, the embedding mechanism is realized through enhancing the competitiveness of the manufacturing industry through the modern service industry cluster. The key is to establish an advanced factor input market close to the service targets. For the construction and development of clusters, the relationship between advanced manufacturing and modern service industry is complementary rather than one of competition. More strictly speaking, advanced manufacturing is highly dependent on the input of advanced factors, so we can attract advanced manufacturing with a modern service industry so as to realize co-location and collaboration. Martin (2004) has also confirmed this through study. His study shows that ANote location is a function of the location of the manufacturing industry. The reason is that there is a "supplier–customer" relationship between them. Manufacturers benefit from close proximity of producer services, and therefore time-based "accessibility" is an important variable for the explanation of their co-location. Proximity to ANote can be used to explain the location of manufacturing. However, since producer services are often inputs in the production of other service industries, proximity to manufacturing industry is not a significant statistical factor which can explain ANote location. His study also shows that the flexibility of knowledge-intensive manufacturing industry's proximity to ANote is smaller than that of non-knowledge-intensive manufacturing industry to ANote.

Second, experience shows that FDI is one of the most important factors promoting co-location and collaboration between modern service industry and manufacturing industry. In addition, the co-location and collaboration power generated can create a "self-reinforcing" effect for clusters, thus further attracting FDI and large domestic enterprises.[10] We have found in our recent study on spatial concentration that in the Yangtze River Delta: (1) The higher the collaborative cluster level between the manufacturing industry and the service industry is, the higher agglomeration level of the manufacturing industry is. (2) The higher the collaborative cluster level between the service industry and the manufacturing industry is, the higher the agglomeration level of the service industry is. Therefore the collaborative cluster has promoted the industry cluster. (3) FDI is related to the gathering of manufacturing and service industry. After the collaborative cluster level is improved, its significance is increased. (4) The agglomeration level of service industry and manufacturing industry in all places is affected by distance from Shanghai, the central city. The closer to Shanghai they are, the higher collaborative cluster level they have. Therefore the radiation effect of central cities is obvious.[11]

Third, it is necessary to effectively embed advanced factors into the production process of goods and services. In the past we put more emphasis on the common effect of "production, study, and research." In line with the background of the transition economy of China, now we strongly advocate technology innovation and a transfer mechanism which promotes the integration of "production, study, research, and policy." But practice has proved that to realize technology innovation and transfer through integration of "production, study, research, and policy," a "non-technology innovation mechanism" is required to support the industrial or commercial process, otherwise it will definitely fall into the "European Paradox" of technological innovation (Veugelers et al., 2007).[12] That is to say that although the technology innovation model and mechanism of integrating "production, study, research, and policy" is the most important content and the main way forward for the new national technology innovation system, if there is lack of support from the "non-technology innovation mechanism," then high-level innovation results cannot be translated into technological progress or the competitiveness of enterprises. We believe that such a "non-technology innovation mechanism" in the spatial relationship is the cooperative location and agglomeration mechanism between the modern service industry and the manufacturing industry. Market operation and resources integration with enterprises as the main body and service cluster with ANote as the leading part has gathered forces from the foreign and domestic industrial field, research institutions, universities, the financial field, other intermediaries, and government with the same goal, thus effectively reducing the risks from technology innovation and uncertainty.

Fourth, the operation experience of the Jintong International Industrial Park has reminded us that in the GVC labor division system, there is causality between value chain governance and upgrading of clusters and perhaNote there is more than one way. In the past, representatives of the GVC theory such as Gereffi (1999) emphasized that enterprises in developing countries must gradually realize product and technology upgrading through joining in the value chain "captured" by, and the governance mechanism controlled by, large buyers. China's experience shows that in the "captured" value chain, domestic companies generally can only realize initial product and technology upgrading through "learning while working" and "working while learning" due to the governance mechanism controlled by international buyers. It is very difficult to realize function upgrading (namely, two ends of high value magnitudes in the rising "smile curve"). It is determined by asymmetry in the core capabilities of two parties and the nature of interest conflict. We not only have independently developed the functions at the two ends of the value chain, but also have realized its organic integration with modern manufacturing through development of clusters with the modern service industry as the leading part and through its co-location and collaborative gathering with manufacturing in space.

Conclusion and Policy Recommendations

From the interaction between ANote and advanced manufacturing industry, we have described that attention must be paid to advanced producer services as an input of "advanced factors," on the basis of industry upgrading of the industrial cluster or in rising to the peak of industrial chain in the GVC labor division system.

Through on-site research, we have found that we need to establish a co-location and collaboration mechanism between the modern service industry and the manufacturing industry in the large-scale investment in and construction of industrial clusters in all places, and in particular pay attention to the attraction of advanced manufacturing with ANote gathering, realizing the "two-wheel drive of the modern service industry and advanced manufacturing industry," in order not only to fully utilize the factor endowment difference between China and developed countries to obtain trade profits, but also to gradually improve the input structure in dynamic development and get rid of the "comparative advantage trap."

Our recommendation on policy is: industrial policy should be redefined so as to make China develoNote from being the world's manufacturing center to the differentiated survival and high end of the value chain. Obviously, exclusive attention to industrial policy, the weakest link in the value chain, cannot support China's future economic development. In the global manufacturing transfer trend, China needs to promote integration and interaction of ANote and manufacturing industry in industrial clusters and seek its due position in the value chain, with outstanding entrepreneurs and enterprises as the main bodies, if it wants to concentrate on improvement of its own core competitive power on the basis of independent innovation.

In the past, China won a primary step and an entry point into the GVC by relying on hard work and cheap products. With the establishment of large-scale production capacity, China's industrial policy should encourage various features and functions of manufacturing clusters in order to make China's industrial clusters not only have excellent production systems but also have matching technology innovation systems, market innovation systems and institutions, and management innovation systems, on the basis of ensuring product quality stability, delivery reliability and cost-competitive advantages while being based on the technology innovation and non-technology innovation in cluster areas. In addition, China should develop further self-learning and continuous improvement so as to support and realize the goals of upgrading industrial clusters. To this end, we should support companies within the cluster to enter the global manufacturing network system in a more effective manner, continuously rise up the value chain, and seize the top position in the value chain through cooperation and competition with multinational companies.

Liu Zhibiao

1

Chapter

The Influence of the Service Sector on the Industrialization Process in the Yangtze River Delta

Statement of Problems

Resources and historical environment vary in different countries and regions, so there are significant differences in the form and process of industrialization. The traditional industrialization process in Western countries such as Britain often follows agricultural reform. Agricultural revolution, a catalyst for the industrialization process (Lewis, 1978), can provide the industrialization process thereafter with a market, capital, human resources, and other necessary factors. In a closed economy, high-level agricultural output can support the industrialization process through creation of demand for industrial products. Industrial sectors then gradually expand by way of learning while working. But in an open economy, if a country's agriculture is at a comparative advantage, it will hinder the realization of industrialization and promote the industrialization process of neighboring countries, since neighboring countries have more comparative advantages in the production of industrial goods. For example, Belgium, Switzerland and other natural resource-poor countries realized industrialization earlier than their neighboring countries. In this case, countries with comparative advantages in agricultural endowment can often promote the realization of the industrialization process (Matsuyama, 1992) by protecting industrial sectors. There is also a situation in which countries rich in natural resources such as Canada have also achieved industrialization, although they have a comparative advantage in agricultural production, due to failure to take protective measures for industrial sector. It is found in relevant research that in the aforesaid industrialization process, the service industry has played a very important role. The realization of the industrialization process is promoted through division of labor and specialization of the service industry and effective reduction of the industrial sector's production costs (Eswaran, 2000).

Since the reform and opening up, China has made remarkable achievements in the industrialization process. It has maintained macro-economic growth for 20 consecutive years. The outputs of its main industrial products rank in the very forefront in the world. The GDP per capita increased from less than US$100 in 1978 to US$2,000 in 2006. Although China is a traditional agricultural country, its gradually-opened macro environment means agriculture is unable to provide adequate resources for the industrialization process as it does in a closed economy. In recent years, the government has implemented a certain degree of protection for domestic industry, but with the accelerated pace of China's opening up after accession to the WTO, the intensity and scope of such protection will become increasingly small. It can be foreseen that the service industry will assume an increasingly important role in the industrialization process in China. The industrialization in the Yangtze River Delta, a pioneer of modern industry in China, takes a leading position. Over the recent decade, the GDP per capita level in the Yangtze River Delta has always the highest in the country. The industrialization index is 35 percentage points higher than the national average industrialization index. The industrialization process has entered the second half of late industrialization, ranking the first among the seven largest economic regions in China (Chen Jiagui, 2007). Taking into account the important role of the service industry in the industrialization process in the Yangtze River Delta in an open economy, analysis of the current status, characteristics and evolution trend of the service industry in the Yangtze River Delta is of important practical and theoretical value.

Literature Review

Service industry and Industrial sectors

Chen Xian (2004), Gu Naihua (2006), and other scholars have divided the relationship between the service industry, especially producer services, and industry (mainly manufacturing) into four kinds of opinions, covering demand compliance theory, supply-led theory, interaction theory and integration theory.

(1) The "demand compliance theory" believes that industry (manufacturing) is the premise and basis for the development of the service industry (including producer services). The development of the service industry is of a demand compliance status, namely, service demand caused by economic growth especially expansion of manufacturing exerts an influence, and therefore the development of the service industry is affiliated to the development of manufacturing. Other domestic and foreign scholars holding such views include Cohen and Zysman (1987), Klodt (2000), Zhang Shixian (2000) and Jiang Xiaojuan (2004).

(2) Scholars of the "supply-led theory" believe that the service industry, especially the producer service industry, is the premise and basis for improvement of the productivity of industry (manufacturing). Without developed producer services, there is no possibility of forming industry (manufacturing) sectors with high competitiveness (Pappas and Sheehan, 1998; Karaomerlioglu and Carlsson, 1999; Eswaran and Kotwal, 2001).

(3) The "interaction theory" holders believe that producer services and manufacturing show an interactive relation of interdependence and common development. With the expansion of the manufacturing industry, the demand

for producer services such as trade, finance, transportation, social services, etc. will rapidly increase, which is conducive to improving the productivity of the manufacturing industry. Contrarily, the expansion of the producer industry depends on the increase of intermediate inputs in the manufacturing industry. Moreover, with economic development, the degree of interdependence between the service industry and manufacturing continues to deepen (Park and Chan, 1989; Shugan, 1994; Bathla, 2003).

(4) The newly emerging "integration theory" holders stress that with the development and wide application of information and communication technology, the boundaries between producer services and manufacturing will become increasingly blurred. And there is a trend towards integration between them (Lundvall and Borras, 1998; Zhi Caoyi, 2001; Zhou Zhenhua, 2003).

Among the aforesaid four theories, except for the compliance theory which believes that the service industry is subordinate to the industry, the other three theories all support the interaction between the service industry and industry, and even to some extent the idea that the service industry is the basis for industrial development.

The influence of the service industry on industrial sectors

According to the development experience of developed countries, the role of the service industry, especially producer services, in the industry field is a dynamic process of change. Initially the service industry, which is dominated by finance, inventory management and securities trading in the industry sectors is only a lubricant assisting management; thereafter, logistics services, management consulting and financial services become indirect inputs promoting more efficient industrial production and higher output value (high added value). Since the 1990s, the emerging service industry with information technology as the representative has been fully involved in all aspects of economic development, become the main source and distribution channel of new technologies and innovation, and has played the role of "propeller" and strategic function in a better manner (Li Jiangfan, 2004).

At present, most theoretical and empirical studies related to the relationship between the service industry and manufacturing industry believe that the service industry exerts an important influence on industrial development. Specifically, the service industry achieves these aims mainly in two ways: to reducing transaction costs and improving labor productivity (Banga and Goldar, 2004).

First of all, the existence of the service industry, especially the information and communications sector, is important for the reduction of transaction costs in the industry sector. Transaction costs include communication costs, transportation costs, search costs, and contracting costs. Singh (2004) uses a dynamic monopolistic competition model to illustrate how transaction costs are effectively reduced. He assumes that the initial status of the economy is balanced, and transaction costs determine the number of intermediate goods input into industry. Model analysis shows that transaction costs will reduce the long-term equilibrium level of industry, and even hinder the development of the industry sector. While the development of the service industry, especially the information and communications industry, will reduce transport and configuration costs. Meanwhile, as industrial products, the products of the service industry can also be classified as intermediate products and final products. More and more services have been integrated into modern industrial production as intermediate input factors. Improvement of the efficiency of the service industry can reduce prices of industrial intermediate inputs, thereby reducing transaction costs, offsetting the adverse effects of transaction costs on industrial development, and making it move to a new and higher level of balanced growth. This has been confirmed in the practice of industrial development in India.

Secondly, the role of the service industry in promoting the labor productivity of the industry sector is also very obvious. Banga and Goldar (2004) found through analysis of data on industries in India from 1980 to 1998 that in the 1980s India's service industry made very limited contribution to industrial output growth, only 1%; while in the 1990s, the ratio suddenly increased to 25%, and at the same time, it is found through study that input by the service industry significantly promotes the increase of industrial total factor productivity (TFP). Apart from empirical evidence on India, Triplett and Bosworth (2004) also obtained similar results in a study taking the United States as the example. They found in the study that the increase in the efficiency of the service industry, especially information and communications technology (ICT), played a very important role in the improvement of the productivity of the American industry sector in the late 1990s. ICT provides not only a service but also a new product and new process. If using a large-scale factory-style call center can lead to obvious economy of scale, the industry sector will be affected thereby. In addition the service industry cab also exert an influence on the development of the industry sector through affecting the speed of innovation, since innovation plays an important role in economic growth according to the endogenous growth theory, and the service industry mainly achieves the above purpose through accumulation of knowledge (Grossman and Helpman, 1991). Singh (2003) has made a specific analysis of how the information and communications technology industry promotes economic growth through influencing innovation. In Singh's model, ICT is the driver of effective information communication and storage. The core point is that new ideas are often generated on the basis of a combination of previous ideas. The key to whether potential ideas can successfully be turned into a new idea is the so-called success rate, and Singh has proved by his model that the knowledge storage function of ICT can exert an influence on the success rate in an exogenous way.

Among studies by domestic scholars, Gu Naihua (2005) calls the aforesaid functions of China's service industry in the transition economy a "spillover effect" which is divided into "spillover production effect" and the "spillover reform effect." Spillover production effect mainly refers to the development of the service industry, particularly the development of producer services, and for industrial development the effect means professionalism of some essential aspects of industrial production. Industrial enterprises can make use of service outsourcing to capture specialization advantages of the production of service intermediate inputs. At the same time, the service industry can invent new types of intermediate inputs and create endogenous comparative advantages for industrial development. The aforesaid factors are all conducive to improving industrial productivity. Spillover production effects include the fact that the development of the service industry enables industrial enterprises to develop economy of scale and scope through expansion of the production goods market for industrial goods and demand for consumption industrial goods when the degree of openness of the economy in China is low. Spillover reform effects mainly means that the development of the service industry has provided a suitable channel for transfer of the industrial surplus labor force, which is conducive to easing the long-standing problem of redundant employees and eliminating the bottleneck restrictions, which are the most important in improving the property rights reform of industrial enterprises and promoting industrial development.

Analytical Framework and Methods

Analytical thinking

This Chapter, on the basis of describing the characteristics of the service industry and industrialization in the Yangtze River Delta, first makes a general analysis of the influence of the development of the service industry on the industrialization process in this region. It then discusses the influence of the service industry's development in the Yangtze River Delta on transaction costs and productivity of the industry sector in the region to test some theoretical assumptions raised in various domestic and foreign studies; and finally some corresponding countermeasures and suggestions are proposed for the future development of the service industry in the region in combination with the actual situation, according to the empirical results.

Selection of data and variables

We set the range of empirical test as 1990 to 2005. Samples cover Shanghai, Jiangsu and Zhejiang.

The main variables selected include: (1) Development level and pace of the service industry. They are respectively shown by the proportion of the service industry in these regions to the GDP and the growth rate of the proportion. The efficiency indicators of the service industry are shown by labor productivity, namely the per capita added value of the service industry in that year. (2) Industrial indicators. These mainly include the GDP per capita, rate of industrialization, ratio of heavy industry, and population urbanization rate. Among these the GDP per capita is GDP per capita in that region; industrialization rate is the proportion of the output value of secondary industry, including construction, to GDP; the ratio of heavy industry is the proportion of the heavy industry's output value to the total industrial output value; and the population urbanization rate is the proportion of urban population to total population. Transaction cost of the industry sector is shown by the proportion of product sales cost of industry sector in respective regions to sales income in that year. Labor productivity is per capita industrial output of the industry sector. The aforesaid data are all sourced from the *China Statistical Yearbook* and the local statistical yearbook for the corresponding years.

Analytical method

Empirical analysis has been mainly conducted using sample data processing with descriptive statistics analysis and regression analysis and with the software SNoteS10.0.

The basic form of the regression model is as follows: $\ln Y_i=\alpha+\beta\ln X_i$

Y_i are GDP per capita, industrialization rate, the ratio of heavy industry, population urbanization rate, labor productivity of the industry and cost-to-income ratio, and other indicators of the industrialization level; X_i are the growth rate of the proportion of value-added in the service industry to the GDP, labor productivity of the service industry, and other development indicators.

Empirical Analysis of the Service Industry

Industrialization and the development of the service industry

1. The industrialization process

Currently, China's academic community adopts evaluation methods for the level of industrialization mainly according to the per capita income six-stage theory of Chenery, the output value structure of Kuznets, and the industrial structure four-stage theory of Hoffman. So far there is no unified standard. However most scholars basically accept the conclusion that the overall process of industrialization in China is at the second phase of interim industrialization, namely the high processing degree period of heavy industrialization (Chen Jiagui, 2007). An Tongliang reached a similar conclusion in analysis of the industrialization characteristics in the Yangtze River Delta.

In Table 1.1, an overall judgment on the industrialization level of China and of the provinces and municipalities in the Yangtze River Delta in 2005 is made according to the GDP per capita, the output value ratios of three industries, industrial structure, rate of urbanization and other individual indicators (Chen Jiagui, 2007). Among them, the composite score is a comprehensive index value after confirming the weights of all indicators by analytic hierarchy process, with comprehensive consideration of the influence of the aforesaid single indicators; the industrialization stage is divided according to the six-stage theory of Chenery. The period of industrialization lasts from the second stage to the fifth stage. The first stage and the sixth stage are the beginning period and the developed period.

Table 1.1. Industrialization Level of the Yangtze River Delta (2005)

Region	GDP per capita (RMB)	Share of three industries			Industrial Structrue (%)	Urbanization level of population (%)	Score	Phase of Industrialization	Rank
		1st	2nd	3rd					
China	14,040	12.6	47.5	39.9	52.0	43.0	50	3rd (II)	–
Yangtze River Delta	28,901	6.0	53.7	40.3	64.8	57.1	85	4th (II)	1
Shanghai	51,474	0.9	48.6	50.5	86.2	89.1	100	5th	1
Jiangsu	24,560	8.0	56.6	35.4	64.0	50.11	78	4th (I)	2
Zhejiang	27,703	6.6	53.4	40.0	53.9	56.02	79	4th (I)	3

Source: Chen Jiagui et al. 2007.

Generally speaking, China entered the second half of the mid-industrialization period in 2005. The industrialization level in the Yangtze River Delta is significantly ahead of the national average and in the primacy of the major economic regions. Shanghai has realized industrialization as an indicator that it is first in the country. In Shanghai, the GDP per capita reaches RMB 51,474, the proportion of the three industries' output value accounted for by the service sector has exceeded the proportion accounted for by the industrial sectors, the urbanization level of population is close to 90%, and the integrated score of Shanghai ranks first in China. The industrialization level in Jiangsu and Zhejiang, at the first half of the late stage of industrialization, lags behind Shanghai, but is ahead of the national average. The output value proportion of the service industry to the output value of the three industries is significantly higher than the national level and the population urbanization rate exceeds 50%.

Figs. 1.1 to 1.4 are a dynamic comparison of GDP per capita, industrialization rate, industrial structure, population urbanization rate, and other indicators of the industrialization of China and the Yangtze River Delta in 1995, 2000 and 2005.

Fig. 1.1. Evolution trends of GDP per capita in the entire country and in the Yangtze River Delta

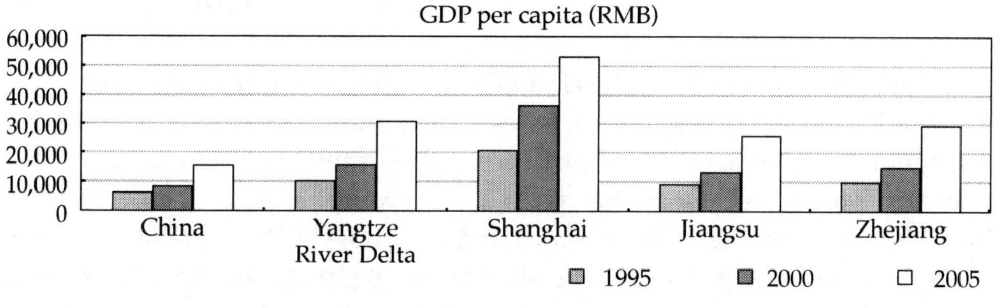

Fig. 1.2. Evolution trends of industrialization level in the entire country and in the Yangtze River Delta

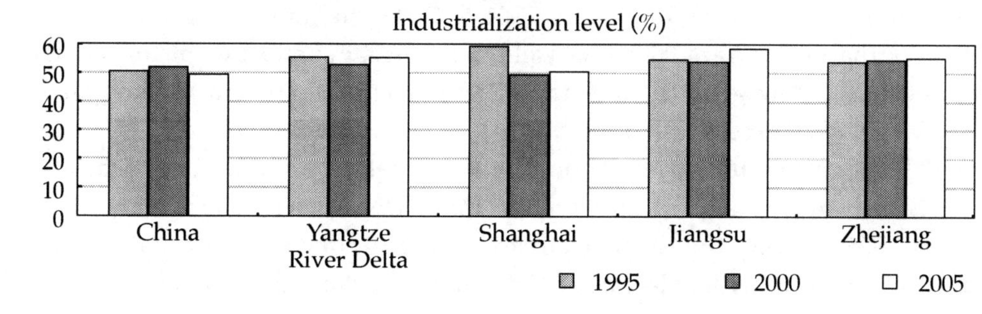

Fig. 1.3. Evolution trends of industrial structure in the entire country and in the Yangtze River Delta

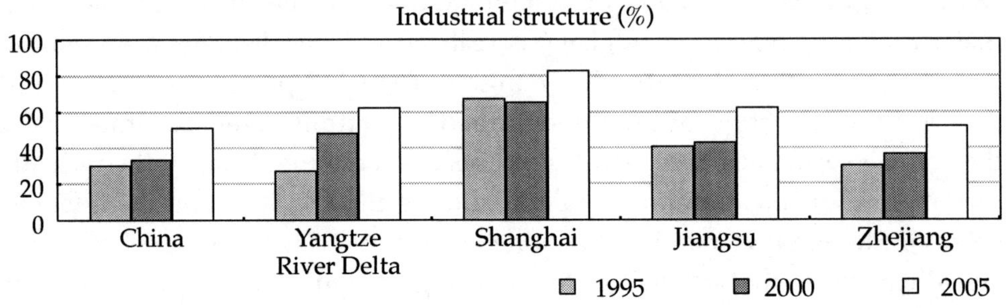

Fig. 1.4. Evolution trends of urbanization level of population in the entire country and in the Yangtze River Delta

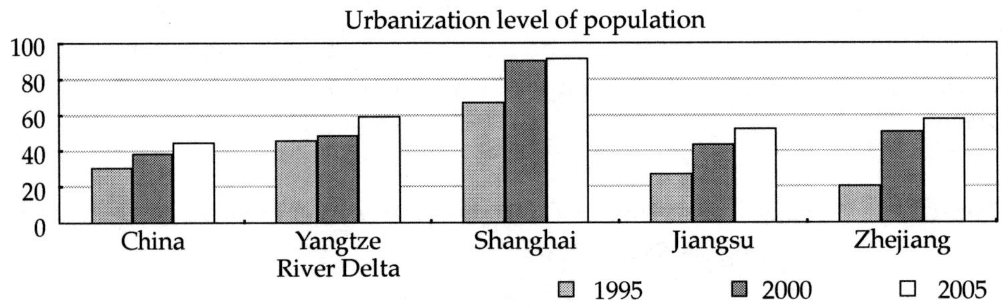

Judging from the absolute level of GDP per capita, the absolute level of the Yangtze River Delta over the years was significantly higher than the national average. Take Shanghai for example. The GDP per capita in 2005 was equivalent to nearly four times the national average. According to the evolution trend of indicators, in 1995 the entire country and the Yangtze River Delta showed a trend of rapid growth, but the overall growth rate of the Yangtze River Delta was higher than the national level. From 1995 to 2000, the national GDP per capita increased by 45.98% on average; the GDP per capita in the Yangtze River Delta increased by 62.35%; and the GDP per capita in Shanghai with the fastest growth increased by 82.37%. From 2001 to 2005, the national growth rate was 98.14%; that in the Yangtze River Delta was 104.49%; and except for Shanghai which had a low growth rate, the GDP per capita growth in Jiangsu and Zhejiang was in excess of 100%.

Change in the industrialization rate was relatively stable. The volatility in the entire country and in the Yangtze River Delta was basically about 10%. From 1995 to 2000, the industrialization rate in Shanghai presented a clear downward trend, with a decline of 17%, mainly because this region had realized industrialization from 1995 to 2000 and the industrial structure was adjusted after entering the post industrial society.

Change in industrial structure can better illustrate the evolution trends of the industrialization process in the entire country and the Yangtze River Delta from 1995 to 2005. Despite insignificant change in industrialization during the sample period, the internal structure of the industry sector had undergone significant changes. The entire country and the Yangtze River Delta had shown significant characteristics of heavy industrialization. This was mainly reflected by a significant improvement in the Cody indicator[1] for the entire country and the Yangtze River Delta from 1995 to 2000. Change in the Yangtze River Delta was particularly prominent. From 1995 to 2000, the Cody indicator for the entire country rose from 30.7% to 33.7%, with an increase of nearly 10%, while that in the Yangtze River Delta soared from 27.2% to 49.6%, with an increase of 82.4%. By 2005, the Cody indicator in the Yangtze River Delta had reached 65%, 52% higher than the national average. That in Shanghai which has the highest indicator had reached 86.2%.

Since 1995 the Yangtze River Delta has showed an obvious trend of rapid urbanization. Before 1995, except in Shanghai, the traditional central city whose population urbanization rate was high, the population urbanization rates in Jiangsu and Zhejiang were both lower than the national average. Especially in Zhejiang, the population urbanization rate in 1995 was only 18.6%, far lower than the national average of 29%. However, since 1995, the population urbanization rates in Jiangsu and Zhejiang have shown a trend of rapid growth. By 2000, the absolute value of population urbanization rate in Jiangsu and Zhejiang was higher than the national average level. From 1995 to 2000, the growth respectively reached 66.67% and 161.83%. In 2005, the population urbanization rate in the Yangtze River Delta exceeded 50%.

2. Development of the service industry

In recent years, while the service industry has achieved certain development both in the entire country and the Yangtze River Delta, the development varies from region to region. In the entire country, the proportion of the GDP accounted for by the added value of the service industry from 1995 to 2005 steadily increased from 30.7% in 1995 to 33.4% in 2000, and further increased to 39.9% in 2005. In terms of the Yangtze River Delta, from 1995 to 2000, the proportion of the GDP accounted for by the added value of the service industry increased significantly from 33.3% to 39.7%, with a growth rate of 19.22%, higher than the national average level. The service industry in Shanghai, Jiangsu and Zhejiang all developed rapidly. But from 2001 to 2005, growth of the service industry in the Yangtze River Delta obviously slowed down as the proportion of the GDP accounted for by the added value of the service industry was only 1.51%. And that in Shanghai and Jiangsu showed negative growth. The growth rate in Zhejiang was also below the national average. Refer to Fig. 1.5.

Fig. 1.5. Evolution trends of proportion of the GDP accounted for by the added value of the service industry in the entire country and in the Yangtze River Delta

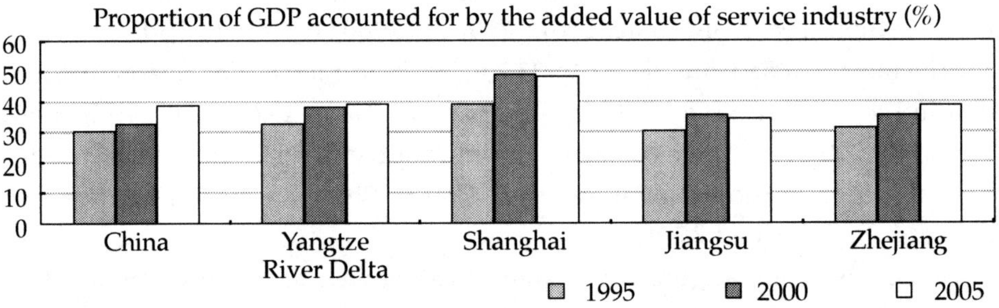

In terms of the proportion of the employed population accounted for by employees in the service industry, both the entire country and the Yangtze River Delta have presented a steady growth. From 1995 to 2005, the growth rates of the proportion of employed population accounted for by employees in the service industry in the entire country and the Yangtze River Delta was never less than 10%. The proportion reached 54.2% in Shanghai while the proportions in Jiangsu and Zhejiang were relatively low, only 2% higher than the national average level. Please refer to Fig. 1.6.

Fig. 1.6. Evolution trends of employed population in the service industry in the entire country and in the Yangtze River Delta

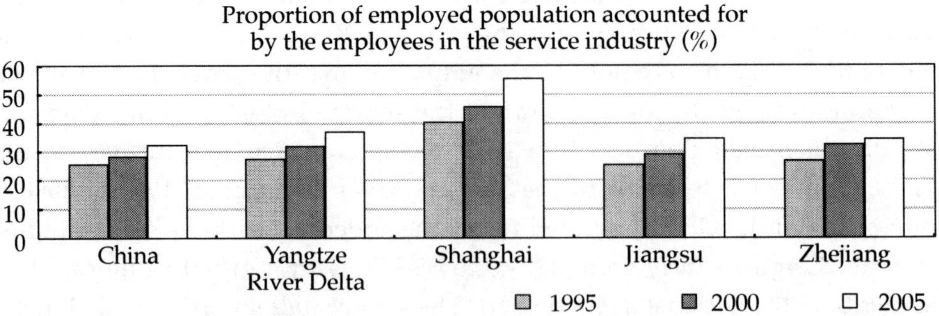

3. The descriptive statistics of main variables

Refer to Table 1.2 for the descriptive statistics of the main variables in the Yangtze River Delta.

Table 1.2. The descriptive statistics of the main variables

Variable		Minimum	Maximum	Mean value	Standard deviation
GDP per capita (10,000 RMB)	Yangtze Delta	0.286 2	2.963 2	1.327 5	0.783 2
	Shanghai	0.713 3	5.934 8	2.941 9	1.626 9
	Jiangsu	0.209 3	2.449 1	1.028 9	0.650 2
	Zhejiang	0.240 9	2.919 9	1.246 4	0.781 5
Industrialization rate (%)	Yangtze Delta	51.31	55.55	53.24	1.47
	Shanghai	48.49	64.27	54.13	4.95
	Jiangsu	43.86	50.99	46.71	2.25
	Zhejiang	48.13	55.59	53.39	1.92
Share of heavy industry (%)	Yangtze Delta	46.52	65.48	54.08	5.54
	Shanghai	50.62	75.58	60.96	7.72
	Jiangsu	47.97	68.70	55.84	6.17
	Zhejiang	38.20	54.01	44.51	4.74
Urbanization rate of population (%)	Shanghai	67.40	84.50	73.30	4.88
	Jiangsu	21.60	50.50	33.90	10.19
	Zhejiang	16.50	56.02	30.80	8.67
Labor productivity of industrial sectors (RMB 10,000/ person)	Yangtze Delta	1.917 7	6.744 5	4.071 6	1.505 5
	Shanghai	1.704 9	13.814 8	7.105 6	3.743 2
	Jiangsu	0.571 2	6.732 5	2.885 1	1.877 7
	Zhejiang	1.849 0	4.542 7	3.138 3	0.791 9

(Con'd)

Variable		Minimum	Maximum	Mean value	Standard deviation
Cost-to-income ratio of the industrial sectors' distribution (%)	Shanghai	80.70	83.73	81.92	0.88
	Jiangsu	83.17	87.81	85.58	1.28
	Zhejiang	82.86	85.99	84.31	0.94
Proportion of GDP accounted for by the service industry (%)	Yangtze Delta	20.84	41.33	35.27	6.57
	Shanghai	37.91	56.84	46.86	5.39 5
	Jiangsu	26.03	37.37	33.16	3.54
	Zhejiang	24.95	40.03	34.06	4.64
Labor productivity of service industry (RMB 10,000/ person)	Yangtze Delta	2.074	5.548 4	3.441 6	1.056 4
	Shanghai	3.497	9.560 0	6.205 6	1.780 2
	Jiangsu	0.591 7	4.207 0	2.195 8	1.079 8
	Zhejiang	1.927 6	5.700 7	3.195 4	1.213 5

Source: Calculated from *China Economics Yearbook*, various years.

The influence of the service industry

1. The influence of the service industry on the level of industrialization

The empirical analysis results of the influence of the service industry on GDP per capita are shown in Fig. 1.3. The Fig. indicates that the proportion of GDP accounted for by the added value of the service industry and the growth of labor productivity play significant roles in promoting the growth of GDP per capita in the Yangtze River Delta. The influence coefficients are all positive. And the determinable coefficients of the regression equation are all above 0.8. Specifically, every 1% increase in the proportion of GDP accounted for by the added value of the service industry is associated with a 2.841% increase in the GDP per capita in the Yangtze River Delta, a 3.786% increase in the GDP per capita in Shanghai, a 6.087% increase in the GDP per capita in Jiangsu, and a 4.901% increase in the GDP per capita in Zhejiang. Every 1% increase in the labor productivity of the service industry can promote the GDP per capita in the Yangtze River Delta, Shanghai, Jiangsu, and Zhejiang to grow by 1.288%, 1.193%, 1.257% and 1.160% respectively.

Table 1.3. Influence of the growth of the service industry on GDP per capita

Variables and regions		C	Coefficient	Adj. R^2
Variable	Region			
Proportions of GDP accounted for by the added service industry	Yangtze Delta	3.109*** (7.991)	2.841*** (7.910)	0.815
	Shanghai	3.978*** (9.777)	3.786*** (7.190)	0.809
	Jiangsu	6.558*** (7.692)	6.087*** (7.959)	0.806
	Zhejiang	5.325*** (9.775)	4.901*** (9.85)	0.873
Labor produstivity of service industry	Yangtze Delta	–1.111*** (-35.7)	1.288*** (50.825)	0.996
	Shanghai	–0.902*** (–6.002)	1.193*** (14.358)	0.954
	Jiangsu	–1.006*** (–50.237)	1.257*** (54.082)	0.995
	Zhejiang	–0.916*** (–15.259)	1.160*** (22.267)	0.980

Note: Figures in parentheses are *P* values of two-tailed test. *, **, *** respectively show statistical significance at 10%, 5% and 1%.

Table 1.4 shows the influence of the growth of the service industry on the industrialization level. Judging from the regression results, the influence of the increase in the proportion of the GDP accounted for by the added value of the service industry and the growth of labor productivity on the industrialization level in the Yangtze River Delta is not really evident. Most of the results of the regression equation fail to pass the statistical tests. Only the influence of the proportion of the GDP accounted for by the added value of the service industry in Shanghai on the industrialization level in Shanghai passes the statistical test, but the influence coefficient is negative, which means that every 1% increase in the proportion of the GDP accounted for can make the industrialization level decrease by 0.47%. The above results show that Shanghai has entered the post-industrial age or service industry industrial age.

Table 1.4. Influence of the growth of the service industry on industrialization level

Variables and regions		C	Coefficient	Adj. R^2
Variable	Region			
Proportions of GDP accounted for by the added value of service industry	Yangtze River Delta	–0.659 *** (–17.895)	–0.026 (–0.777)	–0.029
	Shanghai	–0.998 *** (–10.207)	–0.470 *** (–3.710)	0.515
	Jiangsu	–0.800 *** (–6.236)	–0.034 (–0.296)	–0.065
	Zhejiang	–0.516 *** (–7.099)	0.104 (1.563)	0.093
Labor productivity of service industry	Yangtze River Delta	–0.686 *** (–21.55)	0.042 (1.607)	0.137
	Shanghai	–0.512 *** (–4.681)	–0.083 (–1.372)	0.081
	Jiangsu	–0.774 *** (–42.58)	0.018 (0.851)	–0.019
	Zhejiang	–0.614 *** (–25.643)	–0.0002 (–0.01)	–0.111

Table 1.5 shows the influence of the growth of the service industry on the share of heavy industry. As shown in the figure, the growth of the proportion of the GDP accounted for by the added value of the service industry and the growth of labor productivity in the service industry boost the share of heavy industry in the industrial added value in the Yangtze River Delta. The influence coefficients are all positive. And the determinable coefficients of the regression equation are all large. Specifically, every 1% increase in the proportion of the GDP accounted for by the added value of the service industry is associated with a 0.324% increase in the share of heavy industry in the industrial structure in the Yangtze River Delta, a 0.617% increase in the share of heavy industry in Shanghai, and 0.794% in Jiangsu and 0.606% in Zhejiang. Every 1% increase in the labor productivity of the service industry is associated with a 0.294% increase in the share of heavy industry in industrial structure in the Yangtze River Delta, a 0.365% increase in the share of heavy industry in Shanghai, and 0.178% in Jiangsu and 0.219% in Zhejiang.

Table 1.5. Influence of the growth of the service industry on the share of heavy industry

Variables and regions		C	Coefficient	Adj. R^2
Variable	Region			
Proportions of GDP accounted for by the added value of service industry	Yangtze River Delta	−0.275 ** (−2.923)	0.324 *** (3.734)	0.480
	Shanghai	−0.007 (−0.041)	0.617 ** (2.702)	0.344
	Jiangsu	−0.281 (1.150)	0.794 *** (3.570)	0.456
	Zhejiang	−0.156 (−1.256)	0.606 *** (5.331)	0.662
Labor productivity of service industry	Yangtze River Delta	−0.936 *** (−26.153)	0.294 *** (10.080)	0.910
	Shanghai	−1.118 *** (−10.395)	0.365 *** (6.131)	0.785
	Jiangsu	−0.717 *** (−29.284)	0.178 *** (6.410)	0.741
	Zhejiang	−1.013 *** (−29.554)	0.219 *** (7.374)	0.842

Note: Figures in parentheses are *P* values of two-tailed test. *, **, *** respectively show statistical significance of 10%, 5% and 1%.

Table 1.6 shows the influence of the growth of the service industry on the urbanization level of population. Regression results show that growth of the service industry strongly promotes the urbanization level of population in the Yangtze River Delta. The influence coefficients are all positive. The determinable coefficients of the regression equation are basically above 0.7. Thus the influence of the growth in the service industry on the urbanization level of population in Jiangsu and Zhejiang is stronger than that in Shanghai, probably because of the high urbanization level of population and the low potential for growth in Shanghai. Specifically, a 1% increase in the proportion of the GDP accounted for by the added value of the service industry is associated with a 0.413% increase in the urbanization level of population in Shanghai, a 2.388% increase in Jiangsu and a 1.091% increase in Zhejiang. And a 1% increase in the labor productivity of the service industry is associated with a 0.168% increase in the urbanization level of population in Shanghai, 0.465% in Jiangsu and 0.387% in Zhejiang.

Table 1.6. Influence of the growth of the service industry on the urbanization level of population

Variables and regions		C	Coefficient	Adj. R^2
Variable	Region			
Proportions of GDP accounted for by the added value of service industry	Shanghai	–4.626 *** (71.025)	0.413 *** (4.896)	0.657
	Jiangsu	6.131 *** (16.409)	2.388 ** (7.124)	0.768
	Zhejiang	4.221 *** (29.672)	1.091 *** (8.398)	0.832
Labor productivity of service industry	Shanghai	4.023 *** (93.077)	0.168 *** (7.025)	0.829
	Jiangsu	3.182 *** (70.099)	0.465 *** (8.832)	0.837
	Zhejiang	2.678 *** (72.703)	0.387 *** (12.094)	0.936

Note: Figures in parentheses are *P* values of two-tailed test. *, **, *** respectively show statistical significance of 10%, 5% and 1%.

Generally speaking, the growth of the service industry in the Yangtze River Delta has a significantly positive and active effect on the industrialization process. The increase in the proportion of the GDP accounted for by the added value of the service industry and the increase in the labor productivity of the service industry in the Yangtze River Delta can significantly promote the GDP per capita, the proportion of heavy industry and the urbanization level of the population, but the influence of the above two increases on the industrialization level is not evident. Thus the active effect of the growth of the service industry on the GDP per capita is the most significant, followed by the effect on urbanization level of population and proportion of heavy industry. The empirical results show that the development of the service industry and the enhancement of labor productivity in the service industry in the Yangtze River Delta has had an active effect on the industrialization of the Delta.

2. The influence of the service industry on the production efficiency

Table 1.7 shows the influence of the increase in the service industry on the labor productivity of industrial sectors in the Yangtze River Delta. The empirical results show that the development of the service industry can indeed promote increase in the labor productivity of industrial sectors. A 1% increase in the proportion of the GDP accounted for by the added value of the service industry is associated with a 4.665% increase in the labor productivity of industrial sectors in the Yangtze River Delta, a 5.411% increase in the labor productivity of industrial sectors in Shanghai, a 6.196% increase in the labor productivity of industrial sectors in Jiangsu and a 2.154% increase in the labor productivity of industrial sectors in Zhejiang; a 1% increase in the labor productivity in the service industry could generate 1.262%, 1.941%, 1.274% and 0.653% increases in the labor productivities in the Delta, Shanghai, Jiangsu and Zhejiang respectively. Generally speaking, both the growth of the proportion of the GDP accounted for by the service industry in the Delta and the growth of labor productivity in the service industry have shown significant active and positive effect on the growth of labor productivity in industrial sectors. In the regions in the Delta, the growth of the service industry has a strong promoting effect on the industrial sectors' labor productivities in Shanghai and Jiangsu but a comparatively weak effect on the industrial sectors' labor productivities in Zhejiang.

Table 1.8 shows the influence of the service industry's growth on the labor productivity of industrial sectors. Theoretically speaking, the growth in the service sector could help reduce the cost-to-income ratio of the industrial sectors' distribution, and the two are in negative correlation. However we can observe from the results of the empirical analysis that the growth of the service industry is obviously in positive correlation with the cost-to-income ratio of the industrial sectors' distribution in all regions in the Yangtze River Delta except Shanghai, which shows that the service industry is not explicitly reducing the costs of the industrial sectors and the efficiency of the service sectors needs to be further enhanced. The regression results of the data for Shanghai is not significant, which indicates that the efficiency of the service industry in Shanghai is higher than that in Jiangsu Province and Zhejiang Province.

Table 1.7. The influence of the service industry's growth on the labor productivity of industrial sectors

Variables and regions		C	Coefficient	Adj. R^2
Variable	Region			
Proportions of GDP accounted for by the added value of service industry	Yangtze River Delta	5.818 *** (7.280)	4.665 *** (5.617)	0.753
	Shanghai	5.772 *** (6.157)	5.411 *** (4.499)	0.658
	Jiangsu	7.700 *** (8.979)	6.196 *** (8.054)	0.810
	Zhejiang	3.325 *** (5.639)	2.154 *** (3.765)	0.569
Labor productivity of service industry	Yangtze River Delta	–0.167 * (–2.195)	1.262 *** (20.319)	0.976
	Shanghai	-1.652 *** (–5.421)	1.941 *** (11.526)	0.929
	Jiangsu	0.004 (0.151)	1.274 *** (40.300)	0.911
	Zhejiang	0.393 *** (2.721)	0.653 *** (5.203)	0.723

Note: Figures in parentheses are P values of two-tailed test. *, **, *** respectively show statistical significance of 10%, 5% and 1%.

Table 1.8. The influence of the growth in the service industry on the cost-to-income ratio of the industrial sectors' distribution

Variables and regions		C	Coefficient	Adj. R^2
Variable	Region			
Proportions of GDP accounted for by the added value of service industry	Shanghai	–0.210 *** (–5.794)	–0.014 (–0.295)	–0.113
	Jiangsu	0.038 (0.630)	0.185 ** (3.204)	0.507
	Zhejiang	–0.067 ** (–2.709)	0.099 *** (4.179)	0.647
Labor productivity of service industry	Shanghai	–0.210 *** (–8.607)	0.006 (0.665)	–0.097
	Jiangsu	–0.214 *** (–43.656)	0.062 *** (12.183)	0.942
	Zhejiang	–0.203 *** (–24.241)	0.031 *** (4.004)	0.626

Note: Figures in parentheses are P values of two-tailed test. *, **, *** respectively show statistical significance of 10%, 5% and 1%.

Conclusions and Policy Recommendations

An overview of the relationship between the development of service industry and the industrialization process in the Delta shows that since the 1990s, the growth of service industry has had a significant active effect on the level of GDP per capita and industrialization. The service industry's influence on the industrial sectors is mainly embodied by its active effect on the development of heavy industry, which conforms with the background of the implemented strategies on the development of the heavy industry and chemical industry in China in recent years. The influence of the service sectors on the industrialization is realized mainly in that the service sectors promote the labor productivity of industrial sectors, but we saw little evidence for the hypothesis that the development of service sectors could reduce the transaction costs of industrial sectors, so the efficiency of the service industry still needs to be enhanced. This could be achieved in two ways:

The first is to eliminate monopoly and enhance the operational efficiency of the traditional service sectors. As the infrastructure of economic development, the service sectors, including transportation, telecommunications, commerce, finance and insurance, and public utilities, are likely to become external economies to the development of industrial sectors. The enhancement of these service sectors' efficiencies plays a vital role in reducing the transaction costs of industrial sectors; however, most the above service sectors are still under the inefficient state administrative monopolistic operation; the prices of the services provided are obviously higher than the prices in the international market while the service quality is far from satisfying the demands of the industrial sectors. Therefore in the future we should accelerate reform of monopolistic service sectors and open the service industry more to the market, and promote the reasonable allocation of service resources to enhance the efficiency of the service industry, reduce the division costs of the service industry and further facilitate the growth of the industrial sectors.

The second is to vigorously foster the development of the modern service industry. The modern service industry includes not only the new service forms generated directly due to the development of information industry and informationization, such as computer and software services and information consulting services, but also the service forms evolved and derived from traditional services because of the application of information technology, such as finance and logistics services. The modern service industry, with its high income elasticity of demand, great development potential and few environmental constraints, is an important headspring of sustainable economic growth and a necessity for the conversion of the economic growth model as well as for the remodeling of economic development based on high resource consumption and high environmental pollution. For a long time to come we should energetically promote the development of modern services and transform the industrial growth model from one of extensive growth to one of intensive growth in the Yangtze River Delta, thus making modern intensive services a new source to help to reduce costs, advance technology and enhance the efficiency of the industrial sectors.

2

Chapter

The Economic Growth Driven by the Service Industry: A Review of Economic Growth in the Yangtze River Delta

Service Industry and Economic Growth

As is commonly known technological progress, for its important role in directly promoting economic growth and its indispensability in constantly increasing investment in kind as well as human capital investment, is always considered as the most significant factor to decide and thus the key to accelerate economic growth.

However an in-depth study of the internal part of a country's economy—a detailed analysis of the structural features of the country's economic growth—will show that economic growth is always demonstrated in the total increase and the continuous evolvement of the industrial structure, and the most representative feature of the industrial structural transformation is that with the increase of the GDP per capita, the proportion of the GDP accounted for by service industry is increasing progressively (correspondingly, the proportions accounted for by agricultural and manufacturing industries are constantly declining). For instance, according to statistics released by the Bureau of Economic Analysis of the US Department of Commerce, the service industry's share of the GDP in the US increased from 58% in 1960 to an unexpected 78% in 2006. Table 2.1 shows the changes in the proportion of the GDP accounted for by the service industry in several OECD countries since 1960, from which we can see clearly that during the years between 1960 and 1995, the average proportion of the GDP accounted for by the service industry among the OECD countries increased by 15.6%; and the proportion in Denmark increased by 25.2% during the 35 years, showing the highest growth rate, while the proportion in South Korea increased by 7.5% which was the lowest growth rate.

Table 2.1. Proportion of GDP accounted for by the service industry in OECD countries during the years between 1960 and 1995 (%)

Year	U.S.	Japan	Germany	France	Britain	Denmark	S Korea	Mexico	Spain	OECD
1960	57.9	42.7	41.0	50.4	53.8	46.9	–	–	45.2	52.6
1968	60.6	47.5	47.5	53.9	59.4	63.0	–	–	51.1	55.7
1974	62.9	49.7	51.2	56.6	60.1	66.3	42.6	55.1	52.2	57.5
1985	66.8	55.8	57.7	65.6	62.9	70.9	46.5	57.6	56.8	62.6
1990	69.9	56.3	59.8	67.4	67.8	72.4	47.9	66.8	60.4	65.3
1991	71.1	56.4	60.8	68.2	70.0	73.0	47.3	67.5	61.4	66.2
1992	72.0	57.4	62.4	69.1	70.8	72.6	48.6	68.2	63.7	67.1
1993	72.3	58.7	64.8	70.2	71.3	73.0	49.4	69.5	64.8	68.0
1994	71.9	59.6	65.4	70.9	71.1	72.9	49.9	70.0	65.0	68.1
1995	72.0	60.0	65.8	71.1	66.0	72.1	50.1	69.5	64.7	68.2

Source: Huang Shaojun 2000: 2.

With the increasingly rapid economic globalization, the industrial structures of the major OECD countries have without exception been undergoing a transformation in which the proportion of service industries are continuously expanding. The transformation results from two aspects of demand and supply: on the one hand, with the development of the social economy, the structure of social needs has been changing due to the flourishing demands for service products such as education, culture, laws and entertainment, which drives the social production structure to change; on the other hand, the advancement of modern technologies represented by electronic communications technology and information technology as well as the development of some new areas including cultural and physical industries, laws and regulations, and financial innovations have drastically changed the quality and supply mix of service products, thus accelerating the development of production in the service sectors. Due to the above two accelerators, the proportions of GDP accounted for by service sectors in the economically developed countries have been constantly increasing.

Since the development of the service industry can reduce the costs of production and trade of goods, the major developed countries are all strategically promoting their service industries to enhance the overall level of their economic development and improve the quality of their economic operations. Domestic economists have become progressively aware of the positive influence of a developing service industry on economic growth (Huang, 2000; Zhai, 2002; Liu, 2005), and they have started to consider the increase in the service sectors' share as a new engine to boost economic growth.

China, as an economically underdeveloped country which mainly functions in the middle and low level sectors in the value chain of the global industry division, has a service industry which accounts for a smaller proportion in its

Fig. 2.1. The changes in the shares of the three industries during the years between 1978 and 2005 (%).[2]

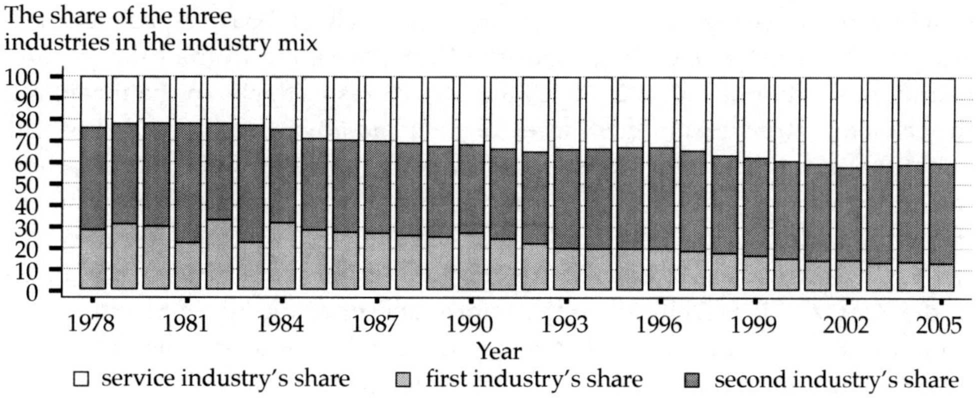

Source: *China Statistical Yearbook 2006.*

industry mix compared to those in the Western countries.[1] Fig. 2.1 shows the change in China's economic structure since the reform and opening up.

The statistics in Fig. 2.1 show that since 1978 when reform and opening up was started, the service industry in China has been developing at a high speed. In the 28 years between 1978 and 2005, the growth rate of the service industry was higher than that of the GDP in 17 different years, and the share of the service industry in the GDP in 2005 had increased by nearly 16% compared to that in 1978. However the proportion of the GDP accounted for by the service industry in 2005 is only 40%, which is far lower than the average level of the OECD countries and is even much lower than low-income countries such as India. According to the statistics of the World Bank, in 2004 the added value of tertiary industry accounted for 52% of the GDP in low-income countries including India, and 56% in middle-income countries.[3] Obviously, the lagging service industry results not only from the international industry division but also from the economic development strategies adopted in China for a long time, and in particular the strategy that treated the development of heavy industry as a top priority during the period of a planned economy directly led to the crippling of service industry at its birth (Lin, 1994; Zhang and Zhang, 2007)[4].

Apart from the two reasons mentioned above, the lagging behind of the service industry in China can be closely linked to the tax system which emphasizes circulating tax, and the distribution system of financial revenue that divides revenue and expenditure between the central and local governments and holds each responsible for balancing their budgets, as these systems strongly motivate local governments to develop the manufacturing industries that will generate more taxes.

The Yangtze River Delta, as the region where the economy has been growing at the highest speed in China since reform and opening up, has maintained its fast economic growth : in 1978, the GDP per capita in Shanghai, Jiangsu Province and Zhejiang Province were RMB 2,497, 430 and 331 respectively; and after the 27 years' economic growth the GDP per capita in the three regions had increased to RMB 67,492, 24,560 and 27,703 respectively. In the meantime, the economic structures in these three regions had advanced considerably with a fast-increasing share of the service industry, and economic development in the regions is transforming from the old model that depended on the industrial sectors to the new model that is driven by both the secondary and tertiary industries. Fig. 2.2 shows the increase in the share of service industry in the Yangtze River Delta since the reform and opening up. In Shanghai, the proportion of the GDP accounted for by the service industry was only 18.6% in 1978, but it increased to 50.5% in 2005, which was equal to that in France in 1960; the proportions accounted for by service industries in Jiangsu Province

Table 2.2. The dynamic change in the economic growth and economic structure in the Yangtze River Delta

	Shanghai			Jiangsu Province			Zhejiang Province		
	GDP per capita (RMB)	Second Industry (%)	Service Industry (%)	GDP per capita (RMB)	Second Industry (%)	Service Industry (%)	GDP per capita (RMB)	Second Industry (%)	Service Industry (%)
1978	2,497	77.4	18.6	430	52.6	19.8	331	43.3	18.7
1985	3,855	69.8	26.0	1,053	52.1	17.9	1,067	46.3	24.8
1990	6,107	64.7	30.9	2,103	48.9	26.0	2,138	45.1	30.0
1995	19,225	56.8	40.8	7,299	52.7	30.9	8,149	52.1	32.4
2000	36,217	46.3	52.1	11,773	51.7	36.3	13,416	53.3	36.4
2003	50,032	47.9	50.9	16,809	54.5	36.6	20,444	52.5	40.1
2004	59,928	48.2	50.8	20,852	56.5	35.0	24,352	53.6	39.4
2005	67,492	48.6	50.5	24,560	56.6	35.4	27,703	53.4	40.0

Sources: *Shanghai Statistical Yearbook 2006*, *Jiangsu Statistical Yearbook 2006*, and *Zhejiang Statistical Yearbook 2006*.

and Zhejiang Province also increased by 15.6% and 21.3% respectively compared to the proportions in 1978.

It is noticeable that in 1978, the service industries' share in Shanghai, Jiangsu and Zhejiang Provinces were similar to each other; however in 2005 the shares in the three regions showed an evident imbalance. Shanghai, as the most economically developed region in China, had witnessed a fast development of service industry and the proportion of the GDP accounted for by the service industry in Shanghai had been around 50% for the last five years while the proportion accounted for by secondary industry had shown a gradual increase instead of a decrease. The proportions accounted for by the service industries in Jiangsu and Zhejiang Provinces, compared to the national average level, was relatively backward and although in 2005 the GDP per capita in these two provinces was nearly double the national average level, the proportions accounted for by the service industries were only 35.4% and 40.0% respectively, which showed that the upgrade of the industrial structure in these two regions fell much behind their economic development levels. If we see the industrial development in the Yangtze River Delta as a reflection of the industry division, the unbalanced development of the economic structure system in the Delta can exactly reflect the comparative superiorities of the three regions in the Delta—different bases of regional developments usually lead to different directions of economic development, thus forming the dissimilar industrial structure features of the three regions.

Certainly, the differences in the industrial structure features in regional economic developments are not unique to the Yangtze River Delta, and they can be exemplified by similar cases in some important economic regions both at home and abroad. Table 2.3 shows the proportions of industry mixes in several major economic regions in the US. As the largest economy in the world, the US has seen great disparities in its regional economic structures. For example, in 1997 the service industry's share in the East-central six states was 12.2% higher than that in the five states in the Great Lakes Area; in 2001, the service industry's share in the East-central Area was 83.6%, which was the highest, and the share in the Southwest Area was the lowest as the average service industry's share in the four states in this area was only 73.5%—the highest was 10.1% higher than the lowest. In 2006 the highest, which was still in the East-central Area, was 15.4% higher than the lowest, which was still in the Southwest Area. We can observe from the GDP per capita in the major regions in the US that the gaps among the economic levels of the regions were not quite evident. For instance, in 2006, the highest regional GDP per capita—which was US$40,952—was found in the West Coast Area, and the lowest—which was US$33,546 was found in the Southeast—which was only US$7,406 less than the highest and the highest was only 22% higher than the lowest.

Table 2.3. The proportions of economic structure accounted for by different regions in the US

	1997			2001			2006		
	First Industry	Second Industry	Service Industry	First Industry	Second Industry	Service Industry	First Industry	Second Industry	Service Industry
US	2.5	21.8	75.7	2.2	20.0	77.8	2.9	19.1	78.0
New England	0.5	20.3	79.2	0.4	18.3	81.3	0.4	16.7	82.9
East-central	0.5	17.0	82.5	0.5	15.9	83.6	0.5	14.4	85.1
Great Lakes	1.3	28.4	70.3	0.9	26.3	72.8	0.9	25.0	74.1
Great Plains	4.0	23.5	72.5	2.5	22.0	75.5	3.1	21.1	75.8
Southeast	2.7	23.8	73.5	2.6	21.6	75.8	2.5	21.0	76.5
Southwest	6.2	22.7	71.1	6.2	20.3	73.5	10.0	20.3	69.7
Rocky Mountains	4.5	18.3	77.2	4.4	16.6	79.0	7.6	16.3	76.1
Far West	2.9	18.1	79.0	2.1	17.1	80.8	2.6	16.5	80.9

Note: First industry includes the agricultural industry and mining industry; the second industry includes public service, the construction industry and manufacturing industry; the service industry includes all the sectors apart from the industries in the first industry and second industry.

Source: The official website of the US Bureau of Economic Analysis (BEA), http://www.bea.gov/regional/gsp/action.cfm

The data in the above table was recalculated by the author using the statistics on the website.

Shanghai, Jiangsu Province and Zhejiang Province in the Yangtze River Delta have arranged their industrial structures in different ways, the influence of which arrangements on the regional economic development has been the focus of much research as the three regions are geographically linked. When discussing how to conduct efficient strategical coordination as well as scientific division to maintain the sustainable development of the Yangtze River Delta in the post-industrialization periods, Liu Zhibiao (2005) pointed out that it was practical for the service industries in different regions in the Delta to seek their particular comparative competitive edges and then exploit to the full their favorable conditions and avoid unfavorable ones: Shanghai should strengthen its function as an economic center and make great efforts to establish its strategic position as a center of the service industry while Jiangsu Province and Zhejiang Province should reinforce their development of modern manufacturing industries in the near future.[5] This concept, which is based on the strategic arrangement of overall regional development, has been well recognized by many scholars and local governmental officials. However, since the current administrative districts are too clearly cut, separation of interests in the real economy must be implemented if the theoretical concept is to be implemented in practice. In other words the local governments, as the managers and spokesmen of the economic interests of the regions, should make the implementation of the strategic concept a voluntary action of the regional governments and we need to study the influence of this kind of division on the overall economic growth of the Yangtze River Delta. But it is regrettable that currently we lack experienced study of the economic structural efficiency in the Yangtze River Delta. In particular, there are few studies concerning the relationship between the service industry and economic growth from the perspective of the interactions among the industries of the three regions in the Delta. This chapter aims to theoretically offer clearer argument of the economic motivation of the service industry's development by studying the interactive relationship between the service industries and manufacturing industries in the three regions in the Yangtze River Delta.

An Analysis of the Service Industry–driven Economic Growth Model

In the modern international division system the inner and inter industries have shown intricate and complicated new division relationships, against which international economic background economists have paid more and more attention to the intermediary function of the service industry's development in economic growth. For example, Zhai (2002) made use of a computable general equilibrium model to evaluate the influence of the service industry's development on the macro-economy in China, and he drew the conclusion that reforms in the regulation of the service industry could greatly enhance economic efficiency. In the ten years from 2000 and 2010 the average growth rate of the GDP would be 0.41% higher than the benchmark, and in all the reforms in the service industry, reform in the financial sectors would have the maximum benefits and could make the real GDP increase to a level about 1.8% higher than the benchmark.[6]

The development of the service industry plays two roles in the driving of economic growth. On the one hand, the service industry itself is an integral part of the domestic GDP, and thus growth in the service industry will surely directly contribute to the GDP; on the other hand, the development of the service industry will reduce the costs of both the production and trade of goods, and from the theoretical perspective of economic growth this "driving" effect is generally realized by promoting the advancement of technology which is the most important factor in the growth of the modern economy, which makes the "driving" effect an indirect one. The active effect of the service industry on the manufacturing sectors is usually more evident in regional economic relations in some manufacturing bases, because the operational efficiency of manufacturing industry is not only subject to the input of material capital and human capital and the improvement of systems in its region but also is promoted by the development level of the producer service industry outside its region. Above all, the producer service industry can bolster the circulation construction of the manufacturing industry and help manufacturing industry enhance its continuity of operation, boost productivity and facilitate large-scale production.

With the adjustments of the global geographical layout of industries, the Yangtze River Delta, as one of the most significant economic centers of manufacturing industries in China, has witnessed dramatic changes in its economic structure. The manufacturing and service sectors have been booming since the reform and opening up. However, development levels of the industrial structures in the three regions in the Delta have been unbalanced with the shares of manufacturing industries in Jiangsu Province and Zhejiang Province being comparatively higher than in Shanghai—in 2005, the secondary industries in the two provinces accounted for 56.6% and 53.4% of their GDPs respectively. In terms of international experience, with the increase of per capita GDP, the proportion accounted for by primary industry would decrease; the proportion accounted for by secondary industry would increase and reach its saturation point at 40–50% and then gradually decrease; and the proportion accounted for by tertiary industry would continuously increase and its share of employment would increase at a rate obviously higher than the growth rate of output value.[7] Chenery and Syrquin divided the transformation of the economic structure into three stages: the primary manufacturing stage, the industrialization stage, and the developed economy stage, and the most essential symbol that marks the transformation into the third stage is that the revenue flexibility of manufactured goods starts to decrease and manufactured goods' share in the total domestic demand also begins to decline at a certain time point and finally the manufacturing industry's share in employment constantly drops.[8] According to the above criterion, the industrial structure in the Yangtze River Delta is undergoing the transformation as even the service industry's share in production in Shanghai—which is the region with the most advanced industrial structure—is not high enough. Fig. 2.2 shows the change in the shares of the secondary industry and service industry in Shanghai since 1978.

Fig. 2.2. Features of the change in the shares of secondary industry and service industry in Shanghai from 1978 to 2005

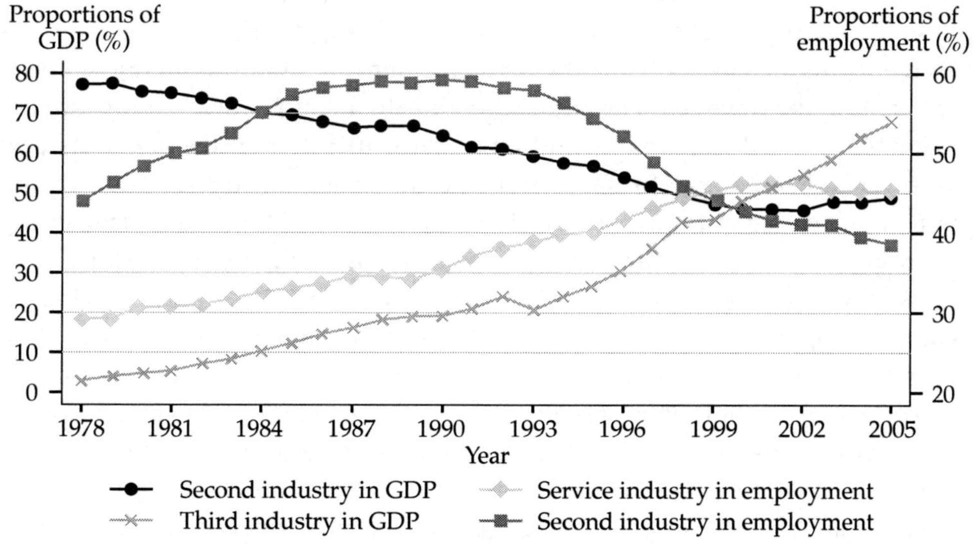

Source: *Comprehensive Statistical Data and Materials on 50 Years of New China* and *China Statistical Yearbook for the relevant years.*

Although since 1978 the proportion accounted for by secondary industry has been declining and the proportion accounted for by the service industry has been increasing in Shanghai, the proportion of secondary industry has never fallen under 46% and the outstanding feature of Shanghai's industrial structure is that secondary industry and service industry have been equally important. The industrial arrangement in Shanghai, observed from the perspective of the overall economic development of the Yangtze River Delta, does not conform with the general theoretical evaluation, as in terms of regional industrial division the three regions in the Delta should implement differentiated industrial development policies and Shanghai should make good use of its central and leading role in the urban cluster of the Yangtze River Delta to promote the fast development of the service industry and especially the modern producer service industry. In other words, Shanghai should be the center for reducing the transaction costs of regional goods and service output in the Yangtze River Delta; and for some time to come, Jiangsu Province and Zhejiang Province should be the regions where the manufacturing costs of goods are reduced. The above strategic arrangement of differentiated industrial development could minimize the "manufacturing costs + transaction costs" in the Delta, thus boosting the global competitive edge of the three regions and attracting more foreign investors into manufacturing.[9]

Although it is important that we emphasize the impetus the service industry gives to economic growth when we consider the positive significance of the promotion of development of the service industry, we cannot ignore the fact that the most important force propelling the development of the service industry comes from the advancement of manufacturing sectors, because it is the development and growth of the manufacturing industry that provides the producer service industry with infinite market demands and space for development. In particular, the detached service function inside the manufacturing enterprises as well as the growth of the newly developing service providers enables the whole producer service industry to develop.

The development of the service industry involves multiple factors including demand, supply and urbanization level, but in this chapter which is focused on the service industry-driven economic growth, we believe that it is necessary to pay special attention to the "servitization" of the economy in the modern post-industrialization society. Unlike the traditional service industry's development which is driven by demand, the service demands in this period are changes of comparative superiority—the changes are always driven by the expansion of the intermediate demands for service which results from technological advancement, the deepening of division and the reform in management style, and the changes take place inside the system of commodity production, are accompanied by the increase in the intermediate consumption of manufactured products and are usually generated by the alteration of different factors' shares.[10] The trend of the modern service industry leads to fast growth in the intermediate demand for manufactured products. And it is exactly the outsourcing[11] by the manufacturing enterprises which aim to cultivate and enhance their core competitiveness that propels the development of many newly developing service industries, and this business process reengineering (BPR) expands the market space for modern logistics, finance and insurance, legal services, accounting services, R&D services and engineering and technological services.

Based on the above analysis, it is natural that in the study of the economic growth in the Yangtze River Delta which is driven by the service industry in the Delta we should never overlook the bidirectional and interactive functioning mechanism, which means that between the development of service industry and the growth of manufacturing industry in the Yangtze River Delta a dynamic evolving relationship should be built up: on the one hand, the development of the manufacturing industry facilitates the demands for the modern service industry; on the other hand, the development of the modern service industry has a positive influence on the increase in the manufacturing industry's efficiency and benefits. In order to deepen our analysis of the progressive relationship between the growth of the service industry and the manufacturing industry, in the following econometric test we will combine panel data analysis with the Granger causality analysis to comprehensively analyze the interactive relation between the development of the service industry and the growth of manufacturing industry in the Yangtze River Delta.

The Empirical Evidence Service Industry and Secondary industry

As the output value of the service industry is an integral part of the GDP in the national income accounting, in our direct discussion of the empirical relation between the service industry and economic growth we cannot avoid the endogenous problems. Therefore the empirical analysis of the service industry-driven economic growth in this chapter is conducted using an alternative approach which is to indirectly deduce the functions of the development of the service industry in economic growth by studying the empirical relationship between the development of the service industry and the growth of the secondary industry in the Yangtze River Delta. Although this indirect research method can generate some deviation, it is a comparatively satisfactory method as it is impossible to find an appropriate instrumental variable (IV). As we have just noted, one of the two functioning ways the development of the service industry drives economic growth is that the development of the service industry would reduce the production and transaction costs of goods. Thus an empirical proof-test of the influence of the service industry's growth rate on the growth rate of secondary industry could provide a clearer picture to enable us to better understand the efficiency of the current inter-provincial industrial structure.

We use the panel data in the three regions in the Yangtze River Delta from 1978 to 2005 to econometrically test the active effect of the service industry's development on the growth of the secondary industry in the Delta. Since we focus on the issue that the economic growth is promoted by the development of the service industry, the dependent variable in the test is the growth rate of the secondary industry and the independent variable is the growth rate of the service industry's output value. As the development of the service industry creates new development space for other industries by reducing transaction costs, it takes some time for this new development opportunity to be recognized and accepted by the market; therefore, in the empirical test, we analyze the growth efficiency of the service industry both in the previous period and the period before the previous one by adding the first-order and second-order lagged variables of the independent variables to the basic analytical model. Additionally in both the booms and the depressions of the business cycle, economic growth could be present as time inertia, which means that the economic growth in the previous period is always an important driver of the economic growth in the current period. Therefore in order to enhance the stability of the analysis, the first-order lagged variable of the secondary industry's growth rate is also taken into the analytical model IV. Table 2.4 shows the results of the analysis.

The analysis results show that in all the four regression models, the service industry's growth rates in the current phase are all conspicuously positive and the regression coefficients are all significant at least on the level of 1%, which means that there is a positive correlation between the development of the service industry and the growth of the secondary industry; a 1% increase in the growth rate of the service industry is associated with a 0.43–0.52% increase in the growth rate of the secondary industry, which demonstrates that the service sectors have a remarkable active effect on the growth of other industrial sectors. This result is generally in accord with the hypothesis about the promoting effect of service industry (Huang, 2000). Also, we are informed by the above

Table 2.4. Analysis results of the active effect of the service industry's development on the secondary industry's growth

Independent Variable	I RE	II FE	III FE	IV RE
C	7.52[a] (2.34)	6.63[a] (2.10)	3.95 (2.62)	2.18 (2.49)
Y_{t-1}				0.34[a] (0.11)
X_t	0.46[a] (0.11)	0.43[a] (0.12)	0.52[a] (0.13)	0.43[a] (0.13)
X_{t-1}		0.09 (0.12)	0.08 (0.12)	–0.03 (0.13)
X_{t-2}			0.10 (0.12)	0.09 (0.12)
R^2	0.62	0.65	0.57	0.92
Hausman X^2	0.85	7.03	25.4	0.96

Notes: 1. In the above table, Y stands for the annual growth rate of the secondary industry, X stands for the annual growth rate of the service industry, and the time subscript t, t–1 and t–2 stand for the current phase, the first lag phase and the second lag phase respectively. The regression dependent variable is the annual growth rate of the second industry Y_{t-1}.

2. The superscript a, b and c represents that the regression coefficients are significant on the levels of 1%, 5% and 10% respectively, and the numbers in parentheses are the standard deviations of the regression coefficients.

3. Whether to adopt the RE or the FE in the panel regression depends on the Hausman test.

4. In the table, R^2 shows the between-column statistic.

Source: Same as Table 2.2.

information that the current acceleration of the service industry's development in the Yangtze River Delta will surely help promote the economic growth in the Delta.

It is worth noticing that the regression coefficients of the lagged growth rate of the service industry turn out to be positive except in the Model IV, and although it cannot pass the common tests of significance level there exists a concurrent change in the development of the service industry and economic growth. If we analyze the inner structures of the service industries of the three regions in the Yangtze River Delta, we will find that currently the added value of the service industries in the three regions are mainly contributed by the transportation and communication/storage/postal sector, wholesale and retail sector, and lodging and catering sector, which service sectors can directly boost market trading efficiency. That is to say, these service sectors will have more remarkably promoted the growth of the second industry in the same period.

The regression results also show that there is an obvious time inertia in the economic growth of the Yangtze River Delta: a 1% increase in the growth rate of the secondary industry in the previous phase is associated with a 0.43% increase in the growth rate of the secondary industry in the current phase, and the regression coefficient is significant on the level of 1%. In terms of the Yangtze River Delta where the economy has been growing rapidly since the reform and opening up, the results accord with the common perception.

Of course, the above analysis of the panel data intrinsically discusses the influence of the service industry's development on the growth of the secondary industry only on the inner-provincial level; however, the geographically linked three regions in the Delta, especially Shanghai which is most economically developed metropolis in China, has a service industry where the development level does not only promote the economic growth of the city but also propels the development of the secondary industries both in Jiangsu Province and Zhejiang Province. In order to observe the promoting effect of the differentiated industrial arrangements in the Delta, Figs. 2.3 and 2.4 illustrate the correlation between the growth rate of the service industry in Shanghai and the growth rates of the secondary industries in Jiangsu Province and Zhejiang Province. From the graphs it is easy for us to see that since the reform and opening up, there basically has been a concurrent change in the growth of the service industry in Shanghai and the growth of the secondary industries in Jiangsu Province and Zhejiang Province. In the sense of theoretical econometrics, this positive correlation could reveal two facts: the first one is that the development of the service industry in Shanghai reduces the transaction costs in both the two provinces thus accelerating the development of the manufacturing industries; the second one is that the continuous increase in the secondary industries in the two provinces creates more demand for the modern service industry in Shanghai thus driving the service sectors in Shanghai to develop fast. To analyze the temporal ensuing correlation between the two, we must make use of the Granger causality analysis. However, theoretically the development of the service industry influences economic growth by reducing the market transaction costs of the industrial sectors, so we will further our analysis of the mutually influential relations between the industrial structural arrangements of Shanghai and the two provinces in the following discussion of the interactive relationship between the modern service sector and the industrial sectors.

Fig. 2.3. Growth rate of the service industry in Shanghai and the growth rate of secondary industry in Jiangsu Province

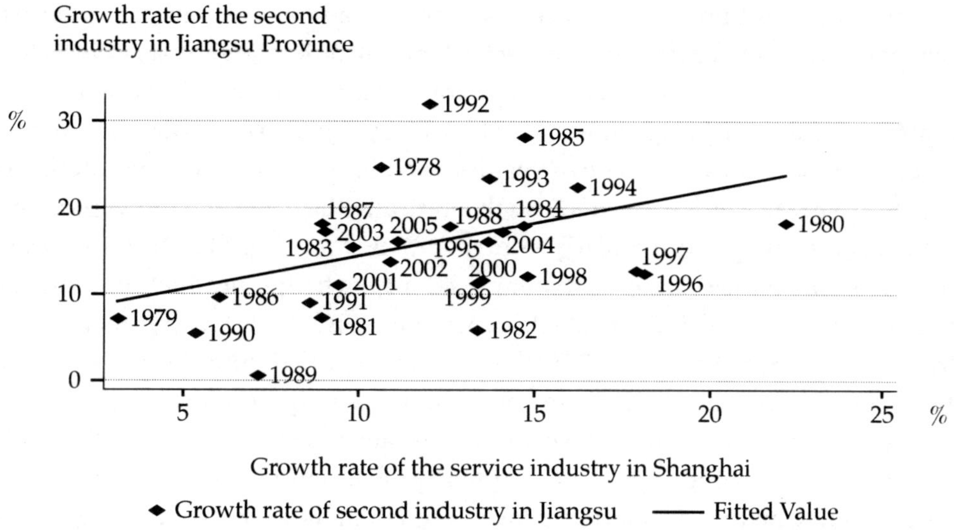

Source: Same as Table 2.2.

Fig. 2.4. Growth rate of the service industry in Shanghai and the growth rate of secondary industry in Zhejiang Province

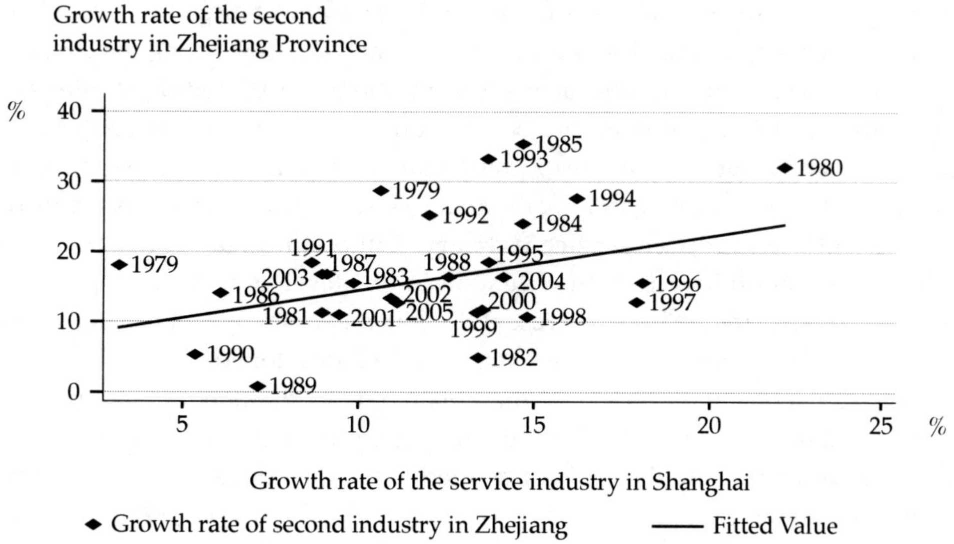

Source: Same as Table 2.2.

Producer service industry and the manufacturing industry

Since the service industry in a pretty comprehensive industry which includes not only the traditional service sectors such as trade and commerce, catering, transportation and communication sectors, but also the modern service sectors such as finance and insurance, real estate, market research, consultancy, planning and designing, agency, technology, law, tax, management and advertising, and all of the above sectors commonly serve the manufacturing sectors to a greater or lesser extent, so theoretically the extension of the producer service industry is academically controversial. Machlup (1962) pointed out that the producer service industry must be a knowledge production industry. And in the "Standard Industrial Classification" (SIC) that was put forward by Browning and Singelman in 1975, the producer service industry is defined as the service to manage enterprises and the knowledge-intensive specialized services such as finance, insurance and real estate services. Marshall (1987) held the view that the producer service industry included the service sectors that are associated with information processing (such as process-handling, R&D, advertising, market research, photography and media etc.), the service sectors that are related to physical commodities (such as sales and storage of goods, waste treatment, and installation, maintenance and repair of equipment etc.) and the service sectors that are linked to individual support (such as welfare services and sanitation etc.),[12] which definition is obvious a comprehensive one.

Undoubtedly, the lack of a consistent definition of "producer service industry" in the theoretical research on producer service brings some problems with the selection of variables in the empirical analysis. Combining the common understandings about the producer service industry in preceding studies and taking the availability of data into consideration, in the following analysis we mainly select the sum of the transportation and communication/storage/postal sector, wholesale and retail sector, and finance and insurance sector as the proxy variables of the producer service industry. Although theoretically the three industries cannot fully reflect the situation in the development of the producer service industry, they can be representative of the Yangtze River Delta where the extroversive manufacturing industries are well developed.

Table 2.5 shows the regression analysis results of the panel data about the active effect of the modern service industry's growth on the industrial sectors in the Yangtze River Delta. It needs to be mentioned that since only the statistics of the finance and insurance sector during the years from 1997 to 2005 are available in related statistical yearbooks, only the growth rates for those eight years are shown in the samples of the analysis. In addition, in *China Statistical*

Yearbooks and the provincial statistical yearbooks only sub-item data about the goods producing industries (the industrial sector and the construction sector), the most direct object of the promoting effect of the modern service industry, are available. Therefore, in our analysis, we have to observe the service industry's active effect on the growth of industrial sectors. According to the current statistical standard adopted by the National Bureau of Statistics of China, the industrial sectors include the mining industry, manufacturing industry, and the production and supply industry of electricity, gas and water.

Table 2.5. Analysis results of the active effect of the producer service industry's development on the industrial sectors' growth

Independent Variable	I	II	III
C	5.98[a] (2.15)	5.50[b] (2.56)	3.28 (2.34)
X_t	0.70[a] (0.12)	0.52[a] (0.16)	0.51[a] (0.14)
X_{t-1}		0.24 (0.16)	–0.16 (0.19)
Y_{t-1}			0.53[a] (0.17)
R^2	0.90	0.84	0.96

Notes: 1. Y stands for the annual growth rate of the manufacturing industry, X stands for the annual growth rate of the producer service industry, the time subscript t and t–1 stand for the current phase and the first lagged phase respectively. The regression dependent variable is the annual growth rate of the manufacturing industry—Y_{t-}.
2. The superscript a, b and c represent that the regression coefficients are significant on the levels of 1%, 5% and 10% respectively, and the numbers in parentheses stand for the standard deviations of the regression coefficients.
3. Since in the Hausman test the null hypotheses cannot be denied, what are applied in the above table are all random-effect regression models.
4. In the figure, R^2 shows the between-column statistic.

Source: *Shanghai Statistical Yearbook 2006*, *Jiangsu Statistical Yearbook 2006*, *Zhejiang Statistical Yearbook 2006* and *Comprehensive Statistical Data and Materials on 50 Years of the New China*.

The regression results of the panel data in Table 2.5 show that in the Yangtze River Delta, the growth of the modern service industry has a significant active effect on the growth of the industrial sectors—a 1% increase in the growth rate of the service industry is associated with a 0.51% increase in the growth rate of industrial sectors. Similarly, our structural analysis also proves that the influence of the growth of the service industry in the previous phase on the growth of industrial sectors in the current phase is ambiguous as in the Model II and Model III, the regression coefficients of the first-order lagged growth rates of the service industry did not pass the general test of significance level.

In the above analysis of total amount and structure, we find that the growth of the service sectors has significant active effect on the growth of other sectors in the same period, but the effect of the lagged variable of the service industry is not clear. The "time lag" of the influence of the service industry's growth on the output of other industries in the Yangtze River Delta is comparatively short, which further proves our hypothesis that in terms of the Yangtze River Delta as a whole, the service sectors in the Delta are still in the basic stage and the sectors' active effect on the enhancement of market transaction efficiency should be further strengthened.

As was emphasized in the earlier part of this chapter, the active effect of the modern service industry's development in the Yangtze River Delta is not only the internal self-promotion of the cities and provinces but it will also develop the mutual promotion between the modern service industry in Shanghai and the manufacturing industry in Jiangsu and Zhejiang as the economic integration in the Delta continues to develop. The typical way to study this interactive relation is certainly the Granger causality test. In the following analysis we will use the Granger test to study the effect of the differentiated division arrangements of the industrial structures in Shanghai and the two provinces.

The Granger causality test that is based on the VAR Model focuses on the explanatory ability of the lag values of independent variables (the annual growth rate of the producer service industry in Shanghai) on the dependent variables (the annual growth rates of the industrial sectors in Jiangsu and Zhejiang). As the analysis samples here are only the data for the years from 1996 to 2005, in order to avoid the loss of degrees of freedom, we only use the first-order lag of each variable in our analysis (Binet, 2003). Table 2.6 is the results of Granger causality test based on the VAR Model.

Table 2.6. Granger causality relationship between the growth of producer service industry in Shanghai (SH) and growth of industrial sectors in Jiangsu (JS) and Zhejiang (ZH)

Null hypothesis	X^2	df	probability
Growth of producer service industry in SH is not the Granger cause of the growth of industrial sectors in JS	0.24	1	0.63
Growth of industrial sectors in JS is not the Granger cause of the growth of producer service industry in SH	1.52	1	0.22
Growth of producer service industry in SH is not the Granger cause of the growth of industrial sectors in ZJ	0.12	1	0.73
Growth of industrial sectors in ZJ is not the Granger cause of the growth of producer service industry in SH	5.36	1	0.02

Note: The period of the sample is from 1996 to 2005. As the degree of freedom is taken into consideration, this Granger causality test is first-order lagged.

Sources: *Shanghai Statistical Yearbook (2000–2006)*, *Jiangsu Statistical Yearbook (2005, 2006)*, *Zhejiang Statistical Yearbook (2006)* and *China Statistical Yearbook* in related years.

According to the Granger causality test results shown in Table 2.6, on the common significance level, there is no causality relationship between Shanghai and Jiangsu; however, the growth of industrial sectors in Zhejiang is the Granger cause of the growth of producer service industry in Shanghai, which shows that in the current industrial structure in the Yangtze River Delta Shanghai does not wholly functioned as the service center of the regional economy and the fast-developing manufacturing industry in Jiangsu and Zhejiang, to some extent, promotes the growth of service sectors in Shanghai. As there are strong correlations among the industries in coastal regions in China (Pan and Li, 2007), the spillover effect of the development of service sectors in Shanghai on the secondary industry in Jiangsu and Zhejiang revealed in the empirical analysis in this chapter is not significant. The conclusion that the growth of industrial sectors in Jiangsu and Zhejiang will promote the development of service sectors in Shanghai is of great importance to the inter-industrial division and coordination inside the Yangtze River Delta, because with the increasing factor costs in the Delta, the development of service sectors plays a vital role in promoting the international competitiveness of the region as a whole. The observation of the history of the relationship between the growth of service sectors and the economic growth in the Delta in this chapter shows that in the current practice of promoting the differentiated development in the

Delta, the key is to strengthen Shanghai's function as a regional economic center and to make great efforts to realize Shanghai's strategic orientation as a service center, during which process we should on the one hand bring Shanghai's comparative advantages into play, and on the other hand we should provide better knowledge and human resources for Jiangsu and Zhejiang to develop their manufacturing sectors and upgrade their industries. In this way we could guide the economic growth in the Delta onto a healthy, stable and positive development path.

Conclusions and Policy Recommendations

There are two main findings in this chapter. Firstly, there exists a positive correlation between the development of the service industry and growth of secondary industry in all regions in the Yangtze River Delta, which shows that the acceleration of the service sectors' development in the Delta will surely promote the economic growth of the Delta; secondly, there is no significant Granger causality relation between the development of the producer service industry in Shanghai and the growth of industrial sectors in Jiangsu, but the growth of industrial sectors in Zhejiang is the Granger cause of the growth of producer service industry in Shanghai.

Although the active effect of the service industry's development on economic growth in the Yangtze River Delta is pretty obvious at present, this positive effect is mainly shown inside the cities and provinces in the Delta and positive inter-city and inter-provincial interactive relations have not yet been formed. In particular, the active effect of the development of the service industry in Shanghai on the growth of manufacturing industry in Jiangsu and Zhejiang needs to be further strengthened. The high-level competition platform of the international economy is gradually shifting to the service industry; meanwhile, the restricting effect of the development level of the service sectors on the manufacturing sectors in a region is getting stronger and stronger. The Yangtze River Delta, with its upgrading manufacturing, in order to maintain its overall international competitive edge and head to the high-end of the industrial value chain, should guide and accelerate the development of its service sectors with related governmental policies. Only when the Delta is structured and polished as an economic zone which enjoys overall competitive advantages and where the service industry and manufacturing industry are in coordinated development can the comprehensive competitive advantages of the Delta in the future international market be maintained. In order to accelerate the development of the service industry in the Delta, we believe it is necessary to resolve problems in two aspects on the macro-policy level.

Firstly, we should facilitate the reform of the tax system and progressively establish a tax system that relies on the income tax. Although there are many reasons why development of the service industry in the Yangtze River Delta lags behind, a tax arrangement that treats the turnover of goods as the major tax base could objectively encourage all regions to develop their manufacturing sectors because in China, where in fact fiscal federalism is practiced, the regional governments are all motivated to encourage the development of manufacturing sectors with more turnover thus restricting the enthusiasm to develop the service sectors. And it is exactly because of the great influence of the tax system on the economic behavior of the regional governments that arousing the regional governments' initiative to develop service sectors and accelerating the improvement of the income tax system in China would have a positive effect on the overall development of the service industry in the Yangtze River Delta. We can observe from the experience of the developed countries that the tax structure is always related to the economic development level. The more economically developed a country is, the higher the proportion of tax earnings are accounted for by income tax. The Yangtze River Delta enjoys a favorable foundation to cultivate sources of income tax, and with the gradual increase in the income tax earnings in the Delta, more financial resources will be funded to the central government to better implement its plan for integrated development of the financial equalization system.

Secondly, the administrative barriers among regions should be broken down without any hesitation. The development of Shanghai as a service center will surely accelerate the development of its economy as a headquarters, during which process it is important to coordinate the fiscal interest relationships involved because the development of the economy in Shanghai will inevitably lead to the transfer of sources of tax from Jiangsu and Zhejiang to Shanghai, which will result in conflicts in the inter-regional fiscal interest relationship in the Delta. From this sense, the industrial division in the Delta does not only concern the strategies of differentiated development in the three regions in the Delta, but also needs the central government to strengthen the inter-regional tax cooperation by improving fiscal and tax systems, and especially to put emphasis on the coordination of distribution of tax interests. In order to break the regional administrative segmentation in the Delta, the adjustment of inter-regional fiscal relations is a problem that we must face and the most economical way at present to solve the problem is to truly practice the interest separation of the real economy on a unified platform. An integration "principle" should be established by the central government, which will help to strengthen the regulatory coordination of the regional governments and effectively solve the inter-regional administrative barriers in the development of modern market service sectors including finance and legal services.

In conclusion, although it is famous for its advanced manufacturing bases, since it is equipped with a strong foundation to develop a modern service industry and encouraged by system innovation, the Shanghai-centered Yangtze River Delta as a whole, which is at the frontier of China's economic development, will surely embrace fast development of a modern service industry. It can be predicted that with the accelerated development of Shanghai as a center of modern service industry, the overall international competitiveness of the Delta will surely be enhanced. Of course, the driving effect between the service industry and the economic growth is not just a macroeconomic issue. It is also associated with the improvement of microeconomic efficiency. Speaking from this sense, we need to study the mechanisms of the development of service industry in the Delta on every micro level, and only when the transaction costs are reduced and resource allocation efficiency is enhanced by developing the service industry can the economic growth of the Delta enjoy a brighter future.

3

Chapter

The Development of the Service Industry and the Enhancement of the Manufacturing Industry's Efficiency

Introduction

Since 2005, economic growth of the Yangtze River Delta showed an overall "drop" for the first time in the last ten years. The statistics for the first half of the year 2005 showed that the growth of the five core economic indicators—total output value, added value of the industrial sectors above the designated size, investment in fixed assets, foreign direct investment (FDI) and credit—all declined, and some even started to fall below the national average level.[1] In 2007, a sample survey of the manufacturing industry in the Yangtze River Delta showed that the enterprises that manufacture final products accounted for over 70%, which means that the economy in the Delta was still lingering at the low-end of the global value chain.[2]

At the enterprise level, the agglomeration of industry structures intensifies the competition among enterprises so that enterprises can only expand their scale of production to reduce costs, which leads to overproduction and price wars and hinders the core competitiveness; at the industrial cluster level, many industrial clusters rely on highly specialized division and the price war has started to reach its nadir. The margins of enterprises are being eroded and the industrial clusters are facing severe crisis, which to some extent leads to the decline of the manufacturing industry; at the globalization level, the manufacturing enterprises in the Yangtze River Delta have shown a tendency toward a "dependent" economy, that is to say that the enterprises are becoming highly dependent on the processing trade, introduction of foreign capital, import of foreign raw materials and equipment, and international big buyers, which dependence results in a weakening of market power and locks the market power at the low-end of the industrial chain for a long time, thus forming a path dependence on the low road. When the Yangtze River Delta focused itself on the specialized production of labor-intensive products, it could not exclude other primary factor-intensive economies (such as India and Vietnam) from the competition. And when the business costs in the Delta increased continuously and the upgrading of industries start to lag behind because of all kinds of reasons, the Delta's efforts to centralize its competitive edge on the original primary factors not achieve a constant increase in export earnings but instead was stuck in the negative situation of "immiserizing growth" (Liu, 2007). Therefore the major problems the Delta is facing now lie in how to help the manufacturing industry rise to the high-end of the global value chain.

In most of the previous research on the upgrade of industries, the analyses were carried out in closed economies. Clark (1935) and Kuznets (1999) expatiated on the upgrade of industries from the perspective of the changes in the industry structures. Their researches show that the evolution of the industry structures follow some general principles. For example, the industry structures must undergo four phases: light industrialization, heavy industrialization, high-processing degree, and knowledge and technology intensification; the factors of production in the industries present the evolvement of "labor-intensive → capital-intensive → knowledge-and technology-intensive" in succession; and the output effects are embodied by the change from low added value to high added value. Generally speaking, the upgrade of industries could be defined as an elevation of enterprises or economies onto a more profitable capital- and technology-intensive economic field, or as a evolutionary process of the industries from low technological levels and low added value to high technological levels and high added value. In accordance with research including that of Kuznets, many domestic scholars equate the upgrade of industries with the upgrading of industry structures. Guo (1996) analyzed the upgrading of the industry structures from the perspectives of the upgrading of production value structures, assets structures, technological structures and labor structures; based on Guo's research, Wang (2004) emphasized that the upgrading of industry structures also included evolution of the industrial organization structures and the deepening of divisions. On the basis of the theoretical explanation of upgrade, Yin (1999), Zhou and Guo (2000) and Wang (2004) made empirical analyses of the upgrade of the manufacturing industry in China at the end of the 20th century and their basic conclusion is that the manufacturing industry in China as a whole is heading towards structural upgrade.

However economic globalization demands that we analyze industrial upgrade from the perspective of the global value chain. In the analytical framework of the global value chain, the production process is only an intermediate link in the chain, and the links of design as well as R&D and brand marketing, which are located at the two ends of the "smiling curve" that shows the added values of all the links in the chain, determine the path of the upgrade of the manufacturing industry. Currently, the manufacturing enterprises in the Yangtze River Delta occupy the production/processing/assembling link which is of comparative low added value, and the design/R&D/marketing link is mainly controlled by the international big buyers. Consequently, the reason why manufacturing industry in the Yangtze River Delta is positioned at the low-end of the value chain lies in the Delta's neglect of the two terminals of the global value chain, which mainly consist of the producer service sectors. Therefore the essential way for the manufacturing industry in the Yangtze River Delta to rise up to the high-end of the global value chain is to develop the modern service industry and especially the advanced producer service industry.

This chapter attempts to analyze the influence of the service industry as a high-level factor input on the rise of the manufacturing industry in the Yangtze River Delta up to the high-end of the global value chain. The layout of this chapter is as follows: the first part is an introduction; the second part expounds the inner mechanisms of the service industry's development as well as the manufacturing industry's upgrade in the Delta; the third part constructs a mathematical model to conduct mathematical deductions on the inner mechanisms of the upgrades of service industry and manufacturing industry; the fourth part makes a descriptive statistic of the intermediate input of the service industry in the Delta on the basis of the input-output table; and the fifth part conducts an empirical test on the basis of the regular statistics on the national economy, which two parts are further demonstrations of the logic analysis and the mathematical model; the sixth part gives conclusions and policy recommendations.

The Service Industry's Development and the Rise of the Manufacturing Industry

Internationally, a conspicuous trend in current economic growth is that the proportion of the GDP accounted for by the service industry is getting higher and higher, and also the service investment and the employers who are engaged in service sectors account for increasing proportions of gross investment and total employers respectively. Many theories attempt to explain this phenomenon from different angles, including the comparatively higher energy consumption elasticity of the final products and the relatively slower productivity growth as well as structural adjustment of the service sectors, which makes the outsourcing service industry more efficient than self-production within enterprises. Multinational research shows that with the increase of the economic development level, both the proportion of gross output accounted for by the service industry and the proportion of total employers accounted for by the employers in the service sectors will continuously increase (Francois and Reinert, 1996; Kongsamut et al., 1997). The increase in the share of the service industry results from two aspects. Firstly, the manufacturing industry keeps outsourcing some nonproductive business, which leads to the increasing share of the service industry; secondly and more importantly, the restructuring of the manufacturing industry increases the demands for intermediate service input in the production process.

Intrinsically, the increasing proportion of the GDP accounted for by the service industry represents the process in which the positive influence of the service industry in the enhancement of the manufacturing industry to the high-end of the global value chain becomes more and more significant, and the process can be embodied by the following two mechanisms.

Mechanism 1: The separation of the production segment and the service segment inside a manufacturing enterprise reduces the set-up cost of the enterprise and helps form the core competitiveness of the enterprise.

The fierce global economic competition forces multinational enterprises to implement industrial strategic arrangements in accordance with the principle of comparative advantage both at home and more importantly, in the whole world. Therefore "outsourcing" has become a main characteristic and an important driver of the flattening of the world in this globalization era. Seen from the analysis framework of the global value chain, the combination of outsourcing and industrial strategic arrangement is shown in the following two aspects:

Firstly, in terms of manufacturing enterprises, they usually focus on manufacturing operations based on core technologies and some service activities such as R&D and marketing, and they outsource their non-core service segments such as legal and financial services to specialized service enterprises, thus gradually separating those service segments from the manufacturing enterprises. The main reason of the above separation lies in the comparatively higher installation costs of the service segments, and the manufacturing enterprises' outsourcing of the service segments in which they are not professionally qualified to specialized service enterprises can shift these fixed costs into variable costs, thus reducing the costs and enhancing the efficiency of the enterprises themselves.

Secondly, some manufacturing enterprises have started to focus on the high-end activities that create value in the industrial chain—they take firm hold of the service businesses that are associated with technological and market activities and take away the manufacturing activities that lack comparative advantages, and in this way can gradually become specialized service providers that are engaged in service added value. The most representative enterprise of this kind is the GE Company in the US. This is an extreme situation of the upgrade of the manufacturing enterprises: the enterprises succeed in transforming from manufacturing enterprises to service enterprises.

Mechanism 2: The socialized specialized division is of help in the formation of the economy and forms the interaction of manufacturing industry and service industry in industrial relevance.

The continual separation of service segments from manufacturing segments enables the service industry as an intermediate factor input to develop constantly and, observed from the perspective of economic operation, the specialized subdivisions of the society make the economy of scale possible. The service industry is in need of a large amount of initial investment, and after the investment the marginal cost will be less; in the service sectors, the economy of scale economy is influential. The costs of the codified and standardized service activities keep decreasing with the expanding scale and this reduces the costs of the intermediate input of the manufacturing industry and to some degree enhances the efficiency of the manufacturing industry. Porter (2002) pointed out that the development of high-end manufacturing industry needs the input of specialized and advanced factors of production, which means that it is in need of a matching high-end producer service industry, and the development of the high-end producer service industry will in turn depend on how much it is needed by the high-end manufacturing industry. Therefore the relationship between the service industry and the manufacturing industry is defined by the level of industrial relevance. As a high-level factor input in the manufacturing industry, technological service of high quality is embedded into the production segment of manufacturing industry and reduces the production costs of the industry through advanced techniques. Furthermore, the "client-supplier" relation between the manufacturing industry and the service industry to some extent reduces the transaction costs of the manufacturing industry. Some scholars including Gu Naihua (2006) worked on empirical analyses on the basis of the panel data and pointed out that the development of producer service industry helps enhance the competitiveness of manufacturing industry, and the more marketized a region is (for example, the regions in the Southern part of China are notably marketized), the more significant the interactive relationship between the producer service industry and the manufacturing industry.

Essentially, the rise of the manufacturing industry to the high-end of the industrial chain is a climbing of the two ends of the chain, and the two ends mainly consist of service sectors. How much the manufacturing industry makes use of the service industry mainly depends on the following aspects. The first one is the pressure faced by manufacturing enterprises to enhance their efficiency, reduce their costs and strengthen their competitive powers, which pressure is determined by the degree of competition at home and abroad; the second one is the availability of the service industry, which is determined by the development degree of the service industry in the process of economic development; the third one is the cheapness of the relative prices when outsourcing to service sectors, which is determined by the production scales of the service enterprises and other factors such as wages for workers.

In the development process of the export-oriented economy in the Yangtze River Delta, the fierce competition between domestic enterprises and foreign enterprises, the foundation of the service industry's development in its region, and the comparatively mature outsourcing experience of the manufacturing industry all enable the service industry to play a more important role in the upgrading process of the manufacturing industry.

The Basic Model

Research on the efficiency of the manufacturing industry in the 1980s was mainly based on the analysis framework of the two factor inputs, in which the added value was used to represent the output and the input was divided into two parts—labor and capital. The key role the service industry plays in the production process was totally ignored. Here we construct a theoretical model to analyze the inner mechanisms of how the service industry enhances the efficiency of the manufacturing industry. We develop the Cobb-Douglas Production Function—we consider the service industry as another input in addition to labor and capital-and we weigh the new input with the input workforce. Taking the model of Ciccone and Hall (1996) for reference, we use the D-S monopolistic competition framework to analyze the service industry. In our analysis, S stands for the combination of all kinds of intermediate inputs:

$$S = \left\{ \int_0^n [x(i)]^{1-1/\sigma} di \right\}^{1/(1-1/\sigma)} \tag{1}$$

Here, σ is the elasticity of substitution among different kinds of services, $\sigma>1$, n stands for the classifications of different services in the production process.

The production function is the Cobb-Douglas Production Function:

$$f(L,S,K)=A(L^{\beta}S^{1-\beta})^{\alpha}K^{1-\alpha} \tag{2}$$

Therefore, there are two functions of the labor input: the first one is manufacture of the final products, and the second one is the intermediate input—the service industry.

In the standard D-S Model, service enterprises in monopolistic competition realize their pricing of marginal cost and they are free to enter the market. The equilibrium profit of the enterprises is zero. Therefore when the market is at equilibrium the mark-up of each service's marginal cost is equal to the reciprocal of the elasticity, and the price of the service industry $p = \frac{mc}{1-1/\sigma}$, in which function "*mc*" stands for the marginal cost of the service industry.

Based on the research results of Ciccone and Hall (1996) we introduce the parameter "a" which reflects the increase in service efficiency that results from technological advancement. We assume that "$ax+v$" units of labor input is needed in the production of "x" units of service (v stands for the fixed cost that in the production of service industry and is weighted by the labor input), and we assume the payment for labor per unit is "w," and $mc=aw$; the profit function of a single service enterprise's maximization of its profit is "$\pi=px-w(ax+v)$", and when the market is in equilibrium, the profit "π" is

$$\pi = px-w(ax+v) = \frac{1}{\sigma-1} wax-wv \tag{3}$$

Let us assume that the enterprises are free to enter the market of the service industry, so $\pi=0$. Therefore,

$$x = \frac{v(\sigma-1)}{a} \tag{4}$$

According to the production function (2), the share of final products distributed to the labor is α, which means that the share distributed to labor that is directly engaged in the manufacturing of final products is $\alpha\beta$, and $wL=\alpha\beta f(L, S, K)$, so the share distributed to all the inputs in addition to labor is $1-\alpha$. In the distribution process, all output except the share distributed to capital is distributed to labor. Let us assume the total labor input in the production process in "N," so $wN=\alpha f(L, S, K)$, thus it can be seen that $L=\beta N$, and the rest "$(1-\beta)N$" labor is engaged in the service activities.

$$n = \frac{(1-\beta)N}{ax+v} \tag{5}$$

If we insert Function (4), we can find that

$$n = \frac{(1-\beta)}{ax}\frac{N}{v} \tag{6}$$

Thus, with the growth of the labor force that is engaged in labor, the more specialized the service industry is the larger the scale is. Assuming that all the service sectors are symmetrical, we can find from Function (1) that

$$S=n^{1/(1-1/\sigma)}x \tag{7}$$

"ax" units of labor is input of each kind of service sectors, and there are totally "n" kinds of service sectors, so the total labor input is "nax." We use the output capacity of the service industry— "R_s" to represent the labor productivity of the industry, so we have

$$R_s=S/nax=n^{(\frac{1}{\sigma-1})}/a \tag{8}$$

Since $\sigma>1$, $\frac{\partial R_s}{\partial n}>0$.

Consequently, we can see that on the one hand, factors such as technological advancement have a direct effect on the service industry by reducing the parameter "*a*," thus enhancing the industry's efficiency; on the other hand, the expansion of market scale[3] resulting from economic integration enhances the output efficiency of the service industry by increasing returns to scale.[4]

In order to observe the influence of the service industry's development on the enhancement of the manufacturing industry's efficiency, we do not directly analyze the influence of the service industry's development on the output of the manufacturing industry but analyze the change in the unit cost of products of manufacturing industry, and a decrease in the unit cost means an increase in the manufacturing industry's efficiency. We assume that the amount of capital needed in the production of a unit of final product is given, and the capital price is exogenously given, so we can exclude changes in the capital cost from our consideration thus simplifying the analysis. As only the inputs of labor and service sectors are considered, the cost of unit production consists of wages of workers—"w," and the input cost of service sectors—"P," so $f(L, S)=L^{\beta}S^{1-\beta}$,

$$\min C(w,P)=wL+PS$$

$$s.t.\ \ f(L,S)=1$$

According to the first-order optimal condition, the cost function is deduced as

$$C(w,P) = \frac{1}{\beta}\left(\frac{1-\beta}{\beta}\right)^{\beta-1} w^{\beta}P^{1-\beta}, \tag{9}$$

Assuming "p_i" as the price of some service sector, and in accordance with the symmetry and former analysis, when it is in equilibrium the price of each kind of service sector is "$p=\mu w$," and the general price index of the service industry is[5]:

$$P(n,p) = (np^{1-\sigma})^{1/(1-\sigma)} = n^{1/(1-\sigma)}p = n^{1/(1-\sigma)}\frac{aw}{1-1/\sigma} \tag{10}$$

Inserting the cost function, we get:

$$C(w,P) = \frac{1}{\beta}\left(\frac{\beta\sigma}{(1-\beta)(\sigma-1)}\right)^{1-\beta} n^{-\left(\frac{1-\beta}{1-\sigma}\right)}w, \tag{11}$$

Solving the partial derivative of "n" in the Function (11), we get:

$$\frac{\partial C(w,P)}{\partial n} = \frac{1-\beta}{n(1-\sigma)}C(w,P) \tag{12}$$

Since $\sigma>1$ *and* $\beta<1$,

$$\frac{\partial C(w,P)}{\partial n}<0 \tag{13}$$

From the above analysis, we can draw the hypothesis of this chapter:

Since the service industry is a high-level factor input into the manufacturing industry, its specialized division and expansion of scale reduce the unit production cost of the manufacturing industry and directly enhance the efficiency and industrial competitiveness of the manufacturing industry.

It follows that the both the specialized division and the expansion of scale of the service industry does not only promote the efficiency of service industry itself but also reduces the production costs of the manufacturing industry as a high-level factor input. The differentiated service products resulting from the specialized division of the service industry to some degree places the industry in monopolistic competition, and thus enhances its pricing competence. However with the indivisibility of the service, generally speaking, the expansion of the service industry's scale brought about by specialized division improves the efficiency of the service industry and finally leads to a decrease in the unit cost of the manufacturing industry.[6]

A Descriptive Statistic

History shows that the most important reason why the developed countries occupy the peak of the global value chain lies in the constant input of technologies, knowledge and human capital which are contained in the modern service industry and enable the industry structure as a whole to adjust towards a "softening." However, statistics show that in 2006, tertiary industry accounted for only 41.1% of the GDP in sixteen cities in the Yangtze River Delta and there was a severe lack of producer service industry. In most regions in the Delta, the local governments focused their upgrades of industry structures on the inner part of the secondary industry, which was a much more serious crisis in the manufacturing industry in the Delta.

Based upon the input-output tables of Shanghai, Jiangsu Province and the whole of China, we can analyze how much the manufacturing industry makes use of the service industry. The input-output table-based analysis could remedy the defects of the regular statistical materials about the national economy, in which calculation is based on the added value, and thus the analysis could reveal the role the service industry as an intermediary plays in the production process of the manufacturing industry. As the input-output tables of statistical departments of different levels were composed at different times—for example, the latest tables for Jiangsu Province and the country as a whole were composed in 2000 while the table for Shanghai was composed in 2002—we base our analysis on the input-output tables made in 2000 about Jiangsu Province and the country in order to maintain the comparability—taking Jiangsu Province as an example, we will compare it with the statistics for China as a whole to observe how much the manufacturing industry makes use of the service industry. Considering the availability of the data, we select the food manufacturing sector, textile/tailoring/leather goods manufacturing sector, coking/gas/ petro processing sector, chemical sector, metal manufacturing sector and mechanical equipment manufacturing sector in the subdivision of manufacturing industry; and we select the transportation/storage/postal and telecommunications sector, commerce and catering sector, finance/insurance sector, social services sector, real estate sector and other sectors in the subdivision of service industry.

Fig. 3.1 shows the input coefficients of intermediate services in each sub-sector in the manufacturing industry both in Jiangsu Province and in China as a whole, which input coefficients are calculated on the basis of the input-output tables. The input of intermediate services in the Yangtze River Delta which is represented by Jiangsu Province is conspicuously higher than the national level. In particular in the food manufacturing sector, coking/gas/petro processing sector and chemical sector, the importance of intermediate services in Jiangsu Province is obviously greater than that in the whole of China. Correspondingly,

Fig. 3.1. The input coefficients of intermediate services in sub-sectors of the manufacturing industry

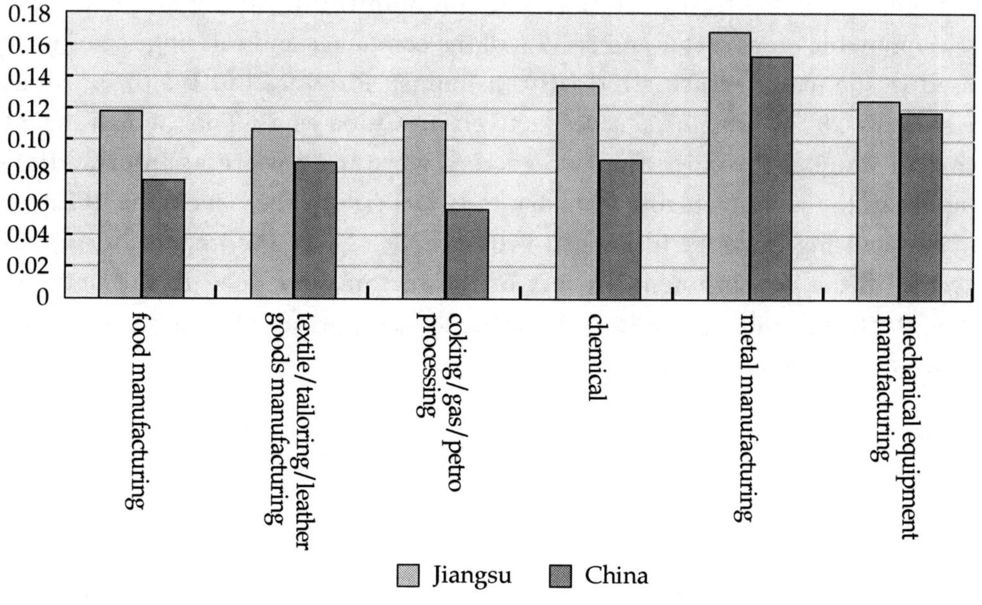

the all-personnel labor productivity in the three sectors in Jiangsu Province is significantly higher than that in other sectors.

Observed from the absolute number, both nationally and in Jiangsu Province, the input coefficients of intermediate services in the chemical sector, metal manufacturing sector and mechanical equipment manufacturing sector are comparatively higher, which means that these sectors are more dependent on the service industry than the traditional food manufacturing sector, textile/ tailoring/leather goods manufacturing sector and coking/gas/petro processing sector. The industry analysis shows that the food manufacturing sector and coking/gas/petro processing sector are comparatively more dependent on raw materials; the food manufacturing sector and textile/ tailoring/leather goods manufacturing sector are both classified as labor-intensive sectors and thus they are comparatively less dependent on the service industry.

Fig. 3.2 shows the proportion of each service sector's gross output that was used in manufacturing industry as intermediate input in 2000. There are four sub-sectors in the graph: transportation/storage/postal and telecommunication sector, commerce and catering sector, finance/insurance sector and service sector (public utilities and local services). From the comparison between Jiangsu and the national situation, what were used in manufacturing industry as intermediate inputs accounted for about 33.06% of the aggregate service sectors in Jiangsu Province while the national proportion was only 19.02%—the Jiangsu level is conspicuously higher than the national level. Fig. 3.2 shows that 44.93% of the transportation and communication/storage/ postal and telecommunications sector and 58.19% of the commerce and catering sector were used in the manufacturing industry in Jiangsu Province but the proportions were only 28.24% and 29.17% respectively in China as a whole, which means that in Jiangsu Province the two sectors were used more as intermediate inputs in the manufacturing industry thus facilitating the development of the manufacturing industry in Jiangsu Province. 28.12% of the finance/insurance sector, in the development process of the sector, were used in the national manufacturing industry, and in Jiangsu, the proportion was 31.3%, showing little gap between the two proportions.

Fig. 3.2. **Proportion of each service sector's gross output that was used in manufacturing industry as intermediate input (2000, %)**

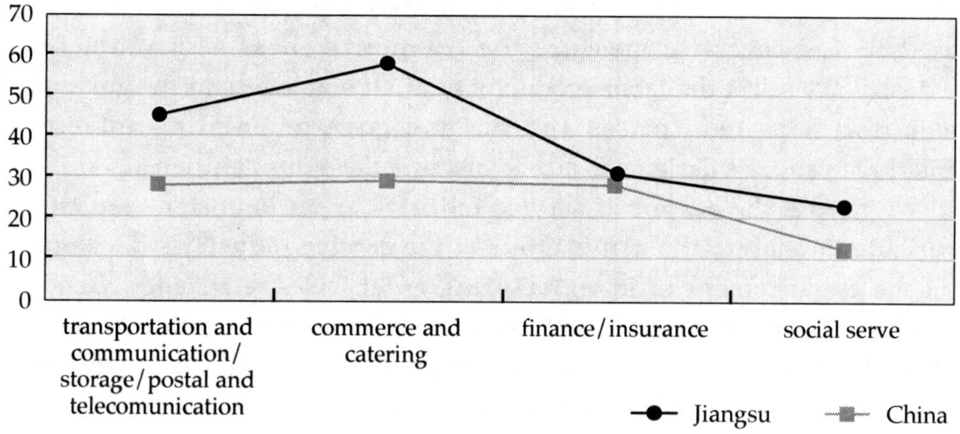

Empirical Test

We have already logically explained the inner mechanisms of the development of service industry and upgrade of manufacturing industry, and we have also worked on an abstract analysis with a mathematical model, but the analysis of the input-output table is only a direct statistical description. In this part, we are about to work on an empirical test with regular statistics on the national economy on the hypothesis drawn from the mathematical models. Considering the availability of the statistics, we mainly analyze whether the service industry as high-level input of the manufacturing industry promotes the enhancement of efficiency of the manufacturing industry in Jiangsu, Shanghai and Zhejiang respectively on the level of sectors. Due to the complexity of economic society, we add some control variables into our empirical analysis to reflect the relationship between the service industry and manufacturing industry in the real economy more objectively.

Indicators, quantitative model and data

There are many differences in the selection of indicators of manufacturing industry's efficiency in various research. The indicators commonly used in foreign research are output capacity (ratio of the added value to output value), efficiency index (ratio of the proportion of national GDP accounted for by an industry to the proportion of national total labor input accounted for by the labor input in the industry), and labor productivity (ratio of the gross output of the industry to the employment volume). However, Chen and Tan (2004) in China selected the industrial profit margin, market share and labor productivity as their indicators to measure the competitiveness of manufacturing industry. We select the labor productivity of all employees in the government manufacturing enterprises and the non-governmental manufacturing enterprises above a designated size to measure the output efficiency.[7]

We choose the output of service industry as an important explanatory variable to analyze the active effect of the service industry's development on the enhancement of manufacturing enterprises' efficiency. Generally speaking, the producer services have a more direct effect on the development of manufacturing industry while the influence of the consumer services on the efficiency of manufacturing industry is indirect. However in the statistics of the real economy, some service sectors (such as the transportation service sector and banking service sector) could be considered as either producer service sectors (serving enterprises) or consumer service sectors (serving citizens and ordinary consumers), but different service sectors have different focuses (Cheng, 2006). In the general analysis, this chapter selects the sum of the outputs of all service sectors listed in the statistical yearbooks. And the quantitative model is as follows:

$$\ln pro_{it}=c_0+c_1\ln Serv_t+c_2\ln Fix_{it}+c_3\ln Comp_{it}+c_4\ln Con_{it}+\varepsilon_{it}$$

In the model, "$\ln pro_{it}$" is the natural logarithm of Sector i on the all-personnel labor productivity of the manufacturing industry in the Year t, and it is the explained variable in the model. The sectors are classified according to the double-digit classification method published by the National Bureau of Statistics, and there are 29 sub-sectors which are numbered from 13 to 42; "$\ln Serv_t$" is the natural logarithm of all sectors in the gross product of service enterprises in Year t, which variable has no subscript "i", denoting that all sub-sectors are influenced; "$\ln Fix_{it}$" is the natural logarithm of Sector i on the annual average balance of the per capita Net Value of Fixed Assets in Year t, which implies the organic composition of capital, and there is a positive correlation between the rise of organic composition of capital and the increase in labor productivity.

In order to analyze the differences in the influences of different sectors of the service industry on the efficiency of manufacturing industry, we will go deeper into the relationship between the sub-sectors of service industry and the efficiency of manufacturing industry. Our model is as follows:

water production and supply sector, gas production and supply sector, and running water production and supply sector—from the industrial sectors of enterprises.

$$\ln pro_{it}=c_0+c_1\ln Tra_t+c_2\ln Sale_t+c_3\ln Fin_t+c_4\ln Est_t+c_5\ln Comp_{it}+c_6\ln Con_{it}+\varepsilon_{it}$$

In the model, "*Tra*", "*Sale*", "*Fin*" and "*Est*" represent transportation, storage and postal communications sector, wholesale and retailing trade sector, catering sector and finance, insurance and real estate sector respectively. The reason why the four sectors are chosen is that we would like to make this analysis consistent with the previous description that is based on the input-output table, so that we can analyze and test some previous conclusions.

In the above two models, we select the following control variables: "$\ln Comp_{it}$" is the natural logarithm of Sector i on the number of enterprises in Year t, reflecting the competition degree in that sector; "$\ln Con_{it}$" is the natural logarithm of Sector i on the proportion of total workers on duty in manufacturing industry accounted for by the workers on duty in the government enterprises and collective enterprises, showing the degree of market liberalization, which is an influence on the level of system.

We select the panel data of the 29 manufacturing sub-sectors in Jiangsu, Shanghai and Zhejiang during the six years from 2000 to 2005.[8] The data come from the *Jiangsu Statistical Yearbooks, Shanghai Statistical Yearbooks, Zhejiang Statistical Yearbooks* and the *China Labor Statistical Yearbooks* of previous years.

Results

Table 3.1 shows the analysis results of the panel data of the 29 manufacturing sub-sectors in Jiangsu, Shanghai and Zhejiang, including the result of the Hausman test. The Hausman test examines whether there are significant differences between the coefficients obtained by the fixed effect method and random effect method and whether the null hypothesis exists. The analysis results show that they all accept null hypothesis, so the random effect model is more suitable.

Table 3.1. Results of the empirical analysis of the factors that influence the efficiency of manufacturing industry in the three regions in the Yangtze River Delta

Explanatory variable	Jiangsu	Shanghai	Zhejiang
c_o	−1.148 (−1.024)	−0.722 *** (−3.394)	3.552 *** (21.385)
Seru	1.793 *** (6.611)	−0.773 *** (11.853)	0.546 *** (12.223)
Fix	0.455 *** (6.161)	0.374 *** (8.360)	0.245 *** (3.672)
Comp	−0.546 *** (−8.221)	−0.456 *** (−10.371)	−0.495 *** (−10.784)
Con	0.122 (1.197)	–	0.107 (1.555)
F Stats	41.482	89.564	59.244
R^2	0.538)	0.772	0.752
n	174	203	168

Notes: The numbers in parentheses are *t* Stats; *** represents significance on the level of 1%; this table is calculated using the econometric software "Eview5.1." The total employment of sub-sectors of manufacturing industry in Shanghai is not available, so it is omitted in the above table.

We can conclude that:

(1) There is a significant positive correlation between the development of service industry and the enhancement of manufacturing industry's efficiency in the Yangtze River Delta. However the service industry's active effects on the manufacturing industry in different regions appears different. According to the statistics, a 1% increase in the output value of service industry is associated with a 1.793% increase in the output of manufacturing industry in Jiangsu, which is significant on the level of 1%; however, a 1% increase in the output value of service industry is associated with only a 0.773% increase in the output of manufacturing industry in Shanghai and 1.546% in Zhejiang. This phenomenon is possibly caused by the function distribution in the Delta. Currently the Delta has shaped a pattern in which Shanghai is the center of service industry and its neighboring Zhejiang and Jiangsu form the periphery of manufacturing industry. As the center of the Delta, Shanghai boasts a service industry that does not just serve Shanghai but also serves its surrounding regions, which results in the comparatively weak effect of the service industry in Shanghai on the manufacturing industry in Shanghai. Seen from another perspective, the active effect of service industry on the development of manufacturing industry in

Jiangsu is especially evident, which effect could have been overestimated partly because Jiangsu is served by the service industry in Shanghai, but we cannot separate this part out in our empirical research.

(2) The per capita annual average balance of net value of fixed assets has significant positive correlation with the enhancement of manufacturing industry in all the three regions. In terms of the coefficients, the highest is in Jiangsu—0.455 and the lowest is in Zhejiang—0.245, and the coefficient in Shanghai is 0.374. The coefficients show that the development of manufacturing industry in Jiangsu is highly dependent on the input of fixed assets while that dependence is weaker in Shanghai and Zhejiang. The per capita annual average balance of net value of fixed assets could also reflect the organic composition of capital, which means that the enhancement of the organic composition of capital could promote the enhancement of labor productivity in manufacturing industry. The upgrading and specialized division of producer services and the increasingly fierce competition set higher demands on technology and knowledge and to some extent advances the innovative competency of the regional enterprises, promotes the continuous progress in technology, leads to the enhancement of capital's organic composition and thus raises labor productivity of the manufacturing industry. Therefore, intrinsically, the constantly enhanced organic composition of capital is a result of the upgrading division of producer services.

(3) The three regions in the Delta are in over-competition because of the evident isomorphism among sectors in the regions combined with the fierce competition among multinational enterprises and lack of an exit system for the enterprises. The results of the empirical analysis shows that when the number of enterprises in the sectors increase by 1%, the efficiencies of sectors decline in various degrees, which are all significant below the level of 1%.

Table 3.2 is an empirical analysis of the influence of the service sub-sectors on the efficiency of manufacturing industry in Jiangsu, Shanghai and Zhejiang, and the results of the Hausman test shows that the random effect model is accepted.

Table 3.2. The influence of the service sub-sectors on the efficiency of manufacturing industry in Jiangsu, Shanghai and Zhejiang

Explanatory variable	Jiangsu	Shanghai	Zhejiang
c	−31.734 *** (−14.030)	−1.296 (−0.930)	−0.850 (−0.160)
Tra	5.288 ** (2.123)	0.184 (0.172)	−1.439 (−1.093)
Sal	0.694 (0.239)	−0.122 (−0.560)	3.501 (0.929)
Fin	22.007 *** (18.630)	0.864 * (1.857)	−0.901 (−0.497)
Est	−14.813 *** (−13.598)	0.354 * (1.740)	0.801 (1.579)
Comp	−0.230 *** (−3.355)	−0.263 *** (−3.467)	−0.397 *** (−8.148)
Con	0.147 * (2.441)	–	0.047 (0.748)
R^2	0.894	0.564	0.662
F Stats	233.702	43.507	52.542
n	174	203	168

Notes: The numbers in parentheses are *t* Stats; *** represents significance on the level of 1%; this table is calculated using the econometric software "Eview5.1." The total employment of sub-sectors of manufacturing industry in Shanghai is not available, so it is omitted in the above table.

The empirical results given in Table 3.2 prove some of the conclusions drawn from the previous analysis of the input-output table.

We find that in Jiangsu, the transportation, storage and postal communications sector promotes the enhancement of manufacturing industry's efficiency: a 1% increase in the output value of the sector is associated with a 5.288% increase in the all-personnel labor productivity in manufacturing industry; however, the influence is not evident in Shanghai and Zhejiang.

The active effect of the finance and insurance sector on the upgrade of manufacturing industry is especially evident in Jiangsu with a coefficient of 22.007 significant on the level of 1%; however, the effect in Shanghai was barely significant as the coefficient was only 0.864. We believe that the finance and insurance sector in Shanghai, which is the financial center of the Yangtze River Delta, has brought its radiation and spillover effect into play instead of only serving Shanghai. We ran a correlation test on the efficiencies of the finance and insurance sector in Shanghai and the manufacturing industry in Jiangsu and found that the correlation coefficient reached 0.95, which proves from another angle the radiation effect of the development of the finance and insurance sector in Shanghai. This conclusion is generally consistent with the conclusion of the previous analysis in the input-output table. There is hardly any correlation between the development of the finance and insurance sector and the upgrade of manufacturing industry in Zhejiang which, we think, is mainly because the manufacturing industry in Zhejiang is focused on privately-run enterprises and their financing channels are always private banks and personal financing which are not included in the official statistics—the incomplete statistics lead to the insignificance in correlation test.

The empirical research on Jiangsu shows that the development of the real estate sector hinders the development of the manufacturing industry. The input-output table for Jiangsu in 2000 shows that only 3.64% of the real estate sector in Jiangsu was used as intermediate input into the manufacturing industry. Therefore the fast development of the real estate sector did not directly or indirectly promote the upgrade of manufacturing industry and it was in fierce rivalry with the manufacturing industry in labor and capital, thus hindering the enhancement and upgrade of the manufacturing industry's efficiency.

Conclusions and Policy Recommendations

The analysis shows that the development of the service industry as a high-level factor input in manufacturing industry enhances the competitiveness of manufacturing industry and promotes the rise of manufacturing industry up to the high-end of the global value chain. The separation of service links from manufacturing links inside manufacturing enterprises reduce the installation costs of the enterprises and will help the enterprises to form their core competitiveness; the socialized and specialized division is helpful to the formation of economy of scale and activates the interaction between manufacturing industry and service industry in the industrial linkage. The analysis of the input-output table and the empirical research on the situation in the Yangtze River Delta from 2000 to 2006 supports the hypothesis deduced by the logical expatiation and mathematical models.

From the perspective of industrial interaction, in the global competition, in order to rise to the high-end of the industrial chain, the manufacturing industry in China represented by the Yangtze River Delta should make great efforts to develop the modern service industry. The development of the service industry, especially the producer service industry in the Yangtze River Delta, is somewhat lagging behind with comparatively small scale and low quality, so it has become an obstacle to the development of manufacturing industry and even to future economic growth. Therefore, at the present stage, we should lay emphasis on the reform of the service industry. The current service industry is mostly occupied by monopolistic sectors that have strict control over entry to the sectors. These sectors include finance, telecommunications, railway transportation, and information. These sectors are either naturally monopolistic or administratively monopolistic, which greatly restricts their competitiveness; meanwhile, the existence of the entrance barriers restrains the employees in these sectors from accounting for a large proportion of the total employment, which reduces the degree of specialized division inside these sectors. Additionally, China's policies on foreign capital at the present stage should no longer focus on attracting FDI with its cheap labor force and land but should put emphasis on the programs and systematic business and commercial services that are of high technology, high output and high added value, and in particular we should bring in the R&D centers and marketing networks of foreign enterprises, offer national treatment to foreign service institutions and provide them with support for the protection of their intellectual property rights. Furthermore, the core of service industry is the input of human capital. Human resources has a high depreciative rate, which is especially evident in the modern producer service industry in which knowledge capital, human capital and technology capital are highly intensive. Therefore further education including professional training seems to be of great importance. In the current fiscal and tax policies in China, the depreciation is only assessed on fixed assets such as equipment and factory buildings but not on intangible assets. One approach for the fiscal and tax system to promote the development of the service industry is to allow the service sectors to depreciate their human capital and charge the depreciation to costs, and allow pre-tax deduction of the depreciation, thus encouraging the service sectors to increase their inputs of human capital (Jiang, Liu & Yu, 2007).

Further research could be done on some points mentioned in this chapter. For example, the study on the relationship of coordinating position and interactive development between the service industry and manufacturing industry would inevitably involve the endogenesis of the relation, which is representative in the analysis on the level of sectors. For instance the transportation, storage and postal communications sector has the most evident influence on the labor-intensive sectors, or we can say that the labor-intensive sectors are greatly dependent on the systematic services of the transportation, storage and postal communications sector. The existence of the endogenesis would make the regression coefficients overestimated, which weakens the stringency of our conclusions. However, to solve the problem of endogenesis, we need comparatively long time series indicators for Granger causality test, but it is difficult to obtain the data for the service industry in China. As a further example, although agreement has been reached on the definition of "service sectors" among the theorists, it is difficult to collect data that are consistent with the definition in empirical analysis. Additionally, as a high-level factor input, the service industry does not only have great influence on the manufacturing industry but also has tremendous effect on the development of the service industry itself and the agricultural industry. The focus of our analysis is the service industry's influence on the manufacturing industry and partly takes the control variables such as organic composition of capitals and competition degrees of sectors into consideration. Research is heading towards the loosening of condition for hypothesis and the analytical framework's embracing of variables such as economic development stage and specialized division.

4

Chapter

The Determining Mechanism of the Yangtze River Delta's Attraction of FDI on the Service Industry

Statement of Problems

FDI can directly facilitate the economic growth of the host country with the spillover of technology and management knowledge and can also activate the export of the host country, thus indirectly promoting the economic growth of the country. The above viewpoint has been commonly recognized by economists such as Markusen (1995), Lui R. De Mello (1999), V. N. Balasubramanyam, M. Salisu and David Sapsford (1996), Ray Barrell and Nigel Pain (1997), Porteria and Lichtenber (2001). And many Chinese scholars, including Sang Xiuguo (2002), Shen Kunrong and Gen Qiang (2001), Xiao Zheng and Shen Yan (2002), Jiang Jingfan (2004) and Zhong Changbiao (2000), have also made detailed analyses of how FDI facilitates economic growth in China. All the research results provide a firm theoretical foundation for developing countries to provide all kinds of preferential policies to attract FDI. However, in this research, the FDI attracted by the host countries was seen as a whole and was not subdivided according to industry. The selection of industries is important in the decision-making of the multinational enterprises concerning FDI. The FDI behavior of both the diversified multinational enterprises which are engaged in many different industries or the simple multinational enterprises which are engaged in a single industry are ultimately direct investment to certain industries in the host countries.

According to the differences among the industries in which FDIs are invested, FDI can be classified as FDI in the manufacturing industry and FDI in the service industry, which is based on the outputs of both the two industries and the differences between the two industries. Firstly, the processes of production, exchange and consumption of services are always closely related to each other and are even simultaneous. However the three processes of the products are always separated from each other. Secondly, the trade in products means the complete transfer of property rights, and the transactional values are the prices of the ownership of the products except when the transaction takes place within an enterprise. But in terms of most services, when they are combined with the material products and then traded, only a part of paid prices represent the transfer of the property rights and the rights transferred are incomplete. For example, when we purchase a cinema ticket to enjoy a movie, the entertainment service brought by the movie is combined with the material equipment in the cinema, and the production of the entertainment service and the consumption are concurrent; a part of the ticket price could be considered as the payment for the temporary transfer of the ownership of the equipment in the cinema such as the chairs, and the rest of the price could be seen as the payment for the entertainment service.

Certainly, the difference between service and product is not absolute. For instance, in transactions to purchase access to products or to obtain the product service (such as car leases), the difference between the service and product is even more ambiguous as the two are closely linked—the paid price includes not only the prices of the services but also the prices of the access to the product. Also, in a certain sense, to purchase a product is to obtain the service brought by the product, and only a few products or services are "pure." Many kinds of services are input in the production process of the products, and the production process of services also relies on many material assets. Furthermore, many products and services are supplied to the customers at the same time.

With the progress of global economic integration, FDI has become one of the major channels for the services to flow across borders and to be changed from non-trade goods into tradable goods, so the increasing proportion of FDI accounted for by the service industry has become an important trend in world economic growth. In 2004, the *World Investment Report* issued by the UNCTAD took "The Shift Towards Services" as its subhead and pointed out that in the world, FDI is shifting towards the service industry and that the share of the service industry in total FDI stock increased from 25% in the 1970s to 60% in 2002, and the FDI in service industry was about US$6 trillion in 2002. Kang and Su (2006) further noted that the flows of FDI in services are increasingly globalized and that the share of FDI attracted by developing countries in total FDI has been continuously increasing.

Against this background, we can observe that the active effect of FDI in service industry and FDI in manufacturing industry on the economic growth of the host countries have shown different characteristics. FDI in the service industry can bring more technological spillover and management knowledge spillover to the host country. For example, FDI in finance can bring advanced foreign risk management techniques. FDI in services are always high tech- and human capital-intensive FDI—such as the R&D centers of multinational enterprises, which raises the demand for high quality of personnel. Meanwhile, FDI in services, especially in the producer service industry, as a must-input high-level factor in the production process, is of high added value, so its employers are always better paid.

So how can developing countries attract FDI in services? What are the factors that decide the FDI in services in host countries? If we can answer these questions well we can help China grasp the core factor in the equalization of policies on foreign investment and then guide the adjustment of foreign investment policies in a more focused way. In the meantime, the developed regions along the east coast of China are the major regions attracting FDI into services, among which regions the Yangtze River Delta is the most important one. In 2005, the contracted FDI in services and the actual FDI in services in Shanghai, Jiangsu Province and Zhejiang Province accounted for 36.78% and 44.72% respectively of the total FDI in China.[1] Therefore the study in this chapter is focused on the Yangtze River Delta and analyzes the key factors in the Delta which attract FDI into services in order to inspire other regions in China. The author believes that the foundation of the services in a country is the core factor determining the inflow of FDI into services. Only when the service industry in a developing country develops to a certain level that meets the requirements of multinational enterprises will FDI flow into the services of the country. Also the market scale, foundation of the manufacturing industry and FDI in the manufacturing industry are factors which influence the attraction of FDI to services.

Literature Review

In foreign economics there is abundant research on FDI in the manufacturing industry. For example, Markusen (1995) gave a detailed overview of FDI theories from the perspective of multinational enterprises. However the foreign research on FDI in services is much less than that on FDI in the manufacturing industry. There is a sharp contrast between the lagging behind of the theoretical research and the trend in global economic development. Of course there are some exceptions. For instance, in the process of its long-term research on multinational enterprises and FDI phenomena, the UNCTC shifted its research focus to multinational enterprises in services and FDI in services in 1989 and published its research results in the following years. Markusen, Rutherford and Tarr (1999) studied the economic effect of FDI in services on the skilled labor force market. Buch (2000) used the regression quantitative approach to study FDI behavior of the banking sector in Germany. Dunning (1989) believed that the OLI paradigm could explain the motive of multinational enterprises in services to directly invest abroad, that is to say, that ownership advantage, internal advantage and location advantage could explain the FDI behavior of multinational enterprises in services. But Raff and Ruhr (2001) thought that producer services are the input into the downstream manufacturing industry, and FDI in the producer service industry appears to follow the manufacturing industry, which leads to the agglomeration of the producer service industry and manufacturing industry. This mainly results from the inadequacy of information between the sellers and buyers of the producer services as well as the moral hazard. The above views accord with the research results of Fujita, Krugman and Venebles (1999).

Researches on FDI in China can be traced back to Zhang and Liu's research (1996). Zhang and Liu summarized and evaluated the policy measures a country could adopt on FDI in services, which measures include market access and national treatment and the measures either encourage or restrict FDI in services to flow into a country. Zhang and Liu also pointed out the issues China should pay attention to in their treatment of FDI in services.

The recent research on FDI in services has focused on the economic effect. In one aspect it is believed that based on the common sense that FDI drives economic growth, FDI in services will promote the economy to grow; in the other aspect it is believed that FDI in services has economic effects apart from that it can drive economic growth.

Research on the first aspect mainly consist of quantitative analyses. Zhuang and He (2005) proved that there is a long-term integration relationship between FDI in services and economic growth in China: the former is the unilateral Granger cause of the latter. Zhuang and He also made use of the trade gravity model to study the three ways of that FDI in services facilitates economic growth in China—via the technology effect, the trade effect and the employment effect. Some scholars have studied the influence of the attraction of FDI in services in particular regions on the economic growth in those regions from the perspective of the regional economy. Zha and Wu (2006) used the statistics of Jiangsu Province in the years between 1998 and 2003 to test the active effect of FDI in different sectors of the service industry on the GDP of the province; He (2005) used the time series to analyze the relationship between economic growth and FDI in services in Guangdong Province; Wu (2007) used the time series data to study the positive effect of FDI in services in the Yangtze River Delta on the economic growth of the Delta and found that FDI in services is the Granger cause of economic growth in the Delta.

Research on the second aspect mainly analyzes the influence of FDI in services in employment, technology and exports of the host country. Xue and Han (2006) found that FDI in services has little effect on employment but significantly facilitates the employment quality in China as it enhances the labor productivity, promotes the development of human capital and optimizes the employment structure. Kang and Su (2006) analyzed the economic effects of FDI in services in its host country, including employment effect and technology spillover effect, and pointed out that FDI in services will influence the balance of payments, service sectors and export competitiveness of the host country. Zhao and Song (2006) overviewed the current situation of the investments of multinational service enterprises in China and analyzed several economic effects of the investments, such as improving the internal structure of the service industry in China and the creation of new jobs directly or indirectly in China. Zhang and Tang (2007) studied FDI in services and in manufacturing industry separately and did comparative research of the two, and they found that the inflow of FDI in the manufacturing industry will increase the total employment volume in the host country and the employment volume in manufacturing sectors in the country while FDI in services will only increase the employment volume in service sectors but reduce the total employment volume in the country.

Additionally, some Chinese scholars have started to study the governing factors of FDI in services in China. Wang and Zhu (2007) studied the factors that decide the location of FDI in service industry in China and found that the openness of the market and concentration effect of FDI in services are the most influential factors in FDI in services in China while market scale, market potential and the cost of labor are not significantly influential. Wang (2006) found that in the finance, retail and transportation sectors, the factor that decided China's attraction of FDI is the degree of concentration of governmental enterprises and the market concentration of the service industry. Li (2004) overviewed the favorable factors for China's attraction of FDI, including the huge market potential and the low threshold to enter the service industry in China, and he also pointed out the restricting factors, such as the backward foundation of the service industry, the lagging behind of urbanization and the lack of human resources.

The above research was generally concerned with the causes, determining factors and economic influence of FDI in services. The author believes that, generally speaking, FDI in services as a part of the total FDI has been the subject of much research at home and abroad, the conclusions of which are partly applicable to FDI in services. However, on the one hand, since FDI in services is becoming increasingly important in real economy, and on the other hand, FDI in services is different from FDI in other industries (such as FDI in the manufacturing industry), so we should study FDI in services separately. The center of study on FDI in the service industry basically includes two aspects: the first one is the analysis of all its economic effects; the second one is analysis of the determining factors of its global distribution, namely, the factors in a host country that determine the inflow of FDI to the service industry. The author believes that of these two aspects, the latter one should be discussed first. Without the relevant supporting conditions, FDI in the service industry would not flow into a country, and then the discussion on the economic effects would be meaningless. Therefore the issues discussed in this chapter emphasize particularly the determining factors of FDI in the service industry, which means that we need to find out the improvement of what factors could help developing countries attract more FDI in the service industry.

Although there has already been some research on the superior topic of this chapter, most of it is based on qualitative analysis which is not thorough enough and which lacks statistical support. Even though some few studies are grounded on quantitative analysis, there are some problems in their selection of quantitative approaches as spurious regression can occur if the time series data are directly used in multiple regression. Moreover most of the current research discusses the determining factors of FDI in the service industry from the perspective of countries, but there are great discrepancies between eastern, central and western China, and the developed cities in eastern China are the major regions in China which attract FDI into the service industry. The Yangtze River Delta is a giant in attracting FDI into the service industry. Consequently, study on the determining factors of the flow of FDI into the service industry in the eastern developed part of China is of practical meaning to the economic growth of China. However so far these kind of studies are rare, so the significance of this chapter lies in that, firstly, it adopts the time series quantitative approach to study the determining factors of FDI in the service industry and finds out that the foundation of the local service industry is the most important factor in deciding the region's attraction for FDI in the service industry; and secondly, as we take the Yangtze River Delta as the subject to study the determining factors of FDI in the service industry, we can review the experience of the Delta and offer better guidance to other regions.

The Econometric Model and Data Processing

According to the differences among consumers of services, the service industry can be subdivided as consumer service industry and producer service industry; correspondingly, we can divide FDI in the service industry as FDI in consumer services and FDI in producer services.

Quantitative model

The quantitative analysis in this chapter is divided into two parts. The first part analyzes whether the foundation of the service industry in the Yangtze River Delta determines FDI in the service industry, in which the time series quantitative analysis is done on three different levels. Firstly, as the time series are not stationary for most of the time, if we regress several columns of time series data directly, "spurious regression" could occur and then our results would be erroneous. Therefore we must test the staticness of the time series first. The ADF Test (Augmented Dicker-Fuller Test) and PP Test (Phillips-Perron Test) will be used.[2] Secondly, when several columns of time series become integrated series of the same order after the stationary test, we use the E-G Two-Step Method for the cointegration analysis.[3] Thirdly, in order to further prove that the foundation of the service industry is a determinant of the inflow of FDI into the service industry, we will do a Granger causality test. The idea is to find out to what extent the current variable "y" can explain the past variable "x," that is to say, we will observe that whether the adding of the lag value of "x" could give a better explanation than the sole use of the lag value of "y" does. If "x" is helpful in the prediction of "y," or the correlation coefficient between "x" and "y" is statistically significant, we can say that "y is Granger caused by x" or "x is the Granger cause of y."[4]

Since in statistics in China foreign investment is always divided between contracted investment and realized investment, so we will test stationaries of the contracted FDI as well as the real FDI in the service industry and the fundamental variable of the local service industry, and conduct integrated analysis as well as the Granger causality test on the three.

In the second part, the major determining factors of the inflow of FDI into the service industry will be analyzed completely, which analysis will be done in two aspects. The first aspect is to use the current approaches to assess the international direct investment environment for reference. As with multinational manufacturing enterprises, multinational service enterprises must carry through a detailed assessment of the environment in the host country in their decision-making and the factors assessed can be considered as the determining factors of the inflow of FDI into the service industry. Currently, in international direct investments, there are many approaches to assessing the environment of the host countries, including the level scoring method created by Robert B. Stobaugh, Ming's assessment method and the Mitsubishi assessment method, which cover many factors of the investment environment of the host countries but emphasize different aspects, and even though some factors are covered by all the methods the significance of a factor in each different method differs quite considerably. Therefore it is impractical to cover all the factors in our quantitative analysis, so we need to find the core economic variables that represent the factors and take the variables as the major factors to decide the inflow of FDI into the service industry.

Generally speaking, the environmental factors include material factors and non-material factors: the former includes transportation, telecommunications and other infrastructures, and the latter includes macroeconomics, public service system, institutional environment and industrial situations. The GDP indicator is classified as a macroeconomic factor and the higher the GDP is, the better the infrastructure and public service system is, so the GDP should be one of the most important factors to determine the inflow of FDI, which theory is also suitable for FDI in the service industry. The industrial situation is also an important factor in the environmental analysis, and the analysis of the service industry can include two aspects: demand and supply. The demand in the service industry refers to the market demand situation faced by the industry. It is necessary for the service industry, especially the consumer service industry, to attach importance to market demand. We can use the target population to effectively reflect the market demand situation: the larger the population is, the stronger service demand is, so the population will determine the inflow of FDI into the service industry. The supply in the service industry, which includes many aspects such as the competition situation of the current production scale and the manufacturers in the industry, can be reflected by the current industrial foundation, namely, the gross output of the industry. The gross output of the industry directly weights the current production scale of the industry. If there is a direct competitive relation between the FDI in service industry and the domestic service industry, the more higher the gross output of the industry is the fiercer the competition faced by FDI after its entrance will be and the more restricted the future development space of the industry will be, which will make it difficult for the profits of FDI after its entrance to be maintained. However, if there is a huge discrepancy between the levels of the local service industry and the foreign service industry, especially when the discrepancy is demonstrated in the technology level and managerial competency of many producer service sectors, it will be hard for the local service industry to establish a competitive relationship with the advanced foreign service industry, and thus regional service sectors mainly assist the multinational enterprises' business operations. At this moment, the bigger the gross output of the local service industry is, the easier the inflow of FDI into the service industry is. Considering the current situation of the service industry in China, the author is inclined to believe that the local service industry will help the inflow of FDI into the service industry. Thus the foundation of the local service industry is one of the determinants of the inflow of FDI into the service industry.

The institutional environment of the service industry is difficult to quantify and it is usually measured by subjective acceptance criteria. In China, the institutional environments of different regions differ little from each other and they have little influence on the flow of FDI into the service industry, so they can be neglected.

The second aspect concerns the special determining factors of the inflow of FDI into the service industry. FDI in the service industry, as a integral part of FDI in all industries, enjoys a particularity which is mainly embodied in the fact that the interactive relationship between the producer service industry and the manufacturing industry could influence the FDI in the service industry. Firstly, the output of the producer service industry is one of the inputs into the manufacturing industry, so the former is the upstream industry of the latter. For example, the management and consultancy, accounting and audit, and investment banking in the producer service industry are all high-level production factors needed in the manufacturing industry. As China is gradually becoming a global production center, the development of the manufacturing industry in China needs to input a large amount of these high-level production factors. In the meantime, in order to find new markets, foreign multinational service enterprises have strong motives to enter the Chinese market. Influenced by the above conditions, the output of the regional manufacturing industry should be another important determinant of the inflow of FDI into the service industry. What is more, Raff and Ruhr (2001) found that FDI behavior in the producer service industry appears to follow the manufacturing industry, the cause of which is that as asymmetry of information exists in the market transactions of the producer service industry, the service providers always take advantage of the manufacturers' inadequate knowledge of the service industry to give false publicity of the quality of their service industry thus bringing about moral hazard. Therefore the manufacturers usually only purchase services from the providers they are familiar with, and FDI in manufacturing will not purchase services from the local service-providers but ask the service providers they are familiar with to provide services by entering the host countries in the form of FDI. This means that FDI in manufacturing also determines the inflow of FDI in the service industry.

In the previous analysis, we found that the GDP is influential on the inflow of FDI in the service industry, but it is worth noting that the output of the service industry and the manufacturing industry constitute the major part of the GDP. Therefore, multicollinearity will show when the two outputs are both taken as independent variables. In view of the above, this chapter only takes the output of the local service industry and the output of manufacturing industry as independent variables, and substitutes the combined effects of the two variables for the GDP's determinant effect on the inflow of FDI in the service industry.

This chapter will carry out OLS regression of the panel data, and take the real FDI (*rsfdi*) as the dependent variable and the service industry's added value (*sgdp*), the GDP of the local manufacturing industry (*mgdp*), FDI in manufacturing (*mfdi*) and the local population (*pop*) as the independent variables to establish the regression equation, which is shown as follows:

$$\ln(rsfdi_i)=c+a_1\ln(sgdp_i)+a_2\ln(mgdp_i)+a_3\ln(mfdi_i)+a_4\ln(pop_i)+\varepsilon_i \quad (1)$$

ε_i is the random perturbation item. In order to eliminate the heteroscedaticity, all the variables take the forms of natural logarithms. The subscript "*i*" refers to different regions. Here, we use the local service industry's added value "*sgdp*" to stand for the foundation of the service industry's development and we predict that its coefficient will be positive; we select the GDP of the local manufacturing industry (*mgdp*) as the indicator to evaluate the foundation of the local manufacturing industry, and we predict that its coefficient will be positive; we predict that the coefficient of FDI in manufacturing will be positive; and we predict that the coefficient of the population variable (*pop*) will be positive.

Sources and processing of data

Scholars, with their difference research purposes, always give different definitions of the "service industry," but generally they agree that the scope of the third industry is approximately equal to that of the service industry. Considering the availability of data, we equate tertiary industry with the service industry.

In the first part—the time series quantitative analysis—the data comes from the statistical yearbooks and the reports of Shanghai (SH), Jiangsu (JS)and Zhejiang (ZJ) in related years. We select the actual FDI in the service industry (*rsfdi*), contracted FDI in the service industry (*csfdi*), service sectors' added value (*sgdp*) of the three regions, in which the spans of time of the data for Shanghai, Jiangsu and Zhejiang are 1999–2006, 1999–2005 and 1997–2005 respectively. All the data has undergone natural logarithm transformation.

Thus, from 1999 to 2004, the amount of the contracted FDI in the service industry in JS is calculated by adding together the data of different sectors in the "new foreign direct investments classified according to sector (old)" in the *Jiangsu Statistical Yearbooks*. And the actual FDI in service industry in the province in the same period is obtained with the same method. The contracted FDI in the service industry in Jiangsu in 2005 is obtained by adding together the data of 13 sectors in the "new foreign direct investments classified according to sector."

The data for the service industry in Zhejiang could not be obtained directly, so they were substituted with indirect and calculated data. The data for real and contracted FDI of service industry in Zhejiang from 1997 to 2002 are substituted by the products of tertiary industry's share in the total output value in Zhejiang and the real and contracted FDI in Zhejiang, which products are higher than the actual real and contracted FDI in the service industry in corresponding years. The data for FDI in the service industry in Zhejiang are substituted by the products of tertiary industry's share in the "above norm investments of foreign economies in different sectors and capital sources" (in the *Zhejiang Statistical Yearbook*) in corresponding years and the contracted and real FDI in Zhejiang. The data of FDI in the service industry in Zhejiang in 2005 and 2006 come from the *2006 Statistical Bulletin of National Economy and Social Development in Zhejiang Province.*

In the second part—the cross-section analysis of data—the data for the service industry's added value (*sgdp*) and the GDP of the local manufacturing industry (*mgdp*), FDI in manufacturing (*mfdi*) and the local population (*pop*) mostly come from the *Yangtze River Delta & Pearl River Delta and Hong Kong & Macao SAR Statistical Yearbook 2005*, and some of the data come from *Shanghai Statistical Yearbook*. The FDI in the service industry is obtained by adding up the data of nine sections. The dependent variable "*sfdi*" is the real FDI in the service industry in the cities in the Delta. In this part, we take 16 cities in the Delta as our research subjects.[5]

Econometric Results and Analysis

The co-integration analysis of the time series and Granger causality test

1. Stationarity test

The results of the stationarity test of the logarithms of the real FDI in the service industry in Shanghai (SH), Jiangsu (JS) Province and Zhejiang (ZJ) Province—"ln(*rsfdi*)," the logarithms of the contracted FDI in the service industry in Shanghai, Jiangsu Province and Zhejiang Province—"ln(*csfdi*)" and the logarithms of the service industries' added values in the three regions are shown in Table 4.1.

Table 4.1. Stationarity test of the data of the Yangtze River Delta

Region	Variables	ADF Value	ADF CriticalValue	Lag Period	PP Value	PP Critical Value	Stationary Series or Not
SH	ln(*rsfdi*)	–0.69	–2.89 ***	1	–0.39	–2.84 ***	No
	ln(*csfdi*)	0.28	–2.84 ***	0	1.48	–2.84 ***	No
	ln(*sgdp*)	–0.04	–2.84 ***	0	0.65	–2.84 ***	No
	Δln(*rsfdi*)	–5.42	–5.12 *	0	–9.69	–5.12 *	Yes
	Δln(*csfdi*)	–11.1	–5.6 *	1	–7.67	–5.12 *	Yes
	Δln(*sgdp*)	–6.71	–5.34 **	1	–2.97	–2.89 ***	Yes
JS	ln(*rsfdi*)	–1.66	–2.98 ***	1	–0.44	–2.89 ***	No
	ln(*csfdi*)	–0.13	–2.89 ***	0	0.45	–2.89 ***	No
	ln(*sgdp*)	3.59	–2.89 ***	0	4.46	–2.89 ***	No
	Δln(*rsfdi*)	–40.6	–6.42 *	1	–1.71	–1.59 ***	Yes
	Δln(*csfdi*)	–3.89	–3.69 **	0	–5.21	–5.6 *	Yes
	Δln(*sgdp*)	7.89	–3.12 ***	1	4.22	–2.98 ***	No
ZJ	ln(*rsfdi*)	–2.67	–3.59 ***	1	–3.78	–3.52 ***	No
	ln(*csfdi*)	–1.02	–2.77 ***	0	–1.37	–2.77 ***	No
	ln(*sgdp*)	2.06	–2.77 ***	0	2.06	–2.77 ***	No
	Δln(*rsfdi*)	–3.21	–2.8 ***	0	–5.44	–4.58 *	Yes
	Δln(*csfdi*)	–3.51	–3.4 ***	1	–3.49	–3.32 **	Yes
	Δln(*sgdp*)	–2.37	–2.8 ***	0	–3.09	–2.8 ***	Yes
	Δ^2ln(*sgdp*)	–3.22	–2.84	0			Yes

Notes: 1. * stands for the significance on the level of 1%, ** for the significance on 5%, and *** for the significance on 10%.
2. The selection standard of the ADF lag period is SIC Standard, and the model with intercept is adopted.
3. Δ stands for the first-order difference, and Δ2 for the second-order difference.

We can see from Table 4.1 that the logarithm of contracted FDI in the service industry in Shanghai—"ln(*csfdi*)," the logarithm of real FDI in the service industry in Shanghai—"ln(*csfdi*)" and the logarithm of the added value in the service industry—"ln(*sgdp*)" are all I(1) processes under both the ADF method and PP method. The logarithm of contracted FDI in the service industry in Jiangsu—"ln(*csfdi*)" and the logarithm of real FDI in the service industry in Jiangsu —"ln(*csfdi*)"are I(1) processes under both the ADF method and PP method but the logarithm of the added value in the service industry in Jiangsu—"ln(*sgdp*)"—is not a I(1) process. The series is a I(2) process only under the PP method that uses the model with intercept and trend variable. The logarithm of the added value of the service industry in Zhejiang is a I(2) process under the ADF method but a I(1) process in the PP method. The logarithm of contracted FDI in service industry in Zhejiang—"ln(csfdi)"—and the logarithm of real FDI in the service industry in Zhejiang—"ln(csfdi)"—are I(1) processes under both the ADF method and the PP method

2. Co-integration analysis

According to the results in Table 4.1, we can see that the three variables of Shanghai are all first-order integrated processes and meet the requirements of co-integration analysis; both the Zhejiang ln(*rsfdi*) and ln(*csfdi*) are I(1) processes and ln(*sgdp*) is a I(1) process under the PP method, which basically meet the requirements of co-integration analysis. However, as the Jiangsu ln(*sgdp*) is not in the same order as the two other variables the three variables of Jiangsu cannot be co-integrated, that is to say, there is no long-term equilibrium relationship. Therefore only the data of Shanghai and Zhejiang are used in the co-integration analysis with the E-G Two-Step Method.

In the first step, we use the ln(*rsfdi*) and ln(*csfdi*) of Shanghai and Zhejiang as dependent variables and the ln(*sgdp*) as the independent variable, and then we use the OLS regression so we have four regression equations. Then we use the dependent variables to differentiate the equations and get the residual series "$\hat{\mu}_t$." The results are shown in theTable 4.2. Table 4.2 suggests that the coefficients of the added value of service industries in Shanghai and Zhejiang are both significantly not equal to zero, and both have a positive effect on the two dependent variables—real FDI in the service industry and contracted FDI in the service industry, and the fitness degree of the regression is relatively high.

In the second step, the residual series "$\hat{\mu}_t$" of the four regression equations are put into stationarity test. The ADF method is adopted here without considering intercept and trend variable, and the results are shown in Table 4.3.

Table 4.2. The OLS regression results of Shanghai's and Zhejiang's ln(*rsfdi*), ln(*csfdi*) and ln(*sgdp*)

Region	Dependent variable	Intercept variable coefficient	ln(*sgdp*) coefficient	Adj. R^2
Shanghai	ln(*rsfdi*)	–7.06 (–3.51) **	1.27 (5.07) *	0.78
	ln(*csfdi*)	–0.88 (–4.47) *	1.79 (5.99) *	0.83
Zhejiang	ln(*rsfdi*)	–5.59 (–6.29) *	0,97 (8,72) *	0.89
	ln(*csfdi*)	–9.95 (–7.11) *	1.59 (9.08) *	0.9

Note: The number in the parentheses are *t* stats, * stands for significant level of 1%, ** stands for significant level of 5%, and *** stands for significant level of 10%.

Table 4.3. Stationarity test of residual series "$\hat{\mu}_t$"

Region	Dependent variable	Residual series ADF value	ADF critical value	Lag period	Residual: Stationary or not
Shanghai	ln(*rsfdi*)	–2.91	–2.93 *	0	Yes
	ln(*csfdi*)	–5.48	–3.01 *	1	Yes
Zhejiang	ln(*rsfdi*)	–2.98	–2.89 *	1	Yes
	ln(*csfdi*)	–2.35	–1.99 **	0	Yes

Note: * stands for significant level of 1%, ** stands for significant level of 5%, and *** stands for significant level of 10%.

Table 4.3 tells us that the residuals of all the four regression equations are I (0) processes, which proves that there exist co-integration relationships between the ln(*rsfdi*) and ln(*sgdp*) and between the ln(*csfdi*) and ln(*sgdp*) in Shanghai and Zhejiang. The long-term equilibrium relationship is shown in Table 4.2. From the long term perspective, a 1% increase in the service industry is associated with a 1.79% increase in contracted FDI and a 1.27% increase in real FDI in Shanghai; and a 1% increase in service industry is associated with a 1.59% increase in contracted FDI and a 0.97% increase in real FDI in Zhejiang, which shows that the development foundation of service industries in Shanghai and Zhejiang could positively promote the FDI in service industry to flow into the two regions in the long term.

3. Granger causality test

In order to further illustrate the relationship between the FDI in service industry and the foundation of the service industries in the three regions in the Delta, here the Granger causality test is adopted to analyze whether Granger causality relations exist between ln(*rsfdi*) and ln(*sgdp*) as well as between ln(*csfdi*) and ln(*sgdp*) in Shanghai, Jiangsu and Zhejiang. If the relationship really exists, it can be further proved that the foundation of the service industry in a region in the Delta is a determinant factor of the FDI in service industry flowing into the region. Results of the test are shown in Table 4.4.

Table 4.4. Granger causality test of FDI in service industry and foundations of service industries in the Yangtze River Delta

Region	Null hypothesis	Order of lag	F Stat.	Probability
SH	ln(*rsfdi*) is not ln(*sgdp*)'s Granger cause	1	2.94	0.16
	ln(*sgdp*) is not ln(*rsfdi*)'s Granger cause	1	3.34	0.14
	ln(*csfdi*) is not ln(*sgdp*)'s Granger cause	1	0.67	0.46
	ln(*sgdp*) is not ln(*csfdi*)'s Granger cause	1	24.3	0.008
JS	ln(*rsfdi*) is not ln(*sgdp*)'s Granger cause	1	0.02	0.89
	ln(*sgdp*) is not ln(*rsfdi*)'s Granger cause	1	4.67	0.12
	ln(*csfdi*) is not ln(*sgdp*)'s Granger cause	1	0.32	0.62
	ln(*sgdp*) is not ln(*csfdi*)'s Granger cause	1	5.85	0.09
ZJ	ln(*rsfdi*) is not ln(*sgdp*)'s Granger cause	1	0.17	0.69
	ln(*sgdp*) is not ln(*rsfdi*)'s Granger cause	1	6.29	0.05
	ln(*csfdi*) is not ln(*sgdp*)'s Granger cause	1	1.54	0.26
	ln(*sgdp*) is not ln(*csfdi*)'s Granger cause	1	2.19	0.19

Table 4.4 indicates that on the significance level of 1%, the natural logarithm of added value of the service industry in Shanghai—ln(*sgdp*) —is the Granger cause of the natural logarithm of contracted FDI in the service industry—ln(*csfdi*), but the converse is inaccurate. On the significance level of 10%, the natural logarithm of added value of the service industry in Jiangsu—ln(*sgdp*) —is the Granger cause of the natural logarithm of contracted FDI in the service industry—ln(*csfdi*), but the converse is inaccurate. There are no Granger causality relations between the natural logarithms of added values of service industries—ln(*sgdp*)—and the natural logarithms of real FDIs in the service industry in Shanghai and Jiangsu, and in particular there is no co-integration between FDI in service industry and the foundation of service industry in Jiangsu. This is, however, not an obstacle to the fact that the foundation of service industry is the Granger cause of contracted FDI in the service industry in Jiangsu. On the significance level of 5%, the natural logarithm of added value of service industry—ln(*sgdp*)—is the Granger cause of the natural logarithm of real FDI in the service industry—ln(*rsfdi*)—in Zhejiang, but the converse is not accurate. There is no Granger causality relation between the natural logarithm of added value of service industry—ln(*sgdp*)—and the logarithm of the contracted FDI in the service industry—ln(*csfdi*)—in Zhejiang, which further proves that in the three regions in the Delta, the foundations of local service industries have determinant influences on the inflow of FDI into the service industry.

Analysis of Cross-section Data

The above analysis of time series has fully proved the determinant influence of the development level of local service industry on the inflow of FDI into service industry. However, besides this determinant factor, are there any other determinant factors in the inflow of FDI into service industry? Will the determinant influence of the development level of local service industry on the inflow of FDI in the service industry change after we take other factors into consideration? All these questions will be answered by the analysis of cross-section data. We use the equation (1) as the basic model of our cross-section data and then build and test eight models. The results are shown in Table 4.5.

The former four models in Table 4.5 indicate that there exists a positive correlation between the inflow of FDI into the service industry and the four variables—the foundation of service industry in the region, foundation of manufacturing industry in the region, FDI in manufacturing, and the local market scale.

Table 4.5. Analysis of cross-section data model of real FDI in the service industry in the Yangtze River Delta

Independent variable	Model One	Model Two	Model Three	Model Four	Model Five	Model Six	Model Seven	Model Eight
ln(*sgdp*)	1.71 (6.92) *				1.91 (1.98) ***	1.45 (3.02) **	2.17 (2.04) ***	2.49 (2.30) **
ln(*mgdp*)		1.58 (5.6) *			−2.18 (−1.83)		−0.45 (−0.45)	−1.37 (−1.07)
ln(*rsfdi*)			1.02 (4.69) *		0.54 (1.54)	0.19 (0.65)		0.46 (1.15)
ln(*pop*)				2.59 (7.15) *	2.05 (1.95) ***			
Adj. R^2	0.79	0.72	0.68	0.81	0.84	0.78	0.78	0.78
D.W.	2.26	2.07	2.32	2.34	2.38	2.25	2.23	2.11

Note: * stands for significant level of 1%, ** stands for significant level of 5%, and *** stands for significant level of 10%.

A 1% increase in each of the four variables will lead to a 1.71% increase, a 1.58% increase, a 1.02% increase and a 2.59% increase in inflow of FDI into the service industry respectively. So the conclusion of the four models is consistent with our hypothesis—the inflow of FDI into the service industry is positively promoted by four major factors including the foundation of the local service industry.

As the former four models in Table 4.5 are all simple regression models with certain limitations, the models need to be extended and multiple regression models are used to analyze the four factors' integrated effect on the inflow of FDI into the service industry. Model Five in the figure is a direct test of Equation (1) and uses the four variables in analysis of inflow of FDI. In Model Five, the coefficients of two variables—foundation of local service industry and market scale are not equal to zero on the significance level of 10%, and 1% increases in the two variables could generate a 1.91% increase and a 2.05% increase respectively in FDI in the service industry flowing into the Yangtze River Delta. Model Six takes the foundation of service industry and FDI in manufacturing industry as independent variables and it is found that the coefficient of the former independent variable is not zero on the significance level of 5%, and a 1% improvement in foundation of service industry could bring a 1.45% increase in the inflow of FDI into the service industry in the Delta. Model Seven takes the foundation of service industry and foundation of manufacturing industry as independent variables and it is found that only the coefficient of the former of the two variables is not zero on the significance level of 10%, and a 1% improvement in foundation of service industry could bring a 2.17% increase in inflow of FDI. Model Eight takes the foundation of service industry, foundation of manufacturing industry and FDI in manufacturing industry as independent variables and the results also show that only the coefficient of the foundation of service industry is not zero on the significance level of 5%, and a 1% improvement in foundation of service industry could bring a 2.49% increase in inflow of FDI.

The conclusions reached in Model Five to Model Eight tell us that the variable—foundation of the service industry in the Delta—pass the significance tests of 5% or 10%, and the improvement of service industry's foundation could positively promote the inflow of FDI into the service industry with a elasticity coefficient between 1.45 and 2.49. Compared to the foundation of the service industry, the expected effect of the other variables on the inflow of FDI is not significant, and only the market scale shows a positive effect in the Model Four. That is to say, a 1% increase in the local population is associated with a 2.59% increase in the FDI in service industry. The influences of other variables on the inflow of FDI are not evident, which is inconsistent with our theoretical hypothesis. The inconsistency can be understood from two aspects:

The first aspect is that the inconsistency explains the particularity of multinational enterprises' investment decisions when the enterprises enter the Chinese market. Multinational enterprises in the service industry attach most importance to the foundation of the local service industry, and then the market scale, but they do not take much consideration of the foundation of manufacturing industry or the inflow of FDI into manufacturing industry. Of course, the explanation in this aspect is not convincing enough.

The second aspect is that the limitation of data leads to inconsistency. The multinational enterprises in the service industry could be divided into multinational enterprises in the consumer service industry and multinational enterprises in the producer service industry, and the foundation of local manufacturing industry and the inflow of FDI in manufacturing would not significantly influence the investment decisions of the multinational enterprises in consumer services while the enterprises in producer service industry are sensitive to the two variables. In reality, the selected data on the total volume of inflow of FDI in service industry was not subdivided into FDI in consumer service industry and FDI in producer service industry, so it is hard to understand our analysis conclusion that the foundation of the local manufacturing industry and FDI in manufacturing do not have significant effect on the total volume of FDI in the service industry. It needs to be further pointed out that although some of the statistics for the sub-sectors are collectable, since some of the service sectors are both consumer service sectors and producer service sectors it is difficult to accurately distinguish the two kinds of service industry from each other.

In these circumstances, if we review the history of the gradual opening up to the outside world of the service industry in China, we can find that it was the multinational enterprises in consumer services that entered China first and the multinational enterprises in producer services, due to the limitations on their industrial investments, entered the Chinese market much later. Of course this problem has been gradually solved after China's entrance into the WTO. To take the statistics used in this chapter about the FDI flowing into the Yangtze River in 2004 for an example, the wholesale and retailing sector, real estate sector and social services sector accounted for comparatively high proportions of the total volume of FDI in the service industry in the Delta. For instance, these three sectors in Nanjing accounted for 12.06%, 37.85% and 42.35% respectively of the total FDI in the service industry. However the three sectors cannot be classified as pure producer service sectors and in fact are closer to consumer service sectors. Therefore, on the basis of existing research, the insignificant coefficients of the two variables—foundation of local manufacturing industry and FDI in manufacturing in the research based on the total volume of FDI in the service industry—are reasonable.

With the empirical test of the above model, we find that if we observe from the perspective of attracting overall inflow of FDI to the service industry, the foundation of the service industry in a region is the most important factor in attracting FDI in the service industry to that region, and the second important factor is market scale. The effects of other factors are not significant. This conclusion should greatly inspire China's designing of its foreign capital policies, especially the policies to attract FDI into the service industry. As there are few choices for population policies in China, to encourage the development of local service industry and to accelerate the industrial structural transformation in which the focus of the industrial structure shifts from manufacturing industry to service industry should become the guideline of policies.

Conclusion

In the Yangtze River Delta, the foundation of service industry has an irreplaceably important influence on the inflow of FDI into the service industry. From the analysis of time series and intercept data, we find that there exists co-integration both between real FDI and foundation of the service industry and between contracted FDI and foundation of the service industry in Shanghai and Zhejiang. In Shanghai and Jiangsu, the foundations of service industries are the Granger cause of contracted FDI, and in Zhejiang the foundation of the service industry is the Granger cause of real FDI; the added value of service industry is the core factor promoting the inflow of FDI into the service industry, and a 1% increase in the added value of service industry is associated with a 1.45% to 2.49% increase in the inflow of FDI. The market scale has some effect on the inflow of FDI into the service industry.

At present, the development of the service industry is of significance to the economic transformation and sustainable development of China. Against the global background, introducing foreign service enterprises is one of the ways to develop the service industry in China. However, on the other hand, the research in this chapter shows that only when the service industry is developed could it attract FDI into the industry, which demonstrates the mutually supplementary relationship between the development of the service industry and inflow of FDI into the service industry, and it is impractical to expect FDI in the service industry to flow in to drive the development of the service industry in our country. Although theoretically, factors including market scale, foundation of manufacturing industry and FDI in manufacturing industry would facilitate the inflow of FDI into the service industry, in our analysis of existing data for the Delta these factors are far less important than the foundation of service industry in our country. As the data are inadequate, the research of this chapter does not focus on proving that other factors are not determinants of inflow of FDI into the service industry but on proving that the foundation of service industry promotes the inflow of FDI into the industry and thus clarifying the relationship between the two. Thus it can be seen that to build a fair competition environment for the service industry to develop, to gradually break the barriers hindering the entrance into China's service market and to reduce the restrictions on the private economy should be included in our policies designed to attract more foreign capital.

Appendix 1: ADF Test and PP Test

ADF test has three different regression models for us to choose, which are shown as follows:

$$\Delta y_t=\gamma y_{t-1}+\sum_{i=1}^{p}\beta_i\Delta y_{t-i}+\mu_t \quad \text{(a1)}$$

$$\Delta y_t=\gamma y_{t-1}+a+\sum_{i=1}^{p}\beta_i\Delta y_{t-i}+u_i \quad \text{(a2)}$$

$$\Delta y_t=\gamma y_{t-1}+a+\delta_t+\sum_{i=1}^{p}\beta_i\Delta y_{t-i}+u_i \quad \text{(a3)}$$

In the models, $t=1,2,\ldots,T$, and the models (a1), (a2) and (a3) represent the model with neither intercept nor trend variable, the model with intercept variable and the model with both intercept and trend variables respectively. The three models are generally chosen in accordance with figures of the time series. In the ADF test, the null hypothesis is "H_0:$\gamma=0$" and the alternative hypothesis is "H_1:$\gamma<0$." When the null hypothesis is rejected and the alternative hypothesis is accepted, there exists no unit root, implying that the time series are stationary. If the initial time series do not pass the hypothesis test, the time series are stationary and are called I(0) processes. Otherwise the first-order differences should be taken and then the ADF test should be done again; if the time series pass the hypothesis test, the time series are called I(0) processes. The rest can be deduced by analogy.

The PP test take (a4) as the test equation. The null hypothesis is "H_0:$\gamma=0$" and the alternative hypothesis is "H_1:$\gamma<0$." When the null hypothesis is rejected and the alternative hypothesis is accepted, there exists no unit root, implying that the time series are stationary. The method used to evaluate the integrated order of time series in similar to that of ADF test.

$$\Delta y_t=\gamma y_{t-1}+a+u_i,t=1,2,\ldots,T \quad \text{(a4)}$$

Appendix 2: E-G Two-step Method

The steps are as follows:

Step One: if the series "$y_{1t},y_{2t},y_{3t},\ldots, y_{kt}$" are all integrated series of the same order, the regression equation (a5) is established:

$$y_{1t}=\beta_1+\beta_2 y_{2t}+\beta_3 y_{3t}+\ldots+\beta_k y_{kt}+u_t \quad \text{(a5)}$$

The estimated residual error of the model is:

$$\hat{\mu}_t=y_{1t}-\hat{\beta}_1-\hat{\beta}_2 y_{2t}-\hat{\beta}_3 y_{3t}+\ldots+\hat{\beta}_k y_{kt} \quad \text{(a6)}$$

Step Two: use the ADF and PP method to test whether the residual series "$\hat{\mu}_t$" is stationary. If it is, then there is co-integration correlation among the series; otherwise, there is not.

Appendix 3: The Model to Estimate the Granger Causality of Two Variables

As is shown in equation (a7):

$$\begin{pmatrix} y_t \\ x_t \end{pmatrix} = \begin{pmatrix} a_{10} \\ a_{10} \end{pmatrix} + \begin{bmatrix} a_{11}^{(1)} & a_{12}^{(1)} \\ a_{21}^{(1)} & a_{22}^{(1)} \end{bmatrix} \begin{pmatrix} y_{t-1} \\ x_{t-1} \end{pmatrix} + \begin{bmatrix} a_{11}^{(2)} & a_{12}^{(2)} \\ a_{21}^{(2)} & a_{22}^{(2)} \end{bmatrix} \begin{bmatrix} y_{t-2} \\ x_{t-2} \end{bmatrix} + \ldots + \begin{bmatrix} a_{11}^{(p)} & a_{12}^{(p)} \\ a_{21}^{(p)} & a_{22}^{(p)} \end{bmatrix} \begin{bmatrix} y_{t-p} \\ x_{t-p} \end{bmatrix} + \begin{bmatrix} \varepsilon_{1t} \\ \varepsilon_{2t} \end{bmatrix} \quad \text{(a7)}$$

The null hypothesis is "$H_0{:}a_{11}^{(q)}=0, q=1,2,\ldots,p$" and the alternative hypothesis is "$H_1{:}\exists q \in 1,2,\ldots,p, a_{11}^{(q)} \neq 0$"; if and only if the coefficients "$a_{11}^{(q)}$" in the coefficient matrix are all equal to zero, the variable "x" could not be the Granger cause "y."

5 Chapter

To Raise the Status of the Yangtze River Delta in the International Division through Service Trade

The service trade, which is a new field in international trade, refers to the international economic activities that trade in service products. Since the 1980s, with the rising status of the service industry in the world economy, service industry all over the world has increased faster than the trade in goods in corresponding periods. In particular, in recent years, with the wide use of modern Internet information technology and the improvement of the service trade environment, the scope of service trade has been expanding and becoming more and more diversified, and service trade has become an important part of current international trade. Additionally, as economic globalization has blossomed, service trade has become more of a key factor in determining the statuses of countries and regions in the international division, affecting the international competitiveness of countries and regions.

As a base of world manufacturing, the Yangtze River Delta boasts a manufacturing industry that has succeeded in participating in the industrial chain of world manufacturing and it has become an important part of the chain, However, what the Delta takes advantage of to participate in the industrial chain division of world manufacturing is the large amount and cheapness of ordinary labor. In this international division order, although the Yangtze River Delta enjoys a considerable scale of trade every year there is slow growth in the service trade—the trade structure in the Delta is imbalanced and the status of the Delta in the international division cannot be raised. Especially in recent years, since issues including high energy consumption, serious pollution and international market trade frictions have been becoming more and more prominent, the growth model of trade that depends on the import and export of goods is facing increasingly serious challenges.

Against the above background, we need to study the urgency of making use of service trade to raise the status of the Yangtze River Delta in the international division as well as the Delta's external trade competitiveness, and we need to analyze the current situation of the service trade and external trade in the Delta and explore the ways and methods to raise the status of the Delta and to promote the sustainable development of the external trade in the Delta.

The Evolvement of the Service Trade and Its Status in the International Division

According to the definition given by the WTO, the scope of service trade is rather extensive as not only does it include finance and insurance, trade and commerce, logistics, communications, accounting, advertising, management consulting and travel etc. but also the trade forms include cross-border supply, consumption abroad, commercial presence and movement of natural persons. Cross-border supply refers to the services supplied in a country or region to the consumers from other countries or regions; commercial presence refers to the founding of legal entities in other countries or regions to provide services to the local customers; the movement of natural persons refers to natural persons from a country or region providing services in another country or region. Thus it can be seen that in the framework of the WTO, the service trade includes both international trade activities and international direct investment in services.

The sudden rise of the world service trade since the 1980s has been caused by a combination of many factors. In the development process of the world economy, the focus of the industrial structure of the world economy has gradually shifted to the service industry, and in particular the service sectors' participation in the international division is the root cause of the fast development of the service industry. According to the statistics of the OECD, the average proportion of GDP accounted for by the service sectors in the OECD member countries was 43.1% in 1960 but increased to 68.2% in 1995. The data published by the UNCTAD shows that by 2001, the service sectors in the world accounted for 67.7% of the world GDP, and the proportion was 72% in developed countries and 52% in developing countries. In other words, the service industry has become a leading industry in today's world economy.

Against the global background, the international division has started to undergo significant changes. For a long time, the international division was embodied in the division among different industries; however, since the mid-1920s, the international division has developed—not only the division of an industry in different countries but also the division of a product's different production processes or procedures in different countries are included. Particularly, the service procedures and service links have become the objects of international division, which facilitates the development of the service trade including the international service outsourcing.

In recent decades the flourishing and wide-spread use of modern information technology has also directly promoted the development of the service trade. Assisted by modern information technology, the division of the service industry has been upgraded and the former time and spatial obstacles that hinder the development of service trade have been eliminated. For example, by making use of the computer network, we can transfer capital from one country to another swiftly; the engineers and technicians in a country can even do designing and consulting at home for foreign institutions.

The improvement of the trade environment in the 1990s is another important reason for the fast development of service trade. Considering the influence of service trade on the politics, economy, culture and security of a country, for a long time all countries more or less made related laws and regulations to protect the service trade. Compared to the trade in goods, trade in services is more vulnerable to international politics and state policies and is more political and changeable. However, the above situation has improved a lot after the founding of the WTO. More and more countries, in order to better participate in the international division, have sped up their steps to open their service markets, which has created a better institutional environment for the development of the service trade.

According to WTO statistics the gross export of service trade all over the world was US$308.9 billion in 1985, 1.54 trillion in 2002, and in 2005 it was 1.2754 trillion, accounting for 20% of the gross exports of world trade.[1] Currently international transportation, international travel and international finance and insurance are the major contents of the service trade and the developed countries, especially the US, account for a large share of the service trade market. The US is the country with the biggest service trade scale and also with the largest service trade surplus in the world. It is worth mentioning that in recent years, in some developing countries such as China and India, the development of service trade has become faster and faster and the amount of trade in services has conspicuously increased. As a result, the developing countries have become a new force in the world service trade market.

The service industry, with its complicated and uncertain service interests, is different from the trade in goods. However in terms of the relativity between the trade in services and trade in goods, both will facilitate the development of goods trade in the related countries or regions. Thus the service trade has a positive effect on the goods trade. Empirical research shows that the trade in services and trade in goods promote and support each other. The service trade can provide modern transportation services for the goods trade of related countries or regions, which reduces the delay and latency time of the transportation of goods and brings down the transport costs, thus promoting the transfer of goods between the import countries and export countries; modern communication services can save time and costs of the related producers' and traders' searching and processing of information, which enhances the extent and depth of the goods trade; and modern finance and insurance services can provide the goods trade with highly efficient services such as financing, credit and settlement, having a supportive and active effect on the goods trade.

In terms of the exporter of service trade, the trade interest is embodied in that the export of service trade would help the exporting countries increase earnings in foreign exchange, promote employment and activate the development of the service sectors in those countries. In particular the export commodities of service trade, with their high added values, low energy-consumption and little pollution, are advantageous to the sustainable development of the exporting countries. Therefore the developed countries transfer their manufacturing sectors with high pollution and high energy-consumption to the developing countries where the labor is cheap, which places the developing countries in the processing links at the low-end of the value chain and enables the developed countries to focus on the knowledge-intensive and technology-intensive producer service industry that depends on human resources, and thus occupy the high-end of the value chain.

Internationally, the developed countries located at the peak of the global industrial division system are always global or regional service centers and they maximize their economic influences and realize their high revenue by providing other countries with producer services or consumer services of high quality.

In terms of the importing countries of service trade, although a large amount of blind export of foreign service products could have many negative effects on the economies in the importing countries, a proper increase in the service trade import with consideration of the importing structure and method can be beneficial to the raising of the importing countries' status in the international division, which benefits are embodied in that firstly, by importing service trade, the importing countries can bring variety to the domestic service markets and optimize the competitive structures of the domestic markets; and secondly, by importing service trade, the importing countries can bring in advanced modern productive services from other countries thus enhancing the level of their domestic manufacturing industry as well as the competitiveness of their trade in goods.[2]

It can be said that in this era of economic globalization, the development of service trade directly influences the evolution and enhancement of the related countries' or regions' statuses in the international division in industrial chain. To take the manufacturing industry as an example, internationally advanced producer services, such as logistics, finance, insurance, law, accounting, auditing, management, consulting, advertising and technology, are introduced by the service trade and will provide the manufacturing enterprises with support in knowledge, technology and proficiency, which saves transaction costs, increases the output values and enhances the operation efficiency of all production segments, thus effectively boosting the increase in value as well as the international competitiveness of the manufacturing products.

On this issue, Professor Porter has put forward insightful opinions. Porter believes that in the value chain analysis model the competitive edge comes from the R&D at the upstream of the industrial chain, manufacturing and assembling of components are at the midstream of the chain, and many links such as advertising, brand, packing, sale, distribution and after-sale services are at the downstream of the chain, all of which activities influence the relative costs and competitiveness of enterprises. In different parts of the industrial chain, the added value sought by enterprises was different from the influence on industrial competitiveness. Generally speaking, the added values at the upstream and downstream of the industrial chain should exceed that at the midstream of the industrial chain. Therefore, in the current international division system, the enhancement of a country's or region's status is actually embodied in the enhancement of the country or region's status in the international industrial chain or the enhancement of its competency to obtain added value, that is to say, the enhancement is embodied in the country or region's progressive shift from manufacturing links to R&D and brand marketing links. From the perspective of international economic competition, only when they develop towards the producer service industry which is of comparatively high added value can manufacturing enterprises create enduring competitive edges, and the producer service activities will have greater and greater strategic meaning.

The Current Situation of the Service Trade and International Division in the Yangtze River Delta

The service trade is a new thing in the Yangtze River Delta. Service trade in the Delta, just as in other regions in China, had long been on the margins of external trade and it attracted little attention, so its scale was limited. However since the 1990s, especially after China's entrance into the WTO, the service trade in the Delta has developed rapidly. Relevant material shows that through relying on its industrial advantages, location advantages, function advantages and the favorable policies that have given it priority in opening its service industry to the outside world, Shanghai has become one of the regions where the service trade has developed at the highest speed and has the greatest potential in China. In 2004, the volume of import and export of service trade in Shanghai added up to US$24.5 billion, increasing by 52% compared to that in 2003. In this import reached US$12.4 billion, increasing by 49.7% compared to the previous year, and export reached US$12.1 billion with a year-to-year growth of 57%. In 2004, the total volume of import and export of the service trade in Jiangsu Province added up to US$3.1 billion, of which exports reached US$700 million. In Zhejiang during the period of "the tenth five-year plan," the annual gross amount of service trade increased from 800 million to US$6.2 billion, and the total amount for the five years added up to US$15.3 billion with an annual growth rate of 51%, which rate is 20% higher than the annual growth rate of goods trade during the same period. By 2006, the total volume of service trade in Zhejiang had reached US$7.5 billion.

However, we can see from the international comparison that the current trade structure in the Delta still needs improvement. For example, the overall technology level and added value of exported products in the Delta not high, and in particular labor-intensive goods with high resource-consumption and low added value still account for a large share. Therefore, although the foreign trade export in the Delta grows fast and a favorable balance of trade is maintained (Table 5.1), the interests in trade are limited and there is no good measures to solve the increasingly serious problems of energy, environment and international trade frictions. According to statistics, Zhejiang was challenged by 40 trade friction cases brought by 14 countries and regions including the US, the EU, India, Mexico and Columbia, involving nearly US$1 billion.

Table 5.1. The situation of trade in goods in the Yangtze River Delta and in China as a whole

Year	Total volume of export & import			Total volume of export			Total volume of import		
	Yangtze Dalta Area (100 mil USD)	China (100 mil USD)	Share	Yangtze Dalta Area (100 mil USD)	China (100 mil USD)	Share	Yangtze Dalta Area (100 mil USD)	China (100 mil USD)	Share
2000	1,281.7	4,742.9	0.27	705.6	2,492.0	0.28	576.1	2,250.9	0.26
2001	1,450.6	5,096.5	0.28	794.9	2,661.0	0.30	655.7	2,435.5	0.27
2002	1,849.3	6,207.7	0.30	999.5	3,256.0	0.31	849.8	2,951.7	0.29
2003	2,874.8	8,509.9	0.34	1,492.1	4,382.3	0.34	1,382.7	4,127.6	0.33
2004	4,161.0	11,545.5	0.36	2,191.6	5,933.2	0.37	1,969.4	5,612.3	0.35
2005	5,216.9	14,219.0	0.37	2,905.2	7,619.5	0.38	2,311.7	6,599.5	0.35
2006	6,506.4	17,607.0	0.37	3,748.7	9,691.0	0.39	2,757.7	7,916.0	0.35

Sources: *China Statistical Yearbook*, *Jiangsu Statistical Yearbook*, *Zhejiang Statistical Yearbook*, *Shanghai Statistical Yearbook* in related years and the official website of the National Bureau of Statistics of China.

Another prominent feature of the imbalanced trade structure of the Yangtze River Delta is the backward development of service trade—not only is the total amount of service trade in the Delta small but also the comparative scale of the service trade in the Delta in international trade is obviously lower than the average level in the world. To take Shanghai for an example, the current total amount of service trade in Shanghai is only equal to 1/5 of that in Singapore and 1/6 of that in Hong Kong; the average proportion of international trade accounted for by the service trade in Shanghai is below 10%—less than 1/2 of the world average level. In terms of the international investment in services, the Delta does not have a satisfactory performance either. In Jiangsu Province for example the proportion of foreign investment accounted for by foreign investment in services is below 20%, which is not only much lower than the world average level—60%—but also even lower than the national average level.

The backward development level of service trade in the Delta is also embodied in the fact that modern service trade accounts for only a small share in the existing service trade export items and service trade export still depends on the traditional labor-intensive service trade items. The leading trade items in the international service trade export in Shanghai are transportation, travel and consulting; in Jiangsu they are consulting, project contracting, cooperation in labor services and travel; and in Zhejiang they are travel, project contracting, cooperation in labor services and transportation (similar to those in Shanghai and Jiangsu). Thus it can be seen that the technology-intensive service trade of finance, insurance and information, which develop at the highest speed globally, are still in their primary development stage in Yangtze River Delta and they are of great potential there.

The TC Index (trade competition index, also called the export competition index) is an important index to measure a country's or a region's international competitiveness in service trade. The formula of the TC Index is "TC Index = (Export–Import)/ (Export + Import)." A high TC Index means high competitiveness in service trade; conversely, a low TC Index means low competitiveness in service trade. We can use the TC Index to do further quantitative analysis of the current situation of service trade in the Yangtze River Delta. By substituting related data into the formula we can find that the overall TC Indexes of the service trade in the Delta in recent years are all negative, which means that the current service trade in the Delta is in unfavorable balance and is of low competitiveness. Let us take the related data in Jiangsu Province as an example. The calculated TC Indexes of eight trade items (including computer information services, technological services, financial services, consulting, insurance, advertising and postal communications) in service trade in Jiangsu Province all turn out to be approaching the minimum—–1, which means that Jiangsu Province has a lot of imports but little export of the eight items. A comparatively high TC Index shows up for the transportation service, which item profits from the construction of Jiangsu as an international manufacturing base and the fast development of trade in goods in the province. Both the absolute scale and the comparative scale in the service trade in Zhejiang Province are limited. Although Shanghai is the most important port opened to the outside world in China and has many advantageous conditions to develop service trade, the overall TC Index of the service trade in Shanghai is still negative. In particular, Shanghai's lag in the service trade items of high added value is rather significant and the unfavorable trade balance is serious in Shanghai (Please refer to Table 5.2).

There are many reasons causing the current low development level of service trade in the Yangtze River Delta, both direct reasons and indirect reasons. Observed from the perspective of direct reasons, the service trade in the Delta has developed for only a short time, service trade enterprises are in small in size, the technology level is not high enough and there is a lack of professional skills, and especially the famous service enterprises that could supply service products of high added value to other countries are limited in the Delta. These are all major factors that obstruct development of service trade in the Delta. Additionally, the degree of opening up of the Delta needs to be enhanced, which in some degree influences the development of service trade. From the perspective of indirect reasons, the service industry and especially the modern service industry started at a very low level and has a weak foundation, which results in the lack of industrial base and scale needed in the development of the industry. According to statistics, the proportion of the GDP accounted for by service industry in the Delta is lower than 50%, far less than the average level in developed countries, and even lower than the average level of developing countries. In addition, due to many reasons, the socialization, marketization and industrialization reforms in the service industry in the Delta have not been completed, and monopoly still exists in the service trade activities and the service market in the Delta. Laws, regulations and policy systems that regulate the service market competition have not been well established, which combined with the imbalanced internal structure of the service industry, hinders the development of service trade in the Delta.

Table 5.2. Competition index of service trade in Shanghai (2000–2002)

Item	Service trade export (100 mil USD)			Service trade export (100 mil USD)			TC Index		
	2000	2001	2002	2000	2001	2002	2000	2001	2002
Total	35.93	43.89	52.25	42.67	46.43	54.47	–0.085 8	–0.028 1	–0.020 8
Transportation	19.25	24.2	24.88	22.40	26.23	28.24	–0.075 6	–0.040 3	–0.063 3
Insurance	1.71	1.68	1.71	1.56	1.73	1.72	0.045 9	–0.014 7	–0.029 2
Travelling	7.43	9.87	14.34	8.25	6.28	3.66	–0.052 3	0.222 3	0.593 3
Finance	0.09	0.15	0.09	0.13	0.22	0.22	–0.181 8	–0.189 2	–0.419 4
Postal communication	0.25	0.26	0.20	0.10	0.13	0.33	0.428 6	0.333 3	–0.245 3
Project contracting	1.32	1.56	1.02	1.28	0.70	0.36	0.015 4	0.380 5	0.478 3
Computer information	1.06	0.34	0.73	0.96	0.63	0.42	0.049 5	–0.299 0	0.269 6
Patent license & franchise	0.36	0.41	0.39	2.51	5.38	8.71	–0.749 1	–0.858 4	-0.914 3
Consulting	3.00	4.78	6.57	2.86	1.99	7.18	0.023 9	0.412 1	–0.044 4
Education & Medical care	0.38	0.41	0.54	2.04	2.58	3.23	–0.686 0	–0.725 8	–0.713 5
Advertising	1.00	0.06	1.53	0.54	0.49	0.08	0.298 7	–0.781 8	0.900 6
Movie & Video	0.02	0.12	0.15	0.04	0.05	0.30	–0.333 3	0.411 8	–0.333 3
Others	0.06	0.05	0.10	0.000 4	0.02	0.02	0.986 8	0.428 6	0.666 7

Source: Fan Chunzeng and Yu Guang 2005.

The Path to Enhance the Status of the Yangtze River

To develop service trade and to expand the FDI in services is not only an important path for the Delta to vigorously participate in the new international division system and enhance its status in the international division, it is a necessary condition for the Delta to break the passive situation in which manufacturing industry in the Delta lacks technological innovative competence, independent intellectual property and famous brands and to succeed in transformation and upgrading. We think that the deficiencies of service trade in the Delta need to be resolved from many aspects. To conclude, the corresponding policies and measures are on the government level and on the enterprise level.

Firstly, on the level of government, the regional governments in the Delta should make great efforts to establish a more favorable policy environment to accelerate of service trade's development, aiming to enhance the Delta's status in the international division and international competition.

In more specific terms, the government should accelerate the reform of monopolistic sectors and actively eliminate the system obstacles that hinder the development of service industry in the Delta. Opening up to the inside and to the outside should be strengthened and multiple channels should be used to attract high quality factors to the modern service sectors in the Delta to promote the upgrade of the service industry. The governments should offer more support to the service trade and service industry by establishing a preferential tax system, relaxing examination of qualification for loans and setting up industrial investment funds. Also, the governments should strengthen overall planning and unified management, and make good use of the opportunities brought by the current international transfer of service industry to vigorously attract modern service international investment including new investment, merger and acquisition and risk investment, thus continuously expanding the new forms and new areas of the service industry's use of foreign capitals in the Delta. And the governments should use foreign experience for reference and adopt corresponding measures to promote the service trade, and try to improve the law, criteria and supervision mechanisms related to the service trade. Moreover, the governments should improve the related infrastructure, strengthen the training and exploitation of human resources in the service trade and service industry, and emphasize the introduction and cultivation of skills. The governments should establish an open, transparent and highly regulated market supervision system to enhance the quality of services, standardize service behaviors, strengthen protection of intellectual property rights, set up and perfect a self-discipline mechanism for the service industry, and actively facilitate the standardization of the industry.

As the Delta includes Shanghai and more than ten cities in Jiangsu Province and Zhejiang Province, "segmentation" is an inevitable phenomenon in the development of service trade and service industry, which development model is inconsistent with the general trend of international development. Therefore an important breakthrough point of the acceleration of the service trade's and the service industry's development is to strengthen the coordination among different administrative regions as soon as possible and make every effort to construct a hierarchical regional division model in which the functions are properly divided and comparative advantages are emphasized. Therefore we need to energetically explore an interest-adjustment mechanism for regional development and nail down the functional orientation of different cities in accordance with their natural resources and comparative advantages. For example, in terms of Shanghai—a metropolis which is highly internationalized, we need to emphasize its factor agglomeration and radiation function in the service sectors of finance, logistics, commerce and information; in terms of Nanjing and Hangzhou—the regional and integrated modern service centers—we need to strengthen their function to deliver the radiation effect of the metropolis and to put more pressure on their regions; and in terms of the medium- and small-sized cities, we need to enhance their competence to make use of the industrial vertical division and the extension of industrial value and to embrace the opportunities brought by the radiation effect of the big cities. In this way we can establish a development model in which the cities cooperate and coordinate with each other, differentiated division is implemented, and comparative advantages are complementary.

The measures at the level of government to develop service trade also include the integration of service trade and service industry resources in different regions in the Delta. In terms of the transportation sector, the governments should further design and implement the planning of the transportation sector in the Delta, improve the coordination mechanism between Shanghai, Jiangsu and Zhejiang, reinforce the construction of important infrastructure and transportation service management systems, coordinate the standards in different regions on the construction of highways, harbors and inland navigation, realize the potential of the integration of the inter-provincial and inter-regional information resources, achieve the fast delivery of information among traffic departments at all levels in the Delta and carry out online interactive processing of transportation, navigation and highways.

In terms of the finance sector, the governments should clarify the financial cooperation strategy in the Delta and carry out market-oriented cross-regional re-organization of financial institutions to reduce the obstacles to market operation. In decision-making associated with construction of infrastructure, the governments should plan strategically from the perspective of the Delta as a whole and establish a well-designed organizational system and a scientific information-decision system.

Furthermore, the governments should reinforce the internal interactive mechanism in which the service trade and goods trade promote each other. In recent years, the annual total volume of foreign trade in goods in the Delta has ranked the first all the time, maintaining a high growth rate. Meanwhile a large quantity of high quality skills in computers, software, transportation, insurance, finance, accounting, auditing and laws in the country have gathered in the Delta. So the governments should actively make use of these existing resources and advantages—on the one hand, promoting the goods trade to drive the growth of related service trade, and on the other hand, encouraging and developing the producer services, so as to actively guide the mutual penetration and combination of the service enterprises and manufacturing enterprises, seeking for business opportunities for service trade and the trade in goods and further raising the status in the international division and added value of the manufacturing industry in the Delta.

Secondly, on the level of enterprises, the enterprises in the Delta should accelerate the updating and modernization of their production models, energetically promote the marketization and socialization of the internal services of the enterprises, facilitate the separation of "major links" and "auxiliary links," and hive off and socialize their non-core producer service links by innovating management and rearranging procedures. In order to solve the small scale of the service enterprises in the Delta as soon as possible, the enterprises should form an alliance to seek the expansion of enterprise scales. They should break administrative and regional barriers to vigorously discuss inter-regional and inter-sector merger and reorganization of the enterprises that are linked by trademarks and patents.

The enterprises should strengthen their marketing concept—they should be engaged in brand establishment, management and extension planning to achieve the shift from traditional order-undertaking business to brand operation business. In terms of the medium- and small-sized enterprises, they should flexibly adopt the models of franchised brand operation, brand lease and combination of OEM and brand establishment to achieve the organic integration of their own advantages including labor costs, marketing channels, client resources and famous brands, taking advantage of the famous brands to expand their own scale and capabilities.

The enterprises should actively launch service trade business, make efforts to expand the scope of service trade and international economic cooperation, and vigorously develop foreign investment in services to enhance the capability to expand the offshore market and the market competitiveness of the service enterprises in the Delta. International service outsourcing is an outcome of upgrading in the international division, so we should reinforce our research on the global trend of international service outsourcing as well as our study of the experience of other countries, make the right choice of the breakthrough point to develop international service outsourcing, accelerate the cultivation of the skills in international service outsourcing using personnel who do not only have knowledge of software and related technologies but also have already acquired a good command of foreign languages.

The service trade enterprises in the Delta should, under the guidance of related government departments, establish service trade guilds which are really dominated by the enterprises inside the guild and managed by the entrepreneurs, and encourage the guild to play a more important role in the designing of industrial development, in communication and discussion with governments and the public, in the establishment of an industrial database and in the regular trade fairs and promotion seminars. The guilds would effectively potentiate the coordination and management of enterprises, and they can not only bring the administrative function (that used to be played by the governments) into play but also better understand the situation of technology and market in the sectors. Proper guild regulations (including a qualification verification system, charging standards for consulting services, criteria on service quality assurance and penalties for the improper behaviors of enterprises in the sector) should be formulated to raise the self-discipline level of the enterprises in the sector.

6

Chapter

The International Transfer of Service Business and the Construction of an Outsourcing Center

With the upgrading of global industrial transfer and the fast development of communication technology, the outsourcing of service business has become the focus of the new round of international industrial shift. What role will the Yangtze River Delta play in the new round of construction of service business outsourcing centers? What internal and external conditions do we need in our construction of service outsourcing centers? Does the Yangtze River Delta enjoy the necessary conditions? Or does the Delta have the potential to create those conditions? This chapter aims to answer the above questions.

Service Business Outsourcing, which is one of the important strategies in the modern operation and management of enterprises, refers to the business model in which the contractees outsource some business process or management functions that are administered by the insiders of the enterprises in convention to the domestic or foreign specialized and highly efficient service providers by signing contracts with the contractors. The outsourcing model is considered as an effective method for modern enterprises to attract and make use of external technologies and human resources to improve enterprise management, raise the professional level of their procedures and enhance the operational efficiency of the enterprises.

By the content of the service provided, service business outsourcing can be classified as Information Technology Outsourcing (ITO), Business Process Outsourcing (BPO) and Knowledge Process Outsourcing (KPO), etc. ITO includes basic knowledge, IT services, R&D of software, technological R&D, integration of the basic technology platform and management integration; BPO includes the outsourcing of many commercial applications such as business improvement, business processing service, applied management and applied services; KPO includes legal services for intellectual property rights, financial and insurance consulting, data analysis, human resources management, business market research, call services web and animation design, legal consulting, remote medical treatment, remote education and publishing, network management and decision-making etc.

From the locations of the contractees and contractors and the relationship between the two, service business outsourcing can be classified as Onshore Outsourcing and Offshore Outsourcing. The former refers to the business process cooperative relation between different legal entities in the same country, and includes Inter-Group Outsourcing—outsourcing between two different groups and Intra-Group Outsourcing—the outsourcing inside a group. The latter refers to the business process cooperative relation between legal entities in different countries, and also includes Inter-Group Outsourcing and Intra-Group Outsourcing.[1]

Table 6.1. The domains and geographical locations of the outsourcing services of the developing countries and regions as contractors

Outsourcing services	Major contents	Major contractor regions
Movie, television and cultural services	Production and distribution of animation and video products; animation projection; broadcast and TV transmission; recording; entertainment, culture and sports services; media organization services	Argentina, Brazil, Hong Kong, India, Mexico and Venezuela
Commercial services	All kinds of office support services, customer transaction and technological support, including designing of abstracts and tables of contents, data entry and processing, electronic publication, law translation, litigation support, post directory management, remote secretary services, technical writing, electronic marketing, electronic support and website designing	So far, India has been the biggest exporting country of the commercial services.
Computer and related services	Computer hardware and software tool installation service; data processing, maintenance and repair of office equipments including computers; other computer services	Ireland, India and Israel account for a large share of the export market of this kind of services
Higher education and training services	Delivery of educational and video materials, course wares, test questions via Internet; online paper-examining, scoring and GPA assessment; technical training, etc.	A few developing countries, e.g. India
Financial services	Insurance and insurance-related consulting; business service, banking and financial information service, and other financial services	India plays an important role in this domain. In South America, reinsurance enterprises are cooperating with financial service providers and insurance companies to provide a series of competitive new financial products.
Medical services	Medical care, dentistry, nursing, paramedical services, hospitals, social and other human health services, including transport, diagnosis and identification of lab specimens and supply of consulting, online diagnosis, professional X-ray radiodiagnosis by post or electronic approaches	China, Bengal, India, Pakistan, the Philippines and Zimbabwe
Internet and related services	Internet, communication services, Internet contents, mixed business services, audio-video services, computer and related services	Based on the establishment of common language, many dotcoms in South America have expanded their business to other countries; Hong Kong, Lebanon and Singapore are exporting these sorts of services to neighboring countries.

(Con'd)

Other kinds of specialized services	Legal services, accounting services, auditing services, tax services, architectural design etc., which represent the top field of service business outsourcing.	The usual outsourcing processes include book-keeping for customers, document management, manning and IT services. Architectural and other services are also included in specialized service export. India, Singapore and other CEE countries are the major exporters of this sort of services.

Source: Zhan Xiaoning and Xing Houyuan 2005.

Table 6.1 describes in detail the domains and regional distribution of the outsourcing services of the developing countries and regions as contractors. It is clearly shown in the Figure that China has entered into some areas of service business outsourcing and is vigorously developing into other areas.

The International and Domestic Background to the Construction of Service Outsourcing Centers

Assisted by the highly-developed global communications network, multinational enterprises proceed from the strategy of "Refocusing" to reduce costs by fragmentation, slicing the traditional industrial chain and value chain to meet the increasingly diversified market needs, which activities inevitably result in the emergence of service business outsourcing. In recent years multinational enterprises have been more likely to set up offshore subsidiary companies or controllable offshore centers in the developing countries where labor is qualified but cheap to provide services for third parties, or they outsource their business processes to qualified offshore contractors, which is Offshore Outsourcing. Intrinsically, the development of service outsourcing is a consequence of the multinational enterprises' resource factor integration and allocation optimization globally and it is a natural outcome and ultimate trend of the countries' participation in the international production specialized division and fragmentation production in accordance with comparative advantages.

So far, compared to the research on manufacturing outsourcing, research on service outsourcing is rather limited and the existing literature on service outsourcing is focused on the influence of service outsourcing on productivity and employment. However the prime mover of service outsourcing is similar to that of manufacturing outsourcing as in a mature economy, the market entities commonly approve of the model of "outsource when somebody can do it better than you," which model is suitable for R&D, production, marketing, after-sales service and enterprise management. This model is embraced because outsourcing service is more selective[2] in the market than the service provided by the employees inside the enterprises. It is easier for service outsourcing companies with better records to get outsourcing orders and the outsourcing contractees could select more flexibly.

Research on service business outsourcing is rather limited. Mann (2004) studied the IT sector in the US and he proved that globalization, especially the international outsourcing of IT hardware, lead to a 10–30% drop in the prices of the IT hardware. Later, Mann proved that the service business international outsourcing of IT software could also be beneficial to the economy. If we assume that the price elasticity of IT software is higher than that of hardware, the outsourcing of IT software will generate more profits. Finally, Mann pointed out that employment in the IT sector is also increasing, which means that service business outsourcing does no harm to the employment in the outsourcing sector. Amiti and Wei (2004) used data on all manufacturing sectors in the US to show that there exists a strong correlativity between service business outsourcing and labor productivity while manufacturing outsourcing has little effect on labor productivity. Gorg and Hanley (2003) analyzed the statistics for Ireland in the years from 1990 to 1995 and found that service outsourcing had an active effect on the productivity of the electronics sector. They also found that the outsourcing of tangible products in the same period had insignificant effect on productivity. Girma and Gorg (2003) found that during the years between 1980 and 1992, service business outsourcing in Britain had a positive effect on both labor productivity and total factor productivity, but they did not clarify whether the outsourcing was domestic or international.

Analysis of the international background

Firstly, the Internet—which is a transmission medium highly depended on in the construction of service business outsourcing centers—has entered its "obstacle-free" era where it can develop "smoothly."

Currently there are nearly 800 satellites all different kinds orbiting the Earth, which satellites are making meteorological observations, controlling soil erosion, delivering music, news and information, carrying out military observations, collecting civil data, offering GPS navigation and predicting forest coverage. China has 34 of the 800 satellites, including communication and broadcast satellites, earth resource satellites, meteorological satellites, navigation satellites and scientific experimentation satellites. In 1993, China's first international submarine optical fiber cable system was established, and now China has 18 optical fiber cables of 7 systems with a total length of more than 120 thousand kilometers, and China is establishing more international optical fiber cables, all of which cables connect China with Japan, Korea and the US, connect Asia and Europe, and connect the Asia-Pacific with all the big cities in the world. The International Mobile Satellite Company (INMARSAT) was the first provider of broadband BGAN business on land, and it has been expanding its business to the marine and aviation sectors. In the third quarter of 2007, INMARSAT realized complete informationization in the air and on the sea, and it succeeded in complete coverage of broadband communications business on the Earth except for the North and South Poles. An Iresearch Market Consulting Survey shows that by June of 2006, more than 400 cities in the world had realized or were realizing full WLAN coverage. The reports of an American market survey institution—ComScore Networks—show that by the end of 2006, the total number of the people no younger than 15 years old who use the Internet had reached 747 million with a year-to-year growth rate of 10%. On January 23, 2007, the China Internet Network Information Center (CNNIC) released the *Nineteenth Statistical Report on China Internet Development*, which shows that by the end of 2006 the total number of netizens in China was 137 million, accounting for 10.5% of the population in China, and the number increased by 23.4% (260 million) compared to the number at the end of 2005. The authoritative report also analyzed in detail the service functions of the Internet among the netizens, which is shown in Table 6.2.

Table 6.2. The services/functions of the Internet used by netizens in China and the shares of the services/functions

Internet service/funtion	Share	Internet service/funtion	Share
Sending and receiving emails	56.1%	Online recruiting	20.8%
Reading News	53.5%	Online chat room	20.8%
Search engine	51.5%	Personal homepage and space	20.3%
Acquiring information (product and service query, work information query, medical and health service query, govemmental information query)	41.0%	Electronic magazine	17.1%
Forum/BBS discussion group	36.9%	Online education	14.3%
Watching and downloading online video (online TV)	36.3%	Online marketing (including online promition and online auction)	13.3%

(Con'd)

Instant messaging	34.5%	Online phone (including online IP phones and PC to Phone)	11.2%
Listening to and downloading online music (online radio)	34.4%	Online finance (including banking and online stock)	10.5%
Uploading and downloading files (video and music excluded)	32.9%	Text message/multimedia message	9.7%
Online games	26.6%	Online booking (hotel, tickets, registration)	8.6%
Online alumni community	25.6%	Online govement affairs (online complaint, online examinication, online supervision)	7.7%
Blog	25.3%	Marriage Advertisements, friends-making, commumity	6.4%
Online shopping	23.6%	Others	6.4%

Source: *The Nineteenth Statistical Report on China Internet Development*, CNNIC.

It can be seen from Table 6.2 that with the increasing coverage rate of the Internet and the permeation of the Internet, more and more people are making use of the convenient Internet to enhance their life qualities and working efficiencies. In terms of commercial institutions, the highly-developed network system means higher efficiency and profits.

The survey results also show that the total number of domain names in China (including the national top-level domain name CN and the commonly used top-level domain names—COM, NET and ORG) was 4,109,020, of which the number of domain names that finish with "com" was 1,939,343, accounting for 47.2% of the total; the number of domain names that finish with "cn" was 1,803,393, accounting for 43.9% of the total; the number of the domain names that finish with "net" was 299,108, accounting for 7.3% of the total; and the number of the domain names that finish with "org" was 67,176, accounting for 1.6% of the total. English domain names that finish with "com," which reflect the situation of commercial institutions' use of Internet, come first among all the names, accounting for 47.2% of the total, which shows that the Internet service is playing an increasingly important role in social and economic activities.

Fig. 6.1. The classification and distribution of Internet domain names in China

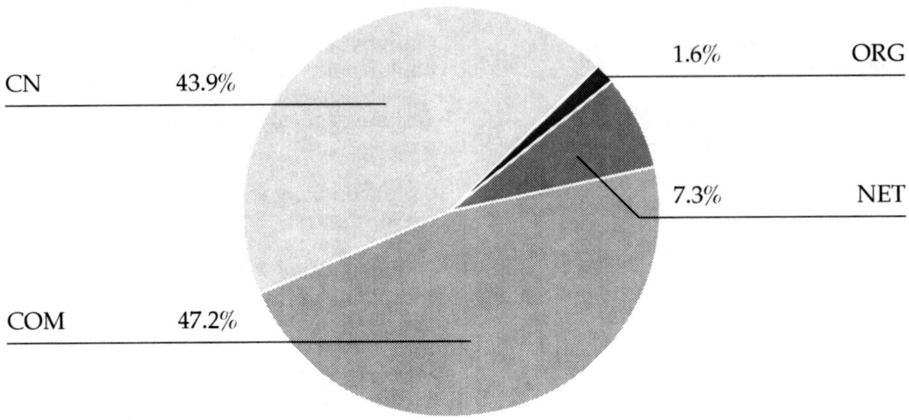

Source: CNNIC.

Nowadays, as the global network communication services are becoming increasingly mature and expanding in function, communication in space has become obstacle-free and smooth; synchronization and non-differentiation has also been achieved in communication in time, which means that in today's world that is interconnected closely and conveniently by information technology, the global market, labor force and products can all be shared by the whole world, and all can be realized in the most efficient and least expensive ways. Nothing can hinder globalization. The workers, accountants, engineers and programmers in the US have to compete with a labor force which is as good or as bad as they are and the more competitive ones will be the winners.[3]

Secondly, the economic foundation which is highly depended on for the construction of service outsourcing centers—the international production structure—has developed to the stage of "specialized distribution" and "fragmentation production."

With scientific and technological innovation, the improvement of manufacturing techniques and the expansion of offshore manufacturing and marketing systems, the strategies of multinational enterprises have been progressively shifting from regional integration to global integration, that is to say, shifting from the partial transfer of links at the low-end of the value chain to the whole transfer of the complete value chain. The specialization of the international production structure has made fragmentation manufacturing as well as inner-product division possible for multinational enterprises, and more importantly, the modern international Internet and logistics delivery system have enabled the across-space manufacturing—marketing—service model that involves global designing, global manufacturing, global purchasing, relocated assembling and global service to come true. What is more important is that with the speeding up of world-flattening, more and more nonproductive links are being outsourced to a third party to optimize the service quality, minimize the service price and make the service more convenient and faster, thus the globalized production structure is developing at an ultra high speed.

It needs to be mentioned that outsourcing is fundamentally different from offshore production. Outsourcing refers to when an enterprise contracts a third party implement some of the links—including R&D, call transits, accounting, data analysis and market surveys—that used to be done inside the enterprise, and then integrates those links into the original business procedure. Offshore production refers to when an enterprise transfers part of or an entire factory which used to be in its homeland to another country by external direct investment through merger and acquisition. The product standards and modes of production of outsourcing and offshore production are exactly the same, but the added labor costs, taxes and even the costs of employee welfare of offshore production are lower and enterprises can obtain more subsidies on raw materials in offshore production. Thus by setting up subsidiary companies or branch institutions enterprises are able to form a huge global production network and then they can bring their products into their global supply system.

Not all service business outsourcing takes place in the service sectors, and the service processes needed by manufacturing sectors and other sectors are more likely to be outsourced. What can be outsourced are the service links in the service sectors and production sectors, but the transmission of their semi-finished products or phase-finished products can rely on the developed global data and information transmission systems—the international interconnected network and communication system. What can be produced offshore could be productive sectors or the productive links in other sectors, and their semi-finished products or finished products are transported or transmitted by the international logistics system; and can also be nonproductive sectors. For example, the biggest enterprise application software vendor—SAP—has set up subsidiary companies in Xi'an, Chengdu and Wuhan in China to provide services to its contractees throughout the world; the biggest Indian IT consulting company—TCS – has built a base in Hangzhou; and Infosys and Wipro have settled in Shanghai and Beijing respectively. The only difference lies in that the former produces physical products and the latter produces services or virtual products.

Thirdly, the economic structure that is highly depended on for the construction of service outsourcing centers—the international economic structure—has developed into the stage of "integration" and "globalization."

With the internationalization of the micro economic entities—the enterprises—economic relations among countries have eliminated national boundaries as the multinational enterprises' globalized R&D team, purchasing network, production system and marketing network blurs the national concept that used to be strictly set by national territory and customs borders. The entities of trade interests and specialized division have shifted from the traditional countries to multinational enterprises; the interests of the multinational interests, to some degree, are no longer consistent with those of their mother countries' interests but with the interests of their host countries; further, by lobbying, multinational enterprises are able to make their mother countries carry out external economic policies or political and military action that is advantageous to the enterprises' implementation of globalization strategies, thus indirectly influencing the host countries.

With the development of offshore finance, the behaviors of micro-entities in different countries can generate the "butterfly effect," so all countries are making efforts to maintain a comparatively stable financial system and monetary system, and thus the global financial and monetary market is relatively stable. The development and maturing of financial derivatives further strengthens the economic relationship between countries, and all the open countries are in symbiosis.

Developed modern trade brings unprecedented "high quality and inexpensive" enjoyment and extremely favorable services to consumers in all countries, and every detail in consumers' daily lives is to a great extent dependent on smooth logistics systems, information systems and interconnected networks—the whole world has become an organism that consists of interconnected micro-entities. The international economic structure has developed to the stage of high "integration" and "globalization." All the above provides a firm macro-foundation for the further integration of the world economy, against which macro-background service business outsourcing is the real reflection and objective demonstration of the micro-entities' pursuit of highly-efficient, convenient and specialized division.

Fourthly, all countries in the world, especially the developing market economies, are actively adopting all measures to accelerate construction of service business outsourcing centers.

Since the end of the 1980s, there have been two rounds of industrial shifts internationally. The first one was the international industrial shift that featured processing trade in the end of the 1980s; the second one is the transfer of world manufacturing sectors from developed countries to developing countries such as China. Nowadays, with the development of information technology, the new round of world industrial structural shift that features the transfer of service trade, high-end manufacturing and technology R&D is sweeping the world, which provides new opportunities for the international market-oriented development of the modern service industry of the developing countries with high quality and cheap human resources, and service business outsourcing, as an important part of the high-end service industry, is booming. Statistics show that the market scale of the current global service outsourcing is between US$300 million and US$500 million, and in the several years to come the scale will maintain a growth rate of 20–30%. In the process of undertaking BPO, the most shining star is India. The statistics from the International Data Group (IDG) show that in the international trend of service business outsourcing India, with its unique advantages, has become the top contractor of software outsourcing and it has monopolized the American market. The latest statistics from India's National Association of Software and Service Companies show that from 2004 to 2005, the BPO earnings in India added up to US$50 billion. It was detected by experts that in 2007, the growth rate of BPO in India could reach 56%, the earnings could add up to US$60 billion and the number of employees could reach 1 million, and at the same time the BPO could create 3 million to 4 million job opportunities in related sectors. In 2008 India accounted for 51% of the market share of software and back-end office service outsourcing in the world, and the annual sales income of this sector added up to US$80 billion. The Deloitte Consulting Company asserted in its report in April 2007 that in 2008, the top 100 financial companies in the world would offer to India 1 million job positions on backstage and technology services, which accounts for 1/5 of the total related job positions in the world. Prabhu, a director in the Bangalore Campus Indian Institutes of Management who is in charge of post-school placement, said: "The wages in India are generally equal to 1/10 to 1/4 of the wages in NYC, London and HK." Therefore when the multinational banks intend to outsource some of their business, India is likely to become the banks' best choice as there are a large amount of skilled workers who can speak English well in India. JPMorgan Chase & Co, Lehman Brothers, ABN AMRO, Citibank, Deutsche Bank and HSBC Holdings recruited a large amount of skilled workers from the top MBA business schools in India in the past three years. China, although it is a world manufacturing magnate, only accounts for a share of US$2 billion in the IT outsourcing market in the world.

Analysis of the domestic background

In our embracing of the international transfer of service capital, we enjoy obvious advantages in policies and labor. Internationally, we are faced with big opportunities; but meanwhile there still exists a gap in our comparison with the contractees and rivals, which confronts us with severe and inevitable challenges.

After the reform and opening up, the competitive edge of China in the global economy lies in its low manufacturing costs. The rise of China is embodied in that China, in some degree, has become the center of global production and manufacturing. Internationally-renowned enterprises have moved their manufacturing bases to China one after another, and China has gradually become a specialized world factory. There are several reasons for this. Firstly, China boasts abundant natural resources and human resources, which provides a firm material foundation for China's turning into a world factory; secondly, the labor force in China is extremely cheap, which can reduce manufacturing costs for global enterprises; thirdly, the production/ manufacturing/ processing/ assembling procedures mainly rely on the workers and as there is little technology involved, so ordinary workers are able to be competent in the procedures; fourthly, the policy on attracting of merchants and investments after the reform and opening up are beneficial to the entrance of multinational manufacturing enterprises. In comparison with India China, in its process of becoming a world factory, has not well developed its service business outsourcing which enjoys comparative high added value. In 2005, China remained the third top trading country in the world with its US$1.42 trillion of goods import and export. However China's service trade rather lagged behind as it only accounted for 10.9% of China's trade volume, far below the international average level of 19%. To take the outsourcing of software in the world for an example, in 2005 the total volume of software outsourcing in China was US$960 million, accounting for only 2.3% of the global total volume. China is stuck in the bottom of the "smiling curve" which traps China in a depression in terms of income distribution.

Firstly, governments at all levels from the central to the regional, are well aware of the importance of undertaking the transfer of service sectors and have issued related encouraging and supporting policies to promote the development of BPO.

After 2000, the issue of *Document of the State Council. No. 18* and *Document of the State Council. No. 47* created a good external environment for the development of the software industry. From 2001 to 2005, the scale of the software industry has more than quadrupled, increasing from US$9.63 billion to US$48.4 billion, and has become the fastest-developing sector in the electronic information industry.

Faced with the opportunity of the international transfer of service business outsourcing industry, the Ministry of Commerce of the People's Republic of China has decided to carry out the "thousand-hundred-ten project" which aims, during the period of "the eleventh five-year plan," to construct 10 internationally competitive service outsourcing base cities, encourage 100 famous multinational enterprises to transfer considerable service outsourcing businesses into China, foster 1,000 large or medium sized service outsourcing enterprises that obtain international certifications in China, and by 2010 to make the export of service outsourcing, based on the level of 2005, quadruple in volume. The Ministry of Commerce and Ministry of Finance will work together to provide funds to support the project and also offer support for the manpower training of the service outsourcing, for the service outsourcing enterprises' obtaining of related international certification, and for the public service platform, public technology service platform construction, base city system and property rights protection system that are needed by service outsourcing. For example, the two ministries, together with the China Development Bank, will provide the service outsourcing base cities and service outsourcing enterprises with preferential policy loans; the China Export & Credit Insurance Corporation will also provide the service outsourcing enterprises with financing guarantee and credit insurance, assisting the enterprises to establish a credit risk management and evaluation system.

The Ministry of Information Industry (now restructured as the Ministry of Industry and Information Technology) has long been considering software development and service outsourcing as a new growing sector in the development of industries, and the Ministry of Commerce has been treating service outsourcing as an important part of the optimization of the export structure. Chen Ying—a deputy director of the Department of Electronic and Information Products Management in the Ministry of Information Industry said that the Ministry is working with other departments including the National Development and Reform Commission on the designing of policies to further encourage the software industry and integrated circuit industry to develop, and the Ministry of Information Industry is also working with the Ministry of Commerce, the Ministry of Science and Technology and the Ministry of Finance on the implementation of preferential policies associated with the technologically advanced modern service industry. Both domestic and foreign certified service outsourcing enterprises can enjoy the related preferential tax policies. The administrative legislation associated with the software and integrated circuit industries is being promoted, and 11 national software industry bases and 6 national software export bases have been approved. Recently, the Ministry of Information Industry together with the Ministry of Commerce and the Ministry of Science and Technology identified a group of cities to boost the foundation and potential to develop service outsourcing; Dalian, Shanghai, Xi'an, Shenzhen and Chengdu became the first five service outsourcing base cities in China.

Secondly, compared to other countries, especially India, China has more advantages in the labor price of BPO.

The labor force in India used to be cheaper, but the wages of college graduates, engineers and programmers increased fast and so the expenses on human resources account for 30–40% of the total annual expenses. However, in China, the monthly wage of a starter in BPO is about only US$300—1/10 of the starter's wage in the US, so the low wages now make China competitive. Henning Kagermann— CEO of SAP—the biggest producer of enterprise software in the world warned in January this year that costs in India are so high that India is no longer suitable for outsourcing business. The labor costs in big coastal cities in China are also increasing, but the low labor costs in inner areas of China are still attractive to enterprises. As well as Xi'an, foreign enterprises are happy with Chengdu and Wuhan. Kaoru Miyata, the director of NEC in Xi'an, said that the rents and wages in Xi'an are 40–50% lower than those in Beijing and Shanghai; Yasuo Noshiro, the director of systems engineering of Fujitsu in Xi'an, said that the costs in Xi'an are even lower than the fast-developing Dalian, and that the residents in Xi'an, who do not have many opportunities to change their jobs, are more loyal to their companies.

In this process, it is worth noticing and extremely convincing that Tata, the biggest IT consulting company in India, has built a base in Hangzhou; Infosys and Wipro have settled in Shanghai and Beijing respectively and they plan to increase the number of their employees in China from a couple of hundred to 5–6,000; Genpact used to be a process outsourcing subsidiary company of GE and now it has set up headquarters in India and Dalian and plans to increase the number of its employees in Dalian from 1,800 to more than 5,000.

The expansion of these enterprises is motivated by the fast increase in foreign customers' demands, and these enterprises hope to reduce their costs, apportion risks and seek for domestic support for their business in China. Meanwhile, Chinese enterprises also have some demands of the same kind. For example, TCS is designing and installing a new software system for Huaxia Bank—the twelfth largest bank in China.

Thirdly, China's established reputation as a "world factory" provides incomparable advantages for the construction of service outsourcing centers. It is particularly emphasized that service outsourcing does not need to happen in the service sectors, and the service processes needed in manufacturing sectors and other sectors are more likely to be outsourced. That is to say that after the industrial base in China succeeded in becoming the world manufacturing outsourcing transfer base in 1992, its status as a "world factory" and its competitive advantages embodied in its low manufacturing costs are favorable conditions for China to undertake the new round of international service outsourcing transfer. Most of the FDI of more than US$600 billion flowing into China and most of the more than 600,000 foreign enterprises are in the manufacturing sectors, and most of them are located in the coastal areas. These enterprises deal with manufacturing orders in the outsourcing model based on FDI and satisfy the needs of foreign markets by processing and assembling, mainly involving the production and operation links that need intensive labor in the production of high-tech products. All the above conditions will progressively promote the development and transformation of China's economy as well as the development of modern services including service outsourcing.

The Construction of Service Business Outsourcing Centers in the Yangtze River Delta

China's achievements in its embracing of international capital transfer in the manufacturing industry has attracted the world's attention, and the Yangtze River Delta has succeeded in playing the important role of "world factory." The Delta'a intact industrial supporting facilities and extension of the industrial chain both enable the Delta to boast overwhelming advantages in the next round of international competition. In the new trend of BPO, it is necessary and possible for the Delta to be the biggest service business outsourcing center in China and even in the world.

The necessity

Firstly, the development of tertiary industry in the area ranks the first in China, so it is necessary for the Delta to further strengthen its overall advantages in service industry thus driving fast development of the economic society.

Currently the proportions of the GDP accounted for by service industry in developed countries are all above 70%, and the proportion of the GDP in the world accounted for by service industry reaches 50%. However the proportion in China is only 32%. In 2006, the added value of tertiary industry in the 16 cities in the Delta reached RMB1.629991 trillion, an increase of RMB242.457 billion compared to 2005, and the share of service industry in the added value in 2006 was 41.3%. And in 2006, except in Shanghai and Zhoushan, the industrial structures in the 14 cities all revealed the model of "the second industry, the third industry, the first industry"—the share of the second industry in the structure is the largest, the third industry the middle and the first industry the lowest.

We can see from the situation in the 16 cities in the Delta that Shanghai's advantage in industrial structure is evident as the share of tertiary industry in the structure in Shanghai reached 50.6%; the share in Nanjing is 47.5%, ranking second in the Delta; and due to the geographic location and natural resources of Zhoushan, the share in Zhoushan is 46.1%, ranking third in the Delta. The shares in Hangzhou (44.9%) and Ningbo (40.1%) are both above 40%. The lowest share is found in Taizhou (32.1%). It can be seen from the development trends of tertiary industry in different regions, the cities in Zhejiang Province, except Jiaxing and Huzhou, boast the tertiary industries which develop faster than the economy and the shares of the industry in the GDP in these cities have been more or less increasing. The cities in Jiangsu Province, except Changzhou, boast tertiary industries that are developing at a speed higher than the economic growth rate, and the share of the industry in all the eight cities in Jiangsu, including Changzhou, has increased compared to that in 2005. The share in Suzhou increased by 1.5% compared to that in the previous year, which growth rate ranks the first in the 16 cities.

In the national comparison, the national GDP reached RMB20.9407 trillion which, in comparable prices, was an increase of 10.7% compared to that in 2005. Of this the added value of primary industry was RMB2.47 trillion with a year-to-year growth of 5%, the added value of secondary industry was RMB10.2004 trillion with a year-to-year growth of 12.5% and that of tertiary industry was RMB8.2703 trillion with a year-to-year growth of 10.3%. The ratio of the primary, secondary and tertiary industries is 11.8:48.7:39.5. Primary industry's share in the Delta is 8.1% lower than the national level, secondary industry's share in the Delta is 6.3% higher than the national level and tertiary industry's share in the Delta is 1.8% higher than the national level.

In Jiangsu Province the ratio of the three industries changed from "7.6:56.6:35.8" to "7.2:56.5:36.3" in 2006. The share of primary industry in the Yangtze River Delta is 3.5% lower than the Jiangsu level and the share of secondary industry in the Delta is 1.5% lower than the Jiangsu level, but the share of the first industry in the Delta is 5.0% higher than the Jiangsu level.

In terms of the comparison with Jiangsu Province, the ratio of the three industries in Jiangsu changed from the "6.5:53.5:40" to the "5.9:53.9:40.2" in 2006. The share of the first industry in the Yangtze River Delta is 2.2% lower than the Zhejiang level but the share of second industry in the Delta is 1.1% higher than the Jiangsu level and the share of the first industry in the Delta is 1.1% higher than the Jiangsu level.

Secondly, the science education in the Delta is of great importance in China, so it is necessary to retain and further attract high-tech skills by strengthening the modern service industry and building service business outsourcing centers.

In Nanjing, the numbers of universities and full-time undergraduate students rank in the front row in China. In 2006, in Jiangsu Province, there were 119 universities and 1.3062 million undergraduate students. 3,591,000 students were enrolled into universities and 2,573,000 students graduated from universities in that year. There were 891,000 postgraduate students in universities; 318,000 students were enrolled into postgraduate programs and 193,000 postgraduate students graduated from universities in that year. The enrollment rate in higher education reached 35.6%. In 2006, the expenses for R&D activities in Nanjing accounted for 2.45% of the total output value of the city. A total of 7,858 technology contracts were signed with a volume of RMB5.248 billion, an increase of 17.5% compared to 2005. There were 16 technological trade institutions started in 2006. At the end of 2006, the number of academicians of the CAS (Chinese Academy of Sciences) and the number of academicians of the CAE (Chinese Academy of Engineering) were 45 and 31 respectively. During the year, 6,793 patents were applied for, an increase of 29.9% compared to 2005. Of these the number of patents for inventions was 3,360, an increase of 44.9% and accounting for 49.5% of the total patents applications; the number of patent grants was 2,890, an increase of 33.7%. There were 366 high-tech enterprises above designated size. The industrial output value of the high-tech sector was RMB194.04 billion, accounting for 41.3% of the total industrial output value of the sectors above designated size in the city. Nanjing further implemented the strategy of "developing agriculture by applying scientific and technological advances": 50 new agricultural species were introduced, 45 agricultural technology demonstration parks were built, three modern agricultural demonstration parks were approved by the provincial government and 6 international cooperation programs were carried out. There were 200 agencies for examination of product quality, 8 state inspection centers, 3 institutions for certification of product qualities and systems, 1 legally-set measurement inspection institution and 13 legally-authorized measurement inspection institutions in Nanjing. An amount of 6,019 batches of products were inspected and spot checked, increasing by 10.2% compared to 2005. A total of 25 local standards were formulated or amended, increasing by 47.1%. There were 62 kinds of national, provincial and municipal brand-name products and national inspection-exempt products in Nanjing, including 4 kinds of new China Top Brand Products and 16 kinds of national inspection-exempt products. 1,464 quality engineers were trained and 1,147 were registered in 2006. There were 41 universities (excluding military colleges) in Nanjing, accounting for 1/3 of the universities in Jiangsu Province. In Nanjing in 2006, 1,383,000 students were enrolled into undergraduate programs in universities, 6,100 less than that in 2005, and there were 5,571,000 undergraduate students, increasing by 534,000 compared to 2005; 222,000 students were enrolled in postgraduate programs, increasing by 1,800 compared to that in the previous year and there were 637,000 postgraduate students in universities in Nanjing, 6,200 more than that in 2005.

However although there are abundant educational and high-tech resources in Nanjing, the city is still facing an important problem—the severe brain drain resulting from the incomplete skills-retaining mechanism. Among the various excellent talented people educated by the universities in Nanjing, those above the middle level, when deciding their final working location, always choose Shanghai instead of Nanjing and those below the middle level always choose Nanjing instead of other cities. If Nanjing could succeed in establishing its status as a BPO center, the high-level service industry would to great degree alleviate the "brain drain" and enable the overall structure of human resources in Nanjing to be promoted and optimized, thus providing constant intellectual support for the development of other related industries.

The imbalance caused by the flow of personnel inside the region stems from the differences in average wages and the development space of different job positions. In order to construct high-level service business outsourcing centers we must solve the imbalance of personnel. We need all member regions to coordinate in resource distribution and differences in policies in the development process and to take everything into account and so optimize allocation of human resources.

Thirdly, compared to the manufacturing industry in the Delta which boasts overall advantages in introducing foreign investment, the service industry is lagging behind. Especially in the industrial structure, the function of foreign capital as a promoter of service industry is hardly conspicuous. It is necessary for the Delta to take advantage of the high share of tertiary industry in the industrial structure to seize opportunities to facilitate the construction of service business outsourcing centers.

The development of manufacturing business outsourcing and development of service business outsourcing are the natural evolution and strategic choices for China in two different stages of industrialization in the increasingly open market. The former development is not purely replaced by the latter, instead, on a certain basis, the two promote each other as they depend on and complement each other.

The development of manufacturing business outsourcing is an inner foundation and condition for the development of service business outsourcing. The upgrade of the inner division of manufacturing industry and enhancement of manufacturing efficiency is a precondition for the externalization and independent development of modern service business outsourcing; the modern service industry, as an input into the manufacturing industry, contains human capital, knowledge capital and technology capital which are key to the enhancement of manufacturing industry's international competitiveness. Geographically, the service industry and manufacturing industry have the features of cooperative location and agglomeration, and the convergence of developed manufacturing sectors can optimize the spatial distribution of the service industry and then develop service industry clusters. In particular, it needs to be mentioned that FDI in services and FDI in manufacturing always follow each other. That is to say, when FDI in services enters a new country, it selects the area where the FDI in manufacturing is concentrated as its location or selects the supply chain enterprises with which it has already had a business relationship for a long time, the inner logic of which is that the enterprises want to bring their advantages associated with information into play and the advantages come from the transparent service prices and quality services that the enterprises are already familiar with. The existence of the information barrier shows that in distribution, the FDI in services tends to follow the FDI in the downstream industries, which does not only offer a possible explanation for what we have observed in our practice but also provides policy guidance for the encouragement of service business outsourcing.

Generally speaking, a developed service industry is based on a developed secondary industry. However, if the converse is also true we can develop the service industry first, which will promote the level-enhancement and structure-optimization of related industries on the level of external supporting environment and specialized division. A convenient service business supporting environment does not only provide a favorable industrial incubation and growth environment for local enterprises, but also attracts a large amount of external enterprises into the local market in the modes of direct investment, financing or merger, thus extending or optimizing the local industrial structure.

Certainly, rational analysis, policy support and adjustment of industrial arrangement are needed in the real construction of service business outsourcing centers.

At present, the tremendous advantages inside the Delta are the highly developed manufacturing industry strip in Jiangsu and Zhejiang and the highly developed tertiary industry in Shanghai, especially the finance, insurance, logistics and high-end R&D centers. The rational integration of these two advantages will offer much help to the construction of BPO centers in the Delta. As we have mentioned, outsourcing is not limited to service industry, and many service links in the manufacturing sectors, such as program design, procedure control and management service could be outsourced. The service business center needs to be organically integrated with the manufacturing center to bring the industrial correlation effect properly into play.

It is also necessary for the Delta to make use of BPO to increase the service business export with high added value and so enhance the humanized competitive edge of the service industry, to create more job opportunities and to raise the levels of wages and skills. For example, the 2003 McKensey report predicted the volume of unemployment caused by service business outsourcing from 2003 to 2015, and estimated the interest distribution between the contractors and contractees of outsourcing. However since the calculation method was not clear enough, it was difficult to estimate the standard deviation. The report also pointed out that in the common business cycle, the unemployment caused by outsourcing only accounts for a small proportion of the total unemployment. There is a huge difference between the demands for skills in construction of service business outsourcing centers and manufacturing business outsourcing centers as the latter demands skilled techniques as well as continuous and simple consumption of physical strength, which could be achieved by short-term training, while the former demands not just techniques in working procedures but more intellectual support, including adaptability to a multi-language environment, specialties in computer and software operation and proficiency in controlling specific industrial procedures, which capabilities cannot be acquired only in a short-term training program but need high educational accumulation. The demands of service business outsourcing could be combined with the education system in the Delta: while the general skills are cultivated, education in professional skills should be emphasized in accordance with the needs of BPO center construction.

The possibility

The development of service business outsourcing started with software services in the 1980s and began its fast development due to the "Millennium Bug." From 2001 to 2003, the decision-makers in American enterprises all started to use BPO one after another, which led to the fast development of BPO, and now BPO has become an important factor in promoting the development of enterprises. According to statistics, the global volume of the outsourcing market increased from US$150 trillion in 2001 to US$300 trillion in 2004.

Firstly, from the point of view of the external environment of service business outsourcing, although the service business outsourcing develops at a high speed its development is still in the primary stage.

Among the 1,000 biggest companies in the world, about 70% have not outsourced any of their business procedures to countries where the costs are low. A survey by the UACTAD in 2004 on the top 500 enterprises in Europe showed that only 39% of the enterprises had ever implemented offshore outsourcing but the enterprises had already created 20,000 offshore job opportunities; another 44% of the enterprises planned to begin their outsourcing in the next few years.

At present, we are still uncertain of the development scale and degree of service business outsourcing; it is still far from maturity and it has a long way to go before the models and characteristics of location are settled. Even in the finance and IT sector in which the service business outsourcing was launched earlier than in other sectors, service outsourcing is still in the primary stage of international industrial restructuring. For example, in the banking sector, there are still a large amount of opportunities in the regional or global restructuring operation. It can be seen that the extension of service outsourcing has shown an irreversible tendency and that it is likely to spread fast in many sectors and many countries. The essence of service business outsourcing is the enterprises' contracting out or subcontracting of their non-core business to other service providers on the basis of value chain management to enhance the production factor and resource allocation efficiency of the cross-border production organization model. As the outsourcing is mainly focused on the multinational enterprises' non-core business procedures with comparatively low technological content and added value, the developing countries have the advantage of low costs in their undertaking of outsourcing services.

Secondly, the producer service industry that boasts absolute advantages gives the Yangtze River Delta more potential than the Beijing Golden Triangle and the Pearl River Delta to become a service business outsourcing center.

Why could the Yangtze River Delta headed by Shanghai accumulate so many manufacturing sectors and create so many miracles in manufacturing that other regions centered on Beijing, Xi'an, Chengdu and Chongqing could not? Some may use the location advantage, favorable foundation of manufacturing industry, high quality labor force and preferential governmental policies to explain this. However it needs to be pointed out that besides the Yangtze River Delta there are many areas in China, especially in the Southern and Eastern coastal parts of China, which are similar in these respects so why have none of those areas, except the Pearl River Delta, managed to concentrate so many manufacturing sectors and make as prominent achievements as the Yangtze River Delta? Moreover even though the Pearl River Delta does not enjoy favorable foundation of manufacturing industry and high quality labor resources, it has agglomerated a large number of manufacturing sectors and has performed very well in manufacturing industry. Therefore the above factors are not the key factors that can explain the accumulation and development of manufacturing sectors in the Yangtze River Delta.

Our opinion is that it is the comparatively developed service industry in the Yangtze River Delta that enables the Delta to agglomerate so many manufacturing sectors and make such prominent achievements in manufacturing. According to the input-output tables in the *Shanghai Statistical Yearbook*, we have worked out that the proportion of gross output of services in Shanghai accounted for by producer services was 58.99% in 2000 and 56.30% in 2002, the proportions of which, although far lower than the average level of 70% in developed countries, were of a high level in China. According to the input-output tables in the *China Statistical Yearbook*, the proportion of gross output of services in China accounted for by the producer services was 53.86% in 2000, which shows that the Shanghai level was 5.13% higher than the national level in 2000.

Thirdly, the agglomeration of manufacturing sectors can reduce the transaction costs of service industry, especially the producer service industry, which externally promotes the concentration and development of service industry in the Delta. The agglomeration of related industries and supporting industries can reduce the transaction costs inside the industry, thus restricting the entrance space of some service sectors like logistics and storage. However service business outsourcing covers not only the producer service industry but also the service links of the manufacturing industry. The agglomeration of target consumers of services would to great extent facilitate the agglomeration of the service industry, thus forming a center.

The manufacturing industry and producer service industry are

complementary to each other. On the one hand, the development of manufacturing industry will naturally lead to the increase in demand for producer services, and just as the Smith theorem pointed out, increase in demand in the market economy will promote the marketization and specialized development of the producer service industry by enhancing the economy of scale. Many producer services that have been internalized inside the manufacturing industry will now be gradually externalized or vertically disintegrated from the manufacturing industry thus forming many specialized service organizations, such as accountancy firms, law firms, advertising and marketing companies, trade companies and R&D centers. According to the specialized theory of roundabout production and enhancement put forward by the Austrian school of economics, the representative characteristic of the deepening process of capital is that the process is accompanied by roundabout and enhanced specialization. And the growth and development is undoubtedly an important demonstration of the increased roundabout production and enhanced specialization. On the other hand, the growth of the producer service industry promotes the enhancement both of the production efficiency and operational efficiency of the manufacturing industry, the rise in output added value and the enhancement of competitiveness by deepening and extending the specialized division. According to the Smith theorem, division boosts productivity via specialization. The development of the producer service industry is not only propitious to the deepening and extending of the specialized division (Jone and Kierzkowski, 1988; Francois, 1990), but also fosters the development of manufacturing industry by reducing the real costs of service input in the manufacturing. Generally, the real costs of services can be represented by sorts: the more sorts of competitive services are the lower the real costs, because the large number of sorts provide the producers with more flexibility and more opportunities to minimize their costs under some certain output levels. If the service production has no fixed costs, then there will be numerous sorts of services because every enterprise in every industrial sector may be in need of a tiny amount of services. If fixed costs exist, the sorts of services are restricted by the market scale.

The development of producer service industry in Shanghai and the agglomeration and development of manufacturing industry in the Yangtze River Delta are complementary to each other. As a famous economic, financial, trade and navigation center in China, Shanghai undoubtedly enjoys the most developed producer service industry in China. The number of accountancy firms in Shanghai rank first in China, and there are many internationally renowned accountancy firms; the financial system and navigation in Shanghai also top the country. Consequently, the Delta could attract a great amount of FDI and industrial transfer both at home and abroad, and the increasing number of countries involved further promotes the development and growth of the producer service industry.

In terms of human resources, the Yangtze River Delta boasts overwhelming advantages, especially in the high-level software skills needed in the construction of a service business outsourcing center. There are a large number of universities and high-tech enterprises in the Delta, endowing the Delta with sufficient science and education resources, specialized technical personnel and intellectual enterprises, which cultivates the technology innovation process.

With its sufficient resources in science and education as well as its cultural background, one of the most important members—Nanjing—enjoys advantageous conditions in the development of "intellectual industry," which conditions have provided the development of intellectual industry with a favorable operation platform. According to statistics there are 48 universities, 16 state key labs, 10 national engineering research centers, 131 post-doctoral mobile research centers and working stations, 271 institutions of higher learning and research institutes, and 174 institutions of large and medium industrial enterprise technical development. In terms of specialized technical personnel, in Nanjing there are 76 academicians of CAS and CAE, 545,000 professionals with senior technical titles and 5,654,000 specialized technical personnel, and a training system for specialized technical personnel is well established. There are 85 software training institutions which train 45,000 technical personnel in software. Twenty-two of the training institutions are non-governmental, and these institutions train 16,000 personnel each year. 704 high-tech enterprises in Nanjing have been certified, among which 23 are listed. Thirty-five enterprises in Nanjing boast a university background and 38 enjoy research institutions as their backup. One hundred and thirty-five enterprises were founded by technical personnel, which shows that the "Nanjing mode" of independent innovation has been established.

As the leader of the intellectual industry, the software industry in Nanjing boasts a year-to-year growth rate of above 50% in the proceeds from sales in five successive years, and the total revenue of the software industry added up to RMB25.8 billion in 2006, ranking the first among the provincial capitals. There are five enterprises with revenue of more than RMB100 million, and seven of the software enterprises in Nanjing are among the top 100 software enterprises in China. Ten of the software enterprises in Nanjing have been successfully listed. Statistics also show that the total revenue of the software industry in Nanjing reached RMB1.8 billion in 2000 and increased to RMB25.8 billion in 2006. The software industry has shown its potential and competence to be the bellwether of the intellectual industry. The output value of the software industry in Nanjing was about RMB30 billion in 2007 and will increase to RMB80 billion in 2010. Currently, the scale of the software industry in Nanjing is preceded only by that in Beijing, Shanghai and Shenzhen, ranking the fourth in China. And in several years to come, the software industry in Nanjing will make efforts to exceed that in Shenzhen to become the third in China. During the period of the "tenth five-year plan," Nanjing will set a base of RMB 12 million and arrange a special fund with an annual growth rate of no less than 20% for the development of the software industry. Meanwhile, the construction of four centers on the level of a city as a whole should be accelerated, which four centers are: software services center, software manpower training and trading center, software test center and a service center for the investment and financing of the software industry. We are also optimistic about the future development of the comic design industry and industrial design industry as important supporters of the intellectual industry. And the largest industrial design center has been built in the National University Science Park of Nanjing University and Colleges in Gulou District.

In Shanghai, after the construction of Jinqiao and Zhangjiang development zone, a new park—Pujiang Intellectual Valley—has been built in Pudong to attract the headquarters of both domestic and foreign famous enterprises. Recently the valley, which boasts a construction area of 300,000 square meters, was praised by the parties concerned as an energy-economical and ecological business park most suitable for working, and the valley was also conferred with the first architectural energy-saving certificate issued by the German government outside Germany.

The Pujiang Intellectual Valley covers an area of about 1,100 mu (1 mu=666.7 square meters) and is focused on the introduction of headquarters of internationally famous enterprises. The valley is devoted in developing intellectual economy and an all-round IT industry of broad scope and multiple layers.

Pujiang Intellectual Valley is located in Pujiang Town, which is one of the nine towns that the Shanghai government is going to attach importance to. In order to further develop the economy in Pujiang, the Pujiang High-Tech Park of Caohejing New-Tech Technological Development Zone, which enjoys a planning area of 8.3 square kilometres, was launched recently. Due to the current demands the Park was elevated from a municipal development park to a national development zone, raising the level of industrial competence.

In Zhejiang, with the fast economic development and expanding opening-up, the international service trade in Zhejiang has moved from the starting period into the accelerating period. During the five years from 2000 to 2004, the total volume of foreign trade in service in Zhejiang increased from US$790 million to US$4.37 billion, increasing by 453%, the growth rate of which was 340% higher than that of the total volume of foreign trade in goods. The service trade export increased from US$260 million to US$2.67 billion, increasing 821% with an annual growth rate of 55.9% which was much higher than the growth rate of goods trade in Zhejiang (26.2%). In 2004 Zhejiang witnessed a favorable balance in service trade for the first time, changing the trend of an expanding unfavorable balance in the previous years. With its growing competency, Zhejiang has acquired the foundations and conditions to accelerate the development of international service trade.

All the above are not only the overwhelming competitive edges of Nanjing, Shanghai and Zhejiang, but also the embodiment of the integrated advantages of the Delta. All these advantages are the "infrastructure" needed in the construction of modern service business outsourcing centers. We believe that the Delta definitely has the potential and competence to build nationally and even internationally famous BPO centers.

The Problems Existing in the Process of Building Service Business Outsourcing Centers

In the process of our construction of a "world office," there still exist many problems and deficiencies for us to solve and improve.

Firstly, generally speaking, the overall scale of the software industry in China is currently too small. For the contractees, any business of which the content can be digitized, of which the procedures can be sliced and of which every part can be removed flexibly could be outsourced to other countries. How to assure the contractees that you can secure and succeed with their outsourced business is a key question, and the most important factors in achieving this goal are scientific and rational software designing and fast but accurate transmission. In 2005, the software industry only accounted for 5.9% of the global market share, but the shares of the US, Western Europe and Japan were 39%, 29.5% and 10.4% respectively. Most of software enterprises in China are medium and small sized, and the average income of the top 100 software enterprises in China is only US$100 million. Moreover the software enterprises in China are mainly focused on made-to-order programs and the development of common application software. For most software enterprises it is relatively hard to develop independently without a good breakthrough point. The low competitiveness of the enterprises and the lack of industrial competitive edge lead to the unclear status of China's software industry in the international software industrial division.

Secondly, at present, the biggest problem in developing BPO is that there are not enough people with both professional skills and English language. For example, in Xi'an, although each year there are more than 300,000 new college graduates, the number of professionally skilled are limited. Consequently foreign enterprises in China have to spend money to "complement the Chinese educational system." Nishiro, the CEO of Fujitsu Xi'an System Engineering Company, sent 40 Chinese employees to Japan to receive training and the annual expense for each person was US$30,000. Nishiro said: "they need to receive two years full-time training to become middle-level engineers and four years to become project managers." James, the director of GrapeCity (an Japanese IT outsourcing company) in Xi'an said: "Even after three years training only 10% to 20% of the programmers could really meet the requirements to be program designers. There are so many universities and college graduates in China, but they are not as good as their diplomas say." The lack of skills and disadvantages in language abilities are the most serious problems in China's competition with other countries, especially with India.

Thirdly, it is of great importance to build a favorable trust relationship with the customers. Mark A. Boyle, Vice-President of Accenture (a famous global management consulting, technology services and outsourcing company), in Greater China thinks that China has the potential to develop into a global BPO market and become the largest outsourcing service provider in the next 5–10 years. However the Chinese enterprises in service sectors and outsourcing sectors are facing many difficulties and challenges. The most important thing for the enterprises is to have excellent credit that would give the customers trust in the enterprises, and on this point China should learn from India. David Tapper, management director of IDC (a globally famous specialized provider of consulting, counseling and activity services of information technology and telecommunication sectors and consumer technology markets), in Greater China thinks that the challenge China is facing is how to elevate the enterprises that already have IT infrastructures into higher processes, how to make the enterprises more efficient and simpler, and how to really implement the BPO strategies. The enterprises need to have the right people to do the right things in the right places at the right times, but they should be not only technologically skilled but also competent in coordination and communication so that they can properly coordinate the whole process.

Fourthly, protection for intellectual property rights is another important precondition for BPO and it is also one of the existing problems we are confronted with. The lack of balancing strategies during transactions can lead to many problems, including hurried agreements. Many enterprises in the EU have their own methods of protecting their intellectual property rights. Intellectual property rights protection is of great importance for multinational enterprises, and only when China attaches more importance to this protection can it attract more international clients. Additionally, government control and management by contract also need a favorable environment to support them. Mark Robinson from Simmons & Simmons Law Firm reminded Chinese enterprises that success could be achieved only when the enterprises give proper consideration of how to minimize the risks, and the issues including capital, business scale and specific objectives should be settled in the early period and precautionary measures should be adopted before the real problems emerge. Mark Robinson pointed out that the tax policies and financing policies should be taken into consideration in the early period, and the services should be clearly described in the contracts, including handling of mechanisms, recomposition competency and integration competency, in order to ensure that the clients are heading in the right direction.

Measures and Suggestions

In recent years, with the expansion of processing trade and manufacturing industry's attraction of foreign capital to China, the status of China as a world manufacturing center has been constantly enhanced. However we need to be aware that the manufacturing industry in China mainly relies on it advantages in labor resources and that with the further development of some industrial sectors, especially heavy industry and the chemical industry, both energy consumption and the costs of environmental protection will increase. Therefore the status of "world factory" will not only make it difficult to optimize the industrial structure in China but will also hinder the sustainable development of the economy and society in China.

The Yangtze River Delta is faced with the same problems—we need new growth points to ensure the fast and healthy development of the economy in the Delta. Developing service industry is the best strategic choice. The modern service industry includes not only the traditional sectors such as banking, insurance and trade but also the new sectors such as telecommunications, commercial services, audio and video, medical care and sanitation, distance learning, information management and technological services. Different from the manufacturing industry, the modern service industry is a "smokeless industry" as it generates no pollution and consumes little resources, and can offer a large amount of job opportunities. With the coming end of China's transitional period after its entrance into the WTO, the service market in China is more open to the outside world. Foreign capital pours into the service market in China and service outsourcing is practiced here in accordance to the enterprises' value chain management concepts, which confront the economic structural adjustment with new opportunities. Without any doubt, to develop the service industry in the Delta and enhance the industrial quality is a strategic choice for the Delta to undertake the new round of industrial transfer.

Firstly, we need to improve the construction of the infrastructure of service industry and reinforce training in international skills. The modern and internationalized centers of the service industry are based on advanced modern information communication systems and data-transmission networks, so BPO cannot be achieved and the construction of high-level service outsourcing centers can never been done without telecommunications satellites, submarine optical fiber cables of high capability and an information expressway system. Therefore the related governments and regional coordination institutions should invest more in the construction of service infrastructure and properly design the information sector as well as the software sector in order to ultimately set up reasonable industrial clusters of service outsourcing.

Internationalized skills of high quality are needed in the construction of international BPO centers. The Indian enterprises that are successful in BPO have completely stepped out of the traditional structure in their demands for skills as they require personnel to know several languages and have knowledge of financial affairs, the financial systems in different countries and laws (especially the laws in the countries of the outsourcing contractees). Therefore outsourcing is a seemingly simple but intrinsically complicated industry. The challenges we will face will be real and severe.[4]

The biggest issue we are facing is how to change the links in the current education system which do not meet the real requirements. We can deal with the issue in this way. We could provide IT training services and online education services by setting up a platform for sharing the educational resources of enterprises and schools, we could lay emphasis on education that focuses on the cultivation of students' techniques, establish an advanced and open lab environment, offer abundant online educational resources, enable every student to have one PC and implement the teaching mode in which the face-to-face teaching is complemented by e-Learning, and also we could use real projects in enterprises to increase the amount of practical training and launch case teaching.

By vigorously developing IBT skills training, enterprises could participate in the whole process of schools' curriculum designing, training objectives setting, teaching plan designing and job training for students, which would enable the students to recognize corporate culture and to be familiar with enterprise business so that they could undergo the transition from students to employees smoothly.

We should build "incubators" for college students to start up their own business, and organize the students who apply to be a member in the form of a "virtual company"; we could introduce practical training from enterprises and develop training programs under the guidance of the schools and tutors from the enterprises. In this way could we enhance the students' practical ability, initiative, and ability to organize and manage.

Secondly, we should vigorously undertake service outsourcing to enhance the overall competitiveness of the industries in the Yangtze River Delta. Industries globally have welcomed a new round of transfers, and the Delta should demonstrate an overwhelming performance during the new round of industrial transfers and construct service business outsourcing centers. The undertaking of service business outsourcing will profoundly influence the development of related industries. Service outsourcing is an intrinsically real embodiment and inevitable outcome of the international industrial specialized division, so the fragmentation slicing off of production processes will make all the service links which are dissociated with the production links available for outsourcing to other regions by networks. The outsourcing undertaking is not only a reflection of high service quality level but also genuine realization of production processes' modernized model and the real embodiment of the complete industrial chain and systematic industrial linkage. The construction of high-level BPO centers will promote the enhancement of the overall level of the industries in the Yangtze River Delta on the level of production technology, managerial skill, managerial efficiency and service quality.

Thirdly, we should adjust our objectives for our attraction of foreign capital and merchants and make great efforts to attract foreign capital into services. With the ending of China's transitional period after its entrance into the WTO, the restrictions in the domestic market on opening to foreign capital will be gradually reduced and the foreign capital in services will enter into China in more active ways. The Yangtze River Delta enjoys favorable industrial supporting facilities and according to the agglomeration theory, the enterprises that provide supporting services to other sectors or other links in the same sector will select their location and make arrangements in the areas in or surrounding the existing high-tech industrial zones or development zones. The Delta should make good use of its fast-developing and high quality tertiary industry to put the focus of foreign capital attraction on the service sectors and attract more foreign capital into services in more active ways.

Fourthly, we should energetically cultivate the local service business entities and enhance the competitiveness of local enterprises. The Yangtze River Delta boasts robust human resources and a related industrial foundation, and in particular the software skills and software industry in the Delta rank top in China. Considered from the perspective of the long-term development of the national economy we cannot purely depend on foreign enterprises and we should enhance the competitiveness of local enterprises and encourage local enterprises to participate in international competition and cooperation. Related governmental departments should formulate corresponding supporting policies to foster the competitive enterprises on the levels of industrial policy, financial policy and tax policy, trying to cultivate an internationally competitive service business outsourcing brand enterprises.

Fifthly, we should actively improve the related laws and regulations to strengthen our protection of intellectual property rights. In the process of undertaking service business outsourcing and building outsourcing centers, more issues associated with the protection of intellectual property rights will be involved. Since those links that can be done via remote network transmission rely on some professional software to process data, write programs, analyze reports and diagnose procedures, the convenient network will, whilst it transmits the services, accelerate the proliferation of pirate software at an unprecedented speed. Therefore there are new requirements on the protection of intellectual property rights. The laws and regulations that protect innovation are not only an ectogenic driving force for the independently innovative entities in the homelands of the software but also a positive environmental encouragement for foreign-funded enterprises as the laws and regulations maintain a fair, reasonable and orderly competition environment while protecting the real benefits of the innovative entities.

7

Chapter

The Optimization of the Distribution of the Productive Force in the Yangtze River Delta

Introduction

Based on the in-depth thinking on the mutually dependent relationship between the manufacturing industry and the service industry, especially the producer service industry, we adopt a new economic geographical analytical method to study the optimization of the spatial distribution of service sectors in the Yangtze River Delta. According to related theories in economic geography, the service industry could coordinate the optimization of the spatial distribution of the productive force in the Yangtze River Delta in two aspects: firstly, when factors can flow freely between the regions, regional economic growth can be achieved by two mechanisms—agglomeration and radiation; secondly, when the factors cannot flow freely between the regions, regional economic growth can be achieved through the relationship between the input and output of inter-regional economic activities.

The above two mechanisms realize regional economic growth through three effects. The first effect is the market approach effect, or the local market effect, which refers to the fact that monopolistic enterprises tend to select a large-scale location for their manufacturing and a small-scale location for their sales; the second effect is the living cost effect, or price index effect, which refers to the influence of enterprises' selection of location on the living costs of the local consumers; the third effect is the market crowding effect, also called the local competition effect, which refers to the fact that over-concentration would do harm to the enterprises and that less competitive enterprises tend to select locations where there are comparatively fewer rivals. In the three effects, the former two effects combined with inter-regional movement of population form an inter-regional circulation-accumulation causality relationship, or the backward-forward linkage, and the former two effects are convergent while the third one is radiative.

At present, as the international production system led by the multinational enterprises has changed a lot, not only has enterprises' organizational structure inside the manufacturing industry disintegrated longitudinally, but also the service industry, especially the producer service industry, has been and will be further separated from the manufacturing industry. It can be said that with the separation of service industry from the manufacturing industry, our era is stepping into the era of the headquarters economy. In the Yangtze River Delta where transportation, logistics and commerce are highly developed, not only the multinational enterprises in manufacturing industry but also some domestic large-sized manufacturing enterprises are strongly motivated internally to realize the spatial strategic separation of their headquarters from their manufacturing factories.

It is exactly because of it extraordinary location advantages and its substantial foundation of manufacturing industry that the Yangtze River Delta has succeeded in establishing itself as a famous modern manufacturing base. However the construction of the modern manufacturing base in the Delta is embodied not only in the spatial distribution of the manufacturing sector, but also and more importantly in the service industry's coordination in the optimization of spatial distribution of the manufacturing industry's productive force, because the producer service industry has been playing an increasingly important role in the construction of modern manufacturing bases. Here the "manufacturing" of manufacturing industry refers to the whole process of creating and providing products for customers, including the development, design, production, circulation and after-sale services of the products. With the constant innovation of the structure of manufacturing industry and the increasingly ambiguous definitions of manufacturing industry and service industry, the future service industry's coordination in the optimization of spatial distribution of manufacturing industry's productive force in the Delta will become more and more comprehensive, and service industry's coordination of the optimization of productive forces' spatial distribution will be more embodied in the construction of modern manufacturing bases and the common development of manufacturing industry and service industry. Only when the two industries integrate to form a combined force can they maintain their competitive advantages in economic development. Moreover as the modern manufacturing base is a regional manufacturing system, the interdependence among the entities in the system demands that manufacturing enterprises strengthen their cooperative interaction with other entities in the system. Therefore the modern manufacturing base as the regional manufacturing system of Yangtze River Delta region as a whole is not only the accumulation of manufacturing enterprises in the region but also a special organizational form in which the manufacturing enterprises are closely linked to the service enterprises in the region, and it is an embodiment of the service industry's coordination of the optimization of productive forces' spatial distribution.

Based on the above theoretical foundation and fundamental reality, by observing the spatial arrangement of service industries' coverage in the Yangtze River Delta, we believe that the agglomeration of service industry will lead to a decrease in transaction costs, which is mainly realized by the spatial flow of factors among the cities and between the cities and villages.

Literature Review

We believe that the study of the service industry's coordination in the optimization of productive forces' spatial distribution should start from the interactive relationship between service industry and manufacturing industry because manufacturing industry and service industry, especially the producer service industry, are mutually supplementary. On the one hand, the development of manufacturing industry is bound to lead to the growth of demands for producer services. The numerous accountancy firms, law firms, advertisement design and marketing firms, trade companies, and R&D institutions in the big cities are good exemplifications. On the other hand, the growth of the producer service industry promotes the enhancement of manufacturing industry's production and operation efficiency, the growth of output added value and the strengthening of competitiveness via the deepening of specialized division. (Gao & Liu, 2005)

There are many methods of measuring the cost of services, but commonly the real cost of service can be shown by the number provided. We have already seen that the more types of competitive services are, the lower the real costs. Diversified types will result in more opportunities offered to producers to optimize their costs on the output level, and flexibility will be enhanced. If service production has no fixed cost, there will be countless sorts of services in the market, because every enterprise in the industrial sector is likely to need a small number of services of every sort. Therefore, as long as the fixed costs exist, the types of services are restricted by the market scale.

Just as the Japanese scholar pointed out, what contend on the stage of international competition are products of manufacturing industry, but the service industry is indirectly regulating the competitiveness of manufacturing industry behind the manufacturing industry's back. Here it is the producer service industry that is indirectly regulating the competitiveness of manufacturing industry behind the manufacturing industry's back. Additionally, according to Porter's competitive strategy theory, the cultivation of competitive advantages should be achieved by differentiation strategy, low costs strategy and target agglomeration strategy. Within this the target agglomeration strategy can be further divided into agglomeration guided by cost and agglomeration guided by differentiation. Therefore the shaping of a region's competitive advantages has actually only two sources—differentiation advantage and low cost advantage. And the service industry's coordination in the optimization of productive forces' spatial distribution is the primary source of these two advantages.

The service industry studied in this chapter is mainly the producer service industry. From the research perspective, research on the service industry's coordination in the optimization of productive forces' spatial distribution can be carried out not only on the level of industry but also on the level of enterprise. In terms of the study on the level of industry, the research focus can be that by analyzing the statistics, we find out the differences among service industries on different regional structures and proportions; and in terms of the study on the enterprise level, we can make good use of model analysis to read the motive of service industry's behavior in the spatial distribution of enterprises. The latter one is the most commonly used analytical method in regional economics concerned with enterprise location theory. If not strictly determined, it is difficult to tell the internal differences between enterprise location theory and industry location theory.

Therefore, in accordance with our research needs, this chapter will review the three theoretical schools of industrial location theory—normative industrial location theory, behavioral location theory and enterprise geographical theory. Normative industry location theory originates from the industrial location theory published by Alfred and Weber in 1909, which theory holds the view that enterprises will locate their factories in the places where the costs are the lowest. The theory also asserts that the factors that influence the industrial enterprises' location selection are mainly transport cost, labor cost and agglomeration economy. On the basis of the theory, scholars have put forward a series of enterprise and industrial location theories. For example, Moses (1958) introduced the fluctuant production functions to further explain how to change the quantitative combination of production scale and production factors to determine the best location for factories. A German scholar, Losch (1954), introduced demands into the spatial economic models for the first time and he put forward the view that the point that determines the lowest production costs of enterprises is not necessarily equal to the point that brings the largest profit (although the former is in pursuit of the latter). Gleenhut (1974) attempted to combine the "lowest cost theory" with the "location interdependence theory," and tried to use the maximum gross profit to integrate the lowest costs with the location interdependence, in order to decide the best location. Additionally, Smith (1981) re-explained the new industrial location theory from the viewpoint of economic geography and developed two important ideas—spatial cost curve and profitable spatial margin.

The behavioral location theory was first put forward by Simon in his work in 1957 and March 1958. Simon found from real observation that no matter whether an economic man is an optimum theoretician or not, his real behavior is always in pursuit of satisfaction. That is to say that in fact the decision makers cannot take everything into consideration so they can only take behavior that satisfies them. Simon defined this kind of behavior as "Bound Rationality." From the perspective of limited rationality and incomplete information, Allen Pred (1967) believed that human wisdom and available information are both limited, so every choice of location is based on information on different levels of completeness and on different competencies to apply information. Generally speaking, the more sufficient the information is and the more competent the decision-maker is in applying the information, the larger the possibility for the decided location to be the optimum is; otherwise, the smaller the possibility is. Allen Pred also combined the above concepts with a behavior matrix and applied the combination in the location-deciding of different new factories. A prominent feature of the behavioral research method is that it emphasizes that the process of decision-making is always influenced by many personal factors. However, in modern society, decisions are no longer made by single persons but by large-sized organizations or the decision-making departments of enterprises, which organizations include governmental departments and private organizations. McNee (1960), in his research of enterprises' geographical location, came to realize the meaning of this kind of large organization and thus named these kind of groups as "Area or Space Organization Institutions."

The trend of using enterprise geography theories to study large-sized enterprises emerged comparatively late—at the end of the 1960s and the beginning of the 1970s. The central concept of enterprise geography lies in how competent the manufacturers are in improving and using the environment they are located in (Hayter and Watts, 1983). A prominent feature of the research styles of the scholars in this school is that they are not restricted to studying how location deciding leads to location distribution, but further discuss some geographical outcomes of some non-spatial deciding factors. Therefore the most significant contribution of the research of enterprise geography is that it shifts the emphasis from the spatial factors of the economic environment in the traditional location researches to the possible impact and change of enterprises' activities in the environment.

In a simple review of the basic viewpoints and research methods of the three theoretical schools, it is easy for us to find that the cost-profit analysis is a primary factor every enterprise should consider when making decisions about location and specific space organization. Institutions are needed in the enterprises' selection of geographical locations, and the decisions made should be in coordination with the environmental space factors. Although the above theories are focused on manufacturing enterprises, they are suitable for the service industry when it comes to selection of spatial location.

Theoretical Models

We use the existing researches of Zhao Hong (2004) and Wu Fuxiang (2006) for reference and adopt the theoretical models to explain how the service industry uses its selection of geographical location to coordinate the optimization of productive forces' spatial distribution. Please refer to Fig. 7.1.

Fig. 7.1. The relationship between the spatial organizational structures of manufacturing industry and service industry

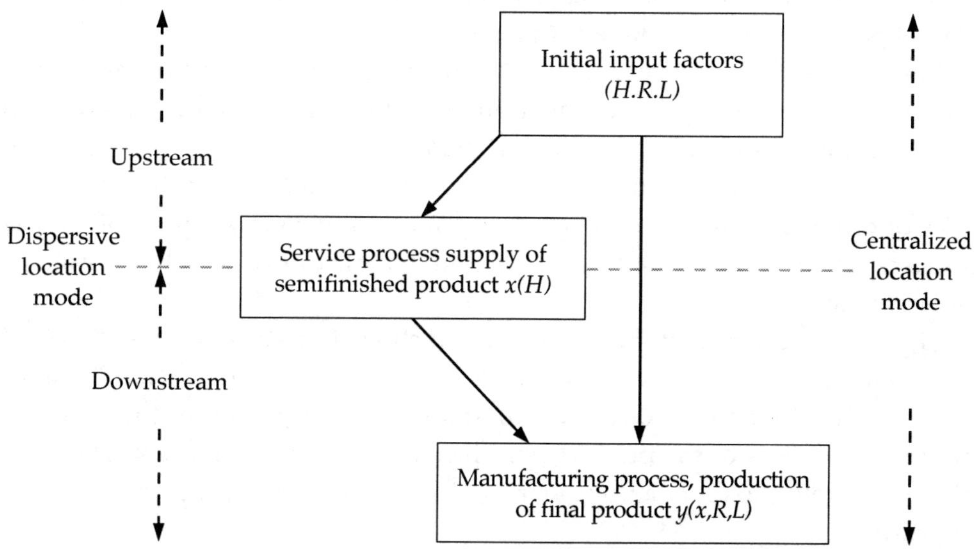

Basic hypotheses

(1) We assume that the enterprises need two value-creating activities in their production of some products: the first activity is the manufacturing process of the products, which is called "y"; and the second is the design, R&D, marketing and management activities provided to the products, which is called "x," and "x" is the intermediate ring used to form the final product "y."

(2) We assume that the production "x" is in need of a high level of intellectual human resources "H," namely, the producer service input; and "y" needs human resource "$x(H)$," natural resource "R" and common labor "L," the production functions of which resources can be expressed as "$x=f(H)$, $y=g(x, R, L)$." We assume the price of the final product "y" as "P_y." Here we do not take the capital factor into our consideration because if the capital could flow freely among the regions thus leading to the similarity of costs of funds among

different regions the capital factor, after its introduction into the model, could not enhance the explanatory capability of the model but would make the model more complicated.

(3) We assume that there are two regions—*A* and *B*. *A* refers to the big cities, such as Shanghai and Nanjing, and *B* refers to the middle- and small-sized cities, such as Suzhou, Wuxi or the suburbs. There exists a natural difference in the structure of resources of the two regions. In region *A*, there are abundant human resources "*H*," and compared with *B*, *A* can obtain human resources "*H*" needed by production "*x*" at lower prices, that is to say, $P_{HA}<P_{HB}$. Here P_{HA} refers to the market price of human resource *H* in region *A*, and P_{HB} refers to the market price of human resource *H* in region *B*.

We assume that *B* is richer than *A* in common labor "*L*" and in the natural resource "*R*" needed by the production "*y*" which is not fluid. According to this assumption, obviously we have $P_{AL}>P_{BL}$ and $P_{AR}>P_{BR}$. Here P_{AL} refers to the market price of common labor "*L*" in region *A* and P_{BL} refers to the market price of common labor "*L*" in region *B*; P_{AR} refers to the market price of natural resource "*R*" in region *A* and P_{BR} refers to the market price of natural resource "*R*" in region *B*.

(4) We also assume that the production function of production "*x*"— "$x=f(H)$" has the basic features of a convex function, so we have "$f'(H)\geq 0$ and $f''(H)<0$," representing that the production of semi-finished products (design and marketing services of the product) will increase with the increase in the input of highly-intellectual human resource "*H*," but its marginal productive force is digressive.

In order to make the discussion more convenient, here we also assume that the character of the production function of final product "*y*" is: $\partial g/\partial x\geq 0$, $\partial g/\partial L\geq 0$, $\partial g/\partial R\geq 0$, which means that the output of final product "*y*" will increase with the increase in the number of inputs and factors. Similarly, in order to make sure of the existence of function solution, we assume here that "$\partial^2 g/\partial x^2\leq 0$, $\partial^2 g/\partial L^2\leq 0$, $\partial^2 g/\partial R^2\leq 0$," which means that the marginal productivities of all production factors are digressive.

(5) Finally, we assume that to the production of final product "*y*," the input of common labor "*L*," input of natural resource "*R*" and the semi-finished product of R&D and marketing "*x*" cannot replace each other, which assumption avoids the discussion of the enterprises' adjustment of input amount of production factor for the production of the same amount of "*y*" under different prices of production factors. Meanwhile the assumption also means that even if the relative prices among the factors change, for the same amount of "*y*," the shares of different factors in the input will not change. Obviously, with

this assumption, there exists "$\frac{\partial^2 g}{\partial R \partial x} = \frac{\partial^2 g}{\partial R \partial L} = \frac{\partial^2 g}{\partial L \partial x} = 0$". In addition, here we also assume that for "x" there exists a minimum input amount "$\underline{x}$," if $x=\underline{x}$, then $y=g(\underline{x},R,L)=0$. Only when $x>\underline{x}$ could the final product "y" be produced. The economic meaning of the assumption, which is obvious, is that the intermediary services "x," including design, R&D, marketing and management, must participate in the production of final product "y." In other words, "y" cannot be produced without "x."

Analysis of the models

Based on the basic hypotheses of the above models, we will deduce and discuss one by one the three spatial distribution models of the value-creating activities of the manufacturing industry and service industry in the Yangtze River Delta.

The first model is that the enterprises put the two links—x and y—of the value-creating activities into the same region—A or B. This model is the centralized location model.

The second model is that the enterprises distribute their value-creating activities in accordance with the comparative advantages of the regions and achieve the vertical disintegration of the enterprise organizations' spatial structures. An important outcome of the second model is that if the property rights of the enterprises are not disintegrated, then the organization communication cost "C (Communication)" inside the enterprises will surely increase; and if the property rights of enterprises are disintegrated, the transaction cost "T (Transanction)" of enterprises in market transactions will surely increase. This model is a dispersed location model.

The third model is that the two activities—x and y are undertaken by two different enterprises. The enterprise which produces the final product "y" purchases the intermediary services from the enterprise which produces the semi-finished product "x," which is what we call "service business outsourcing." The problems brought by the third model concern the market pricing of semi-finished product "x" and then the increase in the transaction cost "T" in other markets. This model could be either a centralized or dispersed location model.

On basis of the basic hypotheses, we will explain the micromechanisms of the service industry's coordination of the optimization of the productive forces' spatial distribution in the Yangtze River Delta by comparing the profits of enterprises in the three different models.

Model One: *x* and *y* are put in by the enterprise in the same region.

If *A* was chosen, the profits of the enterprise in region *A* are:

$$\pi_{1A}=P_y g(x,R,L)-P_{AR}\cdot R-P_{AL}\cdot L-f^{-1}(x)P_{AH} \quad (1)$$

In the above equation, "$f^{-1}(x)$" stands for the input amount of the highly intellectual human resource *H* needed by the semi-finished products of "*x*."

If *B* was chosen, the profits of the enterprise in region *B* are:

$$\pi_{1B}=P_y g(x,R,L)-P_{BR}\cdot R-P_{BL}\cdot L-f^{-1}(x)P_{BH} \quad (2)$$

Obviously, "*y*" is given, and with the assumption of the irreplaceability of input factors, we subtract the Equation (1) and Equation (2), and then we have:

$$\pi_{1A}-\pi_{1B}=[(P_{BR}-P_{AR})\cdot R+(P_{BL}-P_{AL})\cdot L]-(P_{AH}-P_{BH})f^{-1}(x)$$

Therefore, when the enterprise's organizational structure is not spatially disintegrated i.e. the centralized location model was adopted, whether the enterprise will be located in *A* or *B* will depend on the differences between the prices of production factors in the two regions.

Model Two: The enterprise distributes the value-creating activities in accordance with the comparative advantages of the locations to achieve the spatial vertical disintegration of the enterprise's organizational structures.

In this model, restricted by the profit maximization, a rational enterprise will locate their manufacturing links in region *B* and locate the intermediary service links including R&D, designing, marketing and management of the products in region *A*. Therefore, the profit of the enterprise is:

$$\pi_2=P_y\cdot g(x,R,L)-P_{BR}\cdot R-P_{BL}\cdot L-f^{-1}(x)P_{AH}-\Delta C \quad (3)$$

In the above equation, ΔC refers to the increment of "C" caused by the spatial vertical disintegration of the enterprise's organizational structure. We subtract (3) and (1), and then we have:

$$\pi_2-\pi_{1A}=(P_{AR}-P_{BR})\cdot R+(P_{AL}-P_{BL})\cdot L-\Delta C \quad (4)$$

Since $P_{AL}>P_{BL}$ and $P_{AR}>P_{BR}$, so in equation (4) the former two variables are positive. In this circumstance, compared to the centralized location model in which all the value-creating activities will be located in *A*, the dispersed location model in which the organizational structure was vertically disintegrated on the one hand could bring a surplus of "$(P_{AR}-P_{BR})\cdot R+(P_{AL}-P_{BL})\cdot L$," and on the other hand increase ΔC of the enterprise's management coordination cost or market transaction cost "*T*". The question now is changed to how the enterprise decides its location by weighing the costs caused by different regions' comparative advantages and management coordination costs. In this circumstance, so long as $(P_{AR}-P_{BR}) \cdot R+(P_{AL}-P_{BL}) \cdot L>\Delta C$, $\pi_2>\pi_{1A}$, that is to say, the enterprise will get more surplus in the dispersed location than in the centralized location model so long as it makes good use of the comparative advantages of production factors in different regions, and the volume of the surplus is determined by the difference between between the market prices of natural resources and common labor in the two regions—*A* and *B*. Here the factors that influence the prices of production factors, enterprises' organizational communication costs and market transaction costs mainly include the inflow of production factors, transportation costs, inter-regional trade barriers and information technologies etc.

Similarly, we subtract (3) and (2), and then we have:

$$\pi_2-\pi_{1B}=(P_{BH}-P_{AH}) \cdot f^{-1}(x)-\Delta C$$

Since $P_{BH}>P_{AH}$, the first variable in the above equation is positive. As has been discussed, compared to the centralized location in *B*, if the enterprise could vertically disintegrate its value-creating activities in accordance with the regional comparative advantages, on one hand the surplus of "$(P_{BH}-P_{AH}) \cdot f^{-1}(x)$" will be brought to the enterprise, and on the other hand, the management coordination costs and market transaction costs will be increased if $(P_{BH}-P_{AH}) \cdot f^{-1}(x)>\Delta C$, $\pi_2>\pi_{1B}$.

Model Three: *x* and *y* are undertaken by two different enterprises, and the enterprise which produces the final product "*y*" purchases the semi-finished product and services from the producer of "*x*."

As the transaction of the semi-finished product "*x*" between the two enterprises is involved, here we might assume the market transaction costs as "*T*." Actually, since "*x*" is a highly-intellectual value-creating activity, it cannot really be embodied in the form of a product that can be traded in the market, and even though it could be traded in the market its pricing and the protection of its intellectual property rights would be rather expensive. That is to say, the *T* value would be pretty high. For research, here we assume that market transaction is available, and we assume the price of "*x*" as P_x.

We need to note that here, since the production of "*x*" is guided by the production of "*y*," P_x is the result of the two enterprises' negotiations and the enterprises are not the price takers. The share of *T* is decided by the two parties' competencies at negotiating. Let us assume that the contractor (service process) covers the transaction expense of δT (the more competent the enterprise is in the negotiations, the less expense it need to cover), and the contractee (production process) covers the transaction expense of $(1-\delta)T$. To the producer of "*x*," as the prices and transaction expenses are given, obviously they will locate in A and the profits it makes in region A is:

$$\pi_x = P_x \cdot f(H) - P_{AH} \cdot H - \delta T \quad (5)$$

Here, $x=f(H)$. Similarly, to the producer of "y," as the prices and transaction expenses are given, obviously they will locate in B, and the profits it makes in region B is:

$$\pi_y = P_y \cdot g(x,R,L) - P_{BL} \cdot L - P_{BR} \cdot R - P_x \cdot x - (1-\delta)T \quad (6)$$

We can observe from the equations (5) and (6) that the income of the producer of "x" is presented as the cost of the production of "y." And now we add (5) and (6)[1] to see the gross surplus brought by the production of "x" and "y" by different enterprises:

$$\pi_3 = \pi_x + \pi_y = P_y \cdot g(x,R,L) - P_{BL} \cdot L - P_{BR} \cdot R - P_{AH} \cdot H - T \quad (7)$$

Equation (7) is pretty similar to equation (3), and the major difference between the two is that in Model Two, what is subtracted from the gross surplus is the coordination cost (ΔC), but in Model Three, what is subtracted from the total surplus of the two enterprises is the transaction cost (T). If we take equation (7) and subtract equation (3), and take "$x=f(H)$" and "$H=f^{-1}(x)$" into our consideration, then we have:

$$\pi^3 - \pi^2 = \Delta C - T \quad (8)$$

We can see from equation (8) that if $\Delta C>T$, it means that more surplus will be generated if x and y are produced by two different enterprises in two different regions—A and B—and then the product is traded in the market. Conversely, if $\Delta C<T$, it means more gross surplus will be brought in by Model Two as the market transaction cost of x will be higher than the added expense of the enterprise's organization coordination caused by the spatial disintegration of the enterprise's organizational structure.

It can be seen from the model that the study of the spatial distribution of the service industry's productivity changes in nature into weighting of the enterprises' organizational costs and market transaction costs, which seems to take us back to the Coarse theorem. Therefore, in the above three models, Model Two is the representative of the current spatial distribution of manufacturing industry and service industry in the Yangtze River Delta. The large-sized manufacturing enterprises, in order to maximize their profits, would take the initiative in distributing their value-creating activities in accordance with the comparative advantages of different locations and implement the spatial disintegration of organizational structure, which is embodied by: firstly, the enterprises locate the value-creating manufacturing processes in region *B*; and secondly, they locate the value-creating service processes in region *A*, and thus the differentiated location of headquarters and manufacturing factories is realized.

We can see from the above model analysis that whether to separate the service industry from the manufacturing industry spatially is determined by the differences in the prices of production factors in different regions, enterprises' management coordination costs, the tradability of the intermediary value activities such as R&D, designing, marketing and management, and the market transaction costs. This conclusion is basically consistent with the spatial distribution of service industry in the Yangtze River Delta as a prominent feature of the service industry's spatial distribution in the Delta is the coexistence of the domestic OEM enterprises guided by the multinational enterprises and the foreign-funded enterprises. When deciding whether to spatially disintegrate the organizational structure, the enterprises should take into consideration not only the operational strategies of the multinational enterprises, which is a subject factor, but also the geographical factors of the supporting enterprises in the host countries, on which situation the new economic geographical model has strong explanatory competence. The economic policies adopted by the supporting enterprises in host countries have an important influence on the decision-making of whether to spatially disintegrate the multinational enterprises' organizational structures, which can also be explained by the above models, and the main line of the explanation is how to distinguish the two dimensions—property ownership and location. On the one hand, in the same structure of property ownership, both disintegration and non-disintegration of organizational structures of enterprises can be carried out; on the other hand, even though the organizational structures of enterprises are disintegrated spatially, the enterprises' property ownership does not have to be disintegrated.

Among the above three models, the first one is a centralized location model. In this model, the enterprises locates the two kinds of value-creating activities in the same region, which always leads to low efficiency, because if manufacturing industry and service industry are distributed in the same region the enterprises will have to cover comparatively high manufacturing costs as well as service costs and these costs rely on the differences between the prices of production factors in the two regions.

The second model is a dispersed location model. In this model, if the value-creating manufacturing processes and service processes belong to two different property owners, the saved expenses are the costs of the factor location comparative advantages, and the added expenses are mainly the market transaction costs; if the manufacturing processes and service processes belong to the same property owner, then the saved expenses are still the costs of the location comparative advantages but the added expenses are the management and coordination costs. The difference between the two is pretty similar to the difference between the costs in two different organizational structures—the vertical integration and the vertical non-integration. (Wu, 2006).

The third model could either be a centralized location model or a dispersed location model. If the model is dispersed, then no matter whether the property rights are disintegrated the model is equal to the second model; if the model is a centralized location model, then it is equal to the commonly discussed industrial agglomeration model. In the latter model, the profits of the enterprises is not only related to the selection of location but also related to the negotiation competences of the two entities who undertake the manufacturing process and service process respectively. Although the total profits of the two are not influenced by their negotiation abilities, if we consider the profits of the two processes separately, the profit of an enterprise is directly affected by the enterprise's ability in negotiation. For instance, if we solve the derivative of δ with respect to the π_x in equation (5) and π_y in equation (6), then we have: $\frac{\partial \pi_x}{\partial \delta} = -T$, $\frac{\partial \pi_y}{\partial \delta} = T$, from which we can find that the influences of the negotiation competences on the profits of manufacturing industry and service industry are contrary to each other and the two are complementary to each other. Moreover, if we look at equation (7) and equation (3) carefully, we can find that "$\pi_3 - \pi_2 = \Delta C - T$" which can show the contrast between the profit generated when the property rights are not disintegrated and the profit generated when the property rights are disintegrated in the disintegration of manufacturing process and service process. If $\Delta C > T$, then the profit gained in the industrial agglomeration model is obviously larger than the profit gained in the headquarters economy. And as a matter of fact, in today's society where the modern transportation and communication technologies are extraordinarily developed, both the management coordination costs and the transportation costs are likely to digress. Therefore the superiority of the headquarters economy when compared to industrial agglomeration comes from the differences in factor costs of different regions and the vertical economies of scope in different working procedures. The differences in factor prices in different regions are the most important, and the differences can be integrated with the agglomeration of manufacturing industry and agglomeration of service industry in a region. That is to say, the big cities always present agglomeration of service industry but the middle and small cities always present agglomeration of manufacturing industry. Of course the agglomeration of service industry in big cities in the Yangtze River Delta, to a great extent, is driven by the multinational enterprises' vertical disintegration of the enterprises' headquarters and manufacturing factories in geographical space. In other words, the multinational enterprises make use of their market advantages and regional cost advantages of the host countries, and their internalized advantages as multinational enterprises, which results in many multinational enterprises' location of their key producer service activities including R&D centers and marketing centers in the big cities such as Shanghai and location of their manufacturing factories in the small cities surrounding the big cities.

Analysis of Descriptive Statistics

In the last 10 years, while maintaining a comparatively high growth rate, the internal structure of the service industry in the Yangtze River Delta has changed considerably. One of the most prominent features of the change is that the share of the traditional service sectors has started to decline while the share of new service sectors has obviously risen. However, while the internal structure of the service industry is optimized, the mainstay industry of the producer service industry—the financial service industry and science, research and technological services in the new service sectors have shown a severe imbalance.[2] For example, in 2005, in the 16 representative cities in the Delta, the traditional service sectors still accounted for a large proportion of the producer service industry (64.52%). In terms of the proportions of the service industry as a whole, the wholesale and retailing sector accounted for nearly 26%, the transportation, storage and postal services sector accounted for nearly 16%, the finance and insurance sector accounted for about 12% but the real estate sector—one of the new service sectors—only accounted for less than 11%. If we classify the wholesale and retailing sector and the transportation, storage and postal services sector as the traditional producer service sectors and real estate as well as finance and insurance as the new producer service sectors, then we will see that the proportion of service industry accounted for by the traditional producer service industry was nearly 42% but the proportion accounted by the new producer service industry was lower than 24%. (Please refer to Table 7.1)

The above statistics show that currently the traditional services are still dominant in the producer service industry in the Yangtze River Delta, and the transportation, storage and postal service sector and wholesale and retailing

Table 7.1. The shares in added value of producer service industry in the cities in the Yangtze River Delta

City	Proportion of service industry accounted for by the producer service industry	Thereinto			
		Transportation, storage and postal services	Wholesale and retailing services	Finance & insurance services	Real estate services
Shanghai	69.41	10.77	18.10	22.04	18.50
Nanjing	64.66	14.11	22.14	17.84	10.57
Suzhou	70.31	13.12	33.21	11.31	12.67
Wuxi	64.34	11.74	34.75	8.48	9.37
Changzhou	70.56	16.36	31.96	12.23	10.01
Zhenjiang	72.71	21.34	26.46	13.87	11.04
Nantong	69.08	14.87	30.80	10.33	13.08
Yangzhou	66.31	21.31	23.15	9.22	12.63
Taizhou	70.82	22.02	24.13	10.70	13.97
Hangzhou	57.72	13.27	20.99	15.62	17.84
Ningbo	62.96	16.69	24.50	12.99	8.78
Jiaxing	61.19	12.62	25.00	14.19	9.38
Huzhou	62.83	15.41	29.71	6.52	12.19
Shaoxing	62.32	13.13	29.71	12.00	7.48
Zhoushan	48.44	14.86	19.56	8.17	5.85
Taizhou	57.48	19.41	21.00	11.30	5.77
Average	64.45	15.69	25.89	12.30	10.57

Source: Calculated using the data in the *Yangtze River Delta & Pearl River Delta and Hong Kong & Macao SAR Statistical Yearbook 2005*.

sector (which are classified as traditional producer service sectors) accounted for 64.52% of producer service industry. The share of these two sectors' added value in the total value-added of the service industry and in the total added value of the producer service industry has been increasing in recent years.

Further, while dividing the producer service industry into traditional producer service industry and new producer service industry, we divide the traditional producer service industry into transportation and storage industry, postal communication industry and wholesale and retailing trade industry etc, and divide the new service industry into information service industry, finance and insurance industry, agency services industry, scientific research and integrated technological service industry, and real estate industry. After careful examination of the statistics in the statistical yearbooks of the Yangtze River Delta in recent years (as shown in Table 7.2), we find that:

Table 7.2. The shares of producer service sectors in major indicators in the Yangtze River Delta and the changes in the shares

Indicator	Share of traditional producer services (%)			Share of new producer services (%)		
	Beginning of the period	End of the period	Raise in share	Beginning of the period	End of the period	Raise in share
Output added value	47.18	50.03	2.85	21.43	25.19	3.76
Employment	45.54	48.37	2.83	2.39	3.74	1.35
Infrastructure	45.10	38.46	−6.64	6.31	12.17	5.86

Sources: *Yangtze River Delta & Pearl River Delta and Hong Kong & Macao SAR Statistical Yearbook 2005* and statistical yearbooks of different regions. In this table, the share at the beginning of the period is the average of the shares in 2000 and 2001, and the share at the end of the period is the average of the shares in 2003 and 2004.

Firstly, the proportions of the GDP accounted for by the traditional producer service industry and new producer service industry in the Yangtze River Delta are changing, which is demonstrated by the fact that in recent years the share of added value of the traditional producer service industries, including the transportation and storage industry, postal communication industry and wholesale and retailing industry, has been tending towards stability; and the share of the added value of the new producer service industries, including the finance and insurance industry and real estate industry, has been slowly increasing. The growth rate of the share differs a lot in different cities, and one of the prominent features is that a great difference is shown in the shares of the new modern services inside the service industry and the mainstay service sectors, especially the finance and insurance sector, in different cities. The share in Shanghai is the highest, followed by Nanjing and Hangzhou, and the shares in the middle- and small-sized cities are relatively low.

Secondly, the roles the traditional producer service industry and new producer service industry play in employment have been changing. Although the traditional producer service sectors are still the major job providers in the Yangtze River Delta, the capability of the finance and insurance sector—the mainstay industry in the producer service industry and the real estate sector—a new producer service industry in providing job opportunities—has been steadily growing. For instance, in Shanghai and the provincial capitals Nanjing and Hangzhou, although a great majority of jobs are provided by the traditional service sectors, the new producer service sectors are rapidly developing their capabilities to provide more employment opportunities.

Thirdly, the roles of the traditional producer service industry and new producer service industry play in the investment structure of infrastructure have been constantly changing. Currently, although the proportion of investment in infrastructure accounted for by the traditional producer service industry is still higher than the proportion accounted for by the new producer service industry, the new service industry's proportion has been constantly increasing. And in further analysis, we find that the most of the investment in infrastructure is in the real estate industry and less is in the other new producer service industries.

Fourthly, both the traditional producer service industry and new producer service industry have changed a lot from the point of view of labor productivity. Although currently we are not optimistic about the industrial structure of the producer service industry in the Yangtze River Delta, and the correlation effect among the sectors as well as the correlation effect between the structure of output value and structure of the labor force inside the service industry are not evident, the situation has improved a lot in recent years. According to statistics, at present the comparative labor productivity of the traditional producer service industry is far lower than that of the new producer service industry. The comparative labor productivity of the traditional producer service industry is about 1.3 while that of the new producer service industry is about 13.2, and the gap is likely to get wider and wider. Therefore as the cities in the Delta tend to input more into the new producer service industry, the function of the new producer service industry in enhancing the comparative labor productivity of the national economy will be strengthened and better brought into play, and also, the new producer service industry will provide a favorable support system of producer services for the development of manufacturing industry.

Considering identity and comparability, we use the statistics of the most representative eight cities in Jiangsu which are located along the Yangtze River to further our analysis. (Please refer to Tables 7.3 and 7.4). Generally speaking, there are several features shown in the spatial distributions of the service industries in the eight cities: (1) If the Yangtze River is taken as a border to cut the Jiangsu Province into the Southern part and Northern part, we can find that the values of the indicators are much higher in the Southern part. (2) Inside the five cities in Southern Jiangsu, the values of the indicators are higher in the cities at the ends of the city line but lower in the cities at the middle of the city line. These features are closely related to their geographical location advantages and the primary level of industrialization.

Table 7.3. Average values on five indicators of eight cities in Jiangsu that are located along the Yangtze River (1995–2004)

City	Annual added value in service industry (100 million RMB)	Annual growth rate (%)	Service industry's share in GDP (%)	Added value per capita in service industry (100 million RMB)	Annual Employment (10,000)
Changzhou	202.44	12.07	35.37	5,579.7	51.7
Suzhou	534.81	13.88	36.80	8,577.5	93.2
Wuxi	452.07	12.50	38.51	9,688.3	63.3
Nanjing	431.44	13.88	45.16	7,459.0	104.2
Zhenjiang	157.97	11.40	36.39	5,597.3	43.3
Yangzhou	162.09	11.62	36.39	3,836.7	67.2
Taizhou	138.01	10.65	35.91	2,616.3	71.9
Nantong	232.73	11.68	33.43	2,797.8	100.2

Sources: *Yangtze River Delta & Pearl River Delta and Hong Kong & Macao SAR Statistical Yearbook 2005* and statistical yearbooks of different regions.

Table 7.4. Average annual changes in each indicator of the service industries in eight cities in Jiangsu Province which are located along the Yangtze River (1995–2004)

City	Growth rate of share in GDP (%)	Growth in addrd value per capita (RMB)	Growth rate of added value per capita (%)	Annual growth rate of employment (%)	Annual employment elasticity
Changzhou	2.22	606	11.01	2.58	0.21
Suzhou	1.37	1,103	12.94	3.16	0.23
Wuxi	2.50	1,102	11.97	2.08	0.17
Nanjing	2.26	904	12.78	2.92	0.21
Zhenjiang	2.29	593	10.97	1.19	0.10
Yangzhou	3.50	335	9.94	1.42	0.12
Taizhou	1.06	251	10.12	0.92	0.19
Nantong	2.24	304	10.97	0.66	0.16

Sources: *Yangtze River Delta & Pearl River Delta and Hong Kong & Macao SAR Statistical Yearbook 2005* and statistical yearbooks of different regions.

The above differences could be measured by the development level of the service industry in a city, and the specific indicators include the share of added value (%), share of employment in service industry (%), possession of service products per capita (10,000 RMB/person), service density (10,000 RMB/square kilometes), and service export ratio (%) (Jiang and Li, 2004). According to the theory of the "shadow effect" of the service industry in central cities, in the above the most representative cities in the Yangtze River Delta, Suzhou and Wuxi, are inside the tight circle of the Shanghai metropolitan circle, so the development of service industries in the two cities are in the shadow of Shanghai and are inevitably influenced by Shanghai as a central city because theoretically speaking, the development of service industry must depend on the human agglomeration effect resulting from urbanization, and only through this effect can the market demands and scale effect of operation that are needed in the development of service industry be created.

Table 7.5 shows the results for the total economies and the development levels of service industries in the major cities in the Delta. From this we can see that at present, the service industry's shares in added value, in employment, in possession of service products per capita and in density of services in Shanghai are all higher than those in other cities. The reason is that currently the centrality and city scale of other cities are comparatively low, which means that the major investment flow is to the manufacturing industry. Consequently, in those cities, not only is the amount and scale of the service industries and producer service industries insufficienct, but also the development of some big client and differentiated individual customer-oriented producer service industry is seriously restricted.

Table 7.5. Total economies and development levels in major cities in the Yangtze River Delta

Indicator	Shanghai	Nanjing	Hangzhou	Suzhou	Wuxi
Added Value in the Primary Industry (100 million RMB)	96.71	70.00	139.10	77.00	51.80
Added Value in the Second Industry (100 million RMB)	3,788.22	1,005.00	1,332.90	2,268.00	1,353.50
Added Value in the Tertiary Industry (100 million RMB)	3,565.34	835.00	1,043.00	1,105.00	944.70
Share in Added Value in the Service Industry (%)	47.86	43.72	41.47	32.03	40.20
Share in Employment in the Service Industry (%)	54.20	48.71	32.67	28.39	32.43
Possession of Service Product per Capita (RMB10,000/person)	7.86	6.04	6.68	10.73	10.61
Density of Service (RMB10,000/km^2)	5,623.12	1,268.55	628.46	1,301.78	1,973.22

Source: Calculated with the data in the *Yangtze River Delta & Pearl River Delta and Hong Kong & Macao SAR Statistical Yearbook 2005*.

Let us look at the differences in the structure of the sectors inside the producer service industry (Table 7.6). One of the prominent features is that in the cities, the proportion of the GDP accounted for by the producer service industry is highest in Shanghai, and in particular the finance and insurance sector accounts for a considerable proportion of the GDP in Shanghai. This phenomenon is closely related to the international OEM model centered on the foreign capital economy in the Yangtze River Delta. Because the producer services needed by foreign-funded enterprises, especially the high-level producer services, are mainly provided by the producer service institutions at the headquarters of the multinational enterprises, there is a strong replacement and crowding-out effect on the local producer service industry in the host country.

Table 7.6. Shares of the sectors inside the producer service industry in the added value in the Yangtze River Delta

Share in Added Value (%)	Shanghai	Nanjing	Hangzhou	Suzhou	Wuxi
Producer Service Industry's Share in the Output Value of the Tertiary Industry	31.27	24.32	23.16	22.18	22.31
Producer Service Industry's Share in the Service Industry	61.36	59.51	58.44	57.34	56.56
Transportation, Storage and Postal Communication	13.89	15.84	15.66	15.66	12.92
Wholesale and Retailing Services	18.36	21.97	21.76	21.75	32.68
Finance and Insurance	21.22	16.03	15.15	14.25	7.18
Real Estate	4.47	4.31	4.62	4.51	2.66
Scientific Research and Integrated Technological Services	3.42	1.36	1.25	1.17	1.12

Source: Calculated with the data in the *Yangtze River Delta & Pearl River Delta and Hong Kong & Macao SAR Statistical Yearbook* over the past years combined with the definition of the producer service industry.

It is easy to explain the above differences in spatial economics, because differences in inter-regional economic growth can form both when the factors can flow freely and when the factors cannot flow freely. Firstly, when a factor, to take population for an example, can freely flow among the regions, two effects will be generated: the first one is the demand-related accumulation causality effect, that is to say, the transfer of population will lead to transfer of consumption expenditure, and consumption expenditure will lead to transfer of production activities, and further, transfer of production activities will again stimulate the population to transfer; the second effect is the cost-related accumulation causality effect, that is to say, the transfer of population leads to transfer of production activities, and the transfer of production activities reduces the price index, and the reduction of price index will further stimulate the population to transfer. Secondly, when a factor cannot flow freely among the regions, agglomeration of service industry can be achieved in two ways: the first is to achieve the agglomeration of service industry through the economic relationship of input and output in inter-regional production activities, namely, with regional spillover effect, and although the effect declines when spatial distance increases, in the Delta this decline is slow; the second is to achieve through the difference between the capital depreciation of inter-regional investment in fixed assets and the capital formation, and the agglomeration can also be achieved by the "Tiebout choice"[3] of local infrastructure.

Table 7.7. Total economies and development levels in major cities in the Yangtze River Delta

Share in Added Value (%)		Shanghai	Nanjing	Hangzhou	Suzhou	Wuxi
Producer Service Industry's Share in the Service Industry		52.96	14.97	11.97	10.14	8.86
Subsectors	Transportation, Storage and Postal Communication	10.87	6.71	3.57	2.96	2.79
	Wholesale and Retailing Services	26.94	4.28	4.82	3.67	3.64
	Finance and Insurance	4.10	2.41	2.88	2.67	1.93
	Real Estate	9.53	0.51	0.15	0.20	0.10
	Scientific Research and Integrated Technological Services	1.52	1.06	0.55	0.64	0.40

Source: Calculated with the data in the *Yangtze River Delta & Pearl River Delta and Hong Kong & Macao SAR Statistical Yearbook.*

The above differences can be better embodied in the employment structure of all sectors in the producer service industry and the distribution of specialized technical personnel (please refer to Table 7.7). Among the cities in the Delta, the share of employment inside the producer service industry is the highest in Shanghai, one of the reasons for which is that Shanghai is an international metropolis where the producer service industry is highly developed, and the fact that the producer service enterprises in other regions all locate their headquarters in Shanghai enables Shanghai, to a great extent, replace the functions of other regions in producer service industry. Suzhou, Wuxi and Changzhou are neighbors of Shanghai and are inside the tight circle of the Shanghai metropolitan circle, so they cannot avoid being influenced by the "shadow effect" of Shanghai. Another reason may be associated with statistical factors, because the producer service industry in Shanghai can be recalculated by custom in export and export and thus Shanghai's "shadow effect" on other cities may have been magnified since, as is commonly acknowledged, whether the manufacturing industry in a city can develop to a great degree depends on the level of the manufacturing industry' attraction, accumulation and use of the specialized skills of producer service industry. The producer service industry here in the statistics includes not only the traditional labor-intensive services such as transportation, and trade and commerce, but also the modern knowledge-intensive and skills-intensive services such as financial services, all kinds of agency services (including consulting, lawyer, accountancy, logistics, science and technology) and information services.

From the above analysis, we can see that in recent years in the Delta, the share of the modern producer service industry in the industrial structure of tertiary industry in the indicators of added value, employment, infrastructure and comparative labor productivity have been increasing. Compared to that in the cities in the developed countries, the producer service industry in the Delta is small in scale, but on many indicators including the growth rate the producer service industry has performed well.

Furthermore we find that although the manufacturing industry in the Delta is comparatively developed, it has limited demand for producer services except for the traditional logistics and transportation, and the division of the inner service activities is far from complete. The overall level of the local producer services in many cities, especially the specialized services such as accountancy and auditing, is not high, the enterprises which have obtained certification are limited and there is a lack of skills. In many cities the average expenses of the enterprises surveyed on legal services, accounting, auditing and management consulting combined only accounted for less than 1% of their amount of sales. Foreign-invested enterprises and state-owned large-sized enterprises have comparatively high expenses for specialized services, but the service providers these enterprises choose are not local. The expenses of domestic-funded companies of limited liability and companies limited by shares for specialized services make up the major source of demand for local producer service business. Therefore the incompetence of the local producer services seriously restrains the manufacturing enterprises' demands for the producer services.

Of course, we need to see that the robust foundation of the manufacturing industry, especially the structure of manufacturing industry in many cities that is centered on the domestic-funded private manufacturing industry, does not only provide the spatial distribution of the service industry in the Delta with strong support, but also provides the future development of the local producer service industry with potential huge demands. If the local producer service enterprises realize those potential opportunities and actively form strategic alliances with the powerful manufacturing enterprises to enhance the level of their own specialized services and then become the specialized producer server for "manufacturing," not only can the spatial distribution of the service industry and especially the producer service industry be optimized, but also the prospects for spatial distribution will be expansive and bright. We know that there are three totally different relationships between the manufacturing industry and the service industry (Liu, 2006). The first relationship is more like a client-supplier relation. Many service sectors emerge after the manufacturing (service) enterprises separate some of their inner service activities from the manufacturing business. This relation has two implications: the first implication is that if the local manufacturing industry is not developed, then the demands for services will be limited, and although the service enterprises purchase services, most of the main sales turnover comes from the demands from manufacturing industry. The second implication is that the structure of manufacturing industry in a region will influence the form and volume of the manufacturing industry's demands for services and the level of the specialization of the services. Without advanced and insightful manufacturing enterprises, the service industry would lose its industrial foundation from bottom upwards. The second relationship relies on the manufacturing products, that is to say, when a manufacturing product is sold, the demand for related services is created. When manufacturing enterprises in a region succeed in the domestic or international market, it will help the service industry in that region to explore the market outside the region. And the services provided by the service enterprises in the region can generate more cost benefits, because the service enterprises in that region will be familiar with pr have even been in touch with the manufacturing products of that specific kind, and the manufacturing enterprises always actively seek help from local service enterprises. The third relationship is that the sales of the manufacturing products relies on the services, that is to say that the service industry's sale of services, such as engineering or management consulting, can result in the customers' demands for other equipment and other related manufacturing products, and therefore successful trans-regional service enterprises can promote the sales of the manufacturing products in the region.

The above three kinds of relationship differ from each other in terms of strength and durability. The first relationship is one of necessity, and the other two are different in importance and durability. For example, when the technology of the manufactured products can be complementary with the technology of the products' related services, or when it is more convenient to purchase the manufacturing products and the related services at the same time, the relationship between the service industry and the manufacturing industry is the closest. The relationship of dependence between the manufacturing of products and services is strongest mostly in the primary stage of reform of the manufacturing industry and the service industry. If clients become increasingly expert and selective about services they may think that the regional service enterprises do not have to serve the region of the enterprise unless the products are very complicated and the technological relationship between the products and the services is close. However the advantages established earlier than others are always created by the manufacturing industry and service industry together, which advantages could, even when the relations between the two industries decline, still bring benefits to some service sectors. Since the producer service industry is insensitive to costs but highly sensitive to technology and knowledge, the distribution of the producer service industry in highly-developed cities can not only make good use of the production factors in the cities but also bring the cities' radiation effect on their surrounding regions into play and reduce the transaction costs of the manufacturing industry. At the same time, we need to realize that a large amount of manufacturing sectors always accumulate in the regions surrounding cities, which plays an important role in reducing manufacturing costs and increasing the demands for service industry. The outcome of the spatial distribution of the service industry exactly shows that there exists a strong interdependence relationship between the producer service industry and the manufacturing industry, although the two can be separated spatially. Of course, the degree of the service industry's coordination in optimization of the spatial distribution of productive forces in the Delta will undoubtedly be restricted by the spatial distribution of manufacturing industry.

Conclusions

We used the new economic geographical analytical method to do theoretical and empirical research on the spatial distribution of the service industry in the Yangtze River Delta and the rules governing its changes. The research results show that the current spatial distribution of service industry is closely related to the special historic stage and the international background of the productive force in the Delta. At present, the features of the spatial distribution of service industry is that the traditional service sectors in the producer service industry, including the transportation, storage and postal services sector, wholesale and retailing sector and the real estate sector in modern service industry, are well and evenly distributed while many sectors, including the finance and insurance sector as well as the scientific research and integrated technological service sector in the modern service industry are unevenly distributed spatially, which is embodied in that the share of the modern service sectors including the finance and insurance sector as well as the scientific research and integrated technological service sector is much higher in Shanghai than that in other cities and are under the influence of "shadow effect" of Shanghai, and these sectors in other cities in the Delta are constantly agglomerating to Shanghai. This phenomenon can be properly explained by spatial economics. The inner mechanism is that since there exist some differences among the prices and qualities of the production factors in different cities in the Delta and the factors are all profit-driven, this combined with the reduction of the factors' flowing spatial costs drives some of quality factors of the modern producer industry to accumulate in the metropolis.

This process is driven by two forces. The first force is the dispersion force caused by the crowded market, and it is a power that is triggered by primary turbulence and that could eliminate the primary turbulence by itself, so we call it the negative feedback mechanism; the second force is a cycle causality chain of demand relationship and cost relationship, which includes two channels: the first channel is population transfer—consumption expenditure transfer—productive activity transfer—further stimulating population transfer; the second channel is population transfer—productive activity transfer—price index reduction—further stimulating population transfer. In the first channel, the change in the spatial distribution of demand is the lever for the above mechanism, and the mechanism is a negative feedback mechanism or backward linkage mechanism; in the second channel, the change in living costs is the lever for the above mechanism, and the mechanism is a positive feedback mechanism or forward linkage mechanism.

It is exactly through the above two mechanisms that the service industry's coordination of the optimization of productive forces' spatial distribution in the Yangtze River Delta drives the modern service sectors including the finance and insurance sector, scientific research and integrated technological services sector to agglomerate into the big cities and makes the metropolis function more and more as the headquarters of large-sized manufacturing enterprises while the surrounding medium- and small-sized cities become the factories of the manufacturing enterprises, thus achieving the division and optimization of functions. The effective channel for the medium- and small-sized cities to further bring the service industry's function as promoter of productive forces into play is to first develop the mainstay producer service industries, such as the finance and insurance industry, and meanwhile to energetically cultivate specialized technical personnel. Certainly, not only do some quality producer service factors inside the Delta concentrate into big cities like Shanghai, but also some quality factors outside the Delta will continue to agglomerate into the Delta.

Finally, it is worth mentioning that in terms of how the service industry coordinates the optimization of productive forces' spatial distribution, we could also use the spatial econometric analytical method, which is analysis of the spatial weight matrix, spatial lag and spatial error, to reveal the micro-mechanisms of the service industry's optimization of the spatial distribution of productive force in the Yangtze River Delta. This is the focus of further research.

8

Chapter

Agglomeration of Service Cities and Formation of Regional Service Centers

Since the 1990s, the Yangtze River Delta's feature as a "city cluster" has become increasingly conspicuous, and the functional division and functional dependence among the cities has been getting more and more intensified, during which the development of service industry plays a fundamental role. On the one hand, the development constantly improves the transportation and communication situation as well as the information network, thus providing a platform for inter-city direct or indirect industrial relations, and on the other hand the agglomeration of service sectors effectively enhances the functions of cities and achieves the proper distribution of service resources, forms regional service centers and regional sub-service centers and demands that cities reevaluate and adjust their relationships with each other.

Agglomeration of the Service Sectors in the City Cluster of the Yangtze River Delta

Since the reform and opening up, both the traditional service sectors and the modern service sectors have been developing fast, laying a foundation for the urbanization and upgrade of city functions, which enables the cities to be a base for the cultivation, development and agglomeration of service sectors.

Urban concentration of service sectors

Existing research shows that compared to the industrial sectors, the service sectors are more likely to agglomerate. Hong (2003) pointed out that compared to the manufacturing sectors, the production and consumption of service sectors are more inseparable, both immaterial and impossible to inventory both in time and space, so the service sectors are more dependent on the local market and more likely to agglomerate than the manufacturing sectors. Furthermore, the service sectors are typical urban sectors, and the cities are the best places for the service sectors (especially the knowledge-intensive modern service sectors) to concentrate. The characteristics of service sectors determine that they have to be close to the consumers and to agglomerate in the cities. Generally speaking, the major target consumers of the producer service sectors are the enterprises and institutions in the cities, and the major target consumers of the living service sectors are the residents in the cities, so the service sectors cannot develop without the cities. The cities are not only the supply base of service products but also the major consumer sites of service products.

From the perspective of economics, there are several reasons for the urban agglomeration of service sectors:

1. The intensive labor market in the cities provides the service sectors with the necessary human resources.

The service sectors need of a large amount of diversified skilled labor, and the cities are not only the places where professional skills are cultivated but also the major spaces where human resources gather. In the cities there are abundant human resources in various sectors—professionals who work in information, finance and high-tech sectors, skilled service workers and manual labor can all be found in the cities. The favorable development conditions of human resources, labor market and information network transmission saves the cost of seeking for talented personnel. Besides, there are a variety of educational and training institutions in the cities, which institutions provide the professionals with more choices and more opportunities to study, laying the basis of the human factor in the continuous innovation and upgrade of the service sectors.

2. The cities help the service sectors find reasonable information about qualities and prices.

It is rather difficult for the service sectors to ascertain reasonable price levels in accordance with the different situations of service qualities. In order to reduce the costs for acquisition of information about qualities and prices, the service sectors need to agglomerate in some certain areas in the cities. Although the agglomeration increases the competition among service sectors, it helps enterprises provide convenient information to customers. Agglomeration in accordance with different quality standards can even be found inside a service sector. For example, high-level shops where brand products are sold always avoid being adjacent to grocery stores and they always seek to be together with shops of the same level. The agglomeration of high-level shops is also intended to inform customers of the high quality of the goods sold in the shops and reduce the customers' costs in seeking for information about prices. Obviously, the cities offer conditions for services to agglomerate in accordance with sector, quality and scale, which is advantageous to the formation and enhancement of the brands

3. The well-established institutional systems in cities helps reduce the transaction costs of service sectors.

Cities are the places where the organization forms of human beings and institution systems are better, and when the growth of cities and improvement of systems reduce the transaction costs to a certain degree, profitable opportunities will be brought to the service sectors. Although the service industry itself can reduce transaction costs, the clear law systems, highly-efficient judicial performance and mature public administration in cities can reduce the operation costs of service sectors on a much larger scale. Cities are always the places where the government departments, judicial departments and other social administrative departments gather, so both the implementation of systems in due form and the reform of new systems can acclimatize themselves to the development of service industry in a timely way.

4. The dense consumer groups in the cities help to realize the scale effect of the service industry.

The scale of he service industry is highly dependent on the market capacity—the larger the market capacity is, the more the realization of scale effect of the service industry is helped. As there are dense consumer groups in the cities, the larger the cities are, the larger the scales of consumer groups of a certain service sector are. On the one hand, the increase in the consumer groups in the cities will facilitate the formation of new service sectors and the traditional service sectors will gradually be replaced by the modern service sectors; on the other hand, when the consumer groups differentiate from each other because of different income levels and preferences, the service sectors will further be subdivided and upgraded, and the original low-level sectors and the more functional new sectors will agglomerate in different areas to serve consumers of different levels.

5. Favorable urban infrastructures help service industry form external economies.

There are mainly three causes of industrial clusters' external economies: abundant demands and supplies of specialized labor, the existence of specialized suppliers, and the spillover of technological knowledge. In order to realize external economies, the service industry on the one hand needs to rely on the network formed by the large number of medium- and small-sized enterprises and those enterprises' cooperation in the agglomeration areas to carry out high-level cooperation based on division, and on the other hand needs to make good use of the favorable environment created by the cities (including the highly-specialized cooperation of service enterprises of the same kind, which cooperation is enabled by the cities, and the well-established public service facilities in the cities) to enable many enterprises to outsource some of their activities.

The above phenomenon of service sectors' agglomeration is also found in China. Wang and Li (2004), Cheng (2003) and Ni (2004) used data from China and the US to do some empirical research and found that the development level of service industry and agglomeration effect are highly influenced by the factors related to urbanization, which mainly include urbanization level, urban population density, urban population scale and GDP per capita. The research on agglomeration effect in cities in China done by Ji (2004) shows that the expansion of city scale will not significantly lead to the enhancement of the industrial sectors' efficiency. That is to say, the agglomeration effect of service sectors is more evident than that of manufacturing sectors. Li and Qian (2007) studied the service industry and urbanization on the provincial level and found that urbanization has had a significant influence on the development of service industry in Zhejiang Province, where the enhancement of the urbanization rate is propitious to the enhancement of service industry's share in employment and output value and the expansion of city scale is propitious to the increase in gross output of service industry. According to estimates, a 1% increase in city scale is associated with a 0.88% increase in the gross output of service industry in Zhejiang Province. The regression results of another research show that the urbanization level has positive influence on the increase in the per capita added value of the service industry, which means that the higher the urbanization rate is, the higher the per capita added value of service industry is. The development of service industry also shows that with the fast development of information technology, the upgrading of social division and the expansion of the scale of non-basic demands in the city service industry, new service sectors have been emerging constantly in the central cities, the service sectors have been obviously getting more and more diversified, and the agglomeration effect of service sectors has been becoming increasingly evident.

Interactive development of service sectors' agglomeration and urbanization

According to economic geography, the scale effect, increasing returns and industrial agglomeration are important forces that promote the enhancement of urbanization level. In today's highly-developed market economy, the industrial division is further deepened, the industrial structure has been constantly adjusted, and not only has the service industry become an important part of the national economy but also the agglomeration of service sectors has become a prominent factor that promotes urbanization. A close interactive relationship has been formed between the agglomeration of service sectors and the enhancement of the urbanization level.

1. Agglomeration of service sectors has become an important force in promoting the enhancement of urbanization quality.

The basic feature of urbanization is the agglomeration of factors. Since the birth of cities, the service industry has been linked to cities. As early as the pre-industrial society period, the service functions of cities as transaction centers of agricultural and sideline products and administrative management and control centers of the surrounding areas started to be formed. In the period of the industrial society, the development and agglomeration of industrial sectors are the first driving force to activate urbanization. With the increasing share of modern service sectors urbanization, which has gradually taken the leading role in urban industry, has been promoted by both secondary industry and the service industry. Service industry, which has become a follow-up driver of urbanization, has been further reinforced and developed and has become a indispensable economic department. Since the post-industrial society, the service industry in cities has developed rapidly and has gradually replaced manufacturing industry as the leading industry of central cities and the economy has started to be service oriented. In the service sectors, the producer service sectors develop at the highest speed and agglomerate in the international cities and regional central cities.

In the service sectors, the agglomeration and growth of the real estate sector has a fundamental effect on urbanization. The development of the real estate sector can not only satisfy people's basic needs for accommodation and enhancement of life quality but also strengthen the functions of cities by constructing business and office buildings and forming CBD, and provide favorable conditions for the transportation, environment and tourism sectors by improving the construction of infrastructure. The development of the real estate sector also shows that in the process of urbanization there exists a complementary relationship among the service sectors, and the realization of urbanization must rely on the cooperative development of many service sectors. It can be said that the fast agglomeration and growth of the service industry centered on the real estate sector creates the basic factors for urbanization and promotes the constant upgrade of city functions.

The agglomeration of modern service industry does not only facilitate the development of a single city but also is propitious to the emergence of city clusters and the growth of the regional economy. In the formation process of city clusters, there are medium-sized and small-sized cities converging together to form central big cities, and there are also central big cities taking some of their parts into and radiating onto the towns and villages to promote the urbanization of the towns and villages. More importantly, the agglomeration of service industry has greatly strengthened economic relations among the original cities in the region and has intensified the inter-city flow of human resources, capital and technologies, promoting inter-city economic cooperation and competition. Therefore in the era of the service economy, the close cooperation of city clusters is centered on the modern service industry, and the competitive advantages of the cities are reflected in their development levels of the modern service industry.

2. The agglomeration of service sectors is an important carrier for urban modernization.

Hong (2003) pointed out that "the service sectors are the carriers and supporters of urbanization and especially urban modernization. The cities need the service industry to be the leading industry to recover the original model of cities and to transform the industrial cities into trade, service and consumer cities. The strengthening of the cities' market functions is related to the elevation of the service industry's share in the industrial structures of the cities. The cities are the market centers and distributing centers for the factors and products (here, "distributing" includes agglomerating and diffusing). The supporter of concentration and diffusion is the service industry. The modernization of cities, in some sense, demands to be embodied by the socialization, specialization and modernization development of the service sectors in the cities, for example the increase of railways and subways in city transportation and the digitization of information services in the cities. The process of the cities' development and upgrading is a process of the constant development of the service industry. And a major demonstration of cities' development is the overall change and enhancement of people's living mode, behavioral mode, values and cultural quality. The realization of this process is actually the complete permeation of the service industry into all aspects and all fields in the cities. From the perspective of the general principle of urban development, the scale, divergent functions and external effects of city development has a strong correlation with the development of city service industry. Thus the globally influential cities, such as NYC, Tokyo and Hong Kong, are all cities in which the shares of service industry are quite high.

The service industry's agglomeration promotes the modernization of cities, which is reflected by the increase in supporting services for production, the increase in living consumer services and the flow of a large amount of advanced service production factors into the cities, plus the fact that factors agglomerate in the cities, for example, enterprises' headquarter, R&D centers and marketing centers and modern service sectors in the cities, such as banks, insurance and agency services, and the agglomeration of high quality skills, new technology, special working techniques, and highly efficient fund circulation. Therefore we can see that the urbanization driven by the agglomeration of service sectors can not only promote the expansion of city scale as well as the increase in number of cities, but also change the city functions and enhance the cities' core competitiveness. The agglomeration of service industry promotes the improvement of both hardware and software facilities in the cities and enhances the standard of people's living, achieving the upgrade of the "quality".

3. The agglomeration of service industry is an important condition for the cities to bring the diffusion effect into play.

The cities can always bring their function as growth poles into play. The growth of the central cities generally has diffusion effect on the development of the surrounding areas. The modern service industry is an important condition that realizes and influences economic diffusion, and the more developed the service industry is the larger the diffusion areas of the cities' economies. This phenomenon has always been found in Britain, the US and Japan. In today's information age the central cities, with their developed information infrastructure such as transportation and communication facilities, robust economic powers, a large number of high quality skills, complete and highly-efficient economic systems and trade networks that cover the whole world, function in the world or in a region as economic centers, and they are the engines that drive regional development. Thus they have been chosen more and more to be the best locations for enterprises in information-intensive services and producer services. It can be said that the control power and diffusion effect of the central cities on their surrounding areas depend on the development levels and structural levels of the service industries in the central cities, which is why the modern producer service sectors agglomerate more and more in the international cities and regional central cities.

In terms of the Yangtze River Delta, there is a positive interactive relationship between the agglomeration of service industry and the enhancement of urbanization level. On the one hand, the existence of city clusters provides the agglomeration of service industry with a favorable platform and enables all kinds of service sectors to find a suitable "habitat" in the Delta; on the other hand, the agglomeration of service industry accelerates the urbanization of the Delta and strengthens the functions of cities. The data in Table 8.1 show that since the reform and opening up, the urbanization rate of the Delta increased from 23.9% in 1980 to 46.4% in 2004, and the growth of all the major cities in the Delta has increased steadily. Meanwhile the service industry in the Delta has developed at a high speed. Statistics show that the proportion of the GDP accounted for by tertiary industry in the Delta was only 19.8% in the early 1980s, lower than the national average at that time, but increased to 39.5% in 2004, far higher than the national average. In the major 16 cities in the Delta, the urbanization level has been consistent with the growth of the service industry. For example the urbanization rate of Shanghai in 2004 was 81.2%, ranking the first in China, and at the same time the proportion of the GDP accounted for by the service industry in Shanghai was 47.9%, topping the 16 cities. Therefore we can see that the growth of the service industry has been closely related with the urbanization of the Delta, which also reflects the positive effect of the agglomeration of service industry on the urbanization of the cities in the Delta.

Table 8.1. Urbanization rates and growth of service industries in the major cities in the Yangtze River Delta

Region	Proportion of GDP accounted for by the third industry (%)				Urbanization rate (%)			
	1980	1990	2000	2004	1980	1990	2000	2004
China	21.4	31.3	33.4	31.9	19.4[a]	26.4[a]	36.2[a]	41.8[a]
Yangtze Delta	19.8	27.3	41.0	39.5	23.9	30.2	39.5	46.4
Shanghai	21.1	31.9	50.6	47.9	61.3	67.3	74.6	81.2
Nanjing	21.4	36.0	46.2	43.7	42.1	47.1	56.8	71.7
Suzhou	16.7	21.7	37.6	32.1	19.0	24.9	42.6	49.7
Wuxi	17.2	22.0	39.1	40.2	23.0	34.5	42.2	62.5
Changzhou	15.8	20.3	36.4	36.5	18.1	25.1	43.3	45.8
Zhenjiang	15.4	20.8	37.5	36.7	16.3	27.8	37.8	41.4
Nantong	22.3	23.1	34.3	33.7	8.2	19.8	32.2	31.1
Yangzhou	16.7	22.32	37.7	36.6	13.2	18.7	27.2	38.1
Taizhou	17.1	19.6	36.5	34.3	9.3	13.0	24.0	27.0
Hangzhou	17.6	33.0	41.2	41.5	25.0	29.4	36.5	43.3
Ningbo	18.0	24.5	35.8	37.3	15.6	20.2	26.3	31.9
Jiaxing	18.4	19.4	33.5	32.1	13.8	18.5	23.7	32.5
Huzhou	19.6	21.8	32.7	34.2	14.4	17.8	25.6	29.7
Shaoxing	19.8	23.1	30.7	33.1	9.4	13.0	18.6	27.9
Zhoushan	26.2	32.0	39.2	38.9	17.1	21.3	28.8	35.7
Taizhou	22.5	28.5	29.2	33.3	6.8	9.1	16.6	17.4

Note: "a" stands for the proportion of total population accounted for by urban population
Source: China/Jiangsu/Zhejiang/Yangtze River Delta Statistical Yearbook (2005).

Agglomeration of service industry and the functional relationship between the cities in the Yangtze River Delta

The city clusters in the Delta cannot form or develop without the agglomeration of service industry, which shows the interactive influence of the agglomeration and urbanization. However the sub-sectors of service industry differ from each other a lot in different regions in the Delta, as each region has its own advantages and disadvantages. Based on these differences, research on the cities in the Delta has been more focused on the functional features of cities, which research clarifies the relationship between the cities' shares in the sub-sectors and the regional average value by analyzing the amount of employees and added value in each sector, and thus formulates the "superior functions" and "dominant functions" of each city.

For instance, an analysis made by The Institute of Contemporary Shanghai Studies (2006) shows that in the 16 cities in the Delta, the cities' functions in different sectors are very different. In the transportation sector, the most functional cities are Nanjing, Ningbo and Taizhou in that order. In the wholesale and retailing sector, the most functional cities are Wuxi, Shaoxing and Ningbo in that order. In the financial sector, the most functional cities are Shanghai and Ningbo in that order. In the real estate sector, the most functional city is Shanghai. And in the culture, education, and movie and TV sector, the most functional cities are Shanghai, Nanjing and Hangzhou in that order. The above situation reflects the cities' developments and the cities' status in the Delta in different service sectors.

However the functional status only shows the "appearances" of the industrial structures in the cities but cannot reveal the inter-city industrial relationship. Most of the cities in the Delta have advanced service sectors and they cooperate closely with each other by sharing service resources. Additionally, a complicated and diversified relationship has been established among these cities because of the agglomeration and division of the service industry. That is to say, the Yangtze River Delta city cluster as an "agglomeration" is firstly based on the spatial "short distance" and "continuity," but more importantly, there exists a close functional relationship between the cities, which in this era of service economy is realized by agglomeration of service industry and strengthened by the cooperation among service sectors.

For instance, in the Delta, a city which boasts a large amount of financial and insurance institutions can provide capital for the other cities' development and investment; a city where many R&D institutions congregate can provide technological services to another city where the industrial manufacturing factories gather; a city which can function as a "feeding port" can provide a large amount of containers for another city which functions as a "pivot port"; a city that enjoys a large amount of export trade functions can provide marketing services for the products manufactured in another city; a "channel" tourist city can transport a large number of tourists to another "destination" tourist city (The Institute of Contemporary Shanghai Studies, 2006). The development of the city cluster in the Delta profits from the agglomeration and development of the service industry in the regional economy. Without the above inter-city functional relations composed by the service industry, even when the cities are fairly close to each other in distance, it is difficult to form a closely-linked city cluster or regional economy.

The Spatial Distribution of the Service Resources in the City Cluster of the Yangtze River Delta

The inter-city functional relationship shows that the development of the service industry is not isolated. No city has to obtain advantages in all service sectors, and the cities should proceed as a region as a whole to examine and analyze the distribution of service resources and further discover the different roles and functions of the cities in the distribution of service industry.

General principles of the spatial distribution of service industry

Economics always explains industrial agglomeration from two aspects. The first is analysis of the force that promotes geographical and spatial agglomeration, namely the "centripetal force"; the second analysis of the factors that obstruct economic agglomeration, namely the "centrifugal force" (Paul Krugman, 2007). In practice, there are mainly six kinds of factors that influence geographical and spatial agglomeration of economic activities (please refer to Table 8.2.).

Table 8.2. Factors that influence geographical agglomeration

Centripetal Force	Centrifugal Force
Market Scale Effect (correlation effect)	Illiquidity of Production Factors
Intensive Labor Market	Land Rent
Pure External Economy	Pure External Non-economy

Source: Paul Grugman, 2007.

The factors that can be classified as "centripetal force" mainly include: the market scale effect (the "forward linkage" and "backward linkage" effect), a more efficient intensive labor market, and an external economy caused by information spillover. The factors that can be classified as "centrifugal force" mainly include: illiquidity of land, natural resources and human resources, progressively-raised land rent, external non-economics such as traffic congestion. In real life, the distribution of almost all industries are influenced by the above two kinds of forces. For example, some big cities become financial centers because there are a large number of clients and specialized skills in the cities, but with the increase in external non-economics such as land rent and traffic, some financial sectors will divert to medium-sized or small cities.

However the spatial distribution of economic activities is not decided solely by the resources in a city. It is always influenced by the larger economic region the city in located in, and the resources are distributed in the process of competition and cooperation of many cities. For example, many industries form a close, complementary and integrated relationship development in city clusters, metropolitan circles and regional blocks. Not only is this trend found in traditional manufacturing industry but also in the fast growth of modern service industry. Service resources' spatial distribution shows obvious features of division, cooperation and integration. For instance, while the manufacturing sectors agglomerate in city A, the service sectors of logistics and R&D formed in city B are providing powerful and useful support for the economic development in city A, and thus a symbiotic win-win economic system evolves between the two cities. In this circumstance, the inter-city agglomeration of service industry is not isolated but has some certain functional relationship.

In terms of the spatial distribution of service industry, this is not only influenced by the characteristics of the service industry but also restricted by the development of the city, the economic block and the city cluster it is in. When the major "centripetal force" factors co-function with the "centrifugal force" factors, the inter-city distribution of service industry always shows the features of a regional service center when forming the city agglomeration. That is to say, the service sectors always agglomerate in cities, and some service sectors may develop to be the center of a city cluster or economic block and their functions can radiate out to and influence many surrounding cities. The agglomeration of service industry in the cities and the formation of regional service centers are not only determined by the particularity of service industry but are also significantly influenced by the resources in the cities.

The factors that influence the spatial distribution of service industry in the Yangtze River Delta

Apart from the above "centripetal force" and "centrifugal force" factors, the spatial distribution of service industry in the Yangtze River Delta is influenced by the following three factors.

1. The international and national functional orientation of a specific city

The functional orientation of a city directly determines "what type of service industry will agglomerate in the city in what way." For example, when a city is oriented as a global financial center, financial and related service sectors will start to concentrate in the city; when a city is oriented as a tourist city, tourism and related transportation, catering and entertainment service sectors will be emphasized. More importantly, from the perspective of international and domestic economic activities, is how people decide the orientation of a city. In the globalized city system, what a city will be oriented as—a regional industrial and commercial city or a world economic center city—has a determining influence on the industrial structure of the city and will also decide the city's relationship with other cities at home and abroad.

What roles should the cities in the Yangtze River Delta play in the global economic network? In practice, the main feature of the Delta's participation in the international industrial division is the shift from inter-industrial division to intra-industrial division. On the one hand, the agglomeration of manufacturing industry develops constantly in the Delta and thus the Delta has been recognized as a "world factory" and "global manufacturing center"; on the other hand, based on the needs for centralized control and command of the diffuse industrial operations, the multinational enterprises and large domestic enterprises are moving their management headquarters, branch institutions and financial institutions to the big cities such as Shanghai, making these big cities more likely to become modern service centers. However cities which are oriented as manufacturing cities need to closely cooperate with the cities with multiple service functions, especially the cities with a comparatively developed producer service industry, to obtain support and guarantees from the service industry. In the city clusters in the Delta, the service resources will also be spatially distributed in accordance with the functional orientation and core industry of each city.

2. Inter-governmental competition-driven policies to develop the service industry

The development of city industries is significantly guided by governmental policies, because government policies are always accompanied by improvement of the investment environment and reinforcement of infrastructure and thus influence the earning position and investment behavior of enterprises. In the Delta, the competition among different cities has been deepened to the level of policies on industries, and when the service industry becomes the important objective of city policies on industries, the related preferential measures as well as reform of infrastructure and technologies that promote the development of the service industry will be strengthened. Since the original service industries in different cities differ from each other in sorts and advantages, the orientations of the adopted policies to develop service industries in different cities will also differ. The government policies for developing service industry on the one hand strengthens the original agglomeration of service industry and promotes the service sectors that boast advantages, and on the other hand influences the intra-regional flow of service resources and changes the spatial distribution situation of the service industry. During the process, although there exists some significant competition between cities' development of their service industries, the cities' cooperation in the city division can be seen in many service sectors.

3. Other industries which support and supplement the service industry

Observed from the perspective of industrial relations, the development of service industry is based on developed manufacturing industry, and the fast development of the service industry in the Yangtze River Delta is grounded on the rise of manufacturing industry. However the producer service industry does not have to be in the same city as manufacturing industry, as with the improvement of traffic conditions and the advancement in information technology, the producer service industry can be spatially distributed in a more expansive area to maximize its efficiency in providing support for the manufacturing industries in many cities. Observation of the inner part of the service industry tells us that there exist complicated cooperative and complementary relationships among the sub-industries inside the service industry. For example, the consumer service industry provides the producer service industry with a favorable operating environment and is provided by the producer service industry with quality enhancement. In the Delta, those cities with better industrial supporting and supplementary conditions will obtain advantages in the resource allocation of service industry and achieve the agglomeration of some specific service sub-sector or sub-industry.

The features of the spatial distribution of service industry in the Yangtze River Delta

1. With the fast development of the producer service industry, the service industry in the Yangtze River Delta appears to be in close interdependence with manufacturing industry on spatial distribution.

The entity of modern service industry is the producer service industry, which is a sector separated from the manufacturing industry and is the outcome of the productivity growth to a certain level of social division and cooperation. The producer service industry, as an intermediate input of goods-production enterprises and service enterprises, depends much on the manufacturing industry, which dependence is also found in the spatial distribution of the producer service industry. The highly-concentrated modern manufacturing industry also leads to the spatial agglomeration of modern service industry. The producer service industry, on the one hand, should be as close as possible to the manufacturing bases, and on the other hand should make good use of the information, knowledge and technological resources in the cities. Since different value-added links demand different factors and have different preferences on locations, the agglomeration of producer service industry is not always found in the same region as the manufacturing activities (please refer to Table 8.3), which results in a spatial distribution in the Yangtze River Delta in which the manufacturing activities agglomerate in the medium- and small-sized cities or in the suburbs while the service sectors agglomerate in the big cities to provide services.

Table 8.3. The preferences in factors and locations of different value-adding links in the manufacturing industry

Value-adding activity	Possible preferences on factor	Possible preferences on locations
R&D activities	High-level factors: Technological skills, technology, knowledge, information	Close to science and research institutions, close to high-level labor market, close to the users of new products
Production and processing activities	Cheap labor, cheap land, raw materials and components, transportation junction	Close to cheap labor market, close to supply of raw materials, close to transportation junction, regions with strong industry-supporting capabilities
Marketing services	Market, information about demands, flexibility	With large market demands, perfect sales network and convenient transportation

Source: Paul Grugman, 2007.

2. Some service sectors with significant scale economy have formed an oligopolistic competition pattern in the Yangtze River Delta economic block.

One of the prominent features of the modern service industry is economy of scale. The scale effect of the modern service enterprises make a certain regional market only available for a few service enterprises, which leads to two consequences: the first one is that the threshold to enter into the industry is comparatively high. It is very difficult for an enterprise outside the industry to enter into a service market that is already occupied by a few enterprises; and the second consequence is the high threshold to enter the region. The advantages of the existing enterprises as the earlier comers in the region greatly increase the costs of later comers into the region, which means there is no need to develop certain services in every city because the services provided by the regional service center are sufficient.

3. The science and research, human resources and policy support in the cities have a significant influence on the spatial distribution of service resources in the Yangtze River Delta.

The high-tech features of the modern service industry are always determined by the high complexity of the problems the modern service industry is facing with. The modern service industry is always confronted with highly-complex production procedures and demands for high diversification. Therefore, the service products provided by the modern service industry need to be of high efficiency, meticulous and accurate, which puts high requirements on production facilities and especially on management. Only high-tech can assure high service quality and thus provide effective service for production. Consequently, the most prominent feature of the modern service industry is the comparatively high level of knowledge-intensity. Both the finance and securities sector and the information technology and software sector have become the service sectors where the high-level skills are concentrated. As a result, the modern service industry is more likely to agglomerate in the cities with a favorable science and research background, human resources, and policies for starting new business. When the service sectors agglomerate to a certain level this can promote the enhancement of the local science and research foundation and the optimization of policies, further strengthening the "centripetal force" of the agglomeration. This feature is evident in the Yangtze River Delta.

4. Some traditional service industry in the Delta is greatly influenced by the city culture so this always influences the agglomeration of this kind of service industry.

The service industry does not merely aim to support production activities, and satisfying the needs of production activities as a part of the service industry exists to satisfy the psychological and spiritual needs of people, such as the tourism and some cultural industries—which are closely related to cultural heritage. Even if some service industries are more focused on material services, after being combined with the local cultural conventions, they become unreplicable and unique industries, for example, some real estate industry with cultural features. This kind of service industry usually does not generate a regional service center, but they are integrated with the cultural tradition and are more likely to stay in the agglomeration in the cities.

The Formation of Regional Centers in the Yangtze River Delta

The Yangtze River Delta city cluster centered on and headed by Shanghai is one of the largest city clusters in the world. Observed from the orientation of the Delta set by the government, all the major cities in the Delta should strive to seize the opportunity of the international transfer of service industry and vigorously develop the service industry to become regional service centers. However, seen from the perspective of natural resources, city functions and development situation of the service industry, Shanghai has already become the regional service center in the Delta while Nanjing and Hangzhou have the functional features of regional service sub-centers.

Comparson of the development of service industries in the cities in the Yangtze River Delta

At the beginning of 2005, Shanghai put foward the "Outline for Shanghai's Acceleration of Modern Service Industry's Development," which set the new "coordinate system" for Shanghai's service economy. In the same year, the Jiangsu government issued the "Outline Concerning Acceleration of the Modern Service Industry's Development," and then Nanjing formulated the outline for its action to accelerate the development of modern service industry in Nanjing. Nanjing proposed to accelerate the construction of a modern service system suitable for the regional central cities, and to vigorously strengthen the integrated service functions of the cities to make Nanjing a regional modern service center in the Yangtze River Delta. The Hangzhou government also put emphasis on the development of service industry as the government proposed to make Hangzhou into a regional financial center and agency service center that boasts a complete set of institutions, developed market and strong radiation function. Of course, whether the cities can become regional service centers in the Delta depends not only on the governments' objectives and plans but also on the scale and quality of the services provided by the cities.

In terms of the added value in tertiary industry in 2005, the 16 cities in the Yangtze River Delta can be divided into three levels: Shanghai is the only city on the first level with a more than RMB 400 billion of annual added value in tertiary industry; the cities on the second level include Suzhou, Hangzhou, Wuxi, Ningbo and Nanjing, in which cities the annual added values in tertiary industry were all about RMB 100 billion; and the cities on the third level are the other 10 cities in which the annual added value in tertiary industry was less than RMB 50 billion. Although the added value in tertiary industry mainly reflects the scale of the service industry in a city, it also to some extent reflects the sorts and quality of service industries in a city.

In the following analysis, we compare the status quo of the development of manufacturing industry and major service sectors in Shanghai, Nanjing and Hangzhou. (Please refer to Table 8.4). We can see from the figure that no matter whether using the representative indicators of service industry or the functions and strengths of the service industry, the development of service industry in Shanghai is far ahead of that in Nanjing or Hangzhou, and especially on the modern producer service industry Shanghai's advantages are prominent. This makes it clear that in the Delta, only Shanghai is really competent to be the regional service center, and Nanjing and Hangzhou should become more influential regional service sub-centers.

Table 8.4. A comparison of the development levels of some service sectors in Shanghai, Nanjing and Hangzhou

	Items compared	Shanghai	Nanjing	Hangzhou
Producer Service Industry	The number of automobile R&D institutions in 2005	27	4	3
	The number of R&D and design institutions of electronic information products	56	6	7
Transportation Sector	Cargo handling capacity of a port in 2005	44,317	10,500	4,626
	Visitor handling capacity of an airport in 2005	2 Pudong District 4 Hongkou District	15	8
Trade Sector (comparison on types of functions and strengths)	Production Supporting Function	+++++	+++	+++
	Consumption Supporting Function	+++++	+++	+++
	Domestic Transfer Function	++++	++	+++
	Import and Export Transfer Function	+++++		
Financial Sector	Banking: Sum of deposits and loans in 2005 (100 million RMB)	40,119	9,923	12,294
	Securities: The gross volume of issued stocks in 2005 (100 million RMB)	125.3	9.9	8.1
	Insurance: The gross premium earnings in 2004 (100 million RMB)	333.62	71.33	72.53

(Con'd)

Tourism Sector	The number of A-class scenic spots	18	23	20
	Gross earnings of tourism in 2004 (100 million RMB)	1,472.0	319.9	410.6

Note: "+" shows the function of the sector, the more "+," the more functional the sector is.
Source: The Institute of Contemporary Shanghai Studies, *Yangtze River Delta Development Report* (Shanghai: Shanghai People's Publishing House, 2006).

Shanghai: The Regional Service Center of the Yangtze River Delta

Shanghai could become the regional service center of the Yangtze River Delta not only because it boasts high quality human resources, favorable traffic organization, excellent business environment, a standardized information exchange platform and a large concentration of service sectors, but also because Shanghai already has what international cities should have—the basic functions of an economic, trade and financial center. Moreover Shanghai is progressively becoming an international city that enjoys comparatively strong competitiveness and influence.

Its status as an international center decides that Shanghai has special advantages in developing the service industry and endows Shanghai with the natural conditions to become a regional service center. On the one hand, many multinational enterprises, international financial institutions and economic organizations have congregated in Shanghai, making Shanghai one of the international centers for capital collection and distribution. In Lujiazui alone —a district in Shanghai—there are more than 300 foreign-funded financial institutions which exert a certain control over today's world economy. Moreover Shanghai is a highly open region which strictly follows common international practices as well as international law and regulations, and it is one of the international collecting and distributing centers for goods, capital, information and labor force. It is also one of the international innovation bases for new ideas, new technologies and new systems etc. On the other hand, Shanghai's large population and large scale of city spaces enables it to form a continuous metropolitan region with the large number of surrounding medium- and small-sized cities. Shanghai enjoys a modern city infrastructure and highly-developed producer service sectors including communications, science and technology, consultancy, business, and municipal utilities. Shanghai is also equipped with a convenient inter-regional and intra-regional fast transportation system and boasts a modern city management system and first-class ecological environment.

Shanghai is in fact the first city in China to put forward the concept of concentration of service industry and has enriched and developed the connotation of the concept. In the early days of reform and opening up, the construction of the Hongqiao Development Zone which featured an outward-oriented economy was the origin of the modern agglomeration of service industry in Shanghai. The Hongqiao CBD was then gradually formed. The Hongqiao District attracted more than a thousand foreign-invested enterprises and nearly a thousand agency offices of foreign enterprises to locate in the area. In the District, the industries including consultancy, auditing, legal services, corporate planning and advertising have developed particularly fast. The Hongqiao District has taken its primary shape as a modern service agglomeration area. Since the 1990s, the service industry in Shanghai has developed at an increasing speed, and the proportion of Shanghai's GDP accounted for by the added value of service industry in Shanghai increased from 31.9% in 1990 to 51% in 2002.

According to the "eleventh five-year plan," the added value of Shanghai's service industry will be more than RMB750 billion in 2010 with an annual growth rate of above 10%. And the added value of the modern service sectors such as finance, commerce and trade, logistics and real estate added up to RMB480 billion, accounting for more than 60% of the total added value of service industry in Shanghai. The added value of the four new services—information services, navigation services, exhibitions and tourism, and agency services have maintained an annual growth rate of more than 20%, reaching RMB230 billion. And the added value of the potential service sectors—culture and entertainment, education and training, medical care and physical exercise—added up to more than RMB100 billion. Apart from further developing the service sectors such as commerce and trade sector and real estate sector, Shanghai will base its strategic orientation on becoming an international economic, financial, trade and navigation center, to vigorously develop and make breakthroughs in the six major service sectors—finance, cultural services, modern logistics, navigation services, exhibition and tourism, information services and specialized services.

"Shanghai, as the core and leader of the Yangtze River Delta area, in the process of the Delta's development into a world manufacturing base has not only strengthened its relations with other cities at home and abroad but also adjusted its city functions and industrial structures as Shanghai's international economic, financial, trade and transportation functions have become increasingly prominent. Shanghai, as an industrial and commercial city in China, is transforming into a world economic center and is more likely to become the center where the costs of the Yangtze River Delta's participation in the global division are reduced, and the expansive surrounding area of Shanghai has been tranformed into centers where the manufacturing costs are reduced." (Liu, 2006) That is to say, Shanghai is no longer a carrier whose economic function was to reduce manufacturing costs, in the traditional industrial society to support the agglomerating development of manufacturing industry, and realize economy of scale and scope. Instead, Shanghai's economic function has changed into reducing the transaction costs of production activities in the Shanghai circle and its surrounding areas by agglomerating and developing service industry. The service industry in Shanghai has become an important force to radiate out and influence the economic development in the Yangtze River Delta, and Shanghai's function as a regional service center has become increasingly significant.

Nanjing & Hangzhou: Regional service sub-centers in the Yangtze River Delta

Apart from Shanghai's status as the regional service center of the Delta, Nanjing and Hangzhou both boast concentration of service industry to a certain level and the two cities can radiate to other cities in their metropolitan economic circles, so the two cities have become modern service centers that are preceded only by Shanghai.

The service industry in Nanjing has undergone several development stages since the reform and opening up, and especially after the CPC Central Committee made the decision in 1992 to accelerate the development of the third industry, the service industry in Nanjing entered into a stage when its development was accelerated in an all-round way. As a result, the proportion of the total added value accounted for by the service industry increased from 20% in 1978 to 48% in 2006, and also the proportion of the employment accounted for by the service industry increased from less than 20% in 1978 to 46.2% in 2006

In terms of the agglomeration of service sectors in Nanjing, the trade and commerce sector, finance and insurance sector, tourism sector, logistics sector and real estate sector have become the mainstay of Nanjing's service industry, accounting for more than 65% of added value of service industry in the city; the trade and commerce sector as well as finance and insurance sector account for 10% and 9% respectively of the total output value in Nanjing, becoming the city's pillar industry. The exhibition and fair sector, science/education/culture/health sector, social services sector and agency sector have witnessed fast development, becoming the most potential new industries. In terms of the economic blocks, the agglomerating and radiating capabilities of the service industry in Nanjing have been greatly enhanced and the integrated service functions of Nanjing have been constantly strengthened, which enables Nanjing to enjoy the status of a regional service center in some service sectors. In 2004, the total volume of retail sales of social consumption goods in Nanjing accounted for 43% of the total volume in the whole Nanjing business circle. During holidays and vacations, more than 40% of the total volume of consumption was accounted for by the consumption of nonresidents, and the proportion even increased to 60% on big holidays. The enterprises with advantages in some businesses expanded at a rate of 20% to 30% in the Nanjing business circle market, and the chain enterprises in Nanjing have established more than 1,700 branches in other regions and reached a sales amount of RMB37.2 billion

In terms of the development trend, Nanjing has put forward a strategic objective of strengthening its comprehensive service functions and developing to become a regional modern service center in the Yangtze River Area. It has also proposed the specific requirements of "five centers," that is to say, Nanjing will be built as: (1) a regional commerce and trade center. Nanjing will further consolidate the central role of its trade, commerce and circulation sector in the "Nanjing metropolitan circle," and achieve "big market, big circulation and big trade," building a highly radiative regional commerce and trade center; (2) a regional logistics center. Nanjing will focus on promoting the competitiveness of the logistics sector and strengthening the radiation effect of regional logistics to cultivate a position as the international logistics sub-center in the Yangtze River Delta, the regional logistics conversion center of the Yangtze River valley and the logistics dispatch center in the Nanjing metropolitan circle. The center is based on the Nanjing economic circle and directed towards the world, and the center is expandable and energetic; (3) a regional tourism and exhibition center. Nanjing will succeed in developing from a "strong tourist city" to a "super tourist city" and forming a developed exhibition economy, building a tourist exhibition center that can radiate on the Eastern part of China, influence the whole country and boast international quality; (4) a regional financial center. Nanjing will strive to bring its advantages on financial resources into play to build a regional financial center that has excellent performance in banking, securities and insurance, connects the Eastern developed region with the large Western inland, radiates on surrounding areas, and enjoys a well-established system; (5) a regional information service center. Nanjing will focus on its construction of "digital Nanjing" to cultivate the information service and scientific R&D to become forerunning industries in the national economy, enable the breakthrough enhancement of an urban informationization and information service competence and build a regional information service center of which the informationization level tops China and equals the level in mid-developed countries.

The orientation of Nanjing as a regional service sub-center is made out of consideration of the following conditions: Firstly, the service industry in Nanjing already has a favorable foundation: in terms of the sectors involved, all the modern service sectors in Nanjing have developed well; in terms of the comparative scale, Nanjing plays a decisive role in the Delta and even in the whole country. Secondly, the service industry in Nanjing does not occupy absolute superior status in the Delta. Especially when compared with the service industry in Shanghai, the service industry in Nanjing falls behind in the R&D, transportation, finance and trade sectors; and even in comparison with the service industry in Hangzhou, Nanjing's service industry cannot show its absolute superiority. Thirdly, there exists a close complementary and cooperative relationship between Nanjing's service industry and the service industries in other cities. For example, in tourism, transport and producer services, Nanjing plays an important role in linking other medium- and small-sized cities with Shanghai.

Similar to Nanjing, Hangzhou has some advantages in developing service industry, can function as a service center in the metropolitan economic circle, and plays the role of a regional service sub-center in the Yangtze River Delta. In more specific terms, Hangzhou boasts three advantages in developing a modern service industry: the first is that Hangzhou, as the economic, political and cultural center of Zhejiang Province and an international scenic tourist city, is a place where human flow, material flow, information flow and capital flow gather; the second is that the prior development of manufacturing industry expands the space for the producer service industry to develop more extensively and deeply; the third advantage is that the development of service industry in Hangzhou has already established a favorable foundation and has formed close radiation relationships with the surrounding regions.

The focus of Hangzhou's development of modern service industry is embodied in finance and agency. In terms of developing the finance sector, the finance sector in Hangzhou enjoys an excellent foundation and the financial system is well established; all major banks and insurance companies have set up branch institutions in Hangzhou, which has generated many benefits. In 2010, the added value of finance sectors accounted for about 9% of the GDP in Hangzhou. Hangzhou will develop to become a regional financial center which has sufficient and complete institutions, a developed market and strong radiation effect on other regions in the Delta, and to be an important part of the Shanghai international financial market. In terms of the developing agency sector, there are about 16,000 agencies in Hangzhou and the development of the agency sector will be accelerated. The agency service system will be improved under the guidance of marketization and specialization to become a modern agency service system that boasts wide variety, reasonable distribution, standard operation and connections with the other countries, and an agency service center that relies on Zhejiang Province but radiates on the whole country in the southern part of the Yangtze River Delta.

The Integrated Strategic Choices of Regional Service Centers and Regional Service Industry

The growth of regional service centers does not only have a fundamental influence on the economic growth of the Yangtze River Delta, but also significantly influences the functions, industrial structures and directions of service sectors of different cities as it demands that the cities in the Delta re-examine their functional relationship with the regional service centers and make clear the direction of their own service sectors' agglomeration in order to ultimately promote the integrated operation of service resources in the whole area and enhance the competitiveness of the region. From the perspective of agglomerating economy and scale economy, in the economic circles within 1–2 hours' drive where the costs of transportation are relatively low and the cities have close economic links with each other, the advantages of integrated development are inevitable and obvious, which is not only better than the lonely development of a single city but also propitious to the enhancement of the competitiveness of the whole Yangtze River Delta economic block, achieving "complementation" and an "all-win" situation.

Emphasizing the functions of a regional service center

As the regional service center of the Yangtze River Delta, Shanghai is a city where many service sectors congregate. The agglomeration of service sectors in Shanghai functions mainly in three ways. The first one is to create the conditions for other cities to participate in the global economic network with low costs. It is much easier for other cities in the Delta to connect with the global production network and service network with low costs via Shanghai—which acts as a bridgehead and transfer station. The second is to provide the surrounding cities with high quality modern services by reducing transaction costs. The accumulated modern service sectors in Shanghai can reduce the transaction costs of economic activities in both Shanghai and the surrounding areas and expand the scale of divisions and transactions in the areas. The third is to reduce the manufacturing costs as a carrier to support the agglomeration and development of manufacturing sectors.

Bringing the function of regional service sub-centers as a connecting link into play

In general, the development of service industries in different cities in the Yangtze River Delta is on gradient levels. The service industry in Shanghai is fairly well developed and Shanghai's prominent advantages in the capital-intensive and technology-intensive sectors such as finance, information and commerce have become the central links that connect the international market with the Yangtze River Delta and radiate out to the Delta as a whole. Although Nanjing and Hangzhou are defined as the sub-centers of the Delta, the service industries in the two cities do not have to be always attached to Shanghai. Instead differentiated service sectors should be developed in the three cities to form advantages in tourism industry, cultural industry and real estate industry in Nanjing and Hangzhou and to develop the functions of Nanjing and Hangzhou as regional service sub-centers. As the center of commercial services, financial service, information services and cultural and educational services in the Nanjing Economic Circle, Nanjing City can provide high quality services for many cities and counties on its periphery and satisfy their needs in goods, capital, information and ideas. Similarly, as the center of agency and financial services in the southern part of the Delta, Hangzhou functions as a connecting link as on the one hand Hangzhou efficiently introduces the service advantage resources into the metropolitan economic circle, and on the other hand it provides the surrounding areas with diversified service resources.

Promoting integration with functional complementation

Close cooperation exists among the service industries in different cities in the Yangtze River Delta, so an "all-win" situation will be achieved by developing regional cooperation. For example, Nanjing, Zhenjiang and Yangzhou all have good foundations in the transportation, logistics and tourism sectors, but their service functions should be rationally coordinated in the integration process. Specifically, the complementation of the travel resources in the three cities should be brought into play by making use of the "one-hour traffic circle" in the region that involves multiple transportation channels—the roads, waterways, railways, aviation and subways—to intensify the interchangeability of the tourist sources market and attract tourists in the three cities to travel in the whole region; the overlapping of the tourist sources market should be increased to attract the tourists in other regions to travel in the three cities; the cooperation of the tourism circles of the three cities should be developed and the three cities' promotion and publicizing of the tourism sectors should be combined together. On the complementation and cooperation on logistics, transportation and communication, the economic block of the three cities could also achieve an effective division of functions and integrated cooperation. As a further example, in terms of the information industry and trade fairs, the cities in the Delta should also realize the complementation of advantages in both software and hardware to establish a regional brand for the trade fairs. In terms of the environmental protection industry, Nanjing could cooperation with the cities located in the downstream Yangtze River areas in environmental protection and bring the industrial advantages of all cities into play to deal with the water pollution in the Yangtze River valley.

Enhancing the brand effect of characteristic service sectors

All regions should lay emphasis on the particularities of the service sectors closely related to cultural traditions and heritage and insist on enhancing the brand effect on the basis of maintaining traditions. In terms of these sectors, in the process of integration, they should not be simply merged or joined with other sectors. Instead we should attach importance to the enhancement of brand effect and form a characteristic industry in the Yangtze River Delta. For example, Yangzhou could make great use of its traditional resources in commercial industry as well as the real advantages represented by the "Three Knives of Yangzhou" to further polish the brand of "Yangzhou Masters." And Nanjing could base its particular advantages on its reputation as an ancient capital for six dynasties and its abundant cultural relic resources to design high-level travel programs and thus form a nationally influential service brand.

9

Chapter

Cooperative Agglomeration and Growth of the Service Industry and the Manufacturing Industry

Introduction

The agglomeration of industries is not only an important feature of the economic development in the Yangtze River Delta, but also a significant direction for the Delta's current and future industrial competition and integration.[1] To some degree, the high-level industrial agglomeration in the Delta is the carrier of "Made in China" supported by the Delta. Together with the economic growth and development caused by the agglomeration, it provides the regional economists and industrial economists in China with sufficient research materials and space for analysis.

The industrial agglomeration in the Yangtze River Delta is closely related to the centralized FDI behavior in the Delta of domestic and foreign enterprises, especially multinational enterprises, since 1992. For example we note that in Shanghai, those enterprises that invest in the same industry stick to each other in competition and form clusters are international or multinational enterprises that enjoy established reputations in the industry. Nearly all of the thirty enterprises in the Shanghai Chemical Industry Park where the total investment exceeds US$8 billion are foreign-funded enterprises or Chinese-foreign joint ventures. In the Pudong micro-electronics Industry Strip with a planned area of only 22 square kilometers, some famous international chip manufacturers hurried to invest in this small zone one after another, and the total number of the micro-electronics projects constructed or under construction has reached 66. In the Strip, the eight enterprises with investment of more than US$100 million have all been set up by foreign investment.

The high-level industrial agglomeration is one of the major engines that have been driving the industries to update and promoting the economy to develop fast in the Yangtze River Delta since the 1990s. For example, in the area along the Shanghai-Nanjing line which is about 50 kilometers in extension and about 300 kilometers in length, the most important industrial agglomeration area in Jiangsu—the Shanghai-Nanjing Information Industry Strip—has come into being. Currently more than 80% of the output value of the information industry and more than 15% of the output value of the industrial sectors are accounted for by this Information Industry Strip. As a further example, in Zhejiang, all the industries with competitive superiorities have basically been developing on the basis of industrial clusters. According to the statistics in Zhejiang, there are now more than 500 industrial cluster areas in Zhejiang, and among the 28 manufacturing sectors which enjoy characteristic advantages in Zhejiang 4 sectors account for more than 20% of the national proceeds of sale of their sectors and 13 sectors account for more than 10% of the national proceeds of sale of their sectors.

Some questions we need to ask in our analysis of the industrial agglomeration and economic growth in the Yangtze River Delta are: why do the enterprises, especially the multinational enterprises, select the Yangtze River Delta centered on Shanghai but not other inland areas in China to put their FDI into services? Does Shanghai, as the central city in the Delta and in China, form in its periphery some strong force and ability that attracts investment in manufacturing? If so, where do the force and ability behind this come from?

The research hypothesis of Gao and Liu (2005) may offer an answer to these questions as they have pointed out that it is exactly because the Yangtze River Delta headed by Shanghai is supported by Shanghai as an internationalized central city, and especially supported by the highly-developed producer service industry in Shanghai, that the Delta could achieve the tremendous agglomeration and favorable development of manufacturing industry that other areas could not achieve. By reducing the regional transaction costs, deepening the new capital, upgrading and extending the specialized division, cultivating the competitive edges of industries, and strengthening the new business start-up and innovative abilities of the region, the developed producer service industry in Shanghai greatly promotes the intensive agglomeration of manufacturing industry guided by FDI in the Yangtze River Delta. However their empirical research was still in the primary stage, so their conclusions lack convincing empirical support and many things in their research need to be further explored. For example, what influence does the interactive relationship between the service industry (especially the modern service industry) and the manufacturing industry (represented by "cooperative agglomeration" in this chapter) have on the industrial agglomeration and economic growth in the Delta? Does FDI promote industrial cooperative agglomeration or not? Simply speaking, Shanghai's strategic thinking on making development of the service industry a priority and making the service industry the important carrier of Shanghai's construction of international economic, financial, trade and navigation centers, and the strategic thinking of accelerating integration into the world economy and better serving the whole country, do not only support Shanghai's modern service industry in the constant and healthy economic development in Shanghai but also form the "headquarters economy" development pattern in Shanghai, enhance Shanghai's integrated service functions, and spatially reduce the transaction costs in the development of manufacturing industry in the Delta. Therefore this strategic thinking is of great and profound importance.

This chapter intends to reveal the inner cause of the high agglomeration of manufacturing and service industries in the Delta and to analyze the role FDI plays in deciding the cooperative agglomeration of service industry and manufacturing industry as well as in the economic growth of the Delta. Unlike previous research of the same kind, the contribution of the research in this chapter to this research field is embodied by the fact that we do not simply study FDI's influence on regional economic growth but instead we base our research on the perspective of the cooperative agglomeration of service industry and manufacturing industry to focus on the three issues concerning this cooperative agglomeration: firstly, the influence of the cooperative agglomeration of service industry and manufacturing industry on the industrial agglomeration in the Delta; secondly, the relationship between the cooperative agglomeration and FDI; thirdly, whether this cooperative agglomeration effectively promotes the β-convergence and σ-convergence of the economic growth in the Delta.

A Review of Related Theories

About industrial agglomeration, cooperative agglomeration and FDI

The existing research on the determinant factors of industrial agglomeration in a country or a region were commonly done using the following theories: (1) Marshall's theories on external economics. Marshall pointed out that local trade secrets and localized skills are the major reasons for the localization of a certain industrial sector's agglomeration. Marshall believed that the expansion of market scale brings the scale effect of intermediate input, the scale effect of the labor market, and information exchange and technical diffusion, and thus it could lead to the external scale economy. (2) Weber's theories on agglomeration economy. From the perspective of micro enterprises' selection of location, Weber clarified that whether the enterprises gather depends on the benefits of agglomeration and the comparison of costs. (3) Coarse's theories on transaction costs. These theories emphasize that the emergence and growth of industrial agglomeration is an outcome of enterprises' selection after they weigh the internal and external transaction costs. (4) Theories on economic geography, represented by Paul Krugman's theories. Krugman believed that industrial agglomeration is caused by the interactive influence of the progressive increase in enterprises' returns to scale, the transportation costs and movement of production factors in market conduction. (5) Porter's theories on new competitive advantage. Porter brought the supporting related industries into his diamond system of industrial competitiveness (Porter, 2000), and he believed that there exists a strong causality between the correlation effect, agglomeration effect of related industries and industrial development and industrial competitiveness.

In recent years, research on this topic has witnessed a new perspective, which is to study the trend of the industrial agglomeration from the cooperative relationship between the geographical locations of service industry and manufacturing industry. Research of this kind always assumes first that there is "closeness" between the manufacturers and the producer service providers. Hansen (1990) noted that the study of the relationship between the producer services and the regional productivity differences should assume that the producer services and the manufacturing industry are geographically close to each other. Klaesson (2001) assumed that the intermediate industry produces at a place "close" to the final industry. In order to explain the convergence of the final industry, he considered the condition that the intermediate industry is geographically close to the final industry as a necessary factor.

Generally speaking, the reason for the existence of the "closeness" between the manufacturers and producer service providers is that the costs of acquiring services from the service providers, for example, the travelling time for a meeting and the frequency of contacts, would increase with the increase in geographical distance. (O. Farrell and Hitchens, 1990) Coffey and Bailly (1991) emphasized the importance of contact frequency: "The demands for intermediate service contain the most expensive part—on one hand, there are the costs in maintaining face-to-face communication with the service providers and on the other hand, there are inputs for services and market costs." This reasoning implies that the manufacturers can get great benefits in cooperative location with the producer service providers' production. Goe (1990) pointed out that the producer service providers could also gain huge benefits from the manufacturers who are located "close" to them because the manufacturers create the market for the service providers. If it is assumed that the relationship between the manufacturing industry and the producer service industry is a "client—supplier" relationship, Marshall (1982) found that the organizational structure of the producer service industry influences the manufacturers' demands for the services, and meanwhile the organizational structure of the manufacturing industry also influences the provision of the producer services. Marshall, in his research, did not analyze the interactive relationship between the manufacturing industry and the producer service industry with consideration to the geographical locations.

Many scholars have paid attention to the role FDI plays in promoting industrial agglomeration. Bagchi-Sen and Wheeler (1989) analyzed the spatial distribution of FDI in two periods: the first from 1974 to 1978, and the second from 1979 to 1983. They found that during the period from 1974 to 1978, in the Northeastern metropolises, especially in NYC, FDI was highly centralized, but in the period from 1979 to 1983, FDI was diffuse. Consistent with the general trend of the metropolitan economy in the US, during the research periods, FDI evidently transferred from the manufacturing sectors to the service sectors. Landesmann and Petiti (1995) discussed the trend of the producer service trade in the developed countries and they emphasized the relationship between the producer service trade as well as the internationalization of the production of the products and the international direct investment on the products, but they did not study the relationship between trade and the interaction between service industry and manufacturing industry. Markuson (1999) pointed out that FDI could catalyze industrial development through the correlation effect and agglomeration effect of industries. Stare (2000) examined the producer service industry in Slovakia and he believed that FDI is an instrument to promote the development of the producer service industry. Stare's point was supported by his empirical analysis, in other words, in commercial services, the maximum benefit of FDI could be obtained in the FDI's spillover effect in the local economy, which includes transfer of knowledge and techniques, and in the indirect productivity of commercial services and the improvement of the commercial services' quality. However Stare did not use theoretical models to support his idea. In terms of the research in China, Fan (2004) did empirical research and pointed out that the transfer of the rural labor force, FDI agglomeration in Eastern coastal areas and the transfer of the rural labor force from the midwest to coastal areas are the major reasons for the agglomeration of manufacturing industry into the eastern coastal areas after reform and opening up.

We think that it is because of the agglomeration effect of FDI that FDI could significantly influence the agglomeration of some specific industries. Since the reform and opening up, Eastern China has attracted a large amount of FDI with its unique location advantages and natural resources, which has promoted the fast economic development of the eastern coastal areas by facilitating capital formation, capital agglomeration, technology spillover, industrial agglomeration, structural upgrade and agglomeration of human capital; and the fast economic growth of Eastern China has enhanced the income level of residents, expanded the market capacity, helped improve the external economic environment, generated agglomeration economy effect and thus further expanded the entrance scale of FDI, which has established a regional circulation accumulation causality. In the following section we are going to point out that the regional circulation accumulation causality between FDI and industrial agglomeration, to a great extent, is determined by the behavior of multinational enterprises.

About industrial cooperative agglomeration and economic growth

The major effect of regional integration and international integration is to increase the efficiency of the spatial economy. And here the questions we need to clarify are: What is the relationship between economic growth and geographical location? How do the two influence each other? How will the differences between regions change as time goes by (increase or reduce)? What factors increase or reduce those differences? It is of great importance to understand the change trend of the differences. Moreover it is commonly believed that the economic differences among regions are not anticipated by the society, so with respect to policies it is essential to study the topic and answer those questions.

When the transportation cost is low enough, modern industries and innovative industries will accumulate in the same region while the other regions are all occupied with specialized production of traditional products. No matter whether technology can flow inter-regionally, the number of enterprises in modern industries will gradually increase as time goes by. In fact industrial agglomeration and economic growth promote each other. So policies that support scattered distribution always do harm to overall economic growth, and in the circumstance that technology can flow freely, it becomes increasingly difficult to prevent the center—periphery space structure from forming as in this situation, the symmetric spatial distribution pattern is never at equilibrium. By contrast, the existence of flowing technology as obstacles makes it possible for a scattered spatial distribution to be maintained. However, even in this kind of circumstance, the deepening of integration is likely to result in the formation of the space structure of "center—periphery."

Nevertheless, the aggravation of unbalanced regional economic development does not always lead to the improvement of the periphery's economic situation, which happens when the agglomeration cannot promote sufficient economic growth. In this situation the transfer of more economic activities to the central area would definitely bring losses to the people who live in the peripheral areas. In the contrary situation, we cannot be certain that the agglomeration and growth are in confliction with fairness: although the living standard of the unskilled workers in the central areas is higher than that of the unskilled workers in the peripheral areas, in the "center-periphery" space structure the living standard of the people who live in the peripheral areas will definitely be higher than their living standard would be in a totally scattered space structure.

Theories of the new economic geography point out that the unbalanced spatial distribution effect of regional economic growth behavior could generate the so-called "geography—growth equation." Martin and Ottaviano (1999)—two scholars who have been engaged in establishing the relationship between agglomeration and the growing process—have pointed out that agglomeration as a whole could be considered as a factor of growth. After doing a large amount of research they found important results in the analysis of regional growth mechanism: on the one hand, the spatial centralization of economic behaviors is favorable to economic growth and the unbalanced spatial distribution is an effective geographical balancing behavior to economic growth; and on the other hand, economic growth can be seen as another agglomerating force, which means that the growth could intensify the polarization process.

Analysis of the Factors That Influence Industrial Agglomeration and Cooperative Agglomeration

The questions we need to discuss first are: What factors influence the cooperative agglomeration of industries? What key links need to be perfected in order to achieve the cooperative agglomeration of industries? The author thinks that the cooperative agglomeration of industries is influenced by both some of the common factors of industrial agglomerations and some special factors. In practice, the factors that influence industrial agglomerations and cooperative agglomeration are as follows:

Geographical factors

Krugman and Venables (1995) hold the view that industrial agglomeration happens due to the market conductive interaction of the factors including progressive increases in enterprises' returns to scale, transportation costs, and movements of production factors. Porter (2003) also believed that closely-combined supporting industries create an international competitive edge in interrelated industries and that they have the effect of mutual benefit and self-strengthening, and their formation is related with the "closeness" in location. The research on industrial agglomeration in the new economic geography is based on geographical factors, and the cooperative agglomeration itself is a geographic concept, so the geographical factor should have an important place in our discussion of the factors that influence industrial agglomeration and cooperative agglomeration.

Radiation from the central cities

Both modern development economics and the new economic geography lay emphasis on the functions of the central cities. As the leader of the economic development in its region, Shanghai has a great influence on the peripheral cities. From the point of view of local market effect, the super scale of Shanghai will definitely influence the industrial geographical distribution in the whole Delta, and all the industrial agglomeration and cooperative agglomeration must be distributed around the central city—Shanghai. As with the research on industrial agglomeration in the new economic geography, distance is a focus of our examination. The distance from Shanghai will decide the industrial agglomeration level in the peripheral cities and the selection of cooperative agglomeration behavior.

FDI level

The longitudinal agglomeration formed by industrial relationships is more evidently shown in multinational enterprises whose investments all over the world generate a series of international enterprises that serve those multinational enterprises, including the producer service providers that provide the multinational enterprises with intermediary products and many services such as logistics, storage, purchasing, consulting, accountancy and financial services. Since the support and supplementary competence as well as the development level of the service industry of the developing countries are far lower than those of the developed countries, the multinational enterprises which have been accustomed to and dependent on the high quality producer services in their home countries cannot always be satisfied by the service support provided by local service enterprises. In this situation, those service enterprises which are in cooperation with multinational enterprises, or the service support departments of the service enterprises, may follow the multinational enterprises to transfer offshore to further provide supporting services for the multinational enterprises. The joining in of the service enterprises is propitious to the improvement of the agglomerated structure of the manufacturing industry and enables the multinational enterprises to enjoy the same business model and business services as they do in their home countries. Following clients to invest in other countries or regions has become a regular practice of international service enterprises, and sometimes the multinational enterprises may invite their supporting enterprises to expand to other countries with them. This generates a positive feedback ring between FDI and industrial agglomerations as well as their cooperative agglomeration.

The situation of the state-owned economy

In the economically developed regions in China, such as Shanghai and Nanjing, the state-owned economy plays an important role in the economic operation. In these regions the state-owned economy brings its leading role into play in the form of large-sized state-owned enterprises and enterprise groups. With the deepening of the reform and opening up, and with the increasingly fierce global competition, the large-sized state-owned enterprises need to transform. In order to enhance efficiency and to control costs, many service and supporting enterprises and sectors have been separated from the state-owned enterprises and turned into independent service providers to continue to serve the original enterprises. Therefore the model of industrial agglomeration and cooperative agglomeration will inevitably be influenced by the scale of the local state-owned economy and the state-owned economy in the neighboring regions.

Wage levels

In the new economic geographical model, the levels of nominal wages and real wages decide the industrial distribution of short-term equilibrium and long-term equilibrium respectively. As the market integration level in China is not high enough, there exist great disparities among the wage levels in different regions in China. The development of the outward-oriented economy in the Pearl River Delta and Yangtze River Delta, to a great degree, profit from the cheap labor force in other regions. Therefore we can anticipate that the regions with lower wage levels will attract more manufacturers, thus bringing higher agglomeration levels of manufacturing industry and its cooperative industries.

Density of knowledge

Since the producer service industry involves a major input of human capital and knowledge capital, a large amount of the output produced by human capital and knowledge capital is involved in the output of the producer service industry. Intra-industrial and inter-industrial concurrent flows of knowledge and technology are the important sources of innovative cooperation effect of industrial agglomerations and cooperative agglomeration. Therefore the density of knowledge as a factor will also influence the industrial agglomerations and cooperative agglomeration. It is anticipated that in a region with higher density of knowledge, higher cooperative agglomeration level and higher agglomeration levels of manufacturing industry and service industry will be found.

Scale of economy

Since local markets of comparatively large scale can attract more manufacturers and their producer service providers, the effect of the local market should be one of the major observable factors of industrial agglomeration. We anticipate that in the more economically developed regions we will find higher cooperative agglomeration level and higher agglomeration levels of manufacturing industry and service industry.

Definitions of Related Indicators and Statistical Descriptions

FDI

Based on the fact that, on the one hand, the proportion of domestic gross production accounted for by FDI was less than 1% before 1990, which means that the influence of FDI on economic growth was not strong enough, and on the other hand that since the 1990s the market economy system has been basically established, and especially in the mid- and late-1990s China progressively moved from an economy of shortage and transformed from a seller's market to a buyer's market, we principally do the econometric analysis using the data on the economy after 1990 on the basis of the features of China's economic operation.

We select the statistics of FDI in 15 cities (Taizhou excluded) in the Yangtze River Delta in the years from 1988 to 2005. The selected representative years are 1988, 1994, 2000 and 2005.[2] The real FDI situation in the cities in the Delta is shown in Fig. 9.1. From the graph we can see that FDI in each city in the Delta has increased considerably and that the growth of FDI in Shanghai and Suzhou is among the most prominent. The growth model of the two cities has shown evident symbiosis.

Fig. 9.1. Volume of real foreign capital in the Yangtze River Delta (1988–2005) (RMB 10,000)

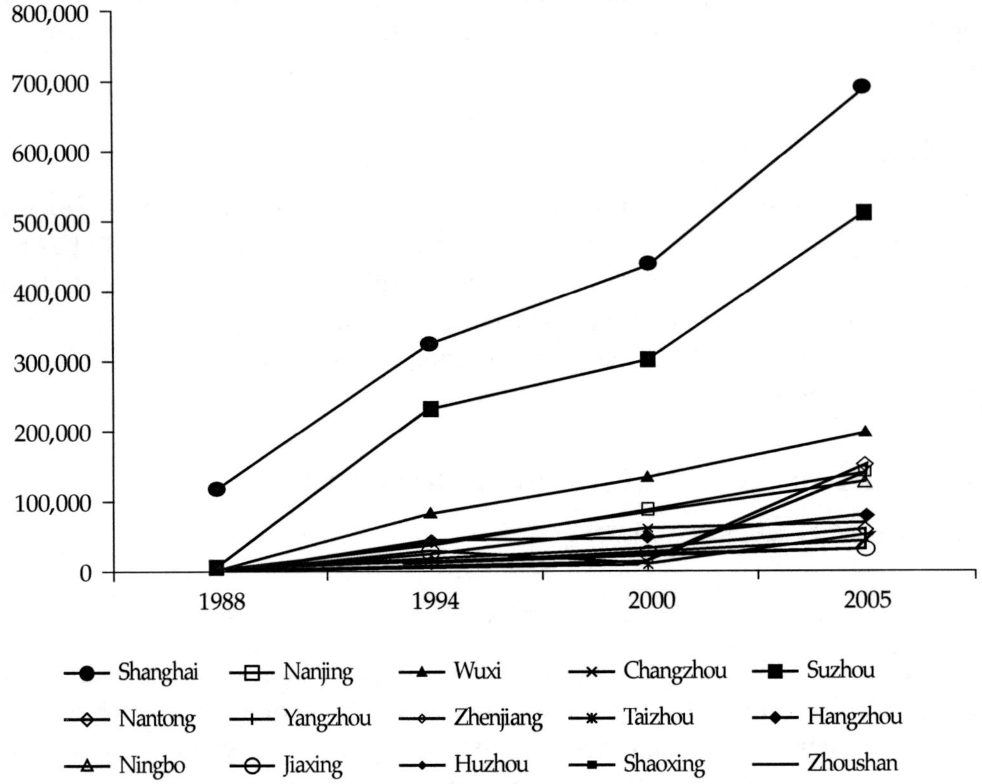

Industrial Agglomeration and Cooperative Agglomeration

In order to maintain the consistency of research, here we select the statistics of the manufacturing industry and employees in the service industry in the 15 cities (Taizhou excluded) in the Yangtze River Delta in 1988, 1994, 2000 and 2005. The related variables are defined as follows:

(1) Agglomeration level of industry.

Based on the regional specialized index, we have constructed the agglomerating index of the Industry "*i*" in Region "*j*":

$$\eta_{ij} = \frac{(\sum_{k} E_{ik} \cdot e^{-T_{jk}} / \sum_{k} e^{-T_{jk}}) / E_{\cdot j}}{E_{i\cdot} / E}$$

In the above equation, E_{ik} is the output value of industry "i" in city "k," "$E_{.j}$" is the output value of city "j," "$E_{i.}$" is the output value of industry "i" in the whole region, and "E" is the gross product of the region. "T_{jk}" is the distance from city "j" to city "k," measured by the hours taken for the trip by train, "T_{ii}"=0. Here we have weighted the output value of industry "i" in city "k" and surrounding cities on the basis of the distance between the cities, in order to obtain the geographical agglomeration level of industries.

(2) Cooperative agglomeration level of industries.

We use the relative difference of agglomeration index to measure the cooperative agglomeration level of industry "i" and industry "m" in region "k":

$$\gamma_{imk}=1-|\eta_{ik}-\eta_{mk}|/\eta_{ik}$$

The larger the index is, the closer the agglomeration levels of industry "i" and industry "m" in region "k" are to each other and the higher the cooperative agglomeration level is.

From Figs. 9.2 and 9.3 we can see that from 1988 to 2005, employment in secondary industry in Shanghai witnessed a significant decline while employment in secondary industry in other cities in the Yangtze River Delta continued to increase. In contrast, employment in tertiary industry in every city in the Yangtze River Delta increased, and the increase was significant in Shanghai.

From Figs. 9.4 and 9.5 we can see that the agglomeration level of service industry in the cities in the Yangtze River Delta all increased. In contrast, the agglomeration level of manufacturing industry in Shanghai, Wuxi and Suzhou decreased considerably and the increase in other cities was not significant.

From Fig. 9.6 we can see that the cooperative agglomeration level in all cities in the Yangtze River Delta showed a significant increase after 2000, which implies that the cooperative agglomeration of service industry and manufacturing industry in the Delta has gradually emerged.

Fig. 9.2. Employment in secondary industry in the Yangtze River Delta (1988–2005)(10,000 people)

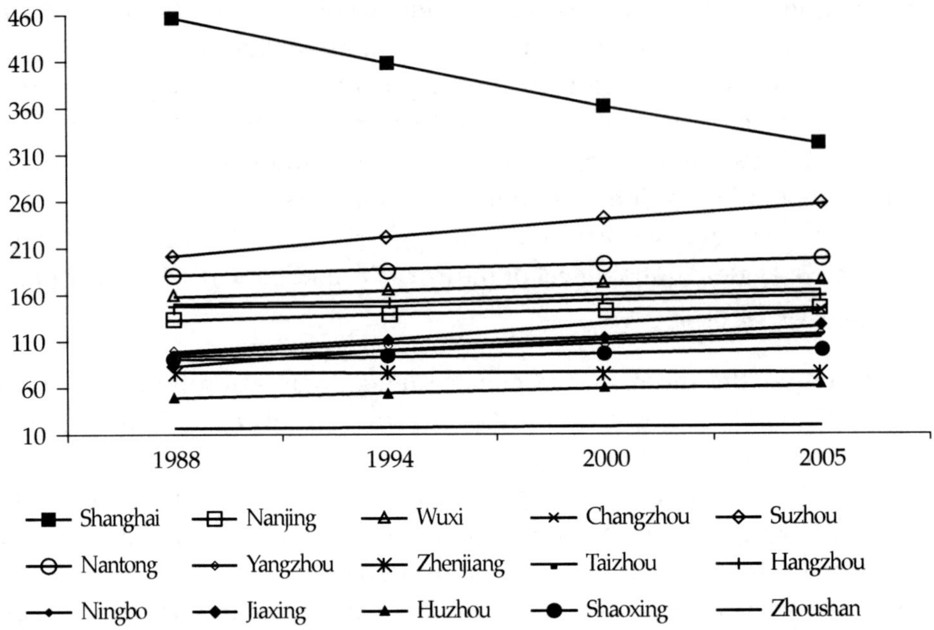

Fig. 9.3. Employment in tertiary industry in the Yangtze River Delta (1988–2005)(10,000 people)

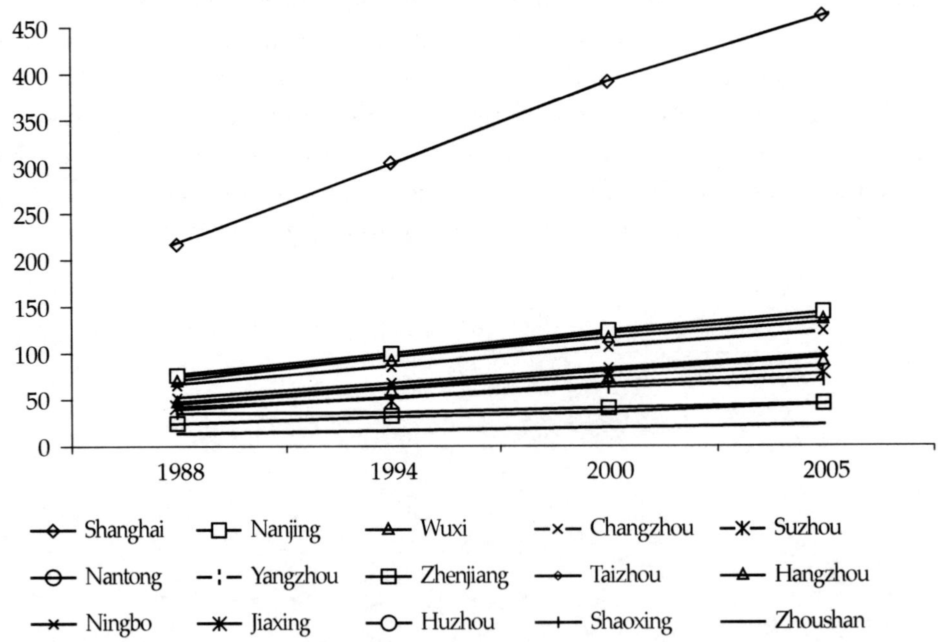

Fig. 9.4. Agglomeration level of service industry in the Yangtze River Delta (1988–2005)

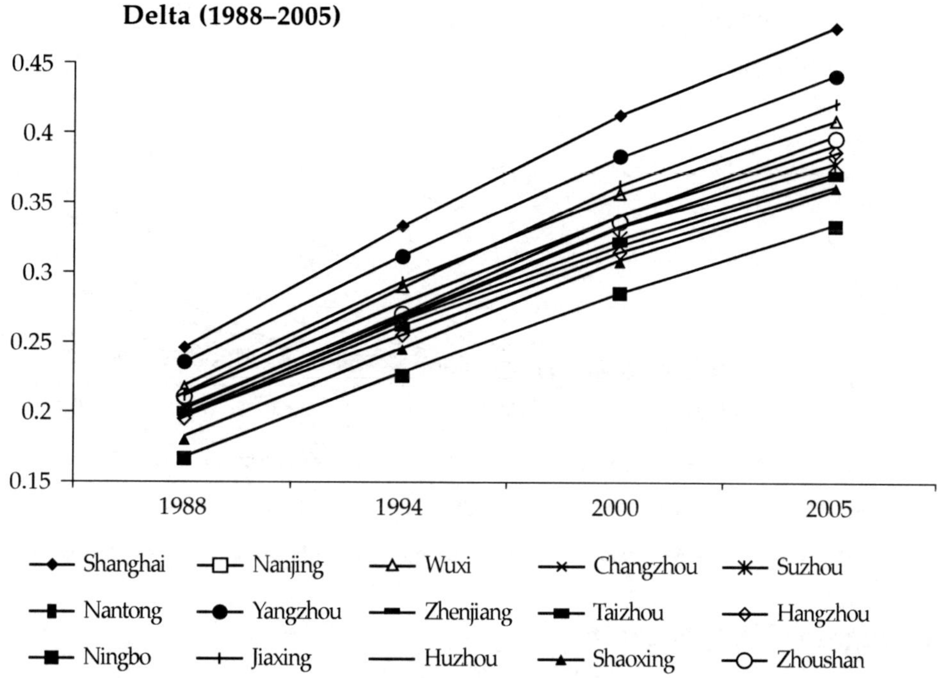

Fig. 9.5. Agglomeration level of manufacturing industry in the Yangtze River Delta (1988–2005)

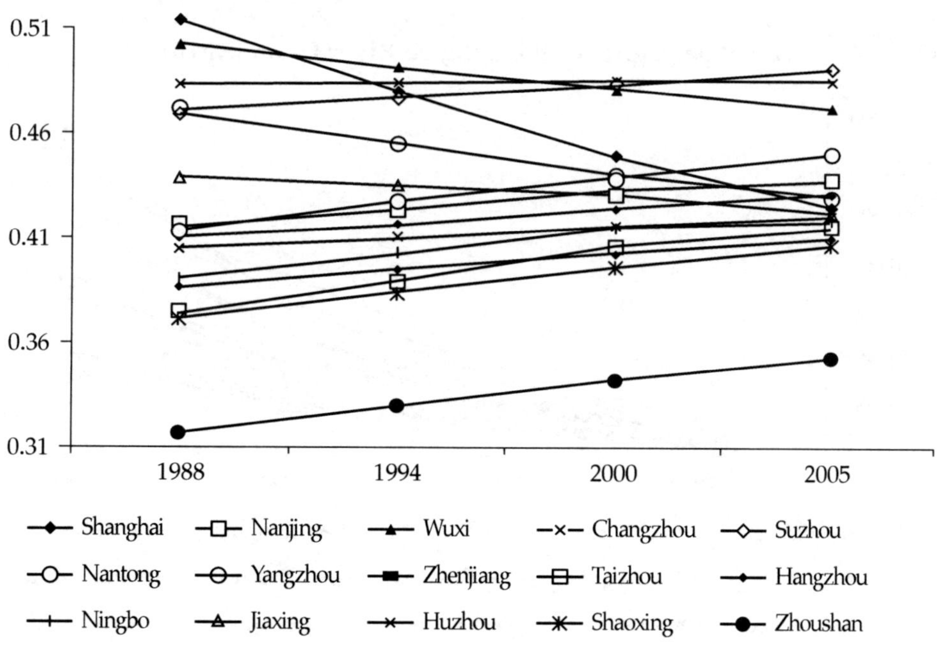

Fig. 9.6. **Cooperative agglomeration level in the Yangtze River Delta (1988–2005)**

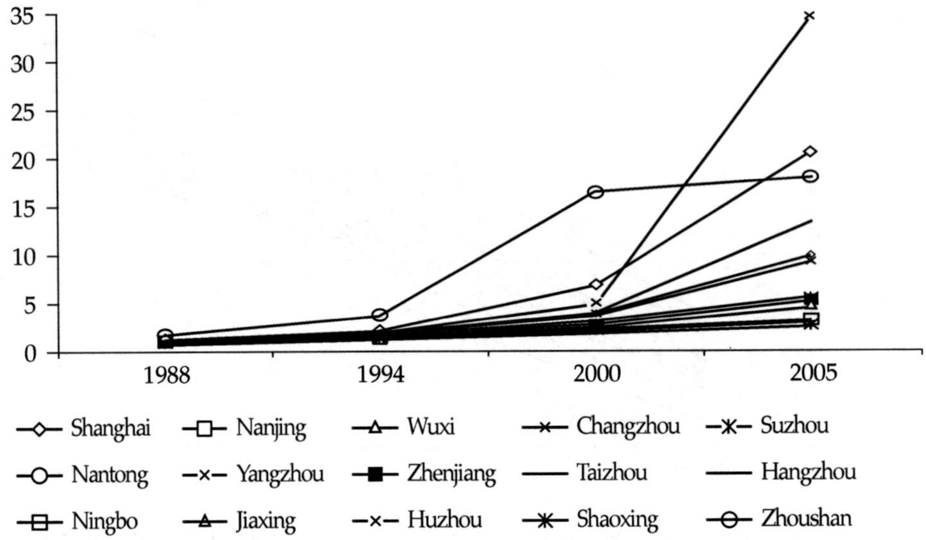

Change in GDP per capita

From Fig. 9.7 we can see the changes in GDP per capita in all cities in the Yangtze River Delta. It can be found that the GDP per capita in all cities showed a trend of "club-convergence," which means that there could exist β-convergence or σ-convergence in all cities in the Yangtze River Delta.

Fig. 9.7. **GDP per capita in the Yangtze River Delta (RMB)**

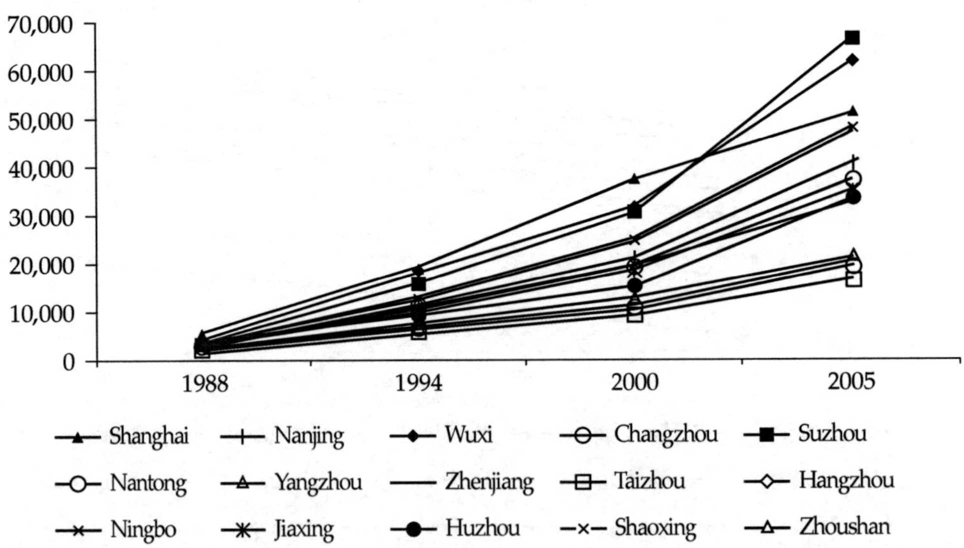

Econometric Test of FDI and Cooperative Agglomeration

Industrial agglomeration and cooperative agglomeration: Simultaneous equations

According to our theoretical hypothesis that the cooperative agglomeration promotes the agglomeration of industries, the simultaneous equations model we construct is as follows:

$$log\eta_{M,j}=\alpha_0+\alpha_1 log\gamma_{M,S,j}+\alpha_2 logFDI_j+\alpha_3 logS_j+\alpha_4 log\omega_j+\alpha_5 logY_j+\alpha_6 T_{j,0}+\mu_j$$

$$log\eta_{S,j}=\beta_0+\beta_1 log\gamma_{S,M,j}+\beta_2 logFDI_j+\beta_3 logS_j+\beta_4 logT_j+\beta_5 logY_j+\beta_6 T_j,0+v_j$$

In the simultaneous equations model, "$\eta_{M,j}$" is the agglomeration index of manufacturing industry in city "j," and "$\eta_{S,j}$" is the agglomeration index of service industry in Ccty "j," "$\gamma_{M,S,j}$ ($\gamma_{S,M,j}$)"is the cooperative agglomeration level of manufacturing industry and service industry in city "j." "FDI_j" is FDI level in city "j," "S_j"is the scale of state-owned economy in city "j," and "T_j, 0" is the distance between city "j" and the central city—Shanghai. We have also controlled other variables: the first one is the average wage of on-the-job employees in city "j"—"ω_j"; the second is the density of knowledge in city "j"—"T_j," which is equal to the proportion of total employees in manufacturing industry accounted for by specialized technical personnel; and the third one is the GDP level in city "j"—"Y_j" (calculated in accordance with the constant price in 2000), which is the proxy variable of scale of economy. According to the hypothesis that cooperative agglomeration promotes the agglomeration of industries, we anticipate that α_1>0 and β_1>0; and also we anticipate that α_2>0 and β_2>0 because of the positive feedback between FDI and industrial agglomeration and between FDI and cooperative agglomeration. According to the relationship between the scale of the state-owned economy and the industrial agglomeration as well as the cooperative agglomeration, we anticipate that both α_3 and β_3 are greater than zero; the manufacturing sectors will be attracted to areas where the wage level is lower, so that α_4 should be negative; as the producer service industry has a relatively high demand for technology and the agglomeration level of the producer service industry is in positive correlation with the knowledge density of the local manufacturing industry, we anticipate that β_4 is greater than zero; moreover, given the local market effect, the aggregation indexes of manufacturing industry and service industry are in positive correlation with the overall economic level, so we anticipate that α_5>0 and β_5>0.

The radiation effect of the central cities make us anticipate that both α_6 and β_6 are less than zero. We use the two-stage least-square method to estimate the hybrid cross-sectional data in the years from 2000 to 2005, and the results of the estimation are shown in Table 9.1.

From the results of the regression analysis of the relevant variables in Table 9.1 we can see that although the coefficient of knowledge density in manufacturing industry is not significant, the coefficients of other variables are all significant on the level of 10%, which may be caused by our replacing the statistics of the producer service industry with the statistics of the third industry. The denotations of all variables are consistent with our expectation, and our conclusions are: (1) The higher the cooperative agglomeration level of manufacturing industry and service industry is, the higher the agglomeration level of manufacturing industry is. (2) The higher the cooperative agglomeration level of service industry and manufacturing industry is, the higher the agglomeration level of service industry is. (3) FDI is in positive correlation with the agglomeration level of manufacturing industry and the agglomeration level of service industry, and after the variable of cooperative agglomeration is introduced, the significance is raised. (4) The scale of state-owned economy is in positive correlation with the agglomeration level of manufacturing industry and the agglomeration level of service industry, and after the variable of cooperative agglomeration is introduced, the significance is raised. (5) The agglomeration level of manufacturing industry is in negative correlation to level of wage, which implies that the competitiveness of manufacturing industry in the Yangtze River Delta is caused by the cheap labor force. (6) The agglomeration levels of service industry and manufacturing industry in a region are influenced by the region's distance from Shanghai; the closer the region is to Shanghai, the higher the agglomeration levels of service industry and manufacturing industry are. Therefore the radiation effect of the central city is evident.

Table 9.1. Result of empirical test of the cooperative agglomeration of service industry and manufacturing industry

Explanatory variable	Explained Variables			
	Agglomeration Level of Manufacturing Industry		Agglomeration Level of Service Industry	
Constant Term (C)	3.68 ** (4.35)	2.345 ** (2.26)	3.68 ** (4.35)	2.738 *** (5.08)
Cooperative Agglomeration Level of Manufacturing Industry and Service Industry		0.310 *** (3.42)		
Cooperative Agglomeration Level of Service Industry and Manufacturing Industry				0.219 * (1.80)
FDI	0.75 *** (14.24)	0.856 *** (15.53)	0.56 *** (9.61)	0.696 *** (11.11)
Scale of State-owned Economy	0.27 * (1.69)	0.387 * (1.71)	0.34 * (1.72)	0.554 * (1.81)
Average Wages of on-the-job Employees	–0.51 *** (–3.86)	–0.626 *** (–5.39)		
Density of Knowledge in Manufacturing Industry			0.126 (0.96)	0.204 (1.04)
Scale of Economy	0.68 *** (5.78)	0.792 *** (6.97)	0.326 * (1.88)	0.444 * (1.97)
Distance from Central City—Shanghai	–0.078 * (–3.2)	–0.089 * (3.64)	–0.082 * (–3.86)	–0.095 * (–4.72)
Adjusted R^2	0.92	0,967	0.89	0.935
Number of Samples	96	96	96	96

Notes: *stands for significance on the level of 10%, ** stands for significance on the level of 5%, ***stands for significance on the level of 1%. Figure in the parentheses are t stats values.

Dynamic panel data models

The basic econometric model is set as follows:

$$y_{it}=x'_{it}\beta+z'_{i}\alpha+\varepsilon_{it}$$

In the model, "y_{it}" is the cooperative agglomeration index of service industry in city "i" in year "t," "x_{it}" is FDI in city "i" in year "t." $z'_{i}\alpha$ is individual effect or heterogenetic variable, including a constant and a group of specific variables of individuals or groups, which are not changeable with time. This model is a classic regression model. If z_i is observable to all individuals, then the whole model could be treated as a common linear model that could fit with the least-square method; if z_i is not observable but is correlated with x_{it}, then the least-squares of α and β are biased and inconsistent, which corresponds with a fixed-effect model; if z_i is not observable and we assume that z_i is not correlated with x_{it}, then we can use the least-square to obtain an estimate that is consistent but without efficiency, which corresponds with the random-effect model.

In this model, the structure of residual items would greatly influence the estimation of the model. Since time change and regional differences could influence the random perturbation items, so we decompose the residual item:

$$\varepsilon_{it}=u_{i}+v_{t}+e_{it}$$

In the above equation ui is the fixed effect of the city, which is not influenced by time change but changes with the changes in the city; v_t is affected by time change. The structure of u_i determines the selection of the estimation model. If u_i is randomly distributed, which means it has no correlation with the explanatory variables, then the random effect model may be more suitable. Conversely if the hypothesis that ui is randomly distributed is rejected, then we prefer the fixed-effect model. The Hausman test provides evidence for our selection of model.

Table 9.2. Hybrid/Panel data model results

	α	β	Adj. R^2	F Stats	Wald Stats
Hybrid Data Model	0.002 5 (1.23)	0.787 2 *** (210.03)	0.286	5.87 ***	
Panel Data Model	0.002 6 (1.35)	0.867 4 *** (212.61)	0.385		23.28 ***

Notes: The Hausman test was run on the panel data model, and we find that the Hausman stats cannot reject the null hypothesis that the fixed effect is not correlated with other explanatory variables, so we choose the random influence panel data model. The figures in parentheses are t stats or z big sample stats.
*stands for significance on the level of 10%, ** stands for significance on the level of 5%, *** stands for significance on the level of 1%.

We then will make a comparison of the hybrid data model and panel data model.

The results are shown in Table 9.2:

Compared to the hybrid data, the panel data is more superior because firstly, observed from the inherent advantage of the panel data model that it is superior to the common hybrid, the panel data model takes the individual heterogeneity—the unique feature factors of each city that do not change with time—into consideration, so we can obtain a more accurate estimation; and secondly, observed from the results, the R^2 value in the panel data model is a little higher than that in the hybrid data model, reflecting that the explanatory competence of the panel model is enhanced; the significance of all coefficients in the panel data model are raised, and the coefficients of the hybrid model are lower than those of the panel data model, which shows that the hybrid data are probably underestimated.

Based on the above analysis, we continue with the panel data analysis on the level of cities. In this section we use the dynamic panel data model and introduce the first lag phase variables of the dependent variables as new independent variables into the model. Our reasons are that the first lag phase variables of the dependent variables can reflect all the historical information and their coefficients reflect the degree of influence of all the past factors in past periods on the current cooperative agglomeration of service industry and manufacturing industry; and the rest of the independent variables in the model independently reflect the degree of influence of the factors in the current phase on the cooperative agglomeration of service industry and manufacturing industry. Thus the model can separate the influence of past factors from the influence of current factors on the current cooperative agglomeration of service industry and manufacturing industry. The model we adopt is as follows:

$$y_{it}=x'_{it}\beta+z'_{i}\alpha+\gamma y_{i,t-1}+\varepsilon_{it}$$

As the first phase variables are related to the error items, if we continue to use the regular LSDV (least-square dummy variable) method or the FGLS (feasible generalized least squares estimator) method to process the panel data model, even though the assumed condition that there exists no serial correlation in the error items is satisfied, the estimated values we obtain are still biased and inconsistent. These problems can be avoided if we adopt the instrumental variable method that is based on GMM and developed by Arellano and Bond (1991). We then get the estimated values of all coefficients in the dynamic panel data model, which results are shown in Table 9.3. As the coefficient of β is significant and above zero, we know that FDI has significant positive effect on the cooperative agglomeration.

Table 9.3. Results of the dynamic panel data model analysis

Model	α	β	γ	R^2	Wald Stats	Sargan Stats
Fixed Influence	0.286 5 *** (9.62)	0.493 6 *** (23.16)	0.002 3 (1.26)	0.458 6		
Dynamic Panel	0.301 8 *** 21.13)	0.001 5 *** (20.53)	0.005 1 (0.18)	0.385	1,128.76 ***	35.68

Note: In the Hausman test, the fixed-effect model is adopted in the regular panel data models; if the model is a dynamic panel data model, then the Arellano and Bond Two-Step estimation method is adopted to estimate the parameters of the models; *stands for significance on the level of 10%, ** stands for significance on the level of 5%, *** stands for significance on the level of 1%; figures in parentheses are t stats or z big sample stats; the Sargan stats is an over-identification restriction test. If all the models pass the test then we believe that all explanatory variables are set accurately.

There exists another possibility, which is that the agglomeration of FDI may not be the reason of the cooperative agglomeration of service industry and manufacturing industry. Instead, FDI may agglomerate in some region which has a relatively high level of cooperative agglomeration. Therefore our next step is to run the Granger causality test, as is shown in Table 9.4. It can be found that on the significance level of 10%; the null hypothesis that FDI is not the Granger cause of the cooperative agglomeration measure $D(M_M)$ can be rejected, which proves that there exists causality between FDI and cooperative agglomeration, and that FDI promotes the cooperative agglomeration of the service industry and the manufacturing industry.

Table 9.4. Granger causality test of relevant variables (order of lag n=1)

Null Hypothesis	Number of Sample	F Stats	Possibility of Hypothesis to be Accepted
FDI is not the Granger cause of $D(M_M)$	392	3.180 05	0.056 58
$D(M_M)$ is not the Granger cause of FDI	392	0.344 85	0.792 91

Note: Determination of the number of samples is based on lag n=1 according to lag numbers from the VEC model.

Spatial Econometric Test of Cooperative Agglomeration and Economic Growth

Except for a few, most of the existing empirical research has overlooked the effect of geographical space (Ying, 2003; Lin, 2005, 2006). As the Yangtze River Delta is undergoing a transformation, it is necessary for us to adopt a more suitable econometric method to analyze the economic growth of the Delta, so we introduce geographical space and agglomeration factor into our test of the effect of the cooperative agglomeration's mechanism on the regional economic convergence (or divergence). We will integrate the simultaneous equations, dynamic panel and spatial econometric model to analyze the relationship between the cooperative agglomeration of the service industry and manufacturing industry and the relationship between the β-convergence as well as σ-convergence of the regional economy and the cooperative agglomeration of service industry and manufacturing industry.

Basis of the construction of the β-convergence model

1. New classic growth β-convergence model

The hypothesis of the convergence of economic growth in different countries or regions originates from the hypothesis of factor marginal diminishing returns in the new classic theories. The analysis of absolute convergence, conditional convergence and some other important concepts are all based on the new classic theories. The model commonly used by the new classic theories in the analysis of convergence is (in order to distinguish this convergence model from the convergence model after spatial dependence is taken into consideration, we call the convergence model here the classic convergence model):

$$\frac{\ln y_{j,T}-\ln y_{j0}}{T} = \alpha+\beta\ln y_{j0}+\varepsilon_i,\ \varepsilon_{it}\sim iid,\ N(0,\sigma^2)$$

If in one region the estimated coefficient β in the above equation is negative and significant, we can know that the average growth rate of the GDP per capita of that region is within the time period "0-T," and the rate is in negative correlation with the GDP per capita at the beginning and there exists β-convergence. That is to say, the economies in backward regions grow faster than those in developed regions. If the coefficient is positive and insignificant on statistics, there is no β-convergence, and the hypothesis should be rejected.

Based on the convergence model, the conditional convergence hypothesis test can also be run, that is to say, we assume that the sub-regions inside the regions are as stationary as the regions and then we introduce the regional dummy variables and then estimate the possibility of the existence of club-convergency by estimating β coefficients, which is reasonable when it comes to China—a country with a large territory and significant regional disparities. Considering that the Yangtze River Delta includes Shanghai, Jiangsu and Zhejiang, and there are huge differences between the regional economic models of Jiangsu and Zhejiang which are represented by the "south Jiangsu model" and the "Wenzhou model" respectively, it is necessary for us to test whether β-convergence exists after the regional dummy variables are introduced into the analysis.[3] The equation that contains the regional dummy variables is:

$$\frac{\ln y_{j,T}-\ln y_{j0}}{T} = \alpha+\beta \ln y_{j0}+\gamma X+\varepsilon_i,\ \varepsilon_{it}\sim iid,\ N(0,\sigma^2)$$

In the equation, γ is the 1×15 order vector of regional dummy variables' coefficients to be measured, and X is the 1×15 vector of regional dummy variables. In the conditional β-convergence model, two effects of economic growth can be anticipated: the first one is the negative effect of starting GDP per capita shown by the estimation of β in our capture of convergence effect, and the second one is the other effect of explanatory X on the growth.

Actually, besides the introduction of dummy variables, the X vector could be some other state variables such as material or human capital storage, and also could be some control or environmental variables such as the proportion of GDP accounted for by public investment, the proportion of GDP accounted for by domestic investment, the improvement of trade conditions, growth rate of population, and political instability etc. Therefore in order to analyze the effect of the cooperative agglomeration of service industry and manufacturing industry on the differences among the economic growths in different cities in the Yangtze River Delta.

However there might exist a correlation between the explanatory variables of the starting GDP per capita and the error items, which would lead to the invalid estimation of OLS and thus the failure of the analysis. So we need to find a new perspective to construct a more reasonable economic growth convergence model. The biggest problem of this research is to assume the independence of the regions. But since the observed intercept region is some economic entity that is obviously spatially dependent on some regions in geography, we should run the spatial correlativity test to judge whether the independent strict hypothesis of error items is reasonable or not. If the null hypothesis is rejected in statistics, we know that the estimation result of OLS is unauthentic and we need to carefully introduce the geographical and spatial dimension into our estimation of the convergence process.

2. Spatial dependence and β-convergence of economic growth

If we assume that there exists spatial dependence between two regions, then the correlated location of a region will influence its own economic performance. In this circumstance there exists β-convergence of the two cities with geographical environments similar to each other. Therefore, if we want to test the hypothesis of the β-convergence, we must test the inter-regional spatial dependence first, because the emergence of spatial correlation will lead to the OLS's failure in estimating or giving the accurate estimation results.

The spatial dependence could be defined as the consistency between the observed value and the location. When a high value or low value of the random variables in the neighboring region show the inclination to agglomerate, there is positive spatial autocorrelation; and when the geographical region tends to be surrounded by neighboring regions with different variable values, there is negative spatial autocorrelation. It is obvious that the spatial dependence means that some observed values agglomerate geographically because of some spatial effect, and these spatial effects that link different regions have a spillover effect and some social economic interaction, such as in trade and communication.

Basis of the construction of the σ-convergence model

σ-convergence suggests the change in the deviation of GDP per capita among different economic systems over time. If the deviation tends to decrease, then there exists σ-convergence in the economic growth of the cities. In order to analyze the change in different economic growth levels in different cities in the Yangtze River Delta, we use the logarithm of real GDP per capita—$\ln(Y_{it})$. The computation formula is as follows: $\sigma_t = \sqrt{\frac{1}{N-1}\sum_{i=1}^{N}(y_{it}-\bar{y}_t)^2}$

In the equation, $y_{it}=\ln(Y_{it}), \bar{y}_t=\frac{1}{N}\sum_{i=1}^{N} y_{it}$; $i=1, 2, \ldots, N$; $t=1, 2, \ldots, T$. The standard deviation index reflects the change in absolute difference, and when $\sigma_t+1<\sigma_t$, there exists σ-convergence among the economic growth of different cities in the Delta. We run the constant regression on the logs of real GDP per capita in different time periods:

$$y_{it}=y_t+\varepsilon_{it}$$

In the equation, $i=1, 2, \ldots, N$; $t=1, 2, \ldots, T$. It can be seen that the estimation for the variance of residual ε_{it} is σ_t^2. It needs to be mentioned that when estimating σ_t^2 by ε_{it}, every city is considered as an individual, implying the assumption that the cities are not correlated with each other. Under this assumption, the form of the logarithm of real per capita GDP variable y_{it} is independent and identically distributed at each time in each city in accordance with the corresponding equation, which means that $y_{it} \sim N(\mu_t, \sigma_t^2)$. Moreover means and variances among the cities are independent. Although the mean and variance of each city changes over time, the means and variances in different cities for the same period are always the same. However this assumption is not consistent with the actual situation. During operation in the real world, any city's economy cannot exist independently; it always has some relationship with other cities. An exogenous shock on the economy of one city also affects the economy of cities around that city. For example, in many studies, technology spillover among cities is often seen as a very important mechanism to promote regional economic convergence. Therefore, under the assumption that there is no correlation of economies among different cities, simply calculating the standard deviation of the convergence of an urban economy will result in inconsistent errors. In other words, the only way to make the correct judgments of the economic convergence among cities is to abandon the independence assumption of the urban economies and introduce the correlation of cities to the model.

Although the interaction between regions arouses widespread attention, most studies which address economic convergence have not introduced the correlation model into the empirical analysis. We use the research idea of Rey and Dev for reference and adopt the econometric methods of Anselin (1988), Anselin and Rey (1991) to introduce the interaction among regional economies in the Yangtze River Delta cities into our study of σ-convergence.

Theoretically speaking, the correlation among different cities is revealed through time differences or spatial relationships. This section focuses on the latter. To avoid the confusion raised by time series among cities, we assume that there is no correlation of the time in each city. The time—spatial econometric model, which takes into account both the space and time relevance among cities, is currently an unsolved problem in econometrics worldwide. In the empirical analysis in the models, the spatial correlation between cities can be attributed to two aspects, which are space related—mean μ_t and space related—variance σ_t^2. Here we mainly discuss how σ-convergence influences the urban economy of the Yangtze River Delta region, when the relevance of some means present.

β-convergence of the regional economy and the cooperative agglomeration of service industry and manufacturing industry

1. Test strategies and model specification

Other than considering the capacity of the cooperative agglomeration of service industry and manufacturing industry, as a control variable, to explain the economic growth, this section will focus on the spatial connection patterns. The information reflected by the economic variables and exogenous variables as the spatial adjacency matrix under pure geographic conditions can better explain the trend of the economic convergence in the Yangtze River Delta. Among the many ways to calculate spatial weight matrix, the first order adjacency method is used here. We also make comparative analysis of the distance between the center of mass of the weight matrix and estimates of various regions based on the latitude and longitude coordinates. Finally, we choose the first-order adjacency matrix as a spatial econometric model of the spatial weight matrix, which has the most significant spatial autocorrelation.

There are several steps involved with the specific inspection process. Firstly, we use the OLS method to estimate the absolute β convergence of the classical model. Then we take the spatial weight matrix method to conduct a variety of spatial auto-correlativity tests of the absolute convergence model in 15 cities on the Yangtze River Delta (except Taizhou). Lastly, we introduce spatial effects and control variables of the cooperative aggregation of service and manufacturing industry into the convergence model to run our spatial econometric estimation and testing.

There are two models for studying the spatial dependence in the analysis of β convergence in the spatial econometric models.

(1) Spatial autoregressive (lag) model. In the spatial autoregressive convergent model, the spatial correlations of observations are treated as endogenous spatial lag variables:

$$(1/T)\ln(z)=\alpha S+\beta\ln(y_0)+\rho W\,[(1/T)\ln(z)]+\gamma X+\mu,\ \mu\sim N(0,\sigma^2 I)$$

In the above equation, z is an interpreted vector in the $n\times1$-order convergence model of unconditional β, which is the growth rate of real per capita GDP in the region i between time 0 and T. $(1/T)\ln(z)$ is the mean of the real per capita GDP growth rate. S stands for the space unit vector. y_0 is real per capita GDP vector during the initial stage time 0 in region i in the $n\times1$ order. X is the explanation vector matrix in order $n\times2$, which contains the mean of the service industry concentration and synergy measures in the $n\times1$ order by the district i between the time 0 and T and the virtual vector in the $n\times1$ order area. μ is the normally distributed error term vector of the $n\times1$ order. α, β, γ and ρ are unknowns to be estimated. ρ stands for the spatial autoregressive parameter, which measures the degree of spatial interactions among the exogenous standardized measure of weight matrix of observations. Endogenous spatial lag variable $W\,[(1/T)\ln(z)]$ is pre-multiplied by the weight matrix of the growth vector. Growth vector $(1/T)\ln(z)$ in region i, the spatial lag vector, reflects the average growth rate of adjacent areas after dealing with the spatial weights.

Even when the residuals are equal and independently distributed, the OLS estimation model will yield inconsistent estimations because the regression vector Wy is related with the error term μ. Therefore, the model generally needs to be estimated by the maximum likelihood (ML) method.

The significance of this model lies in three aspects: firstly, from the perspective of convergence, the information of convergence will be given through the estimated parameter β once the spatial effects are controlled; secondly, from the perspective of economic geography, the spatial effect is highlighted, and when the initial conditions of per capita GDP are determined the model shows the impact of per capita GDP growth rate in a region's adjacent areas on the region through the parameter β; thirdly, from the perspective of the relationship between agglomeration and growth, the model shows how the cooperative agglomeration of manufacturing and service industry would effect the convergent per capita GDP growth rate by estimating the parameter γ.

The model can be rewritten as the following equation through a simple transformation:

$$(I-\rho W)[(1/T)\ln(z)]=\alpha S+\beta\ln(y_0)+\gamma X+\mu$$

$$(1/T)\ln(z)=\alpha(I-\rho W)^{-1}S+\beta(I-\rho W)^{-1}\ln(y_0)$$
$$+\gamma(I-\rho W)^{-1}X+(I-\rho W)^{-1}\mu$$

According to the equation, on average, the growth rate of a region is not only influenced by initial growth rate of GDP per capita level but is also affected by its neighboring regions through spatial transformation and the transposition $(I-\rho W)^{-1}$. Of course, from the perspective of classic convergence, the explanations given by the model hardly conforms with the basic concept of β convergence. Therefore we should be very careful to explain the convergence in case of space-related processes. If we take the role of error into consideration, then the random shocks in a particular area will affect not only the growth rate in the region, but also the growth rate in all other regions through the same $(I-\rho W)^{-1}$.

(2) Spatial Error Model.

When we assume that the spatial dependence functions via the missing variables, the spatial error model is a relatively more accurate one. The model reflects the error process through spatial covariance of different regions, and when the error follows the first-order process, it will be as follows:

$$(1/T)\ln(z)=\alpha S+\beta\ln(y_0)+\gamma X+\varepsilon,\ \varepsilon=\lambda W\varepsilon+\mu,\ \mu\sim N(0,\sigma^2 I)$$

In the equation, λ is the scalar parameter to reveal the relative strength of the spatial correlation among the regression residuals. The non-spherical disturbance error estimated by OLS will give unbiased but not efficient estimations. Moreover, since the estimated parameter variance is biased, results based on the OLS estimation are misleading. Thus the model is the generally required maximum likelihood method or GMM estimation.

2. Test results of the measurement of absolute β convergence

After LM-Error, LM-Lag test and R-LMLAG, R-LMERR test, we select the spatial error model. The results of the sectional regression estimation and econometric test are shown in Table 9.5.

Table 9.5. Results of the sectional regression estimation of the economic growth in the cities in the Yangtze River Delta (SEM)

Variable	Model after the dummy variables are introduced			
	β	Standard deviation	*t* Stats.	*P* Stats.
C (Constant item)	0.014 4	0.028 2	0.510 638	0.475 3
lnRRJGDP (initial per capita GDP)	–0.019 6	0.003 7	–5.297 3	0.000 0
MS (Cooperative Agglomeration index of service industry and manufacturing industry)	0.035 2	0.006 4	5.5	0.000 0
Location Dummy Variable	–0.006 5	0.003 8	–1.710 53	0.045 4
Stats. test	Value	*P*-value		
R^2	0.498 7			
log likelihood	98.657 4			
Space-dependence (Likelihood ratio test) (LR test)	7.243 4	0.010 6		
AIC	–218.907 5			
BIC	–201.843 6			
σ^2	0.000 0			
Breusch-Pagan Heteroskedasticity value	14.839 1	0.637 8		

Note: Calculated using a software called GPE2/Gauss6.0. (Lin, 2001)

From Table 9.5 we can see that the coefficient of the initial GDP per capita is below zero, which shows that after introducing the indicator of cooperative agglomeration there exists β-convergence in the regional economies. The coefficient of the cooperative agglomeration indicator is above zero, showing that the higher the level of cooperative agglomeration in a region is, the higher the growth rate of real GDP per capita in the region is.

The σ-convergence of regional economy and the cooperative agglomeration of service industry and manufacturing industry

We need to conduct a correlativity test on the primary data before we construct the spatial econometric model. Here we run the Moran's I spatial correlativity test on the residuals of the equation. For spatial weight W, we adopt a simple geographical weighting, that is to say, for the 15 cities in Yangtze River Delta region (except Taizhou), the corresponding weight is 1 if the cities are geographically adjacent. Otherwise the weight is 0. The test results in different time periods are shown in Table 9.6. Test results reveal the spatial autocorrelation among cities.

Table 9.6. Results of Moran□s I test in different times

Time	1988	1994	2000	2005
Moran's I	0.315 98	0.317 96	0.341 00	0.357 86
Standard deviation	0.123 68	0.123 68	0.123 68	0.123 68
P value	0.002 157 3	0.002 050 6	0.001 119 7	0.000 704 36

Considering the σ-convergence of the regional economy and the spatial lag model of the cooperative agglomeration of service industry and manufacturing industry, we introduce the lagged spatial variables of the real GDP per capita in each city into the model to illustrate that the level of economic development in a region may be directly related with the economic development in surrounding areas and within the entire system. We set "$y_t = [y_{1t}, y_{2t}, \ldots, y_{Nt}]$," and then the spatial lag model can be expressed as

$$y_{it}=\alpha_i+\lambda_i W y_{t-1}+\beta_i x_{it}+\varepsilon_{it}$$

At the same time, we could express the formula into a model of means:

$$y_{it}=\mu_{it}+\beta_t x_{it}+\varepsilon_{it}$$

$$\mu_{it}=\alpha_t+\lambda_t W_i y_{t-1}=\alpha_t+\lambda_t \sum_{j=1,j\neq i}^{N} W_{ij} y_{jt-1}$$

Table 9.7. Results of the spatial econometric models in different times

Time	1988	1994	2000	2005
α	2.753 5 (1.326 6)	2.776 9 (1.336 0)	2.620 4 (1.297 9)	2.567 4 (1.281 0)
λ	0.607 18 (0.195 87)	0.607 74 (0.195 24)	0.637 02 (0.186 30)	0.650 81 (0.180 54)
β	0.764 94 (0.218 52)	0.761 12 (0.219 55)	0.760 71 (0.219 58)	0.760 77 (0.219 52)
Log-Likelihood	−19.065	−19.337	−19.208	−19.177
Moran's I	0.017 532	0.019 048	0.024 243	0.020 758
Standard deviation	0.118 83	0.118 89	0.118 95	0.118 86
P-value	0.240 29	0.247 87	0.232 73	0.240 29
AIC	−1.333 2	−1.313 8	−1.323 0	−1.325 2
BIC	−1.238 1	−1.218 7	−1.227 8	−1.230 1

Note: The statistics were calculated using the software called GPE2/Gauss6.0 (Lin, 2001).

In the equation, "W_i" is the vectors of "i" row. Therefore the average value is a parameter which is correlated with the level of real GDP per capita in neighboring regions. x_{it} is a measure of the cooperative agglomeration of service industry and manufacturing industry. The results of the econometric test are shown in Table 9.7.

The coefficient of β is above zero and its standard deviation is relatively small, so we can draw the conclusion that there exists a positive correlation between the cooperative agglomeration of service industry and manufacturing industry and the real GDP per capita, which means that in a region where the cooperative agglomeration level of service industry and manufacturing industry is relatively high, the real GDP per capita is relatively higher, which proves that the cooperative agglomeration of service industry and manufacturing industry can promote economic growth.

Conclusions and Policy Recommendations

Since 1998, when 20 years had passed after the reform and opening up started, the cooperative agglomeration of service industry and manufacturing industry in the Yangtze River Delta has not only been promoting the agglomeration of manufacturing industry in the Delta but also has been facilitating the agglomeration of service industry. Therefore the higher the level of cooperative agglomeration of manufacturing industry and service industry is, the higher the level of agglomeration of manufacturing industry or service industry is, and the cooperative agglomeration is one of the important reasons for the industrial agglomeration in the Delta. FDI is the most important factor in realizing the agglomeration of service industry and manufacturing industry, and combined with the cooperative agglomeration the contribution FDI has made to the agglomeration of service industry and manufacturing industry has been significantly enhanced. The scale of the state-owned economy and agglomeration levels of manufacturing industry as well as service industry are in positive correlation, and after the variable—cooperative agglomeration is introduced, the significance level is enhanced. The agglomeration level of manufacturing industry is in negative correlation with the wage level, which implies that the competitive edge of the manufacturing industry in the Yangtze River Delta still rests with the cheap labor force in the area. The agglomerate level of service industry and manufacturing industry in a region in the Delta is influenced by the distance between the region and the central city—Shanghai. The closer the region is to Shanghai, the higher the agglomeration levels of the manufacturing industry and service industry in the region are and the higher the cooperative agglomeration level of the two industries in the region is. Therefore Shanghai, as the central city in the Yangtze River Delta and even the central city of China, has a conspicuous radiation effect.

After the indicator of cooperative agglomeration is introduced, the β convergence exists in the regional economic growth of the Yangtze River Delta. The econometric results show that the higher the cooperative agglomeration level a region is, the higher the growth rate of the GDP per capita in the region is. The cooperative agglomeration level of the service industry and manufacturing industry is in positive correlation with the GDP per capita in the cities. That is to say, the higher the cooperative agglomeration level of a region is, the higher the GDP per capita is, which proves that the cooperative agglomeration of service industry and manufacturing industry can promote the economic growth.

The conclusions we can draw from our analysis are that in order to accelerate the economic development of the cities, the planners and decision-makers of the city development should adopt effective policies to promote industrial agglomeration as well as the cooperative agglomeration of service industry and manufacturing industry and policies to encourage innovations in the cities in order to constantly enhance the external effects of technologies and knowledge and expand the accumulation of human resources.

(1) Specialized industrial zones should be built inside the cities. In the

knowledge economy and global economy, in order to obtain competitive advantages, a city needs the agglomeration of some highly specialized industries in an area where a network of cooperation and competition relationships is established among the large, medium-and small-sized enterprises to accelerate the diffusion of knowledge and technology and to share economy of scale and scope. An urban specialized industrial zone is exactly the sort of "incubator" of innovations in knowledge and technology that we need. Specialized industrial zones can promote a large scale of agglomeration of enterprises which manufacture the same sort of products in some specific geographical area, and then form the super-detailed specialized division and a soft division cooperation system that is rich in externality, strengthening human capital, material capital and industrial agglomeration.

(2) We should attach importance to knowledge, enhance the knowledge accumulation rate, and bring the function of human capital into full play in order to promote economic growth. Therefore we should deepen the reform of the educational system and make policies to encourage lifelong learning. The municipal governments and enterprises also should increase their input into education and technology, enabling the supply of human resources to effectively cooperate with economic growth.

(3) While emphasizing knowledge and strengthening research and development, we should also intensify the application and spread of knowledge. The application of knowledge is of the same importance as the spread of knowledge. In a knowledge economy, the science system yields new knowledge and the enterprises apply the knowledge in the sphere of social production. What a society lacks is not always knowledge but the ability to rapidly and effectively transform the knowledge into productive forces. Therefore, in order to facilitate the transformation of new knowledge from production to application, the enterprises should establish a comprehensive but close relation with universities and science and research institutions, and the municipal governments should play a role in effectively integrating "government, production, education and research."

10

Chapter

The Service Industry and Economic Fluctuation in the Yangtze River Delta

Introduction

According to the global experience, if the economy of a country or of a region is transforming from a middle-low income level to an upper-middle one, the industry structure will undergo a rapid modification and meanwhile the service industry will be at the turning point to fast development. The well-established modern service industry boosts the development of new technological industry. The interaction between service industry and manufacturing industry powers economic growth and increases the competitiveness of regional industry. In 2003 the GDP per capita in the Yangtze River Delta exceeded US$3,000. That is, in accordance with the universal calculating method, considered as a benchmark to estimate whether a country or a region achieves primary modernization. Therefore it can be concluded that the Yangtze River Delta has reached the upper-middle income level and its service industry is rapidly developing.

Economic fluctuation refers to a continuous alteration between prosperity and depression in the course of economic progress. Economists attribute the cause of economic fluctuation to exogenous shocks and endogenous factors. The classical school holds that the change in aggregate supply leads to a change in real output and increase in the cost of production, resulting in recession. Technological improvement then increases and results in prosperity. The Keynes school believes that economic fluctuation is due to the imperfection of market regulation; while the real business cycle theory suggests that economic fluctuation is due to the exogenous shocks of real factors such as technology.

The relationship between service industry and economic increase and fluctuation is the core issue of research on modern service economy but is extremely controversial. Many scholars at home and abroad have done much research on this. In the 1960s both Denison and Kuznets, the American economists, viewed knowledge improvement, increase in knowledge stock and education development as the most important elements for economic growth. As those elements were divided on the basis of the current industry categorization that was offered by service industry, the relation of the development of service industry to the economic growth manifested itself presently. Beyers and Lindahl (1996) believed that the increasing portion of service industry only reflected the change of organization pattern of industrial manufacture. In their opinion, the expansion of service industry was not caused by the economic growth of such a sector or the changes in technology or need, but by the change of systems.

Burns (1960) pointed out that the service industry was not so sensitive to the economic cycle. He proposed several factors which gave rise to the alternation of features of economic fluctuation and one of those factors was the increasing share of service industry. In terms of employment structure in America, the number of employees in some service sectors is relatively stable so the employment fluctuation of the total national economy is weaker than output fluctuation. Burns also definitively discussed the steady effect of the expansion of employment in the service sector on the employment fluctuation cycle in America. But he did not apply any empirical methods to prove the causal relationship between them.

Faulks (1987) worked out that the average net change value of the number of employees in service sectors was far less than that in manufacturing industry. For the value of output, he compared the fluctuation of output value in wholesale and retail with that in manufacturing. The result showed that the fluctuation of output value in those sectors was heavier than in employment and the cyclical fluctuation in manufacturing much heavier than in wholesale and retail.

Roura and Abarca (2001) thought that the springing up of the third industry, especially labor driving other sources transferring from primary and second industries to tertiary ones, was a significant element which leveled the economic fluctuation off gradually. They also discovered that the extent of fluctuation in the service sector was about one third of that in manufacturing and that almost all of industries would present periodicity as well as supervenience.

With respect to domestic research, Bai Zhongrao and Yi Shaohua (2004) emphasized the complexity of the relationship between service industry and the national economy. They considered that in the national economy, service industry played multiple roles in increasing the economy and coordinating industries as well as absorbing labor, and it accordingly could enhance the overall national strength to a great degree. Jiang Xiaojuan and Li Hui (2004) investigated the development and internal structural change of service industry in our country and made a comparison of related data of China's service economic development and data of other countries. They put forward a multiple regression analysis model in order to explore the relationship of economic growth to the development of the service sector. Li Yongjian (2005) stated that although the proportion of the service sector expanded incessantly in pace with the rapid growth of the GDP, the speed of such expansion was restrained by per capita income differences. Xia Qing etc. (2004) showed that the relationship between the service sector and the national economy is not cause-and-effect but a stronger and stronger two-way interaction. The service sector constitutes an important section of industrial production input whereas the external activities of manufacturing promote the development of emerging service industry. At present, the manufacturing and service sectors interconnect with each other, that is, they carry each other and integrate with each other, and consequently impel economic growth. Hua Ercheng (2001) held that the technological upgrading and structural regulation in China's manufacturing depended on the input of more and more effective services of all kinds. The development of service industry supplied the beneficial conditions to maintain the constant growth of the economy and to create opportunities for employment.

Economic fluctuation also exists in the Yangtze River Delta, which is in keeping with the fluctuation of overall national macro-economy to some extent. Moreover issues such as what role the service sector plays in that region and whether it coincides with service sector functioning in the national economy have not yet been studied in detail. This article mainly studies whether the service sector in the Yangtze River Delta plays the role of regulator in economic development and whether it can have an effect of ironing out or buffering economic fluctuation.

Primary Facts on the Service Sector Development and Economic Fluctuation in the Yangtze River Delta

After the founding of the new China, there has been a long period in which tertiary industry developed exceedingly slowly and our country took agriculture and industry as the main driving force of national economic development. Similarly, service industry in the Yangtze River Delta was once subject to the development of primary and secondary industries. Take Jiangsu Province as an example. As indicated in Table 10.1, the industry structure in Jiangsu had been "first-third-second" till the early 1960s, among which the motivation of economic growth came mainly from primary industries. The output value of primary industries in 1952 was as high as 52.7% of the GDP while both secondary and tertiary industries were still underdeveloped. Furthermore, secondary industry because of its weak foundation was even under the level of tertiary industrial development, but at that time the third industry gave priority to the traditional service sector. Later on, China launched a policy of industrialization and in that way secondary industry in Jiangsu developed and became more and more mature. However, restricted by the trend of international investment and personal investing capability, most of manufacturing industries in Jiangsu were inclined to invest in processing supporting sectors with low technical level and low development requirements. Additionally, due to the expansion of investment, it was prone to low-level isomorphism. From the perspective of the international industrial chain, manufacturing in the Yangtze River Delta was in the stage of middle- and low-end; the development and design of products and the marketing network are all controlled by multinational groups; a large number of key materials and accessories needed in the producing process are purchased from abroad; 65% to 70% of advanced production equipment was imported from abroad; and own brand effect and the ability to innovate are lacking. The industry structure was "secondary-primary-tertiary" until 1988 and the proportion of service industry decreased continually to only 17.2% in 1984. During that period, secondary industry became the implicit impetus for economic growth. Subsequently the proportion of tertiary industry increased and even exceeded primary industry in 1989. Just because the development of manufacturing was confronted with potential threats including over-reliance on foreign capital and the tendency of being controlled by advanced firms, the developing service sector was promoted as a growth point to push forward Jiangsu's economy. The industry structure has maintained the mode of "second-third-first" until now.

Table 10.1. Formation of the GDP in Jiangsu Province (%)

Industry	1952	1957	1965	1970	1975	1980	1985	1988	1989
First Industry	52.7	46.0	43.3	39.5	36.7	29.5	30.0	26.4	24.5
Second Industry	17.6	22.1	31.8	35.7	43.2	52.3	52.1	48.5	49.7
Third Industry	29.7	31.9	24.9	24.8	20.1	18.2	17.9	25.1	25.8

Source: *Jiangsu Statistical Yearbook 2006*.

In essence, the changes in the three industries' structure reflect the overall situation in the Yangtze River Delta. Secondary industry in the Yangtze River Delta, represented by manufacturing, has sprung up since the late 1960s. Up until now, manufacturing has always been the basis for economic growth and the pillar of economic growth. In the future it will also play an important part in the Yangtze River Delta. In 2006, the GDP per capita of the region equaled RMB 34,174 (in Shanghai it was RMB 75,990, in Jiangsu RMB 28,685 and in Zhejiang RMB 31,684). In the light of Chenery's theory of stage of economic growth, the region was considered to be in the transitional stage of industrialization from take-off to maturity, which indicated that the level of economic development there had approached that in other moderately developed countries. In addition, the development of regional industrialization would then be in a stable state and the economy would turn to the consumer society which would prompt the fast development of tertiary industry. During the three decades since reform and opening up, a great change in the industrial structure has taken place in the Yangtze River Delta, which mainly refers to the transformation from the original "second-first-third" to "second-third-first" and then gradually to "third-second-first." Meanwhile the service sector in some areas has become the pillar industry. The proportion of added value of the service industry in Shanghai in 2006 was over 50% of the GDP; the added value of tertiary industry in Jiangsu and Zhejiang accounted for more than 35%; and the added value of tertiary industry in the Yangtze River Delta surpassed 40%. Such a tendency coincides with Chenery's theory of the growth of industrialization.

There are various types of competitive service sectors in the Yangtze River Delta and they have had a preliminary combined effect on the service sector. The financial service sector in that region has worked extremely well in that it attracts a lot of financial institutions from at home or abroad. The exhibition industry was at first introduced by Shanghai and has already had a certain scale effect. Moreover not only is the modern information service industry particularly advanced but tourism and real estate also take the lead in China. Meanwhile, as the service trade expands quickly in the region because of its special location, the consequent logistical distribution of industry there is more developed than in other provinces. Dependent upon information technology and modern management, modern service industry also begins to take shape. In the 21st century, a point of view which encourages both the manufacturing and service sectors to facilitate economic advance has been proposed in the Yangtze River Delta and has even been given positive policy support by our country. Thus the added value of service industry has been increasing. As shown in Fig. 10.1, the added value of service industry in the Yangtze River Delta has increased by more than 10% since 1980 and has grown at a rate of more than 30% during the mid-1990s.

Through a general survey of service industry development in the world, we can see that the economic heart of the major developed countries has leaned toward the service sector since the early 1960s and that the industrial structure has tended to transfer from an industrial economy to a service one. The proportion of added value in the global service industry reached more than 60% of the GDP in 2000, amongst which developed countries equaled 70% and low-and middle-income countries even reached 43%. In 2006 the added value of the service industry in the Yangtze River Delta accounted for 41.3% of the GDP, which was obviously lower than that in low-and middle-income countries. Since the GDP per capita of the Yangtze River Delta is so low that service industry

Fig. 10.1. The Growth Rate of Value-added of third industry in the Yangtze River Delta

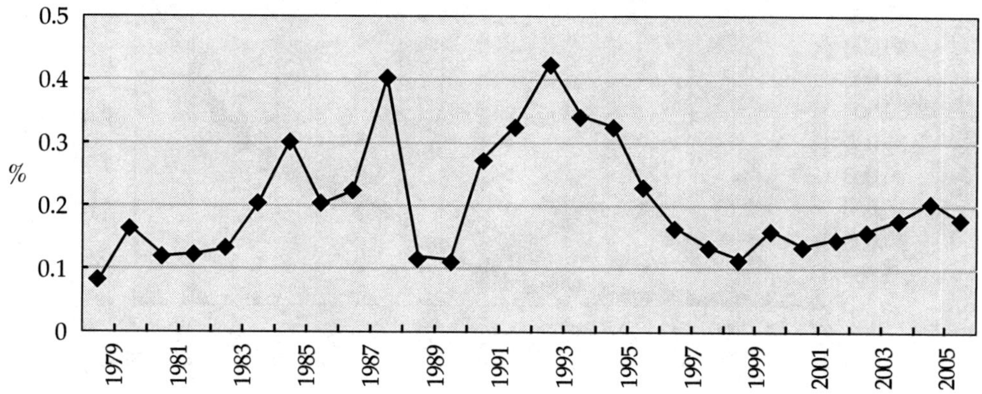

cannot compare with that in other countries at the same level, there is a need to explore ways to develop the service industry.

Primary Facts on Economic Fluctuation in the Yangtze River Delta

For a long time after the founding of the new China, the two provinces and one municipality in the Yangtze River Delta developed independently and there was little balanced development between regions. After the reform and opening up, our country began to pay more attention to the Yangtze River Delta which could be viewed as an integral economic region from then on. In this article, therefore, the analysis of economic fluctuation in the region starts from 1978.

The Yangtze River Delta has never been lacking in economic growth since the reform and opening up. We can see from Fig. 10.2 that the GDP and GDP per capita in that region have been increasing continuously since 1978. In 2006, the GDP reached RMB 4.756 373 trillion, accounting for 22.7% of the nation's GDP; GDP per capita is RMB 34,200, accounting for 2.08 times of nation's per capita GDP. Fig. 10.2 also shows that GDP in the region from 1978 to 2006 has increased by 73.65 times. There is no doubt that the growth of population will definitely bring about the increase in economic aggregate. Furthermore, the fact that GDP per capita has increased by more than 54 times also indicates that both the GDP and GDP per capita have achieved absolute growth, that is, people's living standard has improved.

Fig. 10.2. GDP and GDP per capita in the Yangtze River Delta

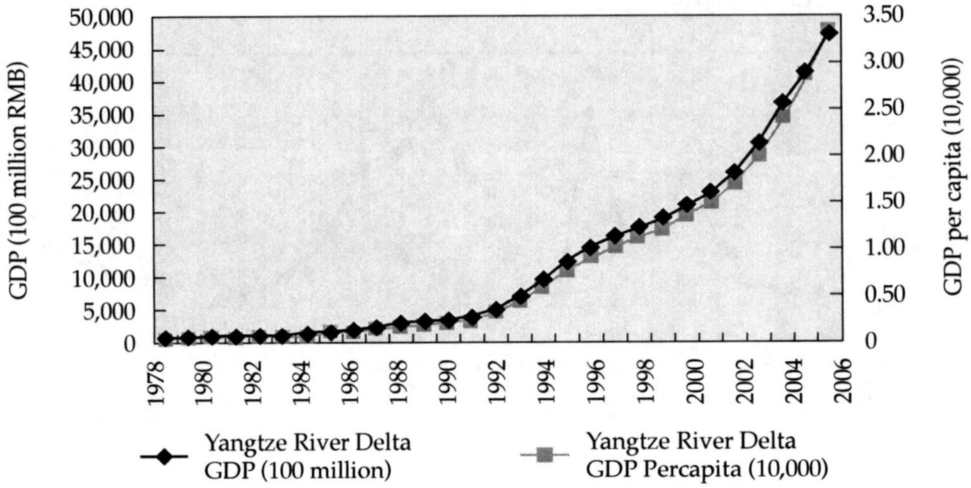

Fig. 10.3. The Growth Rate of the GDP in the Yangtze River Delta

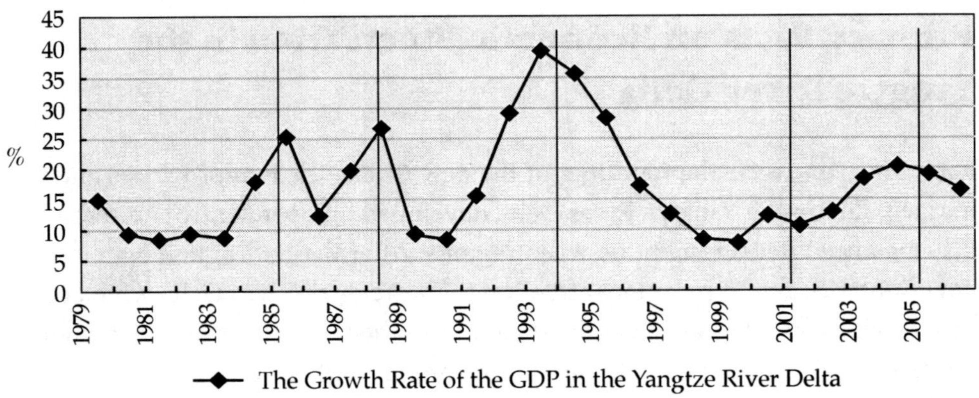

With the enhancement of economic development in the Yangtze River Delta, economic fluctuation the region is inevitable. I will analyze this phenomenon in accordance with change in the growth rate of the GDP.

As shown in Fig. 10.2, the gross economy in the Yangtze River Delta has been rising steadily during for nearly 30 years after the reform and opening up. The growth rate has always presented a positive tendency, which means that there is no classic economic fluctuation (which refers to negative growth when the GDP in an economic depression decreases absolutely). The difference between economic decline and economic boom is connected with the change in rate of economic growth. Therefore such a kind of fluctuation refers to a fluctuation with a growth cycle, that is, that the GDP even in a period of economic depression will not show an absolute decrease but only an obvious slowdown in economic growth.

As shown in Fig. 10.3, I employ the growth rate of the GDP to describe the economic fluctuation in the Yangtze River Delta and take one year as a reference. According to the "peak-peak" method (it refers to a periodic fluctuation from economic depression to economic recovery), the economy in the Yangtze River Delta has been considered to have undergone about 6 cycles of fluctuation since 1978.

(1) 1978–1985

During these 7 years, the economic depression started from 1978 to 1980, in which the growth rate of 15.0% in 1978 decreased to the rock bottom of 8.4% in 1980. It then revived in the following 4 years and reached the peak of 25.5% in 1985. Obviously, the drop between peak and rock-bottom was 17.1%. As the data in the years before 1978 were not taken into calculation, the initial peak in this cycle was unknown and the rate in 1978 was defined as the start point.

(2) 1985–1988

This cycle lasted just 4 years and can also be regarded as an incomplete economic fluctuation. During those 4 years, only in 1986 did the growth rate decline and it reached 12.3% that year. Then the economy started to recover so that the growth rate was up to 19.3% in 1987 and then 26.6% in 1988. In this cycle, the economy did not reach the bottom while it picked up in succession in the following two years. What is more surprising is that the great drop of 14.3% was achieved in only 4 years.

(3) 1988–1993

In the first two years, the rate of economic growth declined and reached the rock bottom of 8.2% in 1990. The economy revived in the following 4 years and reached the peak of 39.2% in 1993. Fig. 10.3 also demonstrates that the peak in 1993 is the summit of the rate of growth from 1979 to 1993. The drop in this period is 31.0%, which is far more than in the former ones.

(4) 1993–2000

This period appears to be much longer and the categorization of it is controversial. Many scholars hold that the period lasts until 2004 as there was only a slight rebound in 2000 but decline afterwards. But it is listed as an independent cycle in this article. The economy in that cycle decreased from the high rate in 1993 to the rock bottom of 7.9% in 1999 and went up to 12.2% in 2000. Due to the high growth rate in 1993, the drop was up to 31.3%.

(5) 2000–2004

The fluctuation in this period is not obvious because the gap between rates of successive two years is not in excess of 10%. In 2000, the growth rate did not reach a peak before it declined. But the rate in 2001 only decreased by 2% before rising again. In 2004, it reached the summit of 20.3% after two years of slow climb. The drop in this cycle is merely 9.6%, which is the smallest in the 5 periods.

(6) The period starting from 2004 has not come to the end and thus both the summit and rock bottom can not be determined. On the basis of data in the past three years, the drop of growth rate in this period is keeping pace with that in last one, that is, the fluctuation in each year is always slight.

The above description of these six cycles shows that the rate of economic growth in the Yangtze River Delta around 1993 has been the highest since the reform and opening up and the region has also been struck with severe inflation these years. Meanwhile two cycles, before and after 1993 respectively, present the greatest drops, and the longest cycle of fluctuation is from 1993 to 2000.

The above analysis shows that the economic fluctuation represented by the growth rate of the GDP in the Yangtze River Delta possesses several features as follows:

(1) The economic fluctuation spread narrows, that is, the sharp fluctuation of growth rate of the GDP decreases. After the reform and opening up, the margin of economic fluctuation was large during the third and fourth cycles but the real growth rate of the GDP was not very high because of inflation. The drops of fluctuation in the other 3 cycles also did not exceed 20%. The growth rates did not show a sharp fluctuation in two successive years, especially in the latest two cycles, in which the drop of fluctuation was 2–3% and there was no obvious great peak or decline.

(2) The economic recovery is prolonged. A cycle of economic fluctuation consists of depression and recovery. Thus "short-term depression and long-term rise" is the most marked feature of fluctuation in the Yangtze River Delta, which means that the rise of growth rate will last for a rather longer time than its decline. In the first cycle, the depression lasted for three years and the recovery for four; in the second one, there was only a one-year decline but a two-year rebound; and in the third one, a two-year decrease was followed with a three-year increase. But the fourth cycle was an exception as its depression was by far longer than the recovery. Besides, it is obvious that the margin of decrease during the first three cycles is rather greater than that of increase thus the increase is undoubtedly slow. A clear tendency of the fifth cycle exhibits a slow decline and rise, that is, both the margins of decline and rise are rather slight. However, the truth that the recovery lasts longer than the depression suggests the increase in growth rate remains slow in the long term.

(3) The duration of the economic cycle is inclined to lengthen. Generally

speaking, the duration of the first five cycles was around six years, among which the first cycle lasted as long as eight years, as long as the fourth, whereas the other three were respectively four, five and six years. Meanwhile such inclination will persist further because the reduction of the growth rate of the GDP and the extension of the period of revival will be bound to cause the longer time spent on reaching the expected growth rate.

Based on the analysis of features of economic fluctuation in the Yangtze River Delta, we can see that the fluctuation in tends to a steady state as expected. It is true that there is no country or region without economic fluctuation but "short-term depression and long-term rise" is the goal in economic development.

Model Analysis of Service Industry and Economic Fluctuation

The share of service industry in the GDP in the Yangtze River Delta is increasing. Correspondingly, the economic fluctuation in the area is apt to be slow in recovery and decline and the economic development enters into a gradually steady stage. In accordance with the practical experience in Western developed countries, an increase in the proportion of the service sector is able to boost a much steadier economy just because the service sector keeps production and marketing in pace. Furthermore, the change in common consumers' needs for services is not great so that the fluctuation of growth rate of the service industry is relatively stabilized. The fluctuation of the gross macro-economy should also be gentle due to the expanding share of the service industry in the economy. In the Yangtze River Delta, the proportion of service industry has grown fast since the reform and opening up. Whether such development orientation of service industry is related to the "slow recovery and depression" of economic fluctuation is the main issue this article will research.

Model Hypothesis

In order to define the relationship between service industry and economic fluctuation in the Yangtze River Delta, we can make several basic hypotheses. First, we can propose a hypothesis that similar with the general macro-economic model, the economy in the Yangtze River Delta is formed by a large number of households and manufacturers and that those households which aim to achieve the maximization of consumption utility earn wages by working so as to guarantee a currency basis for consumption. The production of manufacturers mainly depends on input as well as technology and is aimed at maximizing the output. The performance of households and manufacturers represent the economic situation in the Yangtze River Delta.

(1) The production function is also the Cobb-Douglas production function. We divide the economy in the Yangtze River Delta into two departments: service sector and non-service sector, in which way the function of the service sector in the overall economy can be highlighted. The production functions of these two departments is presented as follows:

$$Y_1(t)=[a_k K(t)]^{\alpha}\,[a_l A_1(t)L(t)]^{1-\alpha} \tag{1}$$

$$Y_2(t)=[(1-a_k)K(t)]^{\beta}\,[(1-a_l)A_2(t)L(t)]^{1-\beta} \tag{2}$$

$Y_1(t)$ and $Y_2(t)$ respectively represent the production functions of the non-service sector and the service sector; a_k and a_l indicate the proportions of the capital K and labour L in the two departments; and A_1 and A_2 separately show the technological levels of the non-service sector and service sector. We also define $K_1(t)=a_k K(t)$, $L_1(t)=a_l L(t)$, $K_2(t)=(1-a_k)K(t)$ *and* $L_2(t)=(1-a_l)L(t)$ for convenience for the succeeding deduction.

According to the experience of the developing economy in the Yangtze River Delta, we can suppose that the contribution to capital output of the non-service sector is greater than that to labor output. Secondary industry dominates the non-service sector in the region, which needs a large amount of fixed assets input and also accumulates a great deal of capital within the industry through decades of development. The major contribution of the service sector is the input of technology and also labor. The traditional service industry is mainly dependent on labor input while the modern service industry relies mainly on input of technology and labor. Thus in the region such hypothesis has its rationality and $\alpha>\beta$ is also meaningful. As service sector relies heavily upon technology, we can assume that the technical level of the service sector is higher than that of the non-service one. Meanwhile, service industries in the Yangtze River Delta infiltrate into other non-service industries such as information services, production services and financial services so we can also assume there is an infiltration of technical levels between the two departments, that is, the advanced technology of the service sector will infiltrate the non-service one. We suppose the technological growth of the two departments as follows:

$$\dot{A}_2(t)=gA_2(t) \tag{3}$$

$$\dot{A}_1(t)=\mu[A_2(t)-A_1(t)],\ \text{in which}\ A_2(t)>A_1(t) \tag{4}$$

g means the growth rate of technical level of the service sector whereas the major technology of the non-service sector is derived from the service sector. Thus μ represents the coefficient of infiltration.

(2) On the basis of the analysis above, we can attribute the major cause of economic fluctuation in the Yangtze River Delta to investment and government purchases. Moreover the fluctuation of investment is presented by the change in capital stock so we ascribe the chief factors of economic fluctuation in the region to the fluctuation of capital stock and government purchases and suppose those fluctuations are subordinated to the first-order autoregressive process.

$$\tilde{K}(t)=\rho_K\tilde{K}(t-1)+\varepsilon_{K,t},\ -1<\rho_K<1 \quad (5)$$

$$\tilde{G}(t)=\rho_G\tilde{G}(t-1)+\varepsilon_{G,t},\ -1<\rho_G<1 \quad (6)$$

In the above formulas, ε is a random disturbance and the mean is 0. Formula (5) suggests the fluctuation of capital stock in the current period influenced by the last fluctuation as the major factor and random disturbance as well. ε just strengthens or weakens the fluctuation inherited from the last one by a small margin, which corresponds to the realistic economic situation in the Yangtze River Delta after 1993. Previously the government imposed uniformity on all cases once an overheated economy occurred, which led to little reciprocity of credit quota and expenditure between two successive periods. After 1993, the slight fluctuations continued in the successive two periods due to the moderate policy, which shows as formulas (5) and (6).

(3) We can assume that if the service and non-service sectors function along the balanced growth path[1] then a worker's salary in the service sector is equal to that in the non-service one. The salary is a kind of reward for working and can be presented by output value of marginal product. Thus salary in the two departments can be presented as:

$$W_1(t)=\frac{\partial Y_1(t)}{\partial L_1(t)}=\frac{1-\alpha}{L_1(t)}\cdot Y_1(t) \quad (7)$$

$$W_2(t)=\frac{\partial Y_2(t)}{\partial L_1(t)}=\frac{1-\beta}{L_2(t)}\cdot Y_2(t) \quad (8)$$

On the balanced growth path:

$$W_1(t)=W_2(t) \quad (9)$$

The three hypotheses above are taken as the basic ones for the argument in this chapter. There are many other hypotheses needed in the model, which will be put forward in the following analysis.

Description of households' performance

Households achieve the maximization of utility by making choices between consumption and work. We have assumed that workers in the two departments earn the same wage, which means that the wages they make do not depend on which industries they are engaged in. Therefore it is not necessary to distinguish the performance models of different households but the overall households' performance can be analyzed using a unified model.

All the households' performance can be described by some representative ones, of which the function of utility can be presented as:

$$U=\sum_{t=0}^{\infty} e^{-\rho t}u(c_t, 1-l_t)\frac{N_t}{H} \qquad (10)$$

ρ represents discount rate, H the total households in the Yangtze River Delta, N_t the population and $\frac{N_t}{H}$ the family members of each representative household. The function of household utility here means the indefinite duration of survival. $u(\cdot)$, which represents the average function of consumption utility of family members and is determined by two independent variables: c_t (per capita consumption of family members) and l_t (average work hours of family members). They can be respectively shown by formulas as $c_t=C_t/N_t$ and $l_t=L_t/N_t$. We suppose the relationship between consumption utility of each member and the two variables as follows:

$$u(c_t, 1-l_t)=\ln c_t+b(1-l_t)^{1-\gamma}/(1-\gamma),\ b>0 \qquad (11)$$

1-l_t represents the spare time of each members (time is simplified as 1) while $b>0$ shows the positive correlation between utility and spare time.

(1) In order to draw a general conclusion about household performance, we begin with the case that the household survives for only one period. For convenience of calculation and the accuracy of the conclusion we assume that there is only one member and no inherited initial wealth in the household. The budget of the household refers to the fact that expenditure cannot exceed salary, shown as $c\leq wl$. We can then get a Lagrange function represented by household object function and constraints function:

$$L=\ln c+b(1-l)^{1-\gamma}/(1-\gamma)+\lambda(wl-c) \qquad (12)$$

The maximization of the Lagrange function is to find out the first-order conditions of c and l, which can be combined as:

$$b(1-l)^{-\gamma}=1/l \qquad (13)$$

Formula (13) reflects the labor supply when survival lasts for one period. If b and γ are given, labor supply as a constant is not determined by wage. Such a situation is considered to be static. Households' consumption can be worked out through consumption constraints if labor supply is fixed. The situation of one-period survival provides a way for more complex analysis but some of the conclusions are untenable in the following analysis.

(2) When a household survives for two periods, we can also make the same hypothesis as in (1) and in the budget constraint consumption also cannot exceed salary, which is represented as $c_1 + \frac{1}{1+r} c_2 \leq w_1 l_1 + \frac{1}{1+r} w_2 l_2$. And then the Lagrange function of household utility is changed into:

$$L = \ln c_1 + \frac{b(1-l_1)^{1-\gamma}}{1-\gamma} + e^{-\rho}\left[\ln c_2 + \frac{b(1-l_2)^{1-\gamma}}{1-\gamma}\right] + \lambda\left[w_2 l_1 + \frac{1}{1+r} w_2 l_2 - c_1 - \frac{1}{1+r} c_2\right] \quad (14)$$

Finding the first-order conditions of 11 and 12, we can combine them into:

$$\frac{1-l_1}{1-l_2} = \left[\frac{w_2}{w_1 e^{-\rho}(1+r)}\right]^{1/r} \quad (15)$$

The above formula suggests that the average spare time and salary of family members are in reverse ratio, that is, labor supply is directly proportional to salary. Such a relationship shows that the substitute of labor supply is determined by wage when a household survives for two periods. In addition, the substitute of labor also can be influenced by the change in interest rate.

From above, we can illustrate the relationship of consumption between two periods as:

$$\frac{c_1}{c_2} = \frac{e^{-\rho}}{1+r} \quad (16)$$

Formula (16) suggests that such a relationship is just related to discount rate. Formula (15) represents how work hours are allocated when family income is maximized. The distribution of consumption of two periods is restrained by wage and affected by the discount rate of consumption utility and income.

(3) Different from the above analysis, if a household survives for more than two periods, we will not pay as much attention to the previous hypothesis. The members in the representative households is not just one but the mean of the members in all households, yet we will also assume there is no initial wealth that can be inherited. The conclusion drawn from the last situation still stands in this case but it presents the substitute of labor supply and consumption substitute between the two successive periods. We focus on analyzing the substitute relationship between working and consumption in each period, that is, the relationship between spare time and consumption. As the source of consumption can only be derived from salary, savings of the first several periods and discount of the last ones, the analysis of substitute of consumption and labor in the current period can indirectly reflect the relationship between labor and consumption in each period.

We employ the most traditional method of cost and profit to analyze such a relationship in each period. Formula (11) suggests the spare time varies directly with utility of family members but is in inverse proportion to labor output. Consumption is also directly proportional to consumption utility, thus working will give birth to the negative consumption utility while consuming bring about the positive one. If we view the negative consumption utility as cost and the positive one as profit, we can conduct the analysis of the substitute relationship.

From formulas (10) and (11), we can calculate the cost of negative marginal utility caused by working as:

$$e^{-\rho t}\frac{N_t}{H}\cdot[\,b(1-l_t)^{-\gamma}\,]\cdot\Delta l \tag{17}$$

The profit of utility increased by consuming is:

$$e^{-\rho t}\frac{N_t}{H}\cdot\frac{1}{c_t}\cdot\Delta c \tag{18}$$

The change in labor supply leading to the change in consumption of each member which can be shown as $w\Delta l$. Therefore we can also find out Δc equal to $w\Delta l$ and the formula above can also be rewritten as:

$$e^{-\rho t}\frac{N_t}{H}\cdot\frac{1}{c_t}\cdot w_t\cdot\Delta l \tag{19}$$

Cost is equal to profit, that is, formula (17) is equal to formula (19):

$$\frac{c_t}{(1-l_t)^{\gamma}}=\frac{w_t}{b} \tag{20}$$

In such formula, the substitute relationship between labor and spare time is mainly influenced by wages in current period.

The three analyses above separately draw three important conclusions, that is, labor supply and consumption in the static state is determined by formula (13), the substitute relation of labor supply and consumption in two successive periods by (15) and (16), and the substitute relation of labor supply and consumption in each period by (20). The relationship reflected in formulas (15), (16) and (20) will be applied in the following discussion.

The cushioning effect of the increase in proportion of service industry

In the macro-economy, C, I, G and EM describe the constitution of aggregate demand while C and L describe the household performance. According to the relationship between C and L concluded in the last sector, we linearize C and L near the balanced growth path. It is easy to find that the fluctuation of consumption and labor supply is represented by fluctuation of capital stock and government purchases as:

$$\tilde{C}_t=b_{CK}\tilde{K}_t+b_{CG}\tilde{G}_t \tag{21}$$

$$\tilde{L}_t=b_{LK}\tilde{K}_t+b_{LG}\tilde{G}_t \tag{22}$$

The capital stock and government purchases will not have an impact on the change in population so $\tilde{c}_t=\tilde{C}_t$ is equal to $\tilde{l}_t=\tilde{L}_t$. With figuring out the logarithm for (20), we can get the formula as follows:

$$\ln c_t-\gamma\ln(1-l_t)=\ln w_t-\ln b \tag{21'}$$

It is supposed that in the Yangtze River Delta wages of the service sector and the non-service one are equal in the static state. Thus if we apply formula (7) and the relationship of K_1 and L_1 and of K and L to the above formula, we can obtain the following:

$$\ln C_t-\gamma\ln(1-L_t)=\alpha(\ln a_k+\ln K_t)+\ln\frac{1-\alpha}{b}+(1-\alpha)\ln A_{1,t}-\alpha a_l-\alpha\ln L_t \tag{22'}$$

Linearize the formula above

$$\tilde{C}_t+\frac{\gamma l^*}{1-l^*}\tilde{L}_t=\alpha\tilde{K}_t-\alpha\tilde{L}_t \tag{23}$$

Apply (21) and (22) to the formula above

$$b_{CK}\tilde{K}_t+b_{CG}\tilde{G}_t+\frac{\gamma l^*}{1-l^*}(b_{LK}\tilde{K}_t+b_{LG}\tilde{G}_t)=\alpha\tilde{K}_t-\alpha(b_{LK}\tilde{K}_t+b_{LG}\tilde{G}_t) \tag{24}$$

The coefficient t on both sides of the above formula is equal.

$$b_{CK}+\left(\frac{\gamma l^*}{1-l^*}+\alpha\right)b_{LK}=\alpha \tag{25}$$

$$b_{CG}+\left(\frac{\gamma l^*}{1-l^*}+1\right)b_{LG}=\alpha \tag{26}$$

The above formula suggests that both capital stock and government purchases are in inverse proportion to coefficients influenced by the fluctuation of consumption and labor supply. Formula (26) presents that the negative utility increases with the increase in workload caused by the fluctuation of households purchase. Only if the growth of consumption promotes the increase in the positive utility, household utility will not decrease. Thus their coefficients are inversely proportional to each other, in which b_{CG} and b_{LG} are respectively positive and negative. Formula (25) also reflects an inverse ratio but the signs of the two coefficients are not determined. If the fluctuation of capital stock is positive, the increase in capital will lead to the increase in the relevant capital of per unit worker as well as the improvement of working efficiency and the increase in wage and then the increase in consumption. The increase in wage adds production effect and wealth effect. That is to say, the increase in wage will cause the increase in labor supply as well as that in consumption. Here b_{CK} and b_{LK} are with opposite signs. Such way of analyzing is the same as formula (26). Moreover the increase in wage leads to the growth of household wealth but the reduction of labor supply so b_{LK} is a positive number. But the reduction of labor supply will bring about the decrease in consumption by a small margin so that those two numbers are positive and b_{CK} decreases.

The economic aggregate in the Yangtze River Delta, excluding service sectors, comes to:

$$Y(t)=Y1(t)+Y2(t) \tag{27}$$

With the logarithm linearization of the above formula, the relationship between the fluctuation of economic aggregate and the two departments is shown as:

$$\tilde{Y}_t=\frac{Y^*_{1,t}}{Y^*_t}\tilde{Y}_{1,t}+\frac{Y^*_{2,t}}{Y^*_t}\tilde{Y}_{2,t} \tag{28}$$

On the basis of relationship drawn from formula (9) and ration relationship between (7) and (8), the relationship of Y^*_1 and t to Y^*_2 and t can be shown as:

$$\frac{Y^*_{1,t}}{Y^*_{2,t}}=\frac{(1-\beta)a_l}{(1-\alpha)(1-a_l)} \tag{29}$$

Applied to formula (28), it becomes:

$$\tilde{Y}_t=\frac{(1-\beta)a_l}{1-\alpha+\alpha a_l-\beta a_l}\tilde{Y}_{1,t}+\frac{(1-\alpha)(1-a_l)}{1-\alpha+\alpha_{al}-\beta_{al}}\tilde{Y}_{2,t} \tag{30}$$

The above formula exhibits the relationship between the fluctuation of the gross economy and that of output value in the two departments. Due to the impact of capital stock and government purchases, fluctuations will come into being inevitably in both departments which have different effects on the fluctuation of the GDP. Such effects on the overall economic fluctuation can be presented by coefficients $\frac{(1-\beta)a_l}{1-\alpha+\alpha a_l-\beta a_l}$ and $\frac{(1-\alpha)(1-a_l)}{1-\alpha+\alpha_{al}-\beta_{al}}$ which have the same denominator but different numerators. α represents the contribution rate of capital input in the non-service sector while β represents that in the service sector. According to hypothesis (1), α is greater than β so $1-\beta>1-\alpha$. The relationship between such two coefficients can also be represented by a_l, which means the proportion of labor in the non-service sector. The approximate value of aL can be drawn from the economic practice in the Yangtze River Delta. The proportions of people working in third industry in Jiangsu and Zhejiang in recent years are listed in the following Table 10.2. In accordance with data in that figure, we can see that the proportion of employees in tertiary industry is about 30%, which has not yet overfulfilled 50%. Therefore, a_L surpasses 0.5 and the economic practice demonstrates $a_l>1-a_l$

Table 10.2. The proportion of people working in third industry in all of employees (%)

Region	1997	1998	1999	2000	2001	2002	2003	2004
Jiangsu	23.4	25.1	26.2	27.0	28.5	30.1	31.5	32.2
Zhejiang	23.9	24.9	29.1	29.0	30.5	31.6	30.5	30.3

Source: *Jiangsu Statistical Yearbook 2006*.

Thus the relationship between two coefficients above is:

$$\frac{(1-\beta)a_l}{1-\alpha+\alpha a_l-\beta a_l} > \frac{(1-\alpha)(1-a_l)}{1-\alpha+\alpha_{al}-\beta_{al}} \quad (31)$$

This obviously suggests that the fluctuation of the service sector has less influence on the overall economic fluctuation than that of the non-service one. Thus the increase in proportion of added value in the service sector in the Yangtze River Delta will lead to the reduction of fluctuation margin of the gross economy, that is, the service industry can cushion the economy.

The cushioning effect of the service industry on economic fluctuation

In the last section we have proved with the influential coefficient of fluctuation in service industry that the increase in the proportion of service industry in the Yangtze River Delta has a cushioning effect on economic fluctuation. In this section we will demonstrate $\tilde{Y}_{2,t}<\tilde{Y}_{1,t}$ to prove that the service industry plays a role as buffer in economic fluctuation only if it exists in the economy.

With the logarithm linearization of formula (1) and (2), we can present the economic fluctuations separately in the non-service sector and the service one as:

$$\tilde{Y}_{1,t}=\alpha\tilde{K}_t+(1-\alpha)\tilde{L}_t \quad (32)$$

$$\tilde{Y}_{2,t}=\beta\tilde{K}_t+(1-\beta)\tilde{L}_t \quad (33)$$

The fluctuations of economic aggregate of the two departments can be respectively represented by linear functions of capital fluctuation and labor fluctuation. If formula (22) is applied to the above two formulas, we obtain:

$$\tilde{Y}_{1,t}=[\alpha+(1-\alpha)b_{LK}]\tilde{K}_t+(1-\alpha)b_{LG}\tilde{G}_t \quad (34)$$

$$\tilde{Y}_{2,t}=[\beta+(1-\beta)b_{LK}]\tilde{K}_t+(1-\beta)b_{LG}t \quad (35)$$

In this way, economic fluctuations in the non-service sector and service sector can be exhibited as linear functions of capital stock and government purchases. With a comparison of $\tilde{K}_t$ and $\tilde{G}_t$ coefficient, we can further compare the margins of fluctuations in the two departments.

Firstly, we can compare them as impacted by government purchases. We have made the hypothesis of $\alpha>\beta$ so $\tilde{G}_t$ has less impact on the non-service sector than on the service one. That is determined by the large amount of government purchase of service.

The impact of $\tilde{K}_t$ on the two departments is not easy to define because there are α, β and (1-α) concluded in coefficients of capital stock. b_{LK} is derived from formula (25) approximately. There is no doubt that wage level in the Yangtze River Delta has not reached the stage of wealth effect, therefore the value of b_{LK} remains negative. By considering the economic level it is easy to find the relationship of influential functions impacted by t between the two departments as:

$$\alpha+(1-\alpha)b_{LK}>\beta+(1-\beta)b_{LK} \quad (36)$$

The impact of capital stock on the non-service sector is greater than that on service sector, which is contrary to the situation reflected by the impact of government purchase. What effect the integrated impact of those two situations has on service sector depends on the relationship between t and its fluctuation.

$$\tilde{Y}_{2,t}<\tilde{Y}_{1,t} \quad (37)$$

Fig. 10.4. Fixed assets investment and expenditure in the Yangtze River Delta

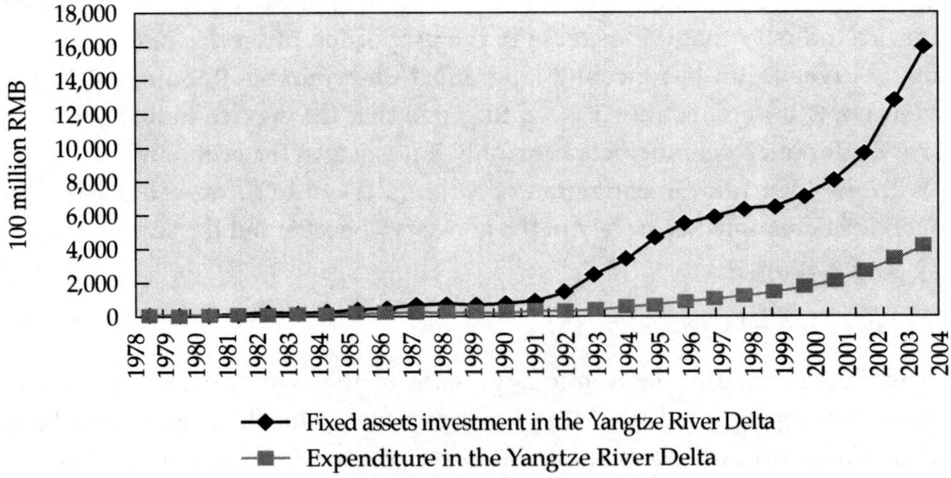

The trend shown by a curve in Fig. 10.4 suggests that in the Yangtze River Delta not only does the gross value of fixed assets investment far exceed expenditure but the growth rate is also sharply higher than that of expenditure. That provides practical evidence for $\tilde{K}_t>\tilde{G}_t$. Thus it can be demonstrated that on the same impact the fluctuation of service sector is greater than that of service one.

Empirical Test

This article employs the growth rate of the GDP, the proportions of service industry and GDP, fixed assets investment and expenditure as variables. All the data used for the analysis is derived from the issues of the relevant statistical yearbooks of 16 cities in the Yangtze River Delta, and the sample data is selected from the annual data from 1978 to 2006.[2]

HP filter analysis

Generally speaking, the economic time queue contains elements of trend and fluctuation. In this article Hodrick-Prescott (HP), a method of filter analysis, is employed to analyze the time queue into protracted trend and cyclical fluctuation and then to investigate the relationship between the development of the service industry and the cyclical fluctuation of economy. Such method was applied by Hodrick, Prescott (1980) for the first time when he analyzed postwar economic cycles in America.

We suppose that $\{Y_t\}$ represents the economic time queue including elements of trend and fluctuation, $\{Y_t^T\}$ the element of trend and $\{Y_t^c\}$ the element of fluctuation, therefore,

$$Y_t=Y_t^T+Y_t^c \quad t=1, 2, \ldots, T$$

Calculating the HP filter refers to drawing $\{Y_t^T\}$ from $\{Y_t\}$. In general, the observable part of $\{Y_t^T\}$ in $\{Y_t\}$ is defined as the solution of minimization as follows:

$$min \sum_{t=1}^{T} \{(Y_t-Y_t^T)^2+\lambda[c(L)Y_t^T]^2\} \tag{38}$$

$c(L)$ is the polynomial of delay factor

$$c(L)= (L^{-1}-1)-(1-L) \tag{39}$$

Formula (39) is applied to (38) and the HP filter is employed to minimize the loss function, that is,

$$min\,\{\sum_{t=1}^{T}(Y_t-Y_t^T)^2+\lambda\sum_{t=1}^{T}[(Y_{t+1}^T-Y_t^T)-(Y_t^T-Y_{t-1}^T)^2]\}$$

λ is a smooth parameter used for balancing interconnection and smoothness of trend and represents the proportion of protracted trend and cyclical fluctuation in such analysis. The bigger λ is, the higher proportion the protracted trend takes up. Meanwhile, the more smooth the curve drawn in accordance with the protracted data is, the greater the fluctuation of the cyclical data is.

The quota investigated in economic cycles employs a relative index, namely, the economic growth rate. It is not represented by an absolute index but by the growth rate of GDP in the statistical yearbooks (it is 100 in the previous year). The development of the service industry is represented by the growth rate of the GDP in service industry. In order to study the trend of increase in economy and service industry and the fluctuation, we will investigate the queue of growth rate of national economy (GY) and that of service industry (GS) as well.

Curves in Figs. 10.5 and 10.6 respectively exhibit the trends of increase in growth rate of the national economy and service industry (drawn through HP filter analysis). From the figures we can see that, in terms of fluctuation of growth rate, the margin of fluctuation in the service industry is smaller than that in the national economy, in which the variance of the former is 2.577 767 while that of the latter is 2.786 797. From the perspective of the uniformity and synchronism of fluctuation, service industry and national economy manifest clockwise periodicity as well as synchronism. Therefore it can be concluded that the service industry has a cushioning effect on economic fluctuation.

Fig. 10.5. The trend of fluctuation of growth rate in the national economy

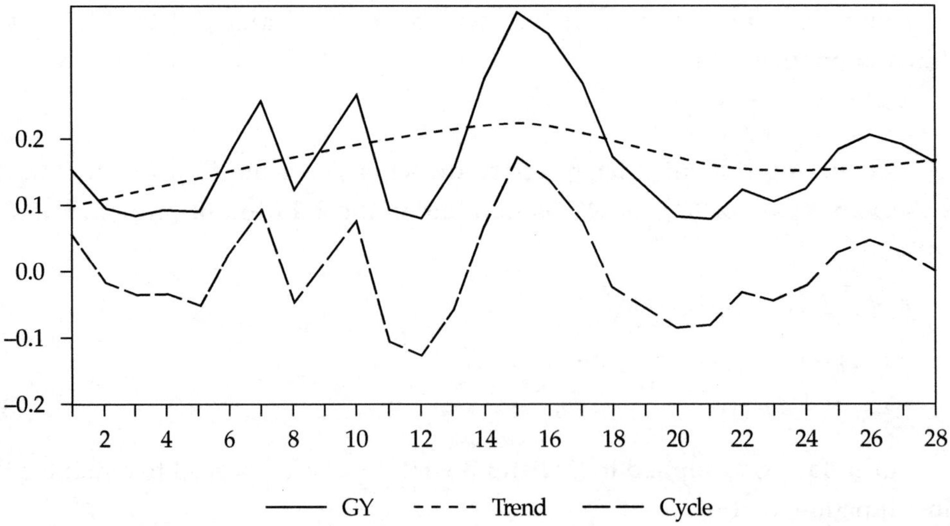

Fig. 10.6. The trend of fluctuation of growth rate in the service industry

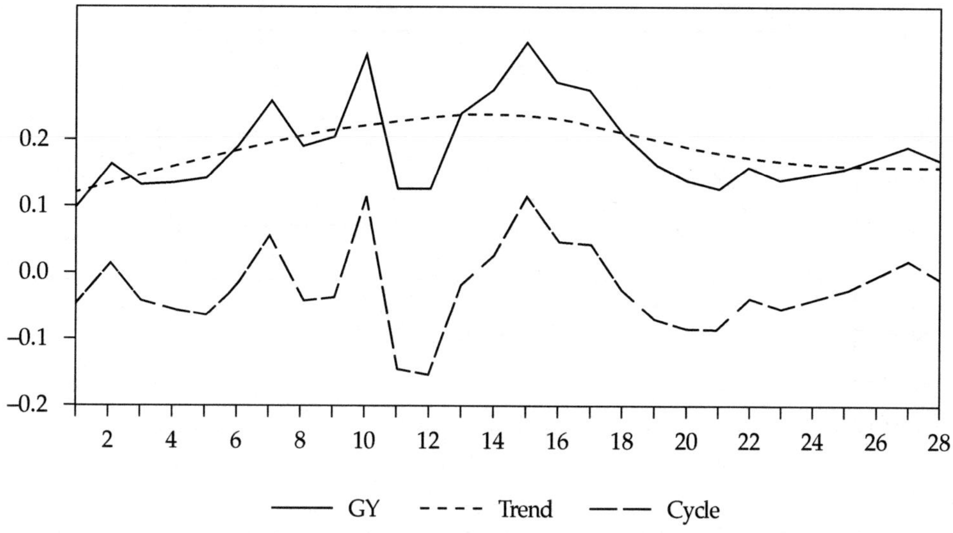

Impulse Response Function

In order to ascertain an exact and meaningful correlation between the national economy and service industry, we should further verify and analyze them. We employ the growth rate of economic aggregate (ΔGDP), the proportion of service industry (S/GDP), fixed estate investment (K) and expenditure (F) to investigate the correlation between the economic fluctuation and the development of service industry in the Yangtze River Delta.

On the basis of vector autoregression (VAR), we apply the impulse response function to study the impact of a standard deviation derived from random disturbance on the current and future values of endogenous variables. The growth rate of GDP in the Yangtze River Delta and the proportion of service industry in the GDP are respectively affected by a impulse response caused by the impact of a standard deviation, which is shown in Figs. 10.7 and 10.8.

Fig. 10.7 suggests that the response of LS/GDP to the impact of one standard deviation of $L\Delta GDP$ is not in a stable state in the initial stage, fluctuating with the lapse of time. However it becomes more distinct after the fourth period and reaches the peak of 0.017 165 in the seventh. And then it falls back gradually and tends to maintain around 0.01, which exhibits a positive convergence effect in the long run. In the beginning, the response of the development of the service industry to the growth rate of economic aggregate is not stable, which can be also considered to present a negative effect. But from a long-term point of view the growth rate of economic aggregate indirectly stimulates the development of the service industry.

Fig. 10.7. **The response function of the proportion of service industry to the impact of growth rate of the GDP**

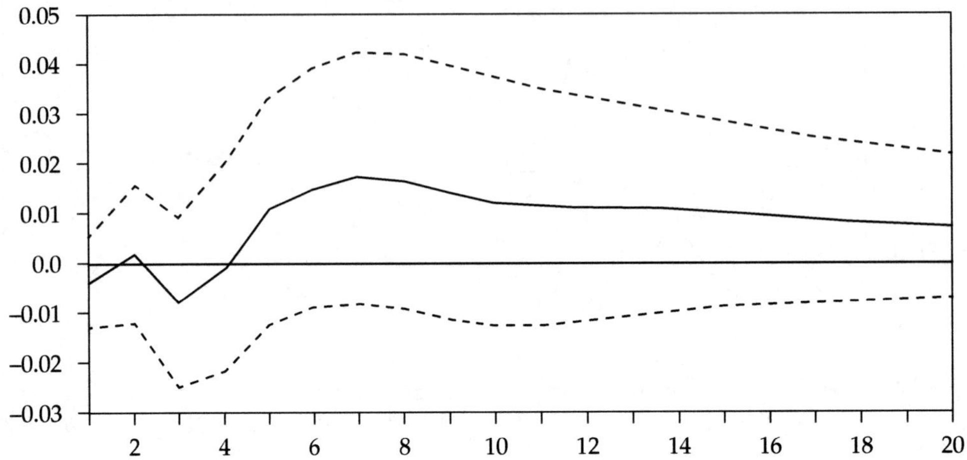

According to Fig. 10.8, we can see that fixed estate investment has a remarkable effect on the growth rate of the GDP and reaches the maximum of 0.335 382 in the fourth period. Afterwards it drops at a slow rate and the margin of its fluctuation is relatively steady.

Fig. 10.8. **The response function of growth rate of GDP to the impact of service industry, fixed estate investment and expenditure**

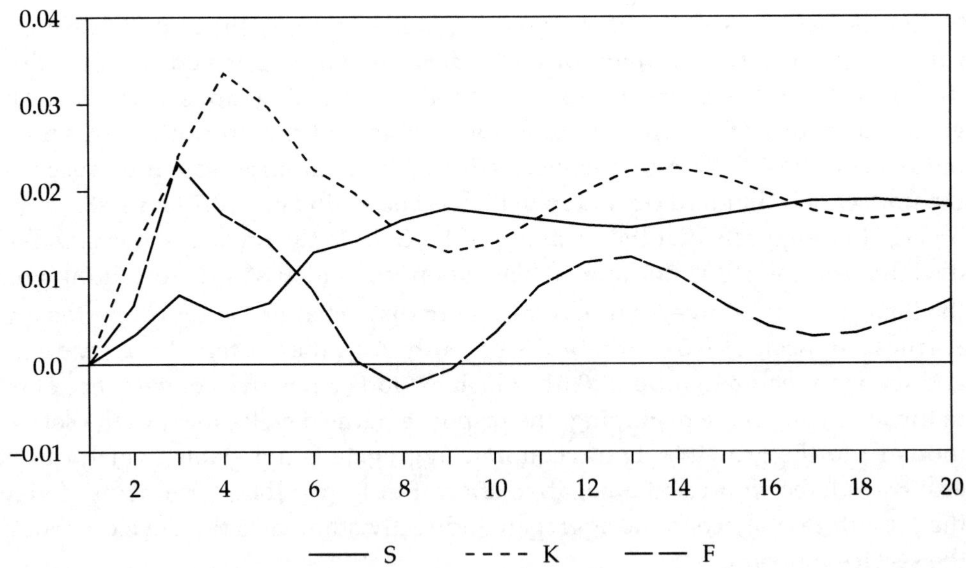

The effect of expenditure on the growth rate of the GDP is not stable and reached a maximum of 0.230 652 in the third period. Then it comes down and has a negative effect in the eighth and ninth periods. But such effect turns positive after the tenth period and begins to fluctuate as time goes on.

The growth rate of the GDP does not show any response to the standard deviation of the proportion of the service sector in the GDP in the first period but becomes positive from the second period, reaching 0.033 606. In time the positive effect spreads gradually and the fluctuation tends to be steady, which shows that the development of service industry has given positive impetus to the growth rate of the GDP.

Conclusions

Based on the analysis above, economic fluctuation is closely related to the service sector in the Yangtze River Delta, which can be concluded as follows:

1. The theoretical model presents that the fluctuations in the two departments are caused by both capital stock and government purchase, in which the fluctuation in the service sector has less influence on the gross economic fluctuation than that in the non-service sector. Thus the increase in the proportion of the added value of the service sector will reduce the fluctuation of the gross economy, which means that the service industry has cushioning effect on the economy.

2. Suffering from the same impact, the margin of fluctuation in the service sector is smaller than that in the non-service one so the service industry plays a role as regulator in economic fluctuation only if it exists in the economy.

3. HP filter analysis suggests that, in terms of the fluctuation of the growth rate, the margin of the fluctuation in the service industry is smaller than that in the national economy. From the perspective of the uniformity and synchronism of fluctuation, both the service industry and the national economy manifest clockwise periodicity as well as synchronism. Therefore it can be concluded that service industry has a cushioning effect on economic fluctuation.

4. In accordance with the analysis of impulse response function, the growth rate of the GDP does not make any response to the standard deviation of the proportion of service sector in the GDP in the first period but obtains a positive effect from the second period. Over of time such a positive effect spreads gradually and the fluctuation tends to be steady, which shows that the development of the service industry gives a positive and steady impetus to the gross economy.

Furthermore, economic growth and fluctuation are subject to various factors such as fixed estate investment, expenditure etc. Therefore to promote steady economic growth is a comprehensive and balanced process. With respect to how to further improve the industrial competitiveness of the Yangtze River Delta, overall consideration is needed on the coordinated development of different industries. Meanwhile we should also realize that the development level and competitiveness of the service industry will become an important pillar for the sustained economic development during the later period of the relatively mature industrialization in the region.

11

Chapter

Income Distribution Effects due to Service Sector Development in the Yangtze River Delta

Introduction

In recent years, the Yangtze River Delta has witnessed optimization of the three industries' structure and a fast growth in the service industry, which has vigorously boosted the economic expansion. The statistics for 2006 shows that the added value of the service industry totaled RMB 1,629.991 billion in the 16 cities of the Yangtze River Delta, accounting for 41.3% of the third industry. The added value of the service industry accounted for 50.6% in Shanghai, over 40% in Nanjing, Zhoushan, Hangzhou and Ningbo and 32.1% in Taizhou. The development of the service industry not only promotes economic growth but also affects the income distribution through changes in the employment structure. In 2005 the employees of the service industry in the 16 cities accounted for 36.2% of the overall workforce, and those in Shanghai stood at 55.6%. Income distribution can be affected by the increase of employees in the service industry and the changes in its employment structure. This chapter will test the research on the income-distribution effect of the service industry in the Yangtze River Delta with empirical methods with a view to exploring its intrinsic mechanism.

According to an American survey made during the Reagan Administration, the expansion of service sectors leads to a relative decline in the number of middle-income groups. This is because employment with low payment and low technology burgeons and the service industries also provide many jobs with high technology and payment, while the increase of traditional jobs with ordinary technological demand and payment is not quite in line with the trend. The uneven development of jobs with high payment and low payment is regarded as a "double peak." The traditional bell-shaped distribution curve will be replaced by a curve that is protruding on both sides and dented in the middle (as shown in Fig. 11.1).

Fig. 11.1. Traditional bell-shaped distribution curve and the double-peak distribution curve

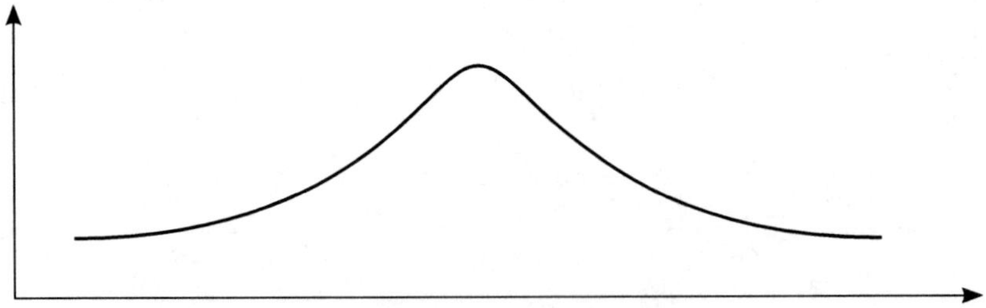

Traditional bell-shaped distribution curve

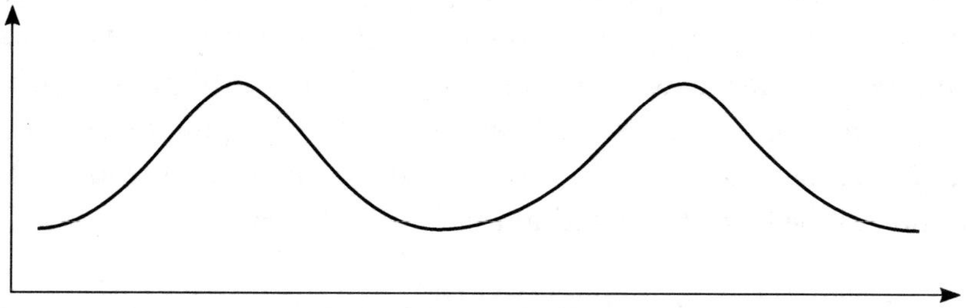

Double-peak distribution curve

Barry Bluestone and Bennett Harrison (1986) conducted research into the data on earning and employment of Americans in 1973, 1979 and 1984 to examine the differences in income distribution over time. They found that 60% of the new jobs from 1979 to 1984 were paid badly, while the number from 1973 to 1979 was less than 20%. And the number of high and middle-income groups increased slightly. Barry Bluestone said that manufacturing is characterized by high average income and narrow income gap, while the service industry by low average income and wide income gap. And the average income decreases and the income gap widens when job opportunities transfer from the manufacturing to the service industry.

Robert Fiala made an empirical test with data of 42 countries, developed or developing, from 1960 to 1980, and concluded that the service industry is more likely to worsen the inequality in income than manufacturing, which is more obvious in less developed countries than in developed countries.

The Development and Structural Change in the Service Industry in the Yangtze River Delta

This chapter will inspect the income-distribution effect mainly through the changes in employment structure of the service industry. Thus the analysis focuses on the development level and structural change in the service industry from the perspective of labor force and employment.

As the economic aggregate and the per-capita income increase, the demand structure of merchandise and labor will also undergo changes. The output structure will unavoidably be adjusted with the rule of maximum output, which can only be achieved by the reallocation of inputs among industry sectors. The labor force is viewed as the most vital and active element of production, and thus the reallocation of input elements among sectors will be achieved by that of labor force among industries, which results in change in the employment structure. With the fast expansion of tertiary industry, enterprises will substitute technology and human capital for labor and material capital respectively, which will guide the labor force to shift to the third industry and lead to changes in distribution of the labor force within the third industry.

The development level and change in the internal structure of the service industry

1. The development level

Firstly, we will explore how the employment level of the service industry has changed in the Yangtze River Delta over the years. As Fig. 11.2 indicates, it has increased steadily from 1992 to 2004; it has increased by 10%, from about 25% to about 35%. This shows that the service industry will provide more job opportunities year by year and more of the labor force will transfer from primary and secondary industry, which will influence the former income-distribution model. This is quite in line with the general development rule of the service industry. In the higher stage of economic development, the demand for physical products will relatively decline while that for services will relatively increase. And the service industry will provide a larger proportion of jobs among the three industries.

Fig. 11.2. The employment level in the service industry in the Yangtze River Delta over the years

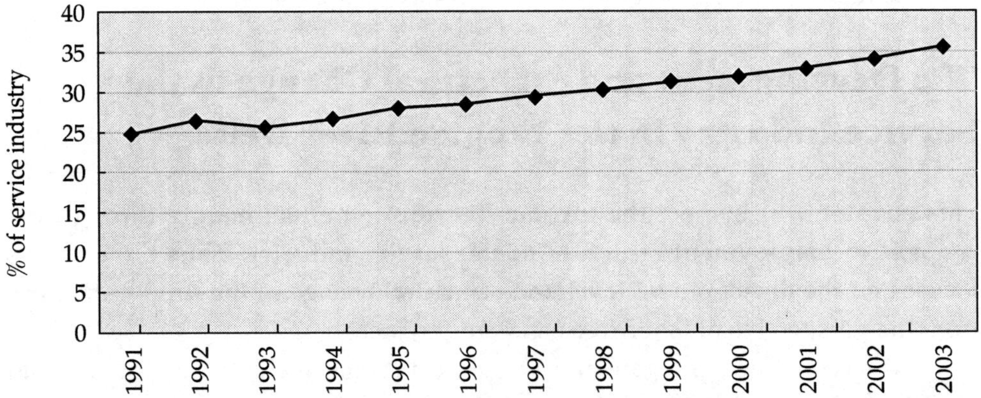

Secondly, even with the 20-year development since the reform and opening up, the employment level is lower than 43.1%, the level of OECD countries in 1960, which is related to the relatively low starting point and the present heavy industrialization.

2. The internal structure

As the proportion of employment increases in the service industry and decreases in primary and secondary industry, sectors within the service industry are undergoing employment structure changes. This chapter will analyze the employment structure before and after the year 2002 when the classification indexes of the service industry changed.

Table 11.1 indicates the employment structure before 2002. The proportion of employment increased in most sectors of the service industry from 1997 to 2002, except in transportation, storage, postal and telecommunications services and wholesale and retail and commercial services. In 1997, the employment proportion of those two types accounted for 59.33% of that of the service industry and only 27.01% in 2002, a dramatic decline.

Although they remain the mainstay of the industry which absorbs most of the labor force, their position and influence in economic growth is constantly decreasing.

Table 11.1. The service employment structure in the Yangtze River Delta (1997–2002)

Industry	1997	1998	1999	2000	2001	2002
Geological prospecting and water conservancy administration industry (%)	0.54 0.15	0.89 0.26	0.82 0.25	0.76 0.24	0.73 0.23	0.83 0.27
Transportation, storage, postal and telecommunications industry (%)	18.05 5.13	11.67 3.40	11.99 3.58	11.30 3.52	10.76 3.41	11.10 3.62
Wholesale and retail and trade industry (%)	41.28 11.72	29.46 8.58	27.03 8.10	24.90 7.75	24.05 7.62	15.91 5.19
Finance and insurance industry (%)	2.44 0.69	4.14 1.21	4.92 1.47	5.08 1.58	5.74 1.82	7.55 2.46
Real estate industry (%)	1.50 0.43	2.24 0.65	2.39 0.71	2.43 0.76	2.62 0.83	3.13 1.02
Social service industry (%)	11.68 3.32	13.18 3.84	13.91 4.17	17.05 5.31	17.60 5.57	14.54 4.74
Health, sports and welfare industry (%)	4.91 1.40	7.62 2.22	7.91 2.37	7.83 2.44	7.87 2.49	9.22 3.01
Education, culture, radio and screen industry (%)	10.94 3.11	18.03 5.25	17.91 5.36	17.66 5.50	17.80 5.64	21.75 7.09
Scientific and integrated technology service industry (%)	2.09 0.59	2.98 0.87	3.12 0.93	3.07 0.96	3.02 0.96	3.57 1.17
Official and social community (%)	6.58 1.87	9.78 2.85	10.01 3.00	9.91 3.09	9.81 3.11	12.40 4.04

Note: The data is based on the *China City Statistical Yearbook*. In each column, the first line is the employment proportion in the service industry, and the second line is that in the three industries.

The share of the finance and insurance and real estate industry (excluding the construction industry) is very small. In 2002, these two modern service industries accounted for a mere 10.68% and 3.48% in the service industry and tertiary industry respectively. However the employment growth has been remarkable in the six years. In particular, that in the finance and insurance industry has doubled. The new service industry will become the main driving force for the employment growth and development of the service industry.

The above changes show that the proportion of modern service industry increases and the traditional service decreases, and the employment structure has been upgraded and optimized from 1997 to 2002. Shifting of employees from traditional service sectors to modern ones improves the utilization efficiency of the labor force and is conductive to economic and social growth.

It also indicates that the service industry in the region does not develop as the double-peak theory suggests. Table 11.1 shows that development takes the form of expansion of high-end service industry (represented by modern service industry) accompanied by the constant decrease of the employment proportion in low-end service industry (represented by traditional service industry).

Table 11.2 shows the distribution of employees in the Yangtze River Delta in service industry and the comparison between it and the distribution of employees of all cities in the service industry. From the figure we can see: of the fifteen classifications of service industry, the top five in the Yangtze River Delta are education (19.36%), public management and social organizations (13.46%), transportation, storage and post and telecommunications (9.6%), wholesale and retail (11.24%), and health, social security and social welfare (10.45%), which accounts for 67.22% of service employees; the top five in all cities are education (27.8%), public management and social organizations (18.83%), wholesale and retail (11.37%), transportation, storage and post and telecommunications (9.69%) and health, social security and social welfare (8.11%), which accounts for 71.78% of service employees. The distribution of employees in the service industry in the Yangtze River Delta is quite in line with that in all cities. But the distribution in all cities is more centralized.

The Yangtze River Delta has many more employees than all other cities in finance, real estate, leasing and business services, scientific research, technology and geological prospecting, transportation, storage and post and telecommunications, accommodation and catering, health, social security and welfare, culture, sports and entertainment. This on the one hand shows that with the higher economic development level, producer services and the entertainment industry are more flourishing in the Yangtze River Delta than in other cities. Moreover the employment structure of the service industry in the Yangtze River Delta needs to be promoted. Traditional service industries such as accommodation and catering absorb much more labor force, while the employment proportion of modern services such as information transmission, computer services and software is relatively low, which is unfavorable to the advanced development of income distribution in the Yangtze River Delta.

Table 11.2. The distribution of employees of the Yangtze River Delta in the service industry (2004)

Project	The total employees of the Yangtze River Delta (10,000 people)	The proportion in service industry (%)	The total employees of all cities (10,000 people)	The proportion in service industry (%)
Total	551.47	100	5,734.14	100
Transportation, storage and post and telecommunications	70.11	12.71	555.8	9.69
Information transmission, computer services and software	11.60	2.10	137.6	2.40
Wholesale and retail	61.99	11.24	651.74	11.37
Accommodation and catering	23.13	4.19	195.23	3.40
Finance	42.38	7.68	340.54	5.94
Real estate	19.88	3.60	140.96	2.46
Leasing and commercial services	27.12	4.92	210.98	3.68
Scientific research, technology and geological prospecting	23.51	4.26	217.54	3.79
Water conservancy, environment and public facility administration	15.42	2.80	166.61	2.91
Residential service and other services	5.75	1.04	87.01	1.52
Education	106.77	19.36	1,363.36	23.78
Health, social security and social welfare	57.61	10.45	464.76	8.11
Culture, sports and entertainment	11.95	2.17	122.38	2.13
Public management and social organizations	74.25	13.46	1,079.63	18.83

Note: Data from *China City Statistical Yearbook 2005.*

The increase in output value of the service industry in the Yangtze River Delta

Table 11.3 shows the development trend of the output value of the service industry in the Yangtze River Delta since the reform and opening up. The output value has been increasing year by year in absolute numbers, from RMB 1.0063 million in 1978 to RMB 162.9991 million in 2006. The proportion of the service industry has grown drastically in relative terms since 1978. In 2006 the proportion of the output value in the GDP was over twice as high as in 1978. However, after 2000, it fluctuated around 40% rather than constantly increasing. The proportion in 2004 was even 2% lower than that in 2002. The reasons for the stagnation are diversified. Some hold that it has something to do with the heavy industrialization policy and stage, and the insufficient service demand caused by the income gap. Some (Baumol and Fuchs) put forward the "theory of cost disease" of the service industry. In 2006 the proportion was slightly higher than that of all cities (39.5%), but obviously lower than OECD countries (68.2% in 1995).

Table 11.3. The increase in output value of the service industry in the Yangtze River Delta

Project	1978	1990	2000	2002	2004	2006
The proportion of output value of service industry in the GDP (%)	18.37	27.16	41.02	41.91	39.54	41.3
The output value of the service industry (RMB 10,000)	100.63	653.46	6,543.97	8,374.20	11,377.36	16,299.91

Empirical Test with Income Data of the Yangtze River Delta

In this chapter, we will use the statistics of the Yangtze River Delta to test the double-peak effect of the income distribution in the service industry. The Gini coefficient of the income level of the Yangtze River Delta is used to indicate the income-distribution gap. The development of the service industry will have a positive effect on the Gini coefficient if it adds to the income inequality.

Statistics and Methods

This article shows the income inequality of the Yangtze River Delta with the Gini coefficient for the past years of the per capita disposable income of urban residents and the per capita net income of farmers. The development of the service industry is indicated by the proportion that the employees of the third industry account for in the overall labor force.

According to the Inverted U Hypothesis of Kuznets, income-distribution inequality is closely related to GDP per capita. The inequality is in proportion with GDP per capita when GDP per capita is rather low; when in a relatively higher stage of GDP per capita, the inequality is in inverse proportion to GDP per capita. The regression analysis will check the income-distribution effect of the service industry and exclude that of GDP per capita.

The regression equation is:

$$G_I = b_0 + b_1 S + b_2 \ln perGDP + b_3 (\ln perGDP)^2$$

G_I is the dependent variable; I refers to the Gini coefficient of the per capita disposable income of urban residents (1) and the per capital net income of farmers (2) respectively; S, In$perGDP$ and (In$perGDP$)^2 are independent variables; S is the proportion that employees of the third industry account for in the overall labor force, In$perGDP$ is the natural logarithm of the GDP per capita, and (In$perGDP$)^2 the square of that. The sample period is from 1994 to 2004.

The empirical results

The conclusion of the regression analysis:

$$G_1 = 79.68 - 0.72S - 55.76 \ln perGDP\ (-1.91)(-2.06) + 11.38 (\text{In} perGDP)^2\ (2.02)$$

$$\text{Adj. } R^2 = 58.55\%,\ F = 5.71 \qquad (1)$$

Figures in brackets are the t statistics of variables. All variables pass the test on the level of 10%.

$$G_2 = 57.25 - 0.49S - 39.68 \ln perGDP\ (-2.12)(-2.38) + 8.00 (\text{In} perGDP)^2\ (2.30)$$

$$\text{Adj. } R^2 = 90.00\%,\ F = 31.20 \qquad (2)$$

Figures in brackets are the t statistics of variables. All variables pass the test on the level of 10%.

The result shows that the mark before (In$perGDP$)^2 is positive in line with the hypothesis of Kuznets. The effects of GDP per capita on distribution inequality have undergone directional changes: at the comparatively low stage of economic development, the higher the GDP per capita is, the broader the income distribution gap is; however, at the relatively advanced stage of economic development, the income distribution gap narrows as the GDP per capita increases.

The coefficient of S is minus. The verse proportion between the development of the service industry and the Gini coefficient (the income inequality) shows that the development of the service industry is quite opposite to the double-peak theory: as the employment proportion of the service industry increases, the income-distribution gap narrows. This corresponds with previous analysis.

A comparison of the two regression results shows that for the coefficient of determination after reregulation, equation (2) is much higher than equation (1).This shows that the development of the service industry and the growth of GDP per capita are more closely related to the per capita income inequality of farmers than to the per capita disposable income inequality of urban residents. A possible reason is that the development of the service industry in the rural areas is accompanied by urbanization, and the growth of service employment shifts labor forces from the low-income industries such as farming, forestry, animal husbandry and fishery. However, in urban areas, the growth of service employment shifts workers from secondary industry and thus has a different effect on income distribution.

Empirical results of different industries

This chapter divides the service industry into traditional service industry and modern service industry to further examine its effect on income distribution. Because of data limitation, we just select several representative industries, such as wholesale and retail, transportation, storage and post and telecommunications in the traditional one and finance and real estate in the modern.

A. the independent variable is wholesale and retail

$G_1=-8.25+0.13S_1+1.59\ln perGDP\ (2.37)(2.82)\ -0.08(\text{In}perGDP)^2\ (-2.77)$

$\text{Adj. } R^2=79.40\%,\ F=10.00$ (3)

Figures in brackets are the t statistics of variables. All variables pass the test on the level of 10%.

$G_2=1.03+0.07S_1-0.21\ln perGDP\ (2.07)(-0.59)\ +0.01(\text{In}perGDP)^2\ (0.66)$

$\text{Adj. } R^2=62.06\%,\ F=4.82$ (4)

Figures in brackets are the t statistics of variables. All variables do not pass the test on the level of 10%.

B. the independent variables are transportation, storage and post and telecommunications

G_1=–9.38+0.002 3S_2+1.85ln*perGDP* (2.71)(3.20) (In*perGDP*)^2 (–3.17)

Adj. R^2=82.53%, *F*=12.03 (5)

Figures in brackets are the t statistics of variables. All variables pass the test on the level of 10%.

G_2=–0.23+0.0016S_2+0.059ln*perGDP* (2.07)(–0.59) –0.030(In*perGDP*)^2 (0.66)

Adj. R^2=84.96%, *F*=14.18 (6)

Figures in brackets are the *t* statistics of variables. In*perGDP* and (In*perGDP*)^2 do not pass the test on the level of 10%, but S_2 passes the test on the level of 5%.

According to the regression results of the two industries, despite the difference in number, the employment proportion of the traditional service industry is in proportion to the income distribution both of urban residents' disposable income and of farmers' per capita net income. Income distribution will tend to be more equal as the proportion of traditional service industries decreases.

C. The independent variable is real estate

G_1=–5.03–0.009 59S_3+0.982 6ln*perGDP* (–1.18)(1.63) –0.047(In*perGDP*)^2 (–1.58)

Adj. R^2=63.36%, *F*=5.03 (7)

Figures in brackets are the *t* statistics of variables. All variables do not pass the test on the level of 10%.

G_2=2.39–0.007 5S_3–0.466ln*perGDP* (–1.85)(–1.55) +0.0237(In*perGDP*)^2 (1.60)

Adj. R^2=57.70%, *F*=4.18 (8)

Figures in brackets are the *t* statistics of variables. All variables do not pass the test on the level of 10%.

D. The independent variable is finance

G_1=–5.96–0.003 1S_4+1.17ln*perGDP* (–0.64)(1.15) –0.056(In*perGDP*)^2 (–1.14)

Adj. R^2=55.11%, *F*=3.86 (9)

Figures in brackets are the *t* statistics of variables. All variables do not pass the test on the level of 10%.

G_2=2.63–0.001 33S_4–0.51ln*perGDP* (–0.46)(–0.84) +0.025 5(In*perGDP*)^2 (0.86)

Adj. R^2=25.32%, *F*=1.79 (10)

Figures in brackets are the *t* statistics of variables. All variables do not pass the test on the level of 10%.

The results of the above two sectors suggest that the mark before the employment proportion of modern service sectors is minus as expected, that is, the growth of modern service sectors reduces the income distribution inequality. But the interconnection of the two equations is relatively low and the variables do not pass the test on the level of 10%, which explains that the effect of modern service industries on income inequality is not very prominent. It may result from two kinds of influence of modern service sectors. On the one hand, the income level of the labor force in modern service industry tends to be higher, which leads to high-end centralization; on the other hand, the income of the labor force moves from low level to high level as it shifts from traditional sectors to modern ones. The interaction of the two influences leads to the unobvious effect of modern service employment growth on the income-distribution inequality.

Moreover in the finance and real estate sectors, variables are more closely related to the income distribution inequality of urban areas than of the rural areas, which shows that in rural areas, modern service industries are not responsible for changing the income-distribution model.

In a word, the development of the service industry has obviously reduced income-distribution inequality, which is the result of two forces: the decrease in the employment proportion of the traditional service sectors and the increase in that of the modern ones. Income will be distributed more equally when labor forces are shifting from traditional service sectors to modern ones.

The Action Mechanism of Service Sector Development on Income Distribution Effect

The knowledge effect

The development of the modern service sector is emerging with high technology and knowledge. Knowledge, regarded as the engine which advances productivity and economic expansion, is playing an increasingly important role in economic growth.

In the knowledge economy, economic activities are more or less based on certain knowledge. Modern service industry shows a stronger demand for knowledge as it is closely associated with highly-specialized knowledge.

Knowledge is the bridge of the income-distribution process of the modern service industry development. Knowledge elements have greatly reduced the economy's dependence on natural resources and have increased the marginal revenue year by year. The knowledge accumulation in workers and production processes mean that they become knowledge-type human capital and innovative production exploration respectively. The combination forms knowledgeable production with double benefits. So knowledge elements will bring a worker higher payment. Knowledge economy promotes the development and application of high technology. It has doubled employment opportunities and improved employment level, which is much higher than that of other industries. The expansion of modern service industry can advance the accumulation and the flow of knowledge. Modern service industry is partially responsible for the production of modern knowledge and is completely responsible for its transfer and spread.

This part section explains the effect of knowledge on the income distribution of the modern service industry by means of the distribution features of labor quality as seen from the level of education. The educational index E is derived from the data on employees' levels of education in all industries of the nation.

$$E=I_1\times 0+I_2\times 6+I_3\times 9+I_4\times 12+I_5\times 15+I_6\times 16+I_7\times 19$$

The signs from I_1 to I_7 refer to the employment proportion of seven educational levels respectively, namely, illiteracy or semi-literacy, primary school, secondary school, senior high school, college, undergraduate and postgraduate. 0, 6, 9, 12, 15, 16 and 19 are respectively their educational years.

Fig. 11.3 is the bar graph based on the educational index of all industries. The three sectors with the longest educational years all belong to the service industry, while the three with the shortest educational years all belong to primary and secondary industry. Inside the service industry, labors with rather low educational level are almost in traditional service sectors like accommodation and catering, wholesale and retail, residential and other service, transportation, storage and postal and telecommunication. Those with high educational level are in modern service sectors like education, scientific research, technological service, geological prospecting, information transmission, computer service, software, finance and real estate.

Fig. 11.3. The distribution features of quality of labor in all industries

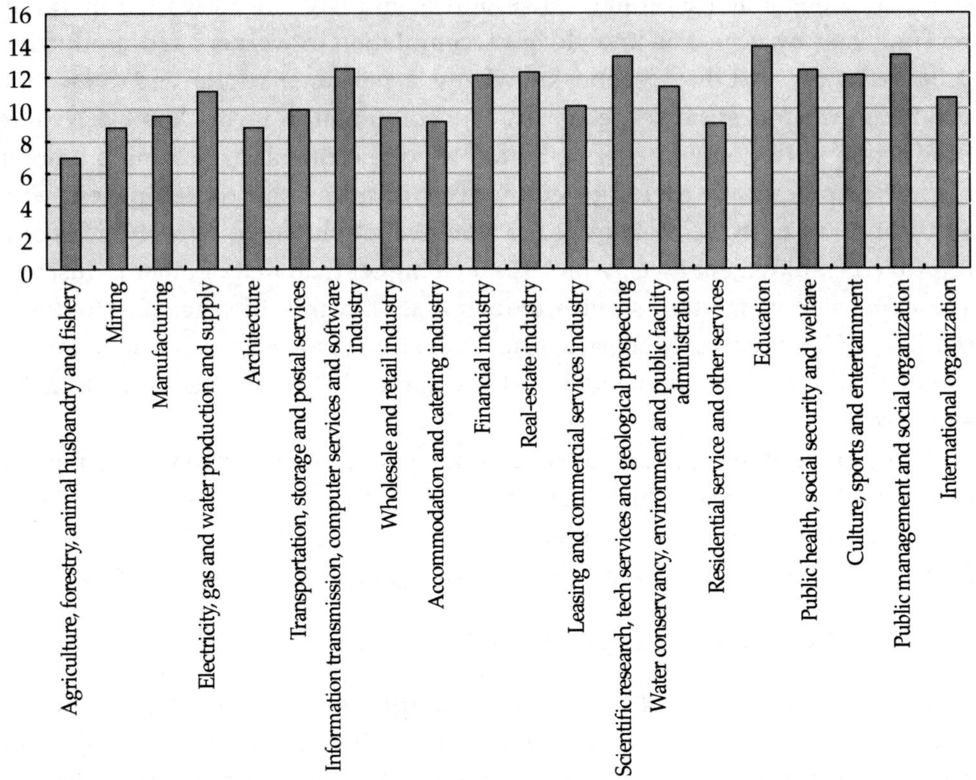

The figure shows that modern service industries with high technology and knowledge have higher requirement on employees' knowledge and techniques when recruiting new employees. Labor with low educational level and techniques have to enter traditional service industries with low requirements and payment. As they shift from primary and secondary industry to tertiary industry, labor with educational limitations is more likely to flow in to traditional service industries instead of modern ones. Although the flow can expand employment, it is obviously harmful to the upgrade of industry structure and the improvement of income level and income distribution equality.

Features of labor productivity

Baumol put forward the famous theory of "cost disease" concerning the labor productivity features of the service industry. He made a distinction between two important sectors of economic activities. One is the technology-oriented "progressive sector" in which innovation, accumulation and scale economy sustain the output growth of single capital; the second is the "nonprogressive sector" in which the labor productivity is stable and the production increases the output of single capital. To his mind, production, in the nonprogressive sector is the final product and there is no room for capital and technology development. The service industry is the representative. In the progressive sector labor is one of the production inputs and capital and technology can bring great increase of productivity, which is typical of manufacturing.

But Baumol only conducted isolated research on the productivity growth of the service industry and neglected the fact that the service industry and especially the modern service industry promoted the productivity growth of agriculture and industry. For example, although it has certain regularities and cannot bring a great leap in productivity, scientific research services play an important role in advancing the productivity of material production. He also ignored the fact that the development of information and technology can increase the productivity of the service industry.

Other sectors such as manufacturing can raise productivity by consuming service products. But the growth in productivity cannot be measured within the service industry. Nusbaumer (1987) holds that service industry sustains the operation of the whole economic system. Service input is accounting for an increasing proportion in the price of material objects. The producer service industry, in particular, plays a significant role in the economic growth. Herbert G. Grubel and Michael A. Walker (1989) found with research that since World War II, the economic growth of developed countries owes mostly to producer services or intermediate input services.

The form of specialization

Production factors are vital in production activities and for creating material wealth. Production activity is a periodic dynamic process which is constantly circulating and expanding. Individual income distribution means that investors like producers and managers in economic practice participate in output distribution on the basis of the amount of invested factors, the degree of scarcity and the real output rate. The history of economic development shows that the human factor was not fully developed in the age both of agriculture and industry. In the agricultural age, human strength and land were the most important production factors. And a flourishing population is crucial to economic growth. In the industrial age, capital, energy and machinery are the most important production factors. However with the exploration of resources and use of machinery, a great number of laborers leave their land and become workers who take up material production beside machines. Mental labor and manual labor are then divided, and mental production is only the patent of the minority. Since the 1950s, with the gradual rise of the knowledge-intensive economy, the source of economic expansion has been gradually shifting from land, capital and labor to labor, capital, technology, knowledge, intellectual, management and education. With the accumulation of knowledge and the application of technology, people can not only gain through labor input but also be paid much more through knowledge and technology input.

Compartmentalization and specialization facilitate the birth of the modern service industry. Market integration and the growth of market capacity, and specialization and diversity of enterprises, have something to do with this. As social division develops towards high specialization and integration, service-oriented labor is separated from production departments and becomes independent and multi-level social service departments of various kinds. The independence, information and standardization of service industry gives it a new face. And the multi-level structure of the service industry needs labor of different qualities. Compartmentalization and specialization highlight the role of modern service industry as the main employment channel. Beneficial interaction has been formed between the development of modern service industry and employment of labor of high quality. According to Stigler, the activities of a company conclude many functions. Compartmentalization and specialization mean those functions are separated from the company and are undertaken by other specialized enterprises. With the growth of the economy and the deepening of division, services which was provided by companies or families in the past can be purchased on the market. There is no difference between the amount of service, but the service is market-oriented. Moreover the increase of specialization brings in high-quality service and low average cost, which adds to the demand and production of those services. Compartmentalization and specialization can help enterprises decrease cost and centralize core business and efficiency of production and trade. Trade efficiency plays a vital role in the evolution of division and the growth of the economy: the lower the coefficient of trade cost, the higher the level of division, which is otherwise lower. Division evolves with the improvement of trade efficiency. The rise and development of modern service industry, which are closely related to the development of information technology and knowledge-intensive economy, are results of specialization and industrial division from the perspective of industrial development. As the division becomes more complicated, the level of specialization increases and the outflanking producing chains of service industry are lengthened. The middle products and the productivity increase on each chain. With the appearance of new technology, there is a growth of commercialization, trade dependence and the diversification of economic structure in the service industry. New service sectors are gradually splitting up the former ones.

Generally speaking, compartmentalization and specialization lead to the separation of modern service industry from the traditional one and its independence, which will disturb the former and even the distribution pattern and enlarge the income distribution gap. An income-distribution system must admit the existence of income gaps resulting from the differences between divisions, specialized production and comparative interests. At the same time, the development of service industry in the Yangtze River Delta, as previously described, has not obviously enlarged the income distribution, which may be a result of the low-income stage, the leading role of traditional agricultural sectors in the national economy, simple economic structure, less industries and greater homogeneity of labor. Income would not be widened with slight labor differences. With economic growth, the modern sectors are expanding gradually; the structure of industries, specialization and occupations will become more complicated and diverse. Consequently there is a growth in the differences of labor and the differences of work efficiency, work quality and income. However, at the advanced stage of economic growth, industry structure is more diversified and the division is more complicated. More sophisticated labor is needed. The differences of labor will decrease as will the income gap. The service industry of the Yangtze River Delta is perhaps in the latter stage.

It is better to support new modern sectors, regulate sunset industries, rationalize the patterns of industrial sectors and enterprises and income distribution, and optimize resource allocation by means of the reasonable transformation of industry structure as guided by industrial polices.

The incentive effect

Income distribution not only can result in equality, but also can spur efficiency. Human capital, with the modern enterprise system, is playing an increasingly important role in creating value and is also a stimulus for the advance in knowledge and technology. Knowledge and technology, the result of innovation, is crucial to modern economic development. The system of income distribution can stimulate knowledge and technology innovation. The effects of modern service industry on income distribution should be conducive to spur the formation of human capital, the increasing growth of individual investment of human capital and the long-term development of our economy. They are also helpful in promoting labor's enthusiasm for innovation and creation and the store of human capital to create more profits and arouse public attention about knowledge. In a knowledge-intensive age, the profits of human capital are mainly from knowledge which is the product of education and innovation of study. Consequently, distribution effect can promote educational development. Income gap results in competition for jobs offering relative high payment. The competition, one the one hand, expands the supply of high-quality elements of some high-profit sectors. Moreover, it encourages those in high-profit sectors to work harder in case they should be replaced by newcomers. It also impels enterprises to make innovations in products and technology. As the effect of income distribution deepens, income distribution, in a market economy, is playing a increasing role as an incentive effect. To sum up, there are three kinds of incentives for individuals which stem from the income gap. Firstly, it directly improves the enthusiasm of individuals in their producing activities. Secondly, it encourages them to be selective and search for new employment or vacations. Thirdly, it provides information on income from different jobs, spurs competition in job selection, and further sustains competition in the investment of human capital to cultivate self quality and specialized technology.

The incentive effect can be discussed from four aspects. Firstly, it arouses the enthusiasm of labor. The income gap is the unavoidable result of the corresponding gap between labor efficiency and payment. Income increase means that the efficiency of labor invested by workers improves, which stimulates them to devote more to economic activities to achieve more payment and so enhances employment. Secondly, the efficiency incentive strengthens awareness of market competition and encourages some workers to innovate and to take risks. Efficiency and payment correspond in distribution and the income gap brought by this correspondence is well admitted. As a result industry, innovation and risks become the primary channels in economic activities and the rational and effective way to gain payment. In a practical economy, the phenomenon is marked by labor and more high-quality skills flow into sectors and enterprises with good benefits to advance the expansion of the national economy. Thirdly, the efficiency incentive strengthens the initiative to actively invest human capital. Efficiency and payment correspond in the process of distribution, which inevitably means that the distribution structure favors high-quality intellectuals and decreases the demand for ordinary labor. This on the one hand encourages laborers to positively add human capital input to pursue high income; and spurs them to study and train in colleges and universities to enhance their human capital cost. The efficiency of human capital is also improved, and so is the income. On the other hand, it provides much more high-quality skilled personnel for future economic growth and the factors necessary for producing technological sophistication and the advanced development of industries. Fourthly, the efficiency incentive stimulates workers to gradually transform their labor income into non-labor producing factors as the income increases, aiming at accumulating non-labor factors for economic expansion. In the current stage, non-labor productive elements are rarer than labor elements. The earning brought by non-labor elements is much higher than that brought by labor elements; the growth speed of non-labor elements is much faster than that of labor elements. This encourages workers to input labor and transform their earnings into non-labor productive elements which will be invested in economic activities to advance economic growth.

The development of the service industry, especially the modern service industry, causes changes in income distribution, which brings an incentive effect. Income distribution starts from benefits, so it provides impetus for the subjects of economic benefits to achieve maximum benefits. Income distribution, through the distribution and redistribution of interests, provides great material incentive for producers, consumers and government, which improves the enthusiasm and creativity, vigor and efficiency of economic activities. Changes in the income distribution pattern contribute to the competition of interest classes centering on high and low economic interests and interest differences. Competition will be center on high-income industries and sectors to gain higher payment with the investment of production elements. The production elements in modern service industry will be allocated more efficiently by survival of the fittest. Production elements shift from industries of low income to those of high income. Modern service industry rises while traditional ones declines, thus meaning that production elements throughout the whole service industry will be distributed more efficiently.

Conclusions

1. Since the 1990s, the Yangtze River Delta has seen a rapid growth of the service industry and the employment proportion of modern service industry, while that of the traditional service industry decreases. However the development level is more backward than that of international level. The absolute and relative amounts of modern service industry are still low.

2. In the Yangtze River Delta, the service industry has led to a more equal income-distribution trend. The decrease of employment in traditional service

industry has remarkably reduced the inequality of income distribution. But the modern service industry has not obviously improved income distribution.

3. Knowledge and technology have played crucial roles both in the development of modern service industry and income distribution. Employees in modern service industry have a higher educational level than those in traditional ones. Correspondingly they account for more shares in income distribution.

4. Compartmentalization and specialization facilitate both the emergence and development of the modern service industry. Employees are separated from former industries which reduces trade cost, advances economic efficiency and leads to the gap in income distribution. The gap, which is caused by compartmatmentalization and specialization, cannot be denied. Due to its unique features in economic transition, compartmatmentalization and specialization undoubtedly result in the enlargement of the income gap.

Policy Recommendations

1. Market readjustment should be given full play. Income distribution should be regulated. Production factors should be effectively allocated to increase the economic interests of the society as a whole. The efficiency of production-factor allocation should be maximized to increase the amount of income distribution as much as possible. The maximum economic benefits provided by the mainstay represented by the market, which efficiently allocates production factors, should be maintained.

2. Positive industrial policies should be implemented. Traditional service should be transformed to expand the modern service industry. New technology, which is applied in traditional service industry, has effectively promoted its technological and knowledge content, economic growth and income distribution. Meanwhile control of modern service industry should be reduced to absorb more labor force.

3. Educational investment and labor quality should be increased. Educational services should be provided. The knowledge-intensive economy has changed industry structure and has deeply impacted on labor structure and character. The income of those who go in for knowledge innovation is multiplied. The income gap between different labor is widened. Labor quality and the ability of knowledge employment and innovation must be strengthened to narrow the gap.

4. The benefits brought by compartmentalization and specialization should

be encouraged. The transforming characteristics of the effects of the service industry on income distribution should be known. The enlargement of the income gap, which is caused by compartmentalization and specialization, should be controlled.

12

Chapter

Employment Effects due to Service Sector Development in the Yangtze River Delta

Introduction

The Yangtze River Delta has always played an important role in absorbing the labor force. A large number of redundant labor forces in rural areas outside this region have worked here for life, some of which have shifted from agriculture to non-agricultural industry in the region. So far, the manufacturing industry has absorbed most of the labor force. However, with the springing up of the service industry in this region, its absorption capacity has been increasingly enhanced.

The development level of the service industry is a key marker of the degree of the economic development and modernization of a region. Since the service industry, which has various kinds of sectors, is labor, capital and technical intensive, it has an enormous capacity to absorb labor forces. Generally speaking, the output value and employees in developed countries or regions account for about 70% of its GDP and the total labor forces respectively.[1] Recently, the proportion of the output value of the service industry has constantly increased in the Yangtze River Delta. In 2006 the industry structure of this region was 5.4: 53.9: 40.7 while it was 19.6: 61.3: 19.1 in 1978. Meanwhile, the number of the employees in the service industry has risen substantially to 30.96 million in 2006 from 12.75 million in 1990. The proportion of employees in the service industry rose from 16.9% in 1990 to 36% in 2006.[2] There are some optimistic views in domestic academic circles that the service industry in the Yangtze River Delta has large room for development and it is gradually replacing manufacturing industry as the main sector to absorb labor forces.[3]

According to the experience of economic development in developed countries, the proportion of employment in the service industry will exceed that in the manufacturing industry. However for the Yangtze River Delta, is now a turning period? What are the prospects for its development and its employment proportion in the future? It is of substantial importance to analyze these issues in order to get a better understanding of the employment market trend as well as to solve problems in the development of service industry.

The Development of the Service Industry and Employment: A Theoretical Review

The rules of the changes in the proportion of employment in the service industry

As early as the 17th century William Petty, an English classical socialist and economist, argued in his masterwork Political Arithmetic that manufacturing would make the most profit, followed by commerce and agriculture. The income gap is a result of the free flow of labor forces between different industries, which urges them to shift to the industry where they can earn more wages. There are also a number of economists conducting theoretical analysis of the evolution of industry structure and the industrial distribution of labor forces. According to the data of time order of the input and output of labor forces in over twenties countries, Clark concludes in his book entitled *The Condition for the Economic Advancement* that the rules of the distribution and shift of labor forces among the three industries in economic development is that as the per capita national income increases, labor forces shift from the primary industry to the secondary, and then to the tertiary when it further improves. When it comes to the distribution of labor forces among the three industries, their proportion in primary industry falls gradually and rises in secondary industry and in the third industry in particular. This point of view is defined as the "Petty Clark Theorem." According to the Theorem, in the countries or regions with a higher per capita national income, the labor force in agriculture accounts for a small proportion of the total labor force compared with the proportion in the second and third industry. In the countries or regions with a lower per capita national income. The opposite is true.

Based on the research results Simon Kuznets, a renowned American economist, conducted empirical analysis of the evolution of national incomes and the distribution structure of labor forces in many countries through much research on the historical economic data. His research results confirm the effectiveness of the Petty Clark Theorem. Chenery, former president of the World Bank and economist, draws a conclusion in line with empirical analysis that with the increase in per capita income, the proportion of employment in the service industry will constantly rise. He believes it is the universal trend in the change in employment structure in every country.

The rules of change in employment structure among various types of service industry

The service industry consists of various types, such as the labor-intensive, technical-intensive, capital-intensive and knowledge-intensive sectors. As their needs for labor forces vary from each other, their capacities of absorbing labor forces are also different. Simon Kuznets points out in his book *Modern Economic Growth* that in the process of economic growth, the amount of labor forces absorbed by commerce and other service industries constantly and orderly increases. The commercial and financial industries are the biggest sectors of the service industry, followed by private services and government departments. Through research on the trend of employment proportion change among various types of service industry in European Community countries during 1963 to 1978, Gershuny and Miles (1983) find that the proportion of employment in the producer service industry and those sectors providing terminal services in a non-market way, such as educational, medical and health care, social welfare and governmental services enjoy a rapid rise, and that other service sectors show little change if not decreasing.

Domestic research on the development of the service industry

The domestic academic world also gives a high priority to research on the service industry. Relatively speaking, they agree on the research method, that is, the service industry will play a key role in absorbing labor forces. For example, through the analysis of input of labor forces in tertiary industry, Li Jiangfan (2003) believes that the rapid development of the third industry helps to absorb more labor forces, compared with the primary and secondary ones. By measuring the elasticity of employment in the service industry, Zhang Shujun (2006) argues that the service industry is the main channel for absorbing labor forces. Although there is little research on the elasticity of employment in the Yangtze River Delta, the domestic academic circle has obtained some results from research on the elasticity of employment in the regional economy and the conclusions they draw are close to those for the whole nation. For example, by measuring the elasticity of tertiary industry to absorb labor force in Guangdong province, Wei Zuolei (2003) concludes that the third industry maintains a high capacity for absorbing labor forces, ranking first; by computing the elasticity of absorbing labor force in each type of the third industry he believes that some industries make a much greater contribution toward increasing employment, such as the residential service industry, financial and insurance industry, real estate industry, public service, wholesale and retail services, catering, health care, sports, and social welfare industries, educational, cultural, art and radio and television industries. Thus he proposes that these industries be given more priority in order to promote employment in Guangdong. However he draws this conclusion in accordance with the elastic analysis without in-depth reasoning.

In my opinion, the industry structure in the Yangtze River Delta is distinct from both that of developed countries and that of other industries in our country, and the employment increase has a close relationship with the change in its industry structure. Therefore through investigating its industry structure and the internal structure of the service industry, I will try to find out the inherent reasons and make clear the potential for employment increase in the service industry.

The Service Industry and Its Employment Structure in the Yangtze River Delta

This chapter focuses on the course of development and the current situation in the employment market in the Yangtze River Delta in terms of statistical data as well as analyzing the characteristics of the changes in the employment market. All of the data in this section is computed from data in the statistical yearbooks of Jiangsu and Zhejiang as well as Shanghai for the relevant years.

The rapid development of the service industry in the Yangtze River Delta

In recent years, the service industry in the Yangtze River Delta has shown a good momentum of development and is moving ahead at a better rate than the secondary industry.[4] In particular from 1990 to 2000 the added value of the service industry increased by 23.5% annually, 4.5% higher than that of secondary industry. The output of service industry increased from RMB 87.533 billion in 1990 to RMB 1,931.03 billion in 2006, accounting for 40.7% of all of the three kinds of industries. Fig. 12.1 shows the changes in structure of the three industries from 1978 to 2006 and the gradually rising service industry in the Yangtze River Delta.

Table 12.1 exhibits the output of the service industry and its proportion in the GDP in the Yangtze River Delta and the three major administrative districts from 1978 to 2006. The service industry in Shanghai is the most flourishing, and in 2006 the total value of its output reached RMB 20.5 billion, accounting for over 50% in the total of the three industries. Since 2000, although the output value of the service industry in Jiangsu has always been greater than that in Zhejiang, its proportion in 2006 was only 36.28%, ranking last among the three administrative districts and 4% lower than that in Zhejiang. All of the above demonstrates that the development of the service industry in the Yangtze River Delta is imbalanced.

The employment proportion of the service industry and manufacturing industry

The development of the service industry in the Yangtze River Delta has led to constantly rising employment. Workers employed in the service industry increased from 9.637 million in 1985 to 30.96 million in 2006. The growth rate of employment in the service industry is 5.7%, 3.3% higher than that in the

Fig. 12.1. The changes in structure of the three industries in the Yangtze River Delta

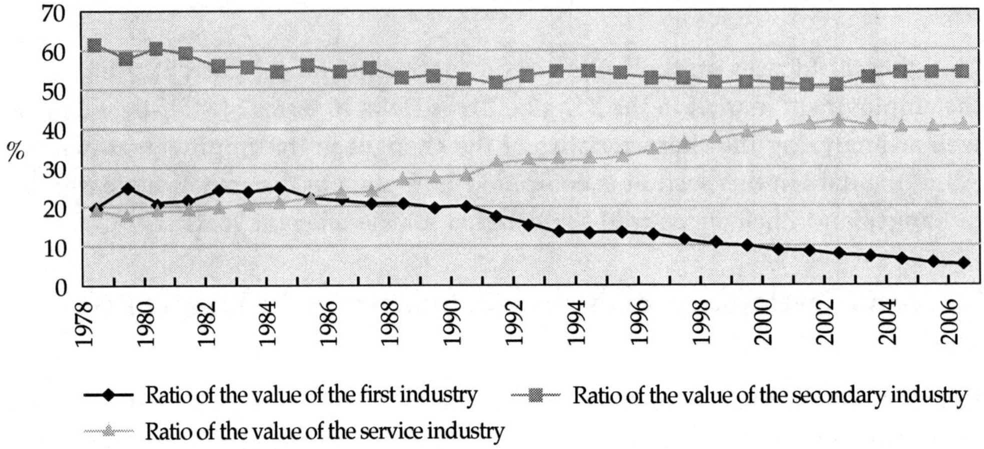

Source: The author has calculated using the statistical yearbooks of Shanghai, Jiangsu and Zhejiang and statistical bulletins of the domestic economy and social development of Shanghai, Jiangsu and Zhejiang in 2006.

Table 12.1. The change in output value of the service industry in the Yangtze River Delta and its proportion in the GDP (1978–2006)

Year	The Yangtze River Delta		Shanghai		Jiangsu		Zhejiang	
	The output value of the service industry (RMB 100 million)	Proportion (%)	The output value of the service industry (RMB 100 million)	Proportion (%)	The output value of the service industry (RMB 100 million)	Proportion (%)	The output value of the service industry (RMB 100 million)	Proportion (%)
1978	123.31	19.10	50.76	18.61	49.44	19.84	23.11	18.68
1979	133.21	17.94	53.83	18.79	53.37	17.88	26.01	16.50
1980	154.84	19.08	65.69	21.06	58.15	18.18	31.00	17.25
1981	173.17	19.70	69.84	21.51	62.62	17.89	40.71	19.91
1982	194.03	20.20	74.44	22.08	69.50	17.81	50.09	21.46
1983	219.62	21.00	82.97	23.58	76.43	17.46	60.22	23.50
1984	263.87	21.42	98.22	25.13	59.46	17.24	76.19	23.66
1985	342.90	22.18	121.59	26.05	116.60	17.89	104.71	24.49
1986	412.36	23.76	135.12	27.53	144.36	19.38	132.88	26.57
1987	504.09	24.33	159.48	29.24	181.78	19.71	162.83	26.97
1988	706.43	26.93	187.89	28.98	302.85	25.05	215.69	28.17

1989	787.86	27.53	200.73	28.82	340.61	25.77	246.52	29.22
1990	875.33	28.27	241.82	30.94	368.74	26.03	264.77	29.48
1991	1,113.81	31.14	309.07	34.58	462.32	28.87	342.42	31.65
1992	1,474.67	31.95	402.77	36.14	622.94	29.16	448.96	32.89
1993	2,099.78	32.67	579.03	38.11	909.52	30.34	611.23	32.01
1994	2,816.37	32.32	794.80	39.92	1,186.64	29.25	834.93	31.31
1995	3,724.47	33.32	1,020.20	40.82	1,573.75	30.53	1,130.52	32.07
1996	4,569.71	34.86	1,292.11	43.69	1,940.91	32.33	1,336.69	32.24
1997	5,316.62	36.03	1,592.74	46.32	2,232.68	33.42	1,491.20	32.15
1998	6,015.16	37.62	1,855.36	48.81	2,512.69	34.90	1,647.11	33.02
1999	6,700.04	38.84	2,129.60	50.84	2,740.30	35.60	1,830.14	34.11
2000	7,745.03	40.00	2,486.86	52.12	3,069.46	35.88	2,188.71	36.26
2001	8,777.09	40.99	2,728.94	52.38	3,454.90	36.53	2,593.25	38.43
2002	10,050.82	41.63	3,038.90	52.93	3,891.92	36.69	3,120.00	40.02
2003	11,623.50	40.74	3,404.19	50.85	4,493.31	36.11	3,726.00	39.66
2004	13,677.29	39.85	4,097.26	50.75	5,198.03	34.65	4,382.00	38.98
2005	16,488.93	40.32	4,620.92	50.48	6,489.14	35.45	5,378.87	40.03
2006	19,310.30	40.66	5,205.30	50.55	7,817.00	36.28	6,288.00	40.18

Source: The author has calculated using the statistical yearbooks of Shanghai, Jiangsu and Zhejiang and statistical bulletins of the domestic economy and social development of Shanghai, Jiangsu and Zhejiang in 2006. The output value in each year is a comparable one.

whole society. The service industry is playing an increasingly significant role in absorbing the work force, which can be seen from Fig. 12.2. In the course of its evolution, the employment structure in the Yangtze River Delta has also changed: the number of the employees in primary industry and the proportion has decreased substantially; the number of employees in secondary industry has increased to some extent but remains stable; the proportion of employment in the service industry has enjoyed a big rise, from 15% in 1985 to 36% in 2006. It should be noted that the employment proportion of the service industry kept rising at a high speed before 2001 while that in secondary industry enjoyed a high but not stable employment proportion. After 2001 the employment proportion of the service industry rose approximately to the level of that in secondary industry but did not surpass it. As the proportion of secondary industry in the GDP is much higher than that of the service industry, the absolute number of employees in secondary industry exceeds that in the service industry by a large margin. Therefore secondary industry is still playing a leading role in the Yangtze River Delta.

Fig. 12.2. The change in the employment structure of the three industries in the Yangtze River Delta

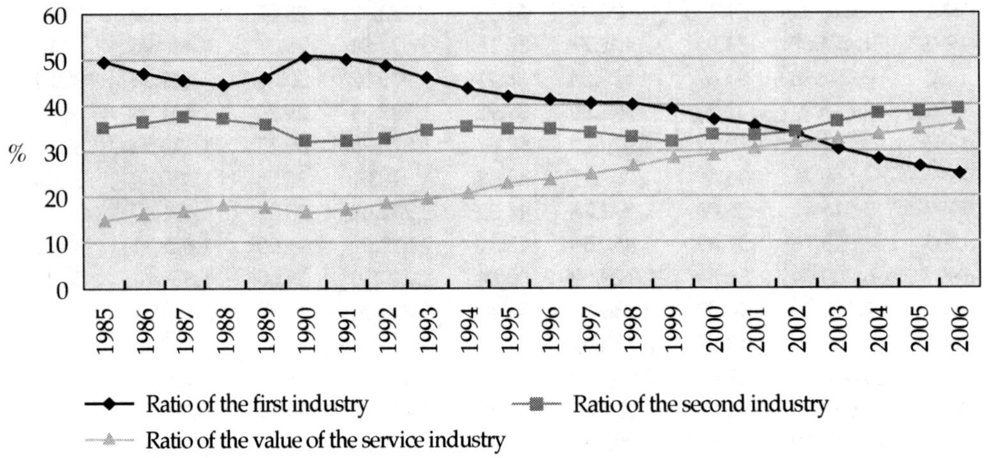

Source: The author calculated using the statistical yearbooks of Shanghai, Jiangsu and Zhejiang and statistical bulletins of the domestic economy and social development of Shanghai, Jiangsu and Zhejiang in 2006.

The factor which drives the growth in the employment proportion of the service industry is that the service industry absorbs the work force from the other two industries, which can be ascribed to three reasons: first, the enhanced productivity in agriculture and some manufacturing sectors leads to surplus work force that may join the service industry; second, the development of the economy in our country and the increased need drives the supply of service products and the development of the service industry enlarges the employment scale; third, as some modern service industries such as financial, legal and consulting services emerge, both the high degree of knowledge intensiveness and the handsome salary attract a large number of high-quality people, which is not an excluding but an absorbing effect of the modern service industry as well as the result of the active transfer of labor.

The Number of Employees Absorbed into Modern Service Industry Is on the Increase

Among the various types of service industry in the Yangtze River Delta, the traditional labor-intensive service industries such as wholesale and retail industry, accommodation and catering industry etc. still make up a high employment proportion. The service industry in Shanghai is the most developed in the Yangtze River Delta and thus we take it as the example to investigate the change in the internal structure of service industry. As shown in Table 12.2, the number of employees in the wholesale and retail industry in Shanghai reached 1.3131 million in 2005, the largest number within the service industry. However, after years of development, the capacity of the traditional service industry to absorb the labor force has reached saturation point. The number of employees in the accommodation and catering industry changed little in the preceding three years and its employment proportion even decreased slightly. All this demonstrates that the capacity of the traditional service industry to absorb the work force is tending to weaken.

Table 12.2. The number of employees in all types of the service industry in Shanghai and its employment structure (the proportion of its employees in the total work force) from 2003 to 2005

Item	The number of employees (10,000)			The proportion of employees in the total work force (%)		
	2003	2004	2005	2003	2004	2005
The total of the service industry	422.22	453.61	479.97	51.93	54.20	55.60
Transportation, storage and postal services	45.90	47.70	48.40	5.65	5.70	5.61
Information transmission, computer and software services	7.10	7.85	9.48	0.87	0.94	1.10
Wholesale and retail service	113.80	125.53	131.31	14.00	15.00	15.21
Accommodation and catering service	23.51	23.05	23.60	2.89	2.75	2.73
Financial service	17.32	15.92	18.24	2.13	1.90	2.11
Real-estate service	28.87	28.94	28.96	3.55	3.46	3.35
Leasing and commercial service	21.60	38.11	45.87	2.66	4.55	5.31
Scientific research, tech service and geological prospecting	12.40	13.35	15.23	1.52	1.60	1.76
Water conservancy, environment and public facility administration	7.72	6.70	6.74	0.95	0.80	0.78
Residential service and other services	73.43	74.73	78.3	9.03	8.93	9.07
Education	27.54	27.30	27.63	3.39	3.26	3.20
Public health, social security and welfare	16.33	17.67	18.29	2.01	2.11	2.12
Culture, sports and entertainment	8.14	8.28	8.25	1.00	0.99	0.96
Public management and social organization	18.56	18.48	19.67	2.28	2.21	2.28

Source: The author calculated based on the data in the *Shanghai Statistical Yearbook 2006*.

In contrast with the sluggish development of the traditional service industry, the modern service industry has developed at a high speed. The modern service industry, based on information technology and modern management ideas, emerged at a time when industrialization has entered an advanced stage. It is a knowledge-intensive and technology-intensive industry, mainly including financial services, information services, leasing and commercial services, logistics and real-estate industry etc. As shown in Fig. 12.2, the number of employees absorbed into such modern service industries as information transmission, computer services and software industry, real-estate industry, and leasing and commercial services shows a rising tendency. The leasing and commercial services industry has enjoyed a particularly rapid development. In just two years the number of employees increased from 216,000 in 2003 to 4,587,000 in 2005, and the employment proportion rose from 2.66–5.31%. Although the development of modern service industry of the Yangtze River Delta headed by Shanghai is still in the initial stage, it has shown a huge potential for absorbing the work force.

The Internal Structure of the Service Industry and Its Employment Structure

The employment structure of the service industry in the Yangtze River Delta lags far behind that of the developed countries. Take Shanghai as an example. In 2005, the employment proportion of the service industry was 55.59% (see Table 12.2), while in most developed countries, it was about 75% (see Table 12.5). This general backwardness is a concentrated expression of the gap between each type of service industry.

Table 12.3. The structure of the output value within the service industry of the Yangtze River Delta in 2005 (the total output value is 100%)

Various types of the service industry	Ratio (%)
Transportation, storage and postal services	11.14
Information transmission, computer services and software industry	6.03
Wholesale and retail industry	23.75
Accommodation and catering industry	4.10
Financial industry	11.60
Real-estate industry	12.75
Leasing and commercial services industry	4.50
Scientific research, tech services and geological prospecting	2.74
Water conservancy, environment and public facility administration	1.20
Residential service and other services	3.00
Education	7.23
Public health, social security and welfare	3.37
Culture, sports and entertainment	1.50
Public management and social organization	7.09

Source: The author had calculated according to the statistical yearbooks of Shanghai, Jiangsu and Zhejiang and statistical bulletins of the domestic economy and social development of Shanghai, Jiangsu and Zhejiang in 2006.

Table 12.4. The structure of the output value within the service industry of America from 2000 to 2003 (the total output value is 100%)

Various types of the service industry	2000	2001	2002	2003
Whole-sale and retail, motor vehicle, private and household goods repairing services	17.00%	16.81%	16.95%	16.73%
Accommodation and catering	3.54%	3.44%	3.46%	3.43%
Transportation, storage and communications	8.63%	8.28%	7.95%	7.93%
Financial brokerage	10.04%	10.13%	10.13%	10.44%
Real-estate, leasing and commercial activities	31.77%	31.82%	31.42%	31.12%
Public management, national defense and social basic security	9.42%	9.46%	9.62%	9.73%
Education	6.39%	6.48%	6.55%	6.51%
Public health and social work	8.12%	8.47%	8.76%	8.94%
Other services for organizations, society and individuals	4.91%	4.96%	5.01%	5.01%
Private residents hiring people	0.18%	0.17%	0.15%	0.16%

Source: The author has calculated using the data in the *International Statistical Yearbook 2005*.

Table 12.5. The employment structure within the service industry in some developed countries (the employment proportion of each type of the service industry in the whole society)

Various types of the service industry	UK	Australia	Canada	US
The total of the service industry	75.32%	75.00%	74.74%	75.62%
Whole-sale and retail, motor vehicle, private and household goods repairing services	15.59%	20.07%	17.30%	20.59%
Accommodation and catering	4.28%	4.92%	6.49%	
Transportation, storage and communication	6.96%	6.34%	7.13%	6.02%
Financial brokerage	4.42%	3.67%	4.22%	12.22%
Real-estate, leasing and commercial activities	11.09%	12.04%	11.93%	
Public management, national defense and social basic security	6.85%	5.84%	5.16%	36.79%
Education	8.55%	7.21%	6.67%	
Public health and social work	11.51%	9.85%	10.69%	
Other services for organizations, society and individuals	5.52%	5.02%	4.66%	
Private residents hiring people	0.50%	0.03%	0.47%	
Organizations and institutions outside the country	0.05%	0.01%	0.01%	

Source: The author has calculated using the data in the *International Statistical Yearbook 2005.*

From the comparison between Tables 12.3 and 12.4, we can see that there are great defects in the service industry of the Yangtze River Delta compared with the US.

For example, as shown in Table 12.3, the proportion of real-estate, leasing and commercial services which represent the modern service industry of the Yangtze River Delta is only 17.25% of the total output value of service industry while it is 31.12% in US as shown in Table 12.4. As shown in Tables 12.2 and 12.5, the proportion of real-estate, leasing and commercial services in Shanghai, the most developed city in the Yangtze Rive Delta, is only 8.66%, and it can be assumed that the general status in the Yangtze River Delta is worse than that; while the proportion in most of the developed countries reaches 12%. This is not a coincidence for the low level of output value inevitably leads to its low employment proportion. In other words, the sluggish development of major types of the modern service industry constrains the employment proportions of service industry in Shanghai. In addition, the employment structure of traditional service industries in Shanghai such as the whole-sale and retail, accommodation, and catering are approximate to that in the UK and US. However, those of modern service industries, such as education, hygiene, social security and welfare lag far behind the developed countries.

Because the emerging industries such as real-estate, leasing and commercial service in the Yangtze River Delta got off to a late start, it is not difficult for us to accept that such industries lag behind those in developed countries. From Table 12.1, however, we can see that since 1999 the service industry structure in the Yangtze River Delta has fluctuated at around 40% of the GDP for seven years. If this situation freezes here for ever or for a stage, the modern service industry of the Yangtze River Delta will not gain great further development. Then we have to admit that there are problems in the internal structure of the service industry in the Yangtze River Delta, which causes the low employment proportion of service industry.

Analysis of Employment Elasticity and Structure Deviation of the Service Industry in the Yangtze River Delta

Analysis of employment elasticity

The employment elasticity referred to here is the ratio of the employment growth rate to economic growth rate. That is, suppose there are no other factors varied, the percentage of the change in the employees keeps pace with one percent point of economic growth. Employment elasticity is a key index for measuring to what degree the economic growth drives the employment effect. The higher the employment elasticity is, the more the economic growth can attract work force and the stronger its effect drives employment. The employment elasticity can be exhibited in the following formula:

$$E = \frac{\Delta L/L}{\Delta Y/Y}$$

of which Y represents the GDP and ΔY represents the growth rate of economy.

Fig. 12.3 shows the employment elasticity in three industries from 1986 to 2006, from which we can see that the employment elasticity of agriculture is not steady and even has a negative value during many years. It means that the agriculture does not absorb work force, instead it sheds a lot of surplus work force. Since the 1980s, the employment elasticity of manufacturing has remained stable at a certain level just as the service industry does after 2002. Manufacturing has always been the main impetus for the economic expansion in the Yangtze River Delta. Although the momentum towards development of manufacturing has not weakened in recent years, manufacturing does not intend to absorb more work force with the advancement of the technology, the rise of the knowledge intensiveness, and the adjustment of the industry structure. The employment elasticity of the service industry has had a slight change since 2002 and the elasticity curves of the service industry and manufacturing basically overlap.

In fact the employment elasticity varies in different countries and at different stages of development. Generally speaking, with the advancement of the economy and the improvement of productivity, the employment elasticity will drop. Economic growth will lead to the enhancement of productivity, which is determined by either technical advancement or change in employment structure in accordance with the economic structure. In the first case, one worker can finish the work that needed two workers so the employment elasticity will certainly drop. In the other case, if the capital-intensive industries grow faster than that the labor-intensive ones, the employment elasticity will also go down.

Fig. 12.3. Comparison of the employment elasticity of three industries in the Yangtze River Delta

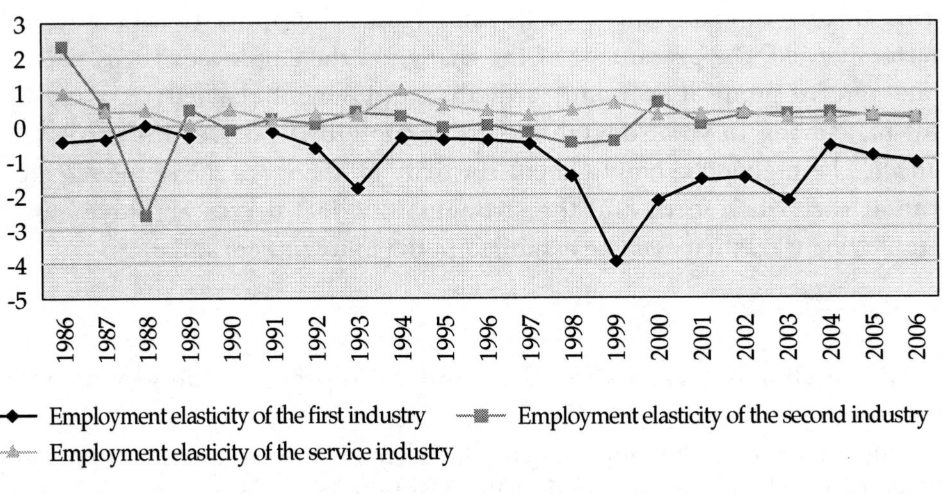

Source: The author calculated using the statistical yearbooks of Shanghai, Jiangsu and Zhejiang and statistical bulletins of the domestic economy and social development of Shanghai, Jiangsu and Zhejiang in 2006.

There is another case as for the reduced employment elasticity: when an industry has reached a certain stage and the need for it is basically met by the market supply, its employment elasticity will go down. Otherwise we cannot explain the reason why the whole service industry cannot be boosted just by the catering trade.

Table 12.6. The evolution of the employment elasticity of service industry in the Yangtze River Delta from 1986 to 2006.

Year	The growth rate of employment of service industry	The growth rate of output value of service industry	The employment elasticity of service industry	The average change in employment elasticity in three years
1986	11.95%	12.70%	0.94	—
1987	5.98%	12.49%	0.48	—
1988	7.63%	15.88%	0.48	0.63
1989	–0.16%	–4.84%	0.03	0.33
1990	3.77%	7.23%	0.52	0.34
1991	4.06%	19.94%	0.20	0.25
1992	8.17%	22.97%	0.36	0.36
1993	6.05%	19.65%	0.31	0.29
1994	8.72%	8.15%	1.07	0.58
1995	8.21%	13.26%	0.62	0.67
1996	5.56%	12.71%	0.44	0.71
1997	4.43%	13.63%	0.32	0.46
1998	6.34%	13.49%	0.47	0.41
1999	7.51%	11.73%	0.64	0.48
2000	4.32%	14.18%	0.30	0.47
2001	4.97%	13.01%	0.38	0.44
2002	6.52%	15.01%	0.43	0.37
2003	3.40%	4.53%	0.23	0.35
2004	3.05%	13.51%	0.23	0.30
2005	5.76%	19.05%	0.30	0.25
2006	4.39%	15.80%	0.28	0.27

Source: The author calculated using the statistical yearbooks of Shanghai, Jiangsu and Zhejiang and statistical bulletins of the domestic economy and social development of Shanghai, Jiangsu and Zhejiang in 2006.

Table 12.6 indicates the change in the employment elasticity of service industry in the Yangtze River Delta from 1986 to 2006. After 1995 the employment elasticity of the service industry in the Yangtze River Delta was on the decrease, from 0.62 in 1995 to 0.28 in 2006. That demonstrates that the driving effect of the output value growth on employment is weakening. It is obvious that the drop of employment elasticity of the service industry has a bearing on its internal structure. According to the analysis in the last chapter we have seen that the traditional service industries in the Yangtze River Delta have reached saturation point while the modern service industries which have a high absorbing capacity have not gained all-round development. The decline of the employment elasticity in the Yangtze River Delta does not only reflect the enhanced productivity driven by the economic growth but also its structural problems to some degree.

Prediction of the Output Value and the Number of Employees of the Service Industry in the Yangtze River Delta in 2010

In 2006 the total output value in the Yangtze River Delta was as much as RMB 4749.4 trillion; the output value of the service industry accounted for 40.66% of the total regional output value; and the number of employees in the service industry was 30.96 million.[5] According to the Eleventh Five-Year Plan of each area, the output value in the Yangtze River Delta will reach about RMB 6400 trillion by 2010, of which the added value of the service industry will account for 45%. In addition, according to Table 12.6, the average employment elasticity was 0.27 from 2004 to 2006. If it stays at that figure until 2010 we can assess the employees of the service industry in that area.

Firstly, we can derive the following formula from the equation of employment elasticity $E = \dfrac{\Delta L/L}{\Delta Y/Y}$:

$$\Delta L = E \cdot L \cdot \Delta Y/Y$$

If we apply the average employment elasticity of the service industry in the Yangtze River Delta, the employees in that industry and the proportion of economic growth in the total output value to the above formula, we can get the number of increased employees of the service industry from 2006 to 2010:

$$\Delta L = 0.27 \times 3\,096 \times (64{,}000 - 47{,}494)/47{,}494$$
$$= 290.5 \text{ (10,000 people)}$$

Adding this it to the 30.96 million employees in the service industry in 2006, we can find that the number of employees in the service industry in the area is approximately 33.865 million in 2010. The ratio of this number to the overall employees in that area is still far lower than that in developed countries.

Analysis of the deviation of employment structure of the service industry

The deviation of employment structure is the differential value between the ratio of the employees of a certain industry to that of the whole society and the ratio of the added value of that industry to the GDP in a country or area, that is,

$$\text{deviation of employment structure} = \frac{\text{employees of a certain industry}}{\text{employees of the whole economy}} - \frac{\text{added value of that industry}}{\text{GDP}}$$

When the degree of structural deviation is greater than zero, that is, a positive deviation, the proportion the employment outweighs the proportion of output value, which suggests that the productivity of that industry is relatively low and the employment within that industry has nearly reached the saturation point so that there is a possibility of workers transferring to other industries. On the contrary, when the deviation degree is smaller than zero, that is, a negative deviation, the productivity of that industry is relatively high and the work force will flow into that industry. When the deviation degree is equal to zero, it means the productivities of various industries are the same and work force will not transfer among different industries. Fig. 12.4 shows the change in deviation of three industries' structure in the Yangtze River Delta since the mid-1980s.

Fig. 12.4. The deviation of employment structure of three industries in the Yangtze River Delta

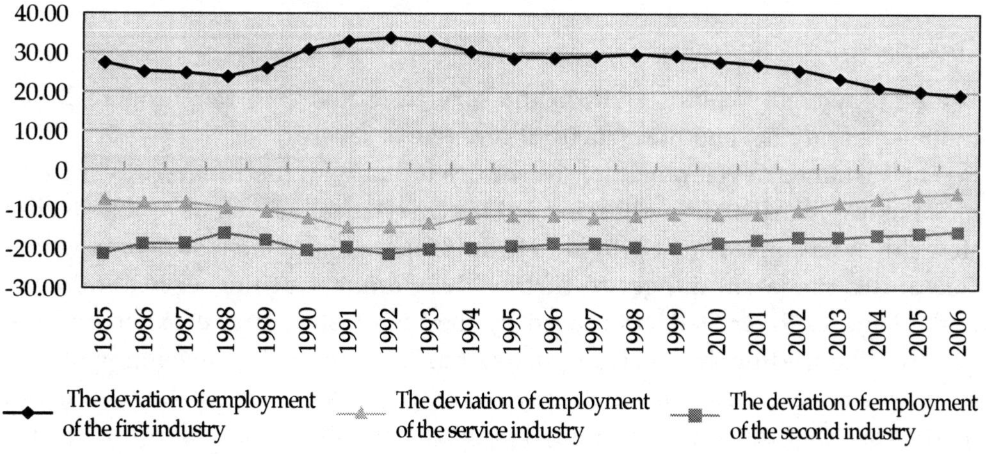

Source: The author calculated using the statistical yearbooks of Shanghai, Jiangsu and Zhejiang and statistical bulletins of the domestic economy and social development of Shanghai, Jiangsu and Zhejiang in 2006.

As shown in Fig. 12.4, since 1985 the deviation of structure of manufacturing was lower than that of the service industry, and both of them were negative. After 2003 in particular, the gap between them began to widen, which will continue if there are no other influences. That is to say, manufacturing is still in urgent need of work force, which suggests that manufacturing was and will be the essential industry to absorb work force for a long time.

The deviation of the structure of service industry in the Yangtze River Delta has risen from –9.2 in 2002 to –4.7 in 2006, which means the capacity of the service industry to absorb work force has declined. It is believed that the major reason for this is the problem with the internal structure of the service industry. As demonstrated in the previous chapter the traditional service industry in the Yangtze River Delta has developed to saturation point; the number of employees absorbed into the service industry does not show an obvious fluctuation; and its absorbing capacity has weakened slightly compared with that in 1990s. But most of the modern service industries are still in an initial development stage thus cannot give full play to their ability to absorb work force, which results in the increased deviation of the employment structure of service industry in the Yangtze River Delta.

Conclusions and policy recommendations

We have analyzed the current situation and prospect of employment in various industries in the Yangtze River Delta through the employment elasticity and deviation of employment structure and drawn two conclusions as follows:

Conclusion 1:

The employment structure within the service industry in the Yangtze River Delta is not rational and the structural problem is severe.

The sustained development of the service industry in the Yangtze River Delta for so many years has brought remarkable achievement as well as problems that slow down its employment growth. The improper employment structure, which constitutes the latent danger to further development of the service industry in the Yangtze River Delta, is caused by the severe structural problem and the fact that the traditional service industry has little scope for development and modern service industry has not fully developed. As discussed above, it is not hard to see that the key to a rational employment structure within the service industry lies in optimizing its internal structure which relies on creating more demands of the market for modern service industry.

Conclusion 2:

Manufacturing will remain the essential part of the employment structure in the Yangtze River Delta.

The service and manufacturing industries are the key drivers for the rapid development of regional economy in the Yangtze River Delta. From the long-term view, the employment proportion of service industry in the Yangtze River Delta will undoubtedly outweigh that of manufacturing. However this does not mean that the service industry will replace manufacturing as the main industry to absorb the work force in the Yangtze River Delta within a short period. As long as the service industry has not made a breakthrough in its expansion, manufacturing will still play a crucial role in the employment structure for a long time in the future. For example, as mentioned in the Eleventh Five-Year Plan of Jiangsu province, we should actively promote manufacturing with a high technological level and high added value, accelerate the construction of the industrial base, cultivate industrial groups, and concentrate our efforts on establishing an advanced manufacturing base with high competitiveness. The added value of manufacturing in the whole province is expected to be over RMB 1,300 trillion and its proportion in the world's manufacturing reach about 2%. Manufacturing in the Yangtze River Delta will maintain its predominance.

Based on the above conclusions, the following policy suggestions are proposed for the relevant departments of the Yangtze River Delta: on the one hand, we should boost the producer service industry so as to ensure the implementation of the economic strategy in the Yangtze River Delta. The general direction of the Yangtze River Delta is to develop a new pattern with high and new technology as the leading factor and advanced manufacturing industry as the mainstay, which should be propped up by a strong modern service industry. On the other hand, the key to solving the structural problems in the service industry in the Yangtze River Delta lies in dealing with its improper internal structure. Hence we suggest developing the producer service industry in order to ensure the implementation of economic strategy in the Yangtze River Delta.

The producer service industry, including financial services, insurance, real-estate, consultation, information services, technological development, commercial services and educational training etc. is designed for production or business activities, not directly for the terminal consumers. There is a comparatively large common area shared by both the producer service industry and modern service industry, but the former has a number of unique economic functions that will support the economic development of manufacturing. The producer service industry develops rapidly in developed countries.

For example, the output value of the producer service industry in America increased by 173.3% from 1970 to 1986, much higher than that of the service industry and the GDP in the same period. In 1992, the proportion of producer service industry in the GDP was over 32% in developed countries.[6] In contrast to developed countries, the producer service industry is fairly backward in the Yangtze River Delta; in 2005, the output value of the producer service in the Yangtze River Delta was RMB 923.151 trillion, accounting for respectively 55.9% and 22.6% of the total output value of the service industry and the GDP that year.[7]

If new market demands do not increase in the Yangtze River Delta in the future, the modern service industry will not expand further, let alone resolving the internal structural problems within the service industry and structural problems of employment. However adhering to the economic policy of taking manufacturing as the leading force can bring about new demands. Focusing on the producer service industry in the Yangtze River Delta can not only serve manufacturing and make new and high technological industry and advanced manufacturing industry the mainstay of manufacturing economy in the Yangtze River Delta as soon as possible, but also supply the necessary market demands for the modern service industry to grow in strength. It can be viewed as a matter of killing two birds with one stone.

13

Chapter

The Service Industry and the Building of a New Countryside in the Yangtze River Delta

The service industry in rural areas holds a decisive strategic position in the building of a new countryside. To expand the service industry in rural areas is the objective demand and safeguard for achieving the industrialization of agriculture, setting up a long-acting mechanism for increasing rural incomes and urbanizing the countryside. It is also an important way to narrow the gap between city and country and to eliminate their dual economy.

Theoretical Analysis of the Service Industry Promoting the Building of a New Countryside

Theoretical foundation of developing the service industry in the building of a new countryside

In terms of economic and social development the rural areas fall far behind the urban areas in our country, which can be attributed to several causes such as history, geography, resources, culture and managerial system. Building a new countryside and expanding the service sector in rural areas have always been key issues which the central government attaches great importance to. General Secretary Hu Jintao has delivered an exposition on the issues of agriculture, rural areas and farmers and the development of the service sector in countryside. He said we need to make resolving the problems faced by agriculture, rural areas, and farmers a top priority in all our work as they are concerned with the building of a moderately prosperous society in all aspects. We should improve the rural infrastructure and strengthen rural markets and service systems for agriculture. With the focus on stimulating the increase in rural incomes, we should develop township enterprises, strengthen county economies, provide more jobs for rural residents through multiple channels and cultivate new-type farmers who are well-educated, skilled and adept in operation. To achieve the above targets of building a new countryside, the most important thing is to expand the service industry in rural areas.

To expand the service industry in rural areas is a fundamental policy the Chinese government pays much attention to. To be specific, there are various factors that determine expanding the service industry in rural areas.

1. Promoting the industrialization of agriculture

We should make joint efforts to develop modern agriculture, improve the output and quality of agricultural products and enhance the competitiveness of China's agricultural products in the markets. We can make plans for comprehensive agriculture development in various regions through the public services of government department; we can adopt modern agricultural technology and advanced modes of agricultural production to breed improved varieties; we can introduce a modern information network to provide diversified market information for agricultural producers; we also can adopt modern rural finance to meet the diverse financial needs of agricultural production and development etc. In short, the development of the service industry in rural areas determines the industrialization of agriculture.

2. Promoting the upgrading of the industrial structure in rural areas

The evolution of the industrial structure suggests that, with the development of the economy, the output value and labor force in primary industry accounts for a decreasing proportion of the gross national economy while the proportion of the secondary and tertiary industries gradually increases. The current industrial structure in China is not rational and it is clear that development of the service industry lags far behind. In 2005, both the proportion of the added value of service industry in the GDP and that of people working in service industry to all of employees were not only far lower than the level of developed countries but also obviously lower than the average level of developing countries (Wang Jin'ao, 2007). Moreover the service industry in rural areas also depresses the development of service industry in our country, which constrains the development of economic society in rural areas and the upgrading of the industrial structure.

3. The development of tertiary industry helps to promote urbanization

The urbanologist Xie Wenhui once claimed that the change in industrial structure would be represented by the change in urbanization (Research Group, 2005). The development of the service sector is conducive to promoting and accelerating urbanization. In the light of development experience in other courtiers, the industrial structure of a country or region is different in each stage of urbanization. Generally speaking, the traditional primary industry occupies a dominant position in the initial stage of urbanization (urbanization is less than 30%); the rapid development of urbanization causes the secondary and tertiary industries to move ahead of primary industry in the medium stage (urbanization is between 30% and 70%); and the service industry holds the most important place in the later stage while there is a great shrinkage in primary industry (urbanization is more than 70%). The service industry and urbanization present a positive correlation to a great degree.

The development of tertiary industry in rural areas contributes to stimulating the interaction between city and countryside and achieving the integrated development of the urban and rural economy and society. The essential interaction between city and countryside, such as selling agricultural products in the city (information, channels, modes et al.) relies on the support of various service industries in rural areas. Meanwhile, after the development of rural and agricultural economy, expanding tourism in the countryside can attract urban residents to go on holiday in rural areas. However, that such interaction can be developed is mainly based on a developed service industry in rural areas (tertiary industry).

It is considered that to develop the service industry in rural areas requires the evolution of the rural social and economic pattern. To build a new countryside means rural people dwelling together, that is, bringing scattered rural people to reside together in a city. Besides urbanization, more settlements of rural people are characterized by housing estates and urbanization which can be viewed as a miniature of urbanization. The evolution of social forms in rural areas presents a demand for service industry. From the perspective of industrial economics, the marked difference between urbanization and the traditional countryside lies in their different industrial positions. To be specific, primary industry dominates the traditional industries in countryside whereas the secondary and tertiary industries are given the priority in urban areas. In addition, tertiary industry occupies the more important place for the more dense the population, the greater the need for the service industry.

4. Moving redundant workers locally and increasing rural incomes

According to a research report from the State Development and Reform Commission, during the Eleventh Five-Year Plan period, redundant workers in rural areas number more than 150 million. Many scholars have drawn the same conclusion (Shang Dongfeng, 2004). There are mainly two traditional ways in which rural workers move. One is that rural workers do temporary work in urban areas; the other is that some of the redundant workers are absorbed locally through developing local agricultural products and industrial products processing. As the capacity of rural industry to absorb redundant agricultural workers is getting weaker and various factors have led to the flow of rural workers slowing down, expanding the service industry in rural areas becomes the major channel to transfer the redundant agricultural workers into non-agricultural industries. Most of the service industries are labor-intensive or labor-capital intensive, therefore the promoting effect of the service industry can increase employment considerably. Moreover in many service industries the labor and capital can be easily absorbed so there is full competition and it is difficult for monopoly to take shape (Wang Jinao, 2007). With the improvement of economic development and per-capita income level, people's need for service industry will increase which provides the conditions for the service industry to absorb a great deal of the labor force.

5. Expanding the service industry and improving rural quality and living conditions

Some service industries in rural areas are closely related to the improvement of rural quality, such as education, culture, public health, sports etc. To accelerate the growth of such industries is conducive to improving ideology and morality, scientific and cultural level, and health conditions. Meanwhile, it can supply high-quality human resources for the sustained development of economic society in rural areas. In rural areas there are many service industries closely associated with people's lives, for example, transportation, communications, finance, trade, catering, repairs, beauty, nursing etc. To vigorously develop the service industry in rural areas also helps to expand the consumption field for the vast numbers of farmers, optimize consumer structure and meet their diverse material and cultural needs.

The Mechanism for the Service Industry in Rural Areas to Facilitate the Building of a New Countryside

Different from the past, the building of a new countryside focuses on the service industry. From the perspective of industrial structure, the traditional industry in rural areas in China is primary industry namely agriculture. The development pattern of traditional agriculture determines the monotonous and seasonal economic structure in rural areas as well as the risks caused by factors other than human, which also leads to a single channel of employment for rural people, the insufficiency of working hours and the low income level. In the building of a new countryside, we should vigorously develop service industry to reverse the above situation at the root. The mechanism of expanding the service industry in rural areas, which can contribute to the building of a new countryside, mainly presents in the following four aspects:

1. To expand modern service industry in rural areas can transform traditional agriculture and change the traditional mode of agricultural production. On the basis of the increase in the input of agricultural technology, we can provide

agricultural production with new varieties, enrich the soil and improve the model of agricultural irrigation. We can also set up service industry for agricultural information to boost the regulation of the industrial structure of agriculture and to alter the model of agricultural production. The service industry in rural areas contributes to the rationalization of the industrial structure of agriculture as well as the enhancement of the quality of agricultural products, and further strengthens the skills of agricultural producers and improves the income of rural people.

2. The modern service industry can play the role of a bridge between town and city and so can narrow the gap between the rural and urban economy and social development. To comprehensively develop various service industries in rural areas can change the conditions of rural infrastructure and the living and productive circumstances fundamentally. A good natural environment helps to expand sightseeing agriculture and the selling of green agricultural products in urban areas can bring a direct increase in rural income. Diversified interaction between city and countryside can narrow the gap in conceptions, income etc. Expanding the service industry in rural areas can promote the development of pluralistic industries in the countryside and provide more employment for rural people in order to enhance the rural income level. The improvement of production and living conditions as well as the growth of income will stimulate consumption of rural people so as to smooth down the distinct contrast between city and town.

3. A developed service industry is conducive to enhancing the educational level of rural people. In this way rural human capital can be increased, which in turn further facilitates the regulation of the industrial structure of agriculture and the improvement of the quality of agricultural products. To expand rural information service and intermediary services such as education and training can greatly raise the overall quality of rural workers. The development of the new-type agriculture presents a high demand for knowledge and skills in rural workers while the traditional rural workers cannot meet the needs of modern agriculture due to the limitation of educational level. Expanding the service industry supplies workers with high quality skills to optimize the industrial structure in the countryside and further provides the development of the modern and new-type agriculture with a good reserve of labor force.

4. A sound service industry in rural areas can upgrade the efficiency of economic and social activity. Thus it can save the cost of economic activity to bring more net profit to rural people. A lot of problems faced in the production and living can be dealt with by sound modern communications. At the same time, the diverse information rural people need can also be fulfilled through

a modern counseling service. The development of service industry can save the corresponding cost in production and living by a big margin and raise the work efficiency so that the rural net income as well as living conditions will be improved.

The construction of service industry in rural areas

The service industry in rural areas mainly consists of agricultural production services, rural cultural services, circulation services, information services, living services, rural intermediary services, public services etc.

1. Agricultural production services

These provide services for modern agricultural production, mainly the supply with the exploitation of seeds and germchit, the means of agricultural production and agricultural technology.

2. Rural circulation services

The major channel for improving the income of agricultural producers is to raise the commodity rate of agricultural products and then to sell those agricultural products at a high price. Therefore there is a need to set up a sound market for the circulation of agricultural products.

3. Rural information services

Compared with urban areas, the rural areas are at a disadvantage in the circulation of information as well as in agricultural production and sales, which is caused by remote geographical position and the constraints of some systems and conditions. Therefore it is significant to set up and provide information services in rural areas. Not only should the means such as the installation of traditional land-line phones and cable televisions be strengthened but the network information services also should be established for modern agricultural production.

4. Rural intermediary services

Rural intermediary service includes legal services, counseling, accounting, finance etc. Taking the rural financial industry as an example, this includes credit financing that supplies capital support to agricultural production and circulation, agricultural insurance that decentralizes the risks of agricultural production as well as exchange services for future agricultural products.

A sound rural intermediary service industry can control or reduce various indefinite risks for rural people.

The intermediary service should also include an organization of agricultural producers, namely, the agricultural guild. Facing the intense conflict between small-scale production and large-scale market, various types of associations are an effective way to guide farmers to markets. Furthermore, integrated associations have much greater influence on the market and give more control on price so that the small-scale producers will not suffer a loss.

5. Public services

Traditionally, town and city have always been governed separately in our country, which has caused a lack of government function in rural areas and a severe lack of rural public services. In contrast to urban areas, it is more common in rural areas that the market does not work. In view of such phenomenon, the rural areas are in urgent need of public facilities and services supplied by the public budget from the government, which consist of diverse infrastructure used in agricultural production and living, public facilities, job training for farmers, various items of social security etc.

6. Rural living services

The flow of workers from towns into cities has been one of the most important channels of increasing employment and income for the mass of redundant workers in rural areas. As a legion of the young and the middle-aged leave home to engage in industrial work or commercial activities, there are only the old and children left in home. In some of families, the old are so weak that they cannot take care of themselves and thus they cannot look after their grandchildren well at all. At present, most of the countryside in China is an ageing society. The transformation of the rural economy and society means there is a great demand for rural living services.

7. Rural cultural services

With the increasingly improvement of rural income level, farmers' need for spiritual civilization is becoming stronger and stronger. Expanding the scientific, educational and cultural services in rural areas helps to upgrade the overall quality of rural people, enrich rural cultural life and form a modern civilized life style.

A General Description of the Development of the Service Industry in Rural Areas in the Yangtze River Delta

The Yangtze River Delta is one of the biggest economic cores of our country. The development of its economy and society suggests that the region does not only maintain an increase of more than 10% in the long term but a dramatic change has taken place in its economic structure during the last 30 years. Most of the regions in the Yangtze River Delta have stepped into the middle stage of industrialization and Shanghai is in the middle-later stage. Compared with other regions in China, the service industry in rural areas in the Yangtze River Delta is relatively developed. I will describe the development situation of service industry in rural areas in the Yangtze River Delta from the following six perspectives.

Agricultural production services

As the input of goods production, producer service plays the role of intermediary to raise the added value and the efficiency of resource operations in different productive stages. The system of agricultural producer services can be divided into pre-production service, mid-production and post-production. Pre-production services mainly supply the means of production including seeds, pesticide, chemical fertilizer, agricultural plastic sheeting, farm machinery and appliances. In accordance with the demands of expanding modern highly-efficient agriculture, Jiangsu Province focuses on fostering a group of leading seeds- and germchit- enterprises, a group of professional organizations providing seeds- and germchit-services and a group of gene pools of agricultural seeds resources. It also promotes a chain operation of agricultural means of production and expands a group of chain operation blocs with a uniform mark, procurement, distribution, accounting and price. The chain operation, to a great extent, can be viewed as brand management, which avoids the inflow of fake and shoddy products in the intermediate link and guarantees the quality of means of production for farmers. Meanwhile the chain operation of agricultural means of production achieves the effective connection between production and the market, reduces circulation and saves costs, and thus prices are lowered. Moreover some technological services and guidance will be provided in the operation which helps farmers to master new agricultural skill and knowledge. Furthermore, the service for renting farm machinery needs to be developed because farmers cannot afford large farm machinery or feel it is unnecessary to purchase one machine on their own. Generally speaking, production is managed by farmer households themselves and therefore the mid-production service mainly supplies information and management knowledge and carries out demonstrations and applications of new technology. The post-production service is mainly to develop processing enterprises for agricultural products, actively seek markets and increase the added value of agricultural products. In the overall system of agricultural producer services, the participation of enterprises can do much to improve the efficiency and quality of service. In Jiangsu Province for example, in 2004 there were 12 enterprises recognized as national key leading enterprises in agricultural industrialization, which meant that Jiangsu ranked second in China. The total national key leading enterprises in agricultural industrialization have reached 28 and achieve annual sales income of RMB 27.9 million, an increase of 22%. In addition, the total profits and taxes have reached RMB 1.98 million, increasing by 14%; and the total of export to earn foreign exchange is US$380 billion, stimulating 974,000 farmer households.

Rural Circulation Services

Recently, the supply of agricultural products has been in surplus and prices have stayed low. The serious truth is that the increase in grain output does not lead to increase in rural incomes and the problem of circulation becomes a bottleneck in the increase in rural incomes. Thus it is necessary to use the agricultural products circulation experience of developed countries for reference. Agriculture in America is the most developed in the world, and Third-Party Logistics is the major model of circulation service. Third-Party Logistics provides a specialized and integrated service, links farmers with the wholesale market, takes on agricultural products processing, packing, transport, safe storage, loading and removal, information and sales, and plans the optimized mode of circulation to save time and exchange costs. The sales of America agricultural products have spread throughout the world, and this relies on its highly efficient system of circulation service. In China the circulation of about 60–70% of agricultural products are undertaken by farmer households themselves, which suggests a low level of socialization and specialization of agriculture.

The Yangtze River Delta has geographical superiority as it is located in the estuary of the Yangtze Valley where the transportation is advanced and infrastructure is completely equipped. By 2004, the length of railways in operation was as long as 2,263 kilometers in the region while the length of highways reached 133,002 kilometers. Shanghai makes use of its prosperous exhibition industry to supply a platform for our country to display and sell agricultural products. At the same time, it also explores new channels of exporting agricultural products depending on its identity as an international metropolis. In 2004, Jiangsu continued to strengthen the development of the agricultural products wholesale market and modern marketing system. The trading volume of 30 provincial key agricultural products wholesale market totaled RMB 39.7 billion, increasing by 28% compared to the same period of 2003. Green channels also are put into operation for the transportation of agricultural products. In the whole province, 1,541 passes for green channels are issued which leads to the remission of toll of more than RMB 30 million so as to promote the circulation of agricultural products. The model of small commodities in Yiwu, Jiangsu Province, is the model of developing commodity circulation service in rural areas. With the thriving development of commodity circulation, capital is accumulated constantly and the operation is extended. Tertiary industry plays the role of a pillar. Commercial capital tends to be invested in fields such as industrial and agricultural production, infrastructure and so on, which stimulates the comprehensive development of economic society. In the procedure above, the model of small commodities has always played an active role as individual economy in order to become an important growing point of the regional economy. Moreover it also facilitates the development of tertiary industry, rural industry, modern agriculture, urban construction and other specialized and production element markets as well.

Information Technology and Education

Information technology has been an indispensable force stimulating the growth of the rural economy. With the globalization of the Internet and the development of electronic commerce, the information industry has infiltrated into various industries and social life. Meanwhile there has been a trend towards employing modern information technology to equip and operate agriculture. Once logged into a Shanghai agricultural website, users can get information such as the updated supply and demand of agricultural products, the sales in the domestic market, the change in the import-export structure of agricultural products, the latest agricultural technology, regulations, and meteorological material etc. Market analysis services supply farmers with information to forecast future prices in order to help them make more profit. However a comprehensive survey of the agricultural information websites of Shanghai, Jiangsu and

Zhejiang show that the platform for agricultural products transaction on the Internet is relatively weak in construction and electronic commerce is not made full use of in its role as a channel to link farmer households and enterprises. That is due to some objective factors. The rural income level in our country is not very high. Even in the Yangtze River Delta, literacy is not extensive in rural areas and people living there do not have an intimate knowledge of computer technology. People in some rural areas have never seen a computer. Although the growth rate of netizens is high in our country, the increase in the application of computers mainly occurs in urban areas. The use in urban areas is 740 times higher than that in the countryside, thus it is necessary to strengthen the infrastructure of information Internet in rural areas.[1]

Education in rural areas does not only provide a steady stream of human resource for urban development but also increases the knowledge of farmers in various aspects such as farming skills, breeding techniques, environmental protection awareness and market-based knowledge. Therefore the development of education, on the basis of the above two points, boosts the agricultural productivity and the increase in per capita incomes. From statistical data in 2005, 10.44 million people graduated from college-level or above, accounting for 9% of the population in the Yangtze River Delta, while the figure for the whole nation was 67.64 million, 6% of the total population. In the Yangtze River Delta, the level of educational equipment and population quality is higher than the average level of the whole country and thus the development of education in rural areas possesses a potential superiority. In pace with the popularization of nine years of compulsory education in rural areas, the vocational education of farmers has come to be the main task of education. Faced with the difficulties in running schools and enrolment, vocational education can adopt the model whereby the government makes overall plans and schools cooperate with the market. That is to say, we should strengthen the responsibility of government to make an overall plan for the management of vocational education and to provide capital, to design a program for long-term development and to implement favorable support policies. Meanwhile each school should absorb outstanding teachers on a wide scale, in which some excellent teacher from other schools can also be allowed to hold a concurrent post. As for the training for farmers, we should uphold the market as orientation and impart knowledge according to the needs of enterprises and professions.

Rural intermediary services

The truth that financial development has the function of promoting economic growth has been proved by many people. Similar research results are also drawn from the perspective of the contribution of financial industry to the development of rural areas. In September 2004, Shanghai Anxin Agricultural Insurance Company, the first professional one in our country, came into operation, which explored the market operation model of agricultural insurance dominated by government. With the ratification of the State Council Shanghai, as the pilot city through which the whole nation deepens reform of rural credit cooperatives, actively boosts such reform and finds radical solutions to problems common in rural credit cooperatives such as unclear ownership rights, imperfect corporate administration and the low standard of management. Furthermore it also makes preparations for the establishment of joint-equity rural commercial banks and creates a pluralistic rural financial service system. Currently, service industries in law, counseling and accounting play little role in rural tertiary industry in the Yangtze River Delta.

In terms of the construction and organization of agricultural industries, associations already established in the Yangtze River Delta are those of agricultural machinery, agricultural information, breeding, the Zhejiang tea industry, green food, Shanghai agricultural industry etc. Nevertheless, these associations do not play a major role at present.

Rural public service industries of culture, living, and infrastructure

Such services mainly include the public commodities and services supplied by government public budget, such as rural infrastructure, rural production services, education in scientific knowledge and job training for farmers, the diffusion of culture in rural areas, the publicity of environmental protection awareness, and various social security systems. Because of the system of the WTO, the distribution of government spending should be shifted from the support of prices to the above aspects. For example, it can provide subsidies for agricultural production, build farmland irrigation projects, raise funds for agricultural development, provide free training in agricultural knowledge and set up a fund for natural disaster and insect control. Rural cultural infrastructure covers the construction of libraries, cultural centers or units, radio stations, schools etc. It also promotes the continuation of folk crafts and traditional folk culture. The new countryside is planned to have sustainable development of production, a prosperous life, a civilized atmosphere, a clean environment as well as a democratic management. However there is no integrated waste recycling system in rural areas. In addition, rivers are seriously polluted by a great amount of plastic waste, and chemical fertilizers and pesticides are dumped into them. Thus only the government can bear the great responsibility of environmental control. On the one hand, it can set up some refuse disposal plants and purify the rivers; on the other hand, it also can publicize environmental protection awareness and take measures concerning rewards and punishment sanctions. Various security systems such as health care in rural areas have been weak until now so we should encourage farmers to buy old-age insurance as well as medical insurance. If rural people are secure using these two types of insurance, they will be more willing to consume. That trend will therefore fuel the consumer demand and further promote economic prosperity in rural areas. The above public services in the Yangtze River Delta are more advanced than in other regions but they have not met the needs of economic and social development in public services.

Rural tourism

To expand tourism is one of the effective ways to achieve the economic growth in poverty-stricken areas. Ecotourism is becoming a new vogue among tourists from urban areas because employees with upper-low incomes or the young prefer to return to nature so as to relieve the pressure of the quick pace of urban life. The net profit of traditional tourism is earned by developers and it is also accompanied with problems such as high-density infrastructure, land use, traffic congestion, air pollution caused by motor vehicles, water and earth pollution and the disturbance to the life of local residents and other living beings. However the profit created by ecotourism will be distributed among developers, the local community and residents. Meanwhile ecotourism provides sustainable employment and boosts relevant industries such as catering, transportation, accommodation, entertainment as well as tourist counseling and booking services that are prepared for ecotourism. Ecotourism lays its emphasis on the perfect harmony of human and nature, therefore local farmers do not only make a profit from their agricultural products but also gain extra returns from the relevant industries.

An Empirical Analysis of the Development of the Service Industry in Rural Areas in the Yangtze River Delta

Expanding rural service industry is the need of the evolution of rural social and economic pattern. To build a new countryside is to make rural people dwell together, that is, to make scattered rural people reside together in the city. Besides urbanization, the more settlements of rural people are characterized by housing estate and urbanization which can be viewed as a miniature of urbanization. The evolution of social form in rural areas presents a demand to service industry. From the perspective of industrial economics, the marked difference between urbanization and traditional countryside lies in their different industrial positions. To be specific, the first industry dominates the traditional industries in countryside whereas the second and third industries are given the priority in urban. The degree of development of service industry is greatly proportional to the population density, that is, the more densely people live, the greater the need for service industry is.

The model of dual economic development

A large number of redundant workers in rural has been created since the reform and opening up, especially with the implementation of management under contract by farmer households, which is an inevitable result of the reform in rural areas. The *Research Report on Chinese Farmer Workers*, released by the Research Office of the State Council suggests that one third of the farmers in China have turned into workers, working in non-agricultural industries. Farmer workers in non-agricultural industries account for 70%, 60% of which work in tertiary industry. In accordance with Louis's theory of dual economy, both the development of urban areas and the income gap encourage the agricultural labor force to move from rural areas to urban areas. Moreover the per capita income in rural areas is less than one third of that in urban areas, which also leads rural people to flock into the cities. People working in the retailing, transportation and building industries earn more than in countryside. On the basis of approximately 30 years of data after the reform and opening up until now the service industry has become a major force driving employment, which can be proved by the following persuasive statistic. Although domestic service is just a small branch of the service industry, it can supply with more than 15 billion job opportunities in the community each year, which is calculated according to investigations of 32 megalopolises and 43 big cities implemented by the Ministry of Labour and Social Security (China). In our country, people above 60 and children under 10 account for 35% of the total population, which means that there is a great demand for domestic service. Thus it is a good choice for farmers to enter the city to work as housemaids. With the reduction in numbers of farmers as well as the improvement of agricultural productivity, per capita income of farmers in primary industry will increase, which can be proved from the following two aspects.

1. The net per capita income of farmers in the Yangtze River Delta and its urbanization level

The relationship between the two aspects can be represented by the model:

$\ln Y = a + b \ln X + u$.

Y presents the net per capita income of rural residents and RMB is taken as the unit. X presents the urbanization level, which is demonstrated by the proportion of non-rural people in the total population. It will be calculated according to data from Shanghai and Jiangsu (Jiangsu did not adopt the uniform method to calculate its urbanization level from 1978 to 2004 so data collected during these years is excluded. Data are drawn from *Shanghai Statistical Yearbook* and *Zhejiang Statistical Yearbook*).

We can see from Table 13.1 that the per capita rural income in the Yangtze River Delta is directly proportional to its urbanization level to a great degree. If the rate of urbanization rises by one percentage point, the per capita rural income in Shanghai will increase by 12.13649% whereas that in Zhejiang will only increase by 4.89319%. It can be concluded that economic development in the urbanized course of Shanghai plays a greater role in upgrading rural income.

The net per capita income of farmers in the Yangtze River Delta and the rate of employment in tertiary industry

The relationship between these can be represented by the model:

$\ln Y = a + b \ln X + u$.

Y presents the net per capital income of rural residents and RMB is taken as the unit. X represents the proportion of employees in tertiary industry, which is demonstrated by the proportion of employees in that industry in the gross employees in the region.

Data are drawn from *Corpus of 55-Year Statistical Data since the Founding of New China*, Shanghai (1978–2004), Jiangsu (1978–2004) and Zhejiang (1985–2004).

From Table 13.2 we can conclude that the per capital rural income in the Yangtze River Delta is directly proportional to the rate of employment in tertiary industry to a great degree. If the rate of employment in the third industry rises by one percentage point, the per capita rural income in Shanghai will increase by 3.634801% whereas that in Jiangsu and Zhejiang will respectively increase by 2.918733% and 2.734425%. It is obvious that the service industry in Shanghai plays a greater role in stimulating agricultural development. Shanghai, the core of the 16 cities in the Yangtze River Delta, makes full use of its identity of an international metropolis to absorb capital from all over the world. Thus its industrial structure updates at a high speed, which brings it the nearest to the standard of developed countries of the three regions. The rapid development of the service industry absorbs a large amount of manpower and material resources and promotes transfer of rural redundant workers into emerging industries or their move from the traditional sectors with low income to the modern one with high income. In that way, the capital and land taken up by traditional sectors will increase and agricultural productivity will also improve, so the real income of farmers in both sectors will be higher than before.

Table 13.1. The data of metrological verification for the net per capita income of rural residents and urbanization level in Shanghai and Zhejiang

	Shanghai	*t* test	Zhejiang	*t* test
a	12.17428	53.13337	15.72495	33.46876
b	12.13649	20.78762	4.89319	18.45915
R^2	0.945310		0.931645	
F-statistic	432.1252		340.7403	

Table 13.2. The data of metrological verification for the net per capita income of rural residents in the Yangtze River Delta and the rate of employment in tertiary industry

	Shanghai	*t* test	Jiangsu	*t* test	Zhejiang	*t* test
a	11.62597	52.64732	12.02803	48.13208	11.88015	52.62107
b	3.634801	19.14425	2.918733	20.63648	2.734425	2.734425
R^2	0.936143		0.944551		952,655	
F-statistic	366.502 1		425.8645		F=362.1917	

Net per capita income of rural residents in Jiangsu and an analysis relative to various service industries in rural areas

Model: $Y=f(X_1, X_2, X_3, X_4, X_5, X_6, X_7, X_8, X_9, X_{10})+u$

In Table 13.3,

Y: per capita rural income (RMB)

X_1: the gross output value of rural transportation in rural social gross output value (RMB 100 million)

X_2: the gross output value of rural commerce in rural social gross output value (RMB 100 million)

X_3: the agricultural credit in financial institutions (RMB 100 million)

X_4: the agricultural spending in the general budget of local finance (RMB 100 million), including in forestry, water conservancy, meteorology and institutional charging in those departments

X_5: rural telephones (10,000)

X_6: agricultural technical personnel (10,000)

X_7: the gross power of agricultural machinery (10,000)

X_8: the effective irrigation area (1,000 hectare)

X_9: the amount of chemical fertilizer (10,000 ton)

X_{10}: electricity consumption in rural areas (100 million kilowatt-hours)

We can find from the regression analysis using EViews's software

$$Y = -1{,}346.462 + 8.326110\ X_1 + 1.390769\ X_2$$

$$(-2.159050)(3.853213)(1.451083)$$

$$-\ 1.647127\ X_3 - 0.131813\ X_4 - 1.181257\ X_5$$

$$(-1.334681)(-0.090840)(-1.376550)$$

$$+\ 157.1150\ X_6 + 0.209667\ X_7 + 0.342421\ X_8$$

$$(2.262437)(1.913477)(1.884518)$$

$$+\ 0.173204\ X_9 - 2.711074\ X_{10}$$

$$(0.497791)(-1.208704) \qquad (1)$$

R^2=0.998

Adj. R^2=0.997

F-statistic=1,164.912

Table 13.3. Factors that influence the geographical agglomeration

Year	Y	X_1	X_2	X_3	X_4	X_5	X_6	X_7	X_8	X_9	X_{10}
1978	155	2.56	7.3	5.52	28.38	2.69	1.36	855.2	3,270.3	371.8	23.28
1979	200	2.62	8.84	5.57	32.06	2.86	1.62	998.6	3,369.5	98	27.75
1980	218	3.09	8.71	6.11	28.95	3.04	1.13	1,113.1	3, 413	118.2	33.74
1981	258	2.97	8.76	7.28	23.79	3.22	1.16	1,204.2	3,455.7	125.3	38.87
1982	309	3.56	8.88	2.33	24.63	3.43	1.32	1,313	3,475.9	146.6	42.61
1983	357	6.64	11.34	5.74	32.29	3.71	1.49	1,430.4	3,495.5	149.8	47.64
1984	448	15.54	15.1	7.51	39.15	4.17	1.71	1,558.1	3,596.3	156.8	53.23
1985	493	19.45	21.42	8.46	50.53	4.91	1.76	1,675.1	3,587.9	157.8	63.57
1986	561	25.45	27.38	11.01	66.16	5.07	1.95	1,811.3	3,537.8	169.7	71.2
1987	627	33.06	35.13	12.15	68	5.65	2.01	1,974.4	3,517.3	178	85.23
1988	797	43.58	48.9	24.37	81.45	6.39	2.16	2,100.9	3,497.3	196.5	94.76
1989	876	46.82	53.45	31.02	92.25	7.3	2.26	2,212.4	3,531.2	204.7	98.39
1990	884	48.27	57.95	39.98	100.97	8.52	2.35	2,004.8	3,970.9	221.8	105.26
1991	921	50.45	63.32	53.16	128.18	9.99	2.39	1,966.6	3,849.8	238.4	121.53

(Con'd)

1992	1,061	69.42	106.24	64.76	125.86	16.21	2.53	2,016.1	3,856.5	246.9	146.46
1993	1,267	103.49	178.18	77.7	163.87	28.85	2.5	2,081.8	3,823.9	249.7	169.2
1994	1,832	160.28	301.02	62.61	200.17	52.76	2.21	2,161.4	3,825.1	271.8	205.99
1995	2,457	229.84	448.96	89.09	253.49	103.63	2.65	2,227	3,832.8	292.8	238.16
1996	3,029	280.74	571.17	125.16	310.94	167.49	3.68	2,297.4	3,821.5	306.7	252.18
1997	3,270	291.97	648.77	164.73	364.36	257.36	3.9	2,499.7	3,839.4	322.7	263.12
1998	3,377	315.6	712.73	235.12	424.9	363.48	4.45	2,594.8	3,855.4	333.3	263.95
1999	3,495	346.84	772.51	224.99	484.65	458.7	4.51	2 ,67.9	3,885.8	335.4	280.5
2000	3,595	375.89	845.95	235.74	591.28	602.63	4.61	2,925.3	3,900.9	335.5	314.6
2001	3,785	417.35	939.37	288.06	729.64	757.2	4.18	2,957.9	3,900	338	345.05
2002	3,996	457.88	1,166.65	368.39	860.25	739	3.74	2,983.9	3,886	337.5	423.61
2003	4,239	541.31	1,455.79	494.04	1,047.68	868	3.74	3,029.1	3,841	334.7	529.5
2004	4,754	615.03	1,787.29	574.58	1,312.04	940.51	3.25	3,052.5	3,839	336.8	679.83

Sources: *Corpus of 55-Year Statistical Data since the Founding of New China, Jiangsu through 50 Years, Jiangsu through 40 Years* and *Jiangsu Statistical Yearbook.*

On the level of α=5%, it can be found that t_2^{α}=2.120. Only the coefficients X_1 and X_6 and the constant terms are verified and the revised model is $Y=f(X_1, X_6)+u$,

From the regression analysis, we can obtain:

$$Y = -238.0522+6.195794X_1+364.5885X_6$$

$$(-2.710138)(23.603\ 38)(8.127\ 730) \qquad (2)$$

R^2=0.992680

Adj. R^2=0.992070

F-statistic=1,627.416

The rise of statistics t and F in the revised model suggests that the rural service industry in Jiangsu remains of the traditional type and only the transportation service is developing relatively well. Nevertheless, we cannot ignore the potential importance of other aspects. Our agricultural production has been backward as yet and thus the contribution of these aspects is not much revealed. However in developed countries such as America and Japan, the contribution of X_3 (finance), X_5 (change from telephone to computer), X_7 (machinery) and X_8 (irrigation) is obviously exhibited. Therefore there is plenty of room for development in the rural service industries in production (pesticide, chemical fertilizer, irrigation, machinery etc.), information, financial intermediation and government farming, forestry, water conservancy and meteorology. Our national policies should also actively guide the transition from traditional agriculture to modern agriculture. On the basis of formula (2), we can conclude the contribution of agricultural technical staff to rural economic growth. If the number of technical staff is increased by 10,000, per capita rural income will increase by RMB 364.5885 equal to 6.195794 (the coefficient of X_1). Such a large contribution suggests the significance of scientific technology and it is the importance of its extension because the techniques can infiltrate into diverse aspects of the service industry and the ultimate result of the infiltration is the improvement of efficiency in all the other aspects. The application of high technology leads to smoother circulation in the commodity and financial markets and also saves costs; biotechnology is adopted in the production service to develop improved varieties, sow seeds in a scientific way and make the most profit with the least cost; and information technology infiltrates almost all the diverse aspects of human life. In the following analysis, we separate the factor of advances in science and technology from other factors in order to investigate its contribution to rural economic development.

Calculation of the rate of contribution of agricultural advances in science and technology

The basic formula of the Cobb-Douglas production function, often used to calculate the rate of advance in science and technology, is $Y=AK^{\alpha}L^{\beta}D^{\gamma}$. Y, K, L, and D respectively represent the gross agricultural output value, the expenditure of material, the number of workers and the cultivated area; α, β and γ respectively represent the output coefficient of the expenditure of material, labor and cultivated area. A is the factor of scientific and technological level and the formula $A=ae^{\delta t}$ is often assumed for the convenience for calculation, in which a is a constant and δ the rate of advances in science and technology. ε is assumed as a stochastic variable. To avoid the influence of inflation, Y is presented by the gross output value of farming, forestry, animal husbandry and fishery, calculated by the fixed prices in 1985. It can be exhibited as "the expenditure of material based on the fixed price = (the expenditure of material based on the price of that year/the gross output value of farming, forestry, animal husbandry and fishery based on the price of that year) × the gross output value of farming, forestry, animal husbandry and fishery based on the fixed price." The number of workers is represented by the number of employees in primary industry and the cultivated area is represented by the effective cultivated areas of each province or city in the end of the year. t, The investigation time, is adopted from 1985 to 2005 in Shanghai and Jiangsu and that in Zhejiang is from 1985–2003.

In this case, the formula through the regression calculation can be shown as:

$$\ln Y=\ln a+\alpha\ln K+\beta\ln L+\gamma\ln D+\delta t+\varepsilon$$

$$\text{The rate of contribution of agricultural advances in science and technology} = \frac{\text{the rate of agricultural advances in science and technology}}{\text{the growth rate of the gross agricultural output value}} = \frac{\delta\Delta t}{\Delta Y/Y}$$

In accordance with the data in the annual statistical yearbooks of rural areas in China, the annual statistical yearbooks of Shanghai, Jiangsu and Zhejiang and the *Corpus of 55-Year Statistical Data since the Founding of New China*, we can draw a conclusion as shown in Table 13.4.

From Table 13.4, we can see that land area in Shanghai and Jiangsu does not make a distinct contribution to the growth of the gross agricultural output value while the contribution of material input of Zhejiang is relatively weak. Excluding these weak factors we can carry out the regression analysis again and obtain Table 13.5.

The statistics in Table 13.5, which are obviously more desirable than those in Table 13.4, are employed to draw conclusions as follows: in Shanghai, the average annual growth rate of the gross output value in farming, forestry, animal husbandry and fishery from 1985 to 2005 is 3.103967% and the rate of contribution of agricultural advances in science and technology (0.024933/0.031 03967×100%) is equal to 80.33%; in Jiangsu, the average annual growth rate of the gross output value in farming, forestry, animal husbandry and fishery from 1985 to 2005 is 5.81975% and the rate of contribution of agricultural advances in science and technology (0.0364/0.0581975×100%) is 62.55%; in Zhejiang, the average annual growth rate of the gross output value in farming, forestry, animal husbandry and fishery from 1985 to 2003 is 4.74589% and the rate of contribution of agricultural advances in science and technology (0.02989/0.047 4589)×100% is 62.98%. In the Yangtze River Delta, the rate of contribution of advances in science and technology to agricultural economy growth exceeds 50%. Moreover the rate in Zhejiang comes near that in Jiangsu while in Shanghai it is rather higher than in Jiangsu and Zhejiang. All the above suggests that science and technology has become the primary productive force.

Table 13.4. Calculation of the contribution of the expenditure of material, labor, land and technology

	Shanghai	*t* test	Jiangsu	*t* test	Zhejiang	*t* test
ln*a*	−70.5631	−4.19328	−39.0656	−0.98907	−36.4651	−2.17917
α	0.306446	4.445763	0.389829	5.691913	0.059119	0.325614
β	0.201861	3.661353	−0.2135	−2.62706	−0.37282	−3.99998
γ	0.479313	1.414498	−1.36801	−0.70504	−1.49606	−1.77583
δ	0.034994	4.549604	0.028225	2.311106	0.027827	3.393184
R^2	0.991088		0.993742		0.993515	
F-statistic	444.8103		635.1606		536.2235	

Table 13.5. Calculation of the contribution of the expenditure of material, labor, land and technology

	Shanghai	*t* test	Jiangsu	*t* test	Zhejiang	*t* test
ln*a*	−48.2053	−8.1137	−66.3967	−8.90507	−38.9407	−2.69397
α	0.374969	7.431157	0.357653	7.109394		
β	0.250949	5.692662	−0.25238	−4.29082	−0.36573	−4.16153
γ					−1.68806	−2.89266
δ	0.024933	8.278234	0.0364	9.626555	0.02989	5.920545
R^2	0.989973		0.993547		0.993466	
F-statistic	559.4766		872.5276		760.2376	

Conclusion

From the perspectives of urbanization, rate of employment in tertiary industry and scientific and technological level, Shanghai is more advanced than Jiangsu and Zhejiang. The upgrading of the industrial structure in its urban district promotes the constant optimization of the primary industry structure in the development of suburbs and agriculture. In 2005 the net per capita income of rural residents reached RMB 8,342 in Shanghai, which was respectively RMB 1,500 and 3,000 higher than in Zhejiang and Jiangsu. In the building of a new countryside in the Yangtze River Delta, we should increase the governmental and collective funds in rural tertiary industry while actively promoting urbanization. Moreover, we should encourage farmers to go into service industries such as entertainment, finance, catering, commerce, real estate, tourism and counseling in small towns. In particular we should increase financial investment in research on agricultural technology and train more and more agricultural technical personnel. Meanwhile the key to becoming better off is to improve the all-round qualities of all farmers through publicizing agricultural knowledge in the countryside.

Policy Recommendations on Improvement of the Rural Service Industry

In our country, the rural areas are vast and the settlements of rural people are relatively scattered. The general income level is also comparatively low. If the market allocates resources arbitrarily, the development of rural service industry will be severely impeded. Therefore guidance from government policy is necessary in the course of development of the various service industries in rural areas. Not only can the government perform its own functions and provide public services for rural areas, it can also guide the flow of social resources into the rural service industry by implementing financial policy. In accordance with conclusions drawn from the empirical analysis of the development of rural service industry in the Yangtze River Delta, I offer the following suggestions in terms of the further development of the rural service industry.

I. The government should fully perform its function in managing public affairs in rural areas and intensify the supply of public service industry.

1. We should set up social security systems covering all rural areas as soon as possible, especially the systems of old-age insurance and cost of living allowances for rural residents.

At present, a new problem is facing the economic and social development of rural areas. On the one hand, there is a need for mechanized, specialized and scale development to pool farmland resources and to accelerate urbanization and the flow of the young from rural areas into urban areas which as well as the aging population in rural areas presents a demand for intensive cultivation and production on farmland. Thus intensive farming will become the trend of the rural economic development and regulation of industrial structure. On the other hand, due to the lack of system and degree of social security, intensive farming means that the old and less educated rural people will lose their necessary means of production. If their problems of social security are not solved properly, the trend of intensive farming will be unable to continue.

To solve such problem depends on the development of public and intermediary service industries in rural areas. Firstly, the central and local governments should create a system of social security in the countryside as soon as possible. Secondly, as there is a problem with the exchange of land for security in the setting up of the social security system in the countryside, the corresponding intermediary should be founded and the land farmers intend to convey should be estimated comprehensively, in which way the interests of both farmers and land contractors can obtain guarantee.

2. We should increase the financial allocations for public facilities in rural areas. In the light of egalitarianism, everyone has a right to essential public facilities. However there is a severe shortage of such facilities in rural areas. Thus, in the building of a new countryside, governments at all levels should completely perform their function in public management and services in rural areas by increasing the budgetary outlay.

3. The development of other public services in rural areas is also sluggish, including rural public services, services in technology, education, culture and health (such as rural comprehensive services in technology, social welfare services and communication services) etc. The public services are not only supplied by the government but the suppliers can vary with the public and private features of public services. While improving the supply of purely public services, the government also should guide the investment of social funds in mixed services by implementing the public financial policy.

II. On the basis of the building of a new countryside we should strengthen the intensiveness and urbanization of rural areas so as to provide good housing conditions for comprehensive services in rural areas. Intensive residence needs various public services, such as community planning, funding support and the supply of diverse information in the building of the community and the management services provided after the founding of a community by local governments and management systems.

III. We should vigorously expand rural finance services, including credit, financing systems, insurance for rural people, future exchange for agricultural products etc. Due to the difficulty of financing for operations with a small capital in rural areas, governments should combine the systems of rural credit and old-age insurance based on the law, that is, that farmers mortgage their endowment certificate to apply to the financial institutions for a loan in order to make achievements in economy and society for all sides (Shang Changfeng, 2007). There are many non-market factors affecting agricultural production which can lead to the commercial insurance market losing efficiency. Therefore the government at various levels should implement the correspondingly preferential policies to guide the commercial insurance market in providing insurance for agricultural production. In that way, the risk in production will be lessened and the income of agricultural producers will be constantly increased.

IV. We should expand rural tourism in an organized way. We should exploit different regions' resource advantages to develop local tourism and also to promote the other relevant services.

V. We should encourage the development of social services in rural areas. Owing to the flow of labor force from town to city, we should supply services to those remaining behind. Meanwhile the aging tendency in rural areas is sharpening which presents an urgent demand for living services. We should set up systems which are similar to those in urban areas for the old so as to ensure that the old in rural areas live in comfort.

14

Chapter

The Upgrading and Optimization of Human Progress by the Service Industry in the Yangtze River Delta

The scientific outlook on development and the demand for constructing a harmonious society determine that we expand our concern from the GDP to the HDI (Human Development Index). Compared with the GDP, the HDI shows that human progress is the ultimate goal of development which covers leading a comfortable life, receiving a good education and having good health as well as living in a nation of democracy and freedom.

The experience of developed countries demonstrates that the development of service industry is not only a crucial channel to raise people's income but also directly relates to human progress. In this chapter, I will explore the relationship between the development of service industry in the Yangtze River Delta and the human progress in this area.

Human Progress in the Yangtze River Delta

The HDI contains the following three indexes: the per capita income, the GDP per capita represented in US dollars, which is used to measure how much material wealth can be utilized to improve the quality of people's lives; the average life expectation which is used to reflect the development of health care; and the educational level which is used to represent educational development.

GDP per capita

1. GDP per capita of Shanghai

According to statistics, the GDP per capital was only US$125 in 1952. With 25 years of development, it surpassed US$1,000 in 1977; and it went up to US$2,000 in 1993. Then it kept rising and reached US$3,000 after just 4 years in 1997, which achieved the first great leap in the economic development of Shanghai and its overall financial strength advanced from the average level of low-income countries to that of middle-low income countries.

The GDP per capita of Shanghai in 2000 made the second stride, exceeding US$4,000, up to US$4,180. And in 2001 the figure was over US$4,500 which meant the comprehensive economic power of Shanghai reach the per capita level of upper-middle income countries. The course of increase in the GDP per capita of Shanghai is shown in Table 14.1.

The total output value of Shanghai in 2006 reached RMB 1,029.697 billion, exceeding RMB 1,000 billion for the first time. Computed in terms of comparable price, it increased by 12% over the previous year, up 0.9%, and maintained a double digit increase for the 15th consecutive year. The added value of tertiary industry accounted for 50% of the aggregate output value in 2006.

Pan Jianxin, the head of Shanghai Statistics Bureau, has confirmed that the GDP per capita of Shanghai exceeded US$7,000 in 2006, which is close to US$7,500 if expressed by the universal calculation method. Thus it is obvious that the GDP per capita of Shanghai grows extremely fast.

2. GDP per capita of Jiangsu

In 2003 the GDP of Jiangsu province totaled RMB 1,245.175 billion, up 13.5% compared to the same period the previous year, which accounted for 10.7% in the national GDP. Meanwhile, it increased by 0.3% over the previous year, ranking only next to Guangdong in the whole nation. From the per capita perspective, the GDP per capita of Jiangsu reached RMB 16,796, up 13.1%; converted in terms of the exchange rate it reached as high as US$2,029 which is US$939 more than the average for the whole nation. Jiangsu succeeds Shanghai, Beijing, Tinajin, Zhejiang and Guangdong as a region where the GDP per capita exceeds US$2,000.

In 2006 the GDP of Jiangsu exceeded RMB 2,100 billion; its GDP per capita was over US$3,500, just 9 years after the GDP per capita surpassed US$1,000 in 1997. The GDP of Jiangsu maintained a double-digit increase for the 15th consecutive year, which is particularly reflected in the remarkable improvement in people's living standard. The per capita disposable income of urban residents was RMB 14,084 and the net per capita income of rural residents was RMB 5,823, up 14.3% and 10.2% respectively. The total output value of Jiangsu and the growth course of GDP per capita are roughly indicated in Table 14.2.

3. GDP per capita of Zhejiang

In 2005 the GDP in Zhejiang was RMB 1,336.5 billion, up 12.4% over the previous year. Computed in terms of the annual average permanent population, the GDP per capita was equal to RMB 27,703, an increase of 10.8% over 2004; based on the exchange rate in 2005 it reached US$3,363, reaching the average level of upper-middle income countries. The GDP per capita of Zhejiang ranked fourth to Shanghai (RMB 51,474), Beijing (RMB 44,969) and Tianjin (RMB 35,405) while its gross GDP came out first.

In 2006 the GDP of Zhejiang totaled RMB 1,564.9 billion, up 11.7% over 2005; its GDP per capita exceeded RMB 30,000, up to RMB 31,684, nearly equal to US$4,000; in particular, the per capita of Hangzhou and Ningbo reached US$6,700 and 6,568 respectively. Zhejiang, the first area in China where the GDP per capita exceeded US$3,000, will witness an excess of US$4,000 which implies that Zhejiang is steadily entering the ranks of upper-middle income countries. In such circumstance, the industrialization and urbanization of Zhejiang will speed up constantly.

Table 14.1 GDP per capita of Shanghai in principal years (RMB)

Index	1978	1990	2000	2005
GDP per capita (computed in terms of census population)	2,497	6,107	36,217	67,492
GDP per capita (computed in terms of permanent population)	2,497	5,910	29,671	51,474

Source: Data from *China City Statistical Yearbook 2005*.

Table 14.2. The total output value of Jiangsu and its GDP per capita in principal years (this figure is expressed in current prices)

Year	GDP of Jiangsu (RMB 100 million)	GDP per capita of Jiangsu (RMB)
1978	249.24	430
1990	1,416.50	2,109
2000	8,553.69	11,765
2004	15,003.60	20,223
2005	18,305.66	24,560

Source: *Jiangsu Statistical Yearbook 2006*.

From the above analysis, we can see that the GDP per capita of the Yangtze River Delta ranks among the first in the whole nation and basically reaches the level of upper-middle income countries.

Life expectancy

The average life expectancy is a comprehensive reflection of the health conditions of the entire population in a country or region. Demographers employ the average life expectancy to measure lifespan, namely, the average age senior people will live to. In 2006 the average life expectancy of our country was 72.6 years, 70.8 for men and 74.6 for women i.e. 3.8 years longer than men. The expectation of life in various areas in the Yangtze River Delta is presented as follows.

1. The average life expectancy in Shanghai

In the early period of the founding of China, the life expectancy of men was only 42.0 years and 45.6 for women in Shanghai. Then it went up rapidly, rising to 74.9 by 1990 with 72.77 and 77.02 years for men and women respectively. It ascended to 77.2 in 1997, 2.3 years longer than in 1990; 75.2 for men and 79.2 for women, respectively 2.43 and 2.18 years longer than in 1990. The life expectancy in Shanghai is above the average level of the world and the level of middle-income countries, and even comes near the level of developed countries.

According to statistics gathered by the department for population census and employment statistics of the Shanghai Statistics Bureau, the life expectancy in Shanghai was as long as 78.77 years in 2000, 76.71 for men and 80.81 for women. In 2003, women's life expectancy in Shanghai reached 81.81; the birth rate there was 4.3‰, hitting a historic low; and infant mortality was stable at a low level that basically reached the level of developed countries. In 2004, the life expectancy of women in Shanghai was 82.48 years, which was 1.67 years longer than at the end of the Ninth Five Year Plan and the highest in the whole country; the mortality of infants, children under five and pregnant women and puerperas was relatively 3.78‰, 5.47‰ and 0.1079‰, all of which attained the targets set in the Tenth Five-year Plan in advance. Shanghai Population and Family Planning Commission, reporting the results of a sample investigation of 1% of the entire population of Shanghai in 2005, claimed that life expectancy in Shanghai was continuously lengthening and that the life expectancy of census residents was 80.13, 1.36 years longer than in 2000.

2. The average life expectancy in Jiangsu

The average life expectancy in Jiangsu in 1990 was 72.87 years (70.39 for men, 75.40 for women), far longer than the world average of 66, the less developed areas of 61 and Asian countries of 64 in 1992. In accordance with the complete life table compiled in 1990, the life expectancy of comparatively developed areas such as Suzhou, Wuxi, Changzhou and Nantong was distinctly longer than that of the less developed areas such as Xuzhou, Huaiyin, Yancheng and Lianyungang.

Based on the fifth national census statistics in 2000, the life expectancy in Jiangsu was 74.13 years (71.88 for men and 76.47 for women). Surprisingly, the life expectancy for women was 11.47 years longer than that of 65 in the whole world as anticipated by the United Nations. Currently the number of centenarians in Jiangsu is increasing year by year; in 2002, there were 112 centenarians in Nanjing and 150 by 2005. The natural population growth rate in Jiangsu decreased from 6.92‰ in 2002 to 2.25‰ while the average life expectancy rose from 72.87 in 1990 to 74.13 in 2000, up 1.26 over ten years.

In 2006 the life expectancy in Nanjing reached 77.45 years, 75.32 for men and 79.84 for women, up 0.34, 0.06 and 0.65 respectively.

3. The average life expectancy in Zhejiang

Before the building of the new China, the average life expectancy in Zhejiang was about 35 years; early in the period it was no more than 50; by 1981 it had increased to 69.51; then by 1990 it had continued to rise to 71.78 years, 69.66 for men, 4.58 years shorter than women's life expectancy of 74.24; it rose to 72.46 in 1995, reaching the level of developed countries; it was 74.7 in 2000, with women's life expectancy being 77.21 years, 4.71 years longer than that for men of 72.5; but it fell to 73.3 in 2005.

On the whole, life expectancy in Zhejiang has increased yearly in pace with the reform and opening up, but it is still varied in different areas. For example, by the end of 2004, there were 299 persons of 100 or more years old in Hangzhou, among whom 227 persons lived in urban districts (including Xiaoshan and Yuhang) which accounted for 75.92% of the total. Thus the average life expectancy in Hangzhou has attained the advanced level of the world. According to statistics, life expectancy in Hangzhou increased by 3.1 from 2000 to 2004, with the increase for men and women being 3.04 and 3.36 respectively; in 2004, it was 78.85 years (76.68 for men and 81.17 for women). *Ningbo's Annual Report on Causes of Residents' Death in 2006* presented that women's life expectancy in Ningbo was 79.47 years in 2006, 0.78 more than the previous year, and was 5.39 years longer than men's (74.08); in 2005, it was 78.60, which was 0.24 longer than 78.36 of 2004 and 4.85 longer than that for men (73.75) in the same year.

Educational level

The educational level is considered as a crucial index for measuring the quality of population in a country or region, including the average years of receiving education, the aggregate enrollment rate as well as the literacy rate.

1. The educational level in Shanghai

The overall educational level in Shanghai is relatively high. The population with all educational levels was 10.720 million and accounted for 78.5% of the total population of Shanghai. This proportion was above the average national level yet still lower than that in Beijing, Tianjin and Liaoning, which was up to 91% in 1997 while the illiteracy rate was 9.03%. In 1990, people with secondary educational level accounted for the largest proportion, which was 39.3% of the total population of Shanghai; then were people with elementary educational level, making up 28.3%; the proportion of people with higher educational level was the smallest, equaling 24.3%. However, in 1997, the proportion of people with secondary, elementary and higher educational level fell to 37%, 21.3% and 23.8% respectively; in 1990, people with higher educational level made up merely 8.4%, which rose slightly to 8.9% in 1997.

From Table 14.3, we can conclude that Shanghai has made substantial achievements in education in primary, junior, high schools and colleges and universities since 2000, which has facilitated the improvement of the per capita educational level in Shanghai by a large margin.

Table 14.3. The educational situation in Shanghai

Index	1990	2000	2004	2005
The number of schools				
Institutions of higher learning	50	37	59	60
Ordinary secondary schools	1,219	1,120	990	966
Ordinary middle schools	712	861	822	807
Primary schools	2,630	1,021	648	640
Special education schools	29	34	29	28
Full-time teachers (10,000)				
Institutions of higher learning	2.58	2.05	2.87	3.18
Ordinary secondary schools	5.62	6.23	6.13	6.08
Ordinary middle schools	4.13	5.01	5.13	5.12
Primary schools	5.88	4.43	3.75	3.74
Special education schools	0.06	0.09	0.10	0.10
The number of students to be enrolled (10,000)				
Institutions of higher learning	3.24	8.13	13.06	13.18
Ordinary secondary schools	22.61	33.58	28.64	26.67
Ordinary middle schools	17.09	26.46	21.81	20.90
Primary schools	18.14	10.28	10.55	10.36
Special education schools	0.06	0.11	0.07	0.07
Students (10,000)				
Institutions of higher learning	12.13	22.68	41.57	44.26
Ordinary secondary schools	62.59	105.28	106.94	99.30
Ordinary middle schools	48.31	79.54	82.7	77.02
Primary schools	110.19	78.86	53.74	53.50
Special education schools	0.33	0.54	0.54	0.52

Source: *Shanghai Statistical Yearbook 2006*.

2. The educational level in Jiangsu

The overall trend in the educational structure of Jiangsu can be illustrated by the fact that the number of people with middle and higher educational level and their proportion in the total population has increased while the number of illiterate and semi-literate people and their proportion has decreased. People with higher educational level increased by 1.56 times from 1982 to 1990; the gross illiteracy rate fell from 22.7% in 1982 to 11.05% in 1990.

Jiangsu's educational situation in the main years from 1990 to 2005 is indicated in Table 14.4. Up to the end of 2005, there were 115 ordinary institutions of higher learning, which had enrolled 1,306,200 college students (including 390,200 new entrants and 257,300 graduates) and 89,100 postgraduates (including 28,700 new entrants and 19,300 graduates); the gross enrollment rate was as high as 35.6%; students attending vocational schools reached 1.45 billion; the proportion of junior school students entering high schools was equal to 93.5% and that of school-age children admitted to primary schools reached 99.8%; special schools admitted 30,000 students including 3,900 new entrants; and there were 1,501,500 enrolled children in kindergartens. The conditions for setting up schools in rural areas had improved further and free compulsory education became available to all rural students.

Table 14.4. The educational situation in Jiangsu

Index	1990	1995	2000	2004	2005
The number of schools					
Ordinary institutions of higher learning	70	67	71	111	115
Ordinary secondary schools	6,377	5,093	4,222	3,561	3,530
Secondary specialized schools	195	213	185	150	150
Ordinary middle schools	5,808	4,439	3,675	3,155	3,141
Primary schools	30,557	27,062	19,110	6,723	6,261
Full-time teachers (10,000)					
Ordinary institutions of higher learning	2.76	2.73	3.31	5.90	6.73
Ordinary secondary schools	19.63	22.16	25.02	30.19	31.13
Secondary specialized schools	1.20	1.30	1.37	1.24	1.42
Ordinary middle schools	17.25	18.91	21.59	27.23	27.98
Primary schools	26.95	27.35	28.90	26.49	26.16
The number of students to be enrolled (10,000)					
Ordinary higher education	4.56	7.13	18.22	34.08	39.02
Postgraduates	0.23	0.38	0.97	2.68	2.87
College students	4.33	6.75	17.25	31.40	36.15
Ordinary secondary schools	109.51	136.80	157.94	203.59	197.19
Secondary specialized schools	4.28	12.27	10.64	21.94	24.45
Ordinary middle schools	99.08	114.03	141.44	168.44	157.55
Primary schools	90.12	130.42	95.53	68.21	61.93

Source: *Jiangsu Statistical Yearbook 2006*.

Thus the tendency of the whole educational structure in Jiangsu can be summed up as the proportion of people with various educational levels rises bit by bit whereas that of illiterate and semi-literate persons falls gradually. In addition, the educational level in Jiangsu also increasingly upgrades which takes the lead in the whole country.

3. The educational level in Zhejiang

On the basis of four census statistics we can see that Zhejiang show a similar trend to Jiangsu, which means that it also has an increase in people with middle and higher educational level and the their proportion, along with a decease in illiterate and semi-literate people and their proportion. The people with a higher educational level in 1990 were respectively 2.1 and 1.67 times more than in 1964 and 1982; the gross illiteracy rate was 37.89% in 1964, falling to 23.93% in 1982 and 17.61% in 1990.

Zhejiang's educational situation in the principal years from 1990 to 2005 is shown in Table 14.5.

Table 14.5. The educational situation in Zhejiang

Index	1990	1995	2000	2004	2005
The number of schools					
Ordinary institutions of higher learning	37	37	35	68	67
Ordinary middle schools	3,353	3,255	2,940	2,609	2,524
Primary schools	31,800	22,600	11,800	6,700	6,100
Special education	43	56	62	62	62
Full-time teachers (10,000)					
Ordinary institutions of higher learning	1.16	1.15	1.90	3.58	3.84
Ordinary middle schools	8.98	10.77	13.93	16.29	16.69
Primary schools	13.46	14.34	16.04	16.01	16.22
Special education	0.05	0.11	0.11	0.12	0.12
Students to be enrolled (10,000)					
Ordinary higher education	—	—	9.76	20.36	22.50
Postgraduates	—	—	0.41	0.80	0.96
College students	1.83	2.81	9.35	19.56	21.54
Ordinary middle schools	64.78	80.67	92.51	84.72	86.45
Primary schools	64.60	66.19	61.58	51.42	48.96
Special education	0.08	0.28	0.24	0.17	0.15
Students (10,000)					
Ordinary higher education	—	—	22.23	59.49	67.69
Postgraduates	—	—	0.99	2.21	2.56
College students	1.83	2.812	1.24	57.28	65.13
Ordinary middle schools	169.62	210.54	249.55	266.14	261.08
Primary schools	372.43	362.98	353.76	344.31	342.40
Special education	0.30	2.37	1.97	1.42	1.29

Source: *Zhejiang Statistical Yearbook 2006.*

In recent years, Zhejiang has vigorously promoted education especially higher education which has led to a great upgrading of educational level in Zhejiang. In the light of the authentic data, we draw a graph to represent the illiteracy rate of various areas in 2000. Therefore, as shown in Fig. 14.1, we can conclude that the illiteracy rate in the Yangtze River Delta was relatively lower than in the other areas, which is closely related to the rapid development of education as well as the great enhancement of educational level.

Fig. 14.1. The illiteracy rate of various areas in 2000 (%)

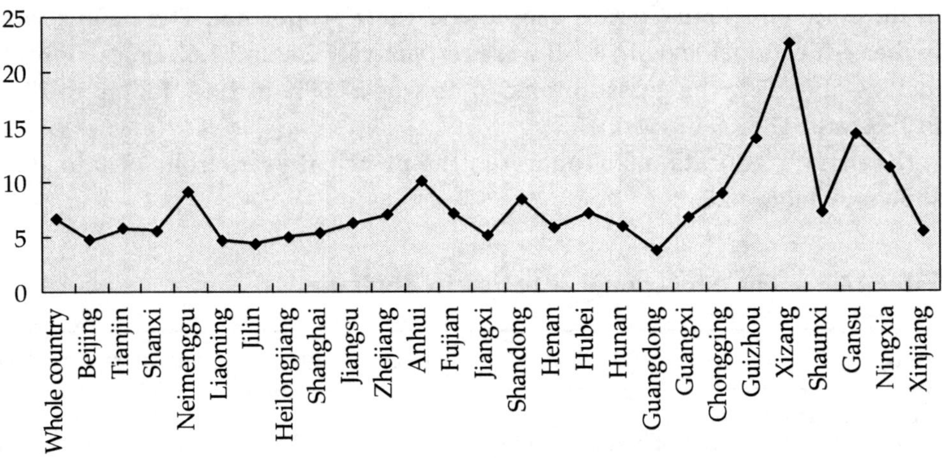

Other aspects

Human progress in the Yangtze River Delta is also reflected in culture, sports, social security, health care, urbanization, the urban unemployment rate registered at the end of each year, per capita residential savings, power consumption and so on. In this section, the social security will be given sole emphasis. Amartya Sen also focuses on the significant influence of social security on human life. He points out that if the responsibility for economic contraction is not shared by the public but completely assumed by the unemployed or by people who have just become redundant (who have the weakest capacity to survive), such contraction will ruin many people's life and even lead to over ten billion people falling into severe poverty.[1]

Take Shanghai as an example. The social security standards and the number of people subscribing to social insurance in the principal years are respectively shown in Tables 14.6 and 14.7.

Table 14.6. The subsidies for social security in Shanghai in principal years (RMB)

Index	2000	2004	2005
The minimum wage of employees	445	635	690
The minimum old-age pension for urban residents	460	460	460
The minimum living subsidy for urban residents	280	290	300

Table 14.7. The number of people subscribing to social insurance in Shanghai in principal years (10,000)

Index	2000	2004	2005
The basic old-age insurance for urban residents			
Urban workers	431.27	435.20	436.52
Self-employed persons and professionals	9.82	20.20	18.26
The retired who receive old-age pension	234.23	264.87	279.72
The basic medical insurance for urban residents			
Urban workers	364.59	433.06	434.51
Self-employed persons and professionals	—	20.20	18.26
The retired who receive old-age pension	202.14	264.16	279.11
The unemployment insurance for urban residents	434.86	488.32	466.06
The maternity insurance for urban residents	—	505.56	539.27
The compensation insurance for urban residents	—	488.32	523.71
The old-age insurance for rural residents	121.00	146.70	101.34
The social insurance for residents in small towns	—	58.74	110.16
The comprehensive insurance for non-native employees	—	209.40	247.70
The subsidies for children receiving hospital treatment	212.47	183.14	181.09

Source: *Shanghai Statistical Yearbook 2006.*

Tables 14.6 and 1.7 show that the coverage of social security in Shanghai is comparatively wide and that policy-holders make up a large proportion, which suggests good living conditions for residents in Shanghai. What needs special attention is that Shanghai also provides social security for non-native employees, which embodies the lead Shanghai takes in social security.

The social security system in Jiangsu has also been further perfected. The system of basic old-age, basic medical and unemployment insurance for urban residents covers 90% of urban areas in Jiangsu. The major types of social insurance have become available to the non-public sectors, rural migrant workers and township enterprises; the basic living subsidy and unemployment insurance for laid-off workers of state-owned enterprises are integrated smoothly; the retired persons from closed and bankrupt state-owned or collective enterprises are covered by basic medical insurance; and the basic living security system for farmers whose land has been expropriated is set up in an all-round way. The recipients of cost of living allowances cover both rural and urban areas in the overall province; people entitled to cost of living allowances, including 401,000 urban residents with financial difficulties and 855,000 farmers, receive them.

By the end of 2005, 8.72 million people in Zhejiang had subscribed to the basic old-age insurance in their own enterprises, up 670,000 people over the previous year; 4.40 million people had subscribed to unemployment insurance, an increase of 120,000 people; 6.32 million people had subscribed to medical insurance, an increase of 630,000; workers buying compensation and maternity insurance were respectively 4.55 million and 2.80 million. Meanwhile there were 610,000 people eligible for cost of living allowances, including 88,000 urban residents and 522,000 farmers; the average monthly minimum living allowances in urban and rural areas were separately RMB 223 and RMB 129 per person. RMB 560 billion was allocated in cost of living allowances in that year, an increase of 26.0% over the previous year.

In recent years the Yangtze River Delta has also made a great contribution to the security system for rural immigrant workers. For example, Jiangsu province actively set up the wage payment security system, strengthened the management of recruitment and workplace safety and health, and constantly intensified services and training related to employment. In Shanghai the minimum wage was extended to rural immigrant workers in the building industry; all the children of rural immigrant workers attended schools; and rural immigrant workers were also supplied with medical security. In short, the sound social security system in the Yangtze River Delta ensures that there is always a sufficient supply of rural immigrant workers even if a shortage of labor occurs in other areas, and therefore it makes a positive contribution to the economic growth and stability of the Yangtze River Delta.

The Influence of the Service Industry on Life Expectancy

The average life expectancy is an indicator reflecting the level of economic development and of medical and health care services, which are influenced by complex factors. Ma Shuluan in his article "An Analysis of Factors Influencing Life Expectancy" states that there are mainly two factors influencing life expectancy, namely, human biology and social economy. The former refers to the influence of physiological structure and law of biology, for instance, the mortality difference in gender influenced by gender difference determined by chromosomes, dying from cerebral apoplexy influenced by one's degenerated cerebrovascular state etc. while the latter mainly refers to the influence of life style, environment and health care service on life expectancy.[2]

The influence of medical and health care services on life expectancy

We believe that the factors influencing the life expectancy cover three major aspects: constitution and inheritance, medical and health care level, and living standard. An economist named Amartya Sen (2002) once claimed that both the increase in public expenditure on medical and health care and the elimination of poverty are the most important factors determining the increase in life expectancy. In the following section the influence of medical and health care services on life expectancy will be explained further.

The following indexes are adopted to represent the level of medical service: (1) the number of employees in the medical services; (2) the number of medical institutions, (3) the number of beds supplied by medical institutions; (4) the numbers of hospitals; and (5) the number of certified doctors.

By the end of 2004 there were 489 hospitals in Shanghai with 85,000 beds for patients and 101,700 health workers including 43,800 certified doctors and 38,100 registered nurses. A total of 94,608,600 patients received diagnostic attention in medical institutions in Shanghai, involving 92,495,600 treated by doctors at outpatient and emergency departments, 1,457,100 discharged from hospitals, 425,700 hospitalized for operations and 230,200 receiving first-aid before being hospitalized.

Jiangsu also achieved a rapid advance in health care service. It increased support for rural health care and transformed rural health centers; the coverage of the new type of rural cooperative medical care system reached 90.5%; pre-job training was provided for 259,00 rural medical technicians and administrators; and it also vigorously expanded community health services which were extended to 65% of urban residents. By the end of 2005 there were also 16,100 health institutions of various types which included 2,504 hospitals and health centers, 203 sanitation and anti-epidemic stations, and 109 maternity and child care centers. Health institutions of various types supplied 205,000 beds including 189,400 beds in hospitals and health centers; the number of health technicians totaled 262,200 which included 110,600 certified doctors and auxiliary doctors, 82,800 registered nurses as well as 7,500 health technicians in sanitation and anti-epidemic stations and 4,000 health technicians in maternity and child care centers; the number of rural health centers reached 14,000, which had 53,000 beds, 60,000 health technicians, and 59,000 country doctors and health workers.

In Zhejiang province, 86 counties and county-level cities and districts in counties had implemented the new type of rural cooperative medical care system by the end of 2005, accounting for 98.8% of those with an agricultural population. 24.6 million farmers subscribed to medical insurance, making up 71% of all the agricultural population. There were 12,549 health institutions, including 2,896 hospitals and health centers, 88 maternity and child care centers and 27 special hospitals (centers and stations); 131,000 beds were provided in hospitals and health centers; and the number of health technicians reached 198,000 of whom 87,700 were certified doctors and auxiliary doctors and 60,300 were registered nurses. Sanitation and anti-epidemic centers (epidemic prevention stations) were as many as 97 employing 3,800 health technicians. Sanitary supervisory organs numbered 105 with 2,300 health technicians employed. The number of rural health centers reached 2,162, in which 20,500 beds were supplied and 35,800 health technicians were employed. The influence of all the achievements above on the life expectancy in the nation as well as the Yangtze River Delta can be summarized in Table 14.8.

Table 14.8. Life expectancy in the whole nation and the Yangtze River Delta

Index	The Nation	Shanghai	Jiangsu	Zhejiang
Life expectancy in the early period of the building of China	35	43.6	—	50
Life expectancy in 1990	68.55	74.90	71.37	71.78
Life expectancy in recent years	72.6	80.13	74.13	73.3

Note: In terms of life expectancy in recent years, data for the nation is from 2006; data for Shanghai and Zhejiang is for 2005; data for Jiangsu is from the fifth census statistics.

The crucial lessons from the development of medical health services in the Yangtze River Delta

With the socio-economic development, residents' need for and utilization of health services have undergone a substantial change. The problem of inadequate and unaffordable medical services has been quite serious in recent years. Therefore the fairness in health services has attracted increasing attention. Particularly in the vast rural areas, the accessibility and fairness of residential health services are in demand, which has had a serious impact on the improvement of residents' health.

A large number of people in our country still live in the countryside. The disintegration of the traditional cooperative medical care system has led the public to be concerned about rural health conditions and the rural areas have become the main force in the self-funded medical care system again. For farmers, the limitation of the current agricultural income makes it impossible for them to afford treatment for serious illness on their own, which results in the problem of poverty caused by illness.

Taking Shanghai as an example, the comprehensive economic power of the suburbs of Shanghai is increasing year by year and the GDP per capita there reached RMB 21,800 (US$3,443) in 2000. At the same time, its health care service has also made great progress. On the whole, a three-stage medical and health care network has been set up and perfected in the suburbs of Shanghai so that 52% of the total population, who live in the suburbs, have access to effective health care and their health continues to improve continuously. However there are still some defects in its health care service, mainly related to imbalanced development which is reflected in both the unfairness and the inefficiency in allocation and utilization of health resources. In the suburbs of Shanghai, particularly in the less-developed areas, the efficiency of utilization of medical care services is fairly low. The proportion of doctors and of nurses in per 1,000 suburb residents is also below the average level of Shanghai.

The expenditure of the suburbs of Shanghai on medical and health care services increases by an absolute value yearly, which was RMB 91 million in 1990 rising to RMB 607 million in 2000, up by 1.66 times in real terms if excluding the price rise factor. Meanwhile the proportion of such expenditure in the total funds used in Shanghai's medical and health care services is also increasing yearly, from 29.7% in 1990 to 42.9% in 2000. In 1990 the per capita fund for medical and health care services for suburb residents was RMB 15.8, just 66.4% of the average level in Shanghai (the per capita fund for medical and health care services was RMB 23.8 for the whole city) while it was up to RMB 87.5 in 2000, 80.3% of the average level in Shanghai (per capita fund on medical and health care services was RMB 108.92 for the whole city). This shows that the per capita fund for medical and health care services for suburban residents is always below the average level for the whole city, but the gap between the former and the latter is gradually narrowing after ten years of development, which means that the local government of Shanghai gives preference to medical and health care services and fairness in allocation of funds for medical and health care services has improved progressively. But in terms of the proportion of funds used for medical and health care services in the total financial expenditure in suburbs of Shanghai, although this gradually increased from

7.68% in 1990 to 3.19% in 2000, and the growth rate was lower than that of the budgetary expenditure of the local government.

Generally speaking, the residents of Jiangsu province have led a relatively comfortable life in pace with many years' progress. However, such a kind of life is low-level and also imbalanced in that social services in rural areas are more backward than in the other areas. The low level of medical care and poverty caused by illness are the most serious problems. As a result, Jiangsu province formulated the "Enforcement Suggestions of Jiangsu Provincial Government for the Set-up of the New Type of Rural Cooperative Medical Care System" in 2003, in line with the "Decisions of the State Council on Further Intensifying Rural Health Care Services." The pilot project has been launched in 10 selected counties and county-level cities and districts since 2004. Even though certain achievements were made, the gap between rural and urban areas in the medical security level was still wide because the latter was nearly three times higher than the former and the per capita level in urban areas was over 16 times as high as that in rural areas.

Jiangsu has witnessed fast socio-economic development as well as a leading medical care level nationwide, yet its development does not keep a balance as rural medical care lags far behind that in the urban areas. Ma Rimin, the director of Shankeng Health Center in Yongjia county, once said: "There are only four health workers including me. As the director, I also should treat patients. Due to the poor medical equipment, the public's needs for medical care cannot be satisfied at all. Even at present, we still rely on the stethoscope, thermometer and sphygmomanometer and thus an exact diagnosis cannot made without the necessary equipment such as type-B ultrasonic, electrocardiogram (ECG) and X-ray." Ye Zhen, the vice-director of Zhejiang Health Department, also admitted that: "In Zhejiang, there are still many country health centers propped up by the three traditional equipments, especially in some remote areas. The imbalanced medical care level in rural areas is primarily restricted by housing, facilities, technology, skills and so on." Therefore, Zhejiang Youth League Committee and Youth Development Foundation promoted another public programme of Project Hope, namely, "Hope Hospital—Relief Operation for Country Health Centers," which was launched last year.

The insiders believe that because of the shortage of wards, medical equipment and skills, the introduction of similar medical relief experiences to the country's medical care system is conducive to resolving the current problems. Non-governmental organizations related to medical care services account for a large proportion all over the world. The aim of such organizations is to serve disadvantaged groups. Members of the organizations should effectively access to those in need of relief and aid and have relief experiences as well as the ability to organize; meanwhile the organizations play a role in founding the infrastructure of medical care services so as to lower the pressure on the government to provide regular medical care services.

Just like Jiangsu province, Zhejiang has conducted a pilot project of the new type of rural cooperative medical care system in 27 selected countries and county-level cities and districts in counties since August 2003. There is no doubt that such a system creates a lot of benefits for farmers but there are still many problems in the practice. For example, the overall medical care plan for serious illness is emphasized while basic medical care service is overlooked. However the medical insurance service aimed at serious illness, related with private belongings remarkably, should be regulated by the market whereas the basic medical care service, related with public property, should be led by the malfunction of the market or the insufficient property and mainly supplied by the government. Moreover the pressure on county-level finances is so heavy that they can not ensure the continuity of public funds raising for the cooperative medical care services. In the process of implementing the cooperative medical care system, the government put undue focus on administrative promotion but little on the security of the legal system and administration. Such a pattern of system promotion, which depends upon the performance orientation and administrative promotion yet lacks legal and administrative security, has a distinct short-term effect but the stability and authority of policy and system are relatively weak.

The comparison between Brazil and East Asia and Southeast Asia illustrated in Amartya Sen's book Basing Development on Liberty can be used to develop the medical care services in the Yangtze River Delta. He claims that the growth rate of gross national product (GNP) in Brazil is roughly as high as that in East Asia and Southeast Asia but per capita life expectancy of Brazil in which the economy grows at a rather high speed increases very slowly because of the long-standing problems with serious social inequality and neglect of public medical care development.[3] Hence we can draw the conclusion that we should balance the development of the medical care services both in cities and towns and should ensure equity in funds for medical care services in the entire Yangtze River Delta; we can take the construction of a harmonious society into consideration only when all people's welfare is increased in the course of economic growth. As Amartya Sen said: "The effect of economic growth, to a great degree, is determined by how the achievement in economic growth is utilized."[4]

The Influence of the Service Industry on the Educational Level

An analysis of factors influencing the educational level

The United Nations Development Program (UNDP, 1990) stated that the HDI represented the average achievement of human progress in the following three aspects: (1) a healthy and long life, (2) education and (3) a comfortable life. Education is measured in terms of the gross enrollment rate and adult literacy rate. The reason for paying close attention to and studying education is that education is essential to an individual's development; and, the more practical reason lies in the crucial role of education in the economic growth. Education can not only improve the efficiency of workers and leaders' administrative ability but also lay the foundations for entrepreneurs to innovate. In addition, the improvement of educational level (especially the educational level of women) contributes to the drop in birth rate and further decreases the growth rate of the population. The reduced number of children in a family can promote parents to raise their investment in labor capital for children.

The factors influencing educational level are diversified but we will address the four major ones.

1. The supply of educational service products

The supply of educational service products includes the quantity and price of educational service products. The former is measured in terms of school size and the number of teachers whereas the latter is measured in terms of tuition and miscellaneous fees. Both aspects have a direct effect on the supply of educational service products. To be specific, the expansion of school size permits the enrollment of more students but it is impossible for there to be a limitless increase in the student-teacher ratio and thus the quantity of education service products will be constrained ultimately if a school is extended but lacks teachers.

From Tables 14.9 and 14.10 we can conclude that the number of colleges, universities and teachers in the Yangtze River Delta was on the increase from 1990 to 2005, which advanced the increase in the gross rate of accession to institutions of higher learning in the area. In 2005, the gross rate of accession to institutions of higher learning in Shanghai, Jiangsu and Zhejiang was 65%, 35.6% and 34% respectively, which suggests that all three areas had moved onto the stage of mass higher education.

Table 14.9. Higher education in the Yangtze River Delta in the principal years

Area	Index	1990	2000	2004	2005
Shanghai	The number of institutions of higher learning	50	37	59	60
	The number of teachers in institutions of higher learning (10,00)	2.58	2.05	2.87	3.18
Jiangsu	The number of institutions of higher learning	70	71	111	115
	The number of teachers in institutions of higher learning (10,000)	2.76	3.31	5.9	6.73
Zhejiang	The number of institutions of higher learning	37	35	68	67
	The number of teachers in institutions of higher learning (10,000)	1.16	1.90	3.58	3.84

Table 14.10. The number of college students per ten thousand people in the Yangtze River Delta in the principal years

Area	1990	2000	2004	2005
Shanghai	94	172	307	325
Jiangsu	21.7	61.7	133.8	155.2
Zhejiang	14.25	14.86	15.49	15.26

Generally speaking, the increase in the price of an article will lead to the increase in the supply of it. Similarly, the increase in the price of an educational service product (tuition) can facilitate an educational institution to provide more educational service products. But the social profit from education (especially basic education) is more than the private profit and thus the improvement of educational level not only relies on charging high tuition but also needs financial support from the government. On the basis of the statistics on the Yangtze River Delta we can see that the financial expenditure on education has been increased by the government over the years. In 2000 the financial expenditure on education in Shanghai, Jiangsu and Zhejiang was RMB 9.379 billion, RMB 11.742 billion and RMB 7.819 billion respectively, which rose to RMB 18.294 billion, RMB 25.824 billion and RMB 23.155 billion respectively in 2005.

2. Per capita income

The enhancement of income stimulates the growth of investment in education. A person's investment in education and his/her income affect and promote each other. On the one hand, the growth of investment in education can raise one's all-round quality including educational level, tastes in life and ability to innovate, which permits a higher income and even higher-quality life; on the other hand, higher income impels one to be willing and able to increase investment in education for oneself as well as for one's children.

With the economic development, the GDP per capita in the Yangtze River Delta has clearly been on the increase. The GDP per capita in Table 14.11 is worked out in terms of prices in the relevant years. The growth of per capita income in the Yangtze River Delta is still remarkable even with the exclusion of the influence of inflation and per capita disposable income of urban and rural resident's advances in varying degrees. At the same time, the increase in income fosters the marked enhancement of per capita educational level in the Yangtze River Delta. Furthermore, the adult literacy rate in Shanghai, Jiangsu and Zhejiang respectively rose from 89%, 83% and 82% in 1990 to 95%, 90% and 88% in 2005.

Table 14.11. The change in GDP per capita in the Yangtze River Delta from 1985 to 2005 (RMB)

Area	1985	1990	1995	2000	2003	2004	2005
Shanghai	3,855	6,107	19,225	36,217	50,032	59,928	67,492
Jiangsu	1,053	2,109	7,319	11,765	16,830	20,223	24,560
Zhejiang	1,067	2,138	8,149	13,416	20,444	24,352	27,703

3. The national policy on education

The educational service is a special kind of article in that its social profit (especially the profit from basic education) is far higher than the private profit. Education plays a crucial role in the foundation of the revival and development of a country. That is because education can enhance the national quality and accumulate labor capital, which gives impetus to and basis for the continued development of the country in the future. Precisely because of the special nature of education, many countries supply nationals with free basic education as a form of welfare. Since the founding of the People's Republic of China, a great number of educational polices have been carried out to promote the expansion of the educational service. It was suggested in the Programme for Reform and Development of Education in China promulgated in 1993 that illiteracy among young and middle-aged people had been basically wiped out and that the nine years of compulsory education had been popularized by the year of 2000. In

Shanghai, Jiangsu and Zhejiang, the enrollment rates for school-age children admitted to primary schools and middle schools were over 99% in 2005, basically fulfilling the popularization of nine-year compulsory education.

4. Socio-economic structure

The socio-economic factor covers the socio-economic structure of a country as well as various institutional plans which influence educational level. The existing dual socio-economic structure, current system of national education and decentralized fiscal system have direct influences on the equal opportunity to receive education and to share educational resources, thereby hampering the improvement of educational level nationwide. Most of the people in our country live in rural areas while a large part of educational resources is secured by urban residents. Moreover due to the insufficient funds for education, the preference given to higher education causes a severe shortage of funds for primary education, which results in the sluggish development of primary education.

The influence of educational institutions on educational level

We will analyze the influence of educational institutions on educational level mainly based on some relevant factors which are convenient for statistics. We will lay emphasis on the following three factors.

1. The number of schools

Not only the quantity but the relative size of schools should be taken into consideration. If the school size is not reduced, an increase in the number of schools will boost the increase in supply of educational service products; if the absolute number of schools decreases while the relative size of schools expands, the ability to supply educational service products will not weaken.

The change in population leads to the year-by-year reduction of the number of school-age children admitted to primary school. In the Yangtze River Delta, the number of students enrolled in primary schools fell from 1995 to 2005, followed by a drop in the number of primary schools. However the enrollment rate for school-age children admitted to primary school remained higher than 99.6% during the ten years. At the same time, student-school ratio was on the increase while student-teacher ratio was on the decrease, which showed that the decreased number of schools and their extended size can advance the improving quality of educational service products as well as intensifying the ability of educational institution to supply such products.

2. The number of teachers

As an educator, the teacher is the direct provider of educational service products and thus the quantity and quality of teachers directly influence the supply of educational service products. The shortage of teachers, on the one hand, constrains the increase in opportunities in education and thus means school-age children are not able to receive educational service products; on the other hand, it leads to the growth of student-teacher ratio and thus overloads teachers and further influences the quality of educational service products to a great degree. Moreover the employment of unqualified teachers just to meet the temporary need will also lower the quality of educational products.

With the socio-economic development, the need for higher education increases year by year. In Jiangsu the intake in ordinary institutions of higher learning rose by 4.5 times from 1995 to 2005. In Zhejiang the number of people with higher-educational level reached 2.5 million in 2005, 1,008,400 more than in the fifth national census statistics. The number of college students in Shanghai roughly doubled from 2000 to 2005, that is, it increased from 226,800 in 2000 to 442,600 in 2005. In addition, the number of both ordinary colleges and universities and the number of teachers in them gradually increased with the increasing need for them. For example, in Jiangsu, the number of teachers was up from 27,300 to 67,300 and the ordinary colleges and universities also increased from 67 to 115; there were similar increases to varying degrees in Jiangsu and Zhejiang.

On the one hand, the growth in the supply of educational service products, particularly the expansion of secondary and higher educational services, boosts the increase in average years of receiving education; on the other hand, it results in the change in the proportion of people with various educational levels in the total population, including an increase in the proportion of people with secondary and higher educational levels as well a decrease in the proportion of people with only elementary educational level.

3. The price of educational service products

At present education is a kind of service product, and therefore people should pay for receiving education or consuming educational service products. However, basic education in numerous developed countries is supplied as a form of welfare for free so citizens of those countries have no idea about the price of basic educational service products. By contrast, citizens in our country have to pay tuition and miscellaneous fees for educational service products and such fees become a part of the cost of educational service products. Hence the price of educational service products affects the quantity of such products supplied by educational institutions to a greater or lesser extent. In theory, the more the fees that are paid for educational service products, the more the cost of such products can be made up and the more such products will be provided by educational institutions. The realistic and potential need for education is greatly expanding in our country. Nevertheless, facing the actual condition that education needs to be implemented in a poor country, residents in our country should pay fees such as tuition and miscellaneous fees to meet the cost of education if they want to enjoy educational services. As a result, the improvement of educational level also accompanies a substantial increase in the price of educational service products and the fees paid for education.

There is still a monopoly on educational resources in our country, which contains the growth in supply of educational service products and the rise in price of such products that leads to increasing expenditure on education. But such a problem cannot be dealt with only by the direct supplier of educational service products or consumers themselves. The strong positive externality of education presents a great demand for more support from the nation. What educational institutions can do at present is to act in accordance with national policies on education, fulfil their duties, stop all irregular charges and provide high-quality educational service products for society.

The significant experience of expanding education services in the Yangtze River Delta

In the light of the statistics of four censuses, it can be concluded that in the Yangtze River Delta, the number of people with secondary and higher educational levels as well as their proportion to the total population goes up while the number of illiterate and semi-literate people and their proportion decreases. Moreover conditions for setting up schools in rural areas are gradually improving.

Jiangsu province perseveres in giving priority to the development of education, accelerates the expansion of strengthening the province through education, promotes the balanced development of education of all types and at all levels, and enhances compulsory, vocational and higher education in rural areas. According to the data of the *Jiangsu Statistical Yearbook 2006*, the enrollment rate for students admitted to senior high schools reached 89%; the gross enrollment rate for students admitted to institutions of higher learning was as high as 35.6%; the institutions of higher learning, college students and students enrolled in vocational schools account for the largest proportion in the whole nation; conditions for setting up schools in rural areas attained further improvement; the problem of releasing provincial subsidies to primary and secondary school teachers in towns in less-developed areas was completely smoothed away; the rate of admission into secondary schools was 93.5%; the enrollment rate for school-age children admitted to primary schools was up to 99.8%.

In Shanghai the rate of admission to compulsory education was always 99.9%, which showed that a balanced, high-quality service was basically supplied there. Enrollment of students admitted to senior high schools reached 98% and an open, diversified pattern of operating schools began to take shape. In 2006, 271,700 students were admitted to ordinary senior high schools. The modification of patterns and structures of schools of all types and at all levels yielded great progress. For example, some schools which had poor operating conditions and were not in line with the socio-economic development were dissolved or merged so that the allocation of educational resources was optimized further and the gains-to-scale of school was also increased. The investment in education by Shanghai municipal government was increased yearly; the aggregate expenditure on local education was equal to RMB 37.073 billion in 2006, an increase of 8.19% over the previous year, which included RMB 22.703 million budgetary expenditure on education, up 9.52% over 2005; the fiscal funds for local education in 2006 made up 2.57% of the total local GDP.

The rate of enrollment in primary and secondary schools in Zhejiang was respectively 99.99% and 99.59% in 2004; the gross rate for pre-school children admitted to kindergartens reached 85.56%; the enrollment rate for handicapped children was 91.02%; the rate for children of the floating population accessing the nine-year compulsory education was 97%; and the proportion of students admitted to senior high schools was up to 91.02%. Therefore it can be concluded that basic education in Zhejiang assumes the lead in various major indexes nationwide. In 1996 Zhejiang became the first province to implement an overall plan to resolve the problems related to non-state employed teachers. It also implemented systems for teachers' certificates and lifelong education and enhanced in-service training, which boosted the great advance in the proportion of qualified teachers and those with higher educational level. In 2005 the full-time teachers in kindergarten, primary school, ordinary middle school, vocational middle schools and ordinary institutions of higher learning reached 58,700, 162,200, 166,900, 22,400 and 38,400 respectively; the acceptance rate of educational background of teachers in kindergarten, primary school, secondary school, ordinary high school and vocational high school was 94.3%, 98.7%, 97.7%, 92.6% and 76.7% respectively; and the number of teachers graduated from college or above in primary schools and teachers graduated from university or above respectively reached 59.8% and 50.9%. The overall investment in education hit RMB 48.03 million in 2004, 2.53% of the local GDP. Zhejiang gave active encouragement to non-governmental sectors to run schools and there are now over ten thousand non-state educational institutions. The mechanism for splitting educational costs is beginning to take shape. Moreover the non-state educational institutions charge at cost and have launched educational credit operations. Owing to the increasing investment, the conditions for running schools of all types and at all levels have distinctly improved; the ordinary primary and secondary school, secondary vocational school and ordinary institutions of higher learning respectively cover areas of 53,304,200, 8,706,100 and 19,726,100 square meters.

The remarkable advance in each index keeps pace with the socio-economic development in the Yangtze River Delta. On the basis of the *China Statistical Yearbook 2006*, Shanghai, Jiangsu and Zhejiang were leading the way in GDP per capita nationwide. The GDP per capita of Shanghai was RMB 51,474, ranking first in our country. According to *The 2005 Report on China's Human Progress*, the HDI of Shanghai, Zhejiang and Jiangsu was 0.909, 0.817 and 0.805 respectively, ranking first, fourth and seventh in the whole nation, all of which were above the national average level (0.755). The economic growth in the Yangtze River Delta fosters the expansion of education so that institutions of higher learning and students admitted to universities in the region accounts for the largest proportion in the whole country. Furthermore the well-developed education system provides for the economic development of the Yangtze River Delta a great amount of labor capital which safeguards the sustained and stable development of the regional economy.

Diverse factors including the increase in governmental investment and social funds, the growth in per capita income, the support of educational policies etc. interact with each other, which facilitates the improvement of educational level in the Yangtze River Delta. By the end of 2005, the adult literacy rate in Jiangsu, Shanghai and Zhejiang was respectively 90%, 95% and 88%. But for all the great progress in education in the Yangtze River Delta, there are still many deficiencies. For example, there is a lack of fairness in the opportunity to receive education as well as in the allocation of educational resources. As shown in Table 14.12, the ratio of men to women is roughly one to one in the composition of population at the age of 15 and above, yet women form the larger proportion in the illiterate population. For instance, in Shanghai, men account for less than 20% of illiterate people. Although the data for Jiangsu and Zhejiang are a little different from Shanghai, all the three areas are almost on a par in the main. The unfairness of education is not only displayed in the difference in educational level between men and women but also in the difference in educational level and quality of education between urban and rural areas, which is less serious in Shanghai than in Jiangsu and Zhejiang. There are also differences in many educational indexes between the southern, central and northern part of Jiangsu; due to the rapid economic development of the southern part of Jiangsu, the adult literacy rate, the gross rate of admission into schools at various levels and the quality of education surpass those in the central and northern part of Jiangsu.

The dual socio-economic structure brings about the distinct difference in income and social status between urban and rural residents, whereas the current national educational system and the decentralized fiscal system promote the close connection of the supply of opportunity to receive education with the family registration system. The Yangtze River Delta takes the lead in socio-economic reform and development nationwide. However fundamental barriers such as the dual society and family registration system have not been broken down and various attendant social problems remain unsolved.

In terms of education, the deficiencies can be concluded as follows. (1) The difference in educational development level between urban and rural areas is marked, which is mainly represented in the following three aspects. Firstly, there are fewer people with good education in rural areas than in urban areas, and most of the illiterate people in Jiangsu come from the rural areas in the northern part of the province; secondly, the gap in opportunity to receive compulsory

Table 14.12. Educational development level in the Yangtze River Delta

Index	Shanghai	Jiangsu	Zhejiang
People at the age of 15 and above (person)	214,169	835,732	545,255
Men (person)	107,344	401,541	274,090
Women (person)	106,825	434,191	271,165
Illiterate people (person)	11,213	83,702	65,172
Men (person)	2,019	17,528	16,687
Women (person)	9,194	66,174	48,485
The proportion of illiterate people to people at the age of 15 and above (%)	5.24	10.02	11.95
The proportion of illiterate men to people at the age of 15 and above (%)	1.88	4.37	6.09
The proportion of illiterate women to people at the age of 15 and above (%)	8.61	15.24	17.88

Source: *China's Census Statistical Yearbook 2006.*

education between urban and rural areas is narrowing but there are still some differences in the quality of schools between urban and rural areas, primarily in conditions for running schools; thirdly, the difference in opportunity to attend school between urban and rural areas is widening in the post phase of compulsory education and the rate of admission into senior high school in rural areas is lower than in urban areas, which exhibits that the bottleneck in the expansion of senior high school is much more serious in rural areas and the opportunity for wider access to higher education is mainly enjoyed by urban residents. (2) The gender difference is notable in education. The illiteracy rate of women is obviously higher than that of men, which is closely related with the gender difference in education. Women have less opportunity to receive education than men because of the impact of culture and customs as well as economic conditions. This is not reflected only in the low ratio of women to men in all types of education but also in the decreased proportion of women students in pace with the improved educational level, which is rather more marked in rural areas. (3) The allocation of public educational resources is imbalanced. Firstly, the overall investment in public education is insufficient. The operation of public education by the government has a rationality of its own because it gives consideration both to the malfunction of the market and reallocation and to equity. However government investment in education is notably lacking at present. Secondly, public educational resources are not equally distributed among education at each level. Imbalance still exists in the allocation of educational expenditure between education at all levels through the shortage of aggregate funds for education. It is mainly reflected in the excessive preference of educational funds to higher education which causes insufficient funds for secondary education. Thirdly, the compulsory educational resources are not equally distributed. Due to the system, per capita educational expenditure in urban areas is remarkably more than in rural areas. There is some research which suggests that the difference in basic educational expenditure between urban and rural areas mainly refers to extra-budgetary expenditure for schools in urban areas, which have more opportunities to obtain extra-budgetary expenditure for education.

Conclusions and Suggestions

There is a sound interaction between human progress and economic growth. On the one hand, the improvement of the preceding human development is conducive to the succeeding economic growth; on the other hand, the preceding performance of economic growth has a striking impact on the succeeding human progress. The expansion of the service industry is subordinate to economic development and thus it also can advance human progress to a great degree. We can further keep abreast of such interaction through analysis of the relationship between the development of service industry and human progress in other countries or areas.

Research on the service industry touches on only one of the factors that affect the HDI. However it is found that the development of the service industry is directly proportional to the HDI. As shown in Fig. 14.2, we adopt the data of the proportion of output value of service industry to GDP and HDI in the Yangtze River Delta from 1990 to 2005. It can be seen from the data that there is a positive correlation between the proportion of the service industry and the HDI. In addition, the HDI is relatively high in areas with a high proportion of service industry such as Shanghai. The data verify the conclusion drawn in this chapter, that is, that the development of service industry does help to advance human development.

Based on the results of research, we put forward the following suggestions.

Fig. 14.2. The relationship between the proportion of service industry and HDI in the Yangtze River Delta

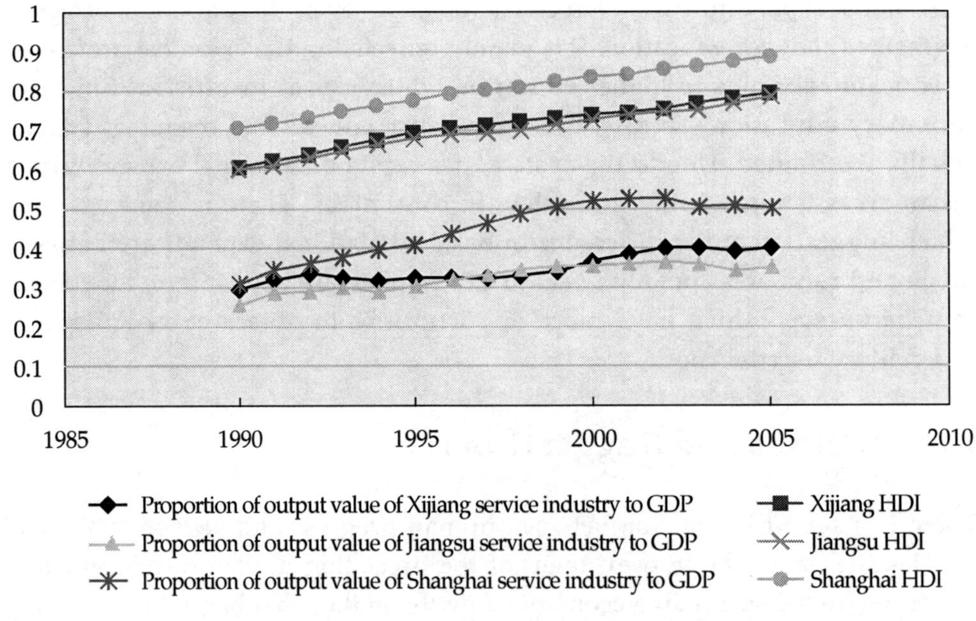

(1) We should accelerate the establishment of a nationwide medical security system so as to set up a unified medical insurance system. Both theory and fact show that only medical insurance can ensure that anyone, not just the rich, can receive medical care services. But it is difficult for private departments to supply such insurance as there is a problem of reverse choice facing health insurance. In order to solve that problem, a lot of developed countries include the health insurance in the function of the government. In Krugman's opinion, public medical insurance shows two predominances of cost. One is that the cost of management is so low that public medical insurance can resolve the problem of reverse choice and the enormous issues about administration in a decentralized medical system can also be avoided; the other is that the government can bargain with the suppliers of public medical insurance (especially medical companies) over costs. Because of the imbalanced development of various areas in our country, it is difficult to set up a nationwide and unified medical security system similar to that in developed countries in the short term. However, based on the economic edge of the Yangtze River Delta, the government can take the lead in making an effort to establish a regional, unified and sound medical security system and set up a multi-level, perfect medical security system for both urban and rural residents, including basic medical insurance for urban employees, medical insurance for urban residents, the new type of rural cooperative medical care system and social medical assistance. Apart from this, the government should further increase funding particularly because of the limited rise in farmers' income and the increasing cost of medical treatment.

(2) A unified medical insurance system relies on good medical and health conditions. Hence the training of health workers in rural areas should be intensified and the improvement of rural medical and health conditions should be expedited. With the imbalanced socio-economic development in our country, there is also an imbalance in the expansion of medical and health care services which is quite distinct between urban and rural areas. Currently, medical technicians and medical facilities are insufficient in rural areas. In 2005 there were 2.3 doctors per 1,000 urban residents and 1.2 doctors per 1,000 rural residents. Such an imbalance should be changed as soon as possible, particularly in the Yangtze River Delta that is one of the most developed areas in China.

(3) We should increase funding for education, especially for basic education. For a developing country the rate of return from primary education is far higher than that from higher education, thus to give priority to the development of basic education can meet the demands of equity and efficiency. Most of the expenditure on basic education should be paid by the nation, and

free compulsory education has become a form of national welfare in many developed countries and even several developing countries. At the same time, the policies relative to vocational and higher education should be liberalized; the monopoly on such education should be broken; and the educational market should be opened up. The Yangtze River Delta has been an area with advanced economy and culture since ancient times, therefore the education there should be more advanced owing to its advanced economy. We also should do our best to dismember the dual economic structure and distribute educational resources more equally. In terms of vocational and higher education, we should make educational resources more accessible to the public and urge more non-governmental sectors to engage in the expansion of education. In line with market needs flexibility is more necessary in offering specialties so that more skills can be fostered to adapt to the demands of economic expansion. Moreover we should increase support to areas with backward basic education such as rural areas, raise investment, improve conditions for operating schools and intensify training for teachers.

15

Chapter

The Role of Institutional Innovations in the Development of the Service Sector: Theories, Empirical Data and Inspiration from the Yangtze River Delta

Introduction

The economic growth of the Yangtze River Delta is a miniature of that of China in the past three decades. Manufacturing is the leading contributor to economic growth in the Yangtze River Delta; the same is true in other cities. Though the GDP per capita has exceeded RMB 40,000 in the 16 cities of the Delta after years of fast development, tertiary industry accounts for a mere 41.3% and secondary industry is up to 55%. The economic development level is already equal to that of moderately developed countries. However, their industry structure differs greatly. The economic expansion of the Yangtze River Delta mainly relies on the export of low-end products from manufacturing. Thus the pressure is increasingly greater on resources, the environment, the upgrading of manufacturing and sustainable development etc. Recently government departments have been well aware that the priority, which the Yangtze River Delta confronts in the process of economic growth and optimization of industry structures, is to accomplish the transition from manufacturing as the leading factor to both manufacturing and service industries as drivers and then to service industries as the dominant contribution.

How does the government promote the development of service industry? According to current theories, the proportion of service industry increases with economic development. On the one hand, the income elasticity of need for the service is higher than that for the material products, therefore the ultimate need for service will be increasingly greater with economic growth and the demand structure will eventually reflect on the industry structure (Fuchs, 1968); on the other hand, the productivity of service industry is increasingly lower than that of manufacturing. The price differences between the two industries will lead to constant growth of the proportion of service industry in statistics (Baumol, 1967). Research on developed countries (Gruber et al. 1991 and Francois et al. 1996) shows that with economic growth, the deepening of social division of labor boosts the producer service industry that mainly meets intermediate demand, which has been the main course of national increase of the proportion of service industry in the last decades. Producer service industry is helpful to the deepening of the social division of labor, which allows industrial chains to be divided up with richer ways in a larger market to improve the overall production efficiency (Liu Zhibiao, 2001; Wu Jinglian, 2006).

To sum up, the above explanation can be regarded as the theory in the development stage of service industry, which is quite in line with the reality. For example, from an international view, the service industry proportion in developed countries is about 70% while that in developing countries is around 50%, and that in some low-income countries is even less. According to the theory, the changes in the industrial structure are the result of economic growth, the policy implication being that the government only needs to care about the level of economic growth since the service industry develops with economic expansion. Recent research (Chen Zhiwu, 2004, Wang Dehua et al. 2007, Mohammad Admin and Aaditya Mattoo, 2006) further indicates that the quality of contracting institution fulfillment will affect the development level of service industry and enrich the public understanding of factors that influence the development of the service industry. Moreover Wang Dehua (2007) said that improper intervention by government would impede the development of the service industry. According to this research, the government should place priority on how to improve the fundamental systems of market economy and to promote service industry by way of structural innovation.

The concern of this chapter is whether the above theories can explain the economic growth and changes in industrial structures in the Yangtze River Delta. The service industry of the area has developed hugely in the past thirty years, however its proportion, as mentioned previously, is still rather lower than that of districts and countries with the same income level. Obviously the stage theory of the development of service industry cannot be used indiscriminately to explain industrial structure. Then what about factors of structural innovation? Firstly, we will conduct theoretical research on how structural innovation influences the development mechanism of service industry. Secondly, factors that affect the development of service industry will be examined based on international data, especially systemic ones. Thirdly, the relationship between structural innovation and the development of the service industry will be explored and analyzed based on the data of the Yangtze River Delta. The last part is our conclusion.

The Mechanism of Institutional Innovation Affecting the Development of the Service Sector

The market economy and the development of the service industry

Generally speaking, the service industry is growing much faster than other sectors in the modern economy. Hence its proportion is increasing year by year. There are three aspects to its growth. Firstly, under the pressure of competition, service functions which were internalized by other industries, have become an independent service industry by means of outsourcing and externalization (Bhagwati, 1984). Thus the proportion of service industry increases in statistical figures. Secondly, with economic growth, real service demands including both ultimate and intermediate ones appear and are satisfied. Relevant research (Gruber et al. 1991; Francois et al. 1984) shows that since the 1970s intermediate demands, which are driven by the producer service, have become the main source of the development of service industry in developed countries. Thirdly, against the background of international division, some countries, using their relative advantages, are concentrating on the production of service industry and moving their manufacturing industry to other countries, which leads to the rapid upgrading of the proportion of service industry (Chen Zhiwu, 2004).

These ways of increase show that the development of the service industry in essence reflects the deepening of production division. As market economy expands, resources are allocated in a larger market sphere and combined in various ways, which makes the role of the service industry increasingly important in the modern economy of each country. With the further deepening of the market economy, the demand for products will be more diversified and complicated. The market becomes both deeper and wider. With the expansion of the market, the service industry needs to create various forms, set up various organizations and promote sales of products and the flow of funds to make deals between buyers and sellers in the market economy. Consequently, both human and material resources are increasing successively in the service industry.

Undoubtedly the government plays an important role in the development of the market economy. Stiglitz (2005) concluded that government should exercise its role in three fields of a market economy. Firstly, the government should define and protect property rights and fulfill contracts; secondly, the government should work in the fields where the role of market fails; thirdly, the government should play its role in redistribution. Government activities, concerning the protection of property rights and the fulfillment of contracts, should be the foundation of the market economy in all countries (Stiglitz, 2005). This is a significant agreement achieved in economic research in recent decades. Redistribution also belongs to the field in which the role of the market fails. So in the last two fields, government intervention works when the market mechanism has defects. The intervening measures and policies are the main aspects of the government management system. However, government intervention also sometimes faces the problem of malfunction of government. Whether it is needed when market cannot work depends on the cost and revenue of intervention.

As analyzed previously, the development of the service industry, which relies on the growth of the market economy and the deepening of social division of labor, is naturally under the constraints of these government actions. In the protection of property rights and the fulfillment of contracts, government should try to improve the quality of the fundamental system on which the market economy depends and which would further the deepening of social division of labor and the development of industries. The following analysis shows that the system of contract fulfillment is more important to the service industry. In the case of government intervention, government should properly define the boundary between government and the market after measuring the consequences of "the malfunction of market and government" to accelerate industrial development with proper intervention methods. Improper government intervention has gained worldwide attention. It is significant to strengthen systemic innovation of government management and reduce improper government intervention for countries such as China transiting from a planned economy to a market economy.

The effect of a contracting institutional system on the development of services

Institutions, as game rules, are mechanisms that humans create to restrict and standardize their interaction (North, 1990). In his opinion (1981), sound institutions can prevent government and elites from destroying private departments and can protect private property in order to further material and human capital investment of private departments and economic growth. Furthermore, those institutions can provide an efficient judicial system as the third party to resolve disputes over how contracts are signed and fulfilled between private departments and public departments to speed up the social division of labor and trade and economic growth. As defined by Acemoglu et al. (2005), the former one is a Property rights institution, the latter a Contracting institution. Many recent papers have provided positively empirical proof on how institutions influence economic expansion. In summarizing those documents, Acemoglu (2004) said that institutions were ultimate reasons for long-term economic growth.

It is necessary to point out that the development of the service industry with its unique characteristics is more dependent on the external environment of the contracting institution than that of other industries. Firstly, as concluded by Hill (1977, 1999), compared with other industries and manufacturing in particular, the invisibility of service output determines that its consumption and supply can go hand in hand. As shown by Holmstrom (1985) and Chen Zhiwu (2004), neither can demanders test the quality of service products before the deal, nor can they evaluate it after the deal. From this point of view, most service products come under the category of "trust products" (Tirole, 1997). To suppliers, it is difficult to protect service outputs due to their invisibility. For example, the results of research and development can only be invisible knowledge and business secrets with low marginal cost for duplication, which will add to protection difficulty in the deal. In such a case, without external force protecting contract fulfillment, it will be more difficult for suppliers and demanders to reach firm expectations on trade revenue and risks in service deals than in other industrial deals. However the independent judicial system, when fully playing its role in protecting contract fulfillment, will greatly reduce the difficulties in service deals.

Secondly, according to common experience, service outputs lack a uniform evaluation standard since most of them are custom-made products. As Eswaran et al. (2002) said, product disparity and diversity are the main features of the service industry. Rauch (1999) said that with disparity, manufacturing products cannot be traded in an organized market like primary products. Thus the service industry is in desperate need of such a market. It can only trade with its unique way. The individuality easily leads to a locking of the two sides in the trade. When laws cannot guarantee the contracting institution, the locking of both sides and the accompanied opportunism easily lead to trading failure and impede the development of the service industry.

To summarize the industrial individuality of the service industry it is that compared with other industries, the service industry, to a larger extent, is a "contract-intensive industry" as Clague et al. said, which means that the production and trade are involved in more intensive and complicated contracting arrangement in service industry. Moreover, as the previous analysis pointed out, the recent worldwide growth of the service industry has mainly stemmed from the expansion of producer service industry as intermediate input. The contract-intensive characteristics are more obvious in producer service industry for it has something to do with extensive contracting arrangements of all kinds. The development of the service industry, as a contract-intensive industry, is in need of sound protection from external institutions. Under otherwise equal conditions, the worse the quality of the contracting institution is, the more likely the potential for opportunism. In anticipation of this, division and trading often fail in the contract-intensive service industry, which impedes the development of the service industry.

It should be noted that, as shown in the analysis, the development of the service industry requires a contracting institution. However according to the international empirical research by Acemoglu et al. (2005), a property rights institution is more important to economic growth. Why is the property rights institution more important to economic growth while the contracting institution is more important to the development of service industry? Both the manufacturing and service industry are vital to economic growth and the development of the two industries requires property rights institution and contracting institution. Although property rights institution is very significant, there are no differences in its effect on the manufacturing and service industry. Thus it has little effect on the formation of industry structure. As analyzed by Acemoglu, when the contracting institution is weak in a country, the manufacturing sectors, with visible products as trading objects, can further trade by other substitution mechanisms, but such mechanisms are difficult to find in the service industry with invisible products as trading objects. Consequently there is no doubt that the trade and effective fulfillment of contracts are greatly dependent on the protection of the formal contract institution.

The effect of government intervention on the development of the service industry

In many relevant documents, the intervention intensity of government on the operation of a market economy is often measured by government size. The larger the government is the more economic resources the government can control, which means that it will more easily penetrate into every aspects of economic operation and can intervene and control market more powerfully. On the one hand, with a larger government scale, government can provide all the necessities for market operation and alleviate market failures to further economic growth. On the other hand, resources will shift from productive sectors to government departments with rather low economic efficiency as government functions. In the process, revenues may lead to certain distortion, and government may do wrong in interfering in the market, which can perhaps lead to excessive growth of government scale and even impede economic expansion (Barro, 1991). Therefore whether the big or small government is conducive to economic growth is still a controversial topic in theory (La Port et al. 1999).

Excessive government size or intervention intensity can impede economic growth due to the characteristics of government and the specialized nature of the service industry. The impedance is more marked in departments of the service industry. First, according to the research of Mattoo et al. (2001), free access and opening-up is crucial to the development of the service industry. However many governments often overvalue other attributes of the service industry instead of economic ones and monopolize its operation, for example, the financial industry with national financial security, the telecommunications industry with national information security, the culture media industry with ideology. In many countries, governments run service departments with a monopoly and restrict the inflow of private and foreign capital, which may stifle their growth. This phenomenon is very striking in China (Wang Xiaojuan et al. 2004; Liu Peilin et al. 2007).

Second, in most countries, the service industry is under more regulation than other industries. Naturally, countries with a large government scale tend to strengthen control over the service industry, which may hamper its development. The research by Eschenbach et al. (2005) on 24 countries with transformed systems in Eastern Europe and Central Asia shows that a loosening of regulations would greatly accelerate the development of the service industry, which indirectly tests the previous point. From China's experience, since 1978, the Chinese government has implemented a series of reforms to relax the regulations on the service industry. For example, in some fields (especially residential services), the regulations have been greatly relaxed and competition is realized perfectly; in fields such as banking, securities, insurance and business retail, competition between different ownerships has been introduced which to some degree has broken the monopoly operation of the state economy. The research of Li Yongjian (2007) shows that the reform has furthered the development of the service industry in China.

Third, when government has strong control over economic operation and can make investment or control the inflow direction of investment, it often has strong motivation to invest in or to provide corresponding preference to large manufacturing enterprises so as to increase economic growth of revenue income. For example, in the development process of East Asian countries such as Japan and South Korea, the governments have supported manufacturing with relevant industrial policies. This is clear also in China where local governments show partiality to and provide preferences to manufacturing (Liu Peilin et al. 2007). Service industry with a small scale cannot instantly promote economic growth and it is difficult for the government to levy tax on the industry. So government is lacking in motivation to offer it the necessary support.

On the basis of the discussion above, excessive government size or too much government intervention leads to market distortion on the whole, which may not only restrict the development of agriculture and manufacturing but also set greater limitations on service industry. In some cases, government even tends to further the development of manufacturing with effective measures while reducing the proportion of service industry.

Relevant Empirical Evidence

Variables and data

The previous analysis has pointed out that the development of service industry can be affected by both the quality of contracting institution and the intensity of government intervention. The chapter designed the following calculating model to test the analysis.

$$SS_i = b_0 + b_1 Inst + b_2 Gov + b_3 Ex + Xc + \varepsilon$$

Because it is difficult to collect the recent measuring index of the contracting institution quality and government intervention intensity in every district of one country, this chapter will conduct a quantitative test with international data. In the equation, *SS* is the proportion the service industry accounts for in the GDP of countries or districts, which is the dependent variable. b_0 is constant. b_1, b_2 and b_3 are unknown parameters; *c* is an unknown parameter vector. The equation contains three main independent variables: the first is *Inst*, the quality score of contracting institutions of all countries; the second is *Gov* i.e. the size of government, used to measure the intensity of government intervention in the economy; the third is *Ex* i.e. the ratio of goods and service exports to the GDP. Apart from that, GDP per capita, the level of urbanization and education are control variables.

We selected scores of nomocracy provided by Kaufmann, Kraay and Mastruzzi as the measure of *Inst*. After comprehensively analyzing over hundreds of indices selected from 37 different data bases, Kaufmann etc. (2005) evaluated government administration in every country including the level of nomocracy. The score measures how the judicial and police systems safeguard the fulfillment of contracts. The higher the score is, the better the quality of the contracting institution is. As previous discussion showed, resolving trade disputes and trading protection is more important in increasing the ratio of service industry. Thus it is reasonable to choose the nomocracy level as the index to measure the quality of the contracting institution.

Gov (the coefficient of government intervention) chooses scores for the size of government from *Economic Freedom of the World: 2005 Annual Report* written by Bwartney and Lawson (2005) as its measure. The index evaluates sizes of governments from the ratio of government consumption expenditure to total consumption, the proportion of transfer payment to GDP, the proportion of investment from governments and government-controlled enterprises to total investment, and the gross marginal tax rate. The index is a comprehensive evaluation of the size of government or the intensity of government intervention in the economy. The higher the score is, the larger the size of government is. That is, the government can control more economic resources and the economic operation more powerfully.[1]

Given the relationship between trading structure and service industry, the model takes E_x (proportion of export to GDP) as a dependent variable which is crucial to understanding the development of the service industry in China, especially in the Yangtze River Delta. In the age of economic globalization, exports in different industries are in essence a shift of industrial demands from domestic to foreign countries so as to increase the proportion of the industry. For example, as the export of material products increases, so does the demand for the output of the primary and secondary industry. And the proportion of these will grow while that of the service industry will decrease relatively. Likewise, an increase in service export will augment the proportion of the service industry. The international competitiveness of products from manufacturing has been greatly improved with the rise of the Yangtze River Delta and China's economy in the past three decades and China has become a "world factory." If the relative proportion is used to measure the development level of the service industry, the export of manufacturing products would have a negative effect according to the previous analysis. With the factor of export, the calculating model is to test whether the analysis is true as well as whether government intervention and institution quality can still affect the development of the service industry. This chapter will examine how exports affects industry structure by the proportion of goods export to the GDP, goods net export to the GDP, service export to the GDP and service net export to the GDP using the World Development Index (WID) provided by World Bank. Thus, the chapter will consider the effect both of the total and net exports of manufacturing and those of the service industry on industry structure.

The control variables in the model are GDP per capita, urbanization level (the proportion of city residents to total population) and evaluation of educational situation. GDP per capita measures the economic development level and urbanization level is generally considered by researchers as an important factor affecting the development of the service industry (Riddle, 1986). The two are by far the most frequently mentioned as factors that influence the development of the service industry (Wang Xiaojuan etc. 2004). The data of variables is from the

WDI. It must be pointed out that b_1 and b_2 with the addition of control variables refer to the marginal influence of independent variables on the proportion of service industry under the same level of per capita income and urbanization. Moreover, nowadays the essence of service-oriented economy is economic informationalization and knowledge industrialization (Liu Zhibiao, 2001; Wu Jinglian, 2006). In such case, the accumulation of human capital plays an increasingly crucial role in the development of the service industry especially producer services. *The 2002 Human Development Report* published by the United Nations made a comprehensive evaluation of education. We regard the score as the measure of human capital accumulation. It includes literacy rate, enrollment rate and the average years of receiving education. The higher the score is, the sounder the education state is.

The research is made based on the international cross-sector data for 2002 when the observations of variables are the most in the data source available, aiming at revealing how contracting institution quality and government intervention intensity influence the development of service industry. We made the first regression with GDP per capita, the level of urbanization and education and the proportion of goods export and service export of the GDP respectively as independent variables, and proportion of the added value in the service industry to the GDP as dependent variable. Then a scatter diagram (Fig. 15.1) was made with regression residuals and coefficient of government intervention as index of y-axis and x-axis respectively. The regression residual is the unknown part of the dependent variables. The coefficient of government intervention is negative dependent to regression residual in the figure, which directly shows that the coefficient can still explain the dependent variable while considering the effect of dependent variables. Fig. 15.2 is the scatter diagram between the first regression residual and quality index of contracting institution, in which they have a positive correlation. The figure shows that even with the effect of the dependent variables, contracting-institution quality can still explain the independent variable.

Fig. 15.1. **The scatter diagram of government-intervention coefficient and regression residual**

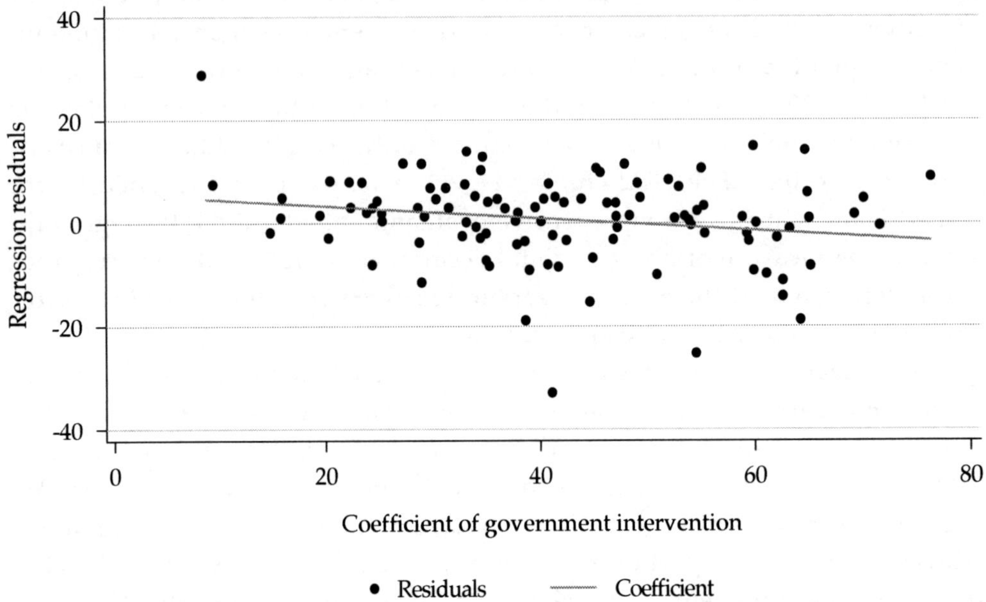

Fig. 15.2. **The scatter diagram of contracting-institution quality and regression residual**

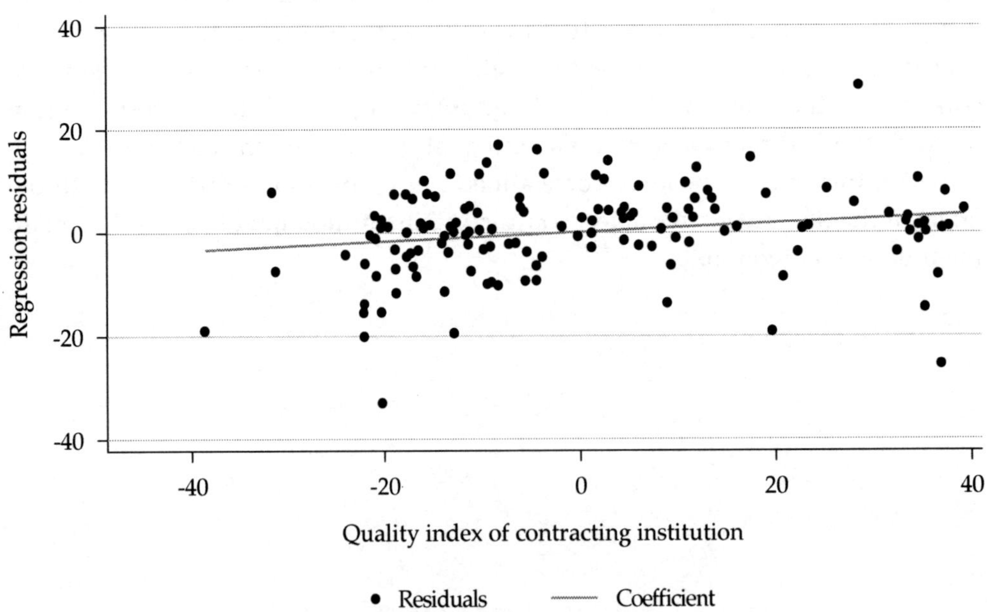

Table 15.1. The results of OLS regression analysis on factors influencing the development of the service industry

Variables	Explained variables: The proportion of added value in the service industry to GDP in 2002					
	1	2	3	4	5	6
Constants	38.3*** (13.35)	35.3*** (6.32)	37.33*** (7.06)	38.10*** (7.02)	29.21*** (5.92)	35.61*** (7.69)
GDP per capital	0.41*** (4.41)	0.03 (0.21)	−0.02 (−0.11)	−0.05 (−0.37)	0.15 (1.39)	0.15 (1.29)
Level of urbanization	0.23*** (4.32)	0.02 (0.34)	0.06 (1.09)	0.11* (1.82)	0.13*** (2.76)	0.13** (2.29)
Level of education		0.32*** (3.68)	0.32*** (3.78)	0.25*** (2.77)	0.26*** (3.10)	0.19** (2.29)
Coefficient of government intervention		−0.19*** (−3.32)	−0.19*** (−3.04)	−0.16*** (−2.63)	−0.12** (−2.57)	−0.11** (−2.28)
Quality of contracting institution		0.23*** (2.79)	0.28*** (3.72)	0.24*** (3.36)	0.16*** (2.70)	0.12** (2.08)
Proportion of goods export to GDP			−0.14*** (−2.91)	−0.16*** (−3.27)		
Proportion of service export to GDP				0.24*** (3.47)		
Proportion of goods net export to GDP					−0.38*** (−7.37)	−0.25** (−2.08)
Proportion of service net export to GDP						0.42** (2.07)
R^2	0.387 3	0.567 0	0.619 4	0.640 1	0.720 2	0.733 2
Number of sample countries	114	114	114	106	114	104

Note: The numbers in the brackets are the statistics figures whose heteroscedasticity is steady. * indicates the statistic is marked on the level of 10%, ** on the level of 5%, *** on the level of 1%.

Results of quantitative test

Table 15.1 shows the results of the quantitative test. In the first line of regression, GDP per capita and level of urbanization are independent variables which are proportional to the dependent variable: If the GDP per capita of one country is 1,000 dollars higher that of another country, the ratio will be 0.41% higher; if the proportion of urban population is 1% larger in one country than in another one, the proportion of service industry will be 0.23% higher. The result tallies with previous research. In the second line of regression, independent variables are level of education, the coefficient of government intervention and quality of contracting institution. The result shows that the dependent variable is proportional to level of education and quality of contracting institution, that is, under identical conditions (GDP per capita and level of urbanization), if their scores are one point higher than those in another country, the dependent variable will be 0.32% and 0.23% higher respectively; if the coefficient of government intervention is one point higher, the proportion of service industry will be 0.19% lower.[2] Due to multicollinearity, the regression coefficients of GDP per capita and urbanization level are positive, but their dominance is not so strong.

From regression 3 to 6, the effect of export on industry structure is taken into consideration, which, as mentioned above, is crucial to analyzing the development of the service industry in China, especially in the Yangtze River Delta. In regression 3, the proportion of goods export to GDP is the independent variable, which is in reverse proportion to the dependent variable. The statistics are marked under 1% of the significance levels. The regression coefficients of educational level, government intervention and contracting institution quality did not change with the addition of the new variable, which matches the conclusion of regression 2. With the addition of a new dependent variable i.e. the proportion of service export to GDP, regression 4 shows that under same conditions, the independent variable is 0.16% lower when the proportion of goods export to GDP is 1% higher, and 0.24% higher when the proportion of service export is 1% higher. Both of the new dependent variables are marked under the level of 1%. Under the level of 1%, the independent variable is remarkably related to educational level, coefficient of government intervention and the quality of contracting institution, which is identical to previous regression results. Urbanization level is in proportion to the dependent variable.

The index in regression 5 and 6 is net export which is different from regression 3 and 4, that is, the proportion of export to GDP reduces import. The change explains the effect of export. Besides the difference in coefficients, the result of regression 5 and 6 is identical to that of regression 3 and 4. With net export as the index, the absolute value of the coefficient of both goods export and service export grows which greatly affects the dependent variable. The regression coefficients of educational level, government intervention and contracting institution quality do not change also much, but there is an increase in the absolute value of the regression coefficient of urbanization level. At the least, these regression coefficients are marked under the level of 5%.

The results of the quantitative test, based on international cross-sector data, have verified two things. One is that export structure has a great influence on industrial structure, as the previous analysis has shown. There has recently been fast development in international trade mainly supported by manufacturing products in the Yangtze River Delta, which is important to the analysis of the development of the service industry in the area. The second is to verify the theory that the development of service industry can be affected by both the contracting institution quality and the government intervention intensity. Table 15.1 shows that the effect is still strong while the export factor is ignored in regressions from 3 to 6. When analyzing the development of the service industry in the Yangtze River Delta, we need to attach importance to structural reform and innovation.

Institutional Innovation and the Development of the Service Sector in the Yangtze River Delta

As a big country shifting from a planned economy to a market economy, China has witnessed constant structural innovation with fast economic growth in the past three decades. The Yangtze River Delta takes the lead in improving the market economy system by structural innovation. Table 15.2 shows the scores of market development in China made by Fan Gang, Wang Xiaolu etc. The indexes for Jiangsu, Zhejiang and Shanghai are still near the top and the development momentum remains good. For example, in 2005 the scores of market development in Shanghai, Zhejiang and Jiangsu ranked first, third and forth respectively among 31 cities, and third, second and fifth respectively in 2001.

Table 15.2. Score sequence of market development in cities of China from 2001 to 2005

Sequence	2001	2002	2003	2004	2005
1	Guangdong	Guangdong	Shanghai	Shanghai	Shanghai
2	Zhejiang	Zhejiang	Zhejiang	Zhejiang	Guangdong
3	Shanghai	Shanghai	Guangdong	Guangdong	Zhejiang
4	Fujian	Fujian	Fujian	Jiangsu	Jiangsu
5	Jiangsu	Jiangsu	Jiangsu	Fujian	Fujian
6	Tianjin	Beijing	Beijing	Beijing	Beijing

Source: Fan Gang, Wang Xiaolu and Zhu Hengpeng 2007.

In the course of market orientation, structural innovation in the area has brought fast economic growth the level of which has approached that of moderately developed countries. However the development of the service industry does not follow the pattern of developed countries since the 1950s and 1960s, and is still in an inferior position. In terms of the proportion of the three industries, the proportion of service industry in the 16 cities is less than that in countries with a similar income level to China and other cities of China. In 2005, the World Bank conducted research on the investment environment in 120 Chinese cities and their proportion of service industry averaged 44.15%, 13 of which are in the Yangtze River Delta with an average proportion of a mere 40.54%. We need to discover why the service industry did not develop at the same high speed as international experience has shown with economic growth and the deepening of the market mechanism? It is, to our mind, mainly due to the special nature of Chinese economic system reform and the export-oriented growth model in the Yangtze River Delta.

Firstly, the economic system reform does not go hand in hand in the manufacturing and service industries: the former is more advanced than the latter, which determines the fast development in manufacturing of those top innovation cities and the very low proportion of service industry.

In China, the service industry has developed in period of transformation of economic system reform. In the past three decades of reform, China has witnessed the shift from a planned economy to a market economy, which plays a decisive role in the fast growth of manufacturing sectors and service sectors. But the shift is more beneficial to manufacturing.

The national economy is under the control of planning departments in a planned economy system where service industry or tertiary industry is traditionally considered not to create value. So there are restrictions of all kinds in policies on the development of service industry instead of realizing its significance. Many modern service industries themselves are fundamental organs supporting the role of the market economy, and are growing as the market economy deepens. It is natural that they did not have enough room to develop in the age of the planned economy. For these reasons, in the planned economy, the service industry did not gain enough development. Also a small part of it is only confined to family services.

Since 1978 the government has been gradually lessening micro-control over the economy, but the relaxation is selective and does not happen backward. Manufacturing saw reforms in price mechanism and entering restrict simultaneously in all industries. At the beginning of reform, the opening up in agricultural industry was striking and then the focus shifted to the industrial field, while that of service industry is option which lead most industries to under great pressure. The inflow of foreign and private capital forces state-owned enterprises to speed up reform. International competition has been greatly strengthened with comprehensive effect. In the service industry, the opening up is only in consumer services such as catering, while that in some important producer services is rather slow. They are even still under state monopoly. For example the reform has always been backward in railways, telecommunications, finance, education etc. although has been speeded up recently. In foreign trade the state monopoly, which began during the planned economy, did not change until 1994. Vocational and business services, which a support market economy, have grown slowly because they are often regarded as public institutions of government.

The industrial structure has been greatly affected by policy restrictions on the development of service industry and the particular competition model in China. In the thirty years of reform, GDP-driven competition has advanced the fast economic growth which is typical of Chinese economic growth (Zhang Jun etc. 2007). There are various policy restrictions on the development of the service industry. Thus local governments that want to speed up economic growth put priority on structural innovation in manufacturing, which gives more preference to enterprises in industry. The development of manufacturing will grow faster in cities that take the lead in structural innovation, while the growth of the service industry is constrained by policies. With policy constrictions, private and foreign capital attracted by structural innovation find it difficult to play a role in service industry. They flow into manufacturing. With this unique economic growth system, although the Yangtze River Delta takes the lead in structural innovation, the development of service industry cannot catch up with that of manufacturing which causes the proportion of service industry to be lower than that in underdeveloped regions.

Secondly, the low proportion of service industry is decided by its position in the global division system. According to the traditional theory of industrial changes, the proportion will increase as an economy develops. But it is difficult to determine whether this fits in a particular region under the background of global division and in service trading in particular. In the system, activities which are necessary to the realization of the ultimate value of output will be deployed internationally with the maximum of output, instead of being confined to one region or area. Thus production activities form a global value chain, in which manufacturing is just a middle part with low added value; the design and development and brand marketing at both ends of the "smiling curve" are with advanced technology and high added value. If the value chain of manufacturing products can be achieved domestically, manufacturing will naturally drive the development of the service industry as the technical level and softening of the economy improve. The position of a region in the value chain of the global division system depends on factors such as development level, resources endowment, institution environment, national policy and opportunities, which will affect its industrial structure. The point is strongly proved by the fact that international data shows that the proportion of goods export to the GDP has a negative effect on the dependent variable.

Since the end of the 1970s when China formulated opening up to the outside world as basic national policy, China emerged into the global production system. After 30 years of fast development, China represented by manufacturing, has occupied an important position in the system. In Fig. 15.3, at the beginning of the 1990s, the proportion of export to GDP reached about 20 and climbed to around 40% recently. In industry, in 2005 the proportion of export value to the total industrial output was 18.97%, and with added value the denominator the proportion will reach 66%; if manufacturing is accounted for separately, the numbers will be 20% and 77% respectively.[3] The numbers show that products of manufacturing in China serve the world to a larger extent. Consequently, China earned the reputation of "made in China."

Fig. 15.3. The proportion of export to GDP in China (1990–2005)

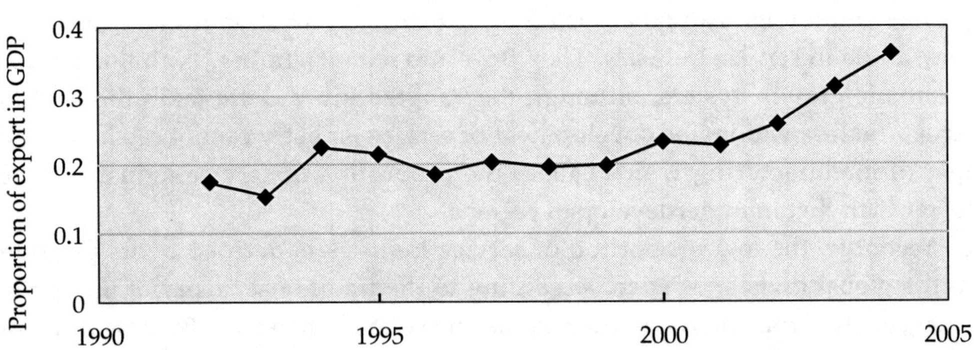

Source: The author used the *China Statistical Yearbook 2006.*

However the achievement in manufacturing is largely due to production, processing and assembling which have low added value and do not need much outside service input, while the producer service input such as design, research and marketing with high added value does not happen domestically. This point is definitely true according to relative statistics: from 1981 to 1985, the exports of the processing trade with processing of supplied and imported materials was 9.373 billion dollars while that of general and other trade was 110.6 billion dollars. The former is less than 10% of the latter. From 2001 to 2005, the figures were 1,313.649 billion dollars and 1,071.5 billion dollars respectively and the former exceeds the latter.[4] China participates global division system mainly by way of processing trade. But Chinese manufacturing engage in production such as simple processing and assembling. The service-intensive parts before and after production are finished by foreign enterprises. For this reason, the service industry in China does not follow the fast growth of manufacturing.

The characteristics of the development of manufacturing in China are more obvious in the Yangtze River Delta. Firstly, the development of manufacturing is typically export-oriented. For example, taking account of the industrial enterprises above the scale, in 2005 the proportion of total exports to total industrial output was 18.97%; in Jiangsu it was 24.09%, in Zhejiang 25.95%, and in Shanghai 3.53%. According to statistics, the three cities accounted for 46.3% of total industrial exports in 2005. Secondly, industrial export is increasingly dependent on processing trade. For example in Jiangsu, general trade accounted for 60.5% of total exports in 1995 while the number dropped to 33% in 2006, the proportion of processing industry mainly with processing of supplied and imported materials was up to 67%, far higher than the national figure of 55.7%. The data shows that manufacturing in the area only participated in the global division system by way of processing and assembling with low service needs. The fast growth of manufacturing has not spurred corresponding development of the service industry.

Conclusions

This chapter tries to reveal why the proportion of service industry in the Yangtze River Delta is low, focusing on whether structural innovation can affect the development of service industry based on recent research papers. According to theories and documents, the development of the service industry will be affected both by the contracting institution quality and improper government intervention on the basis of its development stage theory. Government needs to make structural innovation to solve the two problems. The quantitative test shows that these perspectives are right to some degree. Apart from that, the development can also be greatly influenced by the export structure: the export proportion of the service industry will decrease when that of goods increases.

Since reform and opening up, although the Yangtze River Delta has taken the lead in structural innovation the proportion of service industry is less than that in other cities, which is seemingly contrary to the above theory. The paradox stems from the special model of how China reforms the economic system and participates in the global division system. On the one hand, economic system reform cannot go hand in hand in the manufacturing and service industries: the former is more advanced than the latter, which determines that the growth focus of places like the Yangtze River Delta tends to be on manufacturing and the proportion of service industry is low. Moreover, nowadays while participating in global division, China focuses on low service-density links such as assembling and processing, of which the Yangtze River Delta is the outstanding representative. In such a case, the development of manufacturing cannot promote the growth of producer service industry as much as in a closed production system. Consequently the more it participates in global division, the lower the proportion of service industry is.

In the Yangtze River Delta, the proportion of service industry does not grow as fast with the deepening of the market system as international experience has shown. However this does not mean that structural innovation does not help the development of the service industry. The phenomenon actually demands government to devote much more attention to structural innovation. As previous analysis has shown, the backwardness of service development in the area is mainly because structural innovation in the service industry cannot catch up with global division. In the future, government should make further efforts to improve the basic system of a market economy, to reasonably define the boundary between market and government in the service industry, and to remove systemic restrictions on the development of the service industry. Only by doing this can the restrictions on system and the vicious circle of participation in low-level division be broken. Structural changes can promote the development of high-level producer service industry and the industrial upgrade of the Yangtze River Delta.

16

Chapter

Differences in the Growth of Service Industry in the Yangtze River Delta: On the Basis of Shift-Share Analysis

Introduction

In the 1960s, economic focus began to shift to service industry in developed countries. There has been a constant increase in the proportion service industry accounts for in employment and the GDP, which gradually came to dominate. The world industrial structure also shifted from an "industry-oriented" economy to a "service-oriented" one. Currently the Yangtze River Delta, with less than 3% of the area of China, accomplishes over 25% of China's economic output and is one of the world's manufacturing bases and one of the world's six city groups. On the basis of industrialization and urbanization, the economic growth of cities in the Yangtze River Delta should be furthered with service industry as the leading force, which is an important way to optimize economic structure and promote competitiveness of industries.

In terms of service industry, the main forces that make New York and London, and Singapore and Hong Kong world cities are their financial services and shipping industry respectively, especially with the support of information and network technology. Porter (1990) stressed the supportive role of producer services such as risk investments, colleges and research organizations in industrial groups when advocating that industrial groups are crucial to national or regional competition. Consumption services such as catering are not only necessities for people's life, but also the symbol of prosperity. Yang Wuyang etc. (1997) made an in-depth exploration of the relationship between city level and consumption services based on the classic "central place" theory of Christaller, a German economist. We should not neglect the characteristics of the internal structure in the Yangtze River Delta when considering the overall growth of the service industry. In fact, according to the World Development Report delivered by the World Bank, from 1960 to 2000, in America, the proportion of service industry in the GDP rose from 58% to 74%, in England from 54% to 70%, and in Japan from 42% to 66%. There has been a gradual increase in the proportion of communications, finance, logistics, wholesale and agriculture support services and specific services, which have become the main part of the service industry. For example, in 1998 the proportion in America reached 54.8%, in the European Union 52.3% and in Japan 54.5%. From 2003 to 2005, the additional employment figure was in line with the size of city in the 15 cities (excepting Taizhou) on the basis of absolute number. However the growth rates differed greatly; for example, it is very low in Nanjing. Further growth difference can be found with further analysis of the internal structure (as shown in Table 16.1). This chapter will examine how the service industry grows and how the structure changes. In other words, the chapter will answer the following questions:

(1) In the 15 cities, what is the absolute number of employees in the service industry and how does growth differs in its constitutuant sectors?

(2) Which cities are better for the development of the service industry and the constitutuant sectors? That is to say, which city fits which particular service industry?

(3) What is the relationship between the growth of constitutuant sectors, urban population, economic scale and construction scale?

Table 16.1. A contractive diagram of the employment in the service industry in the 15 cities of the Yangtze River Delta and its changes from 2003 to 2005

City	Number of employees of service industry in 2003 (10,000)	Its proportion in the Delta (2003)	Rank	Number of employees in the service industry in 2005 (10,000)	Its proportion in the Delta (2005)	Rank	The growth rate of employment (%)	Rank
Shanghai	189.78	0.488 004	1	262.88	0.556 171	1	38.518 3	1
Nanjing	47.23	0.121 448	2	48.98	0.103 626	2	3.705 3	8
Hangzhou	41.39	0.106 431	3	46.87	0.099 162	3	13.239 9	2
Ningbo	19.76	0.050 811	4	21.28	0.045 022	4	7.692 3	4
Wuxi	15.88	0.040 834	5	16.5	0.034 909	5	3.904 3	7
Suzhou	14.24	0.036 617	6	14.47	0.030 614	6	1.615 2	11
Changzhou	11.84	0.030 446	7	11.96	0.025 304	7	1.013 5	14
Zhenjiang	9.24	0.023 76	8	9.43	0.019 951	8	2.056 3	10
Nantong	8.43	0.021 677	9	8.55	0.018 089	9	1.423 5	12
Yangzhou	7.29	0.018 746	10	6.82	0.014 429	10	−6.447	15
Jiaxing	5.61	0.014 426	11	5.68	0.012 017	11	1.247 8	13
Zhoushan	5.13	0.013 191	12	5.32	0.011 255	12	3.703 7	9
Huzhou	4.53	0.011 649	13	4.87	0.010 303	13	7.505 5	5
Taizhou	4.33	0.011 134	14	4.51	0.009 542	15	4.157	6
Shaoxing	4.21	0.010 826	15	4.54	0.009 605	14	7.838 5	3

Source: *China City Statistical Yearbook* from 2004 to 2006.

This chapter will analyze how the service industry and its constitutant sectors grow in the 15 cities using the Shift-Share Method (SSM), which is generally used to research growth disparity in regional economics. The research expands the applied scope of the SSM. In the past it mainly focused on how industry and the constitutuant sectors differ in growth or on the industrial growth differences in a certain region. This chapter makes a contrastive study of the growth difference of varied industries in a certain region, which is helpful in revealing how the proportion changes. Combined with the theory of industrial life cycle, the chapter not only vividly analyzes the two-dimensional rectangular relationship between industry and region but also examines their dynamic changes, which makes a helpful addition to the method. Moreover the SSM is combined with regression analysis, that is, the conclusions derived from the SSM will be tested in regression analysis to reveal the relationship between the growth of service industry and the constitutuant sectors, and the scale of urban population, the economy and construction. The chapter is conducive to uncovering the reasons for the growth of the service industry and its structural changes and guiding the selection of the strategic focus of service industry development.

Model and data

Model

The SSM has remained a controversial method since Creamer (1943) created it and Perloff etc. (1960) used it in the analysis of regional economy. The controversy focuses on the feasibility of the model as a tool of expectation and analysis. For example, Praskevopouls (1971), Ashby (1964) and Andrikopoulos et al. (1990) are in favor of it, while Houston (1967) and Brown (1969) are opposed to it. Kalbacher (1979), Klaasen, Paelinck (1972) and McDonough, Sihag (1991) proposed that the method could be improved with the addition of parameters such as multipliers and relative weight. Cui Gonghao (1999), a Chinese scholar, holds that the SSM is a general method to analyze regional economic structure which is comprehensive and dynamic. The method is helpful to reveal the reasons for structural changes of regional sectors and defines the main direction of further development.

This chapter uses the SSM to analyze the dynamic changes in the service industry in the Yangtze River Delta. The changes in urban service industry can be divided into three portions: share portion, structural shift portion and competition shift portion. It is intended to find in which aspects the growth of the service industry exceeds the average level or is less than the average level. The mathematical model is as follows:

$$G_i = N_i + P_i + D_i \tag{1}$$

$$(P+D)_i = P_i + D_i \tag{2}$$

$$N_i = \left(\frac{E_{(t+1)}}{E_t}\right) e_{it} - e_{it} \tag{3}$$

$$P_i = \sum_{j=1}^{n} \left[\left(\frac{E_{j(t+1)}}{E_{jt}}\right) e_{jit}\right] - \left(\frac{E_{(t+1)}}{E_t}\right) e_{jit} \tag{4}$$

$$D_j = e_{i(t+1)} - \sum_{j=1}^{n} \left[\left(\frac{E_{j(t+1)}}{E_{jt}}\right) e_{jit}\right] \tag{5}$$

G_i is the actual growth in employment number in *i* city within the investigation period (in the 15 cities except Taizhou, similarly hereinafter); N_i is share portion, which indicates the growth number of constitutuant sectors should be reached on the basis of average growth rate in *i* city; $(P+D)_i$ is shift portion between the actual growth and the average rate growth (the share portion) in *i* city; P_i is structural shift, which is the shift portion between total growth of internal structure of *i* city on the basis of average rate in the Yangtze River Delta and the average ratio growth of the city; D_i is competition shift, which is the shift portion of the total growth of service industry and of internal structure on the basis of average ratio; ei is the employment number in the city service industry; *E* is the employment number in the service industry in the Yangtze River Delta; *j* is the four internal parts of the service industry (producer services, consumption services, approximate public article services and public article services in this chapter); *j*= 1, 2, 3, 4; *t* is the beginning of the period (2003); *t*+1 is the end of the period (2005).

Data

The data is mainly from the *China City Statistical Yearbook* from 2004 to 2006 and the city statistical yearbooks of the Yangtze River Delta. It covers the classification of service industry, the scope of cities and the selection of time period. The detailed analysis is as follows:

1. The classification of service industry

The classification of service industry is the basis of the research. As for city, a specific space unit, we should first discover how service sectors different from each other in helping the development and operation of cities, and then research on them respectively. The third industry is divided into 15 kinds in *Rules on the Classification of the Three Industries* published by National Bureau of Statistics on May 14, 2003. The research group of service industry divided it into fundamental service, production and market service, individual consumption service and public service in *Outline of the National Plan for the Mediate-long Term Development of Science and Technology* (from 2006 to 2020). Other researches divided it into service industry and service undertaking. The former includes combination of production sectors and enterprises which offer service products for the purpose of added value; the latter is the assembly of governmental behaviors which supply service products to meet public demand. The classification in this chapter is as show in Fig. 16.1.

Fig. 16.1. Classification of service sector on the basis of development power and product nature

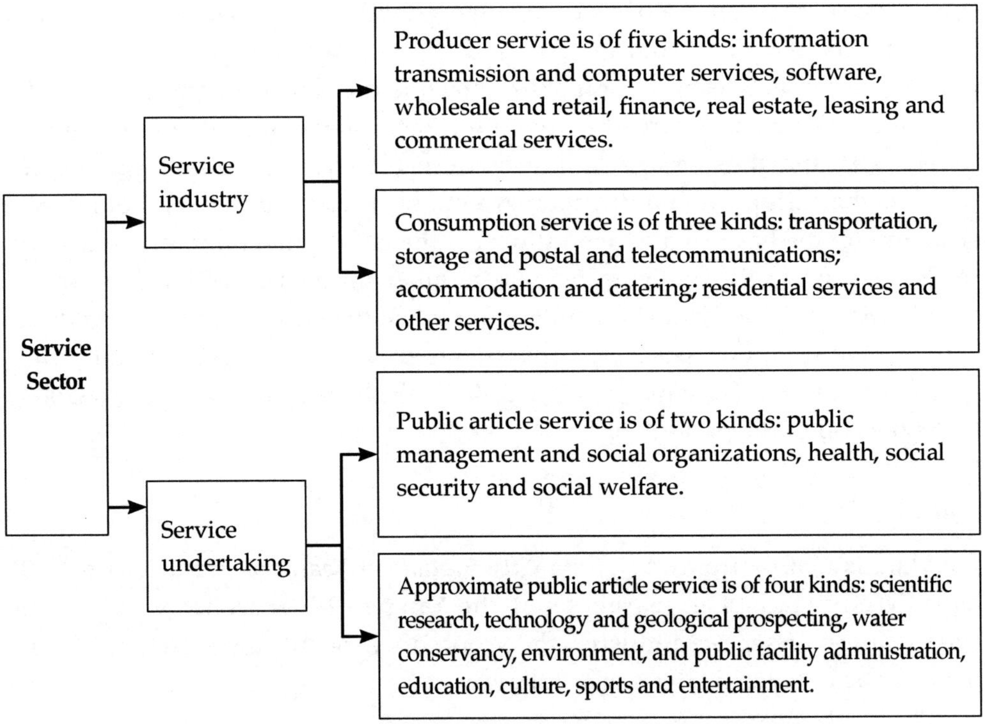

City economics divides the economic activities into two kinds: one is basic activity (export sectors) and the other is non-basic activity (local consumption). The employment growth of basic economic sectors is the main force for expansion of the economy and the size of cities (Zhou Yixing, 1995). So service industry can be divided into service industry and service undertaking; the former is one of the main forces for city development and the latter provides guarantees and support for the former. Service industry can be divided into producer services and consumption services; the former is helpful in strengthening the competitiveness of enterprises; the latter is helpful in increasing the consumption level. The corresponding detailed division is in Fig. 16.1. Service undertaking can be divided into public article service and approximate public article service; the former is the overall service for urban residents (from public financial expenditure); the latter is the service for specific objects (non-profit institutions); the corresponding detailed division is in Fig. 16.1. There are two advantages of such a division. One is that it is helpful in examining the service industry, the producer services in particular, which is the intrinsic power for the growth of cities; the other is that it is conducive to checking the city service level—the service undertaking, the approximate public article service in particular. Relative data is selected on such standards of classification. Because the employment number is the data that statistics yearbook use to classify industries, this is selected as index.

2. The scope of cities

The research involves 15 cities of the Yangtze River Delta (except Taizhou) which differ greatly from each other. They can be divided into three kinds according to the scale of economy, population and construction. The first is exceptionally big cities (or super cities), specifically Shanghai. The second is big cities including Nanjing, Suzhou, Hangzhou and Ningbo, four deputy provincial cities. Wuxi is also one of them with similar scales. The third is intermediate-size cities including nine cities with similar scales, Changzhou, Zhenjiang, Yanghzou, Taizhou, Nantong, Jiaxing, Huzhou, Shaoxing and Zhoushan. The cities differ greatly in the statistical methods of administrative divisions. For example, it is difficult to make a comparison of service industry focusing on the built-on areas of cities in Nantong and Yangzhou which have a great number of villagers. So in data selection, the indexes used are mainly employment, population size and the size of built-on areas in the administrative regions of cities.

3. The selection of time period

The service industry is a big and complicated industry which covers a wide range and has rich content. The different sectors have different characteristics in different cities and at different development stages, but they basically conform to the s-shaped even curve of the industrial life cycle. This chapter will analyze the data from 2003 to 2005 which are the only accessible. It is much better to make detailed research over a long time period which will assist in knowing more about the growth of service industry between cities and its dynamic changes.

Empirical results and explanations

The analysis of different cities

Table 16.2 illustrates the results of the shift-share analysis of the service industry in the 15 cities from 2003 to 2005. The share refers to the growth of each city on the basis of the average growth ratio.

Table 16.2. Results of the shift-share analysis of the service industry in the 15 cities (10,000 people)

City	Share portion	Shift portion			Actual growth
		Structural shift	Competition shift	Total shift	
Shanghai	40.880 13	10.674 42	21.545 45	32.219 87	73.1
Nanjing	10.173 72	−3.999 467	−4.424 253	−8.423 72	1.75
Wuxi	3.420 679	−1.034 312	−1.766 367	−2.800 68	0.62
Changzhou	2.550 430 7	−1.002 211	−1.428 22	−2.430 43	0.12
Suzhou	3.067 409 9	−0.547 314	−2.290 096	−2.837 41	0.23
Nantong	1.815 889 4	−0.544 793	−1.151 096	−1.695 89	0.12
Yangzhou	1.570 324 3	−0.218 591	−1.821 734	−2.040 33	−0.47
Zhenjiang	1.990 369 9	−0.611 489	−1.188 88	−1.800 37	0.19
Taizhou	0.932 716 6	−0.439 734	−0.312 983	−0.752 72	0.18
Hangzhou	8.915 737 1	−0.567 528	−2.868 209	−3.435 74	5.48
Ningbo	4.256 462 1	−0.522 412	−2.214 05	−2.736 46	1.52
Jiaxing	1.208 438 9	−0.113 201	−1.025 237	−1.138 44	0.07
Huzhou	0.975 798 2	−0.567 425	−0.058 373	−0.625 8	0.35
Shaoxing	0.906 867 7	−0.231 097	−0.345 771	−0.576 87	0.33
Zhoushan	1.105 043	−0.264 863	−0.650 18	−0.915 04	0.19

The growth is related to the initial level of service industry, for example, the first ones are Shanghai, Nanjing and Hangzhou; Shanghai ranks first in actual growth and is followed by Hangzhou. The figure for actual growth is small in other cities, and in Yangzhou the growth is even negative. The shift portion constitutes structural shift and competition shift, which indicates the gap between actual growth and share portion. The shift portion is only positive in Shanghai, that is, the actual growth exceeds the growth on the basis of average ratio, while it is negative in other cities, that is, the actual growth is less than the average ratio growth. The changes in shift portion are shown in Fig. 16.2 (on the decreasing order of total shift). Further analysis and explanation are as follows:

Fig. 16.2. The relationship between the proportion of service industry and HDI in the Yangtze River Delta

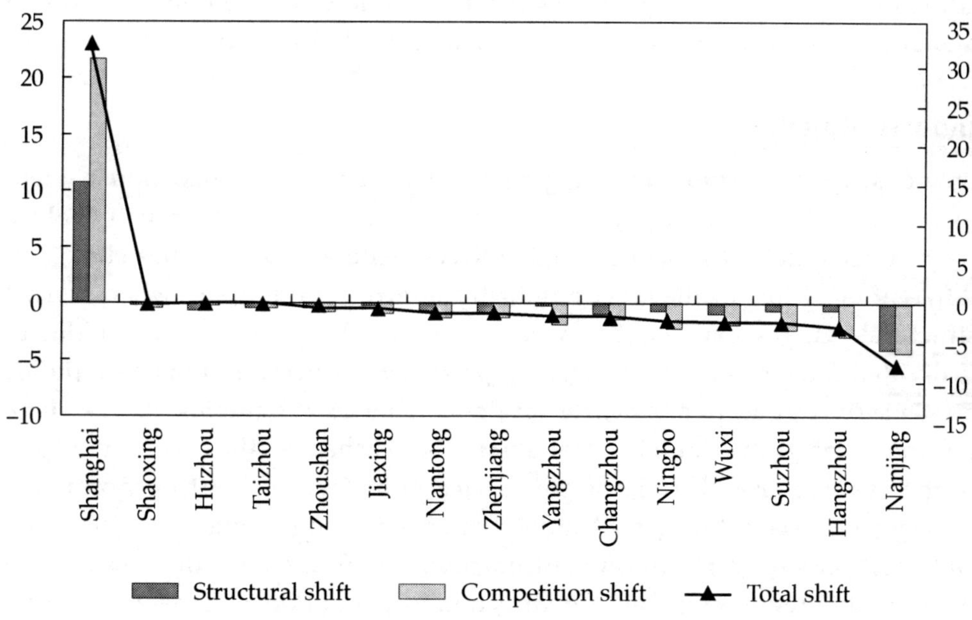

(1) The service industry is in a polarization stage centering on Shanghai. In other words, the service industry of Shanghai covers the whole area of the Yangtze River Delta. Shanghai has a sound foundation of service industry. It ranks first in actual growth and is the only city where the shift portion is positive. This shows that its service industry not only represents the development direction of the Yangtze River Delta in structure, but also has strong competitiveness in sectors such as finance, insurance and real estate.

(2) The radiation range of service industry centering on Shanghai adheres to the decrease of space distance. The shift portion reduces as the distance is lengthened in Suzhou, Wuxi, Changzhou and Zhenjiang (cities on the Shanghai-Nanking line), as it is in Jiaxing, Huzhou and Shaoxing (cities on the Shanghai–Hangzhou-Ningbo line).

(3) From the changes in classification of cities, the sub-center position has relatively declined in Nanjing, Hangzhou, and especially in Nanjing, so it is in Suzhou and Ningbo. There are two reasons for the decline in Nanjing and Hangzhou. First, their former range of service industry has been attracted to Shanghai, a bigger center of service industry; second, some of their former service factors are attracted to Shanghai as well, such as technological services, finance, headquarters of enterprises, and research and development. The decline is more obvious in Nanjing than in Hangzhou because cities within the attraction range of Nanjing such as Anhui have low service demand with an underdeveloped economy and most of its hinterland has disappeared.

Industrial analysis

Previous sections explored the aggregate changes in the service industry and its intrinsic mechanism in different regions or cities. This section will analyze the characteristics of how the Yangtze River Delta and its 15 cities change in different of sectors of the service industry aimed at finding out what internal structural changes service industry has undergone. In Fig. 16.1, service industry is divided into consumption services, producer services, approximate public article services and public article services. Table 16.3 is the result. The share portion is the growth number that should be reached by the end on the basis of the average growth ratio of the service industry; the shift portion is the disparity between actual growth and share portion and it contains the structural shift portion and competition shift portion. The first shows the relationship between different sectors and the direction of overall development; the latter shows the growth trends of different sectors. The conclusions and explanations are as follows:

(1) Consumption service is the main area of growth the in service industry as it is "mature industry" with an even and steady growth trend. The number of its actual growth is 127,700 people. This is slightly less than the employment growth in the producer service, which equals the total employment growth of public article service and approximate public article service. Positive structural shift portion means that the growth rate exceeds that of the whole service industry; when the competition shift portion is negative and its absolute

Table 16.3. Share-shift analysis of the internal structure of service industry in the 15 cities (ten thousand people)

Region or city	Consumption service				Producer service				Approximate public article service				Public article service			
	Share portion	Structural shift	Competition shift	Actual growth	Share portion	Structural shift	Competition shift	Actual growth	Share portion	Structural shift	Competition shift	Actual growth	Share portion	Structural shift	Competition shift	Actual growth
The Yangtze River Delta	18.39	1.717	-7.337	12.77	27.178	2.197	13.935	43.31	22.124	-1.841	-15.493	4.79	16.084	-2.066	-6.378	7.64
Shanghai	10.043	7.915	-5.988	11.97	14.686	11.576	16.638	42.9	9.627	7.587	-14.024	3.19	6.525	5.143	-9.128	2.54
Nanjing	2.439	-2.019	-0.15	0.27	2.515	-2.083	-1.452	-1.02	3.307	-2.738	0.341	0.91	1.913	-1.584	0.611	0.94
Wuxi	0.545	-0.447	-0.248	-0.15	1.046	-0.855	-0.431	-0.24	1.06	-0.868	-0.182	0.01	0.771	-0.632	0.511	0.65
Changzhou	0.403	-0.383	0.02	0.04	0.689	-0.657	-0.122	-0.09	0.796	-0.758	-0.018	0.02	0.663	-0.632	0.049	0.08
Suzhou	0.423	-0.391	0.198	0.23	0.966	-0.894	0.248	0.32	0.918	-0.85	-0.888	-0.82	0.763	-0.705	0.402	0.46
Nantong	0.414	-0.386	-0.068	-0.04	0.557	-0.521	-0.526	-0.49	0.433	-0.404	0.081	0.11	0.411	-0.384	0.363	0.39
Yangzhou	0.258	-0.336	-0.132	-0.21	0.457	-0.594	-0.213	-0.35	0.465	-0.605	0.26	0.12	0.39	-0.507	0.257	0.14
Zhenjiang	0.433	-0.391	-0.152	-0.11	0.567	-0.513	-0.004	0.05	0.527	-0.476	-0.091	-0.04	0.463	-0.419	0.026	0.07
Taizhou	0.14	-0.113	-0.107	-0.08	0.303	-0.244	0.001	0.06	0.24	-0.193	-0.047	0	0.252	-0.203	0.141	0.19
Hangzhou	1.81	-0.698	-0.542	0.57	2.529	-0.974	0.125	1.68	2.562	-0.987	-0.415	1.16	2.016	-0.777	-0.679	0.56
Ningbo	0.895	-0.576	-0.309	0.01	1.419	-0.912	-0.307	0.2	1.053	-0.676	0.113	0.49	0.887	-0.571	0.254	0.57
Jiaxing	0.132	-0.124	-0.068	-0.06	0.487	-0.458	-0.009	0.02	0.323	-0.304	-0.079	-0.06	0.267	-0.252	0.255	0.27
Huzhou	0.12	-0.077	0.147	0.19	0.285	-0.183	0.298	0.4	0.291	-0.186	-0.485	-0.38	0.28	-0.18	0.23	0.33
Shaoxing	0.118	-0.076	0.078	0.12	0.338	-0.215	-0.253	-0.13	0.255	-0.162	-0.033	0.06	0.196	-0.125	0.179	0.25
Zhoushan	0.217	-0.181	-0.016	0.02	0.334	-0.276	-0.058	0	0.267	-0.221	-0.026	0.02	0.287	-0.238	0.151	0.2

Note: Producer services includes information transmission, computer services and software, wholesale and retail, finance, real estate, leasing and commercial services. Consumption services includes transportation, storage and postal and telecommunication, accommodation and catering, residential services and other services. Public article service includes public management and social organizations, health, social security and social welfare. Approximate public article service includes scientific research, technology and geological prospecting, water conservancy, environment, and public facility administration, education, culture, sports and entertainment.

number is larger than the structural shift portion, the growth trend is even. According to the dynamic changes in consumption service in the Yangtze River Delta, the characteristic in Shanghai is similar to those in the Yangtze River Delta: most of the cities are on the decline with negative structural and competition shift portion, but there are certain structural advantages in cities relatively far from Shanghai such as Huzhou, Shaoxing etc.

(2) Producer service is the "growing industry" with a thriving growth trend, and is also the main growth part of the service industry. It will undergo fast expansion in future. In the Yangtze River Delta, the number of actual growth is 433,100 people, exceeding the total of the additional employment in the other three sectors within the service industry. Both the structural shift portion and the competition one are positive in producer service. It not only represents the overall direction of service industry, but has also seen further improvement in structural proportion and position. According to its dynamic changes, the characteristics in Shanghai are similar to those in the Yangtze River Delta; most of the cities are in the embryonic stage with slow development, while Hangzhou and Suzhou have begun to start.

(3) Public article and approximate public article services are "declining sectors" which develop rather slowly. Approximate public article service has a sounder foundation. Its new employment number is 221,240 people on the basis of average ratio, but the number of actual growth is a mere 47,900 people, the smallest number. Public article service is similar to the approximate one but the former has higher growth rate than the latter one with the improvement of local financial ability. According to their dynamic changes, Shanghai is different from other cities, which is perhaps caused by the disparity in statistical methods.

(4) On the whole, producer service and consumption service have become the main growth sectors within service industry in the Yangtze River Delta, the development trend of which will be fast. This shows that activities and functions of service industry there will become the main driving power of economic growth in regions or cities instead of being confined to governmental administration and public service.

The relationship between the growth of service industry and the population, economy and construction scales of the city

According to the shift-share analysis, the service industry in the Yangtze River Delta is developing with Shanghai as the leader, and shows structural growth disparity. As Li Jiangfan (2005) said, the development of tertiary industry is affected by urban population, economy level and city density etc. This chapter gives a further analysis of the service industry in 15 cities and the relationship between internal structural growth and the scales of urban population, economy and construction. It is necessary to point out that the growth of the service industry obviously has something to do with population and economy scales of urban areas; the index of construction scale is used to measure the intensity of service scope. Then the multiple regression equation is:

$$y_{it}=\alpha+\beta_1 x_{1it}+\beta_2 x_{2it}+\beta_3 x_{3it}+\varepsilon \qquad (6)$$

y_{it} is the number of employees in the service industry; x_{1it}, x_{2it} and x_{3it} are scales of urban population, urban economy and urban construction respectively; i and t refer to cities and years respectively. The data is from the *China City Statistics Yearbook* from 2003 to 2006. From the simple analysis before multiple regressions, we can see that there is a certain relationship between the number and the scales.

Table 16.4 is the result of multiple regression analysis. The explanation follows Fig. 16.3 and 16.4:

Table 16.4. Regression results of the relationship between employment growth of the service industry and the scales of urban population, economy and construction

Y	Employment figures in service industry	Employment figures in producer service	Employment figures in consumption service	Employment figures in approximate public article service	Employment figures in public article service
Constants	−10.135 17 (2.176 282)	−4.169 451 (1.391 518)	−3.237 891 (0.530 870 3)	−2.125 16 (0.235 53)	−0.575 010 5 (0.163 595 7)
Scale of urban population (x_1)	0.129 355 5 (0.032 946)	0.031 226 7 (0.021 065 7)	0.038 217 8 (0.008 036 7)	0.038 158 5 (0.003 565 6)	0.020 074 87 (0.002 476 6)
Scale of urban economy (x_2)	0.010 984 9 (0.005 120 6)	0.008 451 4 (0.003 274 1)	0.001 824 5 (0.001 249 1)	−0.00 227 2 (0.000 554 2)	0.001 236 3 (0.000 384 9)
Scale of urban constructions (x_3)	−0.041 853 1 (0.024 729 1)	−0.022 583 3 (0.015 811 8)	−0.013 883 2 (0.006 032 3)	−0.001 272 4 (0.002 676 3)	−0.003 699 6 (0.001 858 9)
Observation figures	45	45	45	45	45

Note: Figure in brackets is the standard deviation.

Fig. 16.3. **Relationship between employment figures of the service industry and the scale of urban population**

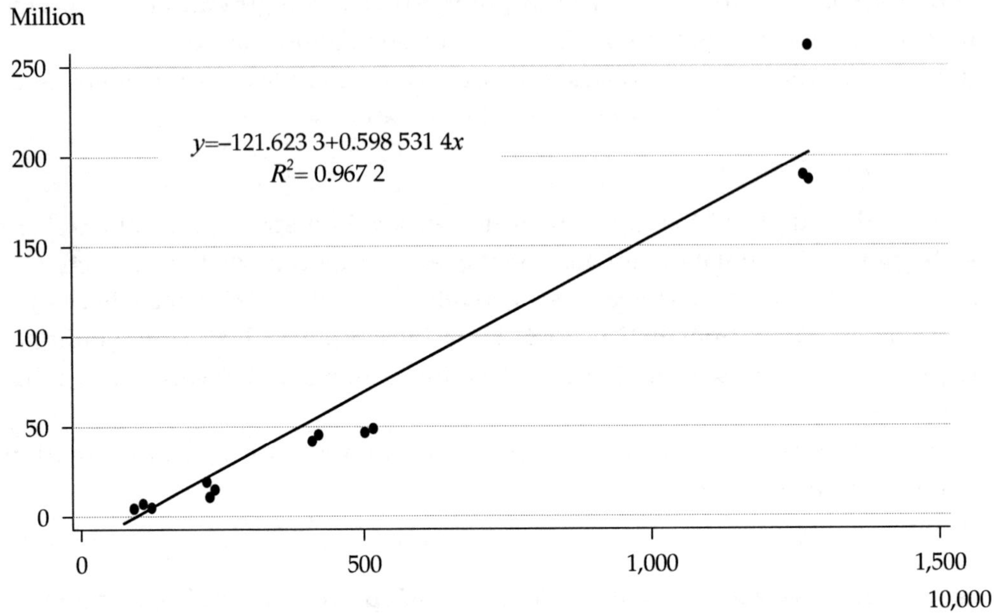

Fig. 16.4. **Relationship between employment figures of the service industry and the scale of urban economy**

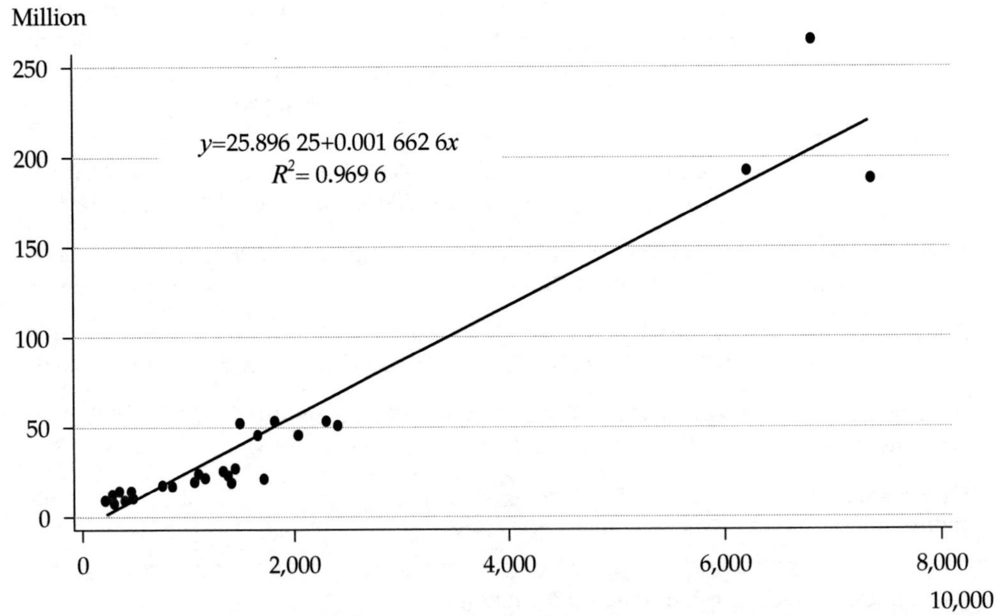

(1) The growth of employment figures in the service industry is in positive proportion to urban population and economy scales while in negative proportion to urban construction scale. The figures are most deeply affected by urban population scale. Because there are a large Registered Permanent Residence resident population as well as a floating population and the population density (the ratio of population to city size) is large in Shanghai, the service industry develops faster in Shanghai than in Suzhou and Hangzhou which have a similar economic level (GDP per capita). This point is helpful in explaining why the service industry in Shanghai is the leader in the Yangtze River Delta according to the shift-share analysis.

(2) There are some differences between the four sectors in internal structure. Employment figures in production, consumption and public article service are in proportion to the scales of urban population and urban economy, which that in approximate public article service is in inverse proportion to urban economy scale. Perhaps the technological development in information and communications particularly promotes its operational efficiency and so reduces employment. Economic scale makes much more contribution to producer service than to consumption service, while population scale has the opposite effect. The producer service is dependent on economic level and the consumption service depends on consumers (the scale of urban population). Employment numbers in public article service grow with the expansion of the scales of urban population and urban economy. This fits the share-deviation analysis that the four sectors are in a different life cycle of the service industry in the Yangtze River Delta.

Conclusions

Regional industrial growth can be researched from the gross number as well as internal structure. And share-deviation is a useful way. Conclusions can be drawn from analysis of the dynamic process of the service industry in 15 cities and the internal structural growth.

First, if the growth of service industry is examined from the city or regional view, we will find in the Yangtze River Delta that the service industry is in a polarization stage centering on Shanghai, which is different from the diffusion stage of manufacturing. The service industry radiates externally centering on Shanghai as the space distance shortens, especially in consumption service sectors. The sub-center position of Nanjing and Hangzhou, and Nanjing in particular, has been weakened because their range of attraction and hinterland has been crippled by Shanghai.

Second, from the dynamic changes in the four sectors of the service industry, consumption service is the main part of growth in service industry but it belongs to "mature industry" with an even and steady growth trend; producer service is the "growing industry" with a thriving growth trend, which is also the main growth part of service industry. It will undergo fast expansion in the future. Public article and approximate public article services are "declining sectors" which develop rather slowly. On the whole, producer service and consumption service have become the main growth sectors within service industry in the Yangtze River Delta and their development trend will be fast. This shows that the activities and functions of service industry there have become the main driving power of economic growth in regions or cities, instead of being confined to governmental administration and public service.

Third, from the combination of the SSM and multivariable regression analysis, we can find: the growth in employment number is in proportion to the scales of city population and city economy while in inverse proportion to the scale of city construction, and is most influenced by scale of city population. That supports the point in the shift-share analysis that the growth of service industry in Shanghai has become the leader and center of the Yangtze River Delta. The marked characteristics of the internal structure of the service industry is as follows: economic scale plays a more important role in producer service than in consumption service, while the role of the size of city population is much slighter in the former than in the latter. In the Yangtze River Delta, a region with fast economic growth and vitality, producer service has taken the lead in the growth of service industry, and consumption service has reached a rather mature stage, which matches the conclusion in the shift-share analysis that in the Yangtze River Delta, the service industry is in different stages of life cycle.

17

Chapter

Boosting the Development of Service Industry in the Structural Adjustment: Experience and Enlightenment from OECD Countries

Against the backdrop of economic globalization, we should promote the development of service industry in the Yangtze River Delta and put especial emphasis on research on the course of the service industry in developed countries (mainly the countries in Organization for Economic Co-operation and Development (OECD for short)). In the economy of OECD countries, the service industry has absorbed 70% of employees up until now, which brings in about 80% of the economic added value. Moreover most of the increase in employment is led by the service industry. The service industry in some OECD countries has contributed to the increase in the gross productivity for more than ten consecutive years. The development level of the service industry has become an important criterion of the comprehensive competitiveness and modernization.

Since the beginning of the 21st century, the economic structural adjustment of countries in the OECD has faced a new challenge by the continuous upgrading of manufacturing, the globalization of service industry and the innovation in information technology. In order to respond to these challenges, OECD countries actively adjusted their policy on the service industry. At the same time, the service industry in the Yangtze River Delta has undergone a rapid modification. Thus there is no doubt that the course and experience of the service industry in OECD countries have great significance in accelerating, improving and optimizing the service industry in the Yangtze River Delta.

The Development Status of Service Industry in OECD Countries

With the development of economic society, the industrial structure in OECD countries has been modified constantly in the past 50 years and the service industry has begun to occupy a dominant position. To be specific, compared with manufacturing, employees in the service industry account for a larger proportion in the gross number of employees in various industries and the GDP created by the service industry is also much higher. In short, the service industry has become the most important economic entity in the OECD, which has upset the hypothesis of balanced improvement that all industries improve steadily. Does the increase in the productivity of service industry in OECD countries determine the development of service industry? Have OECD countries got out of "Baumol Dilemma"[2]? Can the economy increase sustainably? All the questions above require our further empirical investigation on industrial structure, especially the structure of the service industry, in OECD countries.

As the course taken by service industry in all OECD countries is quite different, it is convenient for the analysis to divide OECD countries into five categories: countries with a British or American system (including the UK, America, Canada and Australia), countries with a continental system (France, Germany, Italy and Spain), countries with an emerging market system (Japan and Korea), countries with a transformed system (Hungary, Poland and Slovakia) and small countries (Austria, Belgium, Denmark, Finland, Greece, Luxembourg, The Netherlands, New Zealand, Norway, Portugal and Sweden).[3]

The change in the proportion of added value in service industry

As shown in Table 17.1, the proportion of the added value in service industry in countries with a British or American system is close to that in small countries and is a little higher than in countries with a continental system (that in all three categories of country are close, all higher than 70%).[4] But they are obviously higher than in countries with an emerging market system and with a transformed system (the latter two categories are close but about 8% lower than the former ones).

In terms of the change in the proportion of the added value in the service industry, that in countries with a British or American system, countries with continental system, countries with an emerging market system and small countries increased by 6.3%, 6.8%, 6.0% and 5.3% respectively from the 1980s to the 1990s (the data of countries with a transformed system cannot be obtained so it is not taken into the analysis). Except for small countries, the proportion in other categories of country grew at a high speed and that in countries with a continental system is a little higher.

Comparing the proportion of the added value in the service industry in 2005 with that in 1995, that in countries with a British or American system, countries with a continental system, countries with an emerging market system, countries with a transformed system and small countries has increased by 3.5%, 3.4%, 4.7%, 5.1% and 3.0% respectively. Developing from a low staring point, the service industry in countries with an emerging market system and a transformed system achieved rapid improvement, especially in the latter. The service industry has developed at a relatively high level although on the whole the range of increase in the last ten years has been smaller than in the previous ten years. However, all the above can suggests that the gradual service industrialization of the industry structure in developed countries is the general tendency of development.

Table 17.1. The proportion of the added value in service industry in OECD countries (%)

Country	1980–1990	1990–2001	1995	2005
Australia	62.7	69.3	67.8	68.9
Canada	63.1	67.0	66.4	66.7
UK	60.0	69.0	67.5	75.9
The U.S.	68.1	73.8	72.0	76.0
The average value in countries with British or American system	63.5	69.8	68.4	71.9
France	65.0	71.2	72.6	77.0
Germany	59.3	67.2	66.6	69.7
Italy	61.2	67.8	66.4	71.2
Spain	59.8	66.2	66.1	67.4
The average value in countries with continental system	61.3	68.1	67.9	71.3
Japan	58.0	64.7	64.9	69.9
Korea	45.9	51.3	51.8	56.3
The average value in countries with emerging market system	52.0	58.0	58.4	63.1
Hungary	—	62.1	61.9	65.6
Poland	—	58.7	56.8	64.6
Slovakia	—	59.2	56.3	59.9
The average value in countries with transformed system	—	60.0	58.3	63.4
Austria	62.4	66.5	66.9	68.6
Belgium	65.5	70.8	70.2	74.8
Denmark	68.9	71.7	71.4	73.0
Finland	57.6	64.0	62.8	65.7
Greece	60.1	68.3	70.0	76.6
Luxembourg	69.8	78.7	77.2	83.4
The Netherlands	64.4	69.4	69.2	73.7
New Zealand	62.4	66.7	66.8	69.1
Norway	59.5	62.0	62.8	55.4
Portugal	59.1	65.4	65.9	72.2
Sweden	64.8	69.0	67.0	70.6
The average value in small countries	63.1	68.4	68.2	71.2

As shown in Tables 17.2 and 17.3, the added value in various services in OECD countries except those with an emerging market system (countries with transformed system are not taken into analysis owing to the lack of statistics) accounts for a similar proportion in the 1980s, among which that proportion in wholesale and retail, accommodation and catering is around 15%, in transportation, storage and communications about 7.5%, in community, social and private service as well as finance, insurance, real estate and commercial services about 20%. However in countries with an emerging market system, the proportion in transportation, storage and communication comes close to that in countries in the other three categories while in other services, especially in community, social and private services as well as finance, insurance, real estate and commercial services the proportion is distinctly lower than in countries in the other three categories.

Table 17.2. The proportion of each service industry in the aggregate added value in OECD countries from 1980 to 1990 (%)

Country	Wholesale and retail, accommodation and catering	Transportation, storage and communication	Finance, insurance, real estate and commercial services	Community, social and private services
Australia	12.9	7.7	19.0	20.4
Canada	17.7	6.7	22.7	21.1
UK	12.7	8.7	21.8	19.5
The U.S.	13.9	7.7	20.6	20.9
The average value in countries with British or American system	14.3	7.7	21.0	20.5
France	12.6	6.6	24.8	21.0
Germany	11.3	6.0	22.1	19.9
Italy	17.2	7.2	18.6	18.1
Spain	17.1	7.9	17.2	17.7
The average value in countries with continental system	14.6	6.9	20.7	19.2
Japan	13.3	6.4	19.2	19.1
Korea	14.0	7.5	11.4	12.9
The average value in countries with emerging market system	13.7	7.0	15.3	16.0
Hungary	—	—	—	—
Poland	—	—	—	—
Slovakia	—	—	—	—
The average value in countries with transformed system	—	—	—	—
Austria	17.7	7.6	16.5	20.6
Belgium	13.1	6.9	21.2	24.3
Denmark	15.0	7.0	20.7	26.1
Finland	13.3	8.8	15.2	20.4
Greece	19.5	7.4	16.2	17.1
Luxembourg	14.8	6.9	31.1	17.0
The Netherlands	14.2	6.7	18.4	25.1
New Zealand	17.7	7.9	20.3	16.5
Norway	13.4	9.5	16.7	19.8
Portugal	19.6	7.1	15.0	17.3
Sweden	12.7	8.1	18.8	25.1
The average value in small countries	15.5	7.6	19.1	20.8

Table 17.3. The proportion of each service industry in the aggregate added value in OECD countries from 1990 to 2001 (%)

Country	Wholesale and retail, accommodation and catering	Transportation, storage and communication	Finance, insurance, real estate and commercial services	Community, social and private services
Australia	14.4	7.8	25.0	21.7
Canada	17.7	6.6	27.4	22.1
UK	13.7	8.8	27.1	19.7
The U.S.	13.6	7.2	24.7	21.6
The average value in countries with British or American system	14.9	7.6	26.1	21.3
France	13.0	6.4	28.9	22.9
Germany	11.8	5.8	28.2	21.4
Italy	16.8	7.3	24.2	19.5
Spain	18.9	8.0	18.9	20.4
The average value in countries with continental system	15.1	6.9	25.1	21.1
Japan	14.0	6.4	24.3	20.0
Korea	12.0	6.6	18.0	14.6
The average value in countries with emerging market system	13.0	6.5	21.2	17.3
Hungary	13.3	9.1	19.2	20.5
Poland	20.2	6.9	11.3	20.3
Slovakia	16.1	10.7	17.2	15.2
The average value in countries with transformed system	16.9	7.4	21.3	20.9
Austria	13.7	6.9	26.6	23.7
Belgium	14.4	7.7	23.1	26.5
Denmark	11.7	10.0	19.6	22.8
Finland	20.3	7.2	21.2	19.5
Greece	20.3	7.2	21.2	19.5
Luxembourg	12.9	8.9	40.3	16.6
The Netherlands	15.1	7.2	23.9	23.2
New Zealand	15.4	8.2	26.2	17.0
Norway	11.7	9.9	18.4	22.2
Portugal	17.6	6.4	18.0	23.4
Sweden	12.2	8.4	23.7	24.7
The average value in small countries	14.7	8.0	23.8	21.9

Since the 1990s, the proportion of the above service industries except for finance, insurance, real estate and commercial service in OECD countries has not changed greatly. Such proportion of service industries in finance, insurance, real estate and commerce in countries with British or American system, countries with continental system, countries with emerging market system and small countries perspectively increased by 5.1%, 4.4%, 5.9% and 4.7%. Moreover, that type of service industry in Japan and Korea improved rapidly. According to the statistics, we can further get that in Japan the proportion of financial service raised from 5.2% to 5.6% and that of real estate went up from 9.9% to 11.8%, which suggests that the growth of such industries is mainly promoted by the raise of real estate and commercial service. Meanwhile, in Korea, such proportion of financial service increases from 4.4% to 6.5% and that of real estate is up from 5.0% to 7.7%. It is really amazing that the service industries in finance, real estate and commerce can expand simultaneously in Korea even though struck by the Asian financial crisis previously.

As for the service industry structure in countries with transformed system, it can be concluded from Tables 17.2 and 17.3 that in 1990s countries of such category gave priority to the traditional service industries (domestic trade, transportation et al.) while the service industries in finance and real estate accounted for a low proportion thus were less developed.

Comparing 1995 with 2005 (see Table 17.4), in countries with British or American system, the proportion of service industries in wholesale and retail, accommodation, catering, transportation, storage, communication, education, health care and social works changed a little while that of financial and insurance services increased by 1.3%[5] and services in real estate, leasing and commerce raised by 2.3%, totaling 3.6% that is lower than that in the last ten years. Actually, it coincides with the great prosperity of real estate market led by the low interest in countries with British or American system and continental system after "9·11" terrorism event.

Table 17.4. The proportion of the value-added in each service industry in OECD countries in 1995 and 2005 (%)

Country	Wholesale and retail, accommodation and catering		Transportation, storage and communication		Finance and insurance		Real estate, leasing and commercial services		Public management and national defence		Education, health care, social works and other services	
	2005	1995	2005	1995	2005	1995	2005	1995	2005	1995	2005	1995
Australia	13.5	14.7	7.5	8.8	7.8	6.1	21.0	19.8	4.2	4.3	15.0	14.2
Canada	13.8	13.4	6.9	7.3	7.3	6.6	18.2	17.6	5.8	6.6	14.2	14.8
UK	14.5	13.7	7.1	7.7	8.3	6.4	23.4	18.1	4.8	5.8	17.8	15.7
The U.S.	13.1	13.3	5.6	6.4	7.9	6.8	24.3	21.9	8.7	9.4	16.5	16.0
The average value in countries with British or American system	13.7	13.8	6.8	7.6	7.8	6.5	21.7	19.4	5.9	6.5	15.9	15.2
France	12.9	13.2	6.4	6.2	4.6	4.8	27.2	22.8	7.6	7.9	18.0	16.9
Germany	12.2	12.3	5.9	5.7	5.0	4.6	24.3	21.8	6.0	6.7	16.4	15.5
Italy	15.4	17.2	7.8	7.0	4.6	4.7	22.3	17.7	6.5	6.1	14.3	13.8
Spain	18.4	17.5	7.1	7.0	4.6	4.7	16.7	13.6	6.0	6.6	14.9	14.4
The average value in countries with continental system	14.7	15.1	6.8	6.5	4.7	4.7	22.6	19.0	6.5	6.8	15.9	15.2
Japan	13.0	14.6	6.5	6.8	7.2	6.1	20.3	18.3	5.9	4.3	17.4	15.7
Korea	9.8	11.5	7.3	6.6	8.4	6.9	12.5	11.5	6.3	5.3	12.0	9.9
The average value in countries with emerging market system	11.4	13.1	6.9	6.7	7.8	6.5	16.4	14.9	6.1	4.8	14.7	12.8
Hungary	12.7	13.1	7.7	8.0	4.6	3.8	17.1	14.8	8.7	8.4	14.7	13.9

Table 17.4. Continued (Con'd)

Country	Wholesale and retail, accommodation and catering		Transportation, storage and communication		Finance and insurance		Real estate, leasing and commercial services		Public management and national defence		Education, health care, social works and other services	
	2005	1995	2005	1995	2005	1995	2005	1995	2005	1995	2005	1995
Poland	8.4	7.2	7.2	6.3	4.1	2.6	13.7	10.0	6.2	6.8	13.1	11.8
Slovakia	15.7	14.0	10.4	10.5	4.2	5.7	14.3	11.8	5.6	5.2	9.7	9.1
The average value in countries with transformed system	12.3	11.4	8.4	8.3	4.3	4.0	15.0	12.2	6.8	6.8	12.5	11.6
Austria	17.4	16.8	7.0	7.4	5.4	6.1	18.0	13.8	5.8	6.8	15.0	16.0
Belgium	14.6	13.8	8.4	8.2	5.8	6.4	22.2	19.1	7.3	7.1	16.5	15.6
Denmark	12.8	14.7	9.2	7.6	5.6	5.2	18.2	17.1	6.3	6.8	16.3	20.1
Finland	12.2	11.1	10.4	9.7	2.3	4.3	18.5	14.6	5.0	5.5	17.4	17.7
Greece	23.8	—	8.3	—	4.2	—	15.2	—	7.3	—	17.7	—
Luxembourg	11.4	13.1	10.3	8.2	24.2	22.1	20.0	17.2	5.6	5.6	11.9	11.1
The Netherlands	14.5	14.8	7.1	6.9	7.4	6.3	20.0	17.9	7.3	7.9	17.3	15.3
New Zealand	15.7	16.0	7.4	8.3	6.6	5.8	21.7	19.6	4.4	5.0	13.8	11.3
Norway	9.4	12.3	7.5	10.0	3.9	4.4	14.0	13.1	4.4	6.1	16.2	16.9
Portugal	17.6	17.7	7.0	6.5	6.7	6.3	14.4	13.6	9.1	8.1	16.9	13.6
Sweden	12.2	12.5	8.0	8.1	4.5	4.4	19.8	17.9	5.5	5.9	20.7	18.1
The average value in small countries	14.7	14.3	8.2	8.1	7.0	7.1	18.4	16.4	6.2	6.5	16.3	15.6

Similar with countries with British or American system, the service industries in wholesale and retail, accommodation, catering, transportation, storage, communication, education, health care, social works and others have a slight change in countries with continental system.[6] It is distinct that changes in services in finance and insurance also do not take place in theses countries but the proportion of services in real estate, leasing and commerce increases by 3.6%, totaling 3.6% too that is lower than that in the last ten years.

Different from the countries of the above two categories, in countries with emerging market system, the proportion of industries in wholesale and retail, accommodation and catering drops by 1.7%; there is little change in transportation, storage and communication; the proportion of value-added in other industries has an sharp increase in the recent ten years. That proportion in finance and insurance increases by 1.3% and in real estate, leasing and commerce by 1.5% (totaling 2.8% that is a little lower than in countries of the above two categories). Besides, that in public management and national defence raises by 1.3% and in education, health care, social works and others grows by 1.9%.

The trends of countries with transformed system, small countries and countries with continental system seems to be similar. The industries in real estate, leasing and commerce in countries with transformed system and small countries separately raised by 2.8% and 2.0% whereas there is little change in other industries, which suggests that the economic development in countries with transformed system and small countries (most of all are European Union (EU) countries) is influenced by countries with continental system to a increasingly great degree.

The growth rate of per capital value-added in service industry[7]

In 1980s, the growth rate of per capital value-added in service industries in countries with emerging market system was higher than that in small countries, countries with British or American system and countries with continental system (the growth rates in countries of the latter two categories were on a level), the biggest difference being three to four times (see Table 17.5). And then a split has come into being since 1990s. In contrast to in 1980s, that rate in countries with British or American system grows fast and that in countries with continental system and small countries falls a little but drops more (1.3%) in countries with emerging market system. It is surprising that the growth rate is as high as 2.4% in countries with transformed system.

Table 17.5. The growth rate of per capital value-added in service industry (%)

Country	1980–1990	1990–2001
Australia	0.5	1.8
Canada	0.6	1.3
UK	0.8	1.9
The U.S.	0.6	1.6
The average value in countries with British or American system	0.6	1.7
France	1.6	0.2
Germany	1.0	0.2
Italy	0.1	0.6
Spain	0.4	0.2
The average value in countries with continental system	0.8	0.6
Japan	2.5	1.0
Korea	2.9	1.7
The average value in countries with emerging market system	2.7	1.4
Hungary	—	1.8
Poland	—	1.8
Slovakia	—	3.7
The average value in countries with transformed system	—	2.4
Austria	1.3	0.6
Belgium	0.9	0.7
Denmark	0.9	1.2
Finland	1.6	1.4
Greece	—	2.4
Luxembourg	4.1	0.5
The Netherlands	0.1	0.5
New Zealand	0.7	0.8
Norway	0.8	1.8
Portugal	1.7	1.0
Sweden	0.9	1.6
The average value in small countries	1.3	1.1

In terms of the service industry structure (see Tables 17.6 and 17.7), the per capital value-added in service industry increased primarily in transportation, storage and communication and secondarily in wholesale and retail, accommodation and catering in 1980s. The contribution of other service industries (finance, insurance, real estate, commerce as well as community, social and private services) is generally negative. However, it is special in countries with emerging market system that industries in wholesale and retail, accommodation and catering make the greatest contribution. The situation in 1990s is close to that in 1980s. It is noticeable that in countries with British or American system the growth rates of per capital value-added both in financial, insurance, real estate and commercial services and in community, social and private services shift into positive values while in countries with continental system only the growth rate in community, social and private services changes into positive value.

In terms of countries of different categories, in 1980s, such growth rate in countries with emerging market system was obviously higher than that in countries of other categories. Meanwhile, countries with British or American system and countries with continental system are about level in the rate of each type of service industry.

Table 17.6. The growth rate of per capital value-added in each service industry in OECD countries from 1980 to 1990 (%)

Country	Wholesale and retail, accommodation and catering	Transportation, storage and communication	Finance, insurance, real estate and commercial services	Community, social and private services
Australia	2.0	3.5	−0.5	−0.5
Canada	1.8	1.7	−1.2	0.0
UK	−0.8	2.7	−1.1	0.2
The U.S.	0.5	2.2	−0.1	0.0
The average value in countries with British or American system	0.9	2.5	−0.7	−0.1
France	2.4	4.0	0.5	0.7
Germany	0.8	2.2	1.0	−0.02
Italy	0.1	3.1	−2.3	−0.9
Spain	−0.1	2.2	0.5	0.2
The average value in countries with continental system	0.8	2.9	−0.1	−0.1
Japan	3.9	3.8	4.0	−0.8
Korea	5.4	3.9	−0.3	−0.3
The average value in countries with emerging market system	4.7	3.9	1.9	−0.6
Hungary	—	—	—	—
Poland	—	—	—	—
Slovakia	—	—	—	—
The average value in countries with transformed system	—	—	—	—
Austria	1.9	2.6	1.4	−0.2
Belgium	−0.3	3.3	1.0	0.0
Denmark	0.7	2.7	0.3	0.3
Finland	2.9	2.9	0.2	0.5
Greece	—	—	—	—
Luxembourg	4.9	10.3	−1.1	4.2
The Netherlands	1.4	2.6	−1.5	0.3
New Zealand	−1.4	8.2	1.4	0.4
Norway	1.1	3.0	−1.2	0.3
Portugal	0.7	4.8	1.4	1.2
Sweden	—	—	−2.0	0.4
The average value in small countries	1.3	4.5	0.0	0.7

Table 17.7. The growth rate of per capital value-added in each service industry in OECD countries from 1990 to 2001 (%)

Country	Wholesale and retail, accommodation and catering	Transportation, storage and communication	Finance, insurance, real estate and commercial services	Community, social and private services
Australia	2.1	4.3	1.2	1.0
Canada	3.6	2.7	0.8	–0.4
UK	2.4	4.6	0.9	0.7
The U.S.	2.1	2.5	0.7	0.1
The average value in countries with British or American system	2.6	3.5	0.9	0.4
France	0.5	2.6	–1.2	0.4
Germany	–0.5	7.3	–0.9	0.3
Italy	0.8	3.4	–1.3	0.2
Spain	–0.1	2.3	–1.8	0.6
The average value in countries with continental system	0.2	3.9	–1.3	0.4
Japan	1.6	1.4	2.4	–0.5
Korea	1.9	6.0	–1.0	–0.3
The average value in countries with emerging market system	1.8	3.7	0.7	–0.4
Hungary	0.6	3.0	–0.6	2.5
Poland	2.9	5.5	–2.0	0.8
Slovakia	–2.0	1.2	10.5	6.0
The average value in countries with transformed system	0.5	3.2	2.6	3.1
Austria	0.9	2.1	0.2	–0.8
Belgium	1.0	0.9	–0.1	0.3
Denmark	2.0	4.0	–0.1	0.6
Finland	1.5	4.5	0.9	0.0
Greece	3.0	8.3	–0.8	1.3
Luxembourg	1.5	7.0	–2.8	–0.2
The Netherlands	0.6	2.6	–0.4	–0.2
New Zealand	0.9	5.9	–0.7	0.3
Norway	4.8	3.1	–0.2	0.4
Portugal	1.3	4.9	–1.0	–0.2
Sweden	3.3	3.9	–0.1	0.5
The average value in small countries	1.9	4.3	–0.5	0.2

In the 1990s, the growth rate of per capita added value in the service industry in countries with a British or American system was higher than that in countries in other categories while that in countries with an emerging market system was close to that in small countries. In countries with a transformed system, the rate in wholesale and retail, accommodation, catering, transportation, storage and communications was close to that in countries with a continental system, but the rate in finance, insurance, real estate and commercial services and in community, social and private services 2.6% and 3.1% respectively, both of which were higher than in countries in the other categories. That is why countries with a transformed system play a decisive role in the aggregate growth rate of per capita added value in service industries. Moreover it also suggests that the productivity in service industries in such countries is not as low as imagined but is actually high.

In accordance with the analysis in the above two sections, we can draw several conclusions as follows:

(1) In the last 20 years, the most significant changes in the service industry in OECD countries are mainly represented in finance, insurance, real estate and commercial services whereas both traditional service industries aimed at individuals (wholesale and retail, accommodation, catering, education, health care, social work and other services) and services as intermediate input (transportation, storage and communications) remain steady. This implies that the growth in service industry in OECD countries is mainly promoted by the increase of finance, insurance, real estate and commercial services. As the development of finance, insurance, real estate and commercial services is facilitated by the needs of manufacturing as well as the producer services led by the resolution of the value chain, we can say that the development of the service industry in OECD countries depends on the manufacturing industry.

(2) In the 1980s, the growth rate of per capita added value in finance, insurance, real estate and commercial services was negative in countries with a British or American system and countries with a continental system. In the 1990s that rate in countries with a British or American system turned positive. By contrast, the growth rate of per capita added value in transportation, storage and communications always remained positive and maintained a relatively high increase. The two types of services present different demands for capital intensiveness. The former, as a labor-intensive service, absorbs a great amount of labor force in the course of rapid development. If the investment of capital and the subordinate technology is fixed, the growth rate of per capita added value will decrease; on the contrary, with an increase in capital input and the improvement of the subordinate technical level (mainly the application and

improvement of information technology), the growth rate of per capita added value will be increased. As for the latter, it is obvious that the high demand of such type of service industry for the intensive capital investment leads the growth rate of per capita added value to remain high.

(3) From the perspective of the different development of countries in the various categories, each service industry in countries with an emerging market system exhibits a high degree of improvement, which means that the traditional consumer services or the modern producer services will move into rapid enhancement in pace with the upgrading of industrialization and the deepening of market-orientation. Such an increase in the need for service industry can be not only attributed to the growth in income and manufacturing (the demand for the reduction of cost) but also to the development of manufacturing boosted by the innovation of the service industry itself. It is noticeable that the services in finance and insurance do not achieve a distinct expansion. That is to say that the immature market-orientation impedes the development of the service industry to some extent even though the financial intermediation or liberalization in countries with a transformed system is directly proportional to the productivity of the service industry.[8]

(4) Although the need of OECD countries for communications services tend to increase, the price and output of these are inversely proportional to each other. Without the consideration of the factors affecting the drop of price, the communications services actually developed at a rather high speed. The cause of such a change in communications services can be mainly ascribed to the fact that the rapid innovation of technology and the increasing competitiveness make the production of communications services more and more effective.

(5) Generally speaking, the proportion of added value in service industry in OECD countries and the difference in service industry structures reflect the differences of those countries in aspects of the promotion of employment of labor (especially the employment of women, temporary and full-time employees), the scale supplied by national wealth, the administration policy, and the specialization of trade. To the policy-makers, an important issue is whether the increase in the added value in the service industry and the change in the service industry structure are beneficial to economic growth. The quantitative analysis demonstrates that those two aspects are in reverse ratio implicitly. Nevertheless in countries such as Korea and Ireland, in which the added value in the service industry accounts for a small proportion, the GDP per capita shows a relatively rapid growth.

The change in the proportion of employment in the service industry

On the whole (see Table 17.8), in countries with a high proportion of added value in the service industry, employment in the service industry also accounts for a high proportion of the gross employment. From 1980 to 1990, the proportion of employment in countries with a British or American system was respectively 6.5%, 11.6% and 20.3% higher than that in small countries, countries with a continental system and countries with an emerging market system, while from 1990 to 2001 the proportion in countries with a British or American system was 6.6%, 8.9%, 16.2% and 23.6% higher than that in small countries, countries with a continental system, countries with an emerging market system and countries with a transformed system respectively. The proportion of employment in the service industry in each country kept rising and the gap between countries with a British or American system and countries in other categories remained the same in 1995 and 2005. But the proportion of employment in the service industry in countries with an emerging market system and countries with a transformed system increased rapidly and the gap between the countries in these two categories and countries with a British or American system also narrowed at a high speed.

In terms of the change in the proportion of employment in the service industry in countries of each category, the proportion of employment in service industry in countries with a British or American system, countries with an emerging market system, and small countries has separately risen by 5.2%, 7.9%, 9.3% and 5.1% from the 1980s to the 1990s. The proportion in countries with a continental system and countries with emerging market system, especially the latter, went up relatively fast, which showed that the service industry had an effect on the transformation of the labor force in such countries.

Table 17.8. The proportion of employment in service industry in OECD countries (%)

Country	1980–1990	1990–2001	1995	2005
Australia	66.8	72.5	72.2	75.3
Canada	70.9	75.0	74.0	75.3
UK	67.8	74.8	70.7	76.4
The U.S.	73.4	77.4	73.1	78.6

(Con'd)

The average value in countries with British or American system	69.7	74.9	72.5	76.4
France	63.4	71.4	69.1	73.9
Germany	57.4	65.5	60.5	67.6
Italy	55.9	63.8	59.2	64.6
Spain	55.5	63.4	60.9	64.8
The average value in countries with continental system	58.1	66.0	62.4	67.7
Japan	55.7	61.5	60.8	67.6
Korea	43.1	55.8	54.8	65.2
The average value in countries with emerging market system	49.4	58.7	57.8	66.4
Hungary	—	58.0	58.2	62.2
Poland	—	44.4	45.4	53.4
Slovakia	—	51.4	51.9	56.5
The average value in countries with transformed system	—	51.3	51.8	57.4
Austria	51.3	58.9	60.3	66.9
Belgium	68.5	73.5	71.1	73.3
Denmark	67.2	71.6	68.1	72.8
Finland	57.5	65.4	64.5	69.3
Greece	—	57.8	56.4	65.2
Luxembourg	64.7	71.9	70.4	79.7
The Netherlands	69.7	74.5	73.7	76.6
New Zealand	71.2	74.7	65.2	70.8
Norway	67.4	73.8	71.4	75.8
Portugal	46.6	56.4	56.1	57.3
Sweden	67.8	72.9	71.0	76.0
The average value in small countries	63.2	68.3	66.2	71.2

In 2005 the proportions of employment in service industry in countries with a British or American system, countries with a continental system, countries with an emerging market system, countries with a transformed system and small countries were 3.9%, 5.3%, 8.6%, 5.6% and 5.0% respectively higher than that in 1995. Meanwhile the proportions in countries with an emerging market system and countries with a transformed system increased by the largest margin, which to date has remained very close.

From the perspective of each type of service industry (see Table 17.9 and 17.10), the proportion of employment in service industry does not correspond to the proportion of added value in each country, which is determined by the characteristics of certain types of service industry. That is to say, those with high proportions of added value in service industry do not necessarily have a high proportion of employment, such as service industries in finance, insurance, real estate and commerce. In wholesale and retail, and accommodation and catering services, and in community, social and private services, the proportion of employment is higher than that of added value. Whether in the 1980s or the 1990s, the proportions of employment in the above two types of service industry were relatively high in countries of each category while that in transportation, storage and communications were the lowest, and in finance, insurance, real estate and commercial services in the middle.

From the perspective of different countries, the proportions of employment in transportation, storage and communications were relatively similar in countries of each category in the 1980s. In wholesale and retail, and accommodation and catering services, the proportion of employment in countries with a British or American system was higher than that in countries in other categories (proportions in these countries were close to each other). In finance, insurance, real estate and commercial services, the proportion in countries with a British or American system was higher than that in countries with a continental system and in small countries (that in countries of these two categories was close to each other) and by far higher than in countries with an emerging market system (nearly twice as high as the latter, which shows that such types of service industry were less developed in Japan and Korea, especially in Korea). In community, social and private services, the proportions in small countries and countries with a British or American system were high and close to each other; the proportion in countries with a continental system was a little lower than the former; and that in countries with an emerging market system was 10.3% lower than in small countries. The difference in service industry in countries of each category demonstrates the highly developed community, social and private services in countries with high welfare.

Table 17.9. The proportion of each type of service industry in overall employment in OECD countries from 1980 to 1990 (%)

Country	Wholesale and retail, accommodation and catering	Transportation, storage and communication	Finance, insurance, real estate and commercial services	Community, social and private services
Australia	21.8	6.0	13.3	26.7
Canada	24.9	4.9	12.7	30.8
UK	23.7	7.4	10.8	24.8
The U.S.	24.7	6.2	12.6	27.4
The average value in countries with British or American system	23.8	6.1	12.4	27.4
France	16.8	5.8	11.8	29.0
Germany	18.1	6.0	9.0	24.4
Italy	19.1	5.3	7.5	24.0
Spain	19.5	6.2	6.8	23.0
The average value in countries with continental system	18.4	5.8	8.8	25.1
Japan	17.9	5.7	9.4	22.7
Korea	21.8	4.7	3.8	12.8
The average value in countries with emerging market system	19.9	4.7	3.8	17.8
Hungary	—	—	—	—
Poland	—	—	—	—
Slovakia	—	—	—	—
The average value in countries with transformed system	—	—	—	—
Austria	18.7	5.9	7.0	19.7
Belgium	19.4	6.7	11.2	31.2
Denmark	18.0	6.8	10.0	32.4
Finland	15.9	7.2	7.8	26.7
Greece	—	—	—	—
Luxembourg	21.5	7.1	14.6	21.5
The Netherlands	18.0	5.8	12.8	33.1
New Zealand	25.8	6.8	12.9	25.7
Norway	18.0	9.2	8.2	32.0
Portugal	17.3	3.9	4.4	20.9
Sweden	14.8	7.1	7.9	38.1
The average value in small countries	18.7	6.7	9.7	28.1

Table 17.10. The proportion of each type of service industry in overall employment in OECD countries from 1990 to 2001 (%)

Country	Wholesale and retail, accommodation and catering	Transportation, storage and communication	Finance, insurance, real estate and commercial services	Community, social and private services
Australia	23.0	5.8	17.3	28.6
Canada	24.8	4.9	15.4	32.2
UK	25.3	6.5	13.8	26.8
The U.S.	25.0	5.9	15.5	28.7
The average value in countries with British or American system	24.5	5.8	15.5	29.1
France	17.0	5.9	15	33.3
Germany	19.4	5.7	12.7	27.8
Italy	19.8	4.8	11.4	27.7
Spain	21.2	5.8	8.8	27.5
The average value in countries with continental system	19.4	5.6	12.0	29.1
Japan	17.7	5.8	10.2	27.5
Korea	26.2	5.5	8.3	15.7
The average value in countries with emerging market system	22.0	5.7	9.3	21.6
Hungary	16.6	8.4	6.4	26.5
Poland	14.7	5.7	6.4	17.6
Slovakia	13.2	7.6	5.5	25.3
The average value in countries with transformed system	14.8	7.2	6.0	23.1
Austria	20.6	6.1	9.3	22.9
Belgium	18.7	6.6	15.5	32.7
Denmark	18.5	6.8	11.7	34.6
Finland	15.4	7.5	10.1	32.4
Greece	20.9	6.8	7.7	22.5
Luxembourg	20.1	7.6	22.4	21.8
The Netherlands	20.0	5.7	17.2	31.6
New Zealand	26.5	6.3	13.8	28.1
Norway	17.2	9.0	10.2	37.3
Portugal	19.5	3.4	8	25.5
Sweden	15.4	7.0	11.5	38.9
The average value in small countries	19.3	6.6	12.5	29.8

From the 1980s to the 1990s, the proportion of employment in wholesale and retail, accommodation and catering increased slightly in countries of each category (that in countries with an emerging market system rose by a larger margin). The growth margin of the proportion in transportation, storage and communications was different in countries of various categories. For example, the proportion in countries with an emerging market system and countries with a continental system increased considerable by 4% separately while the increase in countries with a British or American system, countries with a continental system and small countries was close to each other. In finance, insurance, real estate and commercial services, the proportion went up markedly by 3.1%, 3.2%, 2.7% and 2.8% respectively in countries with a British or American system, countries with a continental system, countries with an emerging market system and small countries. Such a growth tendency in the proportion of employment coincides with the rapid development of that type of service in the 1990s.

The statistics of the 1990s also demonstrate that in countries with a transformed system the proportion of employment in community, social and private services was the highest of the service industries and that in wholesale and retail, and accommodation and catering, was the second highest. Such a sequence is the same as in countries in the other categories (but the in the former the proportions are much lower than in the latter). However the proportion in finance, insurance, real estate and commercial services was lower than in transportation, storage and communications in those countries while that was 1.63 to 2.67 times higher than in transportation, storage and communication in countries in the other categories, which suggests that the shift of employment structure in countries with a transformed system lags far behind countries in the other categories.

In the comparison of 1995 to 2005 (see Table 17.11), we can see that the proportion of employment both in real estate, leasing and commercial services and in education, health care, social works and other services respectively rises by 3.3% and 1.2% whereas there is little change in that in other services.

Table 17.11. The proportion of employment in each type of service industry in OECD countries in 1995 and 2005 (%)

Country	Wholesale and retail, accommodation and catering		Transportation, storage and communication		Finance and insurance		Real estate, leasing and commercial services		Public management and national defence		Education, health care, social works and other services	
	2005	1995	2005	1995	2005	1995	2005	1995	2005	1995	2005	1995
Australia	24.7	25.4	6.4	6.5	3.6	3.9	12.1	9.5	5.8	6.2	22.4	20.4
Canada	24.0	23.3	6.8	7.3	5.2	5.4	11.6	8.2	5.2	6.1	21.5	22.2
UK	24.2	23.1	5.9	5.8	4.1	4.4	15.4	12.4	6.4	7.1	23.8	23.8
The U.S.	21.4	24.1	4.8	5.0	4.5	4.7	15.0	10.6	8.4	9.1	24.7	21.0
The average value in countries with British or American system	23.6	24.0	6.0	6.2	4.4	4.6	13.5	10.2	6.5	7.1	23.1	21.9
France	16.9	16.0	6.3	6.1	3.1	3.2	14.8	11.7	8.6	9.5	22.7	21.5
Germany	19.8	18.8	5.4	6.0	3.2	3.4	13.0	8.0	7.0	8.1	21.2	18.0
Italy	20.4	20.2	6.4	6.3	2.4	2.7	11.1	7.3	5.7	6.6	16.7	16.4
Spain	22.4	20.9	5.7	5.9	2.1	2.7	8.5	5.7	7.6	8.8	15.2	19.0
The average value in countries with continental system	19.9	19.0	6.0	6.1	2.7	3.0	11.9	8.2	7.2	8.3	19.0	18.7
Japan	18.0	17.1	5.8	5.9	2.7	3.1	1.5	1.5	3.3	3.3	27.8	23.4
Korea	26.3	26.8	6.2	5.2	3.4	3.5	8.7	4.2	3.4	3.2	16.0	9.9
The average value in countries with emerging market system	22.2	22.0	6.0	5.6	3.1	3.3	5.1	2.9	3.4	3.3	21.9	16.7
Hungary	17.8	15.9	7.7	8.9	2.1	2.3	6.9	3.6	7.8	7.3	19.4	20.3

Country	Wholesale and retail, accommodation and catering		Transportation, storage and communication		Finance and insurance		Real estate, leasing and commercial services		Public management and national defence		Education, health care, social works and other services	
	2005	1995	2005	1995	2005	1995	2005	1995	2005	1995	2005	1995
Poland	17.4	14.2	5.7	5.9	2.1	1.7	7.5	3.2	6.6	2.6	16.0	14.7
Slovakia	20.2	12.1	7.0	7.9	1.7	1.2	7.4	3.9	6.9	6.1	18.1	18.4
The average value in countries with transformed system	18.5	14.1	6.8	7.6	2.0	1.7	7.3	3.6	7.1	5.3	17.8	17.8
Austria	21.9	21.1	6.9	7.2	3.1	3.2	9.6	6.3	6.8	7.2	20.3	18.1
Belgium	17.2	18.0	6.9	7.1	3.3	3.7	15.6	11.7	9.9	9.6	22.6	21.0
Denmark	19.0	17.9	6.5	6.6	3.0	3.0	11.2	7.9	6.0	7.1	29.2	28.5
Finland	15.8	14.8	7.2	7.7	1.6	2.3	10.3	7.4	7.3	7.6	26.4	24.7
Greece	20.5	19.3	6.5	6.6	2.6	2.3	6.8	4.9	7.8	7.4	17.1	14.7
Luxembourg	18.5	21.1	7.5	7.0	11.0	10.3	17.1	9.9	5.4	5.4	15.3	14.6
The Netherlands	19.0	20.0	6.3	5.8	3.8	3.5	15.9	11.5	7.3	7.0	22.4	25.1
New Zealand	26.4	26.3	6.2	6.0	3.0	3.8	12.3	9.3	3.3	4.5	25.7	23.6
Norway	16.4	16.5	9.0	10.0	2.3	2.7	10.3	6.6	7.4	9.0	28.5	26.1
Portugal	22.0	19.3	3.8	3.5	1.8	2.6	5.7	5.7	7.2	8.0	14.7	17.2
Sweden	15.4	15.5	6.6	6.9	2.1	2.1	11.7	8.3	6.2	7.9	32.8	32.4
The average value in small countries	19.3	19.1	6.7	6.8	3.4	3.6	11.5	8.1	6.8	7.3	23.3	22.4

The countries with a continental system had a situation similar to countries with a British or American system. The proportion of employment in real estate, leasing and commercial services increased by 3.7% while that in public management and national defence decreased by 1.1%. Meanwhile, the proportion in other services changed little. Small countries were similar in such proportions to countries with a continental system, in which the proportion in real estate, leasing and commercial services rose by 3.4% and that in other services showed a slight change.

The countries with an emerging market system also showed a similar situation to countries with a British or American system. There was little change in the proportion in all types of service industry except real estate, leasing and commercial services, and education, health care, social works and other services. Moreover the proportions in those two types of services separately increased by 2.2% and 5.2%.

In countries with a transformed system, the proportion of employment rose by 4.4% in wholesale and retail, and accommodation and catering, 3.7% in real estate, leasing and commercial services, and 1.8% in public management and national defence. But that in other services did not change greatly. This implies that the traditional service industry absorbs a large amount of the labor force while the proportion of employment in the producer service industry shows a slight growth (for example, the proportion in finance and insurance services only rose by 0.3%) or even a negative growth (e.g. that in transportation, storage and communications fell 0.8%). The possible reason for this is that, in the course of economic globalization in the recent ten years or more, the division of value chain on a global scale causes countries with an advanced market economy to transfer their manufacturing link to other countries and then focus on producer services as their competitive edge. Furthermore it objectively creates a certain difficulty in transforming employees in countries with a transformed system into producer services.

An analysis of the growth rate of employment in the service industry[9]

From Table 17.12, we can see that in the 1980s the growth rate of employment both in countries with a British or American system and in countries with a continental system was around 2.4% but that in small countries was relatively low. Meanwhile it increased rather quickly in countries with an emerging market system. Up to 1990, the growth rate generally decreased, and was 2.7% in countries with an emerging market system and 1.7% in countries in the other four categories.

Table 17.12. The growth rate of employment in the service industry in OECD countries (%)

Country	1980–1990	1990–2001
Australia	3.2	2.1
Canada	2.5	1.7
UK	1.8	1.1
The U.S.	2.5	1.8
The average value in countries with British or American system	2.5	1.7
France	1.7	1.6
Germany	2.1	1.6
Italy	2.7	1.2
Spain	2.8	2.2
The average value in countries with continental system	2.3	1.7
Japan	1.8	1.2
Korea	5.1	4.1
The average value in countries with emerging market system	3.5	2.7
Hungary	—	0.8
Poland	—	1.5
Slovakia	—	2.8
The average value in countries with transformed system	—	1.7
Austria	1.6	1.6
Belgium	1.1	1.1
Denmark	1.0	0.9
Finland	2.0	0.4
Greece	—	1.4
Luxembourg	4.0	4.7
The Netherlands	1.5	2.6
New Zealand	–0.6	2.5
Norway	1.7	1.6
Portugal	1.9	2.2
Sweden	1.5	0.1
The average value in small countries	1.6	1.7

From the perspective of each type of service industry (as shown in Tables 17.13 and 17.14), in the 1980s the growth rate of employment in finance, insurance, real estate and commercial services was the highest, in community, social and private services, and wholesale and retail, accommodation and catering services the second highest, and in transportation, storage and communications the lowest. However a slight change has taken place since the 1990s. The growth rate in transportation, storage and communications was the highest, in wholesale and retail, accommodation and catering services the second highest, but in finance, insurance, real estate and commercial services and community, social and private services it presented a slow or even negative growth[10].

In terms of different countries, the growth rates in the four types of service industry in small countries were lower than in countries in the other categories in the 1980s. Overall, the growth rate of employment in each type of service industry in countries with an emerging countries system was higher than that in countries with a British or American system and countries with a continental system. This may be attributed to the fact that the proportion of employment in service industry in small countries has been high while that in countries with an emerging market system remained low. Since the 1990s the growth rate of employment in wholesale and retail, accommodation and catering services in countries with a British or American system has been the highest and in countries with a continental system and countries with a transformed system the lowest; countries with emerging market system have had a similar rate to small countries. Each country showed little difference in the growth rate in transportation, storage and communications. In finance, insurance, real estate and commercial service, the growth rate of employment was relatively high in countries with a transformed system; that in countries with a British or American system was close to that in countries with an emerging market system, obviously lower than in countries with a transformed system; the rate in small countries and countries with a continental system showed a negative increase, especially in the latter. In community, social and private services, the growth rate in countries with a transformed system upgraded fast; that in countries with an emerging market system fell; that in other countries showed a slight increase by a similar margin.

Based on the analysis in section (3) and (4), we can draw the following five conclusions in terms of the change in the employment in the service industry in OECD countries since 1980.

1. As economic development or market-based reform leads to the transfer of the labor force from other industries, whether to save trading costs or to make a high profit, this can bring a constant increase in the number of employees absorbed by the service industry.

2. The proportion of employment in the service industry in each country will rise with the growth in the proportion of added value in the industry. However there are some distinctions between various types of service industry in different periods. The change in the proportion of employment is mainly reflected both in finance, insurance, real estate and commercial services and in community, social and private services. Generally speaking, the more developed the service industry is, the higher the proportion of employment in the service

Table 17.13. The growth rate of employment in each type of service industry in OECD countries from 1980 to 1990 (%)

Country	Wholesale and retail, accommodation and catering	Transportation, storage and communication	Finance, insurance, real estate and commercial services	Community, social and private services
Australia	1.4	–0.2	4.0	1.5
Canada	2.3	1.2	4.6	2.1
UK	2.7	1.4	5.8	3.1
The U.S.	2.2	1.4	4.1	2.2
The average value in countries with British or American system	2.2	1.0	4.6	2.2
France	0.9	0.6	3.0	1.8
Germany	1.6	1.1	3.5	2.2
Italy	1.8	0.4	6.6	2.7
Spain	2.0	0.3	3.6	4.0
The average value in countries with continental system	1.6	0.6	4.2	2.7
Japan	0.6	0.5	2.1	3.0
Korea	4.0	4.0	10.5	5.7
The average value in countries with emerging market system	2.3	2.3	6.3	4.4
Hungary	—	—	—	—
Poland	—	—	—	—
Slovakia	—	—	—	—
The average value in countries with transformed system	—	—	—	—
Austria	1.1	0.7	2.9	2.0
Belgium	0.2	–1.1	3.1	1.5
Denmark	0.1	0.6	2.2	1.1
Finland	1.0	0.8	4.3	2.2
Greece	—	—	—	—
Luxembourg	1.7	4.3	9.3	2.7
The Netherlands	1.1	0.6	3.6	1.1
New Zealand	–0.6	–6.3	–1.7	1.5
Norway	0.5	0.5	3.6	2.2
Portugal	1.3	–0.1	3.9	2.4
Sweden	1.0	0.8	4.8	1.2
The average value in small countries	0.7	0.1	3.6	1.8

Table 17.14. The growth rate of employment in each type of service industry in OECD countries from 1990 to 2001 (%)

Country	Wholesale and retail, accommodation and catering	Transportation, storage and communication	Finance, insurance, real estate and commercial services	Community, social and private services
Australia	2.1	4.3	1.2	1.0
Canada	3.6	2.7	0.8	–0.4
UK	2.4	4.6	0.9	0.7
The U.S.	2.1	2.5	0.7	0.1
The average value in countries with British or American system	2.6	3.5	0.9	0.4
France	2.6	3.5	0.9	0.4
Germany	0.5	2.6	–1.2	0.4
Italy	0.8	3.4	–1.3	0.2
Spain	–0.1	2.3	–1.8	0.6
The average value in countries with continental system	0.2	3.9	–1.3	0.4
Japan	1.6	1.4	2.4	–0.5
Korea	1.9	6.0	–1.0	–0.3
The average value in countries with emerging market system	1.8	3.7	0.7	–0.4
Hungary	0.6	3.0	–0.6	2.5
Poland	2.9	5.5	–2.0	0.8
Slovakia	–2.0	1.2	10.5	6.0
The average value in countries with transformed system	0.5	3.2	2.6	3.1
Austria	0.9	2.1	0.2	–0.8
Belgium	1.0	0.9	–0.1	0.3
Denmark	2.0	4.0	–0.1	0.6
Finland	1.5	4.5	0.9	0.0
Greece	3.0	8.3	–0.8	1.3
Luxembourg	1.5	7.0	–2.8	–0.2
The Netherlands	0.6	2.6	–0.4	–0.2
New Zealand	0.9	5.9	–0.7	0.3
Norway	4.8	3.1	–0.2	0.4
Portugal	1.3	4.9	–1.0	–0.2
Sweden	3.3	3.9	–0.1	0.5
The average value in small countries	1.9	4.3	–0.5	0.2

industry is. Moreover the lower the starting point of the service industry, the higher the growth rate of employment in it.

3. The labor-intensiveness of the service industry is fully embodied in wholesale and retail, accommodation and catering services, and community, social and private services, and the proportions of employment in these two types is higher than 20%. However not all types of service industry are labor-intensive. For example, services in transportation, storage and communications attract less labor force because the per capita investment in such services is relatively high. Meanwhile in countries with a British or American system and countries with a continental system, the growth rate of employment in such services presents to be negative from 1990 to 2001. The growth rate in countries with an merging market system is the lowest in all types of service industry although it reaches 9.6%.

4. In the course of economic development, the proportion of employment in producer services shows a rapid growth while that in consumer and social services increases relatively slowly. From Figs. 17.9 and 17.10 we can see that since 1980 the proportion of employment in finance, insurance, real estate and commercial services has risen at the highest speed of each type of services in all the OECD countries[11], among which such a proportion in countries with emerging market system increased by as much as 40.9% and that in countries with a British or American system also rose by 25%. By contrast, the proportion in traditional services such as wholesale and retail, accommodation and catering rises slowly. However, in pace with the upgrading of people's consumption level, the proportion in community, social and private services presents a quick increase, especially in countries with an emerging market system. Services in transportation, storage and communications are viewed as producer services to a great extent, in which the growth rate of proportion of employment is the lowest in all types of service industry and shows negative in countries with a British or American system and countries with a continental system. But because of its capital intensiveness, the development of producer services does not only need the transfer of labor force but also an increase in capital investment and technological innovation.

5. Countries with a British or American system have come out first in expanding service industry, taking the initiative in transforming from an industrialized society into a post-industrialized one. In small countries there are many restrictions on the development of manufacturing and thus they vigorously expand the service industry, almost on a par with countries with a British or American system. Restricted by the international division of labor, countries with a continental system and countries with an emerging market

system have the great preponderance of advanced manufacturing, therefore their service industries fall behind countries in the above two categories. Nevertheless, the economic globalization in the beginning of the 20th century leads the transformation of manufacturing capital on a large scale in those countries and thus their service industry develops more quickly. At present the gap between countries of the former two categories and those of the latter two categories (especially countries with a continental system) is gradually narrowing. Although the starting point of countries with a transformed system is lower than that of the above developed countries, they improve quickly and efficiently owing to their active participation in the integration of the EU. Currently they are roughly the same as countries with an emerging market system. Such case provides a good example for other countries with a transformed system. Additionally, in terms of the course of the service industry, the difference in the basic system in each country has a limited impact on the development of the service industry but the varying level of such development mainly depends on the different economic development policy in each country and the link or place the country takes up in international division of labor in a particular stage. In order to accelerate the development of the service industry, a country has to grasp the opportunity of economic globalization and transfer the previous industries into other regions or countries in a timely way, in which way it can achieve industrial upgrading successfully.

Motivations for the Development of the Service Industry in OECD Coutries

The rapid development of service industry in OECD countries attracts great attention from numerous scholars and professors who present many explanations of the service orientation of the economy in these countries. The following three explanations are comparatively important.

The imbalanced increase in productivity between service industry and manufacturing

In accordance with Baumol's (1967) hypothesis that the growth rate of productivity in service industry is lower than in manufacturing, a possible reason for the increase in service industry in OECD countries is that the growth rate of productivity in manufacturing in OECD countries is comparatively high and thus a large number of the labor force transfer into the service industry in which the productivity rises slowly. This facilitates the increase in employment and added value in the service industry. The empirical analysis suggests that, whether from 1980 to 1990 or from 1990 to 2001, the growth rate of productivity in service industry is 50% lower than in manufacturing in almost all the OECD countries while the rate is less than 30% in Finland, Sweden and America. It also suggests that in OECD countries the gap in the growth rate of productivity between service industry and manufacturing is directly proportional to the growth rate of employment in service industry but is in inverse proportion to the growth rate of employment in manufacturing. In short, all the above validates his hypothesis.

From the perspective of the growth rate of productivity in each type of service industry we can go into more specific explanations for the development of service industry. The labor-intensive services such as community, social and private services and wholesale and retail, accommodation and catering are aimed at the ultimate domestic demand and the increase in productivity will be restricted and obviously slower than in manufacturing. However the productivity in producer services (such as finance, transportation, storage and communications) shows a strong momentum of growth. According to the empirical analysis, the growth rate of productivity was as high as 4.5% in financial services and 10% in postal and communications service from 1995 to 2005, which is close to the growth rate of 5% in manufacturing since 1980. Moreover the producer services varied directly with the growth rate of the economy in the past 20 years[12], which also occurred in wholesale and retail, transportation and storage. The actual cause lies both in the scale economy and competitiveness in the service industry, and in the productivity impact led by the application of information and communications techniques since 1980.

Based on the further analysis of the development of the service industry we can see that the development density of the service industry (measured by the proportion of commercial research funding in the added value in service industry) is lower than that of manufacturing.[13] In terms of the various types of service industry, the development density is comparatively low in wholesale and retail, transportation, storage, financial services etc. In OECD countries the commercial research funding in those services accounted for an average of 0.1% in the aggregate added value in 2001.[14] Conversely, the postal, communications and commercial services (closely related to the developing and computer techniques) are highly technology- and knowledge-intensive industries, of which the development density is higher than 6% and even sometimes exceeds that of manufacturing. The proportion of research funding in service industry in the aggregate commercial research funding in 2005 (see Table 17.15), is

34.1% in countries with a British or American system, 16.9% in countries with a continental system, 8.0% in countries an emerging market system, 26.8% in countries with a transformed system and 22.9% in small countries. Such statistics shows that countries with a British or American system, based on their advanced service industry, keep research funding high and thus they possess strong competitiveness. By contrast, countries with an emerging market system lay more emphasis on the non-service industries, which may be closely concerned with their developed manufacturing. In addition, it is noticeable that the proportion in countries with a transformed system reaches 26.8%, which exceeds that in countries with a continental system and small countries and ranks the second. Therefore it is natural that the service industry has developed rapidly and the growth rate of per capita added value has remained high in the service industry in the last ten years or more.

Table 17.15. The proportion of commercial research funding in service industry in each OECD country in 2005 (%)

Country	The commercial funding in service industry in 2005	Country	The commercial funding in service industry in 2005
Australia	41.1	Hungary	36.9
Canada	37.9	Poland	18.9
UK	21.1	Slovakia	24.7
America	36.1	The average value in countries with a transformed system	26.8
The average value in countries with a British or American system	34.1	Austria	18.0
France	9.4	Belgium	17.8
Germany	8.3	Denmark	33.3
Italy	24.4	Finland	14.5
Spain	25.6	Greece	34.2
The average value in countries with a continental system	16.9	Luxembourg	24.7
		The Netherlands	18.3
		New Zealand	—
Japan	9.1	Norway	35.3
Korea	6.9	Portugal	—
The average value in countries with an emerging market system	8.0	Sweden	10.4
		The average value in small countries	22.9

The change in factors relative to ultimate demand boosts the rapid development of service industry.

Firstly, the flexibility of demand income is great in some types of service industry which means that a certain increase in income will promote the growth in demand by a larger margin. For example, services in entertainment, high-quality health care, higher education and tourism will contribute to the improvement of living standards. With economic development, the increasing demand of citizens in OECD countries for service industry facilitates the rapid development of those types of services and furthers the development of the overall service industry.

Secondly, the change in population composition in OECD countries has influenced the change in demand structure. The constantly decreasing birth rate as well as the longer life expectancy causes the fast aging of the population in OECD countries, especially in countries with high welfare. Moreover this also leads to decrease in demand for some products or services (such as elementary education) while the demand for other products or services (such as health care and private services) increase gradually. Thus this influences the regulation of service industry structure to a great degree.

Thirdly, the demand for some services (such as education and health services) is also closely related with the scale of welfare policy in OECD countries. To expand the scale of social welfare will always lead to an increase in the demand for those services. As the centre-left party is in power and unites with the strong unions, the welfare in developed countries increase steadily. Moreover the welfare is mainly spent on service industry, which also promotes the rapid development of the service industry.

Fourthly, the demand for some services is not restricted by the ultimate domestic demand to some extent. There are also some services involving world trade. The export of services by OECD countries accounted for 6% of the aggregate output at the beginning of the 21st century. In those related to commercial services such as transportation, storage, postal services and communications, 10% to 20% of their output is used to meet the international demand. The expansion of the service trade model facilitates the development of the service trade[15] and further stimulates growth in the domestic service industry.

The role of the service industry as the provider for intermediate demand is more and more important

As the provider of intermediate input the service industry becomes more and more significant, which also suggests close interaction between manufacturing and the service industry.

In OECD countries, the intermediate products respectively supplied by service industry and manufacturing account for almost the same proportion in the gross output (see Fig. 17.1). 24% of output in each of the two industries is respectively used in the intermediate demand of their own and the total of about 34% of output of the two industries is used in intermediate consumption in the whole economic operation. For example, more than half of transportation and communication services are used in the intermediate input while only 20% in the ultimate demand. But 40% to 60% of output in financial and commercial services is used in the intermediate demand.

Fig. 17.1. The demand structure of the gross output in service industry and manufacturing in OECD countries

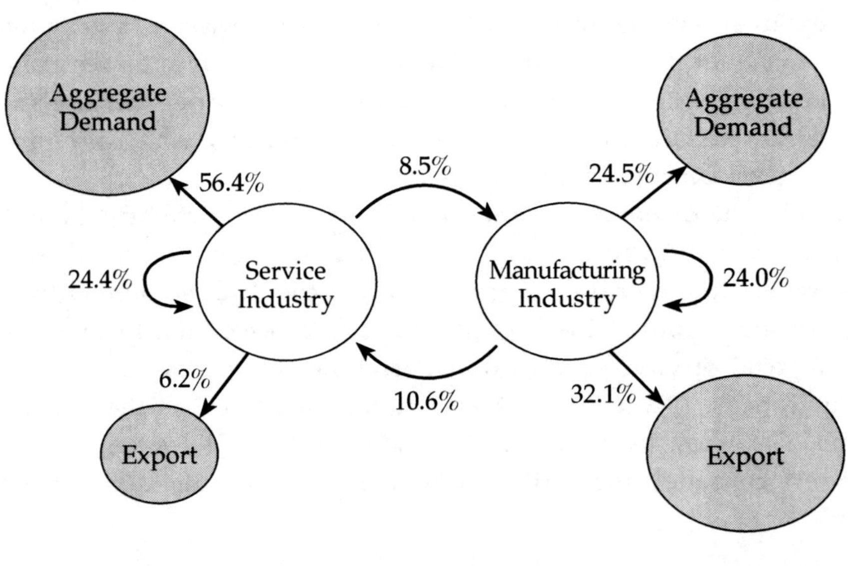

Note: The analysis adopts the data of Italy in 1992, Austria, Germany and the UK in 1995 and Australia, Canada, Japan and America in 1997.
Source: The input-output table of OECD countries.

The following two tendencies can explain the increasing strong interaction between the two industries. Firstly, the necessary or supplementary service activity accounts for a higher and higher proportion in manufacturing. For example, the production of a car cannot be completed without the relevant service activities such as market investigation, technological development, human resources management and business counseling. Moreover cars sold in the form of a package are often accompanied by financing service which can not only be supplied directly to the manufacturers of cars but also can be supplied to them by transferring a deed. Secondly, commercial services such as research and development, financing and general services have tended to be outsourced in the past 20 years. In order to meet the demand for cheaper cost and higher quality service, enterprises can conclude relevant outsourcing contracts with existing specialized service suppliers or sign contracts with newly founded enterprises or enterprises separated from manufacturing. In fact, the above two tendencies suggest that with the development of manufacturing each service link in it will become gradually independent which obviously accelerates the development of the whole service industry.

Policy Orientation for Improvement of the Performance of the Service Industry in OECD Countries

Since the start of the 21st century both the accelerated globalization of manufacturing and service industry and the constant innovation of information and communications technology have presented two challenges to the regulation of the economic structure in OECD countries. One is how to create a trade environment with more vitality and competitiveness so as to encourage service industry to enhance productivity and further provide new services as well as employment opportunities. The other is how to utilize effective policies for technological innovation and spread to carry out structural reform in order to remove the obstacles to technological innovation and spread in the service industry. Thus there are several modification suggestions put forward by the OECD to expand the service industry in each country.

Liberalization of regulations and opening of the domestic service market to create opportunities for investment and employment, facilitate innovation and improve productivity

The regulations governing the service industry in OECD countries mainly consist of general regulations and trade regulations. The former refers to regulations or policies applicable to all industries, including administrative procedures that must be followed when setting up an enterprise. The latter are mainly aimed at a particular industry, including laws or administrative barriers for entrance, scope of business with permission for operating, vertical consolidation, and transnational mergers and acquisitions (M&A).

In the view of the OECD, the restrictive regulations in each country hamper competition and innovation to varying degrees. For example, the regulations for risk capital markets impose restrictions on external financing channels for innovative enterprises, which cause a reduction in investment in innovative projects. Meanwhile the market regulations and tax policies that are aimed at income also place constrain growth in the service industry. The regression carried out by scholars of the OECD in accordance with the panel data from 1986 to 1998 shows that both the average marginal tax rate and regulations for protecting employment have a significant influence on the development of the service industry and such an influence varies with different services. Generally speaking, the relatively strict employment protection acts are always concerned with low proportion of employment, which is rather distinct in the producer service industry. The higher marginal tax rate lowers the proportion of private services to some extent.

In recent years, OECD countries have intensified reform in these two types of regulations. For example, the market-orientation of trade regulations becomes more and more marked but the degree of regulation in various trades are still different. In competitive services (such as highway transport and air transport), the rules usually tend to be relaxed and more and more countries ease the restraints on supply, admittance and pricing of services. However, regulations on network services are obviously less relaxed than those on competitive services. There are also some countries which have intensified regulations in some industries (such as railway transportation).

On the whole, in Australia, Sweden, America and UK, regulations on both competitive and network services are the most relaxed; in Germany, The Netherlands, New Zealand, Finland, Norway, Korea, Canada and Ireland, the rules are relatively liberal. However in Japan, Denmark, Iceland and Belgium, such regulations are comparatively strict; in France, Italy, Austria, Spain,

Portugal, Slovakia, Poland, Hungary, Greece and Turkey, the regulations are rather more strict in both industries.[16]

According to research, the reform of the regulations has had a fairly great influence on the economic performance of the service industry. It is predicted that the profit of analogue efficiency brought by a set of rational reforms of regulations can account for 6% of the GDP in the middle period, which depends upon the initial state of regulations in different countries. The regulation reforms in many industries are related to the technological advance and innovation and the diversity of products. The competitiveness from the open markets helps to stimulate more investment and to upgrade productivity. To open the border of regulations does not only facilitate domestic competition and accelerate the production of high-quality capital but also makes the economic development more attractive to FDI and further stimulates investment in key sectors.

Furthermore, the retailing also creates good welfare since the rules of admittance and pricing are eased. For example, the spread system of products becomes more effective when the restriction on output is removed; after the liberalization of service time, the scope of services provided for consumers is expanded and turnover and number of employees in retailing are increasing. Additionally, the drop in marginal tax rate leads to the reduction of commodity prices and the liberalization of network industry also brings lower prices, stronger competitiveness and higher efficiency in production.

To sum up, the liberalization of regulations can promote the pluralistic supply of services, expand the need for service and investment in it, boost employment, raise the efficiency of production and reduce the cost of production and service.

Open up the international market of service trade through unilateral or multilateral steps

Although the service trade in OECD countries is increasing constantly, the proportion remains lower than that of product trade. It is not only because it is more difficult to develop trade in services than in products but also because the changes in policy on international service trade cannot keep pace with the development of the service industry. Four models of trade proposed in the General Agreement on Trade in Services (GATS) are all restricted by regulations. If the companies, whether at home or abroad, are discriminated, the regulation in the service market will impose restraints on the international trade. For example, most of the OECD countries put restrictions on investment directly from abroad, especially on the amount of foreign investment as well as the approval procedure.

OECD countries are opening the service market gradually in order to further promote economic development and to strengthen the competitiveness of the service industry in each country. Such an opening up includes the reform of market regulations on transportation, communications, finance and some commercial service sectors as well as the removal of barriers for service trade and investment. To open the protected service market vigorously boosts the application of advanced technology (especially ICT) in enterprises to carry forward technical innovation in the service sector. Meanwhile it also drives enterprises to pay more attention to the introduction of innovative products and procedures into the value chain. As the interchangeability between technological advance and service are greatly enhanced, the scope of competition and trans-border trade are increasingly extended in OECD countries.

The EU has made a great contribution to the opening up of the service trade market. On February 16, 2006 the European Parliament voted on the EU Instructions to Services, which was eventually passed (394 votes for, 215 against and 33 abstentions). Such instructions are considered a significant breakthrough in the legislation on EU economy and trade as well as one of the most important laws in the EU in last ten years. In accordance with the instructions passed by parliament, the service trade barriers will be gradually eliminated by EU countries and a uniform service market will be set up in the EU, in which way the economic competitiveness of EU will be strengthened, the economic growth will be promoted and the proportion of employment will be increased. The instructions aroused a wide controversy in the EU and thus the European Parliament made more than 200 amendments that were as long as 15 pages.[18] Nevertheless, the instructions cover something positive, such as the demand of each member country for liberalized admittance to the service market and equal treatment, and the demand for the removal of the restriction that trans-border enterprises must set up independent branch operations in the place of business, which is a significant inspiration for the Yangtze River Delta to accelerate the integration of the service industry.

Carrying forward reform of the labor market and boosting the flow of the labor force so that labor can adapt to the constantly increasing service economy; meanwhile, reforming the policies on education and training in order to meet the demands of society for the immediate acquisition of new skills

The labor market system plays a very important role in the regulation of industrial structure in OECD countries. However, too strict employment protection laws will limit the ability to modify when major change needs to take place in some service sectors (such as tourism and some of the producer services), and will thereby slow down the transfer of the labor force into the service industry. Minimum wage legislation, which is relatively static and involves a high level of payment, may weaken the ability of enterprises to restructure, adopt new methods or use new technology and may further have a negative influence on the growth in productivity. In addition, the development of the service industry may also be restricted by the expensive labor tax rate and indirect taxes, and the latter can reduce the supply of labor. Some service sectors, especially the private services, will be influenced to a great degree.

The OECD, therefore, put forward suggestions that each country should reform the labor market and create many more new job opportunities in the service industry. For example, they can increase the participation of the labor force and improve the flexibility of the market and wages. Each interest group should be committed to providing effective job information rather than supplying negative support to slow the structural regulation. The effective re-employment service can help the unemployed find new work more easily while the wage mechanism can provide the accurate price to contribute to the modification of industrial structure. The flexibility of relative wage is rather important because it can stimulate workers to make the correct response to the change in industrial structure so that they can transfer from one industry to another industry or region and receive training as a labor capital investment. OECD countries also implement many methods to supply the less skillful workers with jobs, such as cutting down the labor tax rate for special groups (e.g. low-income and secondary low-income groups), preparing for the promulgation of policies on employment subsidy and payment of wage etc. In recent years, several countries have also adopted policies on the limit on tax rebate as well as on employment subsidy for housewives.

Besides strengthening the flow of the labor force at home, the OECD also suggests that every country expand this flow throughout the world. The flow of labor force can bring a large amount of potential economic interests to both exporters and importers. The short-term flow of employees within the service sector referred to in the fourth model of the GATS is beneficial to countries of emigration and immigration. For example, it helps some countries to overcome the shortage of workers with major or special skills for the modification of knowledge-intensive industry structure and enhances the demand for modern technology (such as ICT) or a labor force with good research and development skills. The aging population of OECD countries also presents the demand for services such as health care, especially nursing. Moreover immigrants can also invest in and pioneer enterprises, which can strengthen market competitiveness in the countries of immigration. Meanwhile countries such as Germany, Ireland, Korea, the UK and America manage to increase the number of short-term immigrants in particular fields (especially ICT and health care) through special immigration plans.

Furthermore, the international flow of workers in the service industry is featured by short-term employment and thus the social insurance assumed by countries of immigration for the workers is limited. As such short-term mobile workers fill vacancies in the labor force temporarily, it is not necessary to be too worried about the unemployment of workers with the same technical level caused by a surplus supply of labor. At the same time, short-term mobile workers usually return to their own countries when the contract expires, and therefore such kind of immigrants will not lead to a brain drain from countries of emigration. In short, both countries of emigration and immigration can benefit from the knowledge and techniques supplied by short-term mobile workers.

In terms of education and technical training, the technical levels of employees vary in the service industry. But the service industry in OECD countries, especially high-income countries, is filled with employees with high technology skills, which can be measured by the educational levels. The proportion of employees with high technology skills in the service industry, which is between 15% and 40%, is higher than in manufacturing in all the European countries. This kind of employees particularly center on some non-market-based service sectors (such as education, health care and social service).

The OECD believes that the shift of economic development to the service industry needs a corresponding modification of human resources and educational policies for the service industry is also faced with a shortage of technology. For example, there are many service sectors that are in need of experts in ICT. In service enterprises, the development of training is the key to innovation and thus the enterprises, employees and governments should take steps or increase capital to perfect educational policy so as to encourage life-long learning. The measures OECD countries are adopting include: to encourage everyone to increase investment in life-long learning; to ensure equal opportunities for full-time and on-the-job education; to promote vocational certificates and mechanisms of technique expertise; to promote reform in the structure of enterprises etc.

Reforming the policy on innovation of the service industry and removing the obstacles to service sectors profiting from information and communications technology

The OECD points out that there are several possible reasons for both the low density of research and development and the lack of innovation in the service industry in each country. One is that the research and development in service industry have an external effect because the knowledge produced in the innovation of service enterprises is not under the protection of patent law. Another is that the IPR (Intellectual Property Rights) mechanism, used by the service industry, does not have identification based on the information of innovation. However the low density of research and development in the service industry may also relate to its own special innovative process. Innovative enterprises often adopt innovation in marketing or processing. For example, according to the EU's report on innovation, the innovative process and performance of service enterprises are different from manufacturing enterprises in several aspects. Although the two industries are engaged in the innovation of products, the innovative service enterprises lay more emphasis on the innovation of the market in order to introduce new products to the market.[19] Manufacturing enterprises are dependent on internal research and development while service enterprises rely on external resources or other knowledge resources such as training, patent, software and special permission. In fact the service sectors, especially those related to commerce and science and technology, make indirect contribution to the innovation and knowledge accumulation of the overall economy.[20] For example, the legal advisors and commercial consultants provide analysis of the basic legal and financial framework for the innovation; the software providers help to design and implement the innovation; the engineers improve the innovative samples; the market investigators can help discover new demand and services of the market.

In view of the backward state of the research and development in the service industry, the OECD suggests strengthening the competitiveness of the global market and supplying a vigorous environment for the development of service industry so as to contribute to the application of advanced technology and promotion of innovative activities. The innovative activities in the knowledge-based economy are increasingly dependent on the comprehensive function of enterprise management, ICT, innovative elements and human resources. The wide application of ICT is fairly significant to the innovation of service industry in OECD countries, which can promote enterprises to make technological innovations of value chain and develop new equipment to enhance production efficiency. At present the use of information and communications technology in some service sectors, especially in communications, financial intermediation and commercial services, is more frequent than in manufacturing. Service enterprises in some countries do not spend much money on regular research and development. But they do apply new technology, especially ICT, to training and investment in intangible assets as well as to image building, marketing and organizational transformation, and thus various innovations can be achieved.

Although ICT is gradually being put into use, the application of the more complex E-commerce remains limited. Therefore priority should be given to the development of high-efficiency, low-cost and widely publicized networks. Meanwhile each OECD country should start with research on information security strategies in order to ensure the safe use of network services and communications equipment for consumers. Improper regulation may affect enterprises in expanding ICT services or providing services through data and thus the OECD demands that each country modify the framework of regulation so as to balance the interests of users and providers.

The OECD also proposes that each country should supply sufficient financial support for the growth of the service industry. For example, the funding for innovation is still a major barrier to service enterprises, especially small-sized enterprises and those selling immaterial products. Few countries previously implemented special policies aimed at improving the ability to innovate in the service industry. Therefore the government of each country should work out plans for tax credit or tax allowance for the development of financial services so that a developed financial market with regulations can be set up to help enterprises receive private financial services more conveniently. Most OECD countries have drawn up similar plans.

Table 17.16. The tendency of change in industrial structure in the Yangtze River Delta (%)

Category	2002	2003	2004	2005	2006
The proportion of added value in secondary industry	51.87	54.44	55.86	55.24	54.98
The proportion of manufacturing	45.97	48.33	49.80	50.00	50.05
The proportion of service industry	42.32	40.62	39.54	40.68	41.30

Table 17.17. The tendency of change in industrial structure in Shanghai (%)

Category	2002	2003	2004	2005	2006
The proportion of added value in secondary industry	45.7	47.9	48.2	48.6	48.5
The proportion of manufacturing	41.3	43.9	44.5	45.1	45.0
The proportion of service industry	52.9	50.9	50.8	50.4	50.6

The Development of Service Industry in the Yangtze River Delta: Experience and Enlightenment from OECD Countries

Comparison with service industry in OECD countries

Since the reform and opening up, the economic growth in the Yangtze River Delta[21] has maintained a high speed and its industrial structure has also upgraded remarkably; the core of its economy has shifted from primary industry to the secondary and tertiary industries. But the economic growth of the service industry in the Yangtze River Delta has obviously slowed down from 2002 to 2006 (see Tables 17.16, 17.17 and 17.18 respectively). The proportion of employment declined both in 2003 and 2004 but picked up in 2005 and 2006. It was 41.30% in 2006, which is 0.62% higher than in 2005 but still lower than in 2002. The proportion of service industry in Shanghai has decreased after 2002 and rose again to 50.6% in 2006 but has not reached the peak. The proportion in eight cities along the Yangtze River in Jiangsu is lower than in Shanghai but it has also declined recently and only increased 37.02% in 2006, also lower than in 2002.

Not only the comparison of various industries in each country but the comparison of the same industry in different countries suggests that the service

Table 17.18. The tendency of change in industrial structure in eight cities along the Yangtze River in Jiangsu (%)

Category	2002	2003	2004	2005	2006
The proportion of added value in secondary industry	53.44	56.76	58.48	59.61	59.02
The proportion of manufacturing	47.11	49.87	51.70	53.80	53.66
The proportion of service industry	39.53	37.72	36.68	35.94	37.02

Sources: Collected from *Jiangsu Statistical Yearbook 2007* and *Shanghai Statistical Yearbook 2007.*

Table 17.19. The proportion of employment in service industry in OECD countries and the Yangtze River Delta in 2005 (%)

Category	Countries with a British or American system	Countries with a continental system	Countries with an emerging market system	Countries with a transformed system	Small countries	The Yangtze River Delta	Shanghai	8 cities in Jiangsu
The proportion of added value	71.9	71.3	63.1	63.4	71.2	40.7	50.4	35.9
The proportion of employment	76.4	67.7	66.4	57.4	71.2	—	55.6	33.6

industry in the Yangtze River Delta is sluggish. Firstly, the development of the Yangtze River Delta is still backward according to the comparison among different countries (see Table 17.19). The proportion of added value in the region in 2005 was only 40.7%, which is lower than the lowest level of OECD countries in the same year (it was 63.1% in countries with an emerging market system) and lower than that of moderately developed countries (52.7% in 2003). Meanwhile, it is also lower than the average level of low-income countries (49.8% in 2004) and even lower than that of less developed countries (45.5% in 2004). The proportion of employment is roughly the same in each country except for Shanghai which is on a par with countries with a transformed system in the same year.

Secondly, based on the comparison of various industries, we can also conclude that the development of the Yangtze River Delta is relatively sluggish and thus its contribution to economic growth needs further improvement.

(1) The growth rate of secondary industry is always higher than that of the service industry and so is its rate of contribution to economic growth. From

Table 17.20. The three industrial rates in Jiangsu (calculated according to comparable prices, %)

Year	The growth rate of the GDP	Primary industry	Secondary industry	Manufacturing	Tertiary industry
1990	5.0	0.2	2.9	3.0	1.9
1991	8.3	–1.0	4.4	4.0	4.9
1992	25.6	2.4	15.8	14.1	7.4
1993	19.8	0.5	12.2	11.0	7.1
1994	16.5	0.9	12.2	11.4	3.4
1995	15.4	2.1	9.1	7.9	4.2
1996	12.2	1.2	7.0	5.6	4.0
1997	12.0	0.7	7.2	5.8	4.1
1998	11.0	0.3	6.9	5.5	3.8
1999	10.1	0.6	6.5	5.8	3.0
2000	10.6	0.5	6.8	6.3	3.3
2001	10.2	0.4	5.7	5.2	4.1
2002	11.7	0.3	7.2	6.3	4.2
2003	13.6	0.0	9.1	8.3	4.5
2004	14.8	0.6	9.4	8.6	4.8
2005	14.5	0.2	9.0	8.3	5.3
2006	14.9	0.4	9.0	8.4	5.5

Notes: 1. The industrial promotion rate refers to the product of the growth rate of the GDP and the rate of contribution of each industry.
2. Due to the availability, we use the data of Jiangsu Province instead of that of the eight cities.

2002 to 2006, the proportion of added value in the secondary industry rose by 3.11% (by 4.08% in manufacturing) while that in the service industry decreased by 1.02%. Although Shanghai as an international metropolis focuses much more on the service industry, the proportion of added value in its manufacturing increased by as much as 2.51% (see Tables 17.16, 17.17 and 17.18). Therefore in terms of the industrial promotion rate (see Table 17.20), the service industry falls behind the second industry (especially manufacturing). The economic growth in the Yangtze River Delta mainly depends upon secondary industry especially manufacturing, which puts great pressure on resources and the environment in this region.

(2) It can be seen in accordance with the comparison of the various types of service industry that the traditional services develop rapidly while the development of modern producer services is relatively sluggish. From the

Table 17.21. The proportion of added value in each type of service industry in the gross added value in both the Yangtze River Delta and OECD countries in 2005 (%)

Sector	Jiangsu	Shanghai	Countries with a British or American system	Countries with a continental system	Countries with an emerging market system	Countries with a transformed system	Small countries
Wholesale and retail, accommodation and catering	11.49	11.0	13.7	14.7	11.4	12.3	14.7
Transportation, storage and communications	5.79	10.3	6.8	6.8	6.9	8.4	8.2
Financial services	3.07	7.4	7.8	4.7	7.8	4.3	7.0
Real estate, leasing and commercial services	5.21	10.6	21.7	22.6	16.4	15.0	18.4
Public management and social organization (national defence)	2.76	2.0	5.9	6.5	6.1	6.8	6.2
Education, health care, social work and other services	7.12	9.2	15.9	15.9	14.7	12.5	16.3

Note: Due to the availability, we used the data of Jiangsu Province instead of that of the eight cities.

comparison of the proportion of added value of the various types of service industry in Shanghai and OECD countries in 2005 (see Table 17.21), we can see that services in real estate, leasing and commerce are the least developed. The proportion is just half of that in countries with a British or American system and countries with continental system and even lower than countries with a transformed system (15.0%). In face real estate in Shanghai is not backward, and added value accounted for 7.38% of the gross added value in 2005. But that in leasing and commercial services accounted for only 3.19%. There is a lack of data for OECD countries yet the data for 1990s shows that such a proportion in leasing and commercial services exceeds that in real estate. Moreover services in education, health care, social work and others as well as wholesale and retail, accommodation and catering are also less developed.

In terms of financial services, the proportion of added value in Shanghai is close to that of countries with a British or American system and countries with an emerging market system while a little higher than in small countries and far higher than in countries with a continental system as well as countries with a transformed system. This shows that Shanghai is rapidly developing into an international financial center. Moreover the special geographical position of Shanghai and its booming IT industry make this city move ahead of OECD countries in transportation, storage and communications.

Jiangsu has a similar situation with Shanghai yet its services in finance, commerce, education etc. are more backward.

Thirdly, the development of various regions is not at the same level and the correlation among them has to be strengthened. The proportion of service industry in Jiangsu, Zhejiang and Shanghai was roughly the same in 1978 while the service industry in Shanghai has now expanded at high speed and Zhejiang is in balance with the national level, ranking second. However Jiangsu is comparatively backward. It is not only behind Shanghai and Zhejiang but also below the national level.

In addition, the influence of the service industry on economic growth in the Yangtze River Delta is mainly reflected within various provinces and cities but a sound interaction between industrial development in various provinces and cities has not really come into being. The contribution flexibility of the producer service in Shanghai to the industry in the Yangtze River Delta equals 0.918 (Gao Chuansheng & Liu Zhibiao, 2005). However further empirical analysis demonstrates that there is no Granger causality between Shanghai and Jiangsu while the industrial growth in Jiangsu is the Granger cause of the increase in the producer service in Shanghai. At present, in the industrial structure in the Yangtze River Delta, Shanghai does not fully play a role of a service center in the regional economy whereas Jiangsu and Zhejiang, in which manufacturing develops quickly, boost the increase in the service sector in Shanghai to some extent. Thus the function of the service industry in Shanghai, which is to promote both the development of manufacturing and service industry in Jiangsu and Zhejiang, should be strengthened.

On the whole, the development of service industry in the Yangtze River Delta is comparatively sluggish. There are still several problems with the service industry in Shanghai, such as the low degree of its opening up at home and abroad, strict requirements on market access, small-sized enterprises, weak core competitiveness, shortage of personnel with high skills in the service sector etc. In Jiangsu, the overall technological level in the service industry is not high, so productivity and traditional industry occupy the dominant position while emerging industries account for a small proportion. The monopolized lines of business take up a large amount and the constraints on market access are rather high. Industries such as banking, insurance, telecommunications, railways, education and health, press and publishing, and radio and television have maintained relatively strict restrictions on market access. In Zhejiang the ability to innovate is relatively weak in the service industry. In many service sectors government restraints are imposed and the problem of monopolization is fairly serious in some sectors; the socialization and specialization of the service industry are still at a low level; and financial policy provides little support to the service industry. In Jiangsu and Zhejiang, the distinctly sluggish development of the service industry, especially producer services, has become a bottleneck that limits the establishment of modern international manufacturing bases and has influenced the upgrading of economic competitiveness of these two provinces.

Drawing reference from the experience of OECD to boost the service industry in the Yangtze River Delta

The economy of the Yangtze River Delta has moved into a new stage, which means it not only has a rare chance to promote development but is also confronted with the severe challenge that the superiority of its development is weakening. We should learn from the experience of OECD countries in order to boost modern service industry, extend the producer services, provide support for manufacturing to update technology and save cost, to facilitate the optimization of the economic structure and to promote the shift of model of economic development. All the above are of vital strategic significance for the optimal development of the Yangtze River Delta.

The enforcement program and policies for accelerating the development of the service industry have been carried out in the Yangtze River Delta and some achievements have been made in several aspects. However the service industry has not obtained the expected performance in recent years, which may be either because the effect of policy has a time lag or because the focus of development is not clear. Thus in order to speed up the development of service industry in the Yangtze River Delta, each region should draw on some favorable experiences of OECD countries to further formulate the development orientation, to highlight the focus of policies, to coordinate all the industrial polices and to upgrade the competitiveness of the service industry all over the region rapidly.

To accelerate the development of the producer service industry

As stated above the service industry, the provider of intermediate input, becomes increasingly important. At present the added value of the producer service industry accounts for about 50% of the gross added value of service industry in OECD countries, which suggests that the modern service industry[22] in developed countries has become the major impetus behind economic growth. But there is a deepening interaction between the modern service industry and advanced manufacturing. Such an interdependent relationship is mainly shown in the following aspects:

Firstly, the producer service industry, which emerges from manufacturing, is vertically separated from manufacturing and develops into an independent industry. Meanwhile the proportion it represents in the overall economy will become larger and larger in pace with the deepening and extending of the social and specialized division of labor. Secondly, the strong support of the producer service industry comes to be the traction and propeller for the growth of manufacturing, which can supply diverse ways to upgrade the international competitiveness of manufacturing. Thirdly, there is a coordinated positioning effect[23] between manufacturing and the producer service industry. Lastly, the producer service industry has a distinct tendency to follow downstream manufacturing industries.[24]

In terms of the present situation of the Yangtze River Delta, the land use for construction accounted for as much as 17.4% of the national land-use area (excluding water area) by the end of 2006, which proportion is two and a half times higher than that of the 5.05% in America.[25] That implies that the Yangtze River Delta as the manufacturing base is facing the severe challenge of unsustainable development because the land capacity of the Yangtze River Delta cannot bear further expansion of manufacturing. Therefore the potential and room for development mainly relies on the service industry. There are several innovations that should be made for the sustainable development of the Yangtze River Delta: the first is to leave some room for expanding the modern service industry as well as advanced manufacturing; the second is to shift traditional manufacturing out of the region; and the third is to move the production base away from the region while keeping the headquarters and development centers. In the light of the increasingly significant role of the modern producer service industry and the present situation in the Yangtze River Delta, the following essential policies should be particularly implemented in order to boost the development of the modern producer service industry.[26]

As for systems, we should resolutely break through the administrative monopoly that causes the modern service industry not to develop fully and makes its level hard to improve. Therefore the most pressing matter is to lower barriers to admittance through market-oriented reform and to remove the barriers limiting the development of the modern service industry by introducing competitors and competitive mechanisms.

As for mechanisms, we should expedite the setting up of mechanisms for the specialized division of labor for the service industry. From the perspective of economic evolution, the development of the producer service industry represents the deepening and extending of the social and specialized division of labor. Thus to set up an integrated mechanism of specialized division of labor based on the guidance of various policies, measures and the environment is a necessary step to accelerate the development of a modern service industry.

As for policies, we should eliminate both dominant and recessive discrimination as soon as possible so as to balance the development of service industry and manufacturing. The practice of modern economic development exhibits that the commodity production industry without the prop of producer services is difficult to sustain as well as to be competitive. In the view of the present policies and environment in the Yangtze River Delta, the gap in development conditions between service industry and manufacturing is relatively wide and there are still numerous examples of discrimination against the service industry. From the point of promoting coordinated, rapid development among various industries it is vital to provide equal development conditions for the service industry and manufacturing and to eliminate discriminatory policies. Based on the knowledge economy, formulation of the specific policies has to give consideration to the following two aspects: one is that the restrictions on material capital in high-tech enterprises should be eased whether for enterprise registration or for listing on the capital market; the other is that high-tech enterprises should be allowed to raise start-up costs for admittance and training expenses.

As for strategies, we should increase investment in producer service activities. Modern producer services are a kind of labour-, knowledge- and technology-intensive industry. Therefore to speed up the development of a modern service industry in the Yangtze River Delta requires raising the input for labor capital and scientific research and development, even including the importing intensity of important skilled personnel from abroad. Furthermore, in order to enhance the function of a city that can drive the regional economy, we should strengthen the construction of a platform for the development of the service industry, build a collecting center for service industry and facilitate its intensive development.

As for the development model, we should intensify the opening up of the service industry. There are several reasons for this: one is that opening up can break down the administrative monopoly on service industry by introducing competitors and competitive mechanisms; another is that opening up can resolve the shortage of skills facing the modern service industry by importing badly-needed skills; another is that opening up can also push the service enterprises in the Yangtze River Delta into the world market in order to foster their competitiveness.

To vigorously promote service trade, and especially to undertake international services outsourcing

In recent years, service outsourcing has spread in the global service trade. According to the analysis in *The World Trade Report in 2005,* the total of global outsourcing of services reached US$2,850 in 2003. Currently the market scale of global outsourcing of services is between US$300 and 500 billion and it will maintain a growth rate of 20% to 30% in the future. It is expected that the market scale of global outsourcing of services will exceed US$1,000 billion by the end of 2008. Eighty percent of outsourcing is between OECD countries yet some developing countries such as India and China (especially India) have also become important destinations for global services outsourcing. The orientation of service outsourcing is closely related with the application of information and communications technology.[27] Owing to the rapid upgrading of information and communications technology, the opening of source code (Linux effect), the online business of information technological services (Google effect) and the digitization of wideband services lead to increasingly tough competition in service outsourcing all over the world.

From the point of enterprises contracting services, the primary target of services outsourcing is to reduce cost and to sharpen global competitiveness. To be specific, they contract subordinate services to other enterprises and put their focus on key services so as to maintain their core competitiveness. The flow direction of outsourcing mainly depends on a series of conditions in the countries or regions that undertake the outsourcing, especially on the infrastructure of information and communications technological level (including quantity, quality and price), the skills in developing trade through information and communications technology, the complicity of opening procedures, the difficulty of implementing the contract, and the quality and reliability of services. Thus enterprises should determine whether to contract or whom to contract to according to the above conditions. There are also some other essential prerequisites of outsourcing, for example, the stability of the macro-situation such as politics and the macro-economy, the proper protection for intellectual property rights, a good environment for investment, and sound legal systems.

The Yangtze River Delta should not only intensify the division of labor in the internal industry and vigorously develop service business outsourcing but also actively undertake global service outsourcing, which is of great significance for sharpening the competitive edge of the service industry in this region. The expansion of service outsourcing at home and abroad can facilitate the major manufacturing cities around the Yangtze River Delta to improve their technological level and to expand. In this way a service industry center will take shape with the backing of those cities while the neighboring regions will inexorably develop to be manufacturing-intensive. Meanwhile the satellite towns, which become the subordinate peripheral manufacturing bases, foster the regional industrial pattern of "service industry-centered—manufacturing-intensive," which contributes to form a virtuous interactive pattern in which we build up the service industry center to decrease business costs and the manufacturing-intensive neighboring regions to reduce production costs.[28] Such deepening of infiltration level by level will help to narrow the difference in incomes in the Yangtze River Delta and further achieve common prosperity so as to boost the balanced development of the whole region.

Due to the developed manufacturing and the distinct edge it gains from its open economy, the Yangtze River Delta has become one of the most important bases for processing information and communications technological products as well as the biggest export region. Moreover a large number of universities and scientific research institutes are located there. But the ability to undertake global service outsourcing has not been very high in the region because the implementation of protection for intellectual property rights is not strong enough and undue administrative interference influences the strategic decisions of enterprises on contracting outsourcing. In addition, there are also other causes such as the unclear supervision mechanism in information services, the small number of enterprises which have passed the certification of CMM which is necessary for undertaking outsourcing, and the lack of leaders who can keep the whole world in view. On the whole, the Yangtze River Delta is still in the initial stage of undertaking offshore service business outsourcing for transnational enterprises. Therefore it should grasp the chance to expand outsourcing of global services so as to achieve the transformation from "global factory" into "global office." Moreover it should also actively create a particular brand of outsourcing of global services for the Yangtze River Delta to supply a large engine for economic development.

There are many steps which can be taken to promote the undertaking of global service outsourcing, such as human resource development and infrastructure. Furthermore we should give particular importance to both the methods of outsourcing and the protection of intellectual property rights.

First of all, as for the choice of ways of outsourcing, the strategic focus of undertaking outsourcing should be centered on those service programs that have comparative advantages. We can start with the outsourcing of general and peripheral services (mainly aimed at the outsourcing of services in software development and productive business processes, especially in manufacturing). After the learning curve falls we can continue to bid for the outsourcing of high-end, large-scale and non-peripheral services. We should also focus on attracting the world top 500 enterprises as well as international enterprises that have a demonstration effect in offshore service outsourcing, which will help to form the industrial and market environment for offshore outsourcing. Therefore we should strengthen the social control systems for the outsourcing of services, improve the mutual trust and reputation mechanism and manage to lessen the risk undertaken by overseas enterprises, all of which are the key for the Yangtze River Delta to obtain the outsourcing of large-scale, non-peripheral services from overseas enterprises.

Secondly, we should continually perfect the system of protection of intellectual property rights. The protection of intellectual property rights involved in the international service outsourcing is more complicated than in manufacturing and its force has a rather greater effect on the outsourcing of services. Compared with OECD countries, the protection of intellectual property rights is still at a lower level which is considered a barrier to undertaking the outsourcing of global services. Due to the weak protection of intellectual property rights in our country transnational enterprises, which are very concerned about the leakage of patented technology, are not willing to outsource services to us and as a result the development of the service outsourcing is hindered to a great degree.[29] Thus we should intensify the protection of intellectual property rights in the development of service industry in the Yangtze River Delta, which is a significant measure for improving the investment climate.[30]

To accelerate the regional integration of the service industry

In terms of the promotion of regional integration of the service industry OECD countries, especially the EU, have set an example for the Yangtze River Delta. Even though different countries vary in development level as well as profit, the statesmen of each country still adopted the far-reaching *EU Instructions to Services* unanimously in 2006.

From the historical point of view, competitiveness outstrips cooperation in the Yangtze River Delta. In fact the Yangtze River Delta, which is an economic region in our country, satisfies the conditions for speeding up the integration of the service industry because there is no flow of labor force and capital among different countries although it may be interference by factors such as regional interests. Meanwhile economic policies remain consistent owing to the intervention of the central government which also hopes that integration can boost the development of the region and afford an example for the other regions in our country.

Therefore the Yangtze River Delta should grasp the opportunity to give full play to the advantages of each region and further strengthen regional cooperation in the service industry, particularly in removing market barriers, intensifying industrial cooperation and promoting the modern service industry.[31]

As for the regional integration of the service industry Shanghai, the key city of the Yangtze River Delta, should not only expand commercial services and creative industry but also intensify logistics, finance and the establishment of a platform for scientific technological services and make the best of the "overflow effect" to serve the Yangtze River Delta and even the whole nation. In order to achieve this, Shanghai should take both its own interests and the integral interests of the Yangtze River Delta into consideration in the aspects of industrial policy, and focus on development and supporting a program of modern service industry. It also should fully employ its advantages, develop with a dislocated pattern and integrate resources to achieve win-win cooperation as well as the common development of the Yangtze River Delta. On the one hand, it should give a full play to its comparative advantages; on the other hand, it should supply the development and industrial upgrading of manufacturing in Jiangsu and Zhejiang with a large amount of knowledge capital and human resources. Furthermore, in order to strengthen the interactive development of the modern service industry in Shanghai and the whole of the Yangtze River Delta, it should start with industrial integration, strengthen correlated integration and form a closely correlated service-manufacturing industrial chain in which regional market information can be shared and resources can be intensively used. At the same time, it should intensify structural integration and promote the reconstruction of various elements within regions in order to adapt to the high degree of industry structure.

Jiangsu should be based on the local industrial features and actively hasten integration with Shanghai with participation in the functional construction of "four centers" in Shanghai; intensify the division of work and cooperation within the service industry in the Yangtze River Delta; vigorously expand the producer service industry, coordinating manufacturing and set up regional service centers; provide guidance in line with local conditions; and be characterized by differential development. Zhejiang also should make full use of the specialty and advantages of its service industry; take an active part in the regional cooperation in the Yangtze River Delta; and gradually achieve interconnecting transportation, industrial complementation, intercommunicating markets and the sharing of information between Zhejiang and some major cities in the Yangtze River Delta such as Shanghai and Nanjing.

To accelerate the regional integration of the service industry, we should speed up establishment of various types of trans-regional modern service carriers such as regional industry associations. The trans-regional service industry association, which is not restricted by administrative division, can be used as a tool for the integration and interaction of service industry in the Yangtze River Delta and play a part in breaking up the administrative monopoly and in establishing and preserving regional market order. It can also play a major role in keeping close to as well as serving enterprises and fill the gaps in administrative systems. Thus in order to strengthen the integration and interaction of service industry in the Yangtze River Delta we should promote the establishment of a trans-regional service industry association, formulate development plans and market regulations for the regional service industry, standardize the regional market order and explore ways to combine and integrate various types of service market resources in each region.

To relax the regulations on service industry and so stimulate competition

Both theories and facts show that if there are too many restraints on market access and the monopoly is fairly strong, the competitiveness and capacity of the market will inevitably be limited. Furthermore the shortage of competitiveness in the market will cause the insufficient supply of services, low quality and lack of variety, and thereby cause the decreasing need of manufacturing and service industry for services. In addition, the small capacity of the market will restrict the in-depth development of specialized division of work and further influence the increase in production efficiency.

As stated above, the most important reason for the strong growth in service industry in OECD countries is the continuous relaxation of regulations at home and abroad. During the past decades and especially since the beginning of the 21st century, the reform in regulations on service markets related to transportation, communications, finance and commerce, the expansion of service trade and the lowering of barriers for investment have stimulated service enterprises to apply advanced technology especially information and communications technology more actively to raise the efficiency of production. Moreover the sharpening competition also facilitates the access and development of innovative companies.

In contrast to OECD countries, factors hampering major improvement of the service industry in the Yangtze River Delta remain rather severe and include the restrictions on admittance, monopoly on administration and consumers, regional blockage and division of market. Therefore the various regions in the Yangtze River Delta need to relax the regulations on the service industry.[32] The following five proposals should be promptly implemented. (1) We should set up an open regulatory system of market access; break up the administrative monopoly; and encourage and support various kinds of capital especially non-public capital to enter into each type of service industry and field that are not banned by the national laws and regulations. Except for the approval procedure by national regulations before the registration of an enterprise, all of the projects that need the examination and approval should not be classified with those examined and approved before the registration of an enterprise. (2) We should eliminate political discrimination. The service industry should enjoy equal political treatment with manufacturing. Enterprises with different ownership in the same service field should enjoy equal treatment in financing, revenue, land use, foreign trade etc. (3) We should relax the registration requirements for enterprises, especially the restraints on scientific technology service enterprises. (4) We should reform the administrative system of the service industry; correctly define public/non-public, monopolistic/non-monopolistic and profit-making/non-operating services; and carry out classified administration and differential support policies according to attribute differences. (5) We should speed up market-oriented reform in telecommunications, finance, railways, aviation and municipal public services; make the transformation to a standardized corporation system in the monopolistic state-owned service enterprises; and promote the set-up of a market structure in which diverse types of ownership coexist and pluralistic market entities compete with each other moderately.

Notes

Preface

1. The proportion of the total costs of manufacturing enterprises accounted for by this kind of costs tends to increase progressively. For example, Jiangsu Development and Reform Commission made a random questionnaire survey of more than 60 foreign-funded manufacturing enterprises (involving more than ten sectors in the manufacturing industry) in Suzhou Industrial Park, Suzhou High-tech Park and Kunshan Development Zone, and found that the average proportion of the aggregate expenditures of the surveyed enterprises accounted for by their expenses on productive services in 2001 and 2002 were 3.74% and 3.58% respectively; the lowest was 1% and the highest was 5%. It is worth noting that the expenses for productive services accounted for 50–79% of the total costs (raw materials excluded, as the costs of raw materials in manufacturing industry are too high). Most of the expenses for productive services were spent on storage and transportation, advertising, engineering and technological services, intellectual property rights protection, management consulting and postal information transmission.
2. Statistics from *China Statistical Yearbook* and database of the WTO.
3. Official website of Ministry of Commerce of Nation's Republic of China http://fdi.mofcom.gov.cn/aarticle/at/200710/20071005159925.html
4. See Liu Zhibiao and Zhang Jie 2007.
5. The so-called "comparative advantage trap" refers to when a country (especially a developing country) produces and exports primary products and labor-intensive products, completely basing its behavior on its comparative advantage. In international trade which is centered on the economically developed countries and technology- and capital-intensive products, the countries that strictly follow their comparative advantages, although they can make profits, will always be at a disadvantage because of the unstable trade structure.
6. For example, Linhai in Zhejiang Province is an agglomeration center of mold industry as thousands of enterprises that produce molds have gathered in Linhai. The mold industry in Linhai was introduced into the global value chain by Japanese enterprises and some transfer of technology was made in the production process. However, when Linhai later decided to participate in the high-end market, the Japanese enterprises started to blank off the designs, the technologies and even the markets to stop the Linhai mold industry's progress. Examples of this kind can be found everywhere in the Yangtze River Delta. http://www.news365.com.cn/csj/csjzs/200511/t20051104708117.htm
7. From a report in US Business Week: "The China Price." They are the three scariest words in US industry. Cut your prices at least 30% or lose your customers. Nearly every manufacturer is vulnerable—from furniture to networking gear. The result: A massive shift in economic power is under way. For details refer to http://www.businessweek.com/magazine/content/0449/b3911401.htm.
8. Refer to http://news.cnfol.com/070809/101,1281,3234489,00.shtml for news reports such as Boom to Bust of Industrial Clusters in Zhejiang.
9. Please refer to http://www.jinton.com/index.asp
10. For example, in the process of attracting FDI, the Yangtze River Delta has brought a gathering of the manufacturing sector and formed a "world factory." In addition, multinational companies have gradually brought accompanying accumulation of ANote. The synergistic effect between them has made this region attractive to FDI.
11. Refer to Gao Feng and Liu Zhibiao, "Collaborative Clusters and Growth of the Service Sector and the Manufacturing Sector in the Yangtze River Delta," A Working Paper of the School of Business, Nanjing University, 2007.
12. The "European Paradox" refers to a big gap between the high research level of universities and research institutions and low contribution to industrial innovation, namely it refers to insignificant business benefits despite high public spending on research. Many scholars now believe that "commercial failure" is the most important reason leading to the "European Paradox." The policy of promoting commercialization of public research in Europe is not as successful as that in the United States.

Chapter 1

1. Scholars such as John Khodi propose standards for industrialization level which is the share of value-added of manufacturing in the aggregate of the commodity sector. They divide industrialization into four categories: non-industrialization (over 20%), industrializing (20–40%), semi-industrialization (40–60%) and industrialization (over 60%). See Chen Jiagui et al. 2007.
2. Nelson 2001.

Chapter 2

1. Nelson 2001.
2. A study by the National Bureau of Statistics (1994) asserts that in statistics China was underestimated by 5%. Huang hold the view that the service industry has been underestimated by more than 10%, and that so far the service industry in China has developed to a comparatively proper level; therefore, he asserted that "a balanced growth should be implemented between the development of service sectors and that of the agricultural sectors and industrial sectors." See Huang Shaojun 2000: 15.
3. The service industry and tertiary industry are two totally different concepts; although in 2003 the National Bureau of Statistics made it clear that a statistical framework of China's service industry was to be built, so far both the extension and intension of "service industry" have not been given commonly accepted definitions and the statistics for the service industry in a strict sense have not been published. Therefore, in this chapter, we use the statistics for tertiary industry as proxy variables of the service industry.
4. World Bank, *Equity and Development—2006 World Development Report* (Beijing: Tsinghua University Press, 2006).
5. Zhang Shuguang and Zhang Bin (2007) believe that the main reason for the lagging development of the service industry in China lies in that before reform and opening up, in the planned economy system in which the heavy industries were given development priority, production was emphasized while consumption was overlooked. The service industry was hard pressed, which resulted in its seriously backward development; after reform and opening up, although the growth of capital stock and labor inputs of the service industry have been more than those of the manufacturing industry, history makes it difficult to change the service industry's backwardness.
6. The Yangtze River Delta refers to 16 cities—Shanghai, seven cities in South Jiangsu and eight cities in North Zhejiang. Considering the availability of statistics, we use the provincial statistics of Shanghai, Jiangsu and Zhejiang.
7. Liu Zhibiao 2005.
8. Zhai Fan, "The Macroeconomic Influence of Reform in the Service Industry in China," in Li Shantong and Hua Ercheng 2002: 61–73.
9. Li 2005.
10. Chenery 1995: 92–99.
11. Liu 2006: 5.
12. Chenery 1995: 92–99.
13. The enterprise activity outsourcing can either refer to the fact that the enterprises, from the specialized perspective, take away some of the functional departments inside the enterprises and make the departments independent units, or refer to enterprises stopping using the resources or services supplied by the inside departments of the enterprises but start to use those supplied by external but more professional units.
14. 28 Li Jiangfan and Bi Doudou 2004.

Chapter 3

1. "Shedding" or "Cicada Ecdysis"? An Interpretation of the Slowing Down of Economic Growth in the Yangtze River Delta, http://www.xinhua.org, 2 August 2005.
2. The Emergence of Crisis in the Manufacturing Industry in the Yangtze River Delta (http://csj.xinhuanet.com/200707/15/content10582622.htm)
3. This conclusion is drawn from the Equation (6).
4. It needs to be mentioned that here the expansion of the scale of the producer service industry is embodied in the increase in categories, which is a feature of the DS monopoly competition model—the industrial scale economy is embodied in the increase in categories but not in output of a single enterprise.
5. The deduction of price index is similar to the deduction done by Fujita Masahisa.
6. Fujita, Krgman and Venables 2005.
7. It needs to be noted that to what degree the service industry can as an input reduce the costs of manufacturing industry depends on two parameters, which are elasticity of substitution—"σ" and the proportion of total employment accounted for by employment in the service industry—"$(1-\beta)$". A higher "σ" is associated with a stronger elasticity of substitution; a "σ" approaching 0 means that there is more substitution among different kinds of services. Therefore in the elasticity of substitution among services—"σ" is in negative correlation with the reduction degree of costs of manufacturing industry. And "$(1-\beta)$" actually reflects the proportion of total costs of manufacturing industry accounted for by the input costs of producer services; a lower "$(1-\beta)$" is associated with less influence of the growth of producer services on the total costs.
8. The *Jiangsu Statistical Yearbook*, *Shanghai Statistical Yearbook* and *Zhejiang Statistical Yearbook* only give the economic indicators and performance indicators for the government enterprises and the non-government enterprises above a designated size in the provinces and cities, but the statistical yearbooks lack data on the manufacturing statistics standards, so here our indicators of

government and non-government manufacturing enterprises are obtained by excluding nine sectors—the coal mining sector, petroleum and gas sector, ferrous metal mining sector, non-ferrous metal mining sector, nonmetal mining sector, wood and bamboo collecting and delivery sector, electricity, steam and hot water production and supply sector, gas production and supply sector, and running water production and supply sector—from the industrial sectors of enterprises.

9. Data of SH: 2000–2006; Data of ZJ: some part are missing, so the item "handicraft and other sectors" is excluded and there are only 28 manufacturing sub-sectors in ZJ.

Chapter 4

1. This proportion is calculated by the author using the statistics in *China Statistical Yearbook 2006* and the statistical yearbooks and reports in Jiangsu Province, Zhejiang Province and Shanghai.
2. The theories of these two tests are explained in Appendix One.
3. The theories of the E-G two-step method are explained in Appendix Two.
4. The theories of the Granger causality test are explained in Appendix Three.
5. Shanghai, Nanjing, Suzhou, Wuxi, Changzhou, Zhenjiang, Nantong, Yangzhou, Taizhou, Hangzhou, Ningbo, Jiaxing, Huzhou, Shaoxing, Zhoushan and Taishan. However, due to the loss of statistics about the service sectors in Wuxi, Nantong and Taizhou, the actual sample includes only 13 cities.

Chapter 5

1. Due to the complexity of service trade, the volume of service trade reported by the WTO does not include all service trade transactions under the framework of the WTO. In particular service trade that is launched in the form of commercial presence is not included. In other words, the actual current scale of the service trade under the framework of the WTO is larger than the figure published.
2. Historically, the relationship between the producer services and manufacturing industry have undergone an evolution from assistance to support and then to driver. In the early period of the industrial society, the producer services were still in the primary stage and the industrial correlation between producer services and manufacturing industry was comparatively weak. However, with the deepening of the Industrial Revolution, the advantages of producer services began to show, because on the one hand, enterprises' outsourcing of non-core business reduces transaction costs and enhances the core competitiveness of the enterprises, and on the other hand, there is a large demand market for producer services. Thus combined with the upgrading of division, the producer service industry has developed in an unprecedented manner.

Chapter 6

1. Qin (2006) called the business outsourcing inside a company/group "Insourcing" and divides "Insourcing" into onshore insourcing and offshore insourcing. The former refers to the local parent company or a subsidiary company's outsourcing of business to other subsidiary companies inside the company/group, for example, Ford outsourced the components-designing of the factory in Detroit to the factory in Cleveland; the latter refers to the parent company or subsidiary company's outsourcing of business to the subsidary companies in other countries, for example, the IBM parent company outsourced some software development business to its subsidiary companies in India. In order to discuss the consistency between the former and the latter, we do not adopt the term "insourcing."
2. Actually, the emergence of the outsourcing model embodies that the theory of comparative advantage has been widely recognized and used on the micro level.
3. Thomas L. Friedman, Translated by He Fan & Xiao Yingying, *The World Is Flat: A Brief History of the Twenty-first Century.* Changsha: Hunan Science & Technology Press.
4. Let us take a call center for an example, which is commonly called "answering calls." A movie shows how the training for call centers is done in India: a group of children are recruited in the villages to be trained for the call center, and their first lesson is to learn how to change their Indian accent into an American accent, which is difficult. But the Indians practice every day to achieve their goal so that one day the Americans will not know the call receiver is an Indian. If you want to purchase a house in Chicago and you make a phone call, you will not know that the person who answers your call is actually in India. These Indians have never been to America but they can fluently answer the clients' questions in American English. And they have to be able to recite the map of the US so that they can clearly answer the questions about the streets and facilities in the streets in America.

Notes

Chapter 7

1. Notice: although Model Three discusses the situation in which "x" and "y" are undertaken by two different enterprises, here what is examined is the total profit of the two enterprises, which is similar to the profit of a non-disintegrated factory enterprise. Actually, δ represents the shares of transaction costs covered by the two enterprises, and this parameter could further help us analyze whether the property rights have been disintegrated.
2. Generally speaking, the service industry can be divided into the consumer service industry, the government service industry and the producer service industry. The scale of the producer service industry discussed in this chapter mainly includes: transportation, storage and postal services, wholesale and retailing, finance and insurance services, and real estate services.
3. The so-called Tiebout choice is to "vote with your feet," namely the enterprises' or residents' choice to make a move to acquire the public goods they are in need of.

Chapter 9

1. Generally speaking, the agglomeration of industries, as a regional phenomenon, is the process of industries' development and evolution, is a special organization model of manufacturer groups. The regional gathering of manufacturers of the same sector promotes the development of specialized input and services in the region and the scale supply of specialized factors, creates opportunities for communication of ideas and experience, for division with increasing working procedures and for specialization, and thus realizes the accumulated advantages of the growth of the sector and finally brings increasing returns to the scale of production activities and long-term economic growth.
2. The industrial cooperative agglomeration mentioned emphasizes the agglomeration of related industries and supporting industries as well as the cooperative effect among the agglomerating industries generated due to the inter-industrial external economies. A complete industrial cluster includes not only the industrial agglomeration but also the cooperative agglomeration of industries. The cooperative agglomeration of industries is a self-strengthening mechanism. The concept of "cooperative agglomeration of industries" put forward in this chapter emphasizes the external economies among the up-, mid- and down-stream industries, pays attention to the inter-industrial cooperation and restates the importance of related industries and supporting industries.
3. See China City Statistical Yearbook and the official websites of the Bureau of Statistics in Shanghai, Jiangsu and Zhejiang
4. If the city is in Jiangsu, the value taken is 1; if it is in Zhejiang, −1 is taken; and the value taken for Shanghai is 0.

Chapter 10

1. The balanced growth path referred here is in line with the economic growth path in the Solow model. The latter is not the focus of this article and thus the balanced path of economic growth in the Yangtze River Delta will not be solved. The balanced path mentioned below has the same meaning.
2. The statistical accounting of the service industry is a real problem throughout the world. In China, such a problem is more serious and the standard for categorizing service industry does not coincide with the internationally uniform one. Due to the limitation of availability of data, we substitute data on tertiary industry for data on the service industry.

Chapter 12

1. See *International Statistical Yearbook 2005* (Beijing: China Statistics Press, 2005).
2. Data used in this chapter is calculated by the author on the basis of *Shanghai, Jiangsu and Zhejiang Statistical Yearbooks 2006* and data in the national socioeconomic development statistical bulletins of Shanghai, Jiangsu and Zhejiang in 2006.
3. For more information, please refer to Wei 2003; Zhang 2002; Ren 2005; Zhang 2005; Zhu 2006; Clark 1974; Gershuny and Miles 1983.
4. Manufacturing holds the lead in secondary industry in the Yangtze River Delta so the secondary industry referred to here is roughly the same as manufacturing in the Yangtze River Delta, and similarly hereinafter.
5. Computed on the basis of the statistical bulletins of the domestic economy and social development of Shanghai, Jiangsu and Zhejiang in 2006.
6. See Huang Shengli and Zhu Ying 2002.
7. The author takes transportation, storage and postal services, information transmission, computer services and software services, financial services, real-estate, leasing and commercial services, scientific research, technological services and education as representatives of the producer service industry and calculates according to the statistical yearbook of the Yangtze River Delta.

Chapter 13

1. Ma Chongming 2003.

Chapter 14

1. See Amartya Sen 2002.
2. See Ma Shuluan 1989.
3. See Amartya Sen 2002.
4. Ibid.

Chapter 15

1. In the original report, the scores range from 0 to 10. The higher the score is, the smaller the size of government is. For convenience's sake, the new score of government size equals to 10 minus the original score. The higher the new score is, the larger the size of government is. Then the final scores range from 0 to 100 after we multiply each new score by 10.
2. The scores of the three dependent variables range from 0 to 100.
3. Relevant figures are from the calculation of the author based on the data from the *China Industrial Economy Statistical Yearbook-2006*.
4. The data is from the *China Statistical Yearbook-2007*.

Chapter 17

1. The analysis of the development of service industry in OECD countries is mainly adopted from OECD: *Enhancing the Performance of the Services Sector*, Chapter 1, 2005 and Anita Wölfl: *The Service Economy in OECD Countries*, OECD STI Working Paper, 2005.
2. Baumol (1967) indicated that the imbalanced improvement of various industries leads to resources being redistributed to the sluggish industries, and thereby affects the overall economic growth. Based on his experience, he supposed the economy consists of two industries. One is the improving manufacturing, promoted by factors such as advances in technology, accumulation of capital and scale economy; the other is the relatively sluggish service industry, containing industries involved in education, human arts, public administration, health care, social services etc. Due to the particularity of the latter, the advance in technology will not last long but the cost will ultimately be raised. Labor is the input in final products in the manufacturing while it is also the final consumer of services in the service industry. He also supposed that labor is the only input in production and that the aggregate supply of labor force is fixed. He also assumed that wages in the two industries vary with the nominal wages and incomes, of which the growth rate is equal to that of per capita hourly output in manufacturing. According to the above hypothesis, he drew the conclusion that the wage cost in the sluggish industry grows steady whereas that in the industry with a stable increase is invariable. In that case, there may be two results. One is that the output in service industry will decrease if the fluctuation of products price or income in service industry is not very small. The other is that if the fluctuation of products price or income in service industry is slight, the increasing workers will move to the service industry and the labor force allocated to manufacturing will be decrease, which will eventually cause the slow-down of the increase in the aggregate economic productivity.
3. The explanation for the categorization: (1) The economic strength of Canada and Australia falls behind America and UK but the two countries are deeply influenced by the UK. Moreover, we mainly take the relative value of the service industry as the comparison so we classify Canada and Australia among countries with a British or American system; (2) Although Portugal is an old-line capitalist country, it is not classified among countries with a continental system but small countries. This is because its economic indicator shows it is less developed than France, Germany, Italy and Spain and its population is just a little more than ten billion; (3) Mexico should also be classified among countries with anemerging market system but is not taken into the statistics since its model of development is different from that of Korea and Japan; (4) The Czech Republic and Slovakia were the same yet we adopt the statistics of Slovakia in order to keep the uniformity of statistical analysis. If some data cannot found for Slovakia it can be adopted from that of the Czech Republic; (5) Although Iceland, Ireland, Swiss and Turkey are all small countries (the population of small countries is generally less than ten billion), they are not taken into the statistics simply in order to keep the uniformity of statistical analysis.
4. If there is no particular explanation, the following proportions will be considered as the average value of the corresponding category of country.

Notes

5. On November 4, 1999 the America government promulgated *Financial Services Modernization Act* and banned the restrictions on the operation of the mixed financial industry, which indicated that the originally mixed operation in American finance transformed into the mixed mode. Obviously, that boosted the development of financial business in America.
6. Since 1990s, the needs for services in transportation, storage and communication have been increasing, especially in communication. If the price keeps stable, the output value in these services will be much higher than in others, which may cause the proportion of their value-added growing by a large margin. However, the more effective production, the rapid advance in technology and the increasingly intense competitiveness led to the constantly decrease in the relative price of services supplied by those industries thus caused a slight change in the proportion of value-added.
7. As there is a lack of statistics of 1995 and 2005, only the statistics of 1990s and 1980s are taken into comparison in this section.
8. Refer to Ana M. Fernandes, "Structure and Performance of the Services Sector in Transition Economies." World Bank Policy Research Working Paper Series 4357, 2007.
9. There is a lack of statistics for 1995 and 2005 thus the contrastive analysis is only carried out between the 1980s and the 1990s.
10. In most of the OECD countries, if the increase in productivity is high, the growth rate of employment will be low (such as in finance, transportation, storage and communications); conversely if the increase in productivity is relatively low, the growth rate of employment will be much higher (such as in education, health care, social works and other services).
11. According to the proportions of employment in service industry respectively from 1990 to 2001 and from 1980 to 1990, the growth rate of the former to the latter can be calculated.
12. In terms of the whole service industries in OECD countries, if the productivity in service industry increases by 1.1%, the productivity of the gross economy increases by 1%.
13. In 2001 the average proportion of commercial research funding accounted for about 0.4% in the added value of the service industry but 7% in manufacturing.
14. Anita Wölfl, "The Service Economy In OECD Countries," OECO STI Working Papers,2005.
15. It includes trans-border supply, overseas consumption (especially the consumption in tourism), commercial supply (especially supply through foreign organizations) and supply by natural persons.
16. See Li Shantong, 2002, 401.
17. However the rules are not only relaxed but are also intensified. For example, in the aspects of service quality, consumer protection, safety in the work place, labor safety and environmental protection, the rules have not been liberalized but strengthened further. The natural monopoly sector still keeps various regulations such as price rule and improves traditional regulation through incentive methods even though it eases some regulations and introduces competitive factors. For example, the aircraft industry does not relax safety regulations; the telecommunications sector in several countries still imposes restrictions on the structure of the telephone bill rate.
18. For example, they eliminated the controversial "country of origin principle" which provides that trans-border service enterprises shall abide by regulations not in the place of business but in the place of registration; they excluded sectors such as education, public health and social service from the opening up scope of the service industry.
19. On the contrary, manufacturing focuses on the improvement of products, transmission or design, which is more concerned with the innovation of process than service enterprises.
20. There are mainly two channels through which service industry supports innovation activities. Firstly, the service industry purchases knowledge or investment products from manufacturing (stimulating demand); secondly, the service industry provides services or knowledge to manufacturing enterprises or other service enterprises, which is a part of innovators' activities (knowledge promotion).
21. The Yangtze River Delta referred in this chapter covers 16 cities in Jiangsu and Zhejiang, including Shanghai. If certain data is lacked in such regions, we will use the data of two provinces and one city in the Yangtze River Delta instead.
22. Modern service industry is defined as knowledge-, technology- and information-intensive service sectors that rely on the high technology and modern management model of operation and organization and mainly supplies producers with intermediate input, including services related to finance, commerce, information technology, network communications, education, training, health care, third-party logistics and some traditional services transformed by new technology.
23. The coordinate positioning effect between producer service industry and manufacturing suggests that we should implement the principle of productivity allocation in order to avoid the single development of manufacturing or service industry. See Liu Zhibiao.
24. See Liu Zhibiao.
25. See *People's Daily*, December 3, 2007, p. 6.
26. Ibid.
27. The *Prospects for Information Technology of Economic Cooperation and Development Organization in 2006* gives a comprehensive analysis of the development and application of information technology in OECD countries as well as the latest advance in the service outsourcing led by ICT.
28. See Liu Zhibiao, 2007.

29. The developed countries represented by America, directed against China which has lax law enforcement on infringement of copyright and brand, began to appeal to the World Trade Organization that the pirating and counterfeiting level in China is far too high and the insufficient protection for intellectual property rights brings an annual loss of ten of millions US dollars to American companies and employees. The appeal is supported by many famous enterprises including Microsoft and Apple.
30. See Jiang Jing & Liu Zhibiao, 2007.
31. On December 19, 2007, the "Forum for cooperation and development of service industry in the Yangtze River Delta and the first service products exhibition" was held in Shanghai at which Shanghai, Jiangsu and Zhejiang signed an agreement, namely, The agreement on cooperation and development of service industry. Such an agreement marks a good beginning for the integration of service industry in the Yangtze River Delta.
32. The liberalization of regulations does not mean to conniving with the service industry. Just as in OECD countries, the Yangtze River Delta also needs to intensify some regulations for the service industry such as protection for consumers and the examination of malicious amalgamation by foreign service enterprises.

References

Chapter 1

Banga Rashmi and B. N. Goldar. "Contribution of Services to Output Growth Productivity in Indian Manufacturing: Pre and Post Reform." ICRIER Working Paper, no. 139 (2004).

Chen Jiagui 陳佳貴 et al. *Zhongguo gongyehua jincheng baogao* 中國工業化進程報告 (Report on China's Industrialization Process). Beijing: Social Science Academic Press, 2007.

Chen Xian 陳憲 et al. "Fengong, hudong yu yonghe: Fuwuye yu zhizaoye guanxiyanjin de shizheng yanjiu" 分工、互動與融合：服務業與製造業關係演進的實證研究 ("Division of Labor, Interactions and Convergence: Empirical Research on the Evolvement of the Relationship between Service and Manufacturing Industries"). *Zhongguo ruan kexue* 中國軟科學 (China Soft Science), 10 (2004).

Cheng Dazhong 程大中. *Zhongguo fuwu ye de zhengzhang, jishu jinbu yuguoji jingzheng li* 中國服務業的增長、技術進步與國際競爭力 (Growth, Technological Progress and the International Competitiveness of China's Service Industry). Beijing: Economic Management Press, 2006.

Gu Naihua 顧乃華. "Woguo fuwuye dui gongye fazhan waiyi xiaoying de lilunhe shizheng fenxi" 我國服務業對工業發展外溢效應的理論和實證分析. ("The Theoretical and Experimental Analysis of the Spillover Effect of the Service Industry on the Industrial Development of China.") *Tongji yanjiu* 統計研究 (Statistical Research), 12 (2005).

Jiang Xiaojuan 江小涓 et al. "Fuwuye yu Zhongguo jingji: Xiangguanxing he jiakuai zengzhang de qianli" 服務業與中國經濟：相關性和加快增長的潛力 (The Service Industry and China's Economy: the Relevance and the Potential to Accelerate Growth). *Jingji yanjiu* 經濟研究 (Economic Research), 1 (2004).

Li Jiangfan 李江帆. "Guowai shengchan fuwuye yanjiu shuping" 國外生產服務業研究述評 ("A Review of Overseas Producer Service Industry"). *Waiguo jingji yu guanli* 外國經濟與管理 (Foreign Economics & Management), 11 (2004).

Liu Zhibiao 劉志彪. *Changsanjiao tuoqi de Zhongguo zhizao* 長三角托起的中國製造 ("Made in China" Fostered by the Yangtze River Delta). Beijing: China Renmin University Press, 2006.

Lu Zheng 呂政 et al. "Zhongguo shengchanzhe fuwuye fazhan de zhanlüe xuanze" 中國生產者服務業發展的戰略選擇——基於產業互動的研究視角 ("Strategy Selection of China's Producer Services Industries Development—Based on the View of Industrial Interaction"). *Zhongguo gongye jingji* 中國工業經濟 (China Industrial Economy), 8 (2006).

Mukesh Eswaran and Ashok Kotwal. "The Role of the Service Sector in the Process of Industrialization." *Journal of Development Economics*, 68 (2002): 401–420.

Singh Nirvikar. *ICTs and Rural Development in India*. University of California, Santa Cruz, USA. Draft, in progress, 2005.

Chapter 2

Binet, M. E. "Testing Fiscal Competition among French Municipalities: Granger Causality Evidence in a Dynamic Panel Data Model." *Regional Science*, 82 (2003): 277–289.

Chenery, H. (錢納里) et al. *Gongyehua he jingji zengzhang de bejiao yanjiu* 工業化和經濟增長的比較研究 (Industrialization and Growth: A Comparative Study). Shanghai: Sdxjoint Publishing Company & Shanghai People's Publishing House, 1995.

Griliches, Z. "Productivity, R&D and the Data Constraints." *American Economics Review*, 84, no. 1 (1994): 123.

Guojia tongjiju ketizu國家統計局課題組 (Research group of the National Bureau of Statistics of China). *Jiakuai fazhan woguo disan chanye* 加快發展我國第三產業的研究報告 (A Research Report on Accelerating the Development of Service Industry in China). Beijing: China Economy Press House, 1994.

Guojia tongjiju 國家統計局 (National Bureau of Statistics of China). *Zhongguo shouci disan chanye pucha baogao* 中國首次第三產業普查報告 (Report of the First General Survey of Tertiary Industries in China). Beijing: China Statistics Press, 1995.

Huang Fanhua 黃繁華 (Eds.). *Jingji quanqiuhua yu xiandai fuwuye* 經濟全球化與現代服務業 (Economic Globalization and Modern Service Industry). Nanjing: Nanjing Publishing House, 2002.

Huang Gangling 晁鋼令 (Eds.). "Fuwu chanye yu xiandai fuwuye" 服務產業與現代服務業 ("Service Sectors and Modern Service Industry"). Beijing: Shanghai University of Finance & Economics Press, 2004.

Huang Shaojun 黃少軍. *Fuwuye yu jingji zengzhang* 服務業與經濟增長 (Service Industry and Economic Growth). Beijing: Economic Science Press, 2000.

Jiang Xiaojuan 江小涓 and Pei Changhong 裴長洪. *Zhongguo fuwuye fazhan baogao* 中國服務業發展報告 (Report on China's Service Industry). Beijing: Social Sciences Academic Press, 2004.

Li Jiangfan 李江帆 and Bi Doudou 畢斗斗. "Guowai shengchan fuwuye yanjiu shuping" (國外生產服務業研究述評) "A Commentary on the Foreign Producer Service Industry" *Waiguo jingji yu guanli* 外國經濟與管理 (Foreign Economies and Management), 11 (2004): 16–20.

Li Jiangfan 李江帆 and Zeng Guojun 曾國軍. "Zhongguo disan chanye neibu jiegou shengji qushi fenxi" 中國第三產業內部結構升級趨勢分析 ("An Analysis of Upgrading Trends of Tertiary Industry's Internal Structure in China"). *Zhongguo gongye jingji* 中國工業經濟 (China Industrial Economy), 3 (2003): 34–39.

Li Jiangfan 李江帆. *Disan chanye jingji xue* 第三產業經濟學 (Economics of the Third Industry). Guangzhou: Guangdong People's Publishing House, 1990.

Li Shantong 李善同 and Hua Ercheng 華而誠 (Eds.). *21 shiji chu de Zhongguo fuwuye* 21世紀初的中國服務業 (The Service Industry of China at the Beginning of the 21st Century). Beijing: Economic Science Press, 2002.

Liu Wei 劉偉 and Li Shaorong 李紹榮. "Chanye qiegou yu jingji zengzhang 產業結構與經濟增長 ("Industrial Structure and Economic Growth"). *Zhongguo gongye jingji* 中國工業經濟 (China Industrial Economy), 5 (2002).

Liu Zhibiao 劉志彪. "Changsanjiao quyu hezuo jianshe guoji zhizaoye zhongxin de zhidu sheji" 長三角區域合作建設國際製造業中心的制度設計 ("Regional Cooperation to Foster an International Manufacturing Center in the Yangtze River Delta: A Thinking on Its Social Institutions"). *Nanjing daxue xuebao* 南京大學學報 (Journal of Nanjing University (Philosophy, Humanities and Social Sciences), 1 (2005): 47–55.

Liu Zhibiao 劉志彪. "Jingji quanjiuhua zhong de chengshi gongneng bianhua yu fangdichan ye fazhan jiyu—yi Shanghai wei Zhongxin de Changsanjiao diqu weili" 經濟全球化中的城市功能變化與房地產業發展機遇——以上海為中心的長三角地區為例 ("The Changes in City Functions and Development Opportunities of the Real Estate Sector in Economic Globalization—Taking the Shanghai-centered Yangtze River Delta as An Example"). *Nanjing shehui kexue* 南京社會科學 (Social Sciences in Nanjing), 3 (2006): 5.

Mankiw, N. G., D. Romer and D. N. Weil. "A Contribution to the Empirics of Economic Growth." *The Quarterly Journal of Economics*, 107 (1992): 407–437.

Nelson, Richard (理查德 · R · 納爾森). *Jingji zengzhang de yuanchuan* 經濟增長的源泉 (The Source of Economic Growth). Beijing: China Economy Press, 2001.

North, Douglas C. (道格拉斯 · 諾斯) and Robert Paul Thomas (羅伯特 · 托馬斯). *Xifang shijie de xingqi* 西方世界的興起 (The Rise of the Western World). Beijing: Huaxia Publishing House, 1989.

Pan Wenqin 潘文卿 and Li Zinai 李子奈. "Zhongguo yanhai yu neilu jian jingji yingxiang de fangui yu yichu xiaoying" 中國沿海與內陸間經濟影響的反饋與溢出效應 ("Feedback and Spillover Effects between Coastal and Non-coastal Regions of China"). *Jingji yanjiu* 經濟研究 (Economic Research Journal), 5 (2007): 68–77.

Rebelo, Sergio. "Long Run Policy Analysis and Long Run Growth." *Journal of Political Economy*, 94 (October 1991): 1002–1037.

Temple, J. "The New Growth Evidence." *Journal of Economic Literature*, XXXVII (1999): 112–156.

Victor R. Fuchs (維克托 · R · 富克斯). *Fuwu jingji xue* 服務經濟學 (The Service Economy). Beijing: The Commercial Press, 1987.

Wang Xiaolu 王小魯 and Fan Gang 樊綱. "Zhongguo diqu chaju de bianhua" 中國地區差距的變動趨勢和影響因素 ("Analysis of the Regional Disparity in China and the Influential Factors"). *Jingji yanjiu* 經濟研究 (Economic Research Journal), 1 (2004): 33–44.

Wei Feng 魏鋒 and Cao Zhong 曹中. "Woguo fuwuye fazhan yu jingji zengzhang de yinguo guanxi yanjiu—jiyu dong, zhong, xibu mianban suju de shizheng yanjiu 我國服務業發展與經濟增長的因果關係研究——基於東、中、西部面板數據的實證研究 ("The Causality Relationship between the Development of the Services Industry and Economic Growth in China: Based on the Panel Data of Eastern, Central and Western China"). *Tongji yanjiu* 統計研究 (Statistical Research), 2 (2007): 44–46.

Winston, C. "Economic Deregulation: Days of Reckoning for Microeconomists." *Journal of Economic Literature*, 31 (1993): 1263–1289.

Zhang Shuguang 張曙光 and Zhang Bin 張斌. "Waihui chubei chixu zhilei de jingji houguo" 外匯儲備持續積累的經濟後果 ("The Economic Effect of Foreign Exchange Reserve Continual Accumulation"). *Jingji yanjiu* 經濟研究 (Economic Research Journal), 4 (2007): 18–29.

Chapter 3

Chen Limin 陳立敏 and Tan Liwen 譚力文. "Pingjia Zhongguo zhizaoye guoji jingzhengli de shizheng yanjiu fangfa—jianyu Porter zhibiao ji chanye fenleifa bijiao" 評價中國製造業國際競爭力的實證研究方法——兼與波特指標及產業分類法比較 ("Research on an Empirical Method of Valuing the International Competitiveness of Chinese Manufacturing—Comparison with Porter's Index and Industry Taxonomy"). *China Industrial Economy*, 5 (2004).

Cheng Dazhong 程大中. "Zhongguo shengchanzhe fuwuye zhengzhang, jiegou bianhua jiqi yingxiang" 中國生產者服務業的增長、結構變化及其影響 ("China's Producer Services: Growth,Structural Changes,and Effects"). *Caimao jingji* 財貿經濟 (Finance & Trade Economics), 10 (2006).

Ciccone, A. and E. Hall. "Productivity and the Density of Economic Activity." *American Economic Review*, 86, no. 1 (1996): 54–70.

Clark, John Bates (科林 · 克拉克). *Caifu de fenpei* 財富的分配 (The Distribution of Wealth). Shanghai: The Commercial Press, 1935.

Francois, J. F. and K. A. Reinert. "The Role of Services in the Structure of Production and Trade: Stylised Facts from a Cross-Country Analysis." *Asia Pacific Economic Review*, 2, no. 1 (1996): 35–43.

Glasmeier, A. and M. Howland. "Service-led Rural Development: Definitions Theories and Empirical Evidence." *International Regional Science Review*, 16 (1994): 197–229.

Gu Naihua 顧乃華, Bi Doudou 畢斗斗 and Ren Wangbin 任旺兵. "Zhongguo zhuanxingqi shengchanzhe fuwuye jingzhengli guanxi yanjiu 中國轉型期生產者服務業發展與製造業競爭力關係研究 ("The Relationship between Producer Services' Development and Manufacturing's Competence in China during the Transition Period—An Empirical Research Based on Panel Data"). *Zhongguo gongye jingji* 中國工業經濟 (China Industrial Economy), 9 (2006).

Guo Kesha 郭克莎. *Zhongguo: Gaige zhongde jingji zengzhang yu jiegou biandong* 中國：改革中的經濟增長與結構變動 (China: Economic Growth and Structural Change in Reform). Shanghai: Shanghai People's Publishing House, 1996.

Jiang Jing 江靜, Liu Zhibiao 劉志彪 and Yu Mingchao 于明超. "Shengchanzhe fuwuye fazhan yu zhizao ye xiaolü tisheng" 生產者服務業發展與製造業效率提升 ("The Development of the Producer Service Industry and the Enhancement of Manufacturing Industry's Efficiency"). *Shijie jingji* 世界經濟 (The Journal of World Economy), 8 (2007).

Kongsamut, P., S. Rebelo and D. Xie. "Beyond Balanced Growth." NBER Working Paper, No. 6159 (1997).

Liu Zhibiao 劉志彪. "Regional Cooperation to Foster an International Manufacturing Center in the Yangtze River Delta: A Thinking on Its Social

Institutions" *Nanjing daxue xuebao* 南京大學學報 (Journal of Nanjing University (Philosophy, Humanities and Social Sciences), 1 (2005).

Liu Zhibiao 劉志彪. "Fazhan xiandaixing shengchanzhe fuwuye yu tiaozheng youhua zhizaoye jiegou" 發展現代生產者服務業與調整優化製造業結構 ("Upgrade of Outward-oriented Economy Strategies in the Global Value Chain"), *Economic Issues in China*, 1 (2007).

Michael E. Porter (邁克爾・波特). *Guojia jingzheng youshi* 國家競爭優勢 (The Competitive Advantage of Nations). Beijing: Huaxia Publishing House, 2002.

Simon Smith Kuznets (西蒙・庫茲涅茨). *Geguo de jingji zengzhang: Zhongchanzhi he shengchan jiegou* 各國的經濟增長：總產值和生產結構 (Economic Growth of Nations: Total Output and Production Structure). Beijing: The Commercial Press, 1999.

Wang Yueping 王岳平. *Kaifang tiaojianxia de gongye jiegou shengji* 開放條件下的工業結構升級 (Upgrade of Industry Structure in an Opening-up Situation). Beijing: Economic Management Press, 2004.

Yin Xingmin 殷醒民. *Zhizaoye jiegou de zhuanxing yu jingji fazhan* 製造業結構的轉型與經濟發展 (Transformation of Manufacturing Structure and Economic Development). Shanghai: Fudan University Press, 1999.

Zhou Shulian 周叔蓮 and Guo Kesha 郭克莎. *Zhongguo gongye zengzhang yu jiegou biandong yanjiu* 中國工業增長與結構變動研究 (A Study on the Growth and Structural Changes of Industrial Sectors in China). Beijing: Economic Management Press, 2000.

Chapter 4

Balasubramanyam, V. N., M. Salisu and David Sapsford. "Foreign Direct Investment and Growth in EP and IS Countries." *The Economic Journal*, 106, no. 434 (1996): 92–105.

Barrell, Ray and Nigel Pain. "Foreign Direct Investment, Technological Change, and Economic Growth within Europe." *The Economic Journal*, 107, no. 445 (1997): 1770–1786.

Buch, Claudia M. "Why Do Banks Go Abroad? Evidence from German Data." *Financial Markets, Institutions and Instruments*, 2000.

de la Porteria, Bruno van Pottelsberghe and Frank Lichtenberg. "Does Foreign Direct Investment Transfer Technology across Borders?" *Review of Economics and Statistics*, 83, no. 3 (2001): 490–497.

de Mello, Luiz R. "Foreign Direct Investment-led Growth: Evidence from Time Series and Panel Data." Oxford Economic Papers, 1999, 51, no. 1: 133–151.

Dunning, J. H. "Multinational Enterprises and the Growth of Services: some Conceptual and Theoretical Issues," *The Service Industries Journal*, 9, no. 1 (1989): 539.

Fujita, M., P. Krugman and A. Venables. *The Spatial Economy: Cities, Regions and International Trade*. Cambridge: MA, MIT Press, 1999.

He Meiying 賀梅英. "Fuwuye duiwai zhijie touzi yu Guangdong jingji zengzhang de shizheng fenxi" 服務業對外直接投資與廣東經濟增長的實證分析 ("Positive Analysis of FDI in the Service Industry and Economic Growth in Guangdong Province"). *Huanan nongye daxue xuebao* 華南農業大學學報（社會科學版）(Journal of South China Agricultural University [Philosophy, Humanities and Social Sciences]), 2 (2005).

James R. Markusen. "The Boundary of Multinational Enterprises and the Theory of International Trade." *Journal of Economic Perspectives*, 9, no. 2 (Spring 1995): 169–189.

Jiang Jinfan 江錦凡. "Waiguo zhijie touzi zai Zhongguo jingji zengzhang zhongde zuoyong jizhi" 外國直接投資在中國經濟增長中的作用機制 ("Mechanisms of FDI's Effect on Chinese Economic Growth"). *Shijie jingji* 世界經濟 World Economy, 1 (2004).

Kang Canhua 康燦華 and Su Fang 蘇芳. "Fuwuye duiwai zhijie touzi de fazhan jiqi yingxiang" 服務業對外直接投資的發展及其影響 ("The Development of Services FDI and Its Impact"). *Guoji shuangwu* 國際商務 (International Business), 6 (2006).

Li Zhufeng 李珠峰. "Zhongguo fuwuye xiyin guoji zhijie touzi fenxi" 中國服務業吸引國際直接投資分析 ("Analysis of Chinese Service Industry's Attraction of FDI"). *Shijie jingji yanjiu* 世界經濟研究 (World Economy Study), 7 (2004).

Markusen, James R., T. F. Rutherford and D. Tarr. "Foreign Direct Investment in Services and Domestic Market for Expertise," mimeo, 1999.

Raff, Horst and Marc von der Ruhr. "Foreign Direct Investment in Producer Services: Theory and Empirical Evidence." CESifo Working Paper, no. 598 (2001).

Sang Xiuguo 桑秀國. "Liyong waizi yu jingji zengzhang: yige jiyu xin jingji zengzhang lilun de moxing jitui Zhongguo suju de yanzheng" 利用外資與經濟增長：一個基於新經濟增長理論的模型及對中國數據的驗證"Foreign Capital Use and Economic Growth: A Model Based on the New Economic Growth Theory and the Model's Test of Data in China"). *Guanli shijie* 管理世界 (Management World), 9 (2002).

Shen Kunrong 沈坤榮 and Gen Qiang 耿 . "Waiguo zhijie touzi, jishu waiyiyu neisheng jingji zengzhang" 外國直接投資、技術外溢與內生經濟增長

("Foreign Direct Investment, Technical Overflow and Endogenous Economic Growth—An Econometric Test and Empirical Analysis of Chinese Data"). *Zhongguo shehui kexue* 中國社會科學 (Social Sciences in China), 5 (2001).

UNCTC. *The Foreign Direct Investment and Multinational Corporations in Services*. Routledge, 1989.

Wang Jianhua 王建華 and Zhu Yun 朱昀. "Woguo fuwuye waiguo zhijie touzi de quwei yinzi fenxi" 我國服務業外國直接投資的區位因子分析 ("An Analysis of Location Factors on Service Industry FDI in China"). *Guoji shuangwu* 國際商務 (International Business), 1 (2007).

Wang Xiaomei 王小梅. "Woguo fuwuye xiyin FDI di quwei queding yinsu fenxi" 我國服務業吸引FDI的區位決定因素分析 ("Location Determinants of Service FDI Flowing into China"). M.A. Thesis, Shandong University, 2006.

Wu Jing 吳靜. "Fuwuye FDI yu quyu jingji zengzhang guanxi yanjiu—jiyu Changsanjiao diqu suju de shizheng fenxi" 服務業FDI與區域經濟增長關係研究——基於長三角地區數據的實證分析 ("Relationship between Foreign Direct Investment in the Services Sector and Regional Economic Growth—An empirical analysis of the data of Yangtze River Delta"). *Shenji yu jingji yanjiu* 審計與經濟研究 (Audit & Economy Research), 22, no. 2 (2007).

Xiao Zheng 蕭政 and Shen Yan 沈艷. "Waiguo zhijie touzi yu jingji zengzhang de guanxi ji yixiang" 外國直接投資與經濟增長的關係及影響 ("Foreign Direct Investment and Economic Growth"). *Jingji lilun yu jingji guanli* 經濟理論與經濟管理 (Economic Theory and Business Management), 1 (2002).

Xue Jingxiao 薛敬孝 and Han Yan 韓燕. "Fuwuye FDI dui woguo jiuye de yingxiang" 服務業FDI對我國就業的影響 ("The Service FDI Effects on China's Employment"). *Nankai xuebao* 南開學報（哲學社會科學版）(Naikai Journal [Philosophy, Humanities and Social Sciences]), 2 (2006).

Zha Donglan 查冬蘭 and Wu Xiaolan 吳曉蘭. "Fuwuye waiguo zhijie touzi dui fuwuye ge hangye jingji zengzhang de yingxiang fenxi 服務業外國直接投資對服務業各行業經濟增長的影響分析——以江蘇省為例 ("Empirical Research about the Effect of FDI in the Services on the Economic Growth"). *Guoji maoyi wenti* 國際貿易問題 (Journal of International Trade), 11 (2006).

Zhang Cheng 張誠 and Tang Lin 唐琳. "Zhizaoye he fuwuye waiguo zhijie touzi dui dongdaoguo jiuye yingxiang de bijiao fenxi—Yi Meiguo weili) 製造業和服務業外國直接投資對東道國就業影響的比較分析——以美國為例 ("Comparative Study of the Effect of Foreign Direct Investment in Manufacturing Industry and Service Industry in Host Countries: A

Case Study of the USA").*Renkou yu jingji* 人口與經濟 (Population & Economics), 3 (2007).

Zhao Shuhua 趙書華 and Song Zheng 宋征. "Fuwuye kuaguo gongsi zaihua zhijie touzi de jingji xiaoying fenxi" 服務業跨國公司在華直接投資的經濟效應分析("Analyses of the Effects of FDI in the Services Sector on China's Economic Growth"). *Guoji jingmao tansuo* 國際經貿探索 (International Economics and Trade Research), 22, no. 1 (2006).

Zhong Changbiao 鍾昌標. "Waizi yu quyu jingji zengzhang guanxi de lilun yu shizheng" 外資與區域經濟增長關係的理論與實證 ("Theories and Empirical Studies of the Relationship Between Foreign Capital and Regional Economic Growth"). *Suliang jingji jishu jingji yanjiu* 數量經濟技術經濟研究 (Quantitative & Technica Economics), 1 (2000).

Zhuang Lijuan 莊麗娟 and He Meiying 賀梅英. "Fuwuye liyong waishuang zhijie touzi dui Zhongguo jingji zengzhang zuoyong jili de shizheng yanjiu" 服務業利用外商直接投資對中國經濟增長作用機理的實證研究 ("An Empirical Study of the Mechanisms of the Influence of Service Industry's Use of FDI on the Economic Growth of China"). *Shijie jingji yanjiu* 世界經濟研究 (World Economy Study), 8 (2005).

Chapter 5

Chen Xian 陳憲. *Guoji fuwu maoyi—Yuanli, chanye, zhengce* 國際服務貿易——原理、產業、政策 (International Service Trade: Theories, Industries and Policies). Beijing: CITIC Press Corporation, 2000.

Fan Chunzeng 范純增 and Yu Guang 于光. *Fuwu maoyi guoji jingzhengli fazhan yanjiu—Jianlun Shanghai fuwu maoyi guoji jingzhengli fazhan zhanlüe* 服務貿易國際競爭力發展研究——兼論上海服務貿易國際競爭力發展戰略 ("Study on the International Competitiveness of Service Trade—The Case of Shanghai"). Guoji maoyi wenti 國際貿易問題 (International Trade Journal), 2 (2005).

Gu Wenyan 谷文艷. "Shijie maoyi jiegou zongshu" 世界貿易結構綜述 ("An Overview of World Trade Structure"). *Guoji ziliao xinxi* 國際資料信息 (International Materials & Information), 8 (2006).

Huang Fanhua 黃繁華. *Jiaru WTO hou de fuwuye fazhan* 加入WTO 後的服務業發展 (Development of the Service Industry After China's Entrance into the WTO). Beijing: People's Press, 2004.

Zhang Qianjiang張錢江 and Chen Yonghong 陳永紅. "Jiekuai tuidong Zhejiang guoji fuwu maoyi fazhan" 加快推動浙江國際服務貿易發展 ("Acceleration of International Service Trade's Development in Zhejiang"). *Zhejiang jingmao* 浙江經濟 (Zhejiang Economy), 10 (2007).

Zhang Zhihua 張治華 and Liu Shuhua 劉曙華. "Quanqiu shijiao xia quyu jingzhengli de fenxi kuangjia yanjiu" 全球視角下區域競爭力的分析框架研究 ("A Study of the Analysis Framework of Regional Competitiveness from the Global Perspective"). *Xinxi bu* 新西部 (New West), 1 (2007).

Chapter 6

Hu Kai 胡凱 and Zhou Peng 周鵬. "Jiangsu sheng xiandai fuwuye waibao jingying moshi de fazhan ji yingdui caoshi" 江蘇省現代服務業外包經營模式的發展及應對措施 ("Development of an Operation Model of Modern Service Business Outsourcing in Jiangsu Province and Corresponding Measures"). *Xiandai jingji tantao* 現代經濟探討 (Modern Economic Research), 4 (2006).

Liu Jiren 劉積仁, "'Shijie bangongshi' li women duoyuan" 「世界辦公室」離我們多遠？ ("How Far Are We from the 'World Office'"). *Wenhui bao*, 24 July 2005.

Liu Qinglin 劉慶林 and Chen Jinghua 陳景華. "Fuwuye waibao de fuli xiaoying fenxi" 服務業外包的福利效應分析 ("The Welfare Effect Analysis of Service Outsourcing"). *Shandong daxue xuebao* (shehui kexue ban) 山東大學學報 (社會科學版) (Journal of Shandong University [Philosophy and Social Sciences]), 4 (2006).

Liu Qinglin 劉慶林 and Lian Kai 廉凱. "Yindu zhengjie fuwuye waibao dui qi chanye jiegou de yingxiang ji qishi" 印度承接服務業外包對其產業結構的影響及啟示 ("Influence and Inspiration of India's Undertaking Service Business Outsourcing on Its Industrial Structure"). *Guoji jingji hezuo* 國際經濟合作(International Economic Cooperation), 9 (2006).

Qin Yi 秦儀, Li Wenjing 李文靜 and Pan Chundie 潘春蝶. "Kuaguo gongsi fuwuye waibao fazhan qushi yu woguo duice" 跨國公司服務業外包發展趨勢與我國對策 ("Developing Trends of Multinational Enterprises' Service Business Outsourcing and China's Countermeasures"). *Keji jinbu yu dui ce* 科技進步與對策 (Science & Technology Progress and Policy), 4 (2006).

Zhan Xiaoning 詹曉寧 and XingHouyuan 邢厚媛. "Woguo chengjie fuwu waibao de zhanlüe sikao" 我國承接服務外包的戰略思考 ("A Strategic Thinking on China's Undertaking Service Outsourcing"). *Zhongguo duiwai maoyi* 中國對外貿易 (China's Foreign Trade), 5 (2005).

Chapter 7

Ambos, Tina C., Bjorn Ambos and Bodo B. Schlegelmilch. "Learning from Foreign Subsidiaries: An Empirical Investigation of Headquarters Benefits from Reverse Knowledge Transfers." *International Business Review*, 15 (2006): 294–312.

An Husen 安虎森, *Kongjian jingji xue yuanli* 空間經濟學原理 (Principles of Spatial Economics). Beijing: Economic Science Press, 2005.

Bingmu xinyi (日并木信義). *Xiayu hujian: Ri-Mei chanye bijiao* 瑕瑜互見：日美產業比較 (Advantages and Disadvantages: A Comparison of Japanese and American Industries). Beijing: China Financial and Economic Publishing House, 1990.

Gao Chuansheng 高傳勝 and Liu Zhibiao 劉志彪. "Shengchanzhe fuwu yu Changsanjiao zhizaoye jiju he fazhan" 生產者服務與長三角製造業集聚和發展：理論、實證與潛力分析 ("Producer Services and Agglomeration and Development of Manufacturing Sectors in the Yangtze River Delta: Theory, Empirical Research and Analysis of Potential"). *Shanghai jingji yanjiu* 上海經濟研究 (Shanghai Economic Review), 8 (2005).

Grubel, H. G. (格魯伯). *Fuwuye de zengzhang: Yuanyin yu yingxiang* 服務業的增長：原因與影響 (Service Industry Growth). Shanghai: SDX Joint Publishing Company, 1993.

Henderson, J. Vernon and Yukako Ono. "Where do Manufacturing Firms Locate Their Headquarters." *Journal of Urban Economics*, 131 (2007).

Hoover, Edgar M. (胡佛). *Quyu jingjixue daolun* 區域經濟學導論 (An Introduction to Regional Economics). Shanghai: Shanghai Far East Publishing House, 1992.

Lincoln, James R. "The Urban Distribution of Headquarters and Branch Plants in Manufacturing: Mechanisms of Metropolitan Dominance." *Demography*, 15, no.2 (1978), 213–222.

Liu Zhibiao 劉志彪. "Fazhan xiandai shengchanzhe fuwuye yu tiaozheng youhua zhizaoye jiegou" 發展現代生產者服務業與調整優化製造業結構 "Developing Modern Producer Service and Adjusting and Optimizing the Structure of Manufacturing." *Nanjing daxue xuebao* 南京大學學報 (Journal of Nanjing University, 5 (2006).

Mcnee, R. B. *Towards a more Humanistic Economic Geography*. Tijdschrift voor Economische en Socisle Geografie, 1960.

Nijkamp, Peter (彼得 · 尼茨坎普). (Eds.). *Quyu he chengshi jingjixue shouce (di yi juan: Quyu jingjixue)* 區域和城市經濟學手冊 (第1卷：區域經濟學) ("Handbook of Regional and Urban Economics [Volume 1: Regional Economics]). Translated by An Husen (安虎森). Beijing: Economic Science Press, 2001.

Tuan, Chyau and Ng, Linda F. Y. "FDI Facilitated by Agglomeration Economies: Evidence from Manufacturing and Services Joint Ventures in China." *Journal of Asian Economics*, 13, Issue 6 (2003): 749–765.

Wu Fuxiang 吴福象. "Kuaguo gongsi zhizaoye chuizhi fenli: lilun yu zhengju" 跨國公司製造業垂直分離：理論與證據 ("Vertical Disintegration in Multinational Corporations' Manufacturing: Theories and Proofs"). Ph.D. diss., Nanjing University, 2006.

Zhang Peng 張鵬. *Zhongbu jingji shidai* 總部經濟時代 (The Era of the Headquarters Economy). Beijing: Huaxia Publishing House, 2007.

Zhao Hong 趙弘. *Zhongbu jingji* 總部經濟 (Headquarters Economy). Beijing: China Economy Publishing House, 2004.

Chapter 8

Cheng Dazhong 程大中. "Zhongguo fuwuye zengzhang de diqu yu bumen tezheng" 中國服務業增長的地區與部門特徵 ("Regional and Sector Features of China's Service Development"). *Caimao jingji* 財貿經濟 (Finance & Trade Economics), 8 (2003).

Dangdai Shanghai yanjiusuo 當代上海研究所 (The Institute of Contemporary Shanghai Studies). *Changzhang Sanjiaozhou fazhan baogao: 2006* 長江三角洲發展報告：2006 (Yangtze River Delta Development Report: 2006). Shanghai: Shanghai People's Publishing House, 2006.

Grugman, Paul (保羅・克魯格曼). "Dili zai jingji fazhan zhong de zuoyong" 地理在經濟發展中的作用 ("The Role of Geography in Development"). *Bijiao* 比較 (Comparative Studies), 28 (2007).

Hong Yinxing 洪銀興. "Chengshi gongneng yiyi de chengshihua jiqi chanye zhichi" 城市功能意義的城市化及其產業支持 ("Urbanization in its Functional Sense and Corresponding Industrial Support"). *Jingji xuejia* 經濟學家 (Economist), 2 (2003).

Ji Yuhua 吉昱華, Cai Yuezhou 蔡躍洲 and Yang Kequan 楊克泉. "Zhongguo chengshi jiju xiaoyi shizheng fenxi" 中國城市集聚效益實證分析 ("An Empirical Analysis of Urban Agglomeration Effect in China"). *Guanli shijie* 管理世界 (Management World), 3 (2004).

Jiang Xiaojuan 江小涓 and Li Hui 李輝. "Fuwuye yu Zhongguo jingji: Xiangguanxing he jiakuai zengzhang de qianli" 服務業與中國經濟：相關性和加快增長的潛力 ("Service Industry and China's Economy: Correlation and Potential of Faster Growth"). *Jingji yanjiu* 經濟研究 (Economic Research Journal), 1 (2004).

Li Jingkui 李井奎 and Qian Chen 錢陳. "Fuwuye de kongjian fenbu tezheng jiyu chengshihua de xiangguan fenxi—Yi Zhejiang sheng weili" 服務業的空間分布特徵及與城市化的相關性分析——以浙江省為例 ("An Analysis of the Service Industry's Spatial Distribution Features and Its Correlativity with Urbanization: A Case Study of Zhejiang Province"). *Zhejiang xuekan* 浙江學刊 (Zhejiang Academic Journal), 1 (2007).

Liu Zhibiao 劉志彪. "Jingji quanjiuhua zhong de chengshi gongneng bianhua yu fangdichanye fazhan jiyu" 經濟全球化中的城市功能變化與房地產業發展機遇("Change of Cities' Functions and Development Opportunities for the Real Estate Industry in Economic Globalization"). *Nanjing shehui kexue* 南京社會科學 (Social Sciences in Nanjing), 3 (2006).

Ni Pengfei 倪鵬飛. "Zhongguo chengshi fuwuye fazhan: Jieshe yu yanzheng" 中國城市服務業發展：假設與驗證 ("Development of Urban Service Sectors in China"). *Caimao jingji* 財貿經濟 (Finance & Trade Economics), 7 (2004).

Chapter 9

Andersson, M. "Co-location of Manufacturing and Producer Services—A Simultaneous Equations Approach." CESIS Electronic Working Paper Series, Paper No. 8.

Chen Jianjun 陳建軍. "Changjiangsanjiaozhou diqu de chanye tonggou ji chanye dingwei" 長江三角洲地區的產業同構及產業定位 ("A Study on the Same Structure and Position of Industry in Yangtze River Delta"). *Zhongguo gongye jingji* 中國工業經濟 (China Industrial Economy), 2 (2004).

Fan Jianyong 范劍勇. "Shichang yitihua, diqu zhuanyehua yu chanye jiju qushi—Jian lun dui diqu chaju de yingxiang" 市場一體化、地區專業化與產業集聚趨勢——兼談對地區差距的影響 ("Market Integration, Regional Specialization and Tendency of Industrial Agglomeration: An Implication for Regional Disparity"). *Zhongguo shehui kexue* 中國社會科學 (Social Sciences in China), 6 (2004).

Fang Yong 方勇 and Zhang Erzhen 張二震. "Changzhang Sanjiaozhou kuaguo gongsi zhudaoxing chanye jiju yanjiu" 長江三角洲跨國公司主導型產業集聚研究 ("Agglomeration of Industries Lead by Multinational Enterprises in the Yangtze River Delta"). *Shijie jingji yanjiu* 世界經濟研究 (World Economy Study), 10 (2006).

Gao Chuansheng 高傳勝 and Liu Zhibiao 劉志彪. "Shengchanzhe fuwu yu Changsanjiao zhizaoye de jiju yu fazhan" 生產者服務與長三角製造業的集聚與發展 ("Producer Services & Agglomeration and Development of Manufacturing Industry in the Yangtze River Delta"). *Shanghai jingji yanjiu* 上海經濟研究 (Shanghai Economic Review), 8 (2005).

Glaeser E., H. D. Kallal, J. A. Sheinkman and A. Shleifer "Growth in Cities." *Journal of Political Economy*, 100, no. 6 (1992): 1126–1152.

Kang Zhiyong 康志勇. "Changjian Sanjiaozhou waizi chanye jiju yanjiu" 長江三角洲外資產業集聚研究 ("A Study of FDI Industry Clusters in the Yangtze River Delta"). *Nanjing youdian xueyuan xuebao* 南京郵電學院學報 (Journal of Nanjing University of Posts and Telecommunications), 4 (2003).

Krugman, P. and Venables A. J. "Globalization and the Inequality of Nations." The Quarterly Journal of Economics, 110 (1995): 857–880.

Liang Qi 梁琦. "Zhongguo gongye de quwei jinni xisu—Jian lun waishuang zhijie touzi dui zhizaoye de yingxiang" 中國工業的區位基尼系數——兼論外商直接投資對製造業集聚的影響 ("Gini-coefficient of the Chinese Manufacturing Industry"). *Tongji yanjiu* 統計研究 (Statistical Research), 9 (2003).

Lin Guangpin 林光平, Long Zhihe 龍志和 and Wu Mei 吳梅. "Woguo diqu jingji shoulian de kongjian jiliang shizheng fenxi: 1978–2002" 我國地區經濟收斂的空間計量實證分析：1978–2002 ("A Spatial Analysis of Regional Economic Convergence in China: 1978–2002"). *Jingjixue (jikan)* 經濟學（季刊）(China Economic Quarterly), B10 (2005).

Lin Guangpin 林光平, Long Zhihe 龍志和 and Wu Mei 吳梅. "Zhongguo diqu jingji σ- shoulian de kongjian jiliang shizheng fenxi" 中國地區經濟σ-收斂的空間計量實證分析 ("A Spatial investigation of σ-convergence in China"). *Suliang jingji jishu jingji yanjiu* 數量經濟技術經濟研究 (The Journal of Quantitative & Technical Economics), 4 (2006).

Liu Zhibiao 劉志彪 et al. *Changsanjiao tuoqi de Zhongguo zhizao* 長三角托起的中國製造 ("'Made in China' Fostered by the Yangtze River Delta"). Beijing: China Renmin University Press, 2006.

Liu Zhibiao 劉志彪. "Jingji quanqiuhua: Changsanjiaozhou diqu de kaifang wenti siti"經濟全球化：長江三角洲地區的開放問題四題 ("Economic Globalization: Four Questions on the Opening of the Yangtze River Delta"). *Nanjing shehui kexue* 南京社會科學 (Social Sciences in Nanjing), 7 (2003).

Lu Weiqiang 盧衛強 and Wang Qingsong 汪青松. "Fahui 'Changsanjiao' de jiju xiaoying" 發揮「長三角」的集聚效應——論集聚效應與長三角的經濟一體化) ("To Bring the Agglomeration Effect in the Yangtze River Delta into Full Play—A Study of the Agglomeration Effect and Economic Integration in the Yangtze River Delta"). *Shanghai qiye* 上海企業 (Shanghai Enterprise), 6 (2004).

Mao Xinya 毛新雅 and Wang Guixin 王桂新. "FDI Quwei juece zhong de chanye jiju yinsu—Jiyu Changjiang sanjiaozhou (shiliu chengshi) de shizheng yanjiu" FDI區位決策中的產業集聚因素——基於長江三角洲(16城市)的實證研究 ("The Role of Industry Agglomeration in FDI's Location Decision-Making: A Study of the Yangtze River Delta [among its sixteen cities]"). *Caijing kexue* 財經科學 (Finance and Economics), 5 (2005).

Markusen, J. R. "Trade in Producer Services and in Other Specialized Intermediate Inputs." *American Economic Review*, 79 (1989): 85–95.

Martin, P. and Ottaviano, G. I. P. "Growing Locations: Industry Location in a Model of Endogenous Growth." *European Economic Review*, 43 (1999): 281–302.

Phelps, N. A. and Ozawa T. "Contrasts in Agglomeration: Proto-industrial, Industrial and Post-industrial Forms Compared." *Progress in Human Geography*, 27, no. 5 (2003): 583–604.

Porter, M. (邁克爾 · 波特). "Guojia jingzheng youxhi" 國家競爭優勢 ("The Competitive Advantage of Nations"). Beijing: Huaxia Publishing House, 2003.

Porter, M. (邁克爾 · 波特). *Jingzheng lun* 競爭論 (On Competition). Beijing: CITIC Press Corporation, 2003.

Ying, L G. "Understanding China's Recent Growth Experience: A Spatial Econometric Perspective." *The Annals of Regional Science*, 37 (2003): 613–628.

Zhuo Yongliang 卓勇良. "Touzi huanjing junzhihua beijing xia de jiju yu fensan" 投資環境均質化背景下的集聚與分散——長江三角洲地區產業集聚與城市化的若干分析 ("Centralization & Decentralization against the Homogenized Background of the Investment Environment—An Analysis of Industrial Centralization & Urbanization in the Yangtze Delta"). *Zhejiang shuren daxue xuebao* 浙江樹人大學學報 (Journal of Zhejiang Shuren University), 2 (2003).

Chapter 10

Bai Zhongrao白仲堯and Yi Shaohua 依紹華. "Fuwuye yu zonghe guoli de guanxi"服務業與綜合國力的關係 ("The Relationship between Service Industry and Overall National Strength"). *Caimao jingji* 財貿經濟 (Finance and Trade Economy), 4 (2004).

Beyers, W. B. and Lindahl, D. P. 1996. Explaining the Demand for Producer Services, Regional Science.

Burns, Arthur F. "Progress towards Economic Stability." *American Economic Review*, 1960.

References

Cuadrado-Roura, Juan R. and V-Abarca, Alvaro Ortiz. "Business Cycle and Service Industries：General Trends and the Spanish Case." *The Service Industries Journal*, 21, no. 1 (2001): 103–122.

Gao Tiemei 高鐵梅. *Jiliang jingji fenxi yu jianmo: Eview yingyong yu shili* 計量經濟分析與建模：Eview應用與實例 (Analytical Methods and Modeling of Quantitative Economics: Application and Examples of Eview). Tsinghua University Press, 2006.

Hua Ercheng 華而誠. "Lun fuwuye zai guomin jingji fazhanzhong de zhanlüexing diwei 論服務業在國民經濟發展中的戰略性地位 ("On the Strategic Place of Service Industry in National Economic Development"). *Jingji yanjiu* 經濟研究(Economic Research), 12 (2001).

Jiang Xiaojuan 江小涓and Li Hui 李輝. "Fuwuye yu Zhongguo jingji: Xiangguanxing he jiakuai zengzhang de qianli" 服務業與中國經濟：相關性和加快增長的潛力 ("Service Industry and China's Economy: Correlation and Potential to Advance the Growth"), *Jingji yanjiu* 經濟研究 (Economic Research), 1 (2004).

Li Yongjian 李勇堅. "Jingji zengzhang zhong de fuwuye: Lilun zongshu yu shizheng fenxi" 經濟增長中的服務業：理論綜述與實證分析 ("Service Industry in Economic Growth: Theoretical Overview and Empirical Analysis"), *Caijing luncong* 財經論叢 (Collected Essays on Finance and Economic), 5 (2005).

Simon·Kuznets (西蒙・庫滋涅茨). *Xiandai jingji zengzhang* 現代經濟增長 (Modern Economic Growth). Beijing: Beijing Institute of Economics Press, 1989.

Viktor R. Fuchs (維克托・R・富克斯). *Fuwu jingjixue* 服務經濟學 (Service Economics). Beijing: Commercial Press, Ltd., 1987.

Xia Qing 夏晴, Zheng Jichang 鄭吉昌and Jianghong 姜紅. "Lun fuwuye fazhan yu fengong de yanjin" 論服務業發展與分工的演進 ("On the Development of Service Industry and the Evolution of Division of Labour"). *Zhongguo ruan kexue* 中國軟科學 (China Soft Science), 10 (2004).

Yu Dan 于丹. "Meiguo fuwuye de jingji 'wendiqi' zuoyong jiqi dui Zhongguo de qishi" 美國服務業的經濟「穩定器」作用及其對中國的　示 ("The Buffering Effect of US Service Industry on the Economy and Its Inspiration to China"), *Shijie jingji yanjiu* 世界經濟研究 (World Economic Study), 5 (2007).

Chapter 11

Ao Nen 敖嫩. "Dui renli ziben canyu shouru fenpei de jidian renshi" 對人力資本參與收入分配的幾點認識 ("On the Engagement of Labour Capital in Income-distribution"). *Nei Menggu caijing xueyuan xuebao* 內蒙古財經學院學報 (Journal of Inner Mongolia College of Finance and Economics), 3 (2005): 106–108.

Bender, Lloyd D. "The Role of Services in Rural Development Policies." *Land Economics*, 63, no. 1 (February 1987): 62–71.

Bluestone, Barry. "The Impact of Schooling and Industrial Restructuring on Recent Trends in Wage Inequality in the United States." *The American Economic Review*, 80, no. 2 (May 1990): 303–307 (Papers and Proceedings of the 102nd Annual Meeting of the American Economic Association).

Cao Zijian 曹子堅. "Shouyi qunti de zhihui yu chixu tuijin gaige" 受益群體的置換與持續推進改革 ("Displacement of Benefit Groups and Sustained Advance in Reform"). *Gaige* 改革 (Reform). 7 (2005): 13–19.

Chen Jianjun 陳建軍. "Changsanjiao: Cong dianzhou fazhan zouxiang wangle fazhan" 長三角：從點軸發展走向網絡發展 ("The Development Pattern of the Yangtze River Delta: From Pivoting Point to Network"). *Zhejiang shehui kexue* 浙江社會科學 (Zhejiang Social Sciences), 4 (2005): 43–48.

Cheng Dazhong 程大中 and Chen Fujiong 陳福炯. "Zhongguo fuwuye xiangdui mijidu ji duiqi laodong shengchanlü de yingxiang" 中國服務業相對密集度及對其勞動生產率的影響 ("The Relative Density of China's Service Industry and Its Effect on Productivity"). *Guanli shijie* 管理世界 (Management World), 5 (2005): 77–84.

Damesick, Peter J. "Service Industries, Employment and Regional Development in Britain: A Review of Recent Trends and Issues." *Transactions of the Institute of British Geographers*, New Series, 11, no. 2 (1986): 212–226.

Dong Xiaolin 董小麟 and Dong Yuanmei 董苑玫. ("Zhongguo fuwu maoyi jingzhengli ji fuwuye jiegou quexian") 中國服務貿易競爭力及服務業結構缺陷分析 ("Analysis of the Competitiveness of Service Trade and the Defects in Service Industry Structure in China"). 11 (2006): 41–50.

Evans, Peter B. and Michael Timberlake. "Dependence, Inequality, and the Growth of the Tertiary: A Comparative Analysis of Less Developed Countries." *American Sociological Review*, 45, no. 4 (August 1980): 531–552.

Feng Hong 馮虹. "Shouru fenpei yu chengshi liyi jieceng fenhua de xiangguangxing yanjiu" 收入分配與城市利益階層分化的相關性研究 ("Study on the Correlation between Income-distribution and Stratified

Differentiation of Urban Interest"). *Guanli shijie* 管理世界 (Management World), 4 (2006): 142–143.

Fiala, Robert. "Inequality and the Service Sector in Less Developed Countries: A Reanalysis and Respecification." *American Sociological Review*, 48, no. 3 (June 1983): 421–428.

Fiala, Robert. "Labor Force Structure and the Size Distribution of Income within Countries，1960–1980." *International Studies Quarterly*, 31, no. 4 (December 1987): 403–422.

Fiala, Robert. "The International System, Labor-force Structure, and the Growth and Distribution of National Income, 1950–1980." *Sociological Perspectives*, 35, no. 2 (Summer 1992): 249–282 (Studies in the New International Comparative Political Economy).

Gao Mingsen 高明森. "Lun guoren shouru chaju dui jingji zengzhang de xiaoying" 論個人收入差距對經濟增長的效應 ("On the Effect of Difference in Individual Income on Economic Growth"). *Pandeng* 攀登 (Climb), 6 (2003): 26–29.

Kirn, Thomas J. "Growth and Change in the Service Sector of the U.S.: A Spatial Perspective." *Annals of the Association of American Geographers*, 77, no. 3 (September 1987): 353–372.

Li Qi 李琪 and Gai Jianhua 蓋建華. "Woguo xiandai fuwuye fazhan de dongtai yanjin fenxi" 我國現代服務業發展的動態演進分析 ("The Analysis of Dynamic Evolution of the Modern Service Industry in Our Country"). *Weilai yu fazhan* 未來與發展 (Future and Development), 1 (2007): 37–41.

Ma Lili 馬莉莉. *Zhonggong Jinan shiwei dangxiaoxuebao* 中共濟南市委黨校學報 (Journal of the Communist Party School of Jinan Municipal Committee). Shijie jingji daokan 世界經濟導刊 (Guide to World Economy). 8 (2006): 22–26.

Research on the Development Policy of the Emerging Service Industry in China [M], Beijing: China Planning Press, 2003.

Semyonov, Moshe and Richard Ira Scott. "Industrial Shifts, Female Employment, and Occupational Differentiation: A Dynamic Model for American Cities, 1960–1970." *Demography*, 20, no. 2 (May 1983): 163–176.

Udall, Alan T. "The Effects of Rapid Increases in Labor Supply on Service Employment in Developing Countries." *Economic Development and Cultural Change*, 24, no. 4 (July 1976): 765–785.

Wang Jinsong 王勁松, Shi Jinchuan 史晉川 and Li Yingchun 李應春. "Zhongguo minying jingji de chanye jiegou yanjin (zhiyi)—jian lun minying jingji yu guoyou jingji, waiji jingji de jingzheng guanxi 中國民營經濟的產業結構演進〔之一〕——兼論民營經濟與國有經濟、外資經濟的競爭關係 ("On the

Evolution of Industry Structure of Private Economy in China (I)—and also on the Competitive Relationship between the Private Economy and State-owned and Foreign-invested Economy"). *Management World*, 10 (2005): 82–93.

Xu Jiangping 許江萍 and Zhang Hong 張洪. *Woguo xinxing fuwuye fazhan zhengce yanjiu* 我國新興服務業發展政策研究 (The Study of the Development Policy of Newly Established Service Industry). Beijing: China Planning Press, 2003.

Yang Laichun 楊來春 and Liaochun 廖春. "Lun woguo fuwuye de jiegou youhua jizhong dian hangye xuanze—Cong chanye guanliandu, chengzhangxing ji jiuye xinali deng fangmian tanqi" 論我國服務業的結構優化及重點行業選擇——從產業關聯度、成長性及就業吸納力等方面談起 ("On the Structural Optimization of Service Industry and the Selection of Key Industries in Our Country—From the Perspectives of Industrial Correlation, Potentiality and Ability to Absorb Employees"). *Qiushi xuekan* 求實學刊 (Down-to-earth Journal), 1 (2004): 62–67.

Ye Yaoming 葉耀明 and Liu Hong 劉紅. "Shanghai fuwuye neibu jiegou tezheng fenxi" 上海服務業內部結構特徵分析 ("Analysis of the Internal Structural Features of the Service Industry in Shanghai"). *Shanghai jingji yanjiu* 上海經濟研究 (Shanghai Economic Research). 1 (2007): 51–57.

Zeng Fuqiu 曾伏秋. "Lun shouru fenpei yu youxiao jili" 論收入分配與有效激勵 ("On Income-distribution and Effective Inspiration"). *Huxiang luntan* 湖湘論壇 (Huxiang Forum), 3 (2004): 28–29.

Zeng Guang 曾光 and Zhou Weilin 周偉林. "Changsanjiao chengshi jingji zengzhang chayi de shizheng fenxi" 長三角城市經濟增長差異的實證分析 ("Empirical Analysis of Differences in Economic Growth in the Yangtze River Delta"). *Zhejiang Social Sciences*, 6 (2006): 31–39.

Zhao Nonghua 趙農華. Shanghai disanchanye fazhan tuidong laodong jiuye zengzhang de shizheng fenxi 上海第三產業發展推動勞動就業增長的實證分析 ("Empirical Analysis of the Promotion of the Third Industry in Shanghai to the Growth of Employment"). *Tongji yanjiu* 統計研究 (Statistical Research), 2 (2002): 51–53.

Zhao Zhongliang 趙忠良. "Woguo jingji zengzhang, shehui bupingdeng he gonggong zhichu xiangguan guanxi de shizheng fenxi yu zhengce jianyi" 我國經濟增長、社會不平等和公共支出相關關係的實證分析與政策建議 ("Empirical Analysis of the Correlation of Economic Growth, Social Inequity and Public Expenditure and Policy Proposal"). *Hunan shehui kexue* 湖南社會科學 (Hunan Social Sciences), 6 (2006): 105–107, 123.

Zheng Jichang 鄭吉昌. "Shengchanzhe fuwuye yu xiandai jingji zengzhang" 生產者服務業與現代經濟增長 ("Producer Service Industry and Modern Economic Growth"). *Zhejiang Shuren daxue xuebao* 浙江樹人大學學報 (Zhejiang Shuren University Journal), 1 (2005): 27–32.

Zheng Kaijie 鄭凱捷. "Changsanjiao chengshiquan chanye jiegou zhong fuwuye fazhan wenti de fenxi yanjiu" 長三角城市群產業結構中服務業發展問題的分析研究 ("Research on the Development of Service Industry in the Industrial Structure of Cities in the Yangtze River Delta"). *Shanghai touzi* 上海投資 (Shanghai Investment), 12 (2005): 48–53.

Zhong Ruoyu 鍾若愚 (Ed.). *Zouxiang xiandai fuwuye* 走向現代服務業 (Marching to Modern Service Industry). Shanghai: SDX Joint Publishing Company, 2006.

Chapter 12

Chenery, Hollis B. (霍利斯・錢納里) and Moises Syrquin (莫伊斯・賽爾昆). *Fazhande xingshi*: 1950–1970 發展的型式：1950–1970 (Development Pattern: 1950–1970). Beijing: Economy and Sciences Press, 1988.

Clark, M. A. Colin. *The Conditions of Economics Progress*. MacMillan & Co. Ltd., 1974.

Gershuny, J. I. and I. D Miles. *The New Service Economy: The Transformation of Employment in Industrial Societies*. New York: Praeger Publishers, 1983.

Kuznets, Simon (西蒙・庫茲涅茨). *Xiandai jingji zhengzhang* 現代經濟增長 (Modern Economic Growth). Beijing: Beijing Institute of Economics Press, 1989.

Li Jiangfan 李江帆. *Zhongguo disan chanye fenxi* 中國第三產業經濟分析 (Analysis of the Economy of China Third Industry). Guangzhou: Guangdong People's Publishing House, 2003.

Ren Wangbing 任旺兵. *Woguo fuwuye fazhan de guoji bijiao yu shizheng fenxi* 我國服務業發展的國際比較與實證分析 (A Comparison of the Development of Service Industry in China and Other Countries and an Empirical Analysis). Beijing: China Planning Press, 2005.

Wei Zuolei 魏作磊. "Di san chanye fazhan dui Guangdong jiuye chujin de shizheng fenxi" 第三產業發展對廣東就業促進的實證分析 ("Empirical Analysis of the Third Industry Boosting Employment in Guangdong"). *Shangye jingji wenhui* 商業經濟文薈 (Commercial Economics Review), 5 (2003).

Zhang Chewei 張車偉 and Cai Fang 蔡昉. "Jiuye tanxing de bianhua qushi yanjiu" 就業彈性的變化趨勢研究 ("Research on Change in Employment

Elasticity"). *Zhongguo gongye jingji* 中國工業經濟 (China Industrial Economics), 5 (2002).

Zhang Jiangxue 張江雪. *Woguo sanda jingji didai jiuye tanxing de bijiao* 我國三大經濟地帶就業彈性的比較 (Comparison of Employment Elasticity among the Three Economic Zones in China). Beijing: Quantitative and Technological Economic Study, 2005.

Zhang Shujun 張淑君. *Fuwuye jiuye xiaoying yanjiu* 服務業就業效應研究 (A Study of the Employment Effect of Service Industry). Beijing: China Finance and Economy Press, 2006.

Zhao Nonghua 趙農華. "Shanghai disan chanye fazhan tuidong jiuye zengzhang de shizheng fenxi 上海第三產業發展推動勞動就業增長的實證分析 ("Empirical Analysis of Shanghai's Third Industry Promoting Growth in Employment"). *Tongji yanjiu* 統計研究 (Statistical Research), 2 (2002).

Zhu Yueying 朱玥瑩and Jiang Naihua 蔣乃華. "Jiangsu sheng disan chanye jiuye xiaoying fenxi" 江蘇省第三產業就業效應分析 ("An Analysis of the Employment Effect of the Third Industry in Jiangsu"). *Yangzhou daxue xuebao* 揚州大學學報 (Yangzhou University Journal), 7 (2006).

Chapter 13

Cheng Zhiqiang 程智強 and Liu Ming 劉明. "Nongye keji jinbu gongxianlü cexuan zhong de suju chuli wenti" 農業科技進步貢獻率測算中的數據處理問題 ("Data Processing in the Calculation of the Contribution Rate of Agricultural Scientific Technology"), *Yuce* 預測 (Forecasting), 2 (1997).

Huang Shaojun 黃少軍. *Fuwuye yu jingji zengzhang* 服務業與經濟增長 (Service Industry and Economic Growth). Economy and Sciences Press, 2000.

Keti zhu 課題組 (Research Group). "Fuwuye yu chengshihua hudong moshi yanjiu 服務業與城市化互動模式研究 ("Research on the Model of Interaction between Service Industry and Urbanization"). *Zhejiang shuren daxue xuebao* 浙江樹人大學學報 (Zhejiang Shuren University Journal), 2005.

Lewis, Arthur (阿瑟・劉易斯). *Eryuan jingji lun* 二元經濟論 (Dual Economy). Beijing Financial Institute Press, 1989.

Li Guanlin 李冠霖. *Disan chanye touru chanchu fenxi: Cong touru chanchu de jiaodu kan disan chanye de chanye guanlian yu chanye boji texing* 第三產業投入產出分析：從投入產出的角度看第三產業的產業關聯與產業波及特性 (Analysis of Input and Output of the Third Industry: Industrial Correlation and Industrial Ripple-effect from the Perspective of Input and Output). China Commodity Price Press, 2002.

References

Li Jiangfan 李江帆. *Zhongguo disan chanye fenxi* 中國第三產業經濟分析 (Analysis of the Economy of China Third Industry). Guangzhou: Guangdong People's Publishing House, 2003.

Ma Chongming 馬崇明. *Zhongguo xiandaihua jincheng* 中國現代化進程 (The Modernization of China). Economy and Sciences Press, 2003.

Qiao Ying 喬瑛. "Xiandai fuwuye de tezheng ji fazhan qushi" 現代服務業的特徵及發展趨勢 ("Characteristics and Tendencies of the Modern Service Industry"). *Xiandai shuangmao* 現代商貿 (Modern Commerce), 9 (2006): 55–56.

Shang Changfeng 尚長風. *Zhidu yueshu xia de caizheng zhengce zhixiao yanjiu* 制度約束下的財政政策績效研究 (A Study of the Performance of Financial Policy Restrained by Rules). People's Publishing House, 2004.

Shang Changfeng, 尚長風. "Pojie nongcun yanglao baoxian zhidu kunjing de zhidu changxin" 破解農村養老保險制度困境的制度創新 (Innovatiive System for Escaping the Dilemma of the Old-age Insurance System in Rural Areas), *Caizheng yanjiu* 財政研究 (Financial Research), 2007.

Tang Xu 唐旭 and Leng Keping 冷克平. "Woguo xiandai fuwuye de zhuanyi ji duice fenxi 我國現代服務業的轉移及對策分析 ("The Transfer of Modern Service Industry and an Analysis of Countermeasures"). *Keji jinbu yu dui ce* 科技進步與對策 (Advance in Science and Technology and Countermeasures), 12 (2006): 108–110.

Wang Jin'ao 汪金敖. "Tuijin nongcun fuwuye fazhan, jiashu xinnongcun jianshe bufa"推進農村服務業發展·加速新農村建設步伐 ("Promoting the Service Industry in Rural Areas and Accelerating the Building of a New Countryside"), 1 November 2007.

Xu Zuhua 許祖華. "Woguo nongcun fuwuye fazhan xianzhuang ji duice fenxi" 我國農村服務業發展現狀及對策分析 ("The Current Status of the Rural Service Industry in China and an Analysis of Countermeasures"). www.cqagri.gov.cn [25 December 2006].

Yao Yaojun 姚耀軍and He Pichan 和丕禪. "Zhongguo nongcun jinrong fazhan yu jingji zengzhang (1978–2001) shizheng fenxi" 中國農村金融發展與經濟增長 (1978–2001) 實證分析 (Empirical Analysis of Financial Advance and Economic Growth in Rural Areas of China [1978–2001]). *Xibei nonglin keji daxue xuebao (shehui kexue ban)* 西北農林大學學報（社會科學版）(Northwest Agricultural Journal [Social Science Edition]), 6 (2004).

Chapter 14

Lianheguo kaifa jihuashu 聯合國開發計劃署 (United Nations Development Programme). *2005 nian Zhongguo renlei fazhan baogao* (2005年中國人類發展報告The 2005 Report on China's Human Progress). Beijing: China Translation and Publishing Corporation, 2005.

Liu Zhibiao 劉志彪 et al. *Changsanjiao tuoqi de Zhongguo zhizao* 長三角托起的中國製造 (China Manufacturing Propped Up by thc Yangtzc Rivcr Dclta). Beijing: China Renmin University Press, 2006.

Ma Shuluan 馬淑鸞. "Yingxiang yuqi shouming de yinsu fenxi" 影響預期壽命的因素分析 ("An Analysis of Factors Influencing Life Expectancy"). *Renkou yanjiu* 人口研究 *(Research on Populations)*, 3 (1989).

Perkins, Gilliss (吉利斯 · 波金斯) et al. *Fazhan jingjixue* 發展經濟學 (Economics of Development). Beijing: China Renmin University Press, 1998.

Sen, Amartya (阿馬蒂亞 · 森). *Yi ziyou kandai fazhan* 以自由看待發展*(Basing Development on Liberty)*. Beijing: China Renmin University Press, 2002.

Chapter 15

Barro R., and Lee, Jong-Wha. "International Data on Educational Attainment: Updates and Implications." Oxford Economic Papers, 53, no. 3 (2001): 541–563.

Barro, R. "Economic Growth in a Cross Section of Countries." *Quarterly Journal of Economics*, 1991 (106): 407–443

Baumol, W. "Macroeconomics of Unbalanced Growth: The Anatomy of Urban Crisis." *American Economic Review*, 57, no. 4 (1967): 415–426.

Chen Zhiwu 陳志武. "Weishenme Zhongguo ren chumai de shi "yinkuli?" 為什麼中國人出賣的是「硬苦力」? ("Why do Chinese People Offer Their 'Hard Work' for Sale?"). *Xin caifu* 新財富(New Fortune), 9 (2004).

Clague, C., Keefer, P., Knack, S., and Olson M. "Contract-Intensive Money: Contract Enforcement, Property Rights, and Economic Performance." *Journal of Economic Growth*, 4 (1996): 185–211.

Daron, Acemoglu, Johnson, Simon and Robinson, James A. "Institutions as The Fundamental Cause of Long-Run Growth." NBER Working Paper 10481, 2004.

Daron, Acemoglu, Johnson. "Simon.Unbundling Institutions." *Journal of Political Economy*, 113 (2005): 949–995.

Eswaran, M., and Kotwa A. "The Role of the Service Sector in the Process of Industrialization." *Journal of Development Economics*, 68 (2002): 401–420.

Felix, Eschenbach, and Bernard Hoekman. "Services Policy Reform and Economic Growth in Transition Economies, 1990–2004."World Bank Policy Research Working Paper 3663, 2005.

Francois, J. F., and Reinert, K. A. "The Role of Services in the Structure of Production and Trade: Stylized Facts from a Cross-Country Analysis." *Asia-Pacific Economic Review*, 2 (1996).

Fuchs, Victor. *The Service Economy*. New York: Columbia University Press, 1968

Glaeser, E. L, La Porta, R., Lopez-de-Silanes, F. and Shleifer, A. "Do Institutions Cause Growth?" *Journal of Economic Growth*, 9, no. 3 (2004): 271–303.

Gruber (格魯伯) et al. "Fuwuye de zengzhang yuanyin yu yingxiang" 服務業的增長原因與影響 ("Cause and Effect of Growth in Service Industry"). Shanghai: Sdxjoint Publishing Company, 1993.

Gwartney, James, and Robert, Lawson. "Economic Freedom of the World: 2005 Annual Report." Vancouver: The Fraser Institute.Data retrieved from www.Freetheworld.com

Gwartney, James, Randall, Holcombe, and Robert Lawson. "The Scope of Government and the Wealth of Nations." *Cato Journal*, 18, no. 2 (1998): 163–190.

Hill, T. P. "On Goods and Services." *Review of Income and Wealth*, 23, no. 4 (1997): 315–338.

Hill, T. P. "Tangibles, Intangibles and Services: A New Taxonomy for the Classification of Output." *Canadian Journal of Economics*, 32, no. 2 (1999): 426–447.

Holmstrom, Bengt. "The Provisions of Services in a Market Economy." In Robert P. Inman (Ed.), *Managing the Service Economy: Prospects and Problems* (Ch. 7). Cambridge University Press, 1985.

Jagdish, Bhagwati. "Splingtering and Disembodiment of Services and Developing Nations." *World Economy*, 7 (1984): 133–143.

Jiang Xiaojuan 江小涓 and Li Hui 李輝. "Fuwuye yu Zhongguo jingji: Xiangguanxing yu jiakuai zengzhang de qianli" 服務業與中國經濟：相關性與加快增長的潛力 ("Service Industry and China's Economy: Correlation and Potential of Faster Growth"). *Jingji yanjiu* 經濟研究 (Economic Research Journal), 1 (2004).

Kaufmann, D., Kraay, A. and Mastruzzi, M. "Governance Matters IV: Governance Indicators for 1996–2004."World bank Working Papers, 2005.

La Porta, R., Lopez-de-Silanes, F., Shleifer, A., Vishny, R. "The Quality of Government.Journal of Law." *Economics and Organization*, 15, no. 1 (1999): 222–279.

Liu Peilin 劉培林, and Songzhan 宋湛. "Fuwu ye he zhizaoye qiye faren zhixiao bijiao" 服務業和製造業企業法人績效比較 ("A Comparison of Performance of Business Entities between Service Industry and Manufacturing"). *Jingji yanjiu* 經濟研究 (Economic Research), 1 (2007).

Liu Zhibiao 劉志彪. "Lun yi shengchanxing fuwuye weizhudao de xiandai jingji zengzhang." 論以生產性服務業為主導的現代經濟增長. ("On the Growth in Modern Economy Dominated by Producer Service Industry"). *Zhongguo jingji wenti* 中國經濟問題 (China Economic Issues), 1 (2001).

Mattoo, A., Rathindran R., and Subramanian, A. "Measuring Services Trade Liberalization and Its Impact on Economic Growth: An Illustration." World Bank Working Paper No. 2655, 2001.

Mohammad, Admin, and Mattoo, Aaditya. "Do Institions Matter More for Services?." World Bank Working Paper No.4032, 2006.

North, Douglas. *Institutions, Institutional Change and Economic Performance*. Cambridge: Cambridge University Press,1990.

North, Douglas. *Structure and Change in Economic History*. New York: Norton,1981.

Rati, Ram. "Government size and economic growth: A new framework and some evidence from cross-section and time-series data." *American Economic Review*, 76, no. 1 (1986): 191–203.

Riddle. *Service-Led Growth: the Role or the Service sector in World Development*. New York: Prager, 1986.

Stiglitz, Joseph (斯蒂格利茨), *Gonggong bumen jijixue* 公共部門經濟學 (Economics of the Public Sector). Beijing: China Renmin University Press, 2005.

Tirole (泰勒爾). *Chanye zhuzhi lilun* 產業組織理論 (The Theory of Industrial Organization). Beijing: China Renmin University Press, 1997.

United Nations Development Programme. *Human Development Report 2002*. New York, NY: Oxford University Press,2002

Wang Dehua 汪德華, Zhang Zaijin張再金, and Bai Zhongen 白重恩. "Zhengfu guimo, fazhi shuiping yu fuwuye fazhan" 政府規模、法治水平與服務業發展 ("The Governmental Scale, Level of Rule by Law and Expansion of Service Industry"). *Jingji yanjiu* 經濟研究 (Economic Research), 6 (2007).

World Bank (世界銀行). "2002 nian shijie fazhan baogao: Jianli shichagn jizhi" 2002 年世界發展報告：建立市場機制 ("2002 Report on the World Development: Setting up a Market Mechanism"). Beijing: China Finance and Economy Press, 2002.

World Bank. World Development Indicators Online, at http://publications.worldbank.org/subscriptions/WDI.

Wu Jinglian 吳敬璉. *Zhongguo zengzhang moshi jueze* 中國增長模式抉擇 (The Choice of Growth Pattern of China) Shanghai: Far Eastern Publications, 2006.

Zhang Jun 張軍 and Zhou Li'an 周黎安 (Eds.). *Wei zhengzhang er jingzheng: Zhongguo jingji zhengzhang de zhengzhi jingjixue* 為增長而競爭：中國經濟增長的政治經濟學 (Competing for Growth: Political Economics of China's Economic Growth). Shanghai: Shanghai People's Publishing House, 2007.

Chapter 16

Andrikopoulos, A., Brox, J., and Carvalho, E. Shift-share Analysis And The Potential For Predicting Regional Growth Patterns: Some Evidence For The Region of Ontario." *Growth and Change*, 1 (1990): 110.

Ashby, L. D. "The Geographical Redistribution of Employment: An Examination of the Elements of Change." *Survey of Current Business*, 44 (1964): 13–20.

Brown, H. J. "Shift and Share Projections of Regional Economic Growth: An Empirical Test." *Journal of Regional Science*, 9, no. 1 (1969): 118.

Creamer, D. "Shift of Manufacturing Industries, Industrial Location and Natural Resources." US Government Printing Office, Washington DC, 1943.

Cui Gonghao 崔功豪, Wei Qingquan 魏清泉, and Chen Zongxing 陳宗興 (Eds). *Quyu fenxi yu kuihua* 區域分析與規劃 (Regional Analysis and Planning). Beijing: Higher Education Press, 1999.

Houston, D. "The Shift and Share Analysis of Regional Growth." *Southern Economic Journal*, 33 (1967): 577–581.

Kalbacher, J. Z. Shift-share analysis: a modified approach." *Agricultural Economic Research*, 31, no. 1 (1979): 12–25.

Klaasen, L. H., and Paelinck, J. H. H. "Asymmetry in Shift and Share Analysis." *Regional and Urban Economics*, 2, no. 3 (1972): 256–261.

Li Jiangfan 李江帆 (Ed.). *Zhongguo disan chanye fazhan yanjiu* 中國第三產業發展研究 (Analysis of the Development of China Third Industry). Beijing: People's Publishing House, 2005.

McDonough, C. C., and Sihag, B. B. "The Incorporation of Multiple Bases into Shift-Share Analysis." *Growth and Change*, 22, no. 1 (1991): 19.

Perloff, H. S., Dunn, E.S., Lampard, E. E., and Muth, R. F. *Regions, Resources and Economic Growth*. Baltimore, MD: The Johns Hopkins University Press,1960

Porter, Michael. (波特). *Guojia jingzheng youshi* 國家競爭優勢 (Competitive Edge of a Country). Beijing: China CITIC Press, 2000.

Praskevopouls, C. C. "The stability of the regional share component: an empirical test." *Journal of Regional Science*, 11 (1971): 107–112.

Yang Wuyang 楊吾揚, and Liang Jinshe 梁進社. *Gaodeng jingji dilixue* 高等經濟地理學 (Higher Economic Geography). Beijing: Peking University Press, 1997.

Zhou Yixing 周一星. *Chengshi dilixue* 城市地理學 (Urban Geography). Beijing: Commercial Press, Ltd., 1995.

Chapter 17

Dangdai Shanghai yanjiusuo 當代上海研究所 (Research Institute of Contemporary Shanghai). *Changzhang sanjiaozhou fazhan baogao—chengshijian gongneng guanxi de yanjin* 長江三角洲發展報告——城市間功能關係的演進 (Report on the Development of the Yangtze River Delta—The Evolutiont of Functional Relationships among Cities). Shanghai: Shanghai People's Publishing House, 2006.

Guowuyuan fazhan yanjiu zhongxin jishu jingji yanjiubu 國務院發展研究中心技術經濟研究部 (Technological and Economic Research Department of the Development Research Center of the State Council) (Trans.). *Jingji hezuo yu fazhan zuzhi xinxi jishu zhanwang 2006* 經濟合作與發展組織信息技術展望2006 (Prospects for Information Technology of Economic Cooperation and Development Organization in 2006). Beijing: China Finance and Economy Press, 2007.

Huang Fanhua 黃繁華. *Jiaru WTO hou fuwu ye fazhan: yi Jiangsu weili yanjiu* 加入WTO後服務業發展:以江蘇為例研究 (The Development of Service Industry Since the Entrance to the WTO: Taking Jiangsu as an Example to Study). Beijing: People's Publishing House, 2004.

Li Shantong 李善同 and Hua Ercheng 華而誠 (Eds.). *21 shijichu de Zhongguo fuwu ye* 21世紀初的中國服務業 (China's Service Industry in the Beginning of the 21st Century). Beijing: Economy and Sciences Press, 2002.

Liu Zhibiao 劉志彪 and Zheng Jianghuai 鄭江淮 et al. *Changsanjiao jingji zengzhang de xinyinqing* 長三角經濟增長的新引擎 (The New Engine for Economic Growth of the Yangtze River Delta). Beijing: China Renmin University Press, 2007.

Wang Ronghua 王榮華. *2007 nian: Changxin Changsanjiao* 2007年：創新長三角(Reform in the Yangtze River Delta). Beijing: Social Sciences Documentation Publishing House, 2007.

Index

Lightning Source UK Ltd.
Milton Keynes UK
UKOW01n1146160314

228204UK00002B/17/P

9 789814 298209